MIRI RUBIN

Mother of God

A History of the Virgin Mary

Yale University Press

New Haven & London

Published 2009 in the United States by Yale University Press
Published 2009 in the United Kingdom by Allen Lane, an imprint of
Penguin Books

Set in PostScript Adobe Sabon
Typeset by Rowland Phototypesetting Ltd, Bury St Edmunds, Suffolk
Printed in the United States.

Library of Congress Catalog Number: 2008939283
ISBN 978-0-300-10500-1 (hardcover : alk. paper)

A catalogue record for this book is available from the British Library.

This paper meets the requirements of ANSI/NISO Z39.48-1992
(Permanence of Paper).
It contains 30 percent postconsumer waste (PCW) and is certified by the
Forest Stewardship Council (FSC).

10 9 8 7 6 5 4 3 2 1

Contents

v

List of Illustrations

List of Maps

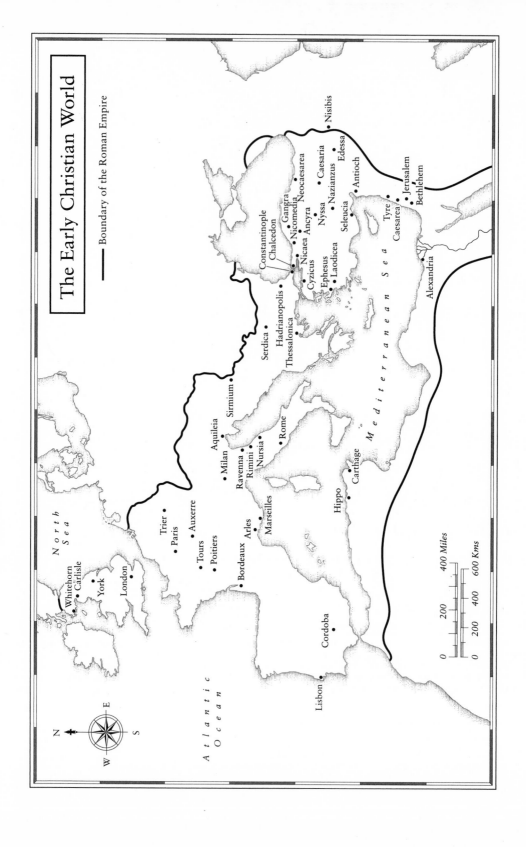

The Early Christian World

—— Boundary of the Roman Empire

Europe and Byzantium, *c*.800

Late Medieval Europe

North Sea

Amsterdam
Leyden
Rotterdam
Veere
Middelburg
Arnemuiden
Bergen-op-Zoom
Bruges
Antwerp
Ghent
Ypres
Schelde
Maria Troon
Louvain
St Omer
Lille

0   20   40 miles
0   30   60 miles

North Sea

Edinburgh
Carlisle
Newcastle
Durham
York · Beverley
Boston
Norwich · Walsingham
Oxford · Cambridge
Bristol · Ipswich
London
Calais
Harfleur · Arras · Douai
Le Havre · Dieppe
Honfleur · Rouen · Soissons
St Malo · Paris
Chartres
Angers
Nantes
Bourges
La Rochelle
Loire
Orléans
Geneva
Lyons
Bordeaux
Rocamadour
Cahors
Bayonne
Bilbao
Toulouse
Orange
Avignon
Montpellier
Marseilles
Perpignan

Santiago de Compostela

0   100   200   300   400 Miles
0   200   400   600 Kms

Atlantic Ocean

Valladolid
Salamanca
Huesca
Lérida
Barcelona
Lisbon
Toledo
Valencia
Monserrat
Seville · Cordova
Granada
Cadiz · Malaga

Medditerranean

Acknowledgements

A number of friends offered their generous and constructive comments on the whole book: Ron Barkaï, Paul Binski, Christopher Brooke, Christopher Clark, Patrick Higgins, Colin Jones, Paul La Hausse de la Louvière, Nils Holger Peterson, Shulamith Shahar, Gareth Stedman Jones and Nigel Yandell. Their insights, so often incisive, were always given with a great deal of grace. The book owes a great deal to them.

Since *Mother of God* covers a long period I also turned to experts who read specific sections: Bart Ehrman, Yitzhak Hen, Racheli Shalomi-Hen on Part I; Ora Limor, Jinty Nelson and Yossi Rapoport on Part II; Julie Barrau, Susan Boynton, Virginia Davis, Rachel Fulton, Fiona Griffiths, Sara Lipton, Jennifer Shea and Ineke van t'Spijker on Part III; John Arnold, Rachel Fulton, Kate Jansen and Sara Lipton on Part IV; John Arnold, Sarah Beckwith, Claire Daunton, Penny Granger, Kate Jansen, Ann Nichols and David Wallace on Part V; David R. M. Irving, Peter Marshall, Michael Questier, Camilla Russell, David Wallace and Anna Whitelock on Part VI; with Eric Foner, Ira Katznelson, Jon Parry and Paul Strohm I was able to discuss the book's general themes, those raised in the Introduction and the Conclusion.

I benefited from the opportunity of presenting sections of this book during a week spent at the Central European University in Budapest in November 2007 as the Natalie Zemon Davis Lecturer of that year. Natalie Zemon Davis, Gabor Klaniczay and György Geréby were particularly generous in sharing materials and expertise. The Humanities Lecture which I prepared for St Mary's College in South Bend, Indiana, and delivered in September 2006 was an occasion not only to address a lively audience but to witness the importance of Mary in the lives of Catholic women, such as the impressive alumnae of St Mary's. I have also enjoyed many chances to speak about the book's many themes in

seminar rooms and lecture halls over almost ten years: in Cambridge and Oxford, Copenhagen, New York, Chicago, Paris, Münster, Jerusalem, Maynooth, Coventry, Birmingham, Southampton, Evanston. In all these places I found that the subject of Mary excited lively responses and inspired collective interest.

I am fortunate in working at Queen Mary, University of London, among inspiring colleagues, within an institution that cherishes diversity and engages in its scholarship with the global city that is London. Thanks to its encouragement I was able to receive the Leverhulme Trust's support and to devote myself fully to research between 2002 and 2005 as the holder of a Major Research Award.

This book owes a great deal to the talented people who help scholars turn their ideas into tangible and beautiful books: to David Watson, an exacting and shrewd copy editor; to Amanda Russell, whose unerring eye helped judge so wisely the pictorial section; and to Catherine Clark for her encouragement and friendship. Simon Winder has read every word and has commented on many; it is a privilege to write for him, historian to historian.

For giving life its meaning and teaching me about the pain and magic of motherhood, this book is dedicated to my families, in three continents.

Cambridge, July 2007

Writing about Mary: An Introduction

For a historian of Europe Mary is a constant presence. Women and men are named after her; so are places, towns, villages and churches. The figure of Mary is imprinted on the medieval fabric of modern Europe: in the images built into houses and walls of Italian towns, on cathedral façades in northern France, on roadside crosses in Austria and Bavaria, or in the icons of Greek churches. Mary is ubiquitous in much of the music of the classical tradition and is frequently portrayed in works of art that form part of the modern grand tour, from the National Galleries of London and Washington to the Uffizi in Florence, the Gemäldegallerie in Berlin, or the Louvre in Paris. Mary is central to western canons of beauty and pleasure in all the historical art forms and in many new ones: painting, sculpture and music, but also conceptual art and advertising. For believers Mary is powerfully present in liturgy and prayer, above all in the Catholic and Orthodox traditions. And since Catholicism is a world religion, the culture of Mary is as diverse as that of the continents that bear her imprint: her many forms include the pomp of celebrations in Mexico City around Our Lady of Guadalupe, the visions of Mary in Kigali in Rwanda or the overwhelming processional dramas so important to the culture of the Philippines. So widely recognizable is Mary all over the world that, when in the late twentieth century a clever young Catholic woman from Detroit sought a persona which would capture her audacity and her towering ambition, she launched herself simply as Madonna.[1]

Mother of God is a history of the ideas, practices and images that developed around the figure of the Virgin Mary from the earliest times until around the year 1600. It is based on a wide range of source materials – music, poetry, theology, art, scripture, miracle tales – and offers an historical understanding of the world in which they were

produced and used. This exploration results in an intimate engagement with Christian cultures, one which does not end with the reading of this book. Part of the pleasure which readers may take away from *Mother of God* is the ability to use its insights to enjoy the heritage which is still around us and to understand the relations between world Christianities, Judaism and Islam.

The making of this book has been a constantly stimulating journey. Wherever I have gone there have been people wanting to discuss Mary: Christians, naturally, but also Jews, Muslims and Buddhists; everyone seems to have a story to tell about Mary, be it funny, adoring or cynical. There are the believers who told me of moments of comfort and illumination, of family eccentricities in which Mary was involved; the art lovers who shared knowledge of unexpected representations of Mary (and who showered me with postcards from their travels); the women who insist that Mary is a fully fledged female deity; and the very many who repeated the tale of a ten-year-old slice of toast with Mary's image imprinted upon it, an item auctioned on eBay for $28,000 in 2004 – Mary marketed with the electronic efficiency of the twenty-first century.[2] Not a dull moment has detracted from the interest of the years spent on writing this book.

The question that animated my interest from the start was this: how did Mary, about whom so little is said in the gospels, become this familiar global figure? This book invites the reader to discover a complex history, to appreciate images and poetry, to reflect on religious experience and the nature of theological discussion, and to enjoy an immersion in European culture and its global extension.

I start by exploring the history of Mary's emergence from the earliest decades of Christianity, a time when Jesus' followers were few, and were little different in outlook and lifestyle from the Jews among whom they were born. While the gospels themselves contained few details about Mary's origins or life, other early writings soon did. A version of Mary's life had evolved by the second century, which endowed her with a fine ancestry, a gracious infancy and a pure childhood. As Christian beliefs were woven from the memories of Jesus cherished by his followers, discussions of his nature – human and divine – necessarily led to a deeper curiosity about the qualities of his mother. Understanding the historical emergence of Mary requires an immersion in the materials and concerns of peoples in the centuries in the world of late antiquity into which

the new religion – Christianity – was born. It was a world full of possibilities for exploring the sacred and one in which religious options were many, and they were strongly held and written about with vigour. In this world the figure of Mary was not just born, but made, by those who cherished the memory of Jesus and who sought to bolster emerging Christianity with powerful arguments and compelling accounts of its origins.

Once Christian ideas gained public endorsement by the Emperor Constantine in the early fourth century, Mary became the subject of theological discussions aimed at establishing an orthodoxy promoted by the imperial state. Mary's stature grew as she became associated with the theological debates in church councils where official formulations of Christian faith and imperial religious policy were being determined. At the heart of discussion was the exact nature of Christ – Man and God – and this often led to formulations about his mother too. From her scant gospel beginnings Mary had become by the fifth century a matter of state: the Council of Ephesus in Asia Minor in 431 decreed that it was seemly to call her Bearer of God – *Theotokos*. Since Mary was a figure of such grandeur, she was depicted as a majestic person: enthroned, facing the viewer with a powerful gaze. This much is clear from the icons made in the eastern Mediterranean, some of the earliest visual representations of Mary.

Christianity first developed with official approval in the eastern, Greek-speaking part of the Roman Empire, Byzantium, with its capital Constantinople, solemnly dedicated in 330. In the eastern Mediterranean theology was conducted in Greek, and western provinces such as the regions around Rome, Gaul and Iberia were deeply marked by this Greek heritage that defined so much of earliest Christian theology and law. Large parts of Europe were yet to become Christian. The story of Europe's conversion over the first millennium is one of painstaking transformation at different paces in different cultures: the Franks, Visigoths, Vandals and Ostrogoths between the fifth and the seventh centuries, the Anglo-Saxons in the seventh and eighth centuries, Scandinavia in the ninth to the eleventh. The stories which most moved Christians were those of martyrs – men as well as women – heroic warriors who suffered as they spread Christianity and professed their faith. The cult of martyrs – in chant, with relics, in edifying heroic tale – was at the core of the Christian identity of the warrior societies settled in the

provinces of the once Roman Empire and beyond. Mary was known from the formulation of the Creed, and the accounts of the gospel, but she did not capture the imagination as martyrs did. This was to change dramatically after the year 1000; for Mary rose to the prominence we now associate with her as Europe itself was born, in the early centuries of the second millennium.

The institutions we most associate with the European heritage – bureaucratic kingdoms, sacred kingship, cathedrals and monastic learning – already existed in the early medieval kingdoms of the Franks and Anglo-Saxons. But it was the dramatic awakening of Europe, based upon a commercial revolution, that saw populations grow, towns and cities founded, in an economy that could feed its numbers and more. This gave Europeans the opportunities to beautify and enhance their environments. Christian culture offered the ideas and practices for understanding and coping with good and evil, life and the afterlife. Its architecture, liturgy, art, music, sacraments all offered the framework for family and community life, for law and rule. There were new monasteries and cathedrals, new feasts and forms of worship, new intellectual expressions of Christian truth. In religious institutions monks strove to magnify God through the pursuit of perfection and the struggle against sin. In them Mary emerged as the perfect companion: mother, bride and consoler. Although monks and nuns were but a minute fraction of the European population, their cultural impact was enormous, and they offered models for emulation. A new interest in Mary, the necessary bearer of an incarnate God, came to the fore in intellectual discussion, artistic design and musical compositions. Moreover, Europe was fast becoming criss-crossed by roads, and these new images travelled fast and widely. The people of Europe now belonged to parishes, and the church aimed to provide meaningful rituals for their lives, from cradle to grave.

This Europe of parishes was also a vast field for experimentation with more demanding – and perhaps rewarding – forms of religious life. There were those who gave up their property and lived the itinerant life of poverty in imitation of Christ and the apostles; and there were those who found religious vocation not in secluded monasteries but in the mission of the streets, preachers who sought to make good Christians in the spoken languages. The Franciscans above all dwelt on the meaning of Mary and her son to simple believers: and they remade the Mary of

monastery and cathedral into a neighbourhood Mary, a woman whose life could be likened to that of the urban wives and daughters of European cities. Since Mary was understood to be both ordinary in her humanity, and unique in her unparalleled purity, she was imagined both as exalted and as modest. The many medieval genres offered ways to explore that contradiction, even to revel in it. The structure of this book reflects these long-term developments: from a limited stock of tales and images in early medieval Europe, to the veritable explosion of possibilities once Mary became available and accessible in the languages that people spoke, and through the poetry, drama and imagery that was created with the aim of making Mary part of their common lives.

There were always those who thought that less elaboration, fewer external displays of devotion and subtler use of colour and texture led to truer religious experience. This book documents several phases when making Mary material and accessible seemed to be close to idolatry or blasphemy. The fifteenth century probably saw simultaneously the greatest production ever known in Europe of feasts, images, liturgies, pilgrimages, poetry and processions around Mary and the most persistent voices of criticism. These coalesced early in the following century into the Protestant onslaught on traditional religion, first that of Luther and then that of Calvin. The book ends with this remaking of Mary by Protestant ideas and practices, and the subsequent Catholic defence of Mary and all that she stood for. The images created over those centuries are still with us today in the portrayal of young motherhood, and in the *pietà*, the quintessential figure of bereavement and loss.

While Europe experienced its internal convulsions over the nature of religious authority and the place of saints – Mary above all – as mediators between believers and God, its religion was becoming a global affair. The years which saw the Lutheran remaking of Mary also saw the introduction of Mary to peoples and places where she had never formerly been known. Catholic missionaries arrived with the conquest of Central America, and the Spanish imperial enterprise brought a religion with Mary at its heart: the Creed, the plays, the miracle tales, developed in Europe, all the ways in which Mary was taught, shared and used, became part of the enterprise of Christianization and conquest. The friars who created the vernacular Mary for the Europeans were now doing so translated into Nahuatl and Tagalog. Even where there was no conquest but relations were forged through trade – as in the Portuguese

settlements in Africa and Asia – Mary was absorbed into the local cultures of converts creating new Christian arts: Mary as an African woman, or an oriental one.

Mary is the most significant feminine presence in Christian cultures, and in her met divinity and humanity. The figure of Mary is one of contradiction, a creative state that challenged poets and theologians and composers who tried to express this quality. While the earliest writings about Mary situated her as a pure young woman from a good Jewish family, Mary developed apace with Christianity itself. The Christian message, of salvation through the grace of an incarnate God, created a space for thinking about and imagining the mother who enabled that very Incarnation. Mary became the mediator between human and the divine, between the here and the hereafter, and to her were attached yearnings for assistance and consolation on earth and in heaven.

The figure of Mary thus emerged through the interlocking efforts of emperors and monks, nuns and priests and lay people in communities and families. Tracing Mary's history over sixteen centuries is not a smooth enterprise: for the earlier centuries we have few images and know little of the sound of the liturgy or the tenor of popular hymns; by the later Middle Ages and the Renaissance there are images aplenty, manuscript as well as print, carved and painted, as well as music and song in tens of dialects and languages. This book offers an historical understanding of the processes which made Mary so utterly available to humans, and utterly desirable as a friendly face of the divine core. It is impossible to imagine the history of Europe, or to understand many world cultures, without the meaning of Mary. The sheer variety of shape and colour, of form and gesture that she ultimately came to embody are reflections of human yearning, ingenuity and creativity. In Mary the feminine became the universal conduit to self-understanding, to learning about emotions and how these might be shared and expressed. By the end of the sixteenth century – and this is where the book ends – Christian cultures had devised ways of living with the magnified Mary of tradition (Catholics), or with a much slimmer Mary based on scripture alone (Protestants); and there were eastern Christianities with some of the most ancient traditions about Mary, living in the lands of Islam.

Here is a history of Mary's rise from a modest ancillary to a global icon.

PART I

From Temple Maiden to the Bearer of God: To the Year 431

I

The Earliest Glimpses of Mary

Most of the stories about Mary known to us from worship in churches or visits to museums were created in the decades following the life of Jesus. But few were told in the gospels. Those versions of Jesus' life that became the gospels of Mark, Matthew, Luke and John provide only scant detail about the life of Mary. They were writings based on the memories of Jesus' followers, which conveyed his message and gave meaning to his death. Yet Mary's life emerged almost in parallel. There was an understandable desire among Jesus' followers to discover the 'back story', to flesh out the details, to understand the provenance of the God made Flesh. There was also a need for answers to questions raised by those who might join them, and from detractors, Jews who were sceptical or scornful of the claim that Jesus was the Messiah.

The world within which the first stories about Mary evolved was a Jewish one, and it was full of difference and variation.[1] For there were Jews who believed that Jesus of Galilee was the Messiah of the House of David and those who did not; there were Jews who practised extreme asceticism according to strict disciplines of body and mind – like the communities that produced the Dead Sea Scrolls and whose rigorous lifestyle inspired John the Baptist – and there were those – the great majority – who followed rabbinical and communal precepts of Jewish life in Palestine. They all lived under Roman rule.

The adherents of Jesus were buoyed by the presence among them of those who could claim affinity to him by blood or by disciplehood. Jesus' followers, those who had appreciated him in his lifetime, passed on this commitment to their sons and daughters, as they mourned his death and remembered his powerful example. Genealogies were composed that linked Jesus with the House of David, and these were included in the gospel of Matthew. The stories about his death and

afterlife expressed the yearnings that the death of beloved leaders inspires: stories of miracles, of appearances and coded messages. To the memory of Jesus were also attached Messianic yearnings, all the more potent after the destruction of the Temple in Jerusalem in 70 CE following the Jewish revolt against Roman rule and the prohibition of Jewish settlement in Jerusalem after the Bar Kochba Revolt of 135.[2] Some Jewish-Christians settled in Trans-Jordan and Syria, others in Egypt, in terrains where long-standing Jewish communities already existed.[3] This was the terrain of conversation and polemic, where fledgling loyalties were tested by scepticism and derision. This was, therefore, a world of narrative, in which memory was cast into tales aimed to solidify the legacy of charisma.

It was a world in which 'Christianity' possessed no dominance, no striving towards doctrinal uniformity, no institutions or offices of popes, bishops and priests. If we are to understand the figure of Mary, we must try to think of this world 'rustling with the presence of many divine beings',[4] an urbanized Roman commonwealth where temples stood alongside synagogues, a Mediterranean world of extraordinary cultural variety that lived under the vigilant eye of local imperial officialdom. Each person in Alexandria, Jerusalem or Ephesus entertained an ethnic predisposition towards a religion but also owed obedience and respect to the emperor.[5] Jesus' followers found themselves at odds with some aspects of public culture of the late ancient city with its sacrifices, worship of ancestors and the cult of the emperor. As early Christian worship was under scrutiny, and its adherents were occasionally persecuted, Christian life took place in homes and even in synagogues.

MARY IN THE GOSPELS

Four accounts of Jesus' life and ministry were written by the end of the first century CE: the three synoptic Gospels of Mark, Luke, Matthew, and the Gospel of John, which differs in structure and style. These were records of memories about Jesus, cherished by his followers. Their interests lie above all in Jesus' dual 'sonship': of David and of God, historic and eternal. None of the gospels offers the story of Mary's early life and provenance; their aim was rather to introduce Jesus, and so Mary enters the frame as a maiden about to receive the Annunciation.

4

Mark's Gospel ($c.65-80$ CE), which was probably composed first, provides no narrative of Jesus' birth, nor does the later gospel of John ($c.90-100$ CE). In the telling of Jesus' coming the circumstances of his birth were all-important, since lineage and affinity were fundamental attributes of a Messiah King. Yet Mark and John introduce Jesus as an adult and steer away from describing his early life. Mary appears only in passing in Mark 6:3: 'Is not this the carpenter, the son of Mary, the brother of James, and Joses, and of Juda, and Simon? and are not his sisters here with us?'[6]

The gospels of Luke and Matthew ($c.80-100$) also support the belief in Jesus as Messiah of the House of David.[7] Followers of Jesus probably provided Matthew's detailed genealogy, which linked Jesus, through Joseph, to the House of David. Luke had access to remarkable sources about the Annunciation and Birth, and the link between Jesus and John the Baptist. He offers these in a language reminiscent of Hebrew poetry. Both Matthew and Luke tend to allegorize Jesus' life, seeing each episode as a fulfilment of a prophecy. In this manner, giving Jesus the deepest possible roots in Jewish prophecy, they aimed to convince other Jews that God was acting through Jesus.[8] The most likely provenance for the idea that Jesus was conceived miraculously by God's spirit is in the circles of Jewish Christians and/or mixed Gentile and Jewish Christians who preferred to articulate the faith in Jesus in the idioms of the Jewish tradition.[9]

The story of the man whose possible divinity was the subject of excited rumour and speculation in the generations that followed his death called for a special kind of beginning. This is where Luke's gospel is so important. Luke chapters 1 and 2 describe Jesus' birth and infancy in keeping with the classical models of biographical writing. It begins in the time of King Herod, with the Annunciation to Zechariah the Priest and his wife Elizabeth – an elderly and childless couple – that a son would be born to them whose name would be John (Luke 1:5-22). Theirs was a son with a mission: 'He shall unite the hearts of all, the fathers with the children, and teach the disobedient the wisdom that makes men just' (Luke 1:17). Elizabeth conceived, aware that God had touched her.

Next Luke tells of another Annunciation, just six months later, in the city of Nazareth, to a virgin named Mary. Luke 1:18 reports that she had been betrothed to Joseph: 'Now the generation of Christ was in this wise. When as his mother Mary was espoused to Joseph, before they

came together, she was found with child, of the Holy Ghost.' Next the Angel Gabriel pronounced the famous words to her: 'Hail, full of grace, the Lord is with thee: blessed art thou among women' (Luke 1:28). Mary was perplexed, so the angel said: 'Fear not, Mary, for thou hast found grace with God. Behold thou shalt conceive in thy womb, and shalt bring forth a son; and thou shalt call his name Jesus' (Luke 1:30–31). Mary protested: 'How shall this be done, because I know not a man?' (Luke 1:34), and in the next verse the angel reassured her that the Holy Spirit would 'come upon her' and 'overshadow' her. When he discovered Mary was pregnant, Joseph wished to send her away, but an angel appeared to him in a dream, and so Joseph took Mary to his house (Matthew 1:19–21). In so many ways Mary's story re-enacted the tale of Sarah, Abraham's aged and barren wife, and the message brought to her by Angels, as told in Genesis 17:17. The testimonies that informed the writers of the gospels surrounded Mary's pregnancy with miracles and wonder.[10]

The consequences of this pair of Annunciations were realized dramatically through the coming together of two women – young and old, Galilean and Judean – Mary and her cousin Elizabeth. At the Annunciation Mary was informed that Elizabeth was already six months pregnant (Luke 1:36), and so she went south to Judea, to visit her kinswoman. The Visitation offers a moment of female friendship and kinship: Elizabeth praises her guest, welcomes her, and feels her own unborn son move. She proclaims loudly: 'Blessed art thou among women, and blessed is the fruit of thy womb. And whence is this to me, that the mother of my Lord should come to me? Blessed art thou amongst women, and blessed is the fruit of thy womb. How have I deserved to be thus visited by the mother of my Lord?' (Luke 1:42–3). This shared experience of song tied the women in friendship, wonder and praise with Mary saying: 'My soul doth magnify the Lord. And my spirit hath rejoiced in God my Saviour' (Luke 1:46–7).

Here the good news of the arrival of a child is accompanied, as it was with Hannah and the birth of Samuel (1 Samuel 2:1–10), by spontaneous singing.[11] The song sounds like a psalm, an intimate appeal to God, an offering of thanks for his remembrance of his 'servant'.[12] Which of the women sang the words was to become a matter for dispute. The Egyptian theologian Origen (c.185–c.254) believed these to have been Mary's words, though he acknowledged that 'in some manuscripts the words

are prophesied by Elizabeth'; indeed the earliest Latin manuscripts of Luke's gospel attribute the Magnificat – as it came to be known – to her.[13] Mary's words of praise, so reminiscent of the sound of the psalms, may have seemed familiar and attractive to Jews who pondered the claims of Jesus' followers.

Mark tells of the arrival of Jesus and his followers at Nazareth, his home town, where he taught at the synagogue and inspired wonder and dismay. When his family appears, the expectation that Jesus would greet his family is dashed. Rather, Jesus teaches the meaning of true disciplehood: the sacrifice of family and kinship:

There came then his brethren and his mother, and, standing without, sent unto him, calling him.

And the multitude sat about him, and they said unto him, Behold, thy mother and thy brethren without seek for thee.

And he answered them, saying, Who is my mother, or my brethren?

And he looked round about on them which sat about him, and said, Behold my mother and my brethren!

For whosoever shall do the will of God, the same is my brother, and my sister, and mother. (Mark 6:31–34)

Mary is not a constant companion to her son in these gospel narratives, though in later centuries it became common to present her among the apostles.

Mary appears rarely in the gospel accounts of Jesus' ministry. John alone mentions Mary's presence at the Marriage at Cana in Galilee (John 2:3–5), and records an exchange between them:

And the wine failing, the mother of Jesus saith to him: They have no wine. And Jesus saith to her: Woman, *what is that to me* and to thee? my hour is not yet come. His mother saith to the waiters: Whatsoever he shall say to you, do ye.

Mary appears at Jesus' first public miracle and is made aware of the fulfilment of prophecy in her son's public work.

Luke, Mark and Matthew tell even the climax of Christ's life, the Crucifixion, without mention of Mary. Only John records Mary's presence at the foot of the cross:

Now there stood by the cross of Jesus, his mother, and his mother's sister, Mary of Cleophas, and Mary Magdalen. When Jesus therefore had seen his mother

and the disciple standing whom he loved, he saith to his mother: Woman, behold thy son. After that, he saith to the disciple: Behold thy mother. And from that hour, the disciple took her to his own. (John 19:25–7)

Mary is presented here as witness and as companion to John, Jesus' favoured disciple.

So, as we see, Mary was situated most prominently within the narratives of Jesus' birth and lineage. Even the genealogy offered by Matthew's gospel is a purely paternal one, and it leads through the generations of fathers to Joseph.[14] Nor is Mary more prominent in the Acts of the Apostles, where she appears only once, in the description of Jesus' followers in prayer after his death. The apostle Paul never discussed Mary in his letters to emergent communities of Christ-followers in the eastern Mediterranean; he referred only once to the fact that Jesus had been born of a woman: 'But when the fulness of the time was come, God sent his Son, made of a woman, made under the law' (Galatians 4:4).[15]

The Jewish world from which Jesus and his first followers had emerged was not accustomed to elaborating complex life-stories for gods, such as those cherished by Greek and Roman writers.[16] But it did have codes for personal piety and moral improvement to which Jesus was seen to adhere. Among the early followers of Christ who emerged from this Jewish world – as yet rightly called Jewish-Christians – the earliest stories about Jesus' mother and his infancy emerged.

The gospels paid scant attention to Mary, but acknowledged her role as recipient of the Annunciation with which the drama of Jesus' life on earth began. Those who cherished Jesus sought to explore his lineage more deeply in support of the emergent claim of his divinity. They were inexorably drawn to the figure of his mother – Mary.

MARY IN THE 'APOCRYPHA'

Among the disciples and followers of Jesus – in Palestine, in Syria, in Egypt – a memory was nurtured not only of an exemplary teacher, but also of a man born of miraculous conception who died, was resurrected and ascended to heaven. This was, however, not the only view of Jesus' life: a robust tradition called Docetism – from the Greek word *dokein*,

to seem – preferred to believe that he had not died on the cross, but rather that he had escaped death by changing places with another person. The rich tradition of exegesis around the story of the Sacrifice of Isaac as well as the Hellenistic myths regarding 'doubles', who suffer in the place of gods, supported a version that imagined Jesus next to or above the cross, laughing as he outwitted his enemies.[17]

The precise formula whereby Jesus was both God and Man was far from established among the followers of Jesus. The tension over such formulations was heightened after the destruction of the Jewish Temple, when apocalyptic anxiety pervaded everyone's lives. Hectic work of persuasion was under way, and it drew from the resources of the Jewish Bible and the tradition of exegesis and accounts of the life of Jesus – the gospels. The deeds of the disciples were collected in the Acts, and this original group included Mary, as in Acts 1:14: 'All these were persevering with one mind in prayer with the women, and Mary the mother of Jesus, and with his brethren'.[18]

The Jewish Bible was full of prophecies which were cherished by the Jewish followers of Jesus. Most important for the figure of Mary was the prophecy of Isaiah 7:14: 'Therefore the Lord himself shall give you a sign; Behold, a virgin shall conceive, and bear a son, and shall call his name Immanuel'. Hence forward attention was directed at the figure of his mother: the Hebrew was *alma*, maiden, but the Greek Septuagint translation, used by Christian writers, was *parthenos*, virgin.

Within this world of Jewish-Christian stories about Mary's early life were composed and they served to 'fill in the gaps in the gospels' for the reassurance of those who followed Jesus and those who might join them.[19] The issue of Jesus' conception and birth possessed some polemical weight. Intense arguments took place in the intimacy of neighbourhood and kinship in Galilee, as well as in cities with large Jewish and Jewish-Christian populations such as Alexandria, Rome and Antioch.

The desire to know more about Mary was fulfilled by the mid-second century. The *Protogospel of James* is a title that was given in the sixteenth century to an account of Mary's life that was probably composed in Syria or Egypt by 150 CE.[20] By the sixth century it was officially deemed to be 'apocryphal' – hidden, not recognized as part of the canonized tradition of scripture. The author was skilled in the Alexandrine style of layered writing and acquainted with Jewish life, though he does not

seem to be a Jewish writer. The story was widely known among early Christians.[21]

The *Protogospel of James* provided Mary with an early life fitting for the mother of a God. It told that Mary came from a very good home; her father, Joachim, was a rich man, noted in the lists of the tribes of Israel.[22] Joachim was renowned for the generous offerings he made to the Temple. Yet he and his wife, Anne, had no children and suffered the shame associated with the failure to make a family. The *Protogospel of James* movingly describes Anne suffering ridicule because she was childless, even by her servant woman Juthine. Joachim and Anne received an annunciation each: like Abraham and Sarah, like Zachary and Elizabeth, they too were to become parents – unexpectedly and wonderfully – at a ripe old age. Theirs would be an unusual daughter: 'You will conceive and give birth, and your child will be spoken of in all the world'. Drawing on the birth narratives of John and Jesus, Mary's birth was announced, caused delight, and augured great things. When Anne was told that she had delivered a girl she responded, like Mary in Luke: 'My Soul is magnified this day'.[23]

Mary was no ordinary child, and the *Protogospel of James* tracks every stage of her precocious development. Her life was watched closely by parents who had promised to offer her to the Temple at the age of three. In her infancy they kept Mary pure and safe at home, in a household where a rigorous regime prevailed. Mary was fed by Anne only after her post-partum purification; she was not allowed to make contact with uncovered ground.[24] The earliest texts about Mary's life are steeped in Midrashic parables – a Jewish literary tradition which elaborated biblical tales in order to elicit from them deeper meaning – and interspersed with mundane observations from the life of virtuous and respectable Jews in Galilee and Judea in Herod's time.[25]

The *Protogospel of James* follows Mary's development stage by stage: at the age of three she was indeed offered to the Temple, and this journey was her first foray into the world. She was delightful and gracious and expressed her elevated spirit in a dance on the temple steps. She lived there quietly until the onset of puberty, when as a nubile woman she could no longer dwell in that holy space. One day, while Mary was working, the high priest Zechariah, guided by prayer, received a message about her future: she was to be handed over to the elderly Joseph, a widower with young children. According to later traditions Zechariah's

vision took place on Yom Kippur, the Jewish festival on which the priest entered into the Holy of Holies.[26] The life of Mary was told in the *Protogospel of James* as a narrative of Jewish cultic excellence refracted through the prism of ascetic values, for there was no institution of celibacy and virginity in the Jewish mainstream. Yet the author of Mary's life chose to endow her with a unique order of physical purity.

Speculation on Mary prompted the author of the *Protogospel of James* to provide her with a lineage and family life. But the figure of Joseph raised questions too. Matthew and Luke provided genealogies of Jesus that led up to or from Joseph but the other gospels mention him very little. The *Protogospel* describes the choice of Joseph among suitable suitors for Mary's hand as a miraculous sign: like Aharon whose rod alone bloomed among those of the Egyptian magi, so Joseph's rod produced a dove, and this marked him for his destiny:

Joseph received the last rod, and behold, a dove came out of the rod and flew to Joseph's head. And the priest said to Joseph: 'Joseph, to you has fallen the good fortune to receive the virgin of the Lord; take her under your care'.[27]

Mary's life as a young woman then moved into a phase of feminine domesticity. Since Joseph, like Mary's father, was a prosperous man, he was often away on business. Mary was summoned by the priestly council to join a group of eight pure maidens, 'pure virgins of the tribe of David'. She and seven others were charged with the task of weaving 'gold, amiant [a gemstone], the linen, the silk, the hyacinth-blue, the scarlet and the purple',[28] and Mary was chosen for the honour of weaving the scarlet and purple. The veil was a sign of holiness, since it was the garment worn by God's angel, who dwelt in the Temple's holy core.[29] The practice of weaving the veil is mentioned in Jewish sources of the period: a commentary on Jewish law describes the making of the veil (*parochet*) by eighty-two maidens.[30] Mary's association with this work suggests she was still of the highest order of purity.[31]

What of Mary's spouse, Joseph? Traditions about Joseph appear later and were combined in *The History of Joseph the Carpenter*, a Greek text of *c*.400, known to us from two later Coptic versions.[32] Joseph emerges in it as a Jewish just man: he was blessed with many children, four sons and two daughters. He worked hard: 'My father Joseph, the blessed old man, worked in carpentry, and we lived by the labour of his hands, and he never ate bread for free'.[33] The *History* agrees with the

Protogospel of James in claiming that Mary was living under Joseph's care 'until the moment of marriage' (4, 3). In his home Mary cared for his youngest son, a sad little orphan. When she became pregnant, Joseph reacted with alarm, a moment he recalled on his deathbed: 'I had never heard of a woman who had conceived without a man, or of a Virgin giving birth while retaining the seal of her Virginity' (17, 8). The *History* offers some particularly touching glimpses of family life. Joseph died in terrible pain, a latter-day Job forced to rue the day of his birth and even curse the body that had nurtured him:

Woe to me today. Woe to the day that my mother bore me into the world! Woe to the maternal body at which I received the seeds of life; woe to the breast from which I sucked milk! Woe to the knees on which I sat! Woe to the hands that gathered me until I grew up to become a sinner![34]

After Joseph's death Jesus led the mourning rituals, as Jewish sons habitually do, and spoke the eulogy: 'That the hair of your head may not fade, the hair which I so often held in my hands'. Joseph's death was not the end; Jesus directed the angels to lay a luminous cloak on his father, for his death was but an invitation to a celestial feast.[35]

The early stories of Mary and Joseph are creations steeped in Jewish family life. They were meant to speak to Jews with the intention of drawing them towards the emergent claim of Jesus' divinity. But in the second and third centuries many more Christians were gentile converts. Arguments and narratives that told of Jesus' life and divinity were developing outside the spheres steeped in the Jewish bible, Midrash, apocalypse and law. Writings by Christian thinkers appealed to pagans in cities of the two great civilizations – the Roman and Persian empires. They proclaimed in Jesus a new order of triumph over sin through control of the body and disciplined virtue.

POLEMIC

The early stories about Mary provided narrative answers to questions that must have vexed each person who retold the story of Jesus – believers and potential believers alike. Jesus' followers accepted that he had not only died a redeeming death on the cross, but that he had risen from his tomb on the third day. If this were true, if Jesus was more than

he had ever claimed to be in his lifetime – if he were a god – then a number of powerful truths followed: every aspect of his life had to agree with the claim of divinity. Jesus' life had to be worthy of his death and of his emergent divinity. None of these assertions about Jesus' nature could be made without reference to the body that had borne him, the person who had nurtured him, Mary.

The claim that Jesus was the Messiah – and gentiles probably understood the Messiah as something like a god – created a need for a suitable mother. Yet claims of miraculous birth also drew attack and derision, especially from Jews. The form of address to Jesus captured in Mark 6:3, 'the carpenter, the son of Mary', may have been a statement of fact, but it could also have been used as a slur. The belief that Jesus had an earthly father is revealed in the *Gospel of Philip*, which argues for a dual parentage: Mary could not have conceived from the Holy Spirit, which in the Syriac tradition was imagined as feminine, so there had to be a human, male father – Joseph.[36] The difficulty in making sense of a god made flesh continued to trouble the followers of Jesus. It is apparent in what came to be called the Docetic view of Jesus' end – that God did not really suffer, that he only seemed to have had a vulnerable body.

These preoccupations were taken up by gentile converts throughout the Empire, men of Greek education, who were attracted to a philosophical understanding of Christianity. Aristides of Antioch, a philosopher who lived during the reign of Hadrian (early second century CE), described Christianity sympathetically; he was impressed by the purity of life and bodily discipline exhibited by Christian men and women, by their simplicity in relation to others.[37] Men like Justin Martyr of Antioch (c.100–165) claimed that Christian truth was outside time, that it was a 'primordial' truth. Justin appreciated the truth-value of Old Testament prophecies, and in his *Dialogue with Trypho*, an educated Jewish interlocutor, offered a Christian reading of the Septuagint, the Greek translation of the Jewish Bible. He deployed classical learning with casual familiarity: some of the myths of pagan gods were, he claimed, far less credible than the claims about Jesus' birth.[38] Knowledge of Mary was peripheral to this type of engagement with Christianity, and she was rarely mentioned in these philosophical debates, though Justin was a committed enough Christian to assert Mary's purity and virginity against all comers.[39] Writing in Carthage,

Tertullian ($c.155–230$) contrasted Jesus' parentage to that of the pagan gods: here was no incest or adultery, but birth from a virgin. He saw a pleasing symmetry between the word (of the serpent) that had led to Eve's fall and the divine word that impregnated Mary.[40]

Some time between 246 and 248 the Christian theologian Origen ($c.185–c.254$) wrote *Contra Celsum*, a polemical defence against the work of the pagan Celsus, which had appeared around 178 and no longer exists in itself. By doing so he preserved a whole array of early objections to emergent Christian beliefs – some attributed by Celsus to Jews, others to pagans – and rebutted them one by one. The following view had been placed by Celsus in the mouth of a Jew:

Jesus had invented his birth from a virgin ... He had been born in a certain Jewish village, of a poor woman of the country, who gained her subsistence by spinning, and who was turned out of doors by her husband, a carpenter by trade, because she was convicted of adultery.

He continued:

When she was pregnant she was turned out of the doors of the carpenter to whom she had been betrothed, as having been guilty of adultery, and that she bore a child to a certain soldier named Pantera ...[41]

Celsus' Jew deployed arguments against virgin birth characteristic of the Jewish milieu; such comments were later evident in the Talmud.[42] But he was a Jew sufficiently familiar with classical culture to compare Jesus' birth to that of the heroes born by the goddesses Danae, Auge or Antiope. The Jew also voices the sort of objections that the *Protogospel of James* had aimed to counter: that Mary was of too humble an origin, lacking in family or possessions, to be the mother of a god.[43]

Pioneering methods were developed by Christians for systematic defence of the claims about Jesus. Inasmuch as polemic with Jews was central to the emergence of Christianity, exegesis – interpretation and commentary – of the Jewish Bible, was central to such work too. Around 240–44 Origen offered a commentary on the Song of Songs and associated homilies, a work he wrote in Athens and Caesarea in Palestine, and which survives in a Latin translation.[44] Origen's approach was quite different from that of the writer of the *Protogospel of James* or the later *History of Joseph the Carpenter*. He dealt only briefly with the circumstances of Jesus' birth, with his family and social milieu. Rather,

14

Origen supported the claims of Jesus' followers by grounding them securely within the text dearest to the Jews: the Jewish Bible. Christian truth was henceforward to be revealed through the inexorable reinterpretation of Jewish scripture, with the tools of exegesis developed by and for the use of Jews, combined with insights gained from a classical Greek education.[45]

Origen immersed himself in the Jewish traditions of commentary on the Song of Songs and appropriated them in support of a new Christian world-view. A Jewish allegorical interpretation of the Song of Songs had developed in the late first century CE that told of the love between Shekhinah (divine presence) and the community of Israel.[46] Origen embraced this scheme but replaced the Christian church as the chosen bride. So powerfully did he attach Christian claims to the Song of Songs that contemporary Jews began to shy away from dealing with the book since it seemed to offer so much solace and inspiration to the followers of Jesus.

The Song of Songs also offered Origen occasion to discuss Mary, though this was subordinated to the task of manifesting Jesus' uniqueness. When expounding the verse 'For thy breasts are better than wine' (Song of Songs 1:1), Origen tells the story of Joseph and Mary searching for their son, only to find him holding forth in the Temple, giving astonishing answers to every question put to him (Luke 2:43–50).[47] Origen suggests that Jesus is to be seen mingling in his breast ancient knowledge with things new. Origen also offered a gloss to the oldest versions of Jesus's life – the gospels. In his Homily on Luke 1:35 he interpreted the message to Mary 'The Holy Spirit shall come upon thee, and the power of the Most High shall overshadow thee' to mean not only birth through the overshadowing (or in-dwelling) of the Holy Spirit in Mary, but also the birth of Jesus in every worthy believer: 'and when you have been made worthy of the shadow, His body from which the shadow is born, will in a manner of speaking come to you'.[48] Mary is also mentioned in passing in Origen's Second Homily on 'For winter is now past, the rain is over and gone' (Song of Songs 2:11). These were seen as Jesus' words, and their meaning as:

In rising from the dead I have curbed the storm and restored calm. And because according to the dispensation of the flesh I grew from a Virgin . . . the flowers have appeared on the earth, the time of spring has come.[49]

At this early stage, when there was so little written about Mary, the Song of Songs commentary offers precious glimpses of the ideas she could inspire.[50]

Beyond the narratives about her birth and early life, Mary drew little attention from the formative thinkers engaged in imagining and writing a Christian universe, a world that could live and believe precepts associated with Jesus. There was clearly a polemical context to which Justin and Origen attest and within which virgin birth 'invited pagan slanders'. There was also an overarching frame of contestation with Jews and Jewish lore over a wide array of issues in areas like Rome, Asia Minor and the Galilee, where these communities met and collided.[51] As Christian beliefs spread throughout the eastern Mediterranean regional styles, grounded in linguistic and literary traditions, affected the understanding of Mary in Syriac, Coptic, Greek, Armenian and Latin. Mary was explored by local faith and language communities, within the scattered and tentative institutions that supported the new religion. Cultic images were scarce in this religious culture born out of Judaism; yet there was always the Bible and its poetry, and hence liturgy aplenty.[52]

The early centuries of Christianity – lived in city communities, worshipped in homes, and the subject of the intellectual work of few committed scholars – possessed a version of the early life of Mary, mother of Jesus, to place alongside the mention of her in the gospels. Talking of Mary was occasionally heated in places that saw the growth of Christian communities out of Jewish ones. The nature of the saving God was alluring and perplexing, and it was his nature and the implications of his example that drew most hope and speculation.

2

Mary in a Christian Empire

The efforts towards understanding and describing the mother of Jesus formed part of the long-term cultural transformation inspired by belief in a god made flesh. This process received significant impetus from the co-emperors Constantine and Licinius, who recognized Christianity as a lawful religion in 313 CE. The essentially local nature of the communities that worshipped Jesus and reverenced his mother was increasingly affected over the fourth century by the will of the sovereign and the power of the Roman state. Constantine built a new capital on the shores of the Bosphorus, a capital for the Greek-speaking, eastern part of the Empire that was in his charge – the Christian city Constantinople.[1] In 380 the Emperor Theodosius made Christianity into the Empire's official religion. Imperial law, officialdom and politics now required a clear sense of what a Christian was, and of the policies aimed at promoting this now imperial cult.

The pagan emperor had been sometimes worshipped as a god, and his cult pervaded most aspects of life.[2] Once Christian emperors linked their prestige and authority to the Christian cult, it was scrutinized and reordered so as to be fitting of imperial dignity. Christianity offered ideas which transcended the local, and which were as ambitiously universal as the Empire itself. Great gatherings were assembled for discussion and legislation on imperial Christianity, and the emperor presided over them as affairs of state. Christian emperors sought to develop an official version of orthodoxy based on the gospels, and on the ideas of the formative thinkers of early Christianity – the Fathers of the Church – some of whom wrote in Greek and others in Latin. Christianity had come to the end of a stage of apologetics, of incessant justification of its beliefs in polemic with other, more ancient religions. It was entering a stage of imagining itself as a political force, a pervasive and hegemonic

17

religion. The complex heritage of how to represent a god made flesh and his mother entered a new stage of intense discussion too. The official aim was to offer clear formulations and rules for public worship, and some for private life.

At the centre of debate was the distinctive Christian understanding of the incarnation of God. The unique mingling of divinity and humanity was variously understood by individual thinkers. As the Empire became a Christian polity intent on defining and promoting Christian orthodoxy, this diversity of regional traditions – Syria, Egypt, Persia – these niches of sentiment and practice were bound to clash. Most prominently, Arianism – developed in the fourth century by Arius of Antioch ($c.250$– 336) – distinguished between the god and the son whom he created. It argued for Jesus' dependence on God the Father.[3]

The imperial church – and the bishop of Constantinople played an increasingly hegemonic role over the ancient sees of Alexandria, Jerusalem, Rome and Antioch – was concerned not only with promoting true religion, but with identifying, and even persecuting, those deemed to be heretics. The central subject for discussion, the most vital and testing area of religion, was the nature of Christ: the relation within him of divinity and humanity and his place within the Trinity, as its second and equal person – the Son. Any discussion of Christ's nature was bound to involve the circumstances of his birth. Inclusion of Mary formed part of these efforts to define and understand God for a Christian Empire.

Constantine created a template for discussion of religious affairs in the Christian Empire. He summoned a gathering of bishops and prominent scholars, alongside his own officials, at Nicaea on the Bosphorus in 325, and he presided over the proceedings. The most urgent matter for discussion was to settle imperial orthodoxy against the teachings of Arius. At Nicaea a statement of faith was formulated which was to bind all Christians in Constantine's Empire, and it insisted on the reality of Christ's divinity alongside his real incarnate nature. This emphatic statement included an important mention of Christ's mother, and it secured a space for Mary in all future debates on Christ's nature. Mary, as Mother of God, reached all Christian communities through the appendix to the letter sent to all bishops in the aftermath of the Council:

For He is the express image, not of the will or of anything else, but of His Father's very substance. This Son, the divine Logos, having been born in flesh from Mary

the Mother of God and made incarnate, having suffered and died, rose again from the dead and was taken up into heaven, and sits on the right hand of the Majesty most high, and will come to judge the living and the dead.[4]

The Council insisted in equal measure that Christ was of the substance of God the Father and born of Mary. The formulation 'Mother of God', which was to become so controversial in the following century, was at this moment introduced without elaborate explanation. The Syriac bishop of Edessa, Aithallah, reported the Council's decisions to Christians in Persia. His letter, which survives in Armenian translation, conveyed the gist of the new creed: 'That Christ was God of God and Man born of a woman, and that just as he dwelt in Mary's pure womb, so he created every foetus in every womb, and inspired each with a little spirit.'[5] The form of the words 'born in flesh of Mary' was like a seed to be sown and to grow in each of the fertile terrains in which Mary was known already.

The Council at Nicaea sought to reach decisions that would be as inclusive as possible of prevalent views and sensibilities. The Empire had always been a fairly flexible political arrangement, which allowed peoples to worship their ancestral gods in their traditional styles. The statement of faith – the Creed – formulated at Nicaea insisted on the dual nature of Christ, but it also left open and relaxed the details of that union of the human and the divine. These questions were to emerge in the heated discussions on Christ's nature in the following century.[6]

The figure of Mary was now bound up with the tastes and interests of the powerful imperial establishment. The terrain that had been her home – the Holy Land – was explored with energy and conviction. Emperor Constantine's mother, Helena – a concubine who had risen to imperial honour – was a much more committed and energetic Christian than her son. She set out to Palestine with a mission: to make the sites which had hitherto lain ruined and neglected into suitable places for Christian worship. The Holy Land had been devastated though in it Jewish communities still flourished, especially in the Galilee.[7] The future martyr Pionius of Smyrna (d.250) described his travel through Palestine as a passage through a country 'scorched by fire, deprived of all produce and water'. All this was caused by divine anger for 'the sins committed by its inhabitants.'[8] With Helena a new age was inaugurated, for she combined pious travel with public works: she visited the Holy Land in

order to find, some 300 years after the events, the sites of Jesus' life and death and to bestow upon them imperial blessing.

Palestine was a very Jewish land: settlements bore Hebrew names and were still inhabited by Jewish populations. Sites sacred to Christians were known and remembered, but they blended into rather than dominated the landscape. Under imperial patronage the stories and memories, the markers of the life of Jesus and his followers, were given official embellishment. The sites most revered were the Holy Sepulchre, the caves in Bethlehem and the Mount of Olives, and Helena had basilicas – vast churches – built on each site.[9] Her impulse sought to relate scripture to location, place-names to narrative; and so the traditions of the Holy Land, hitherto dear just to Christians and maintained by them, received tangible form for all to see. Jerome put it aptly: 'the whole mystery of our faith is native to this country.' The challenge was now to transform a Jewish country, landscape and topography into a beloved terrain that in the fullness of time would reverberate exclusively with Christian echoes and memories. This was a long process, fully achieved only by the fifth century. The Iberian pilgrim Egeria, the earliest Christian writer known to travel to the Holy Land, who visited it in the 380s, knew of no churches or monuments related to Mary's life.[10]

Traditions about Mary's life were meanwhile being explored by all kinds of visitors to the Holy Land who nurtured differing attitudes to Jesus and his message. Athanasius, Patriarch of Alexandria (c.296–373), a promoter of female virginity, records the experience that his female charges recounted after a visit to the Holy Land. The virgins were particularly touched by the fact that they had stepped where Mary and the apostles had lived and in the settings where Jesus had moved.[11] Similarly, when the Roman matron Paula (347–404) visited Bethlehem c.385 she saw 'with the eye of faith' the child Jesus alongside Mary, Joseph and the shepherds.[12] Gregory, bishop of Nyssa in Asia Minor (c.335–94), described in a letter his meeting in Jerusalem in 381 with Christians who lived in the expectation of rebuilding the Temple, and who called Mary 'mother of man'.[13]

Cyril, patriarch of Jerusalem (c.315–86), attempted to offer greater unity and cohesion to the small Christian community there by writing works for new Christians, texts based upon the Jewish Bible. Though Mary was important as the guarantee of Christ's humanity, she was not

unlike other familiar figures. After all, if Sarah, an old, sterile and weak woman, could give birth to a son, surely a maiden could conceive. If Adam and Eve could be created out of nothing, then surely birth from a virgin was not so hard to imagine.[14] Some writers aimed to transform the land and its people by incorporating with care the Jewish biblical heritage and its traces in the landscape, others chose to excise Jewish memory in favour of a newly conceived bond between gospel and land. Mary allowed a combination of old – she was after all a Hebrew woman – and new to take place. She was the mother of a Christian god.

It is hard to know how widely Mary's fame and interest had spread from the eastern Mediterranean and throughout the Mediterranean world. The written sources and the relatively few images surviving from the fourth century tend to reflect the interests of highly committed groups of well-off and educated people who possessed the leisure to indulge in study and to experiment with religious expression. Among more modest Christians it is probably true that the fame of Christian martyrs was the core of Christian identity. Martyrs' fates were described in moving and sensational detail in accounts such as the *Passion of Perpetua and Felicitas*, or the life of an early saint like St Thecla (fl.180), or the extraordinary trials of penitent women, the Harlots of the Desert – St Mary of Egypt and Thais. All of these narratives eclipsed interest in Mary's life.[15]

Many of the earliest ideas about Mary must have been submerged by the emergent official orthodoxy, and have thus left little trace in the records. Some of the range of possible Christian ideas and practices is conveyed in vivacious invective by Epiphanius, bishop of Salamis in Cyprus (310/20–403). His work the *Panarion* – the *Medicine Chest* – aimed at documenting and refuting unorthodox beliefs. It records some eighty Christian 'heresies', large and small. Epiphanius was particularly well informed about the situation in Palestine and Egypt, since he was born in Beit-Govrin (Eleutheropolis) and probably studied in Alexandria. Most of the groups he describes were defined by their understanding of the nature of Christ, a belief which often led to ideas about Mary too. The Nazoraeans were Jews who believed in Christ, born of the Virgin Mary, engendered by the Holy Spirit, but who also lived as Jews. They were thus shunned by both communities.[16] The Cerdonians followed a Syrian scholar called Cerdo who moved to Rome where he taught that 'Christ was not born of Mary, and has not appeared in the

flesh. As he exists in appearance he has also been manifest in appearance, and done all that he has done in appearance.'[17] The Antidicomarians, an Arabian sect, acted

as though they had a grudge against the Virgin and desired to cheapen her reputation, certain Antidicomarians, who are inspired by envy or error . . . have dared to say that St. Mary had relations with a man after Christ's birth, I mean with Joseph himself.[18]

Even more interesting were the Collorydians, who had moved from Thrace to the margins of the Empire, in Arabia, where they followed customs that 'appear laughable and ridiculous to sensible folk'. They practised a cult of Mary:

For certain women decorate a barber's chair or a square seat, spread a cloth on it, set out bread and offer it in Mary's name on a certain day of the year, and all partake of the bread.[19]

Epiphanius was scandalized by the notion that a woman might be worshipped: 'The speculation is entirely feminine, and the malady of the deluded Eve all over again?'[20] No other virgin, such as Elijah and John, nor even the martyr Thecla, was worshipped as Mary was by the Collorydians 'because of the incarnation she was granted to receive'. Epiphanius found the sect puzzling and distasteful, and his sentiments are expressed in a familiar misogynistic tone.

As Christianity spread so did the variety of beliefs that it engendered, not least around Mary, the human mother of God. The voice of Epiphanius was that of a churchman intent on establishing discipline in orthodoxy. Yet even his disapproving sketches of beliefs and practices convey something of the regional variations and personal visions that were developing around Mary.

MARY AND THE LIFE OF VIRGINITY

Having traced the evolution of official attitudes to Mary in the polemical literature of the church and in the formal pronouncements of imperial orthodoxy, let us consider the ways in which Christians incorporated Mary into their lives. Even before Christianity became a tolerated religion Christians were a familiar, if small, group in most cities and

towns of the Roman Empire. Christian communities attracted adherents from the lowest to the highest: prostitutes, the disabled, the sick and the deracinated, alongside some Roman matrons of wealth and status; though most comers were free people, many freed slaves and people of lower social status became Christians too.[21] In North Africa and Syria traditions of Christian virginity, a lifestyle that gained respect from non-Christians had developed amongst men and women. Mary was invoked in writings for such virgins: by Tertullian, Athanasius and by the Cappadocian Fathers of Asia Minor, who dwelt in particular on the nature of Christ's birth of a virgin.[22] Evagrius Ponticus (345–99) shaped monastic living for men and women; his *Exhortation to a Virgin* envisaged communal life in which Mary was loved, as were sisters and servants.[23]

A vast literature in Syriac and in Greek described the trials and the future rewards of the life of virginity. There was a tradition of stoic thought and practice, which elevated the virtues of control of the body and sexual abstention and which created a comfortable environment for the reception of Christian virginity.[24] Mary was the symbol of bodily purity and was developed into a model and companion to those, especially women, who chose a life of Christian striving.

In all parts of Egypt – in the desert, in lively Nile villages and in households of the rich cities of the Delta – experiments in Christian living were many and diverse. The Egyptian desert was the birthplace of institutions of personal and collective renunciation for men. The Egyptian city was made up of closely knit families, ordered patriarchal units of work and devotions. Women were encouraged to experiment with the possibilities of renunciation within accepted boundaries. Athanasius, patriarch of Alexandria (296–373), a leading voice in the fight against Arianism, offered guidance as well as warnings to such women. He recommended Mary as a sufficient model for emulation, and warned against recourse to male teachers. In the *Letter to Virgins*, aimed at the women of Alexandria and its region, he presented a powerful image of Mary. She was not only the epitome of loving motherhood, but also of renunciation, ascetic living and virginal purity:

Thus, Mary was a holy virgin, having the disposition of her soul balanced and doubly increasing. For she desired good works, doing what is proper, having true thoughts in faith and purity. And she did not desire to be seen by people; rather,

she prayed that God be her judge. Nor did she have an eagerness to leave her house, nor was she at all acquainted with the streets; rather, she remained in her house being calm, imitating the fly in honey ... And she did not permit anyone near her body unless it was covered, and she controlled her anger and extinguished the wrath in her inmost thoughts.[25]

In Athanasius' words Mary became a model for the urban ascetic, withdrawn yet dwelling within a family home, hard at work, meek and free of trouble. He used the images of city experience, without recourse to the stories of the apocrypha about Mary. In the colourful language of contemporary life, though echoing St Paul's First Letter to the Corinthians (9:24–27), the virgin was likened to an athlete, committed through hard work and striving towards the ultimate prize:

> The stadium is vast, the course is long!
> The stadium is free, the athlete is ready,
> The victor will be crowned![26]

As befitted a modest virgin living in peace, Mary was horrified at the Annunciation – she wished to escape, or die – but was comforted once Gabriel revealed the divine plan. Athanasius insisted on Mary's enduring virginity with easy scriptural proof: Jesus would not have handed his mother to the care of his disciple John (John 19:25–7) had there been another offspring to care for her. Mary was pure and inclined towards good works; she was humble, spent her days reading scripture, was never distracted, not even casting an eye on the view from her window. Each day was a step in her progress just as each day tested the Alexandrine virgin. Athanasius offered this Mary to women who were considering a change of life:

> She who wishes to be a virgin, should consider this:
> It was for these reasons that the Word chose to take flesh of her
> And become man for us.[27]

The life of the virgin was solitary but not lonely, since she became part of a universal sisterhood of virgins. Their gathering is described by Athanasius as a joyous celebration in which virgins joined Mary at the feet of her son with virtuous women like Sarah and Rebecca, Rachel and Leah, Susanna and Elizabeth.[28]

As Christianity spread in the western and northern parts of the Roman

Empire in the second century, persecutions marked the presence of Christians, by 177 in Lyons and in the next century in Marseille, Arles, Narbonne and Toulouse. The cultures in Gaul, Britain and Iberia had received Romanness, and then Christianity; they had their own versions of mother-deities, expressed as clay and stone figurines.[29] By the early fourth century, in regions further north and west, Latin Christian leaders like Ambrose in Milan aimed to provide in their writings liturgical poetry for Christian communities and guidelines for a Christian life. This cultural production in Latin included polemical encounters with detractors as well as enticing discourses for those who might convert. Latin writers also engaged with the ascetic striving of Christians and, building on the example of Athanasius' guidance to virgins, adapted Mary into a figure of purity of life. Hilary, bishop of Poitiers ($c.$300–368), expressed his confidence that Mary had never borne children after Jesus. Others developed the tropes of 'praise in contradiction', already used by Greek and Syriac writers, like the North African Zeno (d.371), who became bishop of Verona: 'What a wonder: Mary conceived from that which she bore . . . the virgin contained that which the world in its plenitude did not contain.'

The early Christian communities of the Latin-speaking western Mediterranean have left less evidence of ideas about Mary than their eastern counterparts. In Rome anti-Christian edicts had been proclaimed and enforced, Christian martyrs were made, but by the fourth century it was home to vibrant Christian life. Early Christians' art in the spaces where they assembled and buried their dead – the art of the catacombs – represented above all the image of Christ as a good shepherd worthy of the death of martyrs. Wall-paintings from the vault of the Roman Priscilla catacomb depict a statuesque woman dressed in robes and head cover, a child on her knee, faced by a male figure pointing upwards. This image in the older part of the complex may be as early as the third century; and the figure may be a prophet indicating the star of the prophecy of Balaam: 'A star shall come forth out of Jacob, and a sceptre shall rise out of Israel' (Numbers 24:15–17).[30] In the Roman catacomb of Peter and Marcellinus, probably of the early fourth century, the walls were decorated with biblical scenes: Adam and Eve, Daniel in the Lion's Den, Jonah thrown to the Whale, the Mystical Lamb.[31] There is also an image of a seated woman with a child on her lap, her body covered in white robes, and her head with a diaphanous veil. A painting

25

from the Via Latina catacomb in Rome, of before 360, has a similar figure – Mary seated with a child in her lap – facing the Three Magi on her right.[32] Mary is presented as a matron, seated, with no attributes or decorative embellishments. She is a quintessential mother – not an empress, goddess or queen.

AMBROSE'S VISION OF MARY

The possibilities of thinking of Mary from the vantage point of a high-born privileged Christian man in an emergent Christian Empire were realized in the life and work of Ambrose, bishop of Milan (340–97). Through the figure of Mary Ambrose sought to inspire a social revolution. He shaped her into an example of purity, virtue and dignity that might counter the strong demands that marriage made of high-born women. In his tracts of 377–8, De virginibus and De virginitate (On Virgins and On Virginity), Mary epitomized an elegance that bespoke inner dignity and strength:

There was nothing wild in the eyes, nothing wanton in the words, no immodest movement; there was no posture more gentle, no comportment more relaxed, as if the sight of her body was a likeness of the mind, a figure of worth.[33]

Less ascetic perhaps than the hermits who dwelt in the Egyptian desert or in the caves of Cappadocia, the devotees of Ambrose's Italy sought to justify the withdrawal of men and women from productive life, from political responsibility and from the honour of heading a family. The example of Mary served both men and women.

Within this world Mary was embraced as example and companion. Athanasius' vision for the women of Alexandria resonated in the work of later Greek and Latin writers. In the cities of the Roman Empire respectable women of means and influence were attracted to the message of autonomy and virtue enfolded in the ascetic ideal. Ambrose of Milan and his sister Marcellina had grown up in Rome, where they took their first steps along the ascetic's path. The widow Melania the Elder, came to Rome after 364 in search of inspiration; she later ventured as far as the Holy Land. These were tortuous paths that led to rejection of family expectations, and to departure from the safe though limiting world of patrician patriarchy. As Ambrose wrote in his book of advice for Chris-

tian virgins, the battle against family was but the beginning of a life-long struggle, and 'If you conquer your family, you conquer the world.'[34]

Ambrose appreciated how hard it was to maintain Christian virginity, and so he offered Mary as a companion to the celibates who tried. The purity of her body and her decorous comportment were to be emulated by women who strove for virtue, since Mary was a mirror of all virtues. If Athanasius likened Christian virgins to athletes, Ambrose's teachings were full of plenty and riches, a vocabulary often inspired by his work of biblical commentary. The riches of Mary's virginity were like the secret of modesty, a banner of faith.[35] Ambrose delighted in Ezekiel's image of a 'closed gate' in describing Mary's sealed and pure body, because virginity was to him above all a state of separation.[36] Sexual contact blended (*immixtio*) substances best kept apart, but virgin bodies were protected from such sullying and confusion.[37] Mary's body was suitably immune: she was impregnated by the Holy Spirit and was never touched by male seed. Ambrose's reflection on Christ's birth as told by the gospel of Luke emphasizes just how Mary was spared the dreaded mingling with a male body. Her womb was a hall of purity (*aula pudoris*) and in it her son was conceived; nothing of the male had entered her womb.[38] Ambrose admits that the Incarnation was an unnatural act:

Did the process of nature precede when the Lord Jesus was born of Mary? If we seek the usual course, a woman after mingling with a man usually conceives. It is clear then that the Virgin conceived contrary to the course of nature.[39]

While it was a mystery it was also a true Incarnation, as Ambrose emphasizes when he reflects on the Incarnation as a sacrament: yet for all its wonder, Mary gave her flesh to her son as all mothers do:

For childbirth did not change the nature of the Virgin, but established a new method of generating. So flesh was born of flesh. Thus the Virgin had of her own what she gave; for the mother did not give something of another, but she contributed her own from her womb in an unusual manner, but in a usual function.[40]

Mary was used by Ambrose in the effort to secure Christian virtue in an Empire that still tolerated Jews and pagans. The memory of the Emperor Julian (361–3), who had relinquished Christianity and vigorously attempted to re-establish pagan worship, was fresh.[41] Ambrose

thus appealed to women – both virgins and widows – for they could help strengthen a Christian society. Some would become Christian matrons, supporters of Christian values, and others would remain Christian virgins, precious examples to all. Each group had a role to play in the emergent Christian world; to each Ambrose offered a version of Mary, mother and virgin.

Ambrose's acute political sense also led him to the association of Mary with imperial women. His most important oration, delivered at the funeral of Emperor Theodosius I in 395, located the beginning of the Christian Empire not in the deeds of Constantine, but in those of his mother, Empress Helena.[42] Helena's work of holy topography in the Holy Land – above all the finding and identification of the Holy Cross and Nails – were drawn by Ambrose into a providential history of the Empire.[43] Helena nurtured Constantine and saw him rise to imperial dignity. In this she was like Mary: both were mothers of extraordinary sons: 'Mary was visited, so that Eve be liberated; Helena was visited so that the Emperors be redeemed'.[44] At Golgotha, the site of the Crucifixion, Helena berated Satan for hiding the cross. Here was another victory over Satan, already overcome with the birth of Christ in Mary.[45]

Ambrose is strikingly creative in his use of a meagre store of material about Mary, Luke's Gospel and a few references to the early Fathers of the Church. He appreciated greatly Mary's potential appeal to Christian women, mothers and daughters, women noble and imperial. The encounter of Ambrose's imagination with the plethora of imagery contained in the Song of Songs – already a Christian book since Origen – produced something quite new. His commentary, of the years 387–90, built on the basis of Origen's work: the bridegroom of the Song is Christ. But there is more, for the bride is *virgo*, the Christian virgin:

This, this indeed is true beauty, that which lacks nothing, the only one who deserves to hear God saying: Thou art all fair, O my love, and there is no spot in thee. Come from Libanus, come: thou shalt be crowned from the top of Amana, from the top of Sanir and Hermon, from the dens of the lions, from the mountains of the leopards.[46]

Sometimes virgin, sometimes The Virgin, here is a celebration of their unique and interchangeable virtues. In the following years, Ambrose developed further the defence of Mary's life-long virginity.

The decades of the later fourth century saw the creation of Christian

28

cultures which were material and public. Christian answers were now required to questions touching on every area of life: family, the holding of offices, attitudes to slaves and dependents, the human body. As we have seen, the figure of Mary featured in writings about asceticism, but also in those about marriage.

MARY – BETWEEN VIRGINITY AND MARRIAGE

Rome was home to many groups of engaged Christians. Some met in churches for the celebration of ritual and others turned their homes into ascetic households. Those who practised the celibacy that Ambrose had done so much to promote were troubled when a Christian, Helvidius, argued that Mary had not remained a virgin after Christ's birth.[47] Against the growing prestige of celibacy – which was the privilege of well-off Christian women above all – Helvidius claimed that there was no shame in being married and having children, and that earlier Christian thinkers – like Tertullian – had believed that Mary had borne other children with Joseph and that Jesus thus had siblings.[48] Moreover, he believed that to deny Mary and Joseph a conjugal life was to doubt the goodness of God's creation. If the female body repelled the defenders of Mary's virginity, then they should also find Jesus' birth from her body altogether disgusting.

The monk Jovinian similarly found the new emphasis on Mary's virginity to be disturbing. Although his own writings have not survived, but are known through the polemical answers to them, it seems that in the late 380s he denounced the distinction that the cult of virginity created between Christians.[49] Baptism, he argued, made all Christians holy, be they brides, spouses, mothers or sisters, in one great church. If marriage was less than virtuous, then the patriarchs of the Old Testament, much married and fruitful, could no longer be considered as examples of good living. Jovinian sounded a revivalist message, attuned to the diversity of Christian lifestyles and refusing to prefer one over the other. He was probably reacting against the new asceticism, which was turning even the Song of Songs, with which new Christians were welcomed into the church, into a tract about virginity.

These denunciations both of Mary's perpetual virginity, and of the implied superiority of virginity for Christians which followed from it, elicited a stark polemical response from the scholar and church leader Jerome (340–420). Jerome had travelled to Jerusalem and Egypt and finally settled in Bethlehem with a group of female followers, Roman matrons led by Paula. Jerome was a highly energetic scholar and pilgrim. He learned Hebrew and studied the traditions in which Mary had been most powerfully exalted. Jerome's polemical answer was a forthright defence of Mary's perpetual virginity and a vindication of the superiority of the virginal state. He confidently refuted the claim that Mary and Joseph had ever been wife and husband: Joseph was guardian to Mary, hence Jesus had cousins but no siblings.[50]

To the high-born Roman women who chose the life of celibacy or virginity Jerome offered the example of Mary's life: Joseph and Mary had been poor, they travelled modestly and lived so too. Paula and Eustochium wrote to his friend, the Roman matron Marcella: 'Where are the wide porticoes? Where is the gilded panelling? Where are the palaces adorned by the sufferings of the wretched and the labour of the condemned?'[51] In his letter to Laeta on the education of her daughter Paula, Jerome recommends that the girl model herself on Mary. The example of virginity was not for women alone. Christ and Mary – and Joseph too – offered examples of virginity for men and women to follow.[52]

Jerome's greatest contribution to the understanding of Mary was through his biblical work, the work of translation and interpretation. His translation secured the useful – and misleading – translation of Isaiah's prophecy (Isaiah 7:14): 'Behold a virgin [Hebrew *alma*] shall conceive, and bear a son, and his name shall be called Emmanuel.' This became, therefore, a prophecy about a virgin, not simply about a young woman, the usual sense of the Hebrew *alma*. Jerome appropriated the Bible, and the Holy Land itself, as texts to be rewritten in a language that was Christian, and which conveyed truths that were manifest and clear. The Davidic genealogy of Jesus in Matthew linked him to a series of women who were associated with sexual transgression, but who also delivered the Children of Israel from adversity: Tamar, Ruth, Rahab, and Bathsheba. These sinners (*peccatrices*) were, according to Jerome, the epitome of the very sin that Jesus came to atone, as he shared flesh with them in the Davidic line. Each of these women had operated actively

on the stage of Jewish history; each also prefigured Mary's central role in salvation.

MARY BETWEEN CELIBACY AND MARRIAGE

While the monk Jerome provided Christians with a Latin version of the Bible, in North Africa a scholarly bishop was hard at work too, defining Christianity as a universal religion, for the many not just the few. Augustine, bishop of Hippo (354–430), led a tumultuous life which is recounted in dramatic detail in his autobiographical confessional writing. He was attracted early in life to Manichaeism, a religion articulated by the Persian preacher Mani ($c.210$–76), whereby the world is governed by two principles – light and darkness – with the world a product of the invasion of light by darkness. After his conversion to orthodox Christianity in Milan in 387, after hearing Ambrose's sermons to new converts, Augustine became a servant of the religion espoused by emperors, bishops and administrators throughout the Roman world.[53] As bishop of Hippo he offered a vision of a Christian church – a city in the world – that could pave a way out of sin and into the City of God. His Christianity was one of families and marriage, of work and law. Humans strove against the bondage of sin with the aid of the Church militant and its sacraments, and of saints in heaven, among them Mary.[54]

Augustine stated clearly that like all humans Mary was conceived in sin, but that this stain was removed at the moment of her 'ensoulment':

In regard to the Holy Virgin Mary, we must make an exception, concerning whom, because of the honor of the Lord, I do not wish to raise directly the question concerning sins. For whence do we know from him what abundance of grace for triumphing over sin in every particular was extended to her?[55]

Only Jesus was born without sin and he was the source of all grace.[56] Augustine was fairly reticent about the theology of Mary, and shied away from claiming her as Mother of God.[57] On occasion he referred to her in sermons, like that on Mary's motherhood, where he asked: 'Tell me, angel, what is there here of Mary? I have already said, when I

31

saluted her: Hail, full of grace.'[58] Mary served as a model for the church and, as importantly, as a model for Christian marriage and family life.

Augustine wrote his most important tract on Christian marriage in 401, *De bono conjugali* (*On the Good of Marriage*).[59] Procreation was the main good of marriage, and for that purpose sex in marriage was good too. Marriage was an act of free will and of faith; hence it was a binding sacrament. The marriages of Abraham and Sarah and of Mary and Joseph were ones of consent, loyalty and obedience and exemplified the core of Augustine's model of marriage. This model brought Mary into the heart of the discussion, where she exemplified the fundamental unit of Christian life, the family. In the east Mary was attached to the sinews of power, in the churches and liturgies of Constantinople, while from North Africa came the most influential of all visions of Christian life: a vision that has held for all Christian centuries to come. The paradoxical triumphed yet again: Christian marriage imagined through the sexless union of Mary and Joseph.

Augustine celebrated the marriage of Mary and Joseph, and in doing so he rebutted the whole tenor of Manichean morality that abhorred the human body and rejected with disgust the belief in a God born of a 'filthy womb'.[60] Manichaeans attacked the Incarnation, the very notion that a god took on a human body. Augustine addressed the problem of human descent in his commentary on Genesis (401–14), when he confronted the question of generation. In what sense, he asked, was Christ 'in Abraham's loins'? In the sense of having, through Mary, received his flesh from him. Unlike other creatures Christ did not receive his form from any male seed, rather from God alone. Through his mother Christ was present in Adam and Abraham; but as to his formative principle, he was created by God. He thus was never touched by sin, which follows the formative generation.[61]

Augustine thus balanced the principle of human-tainted sinfulness with a divine principle that both shared human carnality, through Mary, and escaped its tainting. Some Manichaean attacks on the Incarnation also attached to the nature of Joseph's parenthood. Augustine addressed these in a polemical tract of 397–8, *Against Faustus the Manichaean*. In answer to the Manichaean attack that Joseph must have been Jesus' biological father since he appears in Jesus' genealogy in the gospel, Augustine retorted that Joseph functioned as Jesus' father. The marriage was a real one, and so was the parenting: 'intercourse of the mind is

more intimate than that of the body.' A few years later Augustine repeated this view in a sermon: Mary and Joseph were married indeed 'without intercourse of the flesh, to be sure, but in virtue of the real union of marriage'. In his polemical writings Augustine defended strongly the conception of a God incarnate, nurtured within a family. Mary and Joseph's family contributed to the development of the Christian family in the decades that saw the rapid spread of Christianity in the Mediterranean world.

3
Versions of Mary

Spread by the system of Empire and by the example of charismatic preachers and exemplary ascetics, Christianity was absorbed into the diverse cultures – in words, images and sound – of the Mediterranean and of regions further east, within the Persian Empire. The region which saw the birth of Christianity in the Near East saw the early and influential development of distinctive styles in thinking about Jesus and of his mother too: these are the culture of the Syriac linguistic sphere and the Christianity which developed in Egypt.

SYRIAC MARY

Between the Mediterranean and the river Tigris, from the mountains of Kurdistan to the Arabian peninsula – between the Roman and the Persian Empires – Aramaic was the language of daily life and of much scholarship and creative writing. It was spoken by Jews even as they used Hebrew, the language of the Bible, for liturgical purposes and for poetic expression. Syriac is the name for the Eastern Aramaic used by Christians in writing and liturgy. Some of the earliest and most evocative writings about Mary were created in Syriac. Syriac Christians dwelt alongside large and ancient Jewish communities in Mesopotamian cities such as Edessa and Nisibis, indeed most converts to Christianity there were Jews. They used Syriac scripture and were highly influenced by Jewish biblical exegesis and by Jewish concepts of the divine.

Syriac Christianity developed its own style and imagery, and its writings survive from around the year 100.[1] It possessed a strong sense of divinity's presence, hence the Holy Spirit was explored in Syriac writings

34

more deeply than in any other Christian culture. Syriac writers built upon the dense Jewish concept of *shekhinah*, God's presence, which was always imagined as feminine.[2] *Shekhinah* interacted comfortably with the notion of a woman – Mary – as the dwelling place of a god. Hence the earliest Syriac Christian writing – the *Odes of Solomon*, probably from the end of the first century CE – expresses some of the ideas that were to be elaborated in future centuries:

> The son is the cup
> And the father is He who was milked;
> And the Holy Spirit is she who milked him . . .
> The womb of the Virgin took it
> And she received conception and gave birth.
> So the Virgin became a mother with great mercies.
> And she laboured and bore the Son, but without pain,
> Because it did not occur without purpose.
> And she did not require a midwife,
> Because He caused her to give life.[3]

The *Odes* have roots in Jewish hymns for public recitation; the poetry resembles the style of the psalms, but it dwells on the idea of a divine love and eternal life.[4] Mary is full of power and love for her son, whom 'she loved with redemption'. She was part of a plan for salvation that saw the birth of the Son from the milk of the Father, brought forth by a feminine Holy Spirit.

Syriac Christianity developed an ascetic style, which emphasized virginity above all virtues. Chastity formed part of the effort to combat sin; purity of body bespoke purity of heart.[5] Merging with *shekhinah*, Mary was imagined as a holy virgin bride; indeed, Syriac poetry often describes her as a 'bridal chamber'.[6] The gospel harmony composed by Tatian (110/20 – after 170), a disciple of Justin Martyr in Edessa around the year 170, omits the genealogies of Luke and Matthew. It also treats Mary's and Joseph's relationship carefully; Mary's pregnancy occurs before her betrothal to him.[7] The Syriac gospels presented both Mary and Joseph as scions of the House of David, but Syriac writers dwelt very little on the details of Jesus' birth to Mary.[8] They delighted in the symbolic possibilities of the merging of a feminine face of divinity and its human emanation in the form of Jesus.

In turn Jewish ideas and sensibilities influenced Syriac Christianity,

35

evident in the avoidance by Syriac writers of excessive preoccupation with the physical nature of Jesus.[9] Another very early text from Antioch, *The Ascension of Isaiah*, is an apocalyptic vision steeped in Jewish mysticism. It expresses the same preoccupations of the Jewish-Christian milieu that the *Protogospel of James* had explored. The *Ascension of Isaiah* considers Mary's and Joseph's union to be most suitable, because of their Davidic kinship. Joseph never touched his virgin wife, and while he was away from home on business she received an angelic message. When he returned, Mary was perturbed to find her son born so miraculously: he appeared after just two months of pregnancy. When Joseph asked her 'What is the matter?', she showed him the boy and praised God, while a voice ordered them to keep it all a secret.[10]

In Jesus some Syriac writers found a unique person, but not a person at one with the ageless God. Paul of Samosata, bishop of Antioch around 260–61, rejected the attribution to the Word – *logos*, God's immanent power – of any human qualities. A later writer cited him, concluding:

Mary did not give birth to the Word since she is not before all ages. Mary received the Word. She gave birth to a man like us, though better in all respects since the grace that is in him is of the Holy Spirit.

For such views Paul was expelled from Antioch, yet his was but an extreme formulation of a much more pervasive Syriac sensibility.[11] It was expressed again in the early fifth century by a great Antiochene teacher, Theodore of Mospuestia (d.428): 'The Word plainly did not have its origin in Mary's womb, for he was begotten before all ages, since the Word was already inhabiting the infant'.[12]

In the face of discomfort with the notion of a human mother for an ageless God, another arrangement of the human and the divine was offered by Syriac writers through the image of 'in-dwelling'. At the Annunciation the divine plan was revealed, as claimed in commentaries on Luke 1:35: 'The spirit shall come and the Power of the Most High shall tabernacle in you in holy fashion'. Syriac authors preferred to think of the spirit that entered Mary rather than of Mary's body itself.[13] The concept of 'in-dwelling' meant that Mary could be comfortably imagined as the body in which divine power operated the work of salvation. Within this redemptive framework Syriac Christians pondered very early on – already in the *Acts of John in Ephesus* of the second century – the

affinity between Mary and Eve. It was considered most fitting that Eve's sin was erased by an act that passed through the female body. It was even imagined that the drama of sin and redemption was located in a single organ: Mary's ear. As Eve had listened to the serpent, so Mary conceived her saving son through her ear.[14]

The Syriac image of Mary finds its most powerful expression in the commentaries and hymns of Ephrem the Syrian (c.306–73). His devotional poetry wove together emergent understanding and symbols into a devotional cosmology.[15] Each of the themes we have just encountered – Eve/Mary, conception through the ear, Mary as dwelling place for the divine – was grist to the mill of Ephrem's poetical imagination. Every aspect of Christianity emerged from a symbolic interpretation of the gospels – and Ephrem knew in addition the *Protogospel of James*, the tradition that celebrated Mary's purity.

Ephrem's Mary was above all the antithesis to Eve, who was so familiar from the Jewish Bible and parable. Mary attracted reflection on repentance and the sacrament of the eucharist:

> Mary has given us bread of rest
> In place of that bread of toil which Eve provided.[16]

Eve's burden was to bear children in pain, and so Mary's own delivery was without any suffering:

> Your womb escaped the pangs of the curse.
> By means of the serpent came the pains of the female;
> Shamed be the Foul one, on seeing that his pangs
> Are not found in your womb![17]

Rather than foul, Mary's womb was a place of great beauty and purity:

> In its brightness I beheld the Bright One Who cannot be clouded,
> And in its pureness a great mystery,
> Even the Body of Our Lord which is well-refined:
> In its undividedness I saw the Truth
> Which is undivided.
>
> . . .
>
> Thy goodly conception was without seed,
> And without wedlock was thy pure generation,
> And without brethren was thy single birth.[18]

The Incarnation in Mary was imaged through a theology of clothing. In a Hymn on Paradise Mary weaves a new robe for Adam, symbolizing the flesh with which she clothed her son:

> Adam had been naked and fair,
>> but his diligent wife
> Laboured and made for him
>> a garment covered with stains.
> The garden, seeing him thus vile,
>> drove him forth.
> Through Mary Adam had
>> another robe
> which adorned the thief;
>> and when he became resplendent at Christ's promise,
> the Garden, looking on,
>> embraced him in Adam's place.[19]

Adam and Eve may have lost their 'garments of glory', but now Mary had undone the harm inflicted by her older sister, Eve.[20]

The question of Mary's virginity, so fundamental to Syriac Christians, was still a subject for polemic, as between Jews and Christians and between Christians and Gnostic Christians, who rejected the physical aspect of the Incarnation and saw in matter an emanation of evil.[21] In his commentary on the second-century Syriac gospel harmony, the *Diatessaron*, which he wrote in late fourth-century Edessa, Ephrem argued polemically:

Because there are those who dare to say that Mary [cohabited] with Joseph after she bore the Redeemer, [we reply], 'How would it have been possible for her who was the home of the indwelling of the Spirit, whom the divine power overshadowed, that she be joined by a mortal being, and give birth filled with birthpangs, in the image of the primeval curse?' If *Mary was blessed of women*, she would have been exempt from the curse from the beginning, and from the bearing of children in birthpangs and curses. It would be impossible therefore to call one who gave birth with these birthpangs blessed.[22]

He also derided those, like Bardaisan of Edessa, who argued that a body had descended from heaven, rather than been born in Mary.[23]

Ephrem realized the polemical potential of Mary, but also her power to signify truth through dramatic oppositions such as Eve–Mary.

Ephrem also used traditional Syriac genres in order to explore Mary further. He set the Annunciation as an ancient Mesopotamian dispute poem; it was, after all, an exchange between Gabriel and Mary.[24] Later, Mary was similarly inserted into a dispute poem of the fifth or sixth century imagined as a debate between the months of the year. The summer month of Iyyar is time for harvest, and it boasts of the beauty of the produce that comes forth, likening Mary to wheat:

'Gorgeous roses appear in me,
sweet and delicately scented;
The king's crown is plaited in me,
and the heart of the labourers rejoices.'
Come and listen to what the months have to say and give praise to their Creator.
'In me the blades of corn sprout forth,

. . .

sprout forth at the top of every spike
at the bidding of the King who so wills.'
Come and listen to what the months have to say and give praise to their Creator.
'He breached his mother and she gave no cry,
he went forth from her and she raised no complaint:
Mary was like the blade of corn
and our Lord Jesus shone forth from her.'
Come and listen to what the months have to say and give praise to their Creator.[25]

Mary and Jesus enter this traditional poem in which roses and sheaves of corn, rebirth, and the beauty of creation are praised.

Syriac Christianity radiated from Antioch and Edessa with the image of Mary as the mother of God, impregnated by the Holy Spirit, redeemer of the sons and daughters of Adam and Eve. Syriac Mary guided the asceticism of monks and was appreciated above all in hymns and poetry recited by communities and read as homilies to fortify Christian souls. Syriac writers shied away from an exploration of the physical and domestic circumstances of Mary and Joseph, and preferred to think of Mary as being at one with the Holy Spirit and ablaze in the eucharist. This was the Christian culture that affected Persia and then India, and it was aware of its proximity to the Jews, who still lived in large numbers in the great cities of Mesopotamia.[26] It remained a religion of praise and of polemic, where some of the most enduring images of Mary were first told. Syriac asceticism also affected the monasticism of Egypt to

the south and Armenia to the north. In western Syriac spheres the subtleties regarding Jesus and his mother confronted the emergent certainties, the orthodoxy of the imperial state. It was an alternative to the faith spread from Constantinople. Syriac Christians had maintained old traditions and subtle ways of weaving humanity and divinity, ways less explicit than the Nicene Creed, and that is how they liked it. This difference led to dramatic future clashes over the nature of Christ and the related nature of his mother.

EGYPTIAN MARY: MOTHER-GODDESS

Jesus was a god who had been mothered. It is, therefore, not surprising that in regions familiar with goddesses as mothers and gods suckled by mothers, local knowledge and traditions merged with thinking about Jesus and Mary. While Judaism had a powerful image of divinity's presence as feminine – *shekhinah* – and this was at work in the writings of Syriac Christians, it had no mothering figure. Egyptian religion, which since the second century BCE had been influenced strongly by encounters with Hellenistic Greek religion and literature, was familiar with a much-loved indigenous figure of that kind: Isis.

Isis, formidable mother-goddess of procreation, childbirth and fertility in nature, had been known since the period of the Egyptian Old Kingdom (twenty-fourth century BCE).[27] She spread beyond Egypt in the centuries following the conquests of Alexander the Great, in the Hellenistic world that spanned the eastern Mediterranean, and then reached westwards. The priests of Isis were her missionaries; they taught the rituals that offered abundance and strength to her adherents. Isis was wife to Osiris and mother to Horus, and one of her many visual forms was as part of this intimate family group. This Egyptian family acquired Greek features in the Hellenistic Mediterranean, to which the Isis cult spread prodigiously. It blended with existing Greek Gods: Isis with Demeter (goddess of fertility), Osiris with Dionysus, and their son Horus with Apollo. In these guises the cult of Isis and her family spread as far as Cologne in the north, Alcazar in Iberia in the west, Carthage in the south, and Syria in the east, with a particularly dense presence in Italy and Greece. She received the patronage of the Flavian emperors of the late first and second centuries.[28] When Christianity began to spread in

the eastern Mediterranean it coincided with the peak of Isis' popularity.

Isis was part of the Graeco-Roman pantheon, familiar in several guises, one of which was as a mother suckling her son.[29] A wall painting from Fayoum, just south of the Nile Delta, has Isis baring a breast, which she offers her son while both look directly at the viewer.[30] Egyptian gods habitually encompassed a variety of identities.[31] Isis was the image of fecundity, which in Egypt was linked most prominently with the water of the Nile. She was, therefore, embedded in Egyptian village religion and was popular, especially among women, as Isis *lochia* – 'she who brought forth a new-born babe'.[32] Her great centre in Egypt was from the fourth century the Temple on the island of Philae, near the first cataract of the Nile, in Upper Egypt.

Isis was also associated with healing and acts of salvation; indeed, one of her titles was *soteria* – saviour. The historian Diodorus Siculus (90–30 BCE) had claimed that Isis was believed by the Egyptians to be the 'Discoverer of many health-giving drugs and was greatly versed in the science of healing ... She finds her greatest delight in the healing of mankind'.[33]

Unlike other Graeco-Roman gods, who were strong but whimsical, Isis was imagined as all-powerful but beneficent. She combined worldly well-being with order, as expressed in a hymn of the first century BCE:

> O Discoverer of Life and Cereal food wherein all
> > mortals delight because of your blessing(s).
> All who pray to you to assist their commerce,
> > Prosper in their piety forever ...
> Persuading the gold-flowing Nile, you lead it in season
> > over the land of Egypt as a blessing for men.
> Then all vegetation flourishes and you apportion to all
> > Whom you favour, a life of unspeakable blessing.[34]

The cult of Isis emphasized mediation, the possible disposition of the divine to incline kindly towards humans. She thus merged easily with Jewish ideas about creative Wisdom and with the Greek *logos*.[35] Above all, with her protective power and her nurturing force, Isis was a much-loved domestic presence, worshipped in domestic shrines, where figures and painted panels were placed.

The reception of early Christianity in Egypt was marked in a number of ways by the presence of this mother goddess. Mary was presented as

a local beauty, reminiscent of the ideal of Isis painted on the wall of a house at Fayoum: with large dark eyes set under strong eyebrows.[36] Very much like the Isis figure, this Mary sits powerfully on a cushioned seat, her body solid under her light garments, her hair intricately braided, her arms energetically fondling the suckled child.[37] The representation of Mary in Egypt benefited from the prevalence and familiarity of this mother-goddess with the powerful attributes of physical prowess and life-giving energy. The fifth-century inscriptions show just how the process of conversion worked: ritual forms used in Hellenistic times to address Isis in spaces previously her own were now used by Christians and for Mary. A later inscription invokes the Egyptian month, yet appeals to the blessing of 'our Lady of all, the holy God-bearing Mary of Philae', the very formula used in temples dedicated to Isis: 'to the Lady Isis of Philae'.[38]

In the monasteries of Egypt Mary was cherished as companion and example. The appellation Mother of God, most commonly used to address Isis, but also attached to other Egyptian goddesses, was evolving as a fitting title for Mary, mother of the Christian god.[39] The image of Mary as nurturing mother was uniquely local and domestic; like Isis Egyptian Mary was situated in a frontal pose, but her eyes drift away from the viewer.[40] She nurtured, fed her son in her lap and thus represented motherhood, protection and care. Not until the year 1200 in Western Europe was the image of a breastfeeding Mary so comfortably represented. It was this commitment to imagining Mary as of the flesh, and more than the flesh, which made Egyptian advocates so central to thinking about Mary as *Theotokos* – the Bearer of God – and to her becoming the unrivalled patron of the imperial family and Constantinople.

4

Mary of the Imperial State

During the first 500 years of Christian life, from its beginning in Naza-reth and Jerusalem, awareness of Mary spread at varying speeds and engendered a wide range of styles. By the Council of Nicaea of 325 Mary had become part of the most solemn formulations of a Christian system and over the next century a central marker of Christian identity. It may even be that texts associated with Emperor Constantine described Mary as 'Mother of God'.[1] Mary continued to demarcate the difference between Christians and Jews, and by the early fifth century also helped to define the style of official imperial religion. Forms of address and forms showing religious dignity, especially those of imperial women, were applied to Mary with increasing ease. Mary's inexorable progress pleased some and troubled others. The tradition which we have seen expressed so well in Syriac, which did not delight in a Mary of flesh, was bound to clash with the triumphant vision of Mary, enthroned, crowned, imperial mother of God.

A clash over the mode of address appropriate for Mary came to a violent climax in Constantinople in the 420s. In 428 Emperor Theo-dosius II appointed as patriarch of Constantinople a Syrian monk, Nestor (381–c.451), who had a reputation for clean living and formid-able scholarship. Nestor was born to Persian parents, was educated in Antioch and joined the monastery of Euprepios, where he became a distinguished biblical scholar. In keeping with both Syrian and imperial sensibilities Nestor espoused the unity of the Trinity as a core divine principle; in it God was one and hegemonic over a Son who took the form of Man. Salvation depended on the Sacrifice of the Son by an all-powerful God for the sake of humanity. There was no space here either for Jesus as both God and Man or for his mother as something approaching a goddess. Nestor was intent on an active policy against

43

'heretics', those who deviated from beliefs laid down by imperial religious policy. He appealed to the emperor to bless his enforcement of true belief: 'Give me, O emperor, the land free of heretics and I will give you heaven in return'.[2]

All strands of religious thinking and devotional practice were seething in the great imperial cities, and so they were in Constantinople too. When a sermon was preached against Mary as *Theotokos* – Bearer of God – Nestor was forced to pronounce. He suggested that the title used to address Mary had become a distinguishing mark between two parties: those who saw Mary as Bearer of God and those who preferred to see her as the bearer of God's humanity alone, or Bearer of Man (*Anthropotokos*). Nestor himself used *Christotokos* – Bearer of Christ – a compromise formulated some years earlier by his own teacher, Theodore of Mopsuestia (d.427). He hoped this would be acceptable to the laity and monks of the city. But it was not. The controversy was reopened when a fiery preacher close to Nestor opined with less subtlety: 'Let no one call Mary *Theotokos*. For Mary was human and it is impossible for God to be born of a human.'[3] When Nestor failed to pacify, but rather rose to condemn the use of *Theotokos*, the capital was split. Politics were moving against Nestor; his opponent Proclus (*c.*390–446), a priest of Constantinople, was becoming closely associated with the emperor's sisters and spoke publicly and emphatically in favour of *Theotokos*.

Proclus delivered his sermon on the Sunday of the Feast of Mary (*partheniki panegyris*) 429. He assembled a variety of verbal images, all of which were to do with mediation and connection, beginning with delight in the fact that a Marian feast had given rise to the gathering:

> She who has called us here is the holy Mary;
> the untarnished vessel of virginity;
> the spiritual paradise of the second Adam;
> the workshop of the union of natures;
> the market-place of the contract of salvation;
> the bride-chamber where the Word took flesh in marriage;
> the living bush, of human nature, which the fire of a divine birth-pang did
> not consume . . .
> handmaid and mother, virgin and heaven,
> the only bridge (for God) to mankind;

the awesome loom of the divine economy upon which the robe of union
  was ineffably woven.
The loom-worker was the Holy Spirit;
the wool-worker the overshadowing power from on high.
the wool was the ancient fleece of Adam;
the interlocking thread the spotless flesh of the Virgin.
The weaver's shuttle was propelled by the immeasurable grace of him who
  wore the robe,
the artisan was the Word who entered through her sense of hearing.[4]

The domestic image of weaving and making of clothing was particularly evocative: the work of women was an act of charity; uncoupled from common household labour, it had become part of a divine plan. Mary was that loom, the worker of the shuttle, and the garment was her own flesh, which her son wore. Proclus also invoked the Jew, in a polemic around Mary: while Mary was employed in weaving and making of cloth, the Jew ripped that cloth asunder. His Homily 2 reminded its hearers that Mary's enemies were to be found not only among the Christians of far-off bishoprics of Syria, but at the heart of Mary's city, among the Jews of Constantinople:

> There may chance to be a Jew in our midst,
> Like the fox from Judah lurking in the vineyard of Christ.
> After the congregation is dismissed
> He might stand outside and mock our words,
> saying such things as these:
> 'Why do you Christians invent such novelties
> and boast of things which cannot be proved.
> When did God ever appear on earth?[5]

A truly formative moment in Christian history then unfolded as Cyril, bishop of Alexandria, entered the fray. His city was a prestigious centre of Christian life, an ancient metropolis, with robust traditions of thought and practice.[6] His Christ was God and Man; the events in Constantinople offered an occasion to diminish, perhaps even unseat, the bishop of Constantinople and gain imperial favour. Cyril wrote to Celestine, bishop of Rome, and lobbied the emperor – Nestor's patron – requesting a gathering at which the issues could be discussed and finally decreed. Theodosius II was probably moved as much by the violence between rival

factions in the streets of Constantinople as by theological conviction; he summoned a council in the ancient city of Ephesus at Pentecost 431. Ephesus was a meaningful choice, for by this time local tradition claimed that Mary had followed the Apostle John to that city and even that she had died there.[7] The Christian exaltation of *Theotokos* occurred in this city still remembered as the centre of the cult of Artemis.

Nestor's legation from Constantinople and Cyril's from Alexandria settled in Ephesus around Easter 431 and conducted a propaganda campaign accompanied by their brutal retinues, who clashed in the streets. Nestor expected a contingent of sixty-eight Syrian bishops to arrive and support his position against *Theotokos*, but the Syrians were delayed on their journey, and so the opening of the Council was delayed too. Nestor's party claimed that he had the support of Roman and African delegates, that he represented a wide array of opinion, but this did not convince the presiding official, who still delayed proceedings.[8] When the Council finally commenced, a fortnight later than planned, Nestor's party was at a real disadvantage.

The Syrian bishops arrived in a city where 'Egyptian' domination was evident in the Council's chambers and in public places. One account reported that Shenoute (371–465), the abbot of the White Monastery at Atripe on the Upper Nile, attacked Nestor physically for his denial of the full divinity of the person born of Mary.[9] Alexandrine bishops were embroidering the figure of Mary as never before: 'Mary the theotokos, the holy ornament of all the universe, the unquenchable lamp, the crown of virginity, the sceptre, the container of the uncontainable, mother and virgin'.[10] The 'holy ornament' is an ancient Egyptian address to a revered woman. Proclus joined in by passionately aligning *Theotokos* with true belief and its defence against all comers, in a homily that became part of the Council's official record:

So he who bought us was no mere man, you Jew! For the nature of man was enslaved to sin. Nor was he solely God, without humanity. For he had a body, you Manichee! Had he not clothed himself in me, he would not have saved me. Rather, when he appeared in the Virgin's womb he clothed himself in him who was condemned; there it was that the awesome contract was concluded. He gave spirit and took flesh. The same one was both with the Virgin and of the Virgin; by his 'overshadowing', he was with her; by becoming incarnate, he was of her ... Do not rend the robe of the incarnation which was 'woven from

46

above'. Do not be the disciple of Arius, for he in his impiety divided the divine essence.[11]

Such outpouring became the way to engage with Mary, through the impossibility of any attempt to describe her fully, and by savouring the contradictions within her person.[12]

Cyril, bishop of Alexandria, was a canny politician; he was aware that Nestor's party would fight back. The Council's achievement had yet to be enforced by the Syrian bishops in their lands and to gain the emperor's support. Cyril mustered the considerable resources – financial as well as diplomatic – of the see of Alexandria and put them to work. He drafted a memorandum to his supporters in Constantinople with a list of sweeteners, gifts and outright bribes to ladies-in-waiting and eunuchs of the imperial court, in an attempt to prevent any backsliding on Mary as *Theotokos*. Luxuries fit for an imperial household, home of the emperor's sisters, were bestowed: 77,760 gold pieces, twenty-four carpets, twenty-five woollen tapestries, twenty-four silken veils, twenty-eight cushions, and thirty-six throne covers. Even the obstinate eunuch Chryseros was softened with tapestries and carpets, ivory stools, Persian drapery and ostrich eggs.[13] Nestor ended his days in exile, and Proclus, the poet of Mary, was the patriarch of Constantinople in waiting.

Cyril's luxurious offerings secured *Theotokos* for Constantinople and for large parts of the Empire. Mary was now inextricably linked to the dynastic identity of the Theodosians, the dynasty that had worked hard to establish orthodoxy and uproot dissent. She was central to the lives of the imperial women. Pulcheria, the eldest of Theodosius II's sisters, took a vow of virginity, and thus positioned herself most aptly as a special devotee of Mary. She founded churches and endowed them with precious gifts, like the gift of her own imperial robe for use at the church of Hagia Sophia. Cyril invoked the long history of imperial Mary worship, even back to the action of Helena, who 'adorned the places where the theotokos gave birth with the most splendid monuments, decorating that cave with the richest ornaments'.[14] According to a sympathizer of Nestor, Cyril was 'working on the sister' with Egyptian flatteries. At stake were issues of decorum, related to the appropriate place of women in the imperial cult around Mary.

Pulcheria's deep identification with the *Theotokos*, through their shared femininity, only compounded the difficulties that Nestorians

encountered in the mingling of woman and God. In the *Bazaar of Heraclides*, written late in his life, Nestor explains his rift with Pulcheria. She was 'A contentious woman, a princess, a young maiden, a virgin, who fought against me because I was not willing to be persuaded that I compare a woman corrupted of men to be the bride of Christ'.[15] Here are words touched by the bitterness of defeat, and so it is hard to assess just how involved Pulcheria had been in the polemic. Yet, as a devotee of Mary, she found *Theotokos* as pleasing as she would be to other and future imperial women.[16]

Two years after Ephesus, in 433, Cyril and the Syrian bishops under imperial inducement accepted a less controversial formulation. They accepted *Theotokos* when accompanied by the affirmation of Christ as 'perfect God and perfect man . . . of one substance with us in his humanity'. A triumphant blast thundered from Proclus (now patriarch of Constantinople) in powerful homilies in praise of Mary. In the imperial capital the human and the divine were publicly fused in the person of the emperor, and in the hallowed mysteries of the virginal lives led – sometimes only for a spell – by the imperial women.

In Constantinople Mary was re-created as a mystery of divinity touching earth, an unexpected female intrusion upon the stage of male world power. The style of preaching that developed around *Theotokos* was overwrought, but it was exciting and uplifting and set the tone for Greek homiletics in future centuries. Mary's title of *Theotokos* emphasized Christ's divinity, but also his humanity nurtured by a mother. *Theotokos* was the symbol of orthodoxy which was increasingly expressed in liturgy and civic display. The council of Chalcedon of 451 explicitly defined this duality, and inserted it into the credal formulation:

begotten before the ages from the Father as regards his divinity, and in the last days the same for us and for our salvation from Mary, the virgin God-Bearer, as regards his humanity; one and the same Christ, Son, Lord, only-begotten, acknowledged in two natures which undergo no confusion, no change, no division, no separation; at no point was the difference between the natures taken away from the union.[17]

This formulation was designed to confound Docetists, who denied Christ's suffering humanity, and Manichaeans, for whom flesh was above all the potential for sin and evil. It was the product of Pulcheria's domination of Constantinople and its liturgy, and of the good relations

she had fostered with Leo, bishop of Rome, through her aunt Galla Placidia (c.392–450), daughter of Theodosius I. It was the orthodoxy of an imperial state, which Pulcheria hoped might reunite the eastern and the western parts of the Empire.[18]

Syriac, Armenian and Coptic writers continued to maintain a less emphatically physical version of Christ's coming, one which celebrated Mary but which speculated very little on the nature of her life as a mother, and of Jesus as a son. Eznik of Kołb, Armenian bishop of Bagrewand (c.430–c.450), wrote a comprehensive apology, a defence of Christian theology against those eastern beliefs contrary to official Orthodoxy. Eznik's vision demonstrates the compromise reached between Syriac distaste for the emphasis on carnality and the Greek and Latin delight in the creative tension between the two natures of Christ. His God was 'true God, Son of God', who became man 'without suffering change, decline or destruction'. His mother 'the Virgin is called and really is Mother of the Lord and Mother of God'.[19] Such a formulation is a far cry from the eruptions of Syriac and from the domesticated humanity of the *Protogospel of James*.

From Constantinople the imperial image of Mary spread throughout the Mediterranean on coins, in liturgies, and in the emergent art of religious panel painting – the icon. Such images represented sacrality powerfully, and often in the image of Mary as *Theotokos*. Thinkers and writers in Greek, Latin and Syriac led the debates about the nature of God the Son and on the qualities of his mother. In the new kingdoms created in the furthest flung provinces of the Roman Empire – in Ireland, Britain and Gaul – Mary would come to be known in her newly proclaimed imperial person.

PART II

From the Eastern Mediterranean to the Irish Sea: To the Year 1000

5

Mary of the Christian Empire

MARY'S REMARKABLE END

The debates between emperors and priests, monks and bishops established a truth to be held by all Christians as orthodoxy – that Christ was born of a woman who was not only a virgin at his conception, but remained intact after his birth for the rest of her life. The Nicene Creed of 325 was supposed to end discussion about the terms of the religion only recently allowed to flourish throughout the Mediterranean and the Near Eastern world. Yet debates continued; in 431 at Ephesus an official view exalted the woman who bore God, *Theotokos*. Mary was deemed to be an agent of God's incarnation, but she was also adopted as patron by the emperors and their families. Mary was now part of court ceremonial; she filled elaborate architectural spaces, was painted and revered. God's joining of himself to humans through Mary seemed to be mirrored in the Emperor's offering of himself through the liturgy of his court.[1]

The battle of words that resulted in a victory for those eager to proclaim Mary as *Theotokos* was followed by a long process by which this understanding took shape and became a palpable reality in Christian life. Mary as *Theotokos* was an imperial vision spread by imperial will and monastic enthusiasm and adopted by individuals and families.

The land where Mary spent her life and nurtured her son attracted the attention of those who now promoted her. Yet this was a land inhabited by Jewish and Samaritans, as well as by Christians. The Jews ranged from the most Hellenized, familiar with Greek learning and enmeshed in local administration, to those who followed the observance of Jewish rituals more strictly under the guidance of the rabbis of Palestine.[2] Samaritans adhered to a literal understanding of the Torah

53

and lived apart in villages surrounding Nablus. There was competition over space, over claims to sacred power, over healing magic, and over hegemony in neighbourhoods, both rural and urban. There was mutual attraction and curiosity between the groups too.

Mary was becoming increasingly vital to the sense of Christian identity. Hesychius, patriarch of Jerusalem (d.450), is a good example of a Christian leader who attended to the pastoral and liturgical needs of his church and community. While the councils wove subtle theological statements on the nature of God and his mother, Hesychius translated these into hymns of praise and sermons. With rhetorical flair and allegorical imagination, in the tradition established by Origen, he coined images for Mary out of the Jewish Bible: Mary was like Noah's ark, a saviour of humans; she resembled the burning bush; and she was as safe as a sealed tower. Here was an image-rich orthodoxy, like that of Proclus: Mary was extolled as the perfect human to bear a perfect Man-God.[3] He was probably the first writer to write about the possibility that Mary's own conception had been without sin, an idea which was amply – and controversially – explored in the later Middle Ages. Hesychius' attachment to Mary is particularly interesting since he had travelled the route from sympathy for monophysitism – belief that Jesus had a sole, divine nature – to the orthodoxy of Ephesus. He was happy to emphasize Mary's nurture of Christ's humanity.[4]

Emperors differed in the zeal which they brought to the conversion of the Holy Land and its people to Christianity. Emperor Zeno (d.c.491) marked the Christianization of the Samaritans with the construction of a church to Mary *Theotokos* on Mount Gerizim, on the site of the Samaritans' holiest temple.[5] This was an act of territorial conquest and of public piety too, as described by the historian Procopius (c.500–c.565):

He drove out the Samaritans from Mt Gerizim and straightaway handed it over to the Christians, and building a church on the summit he dedicated it to the Mother of God, putting a barrier, as it was made to appear, around this church.[6]

Violent revolts continued for almost a century over this rugged terrain, populated by Christian monks and Samaritan villagers. Non-Christians saw the presence of Christian life grow around them. Christianity was now a state religion, the most powerful image of which – in battle, in processions, in new churches – was often the figure of the Mother of God.

Theotokos concentrated thoughts and sentiments upon the Incarnation and the role which it opened to the mother of a god made flesh. Mary was not only a symbol of the Christian polity, but was offered through homilies as a model for virtuous behaviour. A sixth-century Coptic homily praises chaste biblical women, culminating in Mary:

O to the Mother of us all and the Lady of us all, our intercessor, our benefactress, the glorious one, and the perpetual Virgin, Saint Mary, who brought forth the only-begotten of the Father, Jesus Christ, who became redemption and salvation for us.[7]

The woman who had borne Jesus, who had nurtured him and seen him die a terrible death could not have been left to die and putrefy, to the derision of pagans and Jews. So those who sang Mary's praises as the pure container of divinity – men like Proclus – soon turned to the issue of Mary's death. If Mary's birth and childhood were recounted by the mid-second century in the *Protogospel of James*, by the year 500 Mary was endowed with an end in a variety of narratives that emerged in parallel. The reflection on Mary's end inspired writings in all the languages of the Near East: some sixty accounts composed before the year 1000 have survived.[8] Hers was an end, not a death, and it was recounted in versions that drew upon the oral traditions of Palestine. Mary's end was situated in the outskirts of Jerusalem, the holiness of which was marked in the Christian creed, yet a city redolent with memories of acrimonious polemic with its earlier residents, the Jews. Despite their diversity the narratives of Mary's end share two goals: praise of Mary and her miraculous end – a Dormition followed by an Assumption to heaven – and disparagement of the Jews as Mary's enemies.

Those who explored Mary's end appreciated the richness of the knowledge encoded in the Holy Land and its people. In a sermon for the feast of the Assumption the eighth-century preacher John of Damascus claimed that the tradition was based on ancient lore passed on 'from father to son'.[9] Narratives about Mary's end describe her sorrow tenderly and Jewish resentment virulently. Mary bore testimony to her son's message; she visited his tomb and offered guidance to Jesus' followers. Mary continued her son's work through healings and miracles and she nurtured his memory. For this she was resented by the Jews, as one Syriac version tells it: 'the Jews hated the Lady Mary greatly.'[10] The

Coptic version of the story by a writer known as Pseudo-Evodius of Rome, of the mid-sixth century, presents Mary's Dormition – her falling asleep – as a marriage feast: Mary is the 'true bride' and Jesus the 'true spouse'. After a prologue full of praise, cast in images of majesty, the author turns to the Jews:

Where are you now, O ignorant Jew, the murderer of his Lord? This one who does evil to those who do good to him, let him come here today and be ashamed of himself, hearing all of these testimonies, which those of his own people have previously prophesied concerning this Virgin and her blessed birthing.[11]

A whole section follows of confrontation with the Jew as the agent of Christ's crucifixion, witness of his suffering. The author then returns to the subject of Mary's end and her son's reception of her in heaven. A string of appellations follows, redolent of the Song of Songs:

You are exalted above heaven, more esteemed than the earth, because God resided in your holy womb. Blessed are you, O beautiful dove, my bride without blemish. Arise and come beside me, because my time has drawn near, when I will eat my bread with you and drink the sweet-smelling wine in my garden, my holy paradise.[12]

The Dormition saw the exquisite meeting of heaven and earth. It was a special end for a special woman, marked by fine fragrances that rose from her body and from heaven 'a fragrant and sweet odor went forth from the highest heavens of [the Lord's] glory to all places of creation', according to an early Syriac version.[13]

Pseudo-Evodius presents himself as a witness to Christ's life and thus a direct link to Mary's times too. While those around her mourned her passing, Christ reassured them that she had not died. Mary fell into sleep on Mount Zion and was carried by the apostles for burial in a field west of Jerusalem, in the valley of Jehosaphat. When some Jews saw the procession and heard the mournful song, they fell upon the Christians. A miraculous wall of fire protected the procession and blinded the Jews: one Jew, Zephania, who had run towards her bier, was struck by an angel; his hand was cut off and, according to some versions, it remained stuck to Mary's bier. The Jews begged Mary for help, and many converted.[14] The Jews' realization of their error is paralleled in the Dormition sermon of the Palestinian preacher Theoteknos of Livias ($c.550$–$c.650$), in which the Jews say:

'Truly, we have made a mistake "in our foolishness and have considered her life madness" (Wisdom 5:4); we have not plucked the fruit of righteousness, for we had a veil of smoke [before our eyes] . . . Now we know what the prophets meant to reveal to us.'[15]

The emergent traditions on Mary's end display the thrust of polemic that animated early discussions of her. The telling of her death attracted a persistent anti-Jewish emphasis: only one version omits the plot of Jewish disruption at Mary's funeral. This must therefore be an ancient strand in the emergent narrative that was born in the Holy Land, among Jews and Christians, to consider the fate of the woman later called *Theotokos*. Mary's end attracted the greatest interest, for it promised that she had not died, that she was more than just a woman, and that she still resided in heaven alongside her son. Mary's Assumption was to become her most beloved feast.

MARY, THE JEWS, AND THE HOLY LAND

While Christians wrote, preached and heard stories about Mary's end, some Jews created their own versions of the Christian story they witnessed growing around them. As an increasingly exclusive Christian identity was promoted by the Empire, some Jews converted to Christianity. But in the cities of the Mediterranean Jews still lived side by side with Christians and with an ever-dwindling number of pagans. Mary was central to the Christian identity fostered by the Empire; theological effort and political will made her the protector of the capital and the touchstone of orthodoxy. As to the Jews, they were more bemused than intrigued by Mary. Rabbis spent little energy on refutation of the claims about Mary. Occasional mentions of adultery or unusual birth may have had associations with Mary but these are usually too flimsy to assess.[16]

By the fifth century an explicitly polemical version of the gospels, *Toledoth Yeshu*, had evolved: according to it Jesus was a magician, his healings necromancy, his birth illegitimate, his mother an adulteress, his followers a band of 'evil disciples'.[17] In Aramaic and later Hebrew strands, a counter-gospel, a Jewish version of the Life of Jesus, was created. The aim of *Toledoth Yeshu* – the early layers of which may be

as old as the fourth century – was to invert every Christian claim about Jesus.[18] The tradition was transmitted in several versions, but all aim to present Jesus as the product of fornication, and thus a *mamzer*, born to a woman from sexual union with a man who was not her husband. The accusation was older than the tradition of *Toledoth Yeshu*: as we have seen, Origen had rebutted it in his polemical tract against Celsus; he also countered a claim that the father was Panthera, perhaps a Roman soldier. Mary was presented in *Toledoth Yeshu* as a respectable woman, but one who fell victim to a terrible deception.

In Nazareth, the city in the Galilee. In the days of Herod the King there were a man and wife, the man's name was Joseph and his wife's Miriam, and the wife had always been sterile. And Joseph was one of the most pious men of his time, who occupied himself in God's matters in synagogues. Once he quarrelled with an evil man of Israel, who said, 'I am not my father's son if I will not see your end in this world.' Joseph did not suspect that the evil man had decided to fornicate with his wife Miriam, and to separate her from him; and so he did. Once, on Sabbath eve, around midnight, he [Joseph] left the house to pray in the synagogue and the evil man waited for him to leave, and opened the gate and went into his bed and slept with Miriam, who thought it was her husband Joseph. And when he had done his deed, the evil man closed the door and ran off to his house. From that intercourse Miriam conceived Yeshu, and when she was three months pregnant and her belly had grown large, Joseph noticed and said to her, 'Miriam, my beloved, what is this?', and she answered him, 'My lord, on that Sabbath eve when you slept with me I felt that I had conceived.' When Joseph heard his wife's words he said, 'Woe, what are you saying, this never happened' ... And because he loved Miriam who was very beautiful he said nothing about it, lest it all come to court. When the foetus quickened he feared that locals might claim she had always been sterile, so he took her away from Nazareth, their city ... And her time came to give birth, and out of fear she gave birth in her ox's trough. This scared them, so they hired donkeys and went down to Egypt, and the boy grew up there and they called him Yeshu son of Joseph.[19]

Some versions of *Toledoth Yeshu* described Mary's conception even more darkly: in the course of her contact with the neighbour, Joseph ben Pandera, whom Mary thought was her husband, she told him that they should not have intercourse: 'She said to him: "Do not touch me, because I am *niddah*" ... And he did not take this into consideration, and he lay with her and she fell pregnant.'[20] To the fault of birth was

added ritual pollution, *niddah*, the condition of women during the days of menstruation and the seven 'clean' days that followed. So Jews sometimes referred to Jesus as *ben ha-niddah*, the son of the *niddah*.[21] The polemical terrain between Jews and Christians involved the issues of Mary's body, Jesus' birth and, increasingly, the land in which their lives unfolded.

Encounters between Mary and the Jews were most heated in the land of her birth, where strong traditions of polemic and denunciation were attached to the Holy Places. As we have seen, Jerome endeavoured to create a sacred geography of Palestine and identified the sites of Mary's great moments: the Annunciation and the Nativity. The fifth century saw the real thrust towards establishing Mary – now *Theotokos* – in appropriate sites of memory. Following the models of the church of the Holy Sepulchre and the church of the Ascension on the Mount of Olives, three important octagonal churches were built with ambulatories, spaces for circulation by pilgrims and visitors. The church of Mary's tomb in the valley of Joshaphat was built *c.*440, over a rock ledge, and it was decorated with mosaics and inscriptions.[22] The pilgrimage church of the *kathisma* was built at the place where, according to the *Protogospel of James*, Mary sat down to rest on her way to Bethlehem. A site was identified early on between Jerusalem and Bethlehem as that where she bore the Child Jesus.[23] Alongside the monastery of Mar Elias a woman – Hikkelia – founded it around 455, on a site that may have been a cave. The elegant church was situated around the rough rock on which Mary was reputed to have sat.[24] The site also became a relic of sorts; a piece of the rock was used as a side altar in the church of the Holy Sepulchre.[25] A feast of the *kathisma* was celebrated according to the Jerusalem liturgy of the fifth century on 15 August; when a Dormition celebration developed on that date in the sixth century, it forced the move of the feast of the *kathisma* to 13 August.[26]

The efforts of writers who recounted traditions about Mary and of great imperial builders combined to transform the Holy Land into a Christian country redolent with her memory. By 530 the pilgrim Theodosius reported three important Marian sites: the *kathisma* church on the road to Bethlehem, Mary's tomb in the Valley of Jehoshaphat and the place of her birth near Bethesda. The pilgrim Antoninus, who wrote by 570, recorded Justinian's 'new' church for Mary, the Nea. By the seventh century even the place at which the Jews reputedly disrupted

Mary's funeral was shown to pilgrims,[27] and by 724 the route of Mary's funeral procession led pilgrims from the place of her Dormition on Mount Zion to her burial church.[28]

Pilgrims travelled to the Holy Land from all directions. Some of these journeys generated tales, which often express a desire to make the Christian story unfold, rich and compelling, in a land still much occupied by Jews. Artefacts and images were created for the use of pilgrims on their travels but also to be taken back home with them. A reliquary box from Palestine of c.600 described the scenes of Jesus' life, and Mary features in some: resting after the Nativity, attending his baptism, viewing the empty tomb, praying at the Ascension, and on the central panel, viewing the Crucifixion.[29] Arculf, a pilgrim from Gaul in the 680s, described a tapestry he had seen in Jerusalem, depicting Christ and the twelve apostles, and reputed to have been woven by Mary herself.[30] Similarly, in a hoard of some sixty moulds for the making of pilgrim tokens – at Qal'at Sim'an, the shrine of Simeon Stylites the Elder (d.459), some 60 kilometres north-east of Antioch – many including Mary. A third of the tokens depicted the Adoration of the Magi, seven the Nativity, and four the Annunciation.[31] A copper-alloy pendant of c.600 shows the Crucifixion alongside a scene of the Women at Christ's Tomb; an *ampula* – a container of holy liquid, such as oil – of c.600 preserved in the cathedral treasury of Monza depicts Christ's Ascension, with Mary underneath, flanked by John the Baptist and Zacharia.[32] The Flight into Egypt was another popular choice in pilgrim art, as was the Adoration of the Magi. Here was holy travel, divinely protected. But none of these conventional scenes quite conveyed the drama of Mary as *Theotokos* with her unique stature.[33]

Mary's elevation was achieved thanks to the will of emperors, courtiers and churchmen who sought to make their capital, Constantinople, into Mary's city par excellence. In doing so they had to overcome the obvious affinity of the figure of Mary to sites in the Holy Land: Nazareth, Bethlehem, Jerusalem and more. Unlike the buried remains of saints and martyrs, Mary's body had been assumed into heaven, and so veneration was mediated by objects that had been close to that body: her girdle, which she dropped to earth as she was assumed into heaven, and her robe.

The story of Mary's robe is a classic narrative of Christian triumph over Judaism, dramatized as a move from the Holy Land to Constanti-

nople. It is also a story of imperial leadership in pursuit of orthodoxy. The men who found Mary's robe were brothers – Galbius and Candidus – recent converts from Arianism, who chose to bolster their new faith by a visit to the holy places. Passing through Galilee, they took shelter with an elderly woman, a virgin of great beauty. While the brothers dined with her – she did not partake of their fare, but ate her own, Jewish food – conversation turned to a room in her house which was bathed in light and emitted fine odours; in it people experienced miraculous cures. The brothers persuaded her to reveal the secret of the place, and, sworn to secrecy, they heard a tale which had been passed on through her family for generations:

'The Virgin', she said, 'at her death gave to two virgins two of her robes as a benediction; one of these virgins was a member of my family and she took the gift and placed it in a little coffer which was inherited by a virgin successively. within the family. The little coffer is now hidden in the room as you see, and it is the robe within it which is the cause of all the miracles. Sirs, this is the truth which you sought: only let none of those in Jerusalem know.'[34]

Galbius and Candidus thanked the woman and prayed to the *Theotokos* that night for guidance. A scheme to remove the coffer secretly was then put into place. During the brothers' stay in Jerusalem they made a copy of the coffer and on their return to Galilee they exchanged it for the authentic one which they took to Constantinople.[35]

Wishing to keep the knowledge to themselves, the brothers had a church dedicated to St Peter and St Mark built to contain the robe. But they were ultimately led to share their discovery with others. When the imperial couple, Leo I (411–74) and Verena (d.484), heard about the robe they had a church built to house it in the Blachernae palace and offered it a fitting reliquary of silver and gold.[36] One version of the story even claimed that the dress still bore milk-stains, traces of the Child Christ's feeding at Mary's breast.[37] This became the shrine of Constantinople's protective relic, one which in future centuries was credited with saving the city from destruction by the Avars, the Muslims and the Russians.

Unlike the story of the Dormition, in which Jewish men abused and harassed Mary even to her end, the Jewish woman is cast in this narrative as a person close to Christian virtue. Like her female kin before her as guardians of the robe she was a household virgin, like the consecrated

61

maidens that so many well-to-do Christian families produced in those times. Sacred virginity was alien to Jewish social practice, but by creating this hybrid figure, the hagiographer was able to link Mary's past to the robe in latter-day Galilee. Jewish women were never so virulently despised as male Jews; they were considered less 'Jewish', less intent on rejecting Christianity. Mary herself had, after all, been a Galilean Jewish woman. The story of her robe formed part of the process by which every portable vestige of Mary's life in the Holy Land was transported to the political centre of Christianity – Constantinople.

In the Holy Land the ancient patriarchate of Jerusalem ceded primacy to Constantinople over a long period. This involved the movement of relics under the supervision of imperial officials but the lure of the Land itself was still potent. When news of the discovery of St Stephen's remains – he was considered the first Christian martyr – reached Eudoxia herself, the emperor's sister, she decided to make the Holy Land pilgrimage.[38] In the course of the Persian invasion of 614, the church on the site of Mary's 'tomb' was destroyed. The clash between Byzantium – Mary's empire – and Persia, home to Christian as well as Jewish communities, fomented anxiety alongside apocalyptic expectation. Some of the feeling evoked by the now emblematic image of Mary is captured in the narrative of *Sefer Zerubbabel* of *c.*628–30.[39] The author of this Hebrew apocalypse recounts visions of the end of time: the Messiah's mother, Hefzibah, will be given a powerful staff of salvation, made of

almond wood ... This is the staff that the Lord gave Adam and Moses and Aaron and Joshua and King David; it is the staff that blossomed and sprouted in the tent at the time it belonged to Aaron.[40]

Here was a female saviour who would defeat the kings of Yemen and of Antioch. The Messiah's mother had never before been imagined so potently in the Jewish tradition. Hefzibah is here a Jewish counterpart to Mary, an agent of sacred history. The visionary is later transported to a church where he sees

a marble statue in the shape of a virgin. The beauty of her appearance was wonderful to behold. 'This statue is the wife of Belial,' he said, 'Satan will come and lie with her, and she will bear a son named Armilos ... He will rule over all ... He will worship strange gods and speak falsehood ... He will slay by the

sword any one who does not believe in him ... He will make war on the holy ones and destroy them ...'[41]

Armilos is the powerful arm of Antichrist, bringer of strife, probably the figure of Emperor Heraclius, who passed laws that forced the baptism of the Jews.[42] Son and mother, emperor and holy statue, are fused in this Jewish apocalyptic vision. Something of Mary was absorbed even into the Jewish saving heroine.

CONSTANTINOPLE – MARY'S SPECIAL CITY

The many churches of Constantinople came to house Mary's few physical relics, but they also cherished fine and potent images of her – Mary painted on wood, the quintessential icon.[43] With the emergence of the *Theotokos* new forms of address and representation were crafted. Poise and majesty were the keys to the visualization of Mary. Imperial example prompted emulation and so, for example, Cyrus, Prefect of the city, founded a church dedicated to the *Theotokos* around 438.[44] In the regions that followed the capital's example, Mary was presented as an imperial figure: finely dressed, frontal, central and sometimes surrounded by angels and saints as attendants; in Rome she emerged as *Maria Regina*, a queenly figure bedecked in royal costume.

One of the most famous examples is a sixth-century icon made in Constantinople and preserved in the monastery of St Katherine in the Sinai desert: Mary is enthroned with Jesus in her lap flanked by St George and St Theodore in sumptuous court dress with two angels hovering above the group. Mary's eyes are large, and she has strong facial features. This icon is among the finest examples of the aesthetic of late antique art, especially valuable since only eight images of Mary and Child have survived from before the eighth century.[45] It served the monks and pilgrims of this remote outpost of Byzantine asceticism. Of the same tradition, though more resolutely Coptic, is the recently discovered linen painting of Mary with the Child Jesus in her lap surrounded by an almond-shaped sphere – a mandorla.[46]

Carved ivory diptychs were widely manufactured for private devotional and domestic piety of lay people. A late sixth-century

example represents Mary and Jesus on one of its panels, enthroned and accompanied by two figures (apostles for Jesus and angels for Mary), each placed under an ornamental shell-shaped arch. While Jesus raises his right hand in blessing and holds a book in his left, Mary tenderly attends with both hands to the son in her lap.[47] A late sixth-century Coptic tapestry, now in the Cleveland Museum, depicts an arrangement similar to the ivory and icon mentioned above, in a typically Egyptian style. The palette is vivid with reds and blues and there is much decorative vegetation. Mary is enthroned between angels – named here Gabriel and Michael – and her hands secure her son.[48]

Mary's figure was cast in imperial majesty in other cultural spheres too. The title page of the Book of Proverbs in a sixth-century Syriac Bible portrays Mary standing between Solomon to her right and a personification of the church: a woman dressed in white and cloaked in red, carrying a book and cross.[49] Mary is dressed in sumptuous court attire, with red shoes and cloak; her head-gear resembles that of Mary of the Sinai icons. She carries her son in front of her womb.

Egyptian Christians continued to imagine and represent Mary as the breast-feeding mother, God's mother who absorbed the nurture that had for centuries been ascribed to Isis. From the seventh-century monastic complex at Bawit alone four images of Mary suckling Jesus have survived. In chapel 42 mother and son sit enthroned at the centre of the ranks of apostles in the apse scene of the Ascension, while the grown Christ rises just above them.[50] The monastic complex at Saqqara just south of Cairo replaced the immense Egyptian necropolis of the Middle Kingdom. Its cells are decorated with wall paintings, as are several spaces shared by monks. In a wall-niche of cell A, Mary is enthroned, putting her right breast into her son's mouth while looking straight ahead, beyond the viewer. From Egypt too a carving in limestone depicts the large figure of Mary flanked by drawn curtains, holding her son to the breast, with a praying figure at either side.[51] The fragile remains of a papyrus from Antinoe captures a similar gentle image of mother feeding son. The figures are drawn in dark ink: Mary and Child each have a halo on which traces of gold colouring can be identified. The position is frontal: Mary holds the Child in her left hand and places her breast in its mouth.[52] The tradition of Isis putting Horus to the breast influenced these representations of Mary within the Coptic cultural sphere in

papyrus, relief and wall painting. The continuities run deep in Coptic Upper Egypt and Nubia. In the Temple of Isis at Derr (some 200 kilometres south of Aswan) a church was created between the columns; it was dedicated to the *Theotokos*, as the Coptic inscription on a stone makes clear: 'I am Moses, servant of the Holy *Theotokos* Mary. May those who read these lines be so good and pray for me.'[53]

There was an extraordinary vitality in the attachment to Mary exhibited by Coptic writers, some known to have been monks, others anonymous. A collection of Coptic homilies compiled in the seventh and eighth centuries (and ascribed to Archbishop Cyril of Alexandria (d.387)) concentrate on the Passion and Mary. The author opens with the promise that each homily will be an offering like a dish in a banquet: each fine, each different.[54] Mary's humanity is asserted strongly against those – deemed heretics – who claimed that she was but a vital force (*dynamis*) in the form of a woman called Mary who bore a son. Against such a claim the author marshals the full tradition of Mary's genealogy and her ample praises:

O Queen, spouse of truth, and mother of the King of Life; O Queen, wise virgin, show me your people and those of the house of your father, so that we may tell all of your elect parentage. Here I find myself as if the Holy Virgin has taken my hand saying: 'O Cyril, if you wish to know my lineage and those of the house of my father, listen to me: I was a promise of God, which was promised to my parents in faith, that I would be born. My parents were of the tribe of Judah, of the lineage of David ... Search the bible and you will find what you are looking for.'[55]

After her birth Mary lived in the Temple, toiled there and ate only bread, salt and herbs. When she was fourteen she received the Annunciation. The Child Jesus was born to his mother Mary and lived with his guardian Joseph. 'Cyril' adds:

I have told your goodness all these things because of certain godless heretics who say Mary is a vital force. Here, I have exemplified to you the discourse through which I now say: 'Mary is in fact corporeal, the Lamb of God came into the world, stayed in her, and took away the sins of the world'.[56]

A Coptic homily described in detail the intimacy of the child-mother embrace:

Thou didst bend thy neck and let thy hair fall over Him . . . He stretched out his hand, He took thy breast, and He drew into his mouth the milk which was sweeter than manna . . . Having drunk from thy spotless breasts, He called thee 'My Mother'.[57]

Such powerful images were nurtured by local traditions and expressed in local languages.[58] Yet they also interacted powerfully – Egypt quite enthusiastically, while more eastern parts less so – with the imperial orthodoxy that imagined a god made man, dual in nature, and supported by a majestic mother, at once loving and sublime.

While such cultural diversity meant that Mary was experienced differently by Christians of Syriac, Coptic or Greek cultures, Constantinople still exerted a powerful influence on all religious cultures of the Empire. Visitors to Constantinople were faced with an ever more varied and rich experience of Mary's images and liturgies. The fifth and sixth centuries saw the establishment of Mary's shrines in the city, the emergence of the icon, and a body of miracle stories about Mary's interventions in the life of the city, its people, its many monks.[59] The city celebrated the Feast of the Annunciation and the Assumption, and a constant flow of hymnody and homiletics flowed to it from the pens of priests from Constantinople, Alexandria and even Antioch. The preacher Severus of Antioch ($c.467$–$c.538$) chose to emphasize the feasts of the Presentation and the Epiphany.[60] The cult of empire and the cult of saints redefined the mission and the message of imperial rule. Emperors thought as much about religious unity as they did about military strategy, exulted as much in prestigious building and the adornment of churches as they did in fortification or dispensing justice.[61]

Mary became the protector of Constantinople through a process of accumulation. Every misfortune that befell the capital provided occasions for enhanced appeals for Mary's help. These centred on Mary's churches built and continuously embellished by emperors. As we have seen, Mary's robe was housed in the chapel of the Blachernae palace, decorated with a mosaic representing the imperial family around Mary in majesty. The Chalcoprateia church was home to Mary's girdle – believed to have been dropped by her to the apostles in memory of her Assumption into heaven; it was built by Leo and Verena and was completed by Emperor Justin II ($c.520$–78).

The most common form of address to Mary was still that established

by Proclus in the mid-fifth century: strings of appellations, of sacred names, of vivid imagery replete with contradiction. The sacred motherhood merged with signs of imperial greatness and produced an exalted Mary, majestic yet real.[62] Mary accompanied emperors into battle too; when Emperor Heraclius sailed from Africa to Constantinople in spring 610, he carried with him the 'venerable image of the undefiled Virgin'.[63] Even more tortuous was the route travelled by his predecessor's daughter, Maria. When her father, Emperor Maurice, gave her in marriage to the Persian monarch Khosru II (590–628), she was accompanied by priests, and her husband-to-be had two churches built for her – one, fittingly, dedicated to the Mother of God.[64]

From Constantinople spread a particular vision of redemption and authority, at the heart of which was the fusion of the divine and the human, similar to the blend of autocracy and accessibility in the emperor. Mary was also the companion of monks and ascetics.[65] Her comfort and grace demanded and endorsed their often harsh discomfort, as we have seen in the icons of Saint Katherine's monastery in Sinai and in the desert shrines of Bawit. The protector was imagined as being fully attuned, attentive, reserved but not distant. The *Theotokos* was dignified, solemn, but very present and effective. Correspondingly, the homilies addressed to her often used the rhetoric of the court address, known as the encomium.

Rhetoric of empire and the images of sovereignty blended in new and exciting ways in Mary's figure. At the coronation of Emperor Justin II in November 565 the empress Sophia addressed her husband with a prayer for his success, a prayer to Mary.[66] The North African poet Corippus provided a Latin poem for this very Greek occasion, a blend of pagan classical poetics and a Christian devotional hymn:

> Most holy virgin, mother of the creator of the world,
> queen of high heaven, at once and uniquely,
> true parent and ever-virgin, without a father's seed,
> whom God chose for his mother, and who believed in his Word
> and conceived it, and having become pregnant gave birth to our Salvation!
> O merciful love of God, wonderful and terrible at the utterance:
> Our Lord God, the maker of heavens, the one form
> of God the Father, a clothing of real flesh
> took on for himself, and took from a virgin the shape of a servant.[67]

Here are familiar sounds and images – the virginal birth without seed, Christ as 'wearing' flesh. Such a Mary could only be approached by humble adoration and requests for a good reign:

> You, glory of mothers,
> And your help I beseech. May I always adore you
> and call you Lady and preserver of the new rule of Justin.[68]

The imperial couple, beset by invasions and challenges on all sides, put their trust in Mary as protector of the empire and its capital.

Given Mary's centrality to the imperial vision of authority and orthodoxy, it is perhaps not surprising to find that imperial officials occasionally acted brutally against those whose ideas cast doubt on Mary's orthodox dignity. The imperial church tried hard to bring back into the fold those Armenian and Syriac churches that had rejected the formulations of church councils in favour of a Monophysite understanding of Jesus. Money from imperial coffers was spent on building churches in places as far as Sana'a in the Arabian Peninsula in order to bolster orthodoxy there.[69] To those who rejected the dual nature of Christ a formulation was offered – through the concept of *monoenergeia* – one, or single, will in Christ.[70] The monk Maximus the Confessor (580–662), member of an aristocratic family of Constantinople, fell foul of the imperial church by challenging the sense of such a formulation: if there is a sole operation in the Godhead then who was acting in the gospels? Whose will was done on the cross? Such pondering on Christ quickly led to reflection on his mother. Maximus' inquiry into the autonomy of the historic Jesus was interpreted as an attack on Mary, and for these perceived errors he was chastised, exiled to Thrace and physically abused.[71] A soldier from Thrace who heard of Maximus' journey to the place of exile put it bluntly: 'The monk who blasphemes against the Mother of God is on his way here.'[72] Pope Martin I, who had previously supported Maximus, was similarly put on trial in Constantinople and imprisoned. Well-meaning priests attempted to mediate between the exile and Emperor Constans II (630–68), like Theodosius, bishop of Caesarea in Bythinia, who visited Maximus in exile and begged him to explain his difficulty in accepting that there was a sole divine will:

And I'll tell you the reason: because it is a saying foreign to the holy Fathers to speak of one will and activity of two different natures ... If I say that the one

68

will and activity are as of one being, I am forced, even though I do not wish it, to speak of the will and activity as of one Father and as of one Spirit, and the expression will be found to have slipped into a multitude of gods.[73]

Another group of well-wishers linked Maximus' plight with the perceived danger to Mary:

'Father, because certain people have caused a scandal for us against Your Holiness, saying that you do not call Our Lady the most holy Virgin, the Mother of God, I adjure you . . . to tell us the truth, and to turn away this scandal from our hearts . . .'

And after kneeling, he [Maximus] stood up, and stretching out his hands to heaven he said tearfully: 'The one that does not say that Our Lady, who is worthy of all praise, and most holy, inviolate, and venerable to every rational creature was truly made the natural Mother of God who made heaven and earth and the sea, and everything which is in them, let him be anathema . . .'

And they all wept and prayed for him, saying: 'May God strengthen you, Father, and make you worthy to complete this course without stumbling.'[74]

Casting doubt on the delicate balance between Christ's humanity and divinity appeared to soldiers and monks alike not only as a philosophical conundrum, nor even a question on the nature of redemption. The danger was that Mary, the *Theotokos*, who secured the kinship of flesh between humans and God might be diminished.[75] The emperor as her guardian, churchmen as her publicists and lay people as her devotees were quick to respond to any doubt cast on Mary.

Yet later in his life Maximus wrote an astonishing account of Mary's life that was to influence later Byzantine writing. It is the first *Life of the Virgin* to consider at length Mary's part in Jesus' ministry. Based on the *Protogospel of James* in some parts, it is an audacious portrayal of Mary as her son's partner in ministry and even in death.[76] The author exalts Mary's virginity, and as if to dramatize her aloofness, Joseph is said to have stayed at home in Nazareth, being blind, while Mary joined her son in his exciting ministry. Mary is with her son every step of the way and unto his death; Maximus even suggests there that 'I would say, although this may seem audacious, that she suffered more than him, and took upon herself the sorrow of the heart.'[77] There is detailed description of Mary's witness of the Passion and of her involvement in the removal and care of Jesus' body. She is cast in a central role, as

69

apostle among apostles. Far from demoting Mary, Maximus demonstrates how important Mary appeared to him as an example of chastity and of exemplary disciplehood.

Such reflection on Mary's state at the time of the Crucifixion, if not her role in Christ's ministry, was being appreciated in the compositions for use in Constantinople's tens of churches. The sixth-century hymnographer Romanos the Melodist, cantor of the Theotokos church of the city, extended the emotional and psychological range of Marian chant. He wrote long themed hymns – *kontakia* – for public worship often during night vigils which saw large crowds of lay people converge on city churches and experience extended homiletic chant.[78] Among his sixty compositions are hymns on the Nativity, the Presentation at the Temple, the marriage at Cana, and on Mary at the foot of the Cross. Romanos originated from Syria, and was familiar with the rich lore of Syriac poetry. To these he added what seems like Greek poetry of lament, performed by relatives for lost loved ones. The dialogue at the Cross, between mother and son, between human and God, is punctuated by the refrain 'My son and God'. Mary faces her appalling loss by seizing the unfolding paradox: 'Despite the fact that you endure the cross / you remain my son and my God'. Mary's lament is situated in the midst of the social practices of mourning, among the women who accompanied Jesus 'mourning him and lamenting him' (Luke 23:27). She followed 'wearily' with these women, weak and pained. She is not stoical, but suffering:

> I am overcome, my son, overcome by love.
> But I truly cannot bear this: I in my room, you on the cross;
> I in a house, you in the tomb.[79]

But she is reminded of the divine plan, when her son urges her to keep calm:

> Keep calm, if you see the foundations of earth quaking.
> Men's sacrilege will totter all creation.
> The vault of heaven will darken, and not open its eye until I say.[80]

The reassuring assertion of purpose is then shared with the whole community, singing together:

> Come, let us all sing the praise of the one crucified for us,
> For Mary saw him on the wooden beam and cried,

'Even though you endure the torture on the cross, you are my son and my god.'[81]

There were many reasons to grieve in sixth- and seventh-century Byzantium, a polity pressed by the Persian emperors in the east – to which Jerusalem was lost in 614 (though later briefly recovered by Heraclius) – and by the Avars from the north and west. Raids on the city became a matter of course from 619, and they provided the context for imaginative displays of civic and liturgical initiatives that used Mary's icons and relics. A contemporary witness describes the miraculous events wrought by Mary's robe during the Avar raids of 619.[82] A decision was taken to remove into hiding the great treasures of the city's churches, among them Mary's robe in the chapel of the Blachernae. Those appointed to do so opened the reliquary casket in which the robe was kept. This was a highly unusual act, and so once danger had passed a ceremony of restoration was performed from the vigils of 2 July with an incessant flow of prayer issued from the churches of St Laurence and the Blachernae. At dawn the procession was accompanied by lay folk and priests, who chanted psalms and hymns. The patriarch who carried the casket was jostled by people eager to make contact with the holy object. In the safety of the church he broke the seals and opened the casket to reveal the purple cloth that enveloped the holy robe. While the silken imperial cloth had disintegrated, Mary's woollen robe had not – it was intact and indestructible, like the one who had worn it. And this is no wonder, for

how likely it was that this divine and holy garment should partake of grace, when we believe that it not only clothed the Mother of God, but that in it she actually wrapped the Word of God Himself, when he was a little child and gave him milk.[83]

Constantinople was saved again from Avar aggression in 626 by the image of Mary, this time raised by Patriarch Sergius on the city walls. Strings of prayers were instituted, and incessant nightly salutations were directed to Mary by monks who stood and chanted all night. In the church of the Blachernae the *akathistos* tradition was born: an extended mode of singing Mary's praises in short rhythmic stanzas, while standing up, overnight. The *akathistos* mobilized the whole body, it was a discipline, a routine that tested the endurance of holy men:

71

To you, our leader in battle and defender,
O *Theotokos*, I, your city, delivered from sufferings,
ascribe hymns of victory and thanksgiving.
Since you are invincible in power,
free me from all kinds of dangers,
that I may cry to you:
'Hail, bride unwedded'.[84]

The hymn told the story of Mary's life from the Annunciation onwards. It ended with an invocation for acceptance of the hymn-offering:

O mother hymned by all,
you who gave birth to the Word
the Holiest of all Holies:
accepting this present offering,
deliver from every evil and from punishment to come
all those who cry to you:
'Alleluia'.[85]

The appreciation for imperial Mary was couched in a specific style, the product of ancient traditions of rhetoric in which all educated men were schooled. The efforts to describe Mary in poetry and in preaching, to make her visual in illuminated manuscripts and mosaics, to invoke her and praise her in prayer, deployed the well-honed conventions of panegyrics to great men, especially *antithesis* (contradiction) and *hyperbole* (exaggeration and repetition). Contradiction worked particularly well in telling of the Incarnation, for here was a central paradox: a god made flesh, a virgin giving birth, the creator being created. Andrew of Crete, an eighth-century preacher, who described Mary as the 'container of the uncontainable' was inspired by the influential fifth-century homilies of Proclus.[86]

It seemed appropriate to describe Mary with the vocabulary associated with spring and the delights of nature. The Annunciation (25 March), which was celebrated by the early fifth century, coincided with springtime, and so the rebirth of humankind met that of nature. Anastasius, patriarch of Antioch (d.599), even claimed that the Annunciation coincided with the first spring of Creation, while eighth-century patriarch Germanos of Constantinople saw the Annunciation as the 'springtime feast of feasts'.[87] Descriptions of spring amplified the beauty and meaning

72

of the moment when Mary received her message. Descriptive phrases were adumbrated in sequences of attributes of a spring landscape heaped upon Mary: as a fount or a river, as a flowering rod, or as the tree of life. The preacher John of Damascus (*c.*676–749) described her as *more* fragrant than the lily, *redder* than the rose, *more* florid than spring's verdure.[88]

The traditions of rhetoric and display did not preclude creative innovation in singing the praises of Mary. Andrew of Crete stimulated his audience's interest by imagining the anticipated excitement of the feast. In a sermon on Mary's Nativity he likened himself to a rider urging his horse to victory. The audience's sense of occasion was built up in words such as:

> Let us reverence the brightness of the feast,
> Let us apply the honourable title of virginity to the Virgin.
> Let us offer the Queen of the race, as gifts and costly myrrh,
> The revelations of the prophets . . .[89]

He then listed descriptive phrases in a familiar manner. Another rhetorical ploy used in his sermon for the Annunciation was the setting as inner dialogue of Gabriel's own reflection on the manner in which he might deliver his message:

> Shall I enter the chamber quickly?
> – But I shall frighten the soul of the Virgin.
> Shall I go more slowly?
> – But I shall be thought by the girl to have crept secretly into the entrance.
> Shall I knock on the door? And how?
> For this is not customary for angels . . .[90]

Mary's power to intervene miraculously and to protect her devotees was not limited to the imperial capital or the professional religious. Pilgrimage literature described the marvels expressed by visitors to Mary's shrines, while miracle collections recorded Mary's incursions into the daily lives of humans. On his pilgrimage to the Holy Land in the early 680s, Arculf, a bishop from Gaul, reported what his eyes saw, but also hearsay of edifying and amazing tales.[91] We know of his experience because he subsequently went to Ireland and described it to the abbot Adomnán, who wrote it into his book *On the Holy Places* (*De locis sanctis*). A particularly lurid miracle concerns a small image of Mary that once hung on the wall of a house. An 'obtuse and hard-hearted

man', in other words a Jew, inquired about the image, and when he found out that it was an image of 'saint Mary always virgin' he removed it from the wall and took it to a place where people used to empty their bowels while sitting over long perforated planks. He threw the image in and added the contents of his own body. Later a devout Christian passer-by found the image in the stinking mess. He removed it, cleaned it and took it home. The image began to ooze fine oil, and Adomán adds that Arculf had seen this oil with his own eyes. A miracle of the eastern Mediterranean reached the shores of Ireland and then the plains of Gaul through the efforts of this single, engaged pilgrim.

Miracles of Mary abounded by the sixth and seventh centuries. Once her end was established in narratives and in liturgy, it supported the sense that Mary remained in heaven, watching over all Christians, willing to intervene when necessary. The Syrian monastic writer John Moschus ($c.540/50-619/34$) collected tales about the holy men of Egypt and Palestine and other edifying miracles, like so many flowers, in his work *Spiritual Meadow*. Among these was the story of the Jewish Boy.[92] Situated in Constantinople, the account unfolds around a Jewish family that lived among Christians in the city, and whose son went to school near 'the Great Church' – Hagia Sophia:

Now it often happened that the sacristan of [Hagia] Sophia had a great deal left over from the holy table, and he despatched persons to the schoolmaster [asking] for children to be sent to consume what was superfluous from the holy eucharist ... Now when the children came, the Jewish Boy followed too ...[93]

Meanwhile, at home, the Boy's father – a glass blower – was worried at his son's absence. When the boy returned home he explained: 'I went to the Great Church with the other children and ate and drank very well there.' Further interrogation revealed that the son had eaten the communion bread. The angry father violently threw the boy into the furnace in his workshop. The anxious mother arrived home with a sense of foreboding and found her son in the fire. Once she had removed him from it unharmed, the boy explained: 'A woman dressed in purple came to me and gave me water and told me not to be afraid.' The assembled reported the amazing event to the patriarch, seeking the holy man's counsel, and then to Emperor Justinian: the father refused to convert and was burned, while mother and son became Christians: the former a nun and the latter a scholar.[94]

74

The miracle of the Jewish Boy registers several points of tension which could arise between Jews and Christians: it asserted Mary's power against Jewish violence, it contrasted her mercy against the Jew's cruelty and offered the prospect of Jewish recognition in the boy's acknowledgement of Christian truth. It took polemic into the Jewish home, a sphere of paternal tyranny, and offered instead maternal nurture. This story became one of the most popular Mary miracles in future centuries.

A polemical terrain coalesced around Mary, between Christians and other Christians, Christians and Jews, and later between Christians and Muslims. Jews rejected the indignity of a God made flesh and secondarily found unreasonable the notion of a birth that left the mother a virgin. In the polemical tract *The Account of the Disputation of the Priest (Qissat Mujadalat al-Usquf)*, composed in Judaeo-Arabic by the tenth century and later translated into Hebrew, a priest, Nestor, who had converted to Judaism, argues polemically with Christianity. The work is cast as Nestor's letter to a Christian bishop, his sparring partner, and it expresses deep repugnance about the meeting of flesh and God in Mary. Every claim for Mary's purity, such as had been made since the *Protogospel of James*, was met by a counter-claim of pollution and shame:

And when the time came for Mary to give birth at the inn, Joseph the carpenter went out to bring a midwife. He was unable to find anyone other than a harlot named Salome. He brought her and she took care of Jesus. She nursed him, she gave him to suckle, she swaddled him in pieces of cloth and she put him to sleep in the donkey's manger at the inn, as your Gospel claims.[95]

I wonder about you that you are not embarrassed to worship him who dwelled in the oppression of the womb, close enough to hear his mother's flatuses when she moved her bowels like any other woman, remaining in deep darkness for nine months. How can you say that any aspect of divinity dwells in such an ugly place? If you say that there was no aspect of divinity in [that] place, then you are saying that [Jesus] was like any other child, and after he left the womb through the [organ] which receives the penis and the semen, since this is the place from which he emerged with his mouth and nose pulling against the urethra, close to the place from which the stench of excrement exits, then he slept and nursed from his mother's breasts.[96]

Polemical tracts are not witness to daily exchanges, but they do dramatize some of the directions in which discussion could follow in

areas of heated awareness of religious difference or in periods of tension and uncertainty for Jews or Christians. The graphic description of the inner parts of a woman's body is one of the ways in which Mary's humanity was explored by Jews and Christians alike.

MARY AND THE STRUGGLE OVER IMAGES

The confrontation with Islam and the subsequent loss of territory in east and west inspired Byzantine leaders – secular and ecclesiastical – to seek an explanation: wrongful devotion was one of the explanations for the Empire's changing fortunes. As the Byzantine Empire confronted Islam, a religion that rejected imagery, its eastern regions – above all Syria and Eastern Anatolia – became the terrain of heated polemic about the nature of religious practice. One of the questions raised was whether Christ could be represented adequately and appropriately in matter. The Byzantine Church displayed anxiety about the proliferation of practices of representations of saints, Christ and Mary. The decisions of the Church council in Trullo in 692, for example, considered the gifts which believers might offer to the virgin mother and prohibited the making of icons that might be sexually alluring.[97] That council also legislated against rituals that smacked of pagan and Jewish influences. The preacher John of Damascus (675–749) was equally aware that imperial Christianity was closely observed by Muslims and Jews: he countered attacks by both groups on an image worship which was, in their eyes, tantamount to idolatry. The icon, he stated, like the incarnate Christ, is a tangible form of divinity.[98] Images became and remained a terrain for polemic and political competition. Those Christians who attacked traditional veneration of images were, moreover, accused of doing the work of Muslims and Jews.[99]

The primacy of images as channels to the divine was challenged by those who championed the purity of the Word, and this forced the hand of Christian rulers. Emperor Constantine V (741–75) headed a council in 754 in Mary's great church of Blachernae, where the holy relic of her robe was kept.[100] He put to the council a number of questions that he prefaced with a statement of faith and praises of Mary. The council

answered him by rejecting the belief that images could adequately represent divine things, above all the complex and dual nature of Christ. Images could never do justice to, could never share the substance of, divinity and hence they were lacking, even misleading. This failure of images to portray fully the figure of Christ also affected the representation of Mary:

How do they dare to depict, by means of vulgar pagan art, the Mother of God, worthy of all praise, whom the fullness of the Godhead overshadowed, through whom the unapproachable light shone upon us, who is higher than the heavens and is more holy than the Cherubim?[101]

In opposition to this view the preacher John of Damascus insisted that honouring Mary in images was not tantamount to idolatry and that images were even sanctioned by the gospels.[102] But the legislation from the capital tended against images and affected the whole of Asia Minor: icons were removed, whitewashed, burned or hidden away. Images also became the touchstone for emergent world-views that were increasingly separate, eastern Greek and European Latin.

In 787 the Empress Irene reversed the policy on images. She may have been motivated by a personal experience that led her to explore and reinstate Mary's public imagery. She clearly revered Mary and was recorded as a munificent donor to the church of Virgin of the Source (*Tys Pygis*) who granted precious gold veils and curtains, crown and vessels.[103] She convened the Second Council of Nicaea in 787 and used all the political might she could muster to reverse the religious policy against images. Meeting outside Constantinople and supported by troops loyal to her, the Council dealt with several ecclesiastical issues, the most dramatic of which was the full embracing of images. Thinking about Mary helped express the underlying logic of the new tendency:

Prophecy proclaims 'Behold, a virgin shall conceive and bear a son'. When we see this prophecy [made manifest] in an image, namely a virgin with a child in her arms, how can we refrain from adoring and kissing it? Who is so wayward of mind as to dare to resist? With such a kiss let us make ourselves worthy of [this] adoration.[104]

Here was full reversal and a new assertion of imperial will. The return to images now challenged Latin thinkers and rulers to take a position too.

The European power to be reckoned with was the kingdom of the Franks under the leadership of Charlemagne, who, in the year 800, arranged his own coronation by the pope in Rome as the Holy Roman Emperor. The Franks were not invited to attend the Second Council of Nicaea, but they received reports of it. Charlemagne commissioned a response, an assertion of political and cultural autonomy. This resulted in an answer composed by the Carolingian courtier and poet Theodulf, bishop of Orléans (c.760–821). His *Caroline Books* (*Libri Carolini*) provided a clause-by-clause counterblast to the Council's decisions, which had reached him in poor Latin translations. Theodulf took the Greek position to be a full endorsement of the worship of images. He retorted with the argument that God is to be adored not 'through the image, which is created by colours', but rather for his power, through his Word, his son – all of which are ineffable. This power is expressed in the many extraordinary actions of Virgin Birth and miraculous cures. The material signs are the tools by which God's power is adored.[105] Theodulf used such important moments of Mary's life as examples of divine intervention through material objects and expresses how preposterous it would be to deem them all objects of worship:

Surely it cannot be that because the rod of Aaron, which signifies the childbearing of the Blessed Virgin, when the law of nature had been crushed, became fruitful by the irrigation of no human power and flowered and put forth leaves and bore fruit, therefore, rods should be believed things to be worshipped?[106]

Matter carried meaning, but it should not become the object of worship.

Theodulf's position was complex: he maintained, not unlike the Byzantine council, that the true image of Christ in the world is his body and blood on the altar at the mass.[107] But he was willing to concede that images could play a beneficial role in conveying the memory of God's power. The problem was one of discernment and certainty: how could one be sure that the beautiful woman holding a boy in her arms represented Mary? In Theodulf's words:

Even if we suppose that an image of the Holy Mother of God ought to be adored, how are we to identify her image, or differentiate it from other images? When we see a beautiful woman depicted with a child in her arms, with no inscription provided, how are we to know whether it is Sarah holding Isaac, or Rebecca with Jacob, or Bathsheba with Solomon, or Elizabeth with John, or indeed any

other woman with her child? Or if we consider the fables of gentiles, which are often depicted, how are we to know whether it is Venus with Aeneas, or Alcmene with Hercules, or Andromache with Astyanax? For if one is adored [by mistake] for another, that is delusion, and if one is adored that should never have been adored, that is madness.[108]

The *Libri Carolini* was an intellectual exercise aimed at clarifying some central questions in religious belief and practice, and a statement of intellectual and political maturity of the greatest European court. Mary emerged from it as a touchstone of a European devotional style. Writers in Latin were aware of Greek religious traditions in words and images, and they sought to appropriate and re-express them. They were aware of work in ivory, which was widely known in Europe, where it was traded and often received as gifts from the east. Court artists emulated them, producing ivories in which Mary was presented enthroned, powerful and majestic.[109] The Franks knew that their own Roman liturgy was influenced by older Greek ones, and laboured at translation and copying from the Greek. The great hymn of Mary's praise the *Akathistos* was translated into Latin and survives in a ninth-century manuscript from the monastery of St Gall.[110] Nothing quite like the *Akathistos* existed in Latin; strings of Latin Marian praises were yet to come.

MARY'S IMAGES RESTORED

In the resurgent Byzantine east, after a century of soul-searching over the appropriate way of representing Mary, she re-emerged in word and image. By the mid-ninth century icons had regained their place as vehicles for communication with the divine and for contact with saints. A feast-day – the Sunday of Orthodoxy – commemorated the restoration of images, which were now appreciated for their power to protect and inform. The joy in representation affected not only visual imagery but other genres too: visual materials were used in the course of preaching, architectural spaces were made to receive images, and visual metaphors were incorporated into religious poetry. Photios, Patriarch of Constantinople, described the image of Mary in the apse of Hagia Sophia in 867: 'Before our eyes stands motionless the Virgin carrying the creator in her arms as an infant, depicted in painting as she is in writings and visions,

an interceder for our salvation'.[111] The apse mosaic is a fine example of a statuesque *Theotokos*, with her son in her lap, seated upon a gem-encrusted throne, facing forwards, flanked by Emperors Constantine and Justinian, who offer the city and the church to her; her gaze, like that of the St Katherine's icon, trails off to her right.[112] Images of Mary were similarly admired in those parts of the Empire least image-friendly, like the one produced in an Armenian book of gospels of 989 known as the Etchmiadzin Evangeliary.[113] They also spread into new regions, like the kingdom of Kiev, which received its Christianity from Constantinople. When Vladimir of Kiev (980–1015) constructed in 989–96 a church in honour of the *Theotokos*, he employed Greek masons and architects. They had at their disposal a tenth of his possessions to build the Tithe Church (*Desyatinnaya tserkov*) in her honour.[114]

This was not a period of mere restoration of images, but one of innovation and experimentation with representations of the ineffable. From emperor to monastic scribe initiatives were under way: Emperor Michael III (842–67) reinstated Mary on his coins, and manuscript illumination not only represented Mary as part of biblical narrative, but showed her icons to be an essential decoration in churches and domestic interiors. Mary now formed part of the work of biblical commentary in books like the sumptuous collection of homilies by the fourth-century theologian and father of the Church Gregory of Nazianzus (*c.*329–90), lavishly adorned with images in the ninth.[115] The Annunciation and the Visitation are combined in elegant form on folio 3r: Mary leaps out of her seat as she receives the angel's news.[116] The homily on Noah was accompanied not by a discourse on baptism, as was the custom, but by something more esoteric: Noah as a figure of Christ, who saved sinful humanity, and Mary as the ark, which contained him. There was ample scope now for reflection on the rich visual possibilities of Mary, and for innovation too. These settled most frequently on representations of the Incarnation – its necessity and its amplitude. In the ninth-century Pantokrator Psalter, verse 71:6, 'He shall come down as rain upon a fleece; and as drops falling upon earth', was accompanied by David and Gideon contemplating an icon of Mary. David points to an inscription 'in the womb of the Virgin' and Gideon brings to mind the story of the fleece, which soaked up dew but did not wet the ground (Judges 6:36–40). Here is an erudite image aimed at a new telling of the Incarnation:

not a tale but a typological correlation between testaments old and new, a sign of the truthful foretelling of Christ's birth in Mary.[117]

The 'return' to images situated Mary squarely within the Christian story. Mary was often represented in the company of prophets whose words offered support for the claims that she was indeed the *Theotokos*, Bearer of God. In the ninth-century Khludov Psalter, made in Constantinople, sacred word and image combined in portraying Mary as a vehicle of the Incarnation. Psalm 44:2 'My heart has uttered a good word' is interpreted following Hesychius' reading as God's word spoken at the Incarnation of his son through Mary: the scene shows an icon of Mary touched by the hand of God in the presence of the dove of the Holy Spirit.[118] In the apse of the tenth-century cave church of Kaloritissa in Naxos Mary is depicted enthroned, flanked by John the Baptist and the prophet Isaiah.[119] Byzantine ivories of the tenth century, which circulated throughout the Near East and Europe, habitually situated Mary – with John – either side of Christ in scenes of the Crucifixion: Mary gestures with her hands while John often touched his face in sorrow.[120] These were powerful images that were tactile, seen through the light and shimmer of candles and appreciated within the sounds of unfolding liturgy and prayer.

Greek representations of Mary now associated her unambiguously with the story of salvation, with the drama of the Incarnation, supported by biblical prophecy and pre-figuration. A mid-tenth-century ivory of a workshop in Constantinople has Mary as *Hodegetria* ('the one who shows the way'), an iconography known since the sixth century, wherein Mary points at her son – the Way – with her finger. Tall and slender, formal and distant, here is Mary with her son, almost ethereal, though finely carved in ivory.[121] Attributes of celestial majesty were reserved for representations of Mary and Christ alone: archangels dressed in imperial ceremonial garb, like those who accompanied her in the mosaics restored in 843 in the church of the Dormition in Nicaea.[122] Parity between the mother and son is evident in the enamelled cross associated with Pope Paschal I: Mary and her son appear either side of the cross, equal in size and dignity.[123] The central panel of a tenth-century Triptych, deeply carved in ivory, depicts Christ enthroned between the figures of Mary and St John the Baptist; Mary's robes and Christ's throne were painted gold, the colour of majesty.[124]

Together with the strong biblical web woven around Mary there were

even some attempts to express Mary's feelings in gesture. The maker of a small late-ninth-century icon, perhaps from Palestine, chose to emphasize the pathos of the Crucifixion: Christ's eyes are closed and he wears a modest loincloth. Mary's gesture is arresting, she is a pensive, troubled onlooker. Mary was given a rich, secret, intellectual life.[125] Occasionally we are allowed to glimpse the ideas and feelings which beholders and makers of Mary entertained. The anonymous ninth-century *Apocalypse of the Theotokos* imagines Mary on a journey through heaven and hell.[126] Here is no hieratic Mary, nor a grieving mother, but an active Mary who intercedes for sinners by ceaselessly imploring her son on their behalf.

The Byzantine Empire which grew out of the Greek world of late antiquity defined a Christian faith with Mary as Bearer of a God at its heart. To the capital Constantinople relics and tales of Mary travelled from afar, and especially were drawn from the Holy Land. In turn, the city provided models for reflection on the Mother of God, on the contradiction she embodied, on the promise of her assumed presence in heaven, of her protective commitment to the Empire. Greek Christians experienced the trauma of breaking or whitewashing cherished images in order to secure harmony and peace. They ultimately returned to the veneration of images, and so marked in fundamental ways their difference from the Jews of their imagination, and from the Muslims who so often seemed to have God and his mother on their side.

6

Beyond the Greek World

MARY OF ISLAM

In the Near East – Palestine, Syria and Egypt, as well as parts of Mesopotamia – Jews and Christians coexisted in proximity as well as in polemic. The prophetic tradition of Judaism was still attracting converts from among the nomadic and pagan people of the Arabian peninsula. It was out of the religious debates and controversies in the rich desert cities of Arabia that a new stage in the realization of Mary took place, as Mary became one of the holiest woman of a new religion – Islam.

While in the Christian Empire Mary was being thanked and praised, painted and sung with the support and approval of the imperial family, monks and lay people, her figure was being re-evaluated within the sensibility of early Islam. In the Arabian cities a rich variety of influences – Hellenism, Judaism, Christianity (above all of the Monophysite variety) – as well as a pantheon of deities, existed side by side.[1] A new cultural force was unfolding, and its adherents saw in it the final stage of a three-tiered revelation: to Abraham and Moses, to John and Jesus was now added a brother prophet – Mohammed ($c.570$-632). The processes by which one revelation gained authority over others involved a plethora of conversation and debates. Although the Jewish and Christian prophets were acknowledged by Mohammed and his followers, they were given novel interpretations. Allah was the only god, and so Jesus could not be divine; the Trinity was a similarly objectionable concept, just as Jews thought it to be.[2]

The Koran mentions Mary's name more than the gospels do (thirty-four times to nineteen), though it usually cites her name in the phrase 'Isa son of Maryam': she is never called the Virgin Mary. One sura was named after Mary, the *Surat Maryam* (sura 19). The Koran emerged in

83

a world in which Mary was familiar and intriguing; she was cherished by Christians in a variety of ways and was rejected by the Jews. A tradition attributed to 'Alī, Mohammed's cousin and son-in-law, claimed that the Prophet had noted the deep divergence over Mary, and said:

There is a similarity to be seen in 'Isā (Jesus). The Jews hated him so much that they defamed his mother, but the Christians loved him so much that they elevated him to a status that was not rightly his.[3]

In the trading towns of the Arabian peninsula all these influences met – Semitic paganism, Mandeanism, Christianity and Judaism – agitated by deep conflicts and controversies.[4] The Koran refuted some and engages with others.

Like all scripture the Koran is a multi-layered book, and the nature of its references to Mary was determined by the context of its composition. The suras associated with Mecca were aimed above all at pagans and at the establishment of Mohammed's claim to final prophecy. In those suras delivered in Medina, where Mohammed was already surrounded by a following and where he confronted a large Jewish community as well as some Christians, there is a more confrontational tone. Mary appears at both stages, but in different ways. The earlier suras tell the story of Isa, Jesus, in order to establish the lineage of prophets of which Mohammed was the final member. Although the account of Jesus' birth was immersed in the miraculous and the unusual, it stops short of being the birth of a god. Both Christian and Jewish scripture provided models for Mohammed and his followers: God's annunciation to Mohammed on his role as prophet mirrors that to Mary, in sura 19.

The *Surat Maryam* is an extended account of the Annunciation and Nativity, spoken in the words of God:

[16] Make mention in the Book of Mary; when she withdrew from her people to a place, eastward.

[17] And took between herself and them a curtain [or veil]. Then We sent to her Our spirit, who took from her the form of a human being, without fault.

[18] She said: 'Behold, I Take refuge with the Merciful to you, if you are God-fearing.'

[19] He said: 'I am only the messenger of your Lord, that I may give you a faultless boy.'

84

[20] She said: 'How shall I have a boy, seeing that man has not touched me, nor have I been a harlot?'

[21] He said: 'So shall it be! Your Lord has said: "It is easy for me." And in order that we may make him a sign for the people, and a mercy from Us; it has become a thing decided.'

[22] And she conceived him and she withdrew with him to a far place.

[23] And the pains of childbirth drove her to the trunk of a palm tree. She said: 'Would that I had died before this and become a forgotten thing.'

[24] Then there was a cry from below her, saying 'Do not grieve, Your Lord has placed a stream beneath you.

[25] And shake the trunk of the palm tree toward you; you will cause ripe dates to fall upon you.

[26] So eat and drink and be consoled. And if you meet any mortal, say "Behold" I have vowed to fast to the Merciful and may not speak this day to any mortal.'

[27] Then she brought him to her own people, carrying him. And they said, 'O Mary, you have come with something peculiar.

[28] O sister of Aaron, your father was not a wicked man and your mother was not a harlot.'

[29] Then she pointed to him. They said, 'How can we talk to one who is in the cradle, a child?'

[30] He spoke: 'Behold, I am the servant of God. He has given me the Book and appointed me a prophet.

[31] And He has made me blessed wherever I may be, and has enjoined upon me prayer and almsgiving so long as I remain alive.

[32] And He has made me dutiful toward her who bore me and has not made me arrogant, miserable.

[33] Peace be upon me the day I was born, and the day I die, and the day I shall be raised up alive.'

[34] Such was Jesus, son of Mary. A true statement about which they doubt.

The story here told is both familiar and strange. It tells of an angelic annunciation and a troubled acceptance of the unexpected pregnancy. It describes Mary's lonely and painful delivery of a son followed by the forbidding meeting with her disapproving family and friends, which is resolved through the revelation of the son's unusual qualities. One tradition claimed that when some followers of Mohammed fled to Ethiopia and recited this sura, the local Christian king embraced them

as brothers, so similar was their tale to that of Christ's Nativity in the Christian gospels. The *Surat Maryam* emerged as a thoughtful appropriation and remaking of the Christian narrative on Jesus' birth.[5]

Maryam appears in her sura very differently from her portrayal in the early accounts of the gospel and the *Protogospel of James*. She is cast as a woman alone, while in the *Protogospel* she was surrounded by doting parents in childhood and by comfortable domesticity in young adulthood. While the gospels have Mary give birth away from home, she is not alone, as she is in the Koran. God has created Jesus in Maryam through an act of simple will, as the angel put it: 'So shall it be. Your Lord has said: "It is easy for me".' Maryam conceives and is left on her own in the wilderness in pain and hunger. Yet God's consolation is offered in the fine gifts of water and dates, so essential in the desert. When she brings her son to her people – clearly presented as Jews – the polemical thrust is evident. Maryam has brought shame upon her lineage, but even they were convinced when they heard her child speak to them of great things. A prophet was born, one who respected his mother, and whose mission was to offer an example through a life of prayer and good deeds.

The emergent community around Mohammed was gaining in confidence in the 620s after its move to Medina. It attracted converts and so was obliged to defend its position within a world rich with religious possibilities. The years at Medina produced a greater sense of definition; breaking with the Jews became a test of the new religion's autonomy.[6] Moreover, historical narratives of the rejection of a Jew by the Jews offered depth to the reality of Jewish rejection of Mohammed. These narratives brought home the evident truth: just as the Jews had been disobedient in the face of God's messenger Isa, so were they when faced by Mohammed, the ultimate prophet. Sura 3 presents Maryam's story alongside that of John the Baptist. Both were chaste and righteous, and both were rejected by Jews. Sura 4 is even more explicit about Jewish rejection in its polemic against the Jews of Medina:

and for their unbelief, and their uttering against Mary a mighty calumny,

And for their saying, 'We killed the Messiah, Jesus son of Mary, the messenger of God' (verses 153–5).

It goes on to explain that the Jews had not really killed Jesus, who was received by God in heaven like Mohammed after him. The Koran

celebrates Isa's and Maryam's humanity warmly and it vilifies the Jews for abuse of these messengers of God, and for their rejection of Mohammed.[7] Isa and Maryam prefigure the coming of Mohammed and were assumed into his new, unfolding Prophecy.

Islam spread quickly throughout the Mediterranean and further east into Mesopotamia – in Iraq and Iran of today. It resulted in a political space within which a multitude of local Muslim cultures flourished. But it also became the home for hundreds of years – until our own day – to versions of Christianity and Judaism, marked strongly by their Muslim environments. Large Jewish communities resided in Alexandria and Antioch, in Mosul and Nineveh, and alongside them lived Christians. Some of these Christians – in North Africa, in Syria – were followers of the imperial 'orthodoxy' with *Theotokos* at its heart; others were not, and they cherished different versions of Mary. Inasmuch as Muslims respected Mary too, Marian sites and shrines often attracted Muslims to them. The church of Mary in the valley of Jehoshaphat, outside the walls of Jerusalem, was particularly attractive. This Byzantine church was visited as early as 661 by Mu'āwiya (602–80), founder of the Umayyad dynasty, and recurrent discussions of the merits of praying there in the next century show that Muslims were drawn to this, Mary's last resting place.[8] The very multiplicity of religious styles and practices that coexisted in relative peace within the Muslim commonwealth created occasions for cultural encounter and exchange.

Public meetings for intellectual debate provided an interesting space for interaction between Muslims, Jews and Christians in the Caliphate's cities. These *majalis* gathered around prominent scholars or grand patrons, in homes or bookstores. A tenth-century Muslim scholar from Spain describes the public religious disputations in Baghdad as comprising participants of all religions: Muslims, Jews, and Zoroastrians.[9] There were storytellers and performers who wove disparate religious traditions into engaging and edifying tales. Stories about the birth of gods, reciprocal rebuttals of myths of origins characterized this cultural field.

Mary offered an attractive point of intersection: dear to Christians, cherished by Muslims, derided by Jews, she was a figure that sparked the imagination. The Jewish author of the *The Deeds of Ben Sira* (*Toledoth Ben Sira*) in ninth-century Persia told of its protagonist's wondrous birth:

his father Jeremiah had been forced by the evil sons of Ephraim to spill his seed in a public bath, and that seed was preserved in the water until Jeremiah's own daughter was impregnated by it, and bore Ben Sira seven months later. The child was born with his teeth and a wonderful power of speech which explained the circumstances of his virgin birth. He became a teacher to his own master.[10]

This prodigy of birth parallels closely the Infancy Gospel in Arabic, itself based on the early infancy gospels according to which a breath blown into her by the Angel Gabriel impregnated Mary. When Mary was accused of adultery Jesus cried out from her womb and revealed the truth to Joseph. The precocious boy then taught his own master at school. But the author of the *The Deeds of Ben Sira* may also have been exposed to another, Persian, tale of miraculous birth from fallen seed. The *Zend-Avesta*, the principal Zoroastrian scripture, tells of the birth of the God Saoshyant:

Zaratust went near unto Hvôv (Hvôgvi, his wife) three times, and each time the seed went to the ground; the angel Neryôsang received the brilliance and strength of that seed, delivered it with care to the angel Anâhîd and in time will blend it with another ... A maid, Eredat-fedhri, bathing in Lake Kasava, will conceive by that seed and bring forth our Saviour Saoshyant.[11]

Some of Mary's riddles were explored in venues that allowed some limited playful encounter between learned men. Neither political power nor the weight of devotional practices weighed heavily on the version of Mary imagined by Christians and Muslims in Muslim lands.

MARY – ROMAN AND MEDITERRANEAN

The first five centuries of Christian history saw the emergence of Mary from her modest role in the gospels to her heightened position as Bearer of God. Mary was shaped in many different ways as Christianity spread throughout the Roman Empire and beyond. The state religion was firmly embedded in the Greek-speaking lands. In the west, Christianity spread just as the political fortunes of the Empire in the west were waning. Mary was shaped for the use of a Christian Roman elite – its virgin

daughters, its chaste widows, its bookish menfolk – in the cadences of Latin poetry.

Christianity became the religion of the states that absorbed the authority of the western Empire, the kingdoms of Vandals, Visigoths, Ostrogoths and Franks. The first three groups were Arian Christians disinclined to honour the Mother of God. Mary found little favour in the courts of the military, who preferred heroic martyrs to blushing virgins. Mary found her devotees above all among the men who had rejected court and warfare – monks. Proclamations of Mary's purity helped support their efforts to lead a life of chastity. The challenging claims of virgin birth also offered moments for angry denunciation of those imagined or known to be doubters and rejecters – the Jews.

The fifth century, which saw Constantinople's embrace of Mary, coincided with the breakdown of the Empire as a Mediterranean entity. The emperor in Constantinople now ruled the eastern, Greek-speaking parts where Mary was a central theme of Christian devotion and official rites, as the Council of Ephesus (431) demonstrated. The western emperors moved their capital from Rome to Milan, and then to Ravenna, and created a new religious-political order on this terrain. Large sections of the western Empire were carved out as kingdoms ruled by new dynasties of barbaric rulers. They converted to Christianity, developed court cultures that emulated the example of Rome and studied the majesty of the Greek emperors.

The Ostrogoths who ruled Rome and central Italy developed in their capital at Ravenna the cult of their martyr – Apollinaris. In the late fifth century Mary was remembered there too, in a chapel adjacent to the great church of Santa Croce.[12] Hers was a shrine of twelve sides, which was decorated with mosaic narratives – the quintessentially imperial adornment – culminating in a scene of the bishop presenting his church to Mary.[13] Yet Mary's part in the imperial building of Ravenna was small. This held true throughout the western Empire, throughout the area we now call Europe: early medieval devotional experience centred on martyrs and their remains, in the cemeteries of suburban churches, outside city walls and around relics in main city churches.[14] There the remains of martyrs, once cherished in furtive and dangerous worship, now formed the foundations for churches and chapels, some official and others built by pious and prosperous Christians.

Mary's life was not celebrated in the late antique and early medieval west with the abundance and variety practised by her followers in Palestine, Syria, Asia Minor and Egypt. The absorption of Mary deep into European culture occurred later, as we will see. Yet this is not to say that the glories of eastern Mary were not known. Some social and institutional niches were more receptive to the opportunities offered by Mary's sacred poetry and edifying miracles, which were translated from Greek to Latin. Areas which were closely tied to Constantinople or Egypt – like southern Italy – were quicker than others in absorbing Marian practices and ideas. The immensely rich patriarchate of Alexandria was a particular source of inspiration: it was a major Mediterranean trader in grain, which it used for mass distributions to the city's poor.[15] Ships from Alexandria traded throughout the Mediterranean and reached as far as Britain.

Bishops were particularly likely to reflect on Mary. They were charged, after all, with enforcing the policies of the church councils, they supervised the priests who enacted the liturgy and were patrons of vast projects of building and decoration. In the fifth and sixth centuries they tended to be men of senatorial class, sons of privileged and well-connected families who often possessed landed estates, and were trained in classical education. Bishops were involved in the contemporary politics of religion, which occasionally touched upon Mary. So, for example, Gregory, bishop of Tours (538/9–c.594), a great connoisseur of compelling narrative, retold in Latin the Greek Marian miracle of the Jewish Boy in his collection of edifying tales On the Glory of Martyrs.[16] Yet Mary was far from central to the interests of the bishops who led Christian life, just as she was to most devotional activities in early medieval Europe.

Venantius Fortunatus (c.530–609) is an unusual figure on this landscape, in being the only poet active in the Frankish realm whose work has survived. He was born in Treviso, in northern Italy, and was educated in Ravenna, where he became accomplished in both Greek and Latin scholarship. He journeyed in Merovingian Gaul, a land only recently converted to Christianity, where the ruling Christian dynasty endowed and founded religious institutions. Around 566 he entered the court circle of the Frankish King Sigibert at Metz. He travelled to Tours and there made a formative friendship with Bishop Gregory and through him with Radegund, ex-queen and current abbess of the monastery of

the Holy Cross in Poitiers. He served her community by corresponding with the Emperor Justin in Byzantium over the transfer of relics to the nuns' chapel. When some remains of the cross arrived these inspired in the poet devotional hymns and the poems of thanks directed at the imperial couple.

Fortunatus produced a copious flow of elegant verse and communicated through it with a wide circle of spiritual friends. He wrote brilliantly about saints and martyrs, yet in his poetry there is little mention of Mary – no more than two short hymns. Fortunatus uses classical poetical conventions to situate Mary within a cosmos bursting with energy. She was known and recognized; the moon, sun, all things adored her:

> She to whom the moon, the sun, all things,
> are devoted in all time.
> The moist grace of heaven
> brings forth the flesh of the maiden.[17]

The hymn ends with an invocation of Mary as a glorious celestial lady who restores that which sad Eve had removed and offers a window unto heaven.[18]

Fortunatus' poem on Virginity mentions Mary too, but it is above all a roll-call of martyrs who gave their lives in torment and abuse, who could inspire chaste virgins to offer their own lives to Christ. Mary appears among them after the prince of martyrs, Stephen:

> Next, the Mother of God, the pious Virgin Mary gleams
> And she leads the sheep of the virginal flock.
> She, in the midst of the group of maidens
> Towards the light, the shining army of chastity.
> They sing of their happiness in the feast of paradise
> One gathers violets, another plucks roses.[19]

Fortunatus' most prominent reflection on Mary is 'In Praise of St Mary the Virgin and Mother of the Lord' ('In laudem sanctae Mariae Virginis et matris Domini'). It begins with the words of prophets whose tongues reverberate with praise. This is a celebration of divine purpose, in which Mary played so central a role. She was a branch from which the flower Christ was born, in a nice punning alliteration, 'Virgo haec virga fuit', which was to echo in future Marian hymns; Mary was the true

Mother of Zion ('Haec Sion mater, virgo Maria fuit'), and in her a new dispensation was born, a new marriage in flesh.[20] Fortunatus restates the wonders of the Incarnation, and its contradictions:

> Equal to the Father's divinity, and to the mother's body
> And without sin from his mother's flesh.[21]

Her coming is a striking break with the darkness of the past. She is an agent of history, marked by the movement from old to new and from dark to light. Now there was light, and there was cleansing and cure. This poem of Mary, on the Incarnation, became a poem about the cross, to which Fortunatus had already devoted some of his best efforts. It ends with strings of titles and honours:

> Beautiful above jewels, overshadowing the splendour of the sun,
> Higher than heavens, and glittering more than the stars.
> Whiter than snow, more golden than gold itself,
> More radiant than light, sweeter to the mouth than the honeycomb . . .
> Precious, benign, glittering, pious, sacred, worthy of worship, lovely,
> Flower, dignity, monument, brilliance, palm, crown, chastity.[22]

Fortunatus' world was one steeped in the memory of martyrs and the example of recent saints. In an epitaph written following the death of the lady Vilithuta he describes the chariot which descends to judge the souls: led by Elijah and Enoch, followed by the martyrs Peter and Stephen; next comes Mary – crowned with roses – encircled by virgins.[23] Mary's virginity was a model for nuns, some of whom were Fortunatus' close friends. If here Mary was not the focus for piety that she was in Constantinople and Alexandria, she was fitted into the world of liturgical order and religious aspiration among the high-born men and women of sixth-century Europe. The poetry of Fortunatus helped build a Christian polity; it cajoled rulers and competed with the traditional gods and rituals of the Frankish people.

Writers in Frankish Gaul, Ostrogothic Italy and Visigothic Iberia celebrated the heroics of martyrdom; sacred maternity mattered less. In Visigothic Iberia a distinctive style of Christian kingship mirrored some of the initiatives of the Byzantine emperors in the east. The kings summoned church councils and legislated energetically in pursuit of Christian orthodoxy in all areas of life. One area of particular interest was the conversion of the Jews: King Sisibut, who ruled between 612 and

620, required Jews to convert or leave the realm, but it is hard to know how thoroughly this edict was enforced.[24] Within this heated political and religious milieu an important tract about Mary was composed, by Ildefonsus, archbishop of Toledo (607–667). *On the Perpetual Virginity of Saint Mary* (*De virginitate perpetua sanctae Mariae*) affirms Mary's lasting virginity against foes old and new: Helvidius, the fourth-century Roman whom we have already encountered, and the Jews of contemporary Visigothic Iberia. Based on the Latin synonyms compiled by another local scholar, the grammarian Isidore of Seville (c.560–636), Ildefonsus opens with a prayer to Mary, constructed in triplets of synonymous appellations:

> My Lady, my ruler, who rules me,
> Mother of my God, servant of your Son,
> Bearer of the maker of the world
> I beg you, I pray to you, I beseech you . . .[25]

The tract goes on to recount Mary's virtues with lavish use of scripture. It argues against the Jews' rejection of Mary: how could they not appreciate the fact that such a virgin was born amongst them?

> It should be lovely to find a virgin of such glory in your descent
> It should be happy to display the visible sign of such modesty as your own
> It should be joyful to have so great a miracle made public in your family.[26]

Ildefonsus studied closely the gospel words describing the Annunciation and Nativity, linking biblical prophecy and the drama of incarnation and birth. In the western Mediterranean, for a while, some of the polemical style which we have noted in Greek writers of Constantinople is evident in Ildefonsus' passionate defence of Mary. It was much cited in later centuries; a miracle tale associated with him claimed that the Virgin Mary was so delighted by his devotion to her that she gave him the gift of vestments.

Further north Mary was mentioned very little. This fact is reflected dramatically in the choices made for the dedication of churches in Western Europe. In southern France, for example, a region deeply imbued with Roman law and civic remains, in the area around the city of Narbonne, only three dedications of churches and chapels to Mary are known before 800, and only four between 800 and 1000. In the diocese of Autun, only one religious house was dedicated to Mary, the

abbey of St Mary and St John the Great, a late sixth-century foundation. The neighbouring diocese of Auxerre similarly had an abbey of Sainte-Marie, and no other dedication; while the dioceses of Langres, Mâcon, Nevers and Sens had none.[27] Dedications to martyrs clearly ruled the day.[28] Mary posed a poetical challenge to hymn writers and inspired compositions for her feast days, but she was not the central creative spur, nor was she the focus for devotional practice. Even when a rush of monastic foundations followed the conquest of lands in the Iberian Peninsula away from Muslim rule – above all in the frontier kingdom of Oviedo-Leon – the popular choice of patron for the newly founded churches was St Martin, not Mary.[29] Similarly, in the vast ecclesiastical province of Reims special festive liturgical compositions (*historiae*) were created for the local saints – such as Bertin and Omer – but none for Mary.[30] The taste in religion, as in most areas of life, was very local, so the memory of martyrdom, of exemplary saintly lives, prevailed in offering Christians models for life and sources of hope. Anglo-Saxon England followed a rather different trajectory: its history produced fewer martyrs, since Christianity reached southern England by way of mission from Rome at the very end of the sixth century. With such robust Roman influence it had a larger number of dedications to the 'universal' saints, such as Peter and Mary.[31]

Yet even if most European churches and chapels were dedicated to martyrs, whose feast days became the most resonant events of the year, the evolving Christian calendar preserved a place for Mary. Throughout the liturgical year Christ's life was re-enacted. The oldest liturgical pattern available to us is the eighth-century Old Gelasian Sacramentary: autumn and winter experienced Advent and culminated in the Nativity; spring celebrated the Annunciation and led up to Easter; and summer saw outdoor festivities heightened around the feast of John the Baptist.[32] This annual cycle included occasions for reflection on Mary too: as a maiden at the Annunciation, as mother at the Nativity, and as mourner at Christ's tomb. In the Mozarab calendar, observed by Christians under Muslim rule in Iberia, this was realized through the celebration of the Nativity and five Marian feasts: the Purification (2 February), the Incarnation of the Word in Mary (21 March), the Assumption (15 August), the Nativity of Mary (8 September), and the Annunciation of Mary's birth (18 December).[33] Mary's presence was secured through the feasts of her son's life and also though her own

great feast of the Assumption. Wherever Rome influenced liturgical celebration, this feast was soon adopted.

ROME'S MARY — MARIA REGINA

For all its centrality in the history of Christianity and the Mediterranean, Rome has featured relatively little in this story so far. For while Constantinople was the seat of the eastern Roman Emperors from 333 onwards, Rome had suffered severe attacks: the Goths sacked it thoroughly in 410, and in 476 the last emperor of the West, Romulus Augustulus, was deposed. Yet something of the Byzantine association of Mary and imperial dignity which was proclaimed in the art, architecture and liturgy of Constantinople affected this other, troubled, capital, too.

Rome's Christian worship tended to centre on the liturgy of its bishop – later known as the pope – in the basilica of St John Lateran. The city was divided into seven regions, each in the care of a deacon, and it also possessed many chapels in neighbourhoods and cemeteries where martyrs' remains were cherished.[34] The pope's example prevailed over the city, and his festive visits to the churches of Rome wove the city into a single fabric of worship. Papal practice led to the introduction of new feasts and often interpreted and mediated devotional impulses developed in Constantinople.

The first Roman church built in honour of Mary was Santa Maria Maggiore. Pope Sixtus III (432–40) completed the project begun by his predecessor Celestine I (422–32) on a site just outside the Esquiline Gate.[35] The church was adorned with mosaics, and it later housed the early seventh-century image of Mary as Saviour of the Roman People – *Salus populi romani* – a blend of goddess, empress and Mother of God.[36] The mosaics are lively scenes in splendid colour, with Mary at the Annunciation, the Adoration and the Presentation. The Annunciation saw Mary at work, weaving the temple veil in purple yarn, as the *Protogospel of James* had told. Mary is less maternal than matriarchal here: seated on high, dressed in rich and multi-layered garments, her hair is carefully set as befitted a Roman matron and her bearing majestic. The Adoration depicts a formal reception scene in which Mary – enthroned and splendidly dressed – receives the embassy. In Rome, the city of martyrs, if no longer of emperors, Mary was a figure that could

credibly carry imperial memories and representations. A less glamorous version of imperial Mary preserved her saintly comportment without the shiny ornaments. In the catacomb of Comodilla a wall painting of 528 places Mary and son on a sumptuous throne: Mary in black, flanked by Saints Felix and Adauctus with a kneeling widow in whose honour the image was made.[37] Pope Gregory the Great ($c.540-604$) was an early devotee of Mary. In his Rome there were as yet no major Marian feasts to focus attention on her, but he developed Marian themes in his sermons preached at Santa Maria Maggiore, for the Nativity, for Easter and in his homilies on angels.[38]

Gregory's efforts began the remaking of Rome as the centre of the expanding Latin Christianity. Mary's progress was both cause and effect of that process, through acts which transferred the ancient pagan splendour of Rome – still visible in massive, if crumbling, public monuments all over the city – into the spaces and places of a Christian society. A dramatic stage along this route was the rededication around 609 of the great Temple of All Gods – the Pantheon – into the church of St Mary and All Martyrs. A history of the popes recounts Pope Boniface IV's success in gaining the permission of the Emperor Phocas to transform this imperial building – commissioned by Hadrian $c.120$ – into a church of 'the glorious mother of God the ever-virgin St Mary and all holy martyrs'.[39] The ceremony eclipsed any previous event in Christian Rome: the grand ruin in a swampy section of the city was now made into a church fit for Christian worship. The tremendous dome – with its 'eye' (oculus) open skywards – sheltered the multicoloured floor made of fine stones and the vast space of this most impressive Christian edifice within the city's walls.

As a temple, the Pantheon had been dedicated to all Gods; as a church – to all martyrs and Mary. An icon was fittingly made for the church – a Virgin and Child – and relics were deposited at the altar.[40] An elaborate papal mass was celebrated. It opened with the choir's introit: locus iste terribilis est – 'the Lord's hall is an awesome one', taken from Jacob's dream in Genesis, as he recognizes the holiness of the place in which he stood. The Offertory was from the book of Chronicles, where the dedication of Solomon's temple is described; and the Communion antiphon was from Matthew, describing Jesus overthrowing the money-changers' tables. Neither Mary nor martyrs were directly invoked; rather, the themes were those of renewal, purification and transforma-

tion, as temple ceded to church. The colourful icon of the *Theotokos* there may have been prepared for the dedication ceremony, and other ornaments continued to flow. Popes were particularly generous to this church with gifts of golden chalices and purple altarpieces bordered with silk.[41]

Mary's worship did indeed flourish in the city in new and exciting ways: these years saw the composition of the responsory *Gaude Maria* (*Mary, Rejoice*) – a chanted set of biblical verses with soloist and choir – for the office of the Annunciation. Its words invoked Mary as the enemy of heretics and protector of true faith:

> Rejoice, Mary the Virgin,
> You have destroyed all heresies
> When you believed in the words said by Gabriel
> When you bore God and man
> And remained after birth an inviolate Virgin.[42]

To which the versicle answers:

> We believe that the Archangel Gabriel was sent to you divinely.
> We believe that your womb was impregnated by the Holy Spirit.
> May the unhappy Jew blush, who says that Christ
> Was born of Joseph's seed.

Missionaries were sent forth on mission from Rome to Kent, Northumbria, Frisia, wherever there were pagans to be converted. Mary's entry into Roman consciousness was not supported by an elaborate political administration, and so it was achieved by sporadic and occasional boosts, often through the adoption or interpretation of eastern practices. The Greek Pope Sergius I (687–701) incorporated Mary's feasts into the Roman liturgy: Purification, Annunciation, Dormition and the Nativity of Mary.[43] These were to be occasions for collects – gatherings at St Hadrian's church in the Forum – at which the pope and his court met the clergy of the church in which they were to celebrate the festal mass: Santa Maria Maggiore – Saint Mary the Great.[44]

Mary's special relationship with Rome was finally explicitly represented in the title of a fresco in Santa Maria Antiqua, a fifth-century church within the precinct that had once been the Roman Forum.[45] It was constructed as an imperial basilica, and later, in the seventh century, served as the pope's residence. One of its walls contains layers of paint

that are hard to date precisely, yet it is clear that between the sixth and eight centuries artists worked here at the presentation of what can still just be seen: a colourful image of Mary and the Christ Child, attended by angels and servers. One of three representations of Mary in this church shows her enthroned and dressed like a Byzantine princess, seated with her son, just as she was in Hagia Sophia.[46] By the later eighth century the title *Maria Regina* was given to this type of representation. Mary's royalty was realized here in a style that looks Greek, but which belongs to a world outside the Empire, a world whose scholars and liturgy used Latin and whose people had yet to learn much about the *Theotokos*.

The growing interest in Mary's images in Rome meant that when the Byzantine Emperor Leo the Isaurian (*c*.680–741) deemed the use of holy images to be idolatrous and began a century of legislation against images, the bishop of Rome became the defender of iconic representations:

When I enter a church, I contemplate images of Jesus Christ's miracles and his mother suckling Our Lord, and Our Lord in her arms, while angels around them sing a hymn sanctus, sanctus, sanctus . . .[47]

The Byzantine emperors, monks and people were troubled by the heritage of icons; the bishop of Rome was all too willing to make his city Mary's sanctuary for images old and new.

The bishops of Rome revelled in the role of her defenders.[48] Pope John VII probably inspired the famous image of what came to be known as the *Madonna della Clemenza* in the church of Santa Maria in Trastevere, a public gesture in defence of the worship of Mary's icons.[49] The *Madonna della Clemenza* is a powerful statement of the imperial Mary: Mary is enthroned and flanked by saints as she was in the icon of St Katherine's monastery on Mount Sinai. But there is more: Mary's body is extremely long, and she and her son are dressed in the distinctive shade of red/purple reserved for imperial vestments. Like the Empress Theodora portrayed in the mosaics of Ravenna, Mary is decorated with a pearled head-dress, and her neckline, shoulders, wrists and hem are decorated with pearls. So elongated is her imposing figure as to appear standing rather than seated.

A similar appropriation of Greek style is evident in the church of Santa Maria in Domnica, which Pope Paschal I (d.824) rebuilt 'from the foundations bigger and better than it had been before'.[50] This is a

church with three apses, a form rare in Rome but common in the east. The central apse was decorated with a monumental mosaic of Mary enthroned, dressed in a blue gown, seated on a red cushion upon a golden throne, her son in her lap, surrounded by angels.[51] Pope Paschal kneels and touches her feet, in an act of submission within an enhanced imperial court ceremonial. Like elsewhere Mary's Dormition and Assumption received in Rome particular attention; a cycle of paintings on the wall of the church of Santa Maria Egiziaca in Rome depicted around 880 the story of Mary's end, with figures that used lively dramatic gestures.[52] The art of Mary was alive and well in Rome, where her images were revered and her churches were growing in number under the care of the city's bishops. Images were treated like relics, powerful memorials of the sacred, and so they were displayed in processions, received prayers and drew pilgrims.[53] There were regular Marian processions, like that led by the pope, carrying the image of Mary *acheiropita* (Greek 'not made by hand'), and Marian churches featured centrally in the trajectories of thanksgiving processions.[54] With the diminution of Byzantine power after the Muslim conquest of the Mediterranean in the seventh century the bishops of Rome turned to the Frankish rulers for protection; in turn Rome provided guidance on liturgy, art and ecclesiastical governance. Where other than in Rome might the correct ideas about God and his Mother be found?

7

The Emergence of European Mary

MARY AND THE FRANKS

The kingdom of the Franks achieved hegemony in continental Europe and combined administration of the state with leadership in religious matters. So effective was this political vision that in the year 800 Charlemagne, king of the Franks (748–814), was crowned emperor in Rome. Charlemagne's kingdom grew through conquest and in it Christians lived alongside very recent converts. Vast legislative assemblies whose formulations were disseminated widely helped remind people of the tenets of faith. All subjects were required to adhere to certain codes of behaviour. The guidelines (*Admonitio Generalis*) published by Charlemagne in 789 required belief in God the Father, the Son and the Holy Ghost. Such belief was to be bolstered by preaching:

It is to be preached that God's son was incarnated of the Holy Spirit and of Mary always Virgin for the salvation and repair of the human race, that he suffered, was buried and on the third day was resurrected and ascended to heaven.[1]

The Empire's churches used a version of the Roman liturgical calendar. The Feast of the Purification was the main Marian feast, and the Assumption was left to local choice. Masses for Mary's feast days appear in the Old Gelasian Sacramentary (a book of the priest's prayers at the mass), in the Gothic Missal and that of Bobbio, and in the Lectionary (book of gospel readings) of Luxeuil, alongside masses for St Stephen, Peter and Paul, and John the Baptist.[2] Under Charlemagne the feasts of the Purification and Assumption were prescribed for universal observance by church councils which represented his imperial authority.[3] The Purification in 814 may have been the day on which Louis the Pious (778–840), Charlemagne's son, was crowned, and from which he

reckoned his reign-years; many of his annual assemblies met on that day. By the early ninth century several Rhineland and Bavarian dioceses celebrated four Marian feasts: the Purification, Assumption, Nativity and Conception.[4]

Such innovations were probably adopted in a quite haphazard fashion, at a pace which depended on the enthusiasm of local bishops and the support of lay patrons. The feasts were associated with an awareness of the benefits of prayer and liturgy of Mary. When Lupus, abbot of Ferrières, appealed to Emperor Lothar in 840 for the restoration of some property, he reminded the ruler that his monks habitually prayed to Saints Peter, Mary and Paul for the emperor's soul.[5] Rumours of a miracle helped inspire local interest. The introduction of the feast of the Assumption in the diocese of Thérouanne was recounted in the *Annals of St-Bertin* as the result of Mary's own prompting. A slave woman was ironing her master's shirt that was to be worn at mass that day. The more she ironed the more blood-soaked the shirt became. The local bishop treated the shirt as a relic to be kept in his church, and the day's fast was formally adopted by the diocese. Such stories helped the promoters of liturgical innovation make their case; indeed, Hincmar of Reims, who composed this section of the *Annals*, was a keen devotee of Mary.[6] Later in the century the remarkable Charles the Bald (823–77) promoted Mary as the religious theme of his court. Having lost the palace and church which Charlemagne had built in Aachen, he transferred his centre to Compiègne and announced the foundation of his chapel there:

Because our grandfather, to whom divine providence granted the monarchy of this whole empire, established a chapel in honour of the Virgin in the palace of Aachen, we therefore, wanting to imitate the pattern set by him . . . have built and completed within the territory under our sway in the palace of Compiègne, a new monastery, to which we have given the name 'royal', in honour of the most glorious mother of God, and ever-virgin Mary.[7]

Among the Carolingians Marian devotion became a form of commemoration of ancestors, of family piety. It was also an act of imitation of the exultant rituals of the emperors of Constantinople.

The most heated debates about Mary arose when the circumstances of the Incarnation and the nature of a God made flesh were debated. Such discussions were most likely to emerge in the context of mission,

when Christianity followed conquest. Members of Charlemagne's court – bishops, poets, theologians – were obliged to confront non-Franks and their religions following the mass conversion of the Avar people in the 790s. In the late decades of the eighth century the nature of Christ was debated anew, and this led to some discussion of God's mother too. The free-standing, somewhat autonomous Mary – like *Maria Regina* in Rome – became part of the visual world of the interlocking domains ruled by Charlemagne and his successors. On the pages of a beautiful manuscript of the late eighth century – the Gellone Sacramentary – at the opening of the text of the mass, Mary appears, bedecked in fancy ritual garb, almost priestly in manner, with a censer spreading incense smoke in her right hand, and a cross tightly clasped aloft in her left.[8]

It was the Yorkshireman Alcuin (*c*.740–804), the leading intellectual of the Carolingian court, who displayed particular interest in Mary. His compilation *On the Praise of God (De Laude Dei)*, a personal book that travelled with him on his journeys between England and Francia, contains among other sections some 100 antiphons, of which thirteen are dedicated to Mary.[9] This abundance shows just how rich the world of prayer and liturgy around Mary was by the late eighth century in York, where he was educated, and in the north of England more generally.[10] Alcuin invoked Mary in a letter of guidance to the Princess Gisla, with a courtly image of feasting in Mary's chamber.[11] Together with other theologians of Charlemagne's court he was drawn into theological discussions of intensity unmatched in Europe during the preceding centuries. Since these touched on the issue of the Incarnation, Mary became part of their subject-matter too. The debate on the Incarnation was raised by the writing and preaching of an Iberian bishop, Felix of Urgel, who was taken to be reviving the Nestorian error. The belief attributed to him was that Jesus had assumed – adopted – human flesh in an act of willing humility. Felix's teaching denied the coexisting and necessary duality of humanity and divinity in Christ, and since the Spanish Marches formed part of Charlemagne's – the Carolingian – Empire, this polemic became a matter of state.[12] In response Alcuin emphasized Mary's purity and majesty, qualities inseparable from the orthodox view of the Incarnation promoted vigorously by Charlemagne's court. The imperial court and the many monasteries founded and supported by royal and aristocratic families nurtured an intellectual sphere of great distinction and ambition. The abundance of intellectual work – in his-

tory, biography, hymns, legends of saints, painting – provided occasions for representations of Mary, which ranged from the banal to the intense and original.

Mary became the subject of occasional experiments in visual representation, and so she entered spaces never before graced by her. The maker of the Sacramentary for Drogo, the bishop of Metz, around 850 chose to illustrate the initial D with an unusual image of Mary enthroned holding her son, who is seen from the side seated upon the letter I.[13] Mary is also present in the scene with the initial O for the Palm Sunday Prayer 'Almighty Eternal God'; she stands with John to the right of the crucified Christ, her hands held to her face. There is another small female figure, urgently raising a chalice to Christ's side; this is probably *ecclesia* – a figure of the church.[14]

The Carolingian vision was expressed in legislative attempts to spread Christianity of a Latin type. At court, in monasteries and in cathedrals a strong sense of the vast realm of Christian culture – *Christianitas* – evolved. It was associated with Latin learning, a style of heroic male comportment and conventional devotion to Christ. Unlike the situation in the east, only scant attention was directed here at Mary as a figure for ascetic emulation, or even as the fitting patron of imperial majesty. Everywhere Christ's body was to be seen – in the acrostic poems of Hrabanus Maurus (c.780–856), whose letters formed the shape of Christ on the cross, in the works of manuscript illumination, in the hands of priests whose hands made Christ's body at the altar, in bibles which circulated as precious gifts between rulers. The illuminator of the Utrecht Psalter, created in the Benedictine abbey of Hautvillers in northern France between 816 and 834, illustrated Psalm 115 with a scene of the Crucifixion within a broad narrative setting. Mary stands alongside John, gazing at her dead son on the cross, her hands raised in a gesture of distress. Mary is a witness here, rather than a participant.[15] She is almost incidental in this narrative scene, where the Crucifixion occurs strangely off-centre.

The debate over images gave confidence to Latin scholars as they wrestled with the heritage of Greek Christianity. Since Frankish monasteries were spreading Christianity to the north and east, well beyond the borders of the ancient Roman world, Christian thinkers were prompted to re-explore the basic tenets of the Incarnation, and thus of Mary. Around 830 Paschasius Radbert, abbot of the monastery of Corbie,

launched the first systematic reflection on the eucharist, and discussion on Mary too. His letter-tract *On the Assumption of Saint Mary the Virgin* (also known as *Cogitis me)* offered explicit advice to the nuns of Soissons: their devotion should refrain from reliance on the apocryphal accounts which were so central to the narratives of Mary's end. Instead he analysed the liturgy of the feast and penned a work on Mary's birth that was based on the *Gospel of Pseudo-Matthew*.[16] In his commentary on the Gospel of Matthew, Mary and Joseph are depicted as a Christian couple, following Augustine: truly married, though chaste, free of sin and thus fit to nurture Jesus.[17] Mary's prominence in Paschasius Radbert's thought was associated with the eucharist consecrated daily at the altar, since, he explained, 'that which is consecrated in Christ's word by the Holy Spirit is his body born of a virgin'.[18] This work went against the grain of existing Mary-lore: it was not a story or a miracle, not a poem or a litany, but a theological analysis aimed at a new kind of rigour.

Hincmar, archbishop of Rheims, admired Paschasius' letter greatly. Some time in the late 840s he copied it into a sumptuous book used at his cathedral, to accompany Paschasius' tract on Mary's birth. This book has not survived, but a letter by Hincmar has. It defends Paschasius' tract and the Latin story of Mary's birth as being in keeping with the papal stipulation that apocrypha be used 'with care'. He thought so well of it that he had it read as part of the liturgy for the feast of Mary's Nativity at his cathedral at Rheims. The feast was celebrated at the Virgin's altar, recently restored, for which Hincmar wrote the following verses:

> This place dedicated in honour of the Lord's mother,
> Bishop Hincmar, her devotee adorned everywhere
> with holy gifts, having taken service as archbishop in this see.
> When 800 years are now well completed
> and the 45th going by [i.e. 845]
> when Charles as a young man ruled the crowns of the kingdom,
> and the cherished ones of the city sought this man to be their shepherd.[19]

On the flyleaf of the gospel book, his gift to Mary's altar, Hincmar inscribed:

> Holy Mother of God, and ever virgin,
> I Hincmar offer you gifts.

The deeds this pious woman wrought, Jesus Christ taught us,
Having come out of your womb, Chaste maiden.[20]

Inspired by the theology of Paschasius, this poem expressed a new emphasis: Mary was central not only to the Incarnation, but also as partner in the sacrament of Christ's body, ordained for believers.[21]

It was through the work of men like Paschasius and Hincmar, who were personally interested and also sufficiently influential, that some cathedrals began to carve out liturgical spaces for Mary and even to spread her worship in the surrounding dioceses. We have seen that, while writing the Annals of the monastery of St Bertin, Hincmar described how the feast of the Assumption was introduced to the diocese of Thérouanne, within the province of Reims. Like so many occasions around Mary, this was a miraculous event.

MARY OF THE BRITISH ISLES

The British Isles fell out of the administrative reach of the Roman Empire in the early fifth century, but the rich Christian culture of Ireland, which was independent of Rome, continued to contribute to the Christianization of large parts of Scotland and re-entered Anglo-Saxon England from the north and the west, in Northumbria, Mercia and Wessex. Anglo-Saxon dynasts maintained strong marriage and diplomatic links with the Franks and later received the first official Christian mission from Rome in 596.[22] Southern England was converted to Christianity by the efforts of the Archbishop Theodore of Canterbury (602–90), a Greek from Cilicia, and his companions from Rome, all men immersed in Byzantine culture. Irish monks and bishops were also in close contact with Visigothic Spain in the sixth and seventh centuries. The Irish world (which stretched to the west coast of modern Scotland) was in tune with the schools and councils of Visigothic Spain and its capital, Toledo. The British Isles display a trend towards much deeper acquaintance with the liturgy and imagery of Mary than that experienced in other parts of Northern Europe.[23]

The eight-century west-Saxon *Dream of the Rood* (preserved in the Vercelli Book of the mid-to-late tenth century) offers a powerful dramatization of the Crucifixion by turning the cross itself into a dramatic

character. The cross likens itself to Mary, a tangible living being chosen by God for the unfolding of his plan:

> See, the Lord of Glory then honoured me
> over the trees of the forest, guardian of his heaven-kingdom!
> Just as he did his mother, Mary herself,
> Almighty God before all men,
> Honoured her over all woman-kind.[24]

The choice of the tree for the cross was part of a great plan, full of wisdom, just as birth from a woman was. Mary and the cross are brought here into important proximity, for, as we shall see, in future centuries the foot of the cross became the quintessential site for knowing and perceiving Mary. Yet her son's death eclipsed the promise of his miraculous birth.

Some of the earliest surviving representations of Mary in the British Isles are carved in stone. Mary appears on the eighth-century carved crosses found at Monifieth in Angus, the Adoration of the Magi at Sandbach in Cheshire and the Adoration of the Magi on a cross at a 'Chill on the Isle of Canna, in the Hebrides.[25] When the monk of Iona, Cú Chuimne (d.747), wrote in praise of Mary, he knowingly used imagery which Augustine had made familiar: Mary as mother and daughter, creator and created:

> Mary, wondrous mother,
> created her own father,
> by whom, bathed in water
> the whole world came to believe.[26]

Further east was the Northumbrian kingdom, which benefited from an early Irish mission. An intricately carved ivory diptych with scenes of the Life of Christ includes the Annunciation, with Mary seated in a domestic scene of weaving with a basket of wool and the paraphernalia of spinning. Joseph, whose occupation was *faber* in the Latin of the Vulgate, was described in Anglo-Saxon texts as 'smith and skilful artificer', and his son 'smith' or 'smith's son'.[27] The accomplished ninth-century carving at Breedon-on-the-Hill in Leicestershire reverberates with the dignity of imperial Mary, such as we have seen emanating from sixth-century Constantinople. Her drapery is delicately carved, she is frontal and her head-cover is identifiably eastern. She holds a book, an

uncommon local addition.[28] Mary was a combination of Irish tracery and Byzantine decorum.

The poems of the Irish monk and martyr Blathmac ($c.750–835$) demonstrate the wide reach of the story of Mary's infancy and the inspiration it provided. We know little about him except that his father was an associate of the High-King Fergal. Irish monks fulfilled a wide range of pastoral duties, and Blathmac's poem 'to Mary and her Son' is a summary of Christ's life, which adheres closely to scripture and is useful for instruction. Blathmac is creative in dramatizing the narrative by constant appeal to Mary. He recounts to Mary the story of her son, beginning with her foreknowledge of Christ's death:

Come to me, loving Mary, that I may keen with you your very dear one. Alas that your son should go to the cross, he who was a great diadem, a beautiful hero.[29]

Christ's birth is told, and the poem quickly moves to his ministry: he healed and cured people of many miserable conditions:

It is certain that these were the deeds of your great beautiful son, Mary: the ceaseless endowing of each one, bounty and generosity.[30]

The betrayal follows, by Jews who failed in their obligation to one who had bestowed upon them 'every advantage'. Here, again, an aside about Mary maintains the conversational frame:

Jesus, darling son of the virgin, achieved a deed of pure victory; from him the salvation of the human race which great perversity encompassed.[31]

The Crucifixion follows, and after it the destruction of the Jews by Emperor Vespasian. At the end of the narrative Blathmac makes clear the ecclesiological, lasting meaning of the drama. He turns to Mary with three petitions that only she can answer:

Let me have from you my three petitions, beautiful Mary, little bright-necked one; get them, sun of women, from your son who has them in his power.

That I be in the world till old with the Lord who rules starry Heaven, and that thereafter there be a welcome for me into the eternal ever-enduring kingdom.

Everyone who has this as a vigil-prayer at lying down and at rising for unblemished protection in the next world like a breast-plate with helmet;

Everyone, whatever he be, who shall say it fasting on Friday night, provided only that it be with copious tears, Mary, may he not be for Hell.[32]

Finally, the poem's aims are reiterated:

I call you with true words, Mary, beautiful queen, that we may hold converse together to pity your heart's darling.

So that I may keen [lament] the bright Christ with you in the most heartfelt way, shining precious jewel, mother of the great Lord

. . .

Come to me, loving Mary, head of pure faith, that we may hold converse with the compassion of unblemished heart. Come.[33]

While some of the imagery and ideas in this poem are familiar to us – Jewish guilt, strings of praise to Mary, requests for Mary's intercession – some are less common. Christ is the son of a great lady; he is a battling hero (like Blathmac's own father and brother). Heroes are bound to be generous to a fault, but also vindictive towards those who have betrayed them, like the Jews, who failed to offer loyalty in return for his gifts. Both Mary and 'the Lord' are described as physically beautiful. Since Mary is an effective intercessor, the poem-prayer is addressed to her, she who remains with the supplicant after her son's death. Mary was indeed always present in small Irish devotional objects, usually made of metal, which depicted stark scenes of the Crucifixion. A late seventh-century bronze plaque, which had once been gilt, shows Mary and John alongside a much larger Christ, and accompanied by angels. Their bodies turn towards the cross, but their faces gaze at the viewer; Mary's face, especially her mouth, is contorted in pain.[34]

Blathmac's second poem recounts Christ's ministry with an occasional interjection towards Mary, in praise of her offspring:

It is from your son, Mary, that true filial piety is learnt; it is he that unto death on the bright cross was obedient to father.

. . .

Your fair renowned son, Mary, was warm in kin-love; there treads not earth or Heaven an equally renowned youth.[35]

Here again the qualities of loyalty to kin and respect to parents are praised in the example of Christ.

Blathmac was a confident user of a wide range of lore about Mary, aware of the essential meanings they conveyed: virgin birth, Crucifixion, redemption and intercession. All of these were woven into the idiom of closely knit kin-groups, whose men were adept at war, possessors of a

strong tradition of heroic poetry which valued loyal sons and nurturing mothers. Blathmac also appreciated the resonant manner in which the Crucifixion could be described in a conversation with the person most touched by it: the mother of the suffering hero. This representation of Mary was to become in the later medieval centuries the most cherished mode of apprehending her and of approaching the Crucifixion – through the figure of the suffering mother – *mater dolorosa*. But this is yet to come. In early medieval Europe monastic Mary was a partner in prayer. Blathmac was one of the first to realize how effectively the Christian story could be explored through Mary's mediating power of witness. It is hard to assess how widely his poetry was known. Yet it is significant that Irish poetry continued to explore Mary's role in the struggle against sin, as in this late tenth-century poem to 'God incarnate':

> For every holy virgin on the great earth
> For the assemblage of distinguished lay women,
> Forgive me every sin beneath heaven
> For wondrous Mary.[36]

Different emphases coexisted in the materials and genres within which Mary was explored. More pronounced and individualistic than in Blathmac's poem, less dependent on the explicit affinity to her son, is Mary's appearance on a plaque of a Northumbrian ivory diptych of the late eighth century.[37] One panel is devoted wholly to Christ Triumphant, but the other is divided into two registers: above is the Annunciation, with Mary at the centre facing the viewer, while Gabriel enters from her right, energetically conveying his message, and a servant stands at Mary's left. The work is remarkably expressive, especially below, in the Visitation, a moment of female friendship, with a true embrace between Mary and Elizabeth, whose bodies join at the centre of the composition.[38]

Much Anglo-Saxon art was clearly influenced by Byzantine and early Christian modes, but some express new content in local idiom.[39] An ivory Nativity scene of the late tenth century depicts Mary lying on a draped bed alongside her son's crib and two adoring beasts. Joseph occupies the upper right corner, a reflective figure seated in a hunched position.[40] In the hard work of carving stone, in the delicate work of carving ivory, and in the scriptoria that produced illuminated manuscripts, Mary formed part of the biblical story available to the religious of the British Isles and those they instructed and guided. Mary rarely

stood alone; she was an established part of the rich world of biblical tale and liturgical action.

Monastic life flourished in England towards the end of the tenth century, inspired by continental movements of monastic reform and sustained by Anglo-Saxon royal patronage. At the end of the first Christian millennium Anglo-Saxon writers produced an original and dramatic image of Mary, full of human nuance and varied in genre and matter. In the sequence of liturgical poems known as *Christ I* or the *Old English Advent*, of *c.*970, three dwell most particularly on Mary's life-choices. Poem VII, some fifty lines long, offers an exchange between Mary and Joseph. Mary takes the lead by expressing her sadness at being blamed and insulted. Joseph answers:

> 'I suddenly am
> deeply disturbed, despoiled of honor,
> for I have for you heard many words,
> many great sorrows and hurtful speeches,
> much harm, and to me they speak insult,
> many hostile words. Tears I must
> shed, sad in mind. God easily may
> relieve the inner pain of my heart,
> comfort the wretched one. O young girl,
> Mary the virgin!'[41]

While Joseph answers that he had indeed doubted her, there are enemies who claim she is defiled:

> I have too much
> of evil received for this pregnancy.
> How may I refute the hateful talk
> or find my answer
> against my enemies?[42]

Joseph is absorbed in his plight, Mary is troubled though dignified, and her speech closes the poem with an assertion of innocence.

The Crucifixion was understood as a triumphant drama, not only in England, but in other parts of the British Isles. Christ's body hung from the cross and alongside him stood John and Mary, a pair of loving mourners. The unwieldy medium of stone was made into an expressive, if schematic, moment: the Cross of Moridic, found at Llanhamlach in

Breconshire, has Mary on the right and John on the left in positions of prayer either side of a bare cross.[43] The Cross of Conbelin, at Margam Abbey (Glamorgan), has the tiny figures of Mary and John at the foot of a large, abstract cross.[44] An ivory carving of the Crucifixion of $c.$1000 has angels above the cross, and Mary and John gesturing towards it.[45] In manuscript illumination, like the Ramsey Psalter, Mary and John display gestures that are clearly agitated, underscored by the nervous and jagged lines of the drapery hems.[46]

The most prestigious products of Anglo-Saxon art echoed the images of the liturgy and incorporated the details of stories about Mary's life. A late tenth-century ivory associated with Winchester depicts the Nativity. The relief is high, the surface polished and the image immediately recognizable: Mary occupies most of the ivory's surface, with Joseph to her right, the son adored by beasts under her bed, and a midwife arranging the large pillow under her head.[47] The sumptuously decorated Benedictional – a book of prayers to be said by the bishop as he blessed the congregation at mass – commissioned by Bishop Æthelwold of Winchester (963–84) contains nineteen fully decorated pages. Mary appears in the Annunciation, the Nativity, the unusual scene of the Naming of Christ, at the Adoration of the Magi, the Presentation at the Temple, the Purification, among the Women at the Tomb, at the Ascension and the scene of her Dormition and Coronation.[48] The style is deeply indebted to Carolingian manuscripts and to Byzantine ivories; it glows with gold and shimmers with the constant movement of drapery lines and decorative vegetation. In several scenes Mary is accompanied by a cloud of swirling wispy vapour which signals the presence of the Holy Spirit which impregnated her, or of God himself, whose will her life came to fulfil. But Mary's presence is also sensed in scenes devoted to others: the two-page opening at the beginning of the book has two choirs of virgins, all followers of Mary. The full-page image of the royal Æthelthryth (fol. 90v), queen and abbess, faces an image of Christ blessing; Æthelthryth had offered herself as bride to Christ, just as his mother was.[49] These images are extraordinary achievements, yet most people were likely to see Mary on carved stones, finger her on brooch or decorative metal plaque, or hear about her in devotional poetry and improving sermons.

Those who chose to make cult, poetry and art around Mary were clearly also aware of the flimsy origins of the much-cherished stories

of her life. Paschasius' anxiety about the use of apocryphal stories was matched by that of the English homilist Ælfric (fl.987–1010). His *Catholic Homilies* of 990–92 offered a full cycle of sermons for the feasts of saints observed in England around the turn of the millennium. Yet in this comprehensive work of hagiography for use in the liturgy there is no offering for the feast of the Nativity of Mary (8 September).[50] Ælfric divulges the reason for his decision in a note appended to a sermon:

What would we say about Mary's birth, except that she was born of a father and a mother like other people, and that she was born on the day called the Sixth Ides of September. Her father was called Joachim and her mother Anna, pious people in the ancient law. And we do not want to write any more about them lest we fall into error. The gospel these days is very hard for the ignorant people. It is all swollen with the names of holy people . . . Therefore we leave it unsaid.[51]

Ælfric was aware of the sixth-century papal decree that had prohibited the use of 'apocrypha'; it was copied in manuscripts which he used. Yet the lore about Mary was too sparse without these rich and ancient stories.[52] The *Protogospel of James* continued to be copied, often interpolated with sections of the gospel of Luke.[53] Together these accounts formed the basis for the composition of prayers, sermons and devotional poetry, for private use as well as for Mary's feasts. Indeed, the next generation of monks in Ælfric's Abbey of Eynsham would be hard at work formulating materials for a feast of Mary's Conception, an apocryphal tale par excellence.[54] Even Aelfric resolved to absorb other apocryphal materials on occasion, in Assumption narratives woven into his homily for that feast, supported by the authority of Augustine, Jerome and Gregory.

MARY *C.*1000

The millennium is a useful marker for the passage of time, and it was a date that contemporaries considered seriously. The last decade of the century saw the entry into the European sphere of the Magyars in the east. They created a kingdom under their first Christian leader, who was baptised Stephen as a boy of ten. The Kingdom of Hungary was

incorporated into the European domain through a dynastic marriage, but there was more, for Hungary became Mary's fief. Stephen had invoked Mary during his struggles for political hegemony – as he did the military St George, and the saint favoured by converts, St Martin – and to her he commended his kingdom.[55] Stephen may have been influenced by the Marian commitment of St Adalbert of Prague, the missionary who had introduced him to Christianity, but the Magyars also lived in close proximity to the spheres of Greek Christianity to which Mary was so central. Here is a kingdom associated from the perilous years of its birth with Mary, protector and nurturer.

Hungary's lot fits comfortably with the trends we have already noticed in the ninth and tenth centuries, with Mary's growing presence in the courts of rulers, and her insertion into liturgies alongside other well-established saints and martyrs. She was highly prominent in the British Isles, but most parts of Europe also recognized her feasts – the Annunciation and Assumption above all – with elaborate liturgies in religious houses and courts. Some libraries possessed quite a wide range of materials about Mary – liturgies, apocrypha – like Hincmar's Reims, Paschasius' Corbie and Ælfric's Winchester.

The canoness Hrotsvitha found the library at her priory at Gandersheim around 935 to contain sufficient material to form the basis of her *Life of Mary* from birth to the flight to Egypt, which she wrote in racy verse.[56] A cousin of Emperor Otto I, himself an enthusiast for Mary, Hrotsvitha was a very well-connected canoness of the Saxon religious house, where noble women lived lives of scholarship and piety. In these exalted circles there a substantial number of manuscripts containing the wide range of writings about Mary already circulated. In houses such as this a home-grown, contemporary sound emerged. It was increasingly attached to Mary's feasts, through sequences and tropes, short prayers which are evident from around the year 900. These musical contributions to the liturgy were aimed at enriching the distinctive meaning of each feast – and so tropes were composed, unique to each occasion. The main four feasts of Mary benefited from this production. Some of these creations remained the staple of the liturgy for centuries to come. Once heard, such liturgy could be memorized, and thus repeated, and reach wider audiences. Mary's liturgy spread and touched many more than its producers and performers alone.

Hrotsvitha, though, adored poetry and was animated by the heroic

acts of saints and martyrs. She had a wonderful sense of rhythm and was an excellent adaptor of materials far less eloquent than her own. She reworked the history of Mary's early life in elegant verse based on Latin translations of the *Protogospel of James*, stories about Mary's incomparable purity as a baby, girl, maiden, wife and mother. In Hrotsvitha's privileged circle of noble, literate and confident canonesses devoted to the religious life, Mary became a model of good conduct and breeding. Her elegant Latin verse provided Mary's life-story with the elegant expression it deserved.[57] In her stylized preface Hrotsvitha dedicates her work to her fellow nuns: to Rikkardis, her teacher, and to Gerberga, the formidable abbess of Gandersheim, niece of Emperor Otto I.

Throughout the poem there is a sense of joy and splendour. The first third tells of the noble Joachim and Anna, already despairing of having a child. But when their daughter arrives, what joy! After eight days a naming ceremony – equivalent to Jesus' Circumcision – is described:

After eight days the high priests, who had been summoned, came, so that according to custom they might confer a name upon the child and purify the mother. Joachim pouring forth prayers to God said: 'Thou, King of heaven, Who alone dost name the stars, deign to indicate in a heavenly manner by some brilliant sign the name of this tender babe.' When he had said this, a mighty voice sounded suddenly from on high, commanding that the name Mary be bestowed upon the chosen child. 'Stella Maris' [star of the sea] as our Latin tongue has it! Fittingly was this name conferred upon the holy child . . .[58]

The aristocratic Hrotsvitha, a virgin in a house of high-born canonesses, imagined with flair the joy and pride which Mary brought to her family and to all who knew her.[59] Like the female religious of the tenth century, Mary excelled in saying her psalms:

For this child, as soon as she was taken from the cradle, shone resplendently before the whole world because of her matured character, nor did she in her infant frailty ever do anything except what was most just in the commandments of the law, and she was ever zealous in chanting the psalms of David.[60]

Mary's milieu was exalted, and so was to be her adult life. The priests chose her companion – an elderly, worthy man – from among members of the 'royal house of Judeah'. He was humble too and refused the honour of taking away a virgin already consecrated for Christ. Mary

was thus imagined as a noble, chaste woman, a bride of Christ – like Hrotsvitha and her sisters at Gandersheim.

Ever sensitive to the atmosphere of envy that can so easily arise within an enclosed, single-sex community, Hrotsvitha imagined the group around Mary, five maidens of the Temple, who with her wove the Temple veil. Mary was chosen to work in the precious purple, and for that the women taunted her:

It is perhaps decreed that some day thou art to be our Queen because to thee alone is the purple entrusted to be wrought, even though thou art our junior by not a few years?[61]

Hrotsvitha embroidered Mary's life into a precious, delightful narrative of aristocratic and privileged youth. It is perhaps unsurprising, therefore, to find that the events of the Annunciation and the Nativity are described with little detail, over only sixty lines. Joseph was a most helpful spouse, and the decree of cruel Herod sent the family packing on the road to Egypt. Now Hrotsvitha thrusts the boy Jesus centre-stage, following with the many amusing apocryphal tales of the miracles he wrought in order to feed and protect his parents on route. She fittingly ends with thanks and praise to Christ, Mary's son:

O how praiseworthy is the grandeur of Thy power, O Christ! How wonderful are the changes of Thy sacred right Hand! Thou art able to dispose of all things by a mere silent act of Thy Will! . . . Thou, born from the Father before all ages, didst in obedience to His Will take up Thine abode in the womb of Thy mother and didst take from her a human form in the fullness of time . . . Thou didst dutifully take nourishment from Thy Virgin-Mother's breast . . .

For this, may the angelic hosts, I pray, unceasingly praise the Lord.[62]

The stories born in Palestine and Syria during the early centuries of Christianity had made their way by the end of the millennium to the religious houses of Western Europe. Theological reflection and narrative met in Mary and were expressed in poetry, liturgical chant and visual imagery. Much that was most cherished about Mary was not to be found in scripture, and so her admirers – Paschasius, Hrotsvitha – devised ways to make palatable and authoritative stories of purity, nurture and miraculous birth, which were not contained in scripture. Eastern tales – life-narratives as well as miracles – lived on as the favoured terrain for

encounters with Mary. The Mary narratives of the Koran owed much to such narratives too, just as did the liturgy of her most popular feast, the Assumption. Hrotsvitha happily used them, satisfied with an attribution to 'Saint James, the Lord's brother'.

While Ælfric was tormented by his doubts over the story of Mary's Assumption, the tale of her entry into the realm of celestial love was whole-heartedly embraced by the monk-artists who served the Holy Roman Emperor, Otto III (980–1002). Under imperial patronage further glories were in store: a unique ability to describe the movement between heaven and earth was nurtured in the lavishly endowed and protected centres of image-making – the monasteries of Reichenau on Lake Constance and Fulda in Franconia.[63]

Quiet assurance emanated from Mary to her devotees, above all aristocratic men and women in religious houses, whose lips sang her praises and whose eyes saw her every day. Around the year 1000 it was even fitting to decorate the opening leaf of the rule of Saint Benedict, the rule of life which guided most European monks and nuns, with an image of Mary enthroned with Christ the Child in her lap. Together they sat against a background of imperial red and fertile green, within a mandorla, the almond-shaped sphere which usually surrounded the majesty of Christ. Written on its circumference was the inscription 'The prince who rules nature everywhere and at the same time is happy in the lap, is lord of earth and heaven.'[64]

It is striking to see just how ordered is the world these images portray and how important Mary's location is as the apex of hierarchies linking heaven and earth. The Sacramentary of Warmund, bishop of Ivrea, one of Otto III's confidants, has Mary giving Otto his 'diadem of Caesar' – the imperial crown: Mary is larger than the leaning Otto and she touches his crowned head.[65] A Fulda Sacramentary of the late tenth century offered for the feast of All Saints a field of serried ranks of worthies, bishops and monks, with Mary at the centre, raising one hand towards the medallion of the *agnus dei* – Lamb of God, her son – and holding a chalice in the other.[66]

Within the court of the Holy Roman Emperors, rulers of continental Europe, in the years of the Ottonian dynasty, Mary became an essential part of imperial self-understanding: she was the link between heaven and earth; she was the emblem of imperial dignity; she interceded mightily with her son in heaven. These rulers were closely linked to the

Byzantine Court through marriage and trade, while the churchmen looked to theological and devotional inspiration. The powerful themes related to the end of Mary's life on earth were favoured by Ottonian makers of images. A manuscript of Bible commentaries made at Bamberg cathedral $c.1000$ imagines a road from earthly baptism to heavenly glory: Mary led the way, followed by holy women, bishops, apostles, Magi, all climbing towards the crucified Christ.[67] Reassuring above all were images of the Assumption, each frame confidently portraying the Dormition of Mary and her Assumption to heaven. Emperor Otto III's own gospel book was covered with a Byzantine ivory plaque which depicted the Dormition, with the traditional scene of Mary's soul raised by her son: a medallion image carried by angels, as in a Reichenau book of tropes of $c.1001$, resembled the medallion so common in Byzantine representations of Christ, Mary and saints.[68] A decade or two later in that same monastery these scenes were presented across two parchment leaves of another book of collects: on the left side, Christ himself lifts Mary's swaddled soul towards angels while gazing at his mother lovingly; and on the right, in the heavenly scene of her reception, a praying Mary is portrayed within a sphere, supported by angels and drawn up by God's own hand.[69] Alongside these powerful, rich and assertive images we should also note the detail painted into a book made for Bernward, bishop of Hildesheim. The Crucifixion scene in his gospel book of $c.1015$ has Mary and John: tears run down her cheeks.[70] Bernward was led to explore Mary's pain at the death of her son – Mary as *mater dolorosa* – centuries before this became the central theme of European devotion.

Once in heaven, Mary's role was now clear – to pray for her adherents, for those who celebrated her feasts, who remembered her in their prayers, who chanted her hymns and recorded her life. Around 1000 a cross made for the abbess Matilda, head of the religious house for women at Essen, was adorned with an enamel plaque of a woman kneeling at the feet of the enthroned Mary, who is gazing forward, her son on her knee. Precious stones surround the tiny scene, spoils of antique Mediterranean finery. Here is Mary of majesty, but she is not alone. There is a tiny figure at her feet, for Mary had become a subject for supplication, not of adoration alone. The same religious house also commissioned a most sumptuous Mary, of a new kind: a gilt statue of Mary, seated with her son on her lap; Mary, in the round, holding an

orb, or is it an apple? And although she gazes to her right, her son's gaze is turned towards her.[71] In this prestigious and rich religious house, which was home to women of the imperial household, Mary was realized as a patron, but also as an intimate companion. Just as the *Theotokos* was born through the effort of imperial women, so was this shimmering Golden Mary – the *Goldene Madonna*.

PART III

The Emergence of Mary's Hegemony: 1000–1200

8

Mary of the Cloister

The Golden Madonna of Essen displays spectacularly the wealth and interests of a group of high-born nuns at the heart of Europe around the year 1000. This shimmering statue was unique even at its time. Yet it told the story of things to come. Monasteries were the centres of wealth and taste; they set trends in devotion for clergy, the religious and for lay people. This is especially true in all that concerns Mary, for Mary became a central preoccupation of medieval monastic life, expressed in liturgy and art, prayer and miracle tales.

This preoccupation with Mary during the eleventh and twelfth centuries was primarily a monastic engagement with her liturgy and biblical presence, with her images and miracles. But it did not stop there. The spheres of learning and ecclesiastical work brought monks into contact with priests, while the monastic reform movements recruited privileged men who were versed in the ways of the world and often joined religious houses as adults after a life in the world. Bernard of Clairvaux, Mary's great devotee, was not only a great Latin preacher and poet who served the church in political missions all over Europe, but also son to a knightly family of Champagne, a man who understood the culture of chivalry, who had travelled widely and who was acquainted with secular love poetry. The languages and idioms within which Mary was explored were becoming more diverse than ever before, and they offered a variety of moods and approaches to her.

The looming of Mary ever larger in monastic sensibility coincided with a tremendous surge in the intensity and sheer scale of European life. In the two centuries after 1000 the European population probably more than doubled. New settlements were laid out on virgin land, previously marshy or covered with forest.[1] This enterprise was the product of thousands of local initiatives on estates, in villages and in

small towns which saw a considerable growth in Europe's power to grow food and make artefacts by and for its people. Wherever a new village was founded – in Yorkshire, Saxony or on once marshy lands in the Po valley – its people built a church. These churches were consecrated and dedicated to patrons, and, as Mary was familiar and much loved, they were most often dedicated to her.

In these centuries of European integration the thoughts and practices developed in monasteries, nunneries and cathedrals spread far beyond their walls.[2] Through the efforts of churchmen and rulers – and with the prompting of a series of activist popes in Rome – thousands of parishes were coaxed into structures of hierarchy and obedience in dioceses, all of which tended towards the head in Rome. No village or town was so isolated as to be beyond the sound of bells and chants, or without some knowledge of the pomp of Marian processions and the grandeur of buildings built in her honour. As Mary was taught and preached, sung and recited, she was no longer the exclusive possession of a Latin world. Mary lore was a blend of local interpretations with aspirations for universal cohesion within a Christian vision. Mary was produced in many conversations that involved Christians – European and Eastern – and their neighbours.

One of the most famous comments on European society was made by the monk Radulfus Glaber (before 1000–c.1050). He had been offered to the monastic life in Dijon as a boy and subsequently travelled widely before settling around 1044 at the great Burgundian abbey of Cluny. Writing about the changes he saw about him, he commented:

Just before the third year after the millennium, throughout the whole world, but most especially in Italy and Gaul, men began to reconstruct churches, although for the most part the existing ones were properly built and not the least unworthy. But it seemed as though each Christian community were aiming to surpass all others in the splendour of construction. It was as if the whole world were shaking itself free, shrugging off the burden of the past, and cladding itself everywhere in a white mantle of churches. Almost all the episcopal churches and those of monasteries dedicated to various saints, and little village chapels, were rebuilt better than before by the faithful.[3]

Once built, these expensive edifices in (white) stone rather than in wood, were now most often dedicated to Mary. In the ancient city of Narbonne a suburb of St Mary evolved just east of the Roman road,

the Via Domitia, by 1066. The settlement was linked to a new Marian sanctuary and in turn was taken over by a group of religious, so that by 1086 a Benedictine priory, Saint-Marie-La Mourguier, had developed there.[4] Within these churches there was likely to be placed a sculpted figure of Mary enthroned like the very early Imad Madonna, made for the bishop of Paderborn $c.1051/1058$, or the solemn Mary sculptures of the Auvergne, hewn from tree trunks, which became so common in the twelfth century.[5] These are Europe's earliest sculptures in the round, to be seen from all angles, to be touched, transported, adored.[6]

Those who revived old cities or planned new towns and villages rarely omitted a Marian church or shrine. When Bishop Meinwerk ($c.976$–1036) developed the city of Paderborn he had a replica of the Holy Sepulchre in Jerusalem built and dedicated it to Mary and Saints Peter and Andrew. This now existed alongside the older churches dedicated to the local saints St Saviour and St Liborius.[7] The church held relics brought from the Holy Land, memories of the Passion. The conquest of Muslim Iberia was treated as a crusade, and it too heightened awareness of the Holy Land, which was Mary's home. A cache of ancient relics found in a chest opened by King Alfonso VI of Leon-Castille (1065–1109) after the reconquest of Oviedo in 1075 contained a garment rumoured to have belonged to Mary as well as drops of her milk. These were claimed as ancient relics hidden centuries earlier from invading Muslims, alongside pieces of the cross, bread from the Marriage at Cana, soil stirred by Christ and Christ's own tunic. In these zones of conquest – northern and central Iberia – colonization led to the creation of new settlements for Christian colonists. The new churches built and consecrated there were predominantly dedicated to Mary. Mary was not only a universal figure fitting for the devotions of Christian colonizers but a useful and familiar figure for those who converted from Islam under the new, Christian, rule.[8]

Europe's growing prosperity in this period of economic and demographic growth underpinned the stabilization of European states and the creation of networks of towns and cities connected by rivers and roads. This European order allowed schools to flourish, above all in cathedrals built and decorated first in Romanesque and then in Gothic styles. As we have seen the 'old' monastic world was also undergoing change, with a variety of new orders – Cistercians, Premonstratensians,

Gilbertines – each proposing an agenda for vigorous reform. Within these vital institutions – monasteries, cathedrals, priories, schools – and under the patronage of kings, bishops and aristocrats, all aspects of Christian culture were examined afresh. All questions flowed in one way or another from a fundamental reflection on the promise of the Incarnation, the gift of grace, and the ways in which men and women might partake of it.

The twelfth century also saw the incorporation of philosophical terms and questions from the ancient world, which soon formed the framework for discussion of all aspects of the world. Christian culture was considered as an ethical system by some, as a phenomenon in the history of nature by others. Theologians considered the extent of God's will, the requirements of a good Christian life, and the body/mind conundrum. There was little innovation in discussions of Mary within the scholarly curriculum, yet there was great scope for thinking of Mary as a source of wisdom and consolation, both in monasteries and in cathedral schools, and increasingly outside them too. Mary assumed new importance in the spheres of collective action initiated by lay people in villages and towns, with the desire for peace and protection. A carpenter from Le Puy founded a fraternity in the local cathedral of Notre-Dame which grew to a membership of 5,000. The bishop appointed a priest who helped draw up the group's statutes; these required that members wear a white habit adorned with an image of Mary and her son and marked with the inscription 'Lamb of God who bore the sins of the world, give us peace'.[9] The aim was to extend peace in a still violent region through penitential effort aligned with political acts. In twelfth-century Iceland the housewife þorunn Eyjólfsdóttir donated land to St Mary at Staður on condition that its tenant feed three paupers at Easter, Christmas, All Saints and on Mary's feasts and remember the anniversary of her death too.[10] Mary inspired in Europeans many such new gestures of interest and commitment.

MATERIAL MARY

In the early centuries of the second Christian millennium Mary emerges in monastic life as a subject not only for theological reflection, but also of devotional practices. Monastic movements which emphasized

contemplation and personal prayer dedicated a great deal of thought to Mary, and in doing so made her anew. By the year 1200 Mary was deemed by some Europeans to be immaculate in her purity in the face of heretics and Jews. Belief in Mary's purity became the absolute touchstone for membership in the Christian body.

The privilege accorded to Mary in representation went hand in hand with her growing popularity as a patron of religious houses, cathedrals and monastic orders. The Benedictine abbey of Weingarten in Württemberg accorded to its patron, Mary, the central position on the oak-wood binding of its Sacramentary. Mary is shown enthroned, her son on her knee; she erupts from the surface of the binding, larger and more voluminous than any other figure. Her chest and crown are decorated with gemstones – no evangelist, saint, or angel is treated in this way. The preciously bound book – with relics of Mary, George, Oswald, Bartholomew, Peter, Paul and James embedded in its binding – was a powerful object which guided the abbot Berthold through his liturgy.[11] Similarly, the Winchester Psalter, probably made for Bishop Henry of Blois some time in the mid-twelfth century, shows Mary enthroned, her hands raised in prayer, attended by two angels in a Byzantine mode. This may have been inspired by an artefact brought from Sicily – where Byzantine style prevailed – by the bishop's nephew, who was in exile there.[12] Mary's majesty, inspired so early in the bosom of Byzantine Christianity, still appealed to monks, bishops and priests who contemplated her as patron and protector.[13] The lavish prayer book – the Guta-Sintram Codex – was made in 1154 through the combined efforts of the scribe Guta and the illuminator Sintram, for the use of the Augustinian canonesses of Schwartzenthann priory in Alsace. On the dedicatory page Mary is represented dressed in vestments, holding an inscribed ribbon with the artists standing at her sides.[14] They dedicate the manuscript to Mary: 'Sweet, beloved, our hope, blessed Mary, protect us together with motherly feeing'. In turn, Mary answers:

Together, you have adorned this work, which you have dedicated to me, with letters and figures achieved with skill. Together I will make you to share in the same repose.[15]

The abbeys of the congregation of Cluny were among the most ambitious and well connected to Europe's rulers. From Cluny, the mother-house in Burgundy, throughout the tenth and eleventh centuries,

a European network of houses radiated a religious programme of great grandeur and incessant activity. The Cluniac houses maintained liturgy at its most elaborate and ornate, supported by income from landed property, wealth which was protected by papal privileges. At its foundation in the tenth century Cluny had oriented its life under the protection of St Peter and his successors, the popes; by the mid-eleventh century, Mary had become central to its self-image.[16]

Imperial grandeur combined at Cluny with holy chastity. Cluniac houses were protected and endowed by emperors – Henry II (ruled 1002–24) gave Cluny the imperial orb. Early in the new millennium, around 1004, Abbot Odilo of Cluny (994–1049) had a compendium of materials about Mary copied for his private use. Comprising nine sections and amounting to 166 pages, this was a harvest of early Christian and early medieval reflection of Mary: Ambrose on virginity, Jerome on the Assumption, virginity and birth of Mary, Ildefonsus of Toledo on virginity, and more.[17] There was not much that is new in this book; rather, it is a collection of authorities on themes of monastic life, such as virginity and the liturgy of the Assumption. The book was produced for Odilo over some fifteen years; it was a labour of love, not a display of creativity. The sumptuous Cluniac liturgy over which he presided increasingly centred on Marian moments. When Cardinal Peter of Albano visited Cluny in 1080 his entry took place on the feast of Mary's Purification and merged into the day's events.[18]

Awareness of Mary grew not only in prestigious houses like Cluny, it inspired other, more tentative initiatives as well. When St Heribert (c.970–1021), as archbishop of Cologne, sought to repay God for his many mercies he decided to found a monastery dedicated to Mary and All Saints. A suitable site was hard to find, so Heribert prepared himself through fasts and prayers to reveal his intention to Mary. In his sleep he received a vision of her as queen of a starry heaven, and she instructed him:

You know, she said, O Heribert, your prayers have been heard, and so I come here to you, to show you in which place you should achieve what you have in mind. I am, indeed, Mary, Mother of the Lord. So rise and find the castle of Deutz, take hold of it and have it purified, and found a monastery there in honour of God and of me, and so where once sin and the cult of demons had prevailed, now justice will reign in the multitude of saints.[19]

Mary appeared to the abbot and guided his hand through the ambitious project of foundation, which is made to appear like the conquest of land away from sin and evil. Now this account of Heribert was written by Rupert of Deutz, himself a recipient of Marian visions, but it shows at the very least that such experiences could be convincingly turned into tales of foundation. Such visions of Mary were tales of justification, useful support in the mobilization of the good will and resources which great monastic enterprises required.

New foundations and old were full of images. These adorned the spaces of monastic living and edified them too. The very act of making images of sacred figures – and monastic art was often made by monks and nuns themselves – was an act of devotion. Where did craft end and piety begin? We are sometimes able to discern the maker's preoccupation with the challenge of making Mary. Eckhart of St Gall (d.c.1060), a schoolmaster of Mainz who retired to the Benedictine house of St Gall, reported a story that was current in his monastery about a monk-artist, Tutilo (d.913). Tutilo was so talented that he was permitted the unusual privilege of being allowed to work outside the monastery, and the story records his experience in Metz. While Tutilo was carving statues of Mary in that city two poor pilgrims begged him for alms, and he gave them some. A while later the beggars spoke with a clerk about the monk-artist and commented:

'Blessed to God be this man, who has comforted us today. But is that his sister,' they asked, 'the splendid lady, who hands him his scissors so helpfully and instructs him in his work?'[20]

The clerk asked Tutilo who his 'companion' had been, and the artist was so perplexed that he decided to return to the monastery the next day. On the morrow he found a circle incised on the gold leaf he was modelling with a message: Mary had made it herself.[21] By guiding his hand Mary reassured the artist that his project was not only worthy, but correct. Another form of reassurance to those charged with representing the mother of God was offered in scenes, common in Europe from the twelfth century, of the evangelists writing their gospels and Luke painting Mary.[22] The tradition of Mary's images was linked in this way to the earliest moments of Christian history.

The Golden Madonna had been made in a European world which was discovering the power of sacred images, especially those which

inhabited the three dimensions of space. The first widely known cult of a carving/statue of Christ on the cross, the *volto santo*, was at the church of St Martin in Lucca in the eleventh century.[23] Such figures in the round posed acute challenges to their makers and audiences, for they were more audacious and suggestive than pictures on parchment, cloth or wood. They were viewed in the round and summoned the viewer into a physical response. It became expected in these centuries that every church, and increasingly parish churches, possess a statue of Mary. When the penitent Peter of Maule wished to make restitution for a life of sinful gain, he offered the priory of Maule a year's grape harvest for a statue of the Virgin:

shortly afterwards, however, falling sick by divine providence, he confessed his fault and restored it to St Mary quit of all rent. He also gave the grape harvest for that year to the blessed Virgin, for the purchase of a statue.[24]

Those who did not have land could offer the exertion of their bodies. When an acrobat joined the abbey of Clairvaux as a lay brother he knew none of the habitual monastic prayers and so offered his reverence to Mary at night, while the other monks slept, in a series of gyrations, even walking on his hands. When he was found out and denounced to the abbot, Mary interceded; she accepted his sincere offering, his pious if crude art.[25]

Around the year 1000 Mary was most commonly encountered in the celebration of the Nativity, Crucifixion and Assumption.[26] The Crucifixion was the climax of the story of salvation, the fulfilment of the Incarnation's promise. Scenes of the Crucifixion included Mary and John as its privileged and mournful witnesses. An early eleventh-century Psalter from the abbey of Werden, near Essen, contains a line-drawing of Mary and John each gesturing with their hands to Christ nailed to the Cross.[27] The whole Christian story was captured in a relief decoration of that book's binding: the upper scene of Christ in majesty flanked by angels, and the lower scene of the Crucifixion, with Mary and John each with a hand to their face, in a gesture of woe. An increasingly mournful drama unfolded at the foot of the cross, and action often centred on Mary.[28]

Grandeur and autonomy characterized monastic representations of Mary and set her apart from her important established role as witness to the Crucifixion. Mary was frequently presented enthroned; she occupied

increasingly large and more prominent spaces. On the ivory binding of the Gospel Book used by Duchess Judith of Bavaria, of $c.1051-64$, Mary was mounted on a gold plaque. On the dedicatory page of the Svanhild Gospel Book of 1070/80, Mary appears with two religious women, Svanhild and Brigida, who kneel at her feet. The opening page of the Antiphonary of St Peter's monastery in Salzburg, of around 1060, was dipped in purple dye – the imperial colour – and its upper part was illuminated with a scene of Mary's Dormition and Assumption. The scene follows the Byzantine iconography, with mourning apostles around Mary's bier and Mary's rising soul depicted as a small person.[29] On the dedication page of the *Life of Liudger* (around 1100) Mary is not so large, but she sits high up, her son in her arms, against the gold page.[30] The Guda Homiliary, made in the middle-Rhine region in the second half of the twelfth century, boasts a decorated initial for the homily on the Assumption: the figure entitled 'Mary the virgin' (*virgo Maria*) stands alone, raising her hand in blessing, forcefully grasping the intricate foliage which makes the initial letter C.[31] Mary also appears from around 1100 on seals of religious houses dedicated to her: that of Lincoln cathedral of the mid-twelfth century portrays her seated, holding a sceptre and orb. The seal of St Mary's Abbey in York depicts Mary and Child with a fruit-tree and a star.[32] All these examples show how frequently Mary was to be seen in the liturgical books and altar artefacts of monastic houses which formed the backdrop for the daily lives of monks.

In the course of the eleventh and twelfth centuries artists struggled for a balanced representation of Christ's suffering, which included Mary and John as witnesses. Restrained gestures of sadness and mourning were tried out.[33] An English Missal made soon after 1060 includes a representation of Christ on the Cross in the initial 'T' at the beginning of the canon of the mass, but has Mary alone mourning her son on his right.[34] An English monastic ivory from the eleventh century depicts the dramas which followed the Crucifixion, when Mary is depicted twice: with the Holy Women at the Tomb, and at the Ascension, where she leads the group of apostles.[35] An enamel altarpiece made in 1181 by the itinerant enamellist Nicholas of Verdun for the abbot of the Augustinian priory at Klosterneuburg near Vienna has Mary holding a book, inclining her head towards Christ, and John touching his forehead in sadness. The bodies of Mary and her son are linked by gesture as Christ's own

head falls to his right, towards his mother. The inscription reminds the viewer that an act of salvation was unfolding: 'The victim is slaughtered by which our fall is alleviated'.[36]

Mary was increasingly chosen as the focus of religious imagery. Another work by Nicholas of Verdun, a reliquary for Cologne cathedral begun in 1181, is a gilt and bejewelled structure. Christ is shown in it blessing at the upper tier of the relief; at the bottom, Mary sits with her son at the centre under an arch, with the Baptism on their left and the adoring Magi on her right. Mary is both outside the story and within it, as she gestures to her right to receive the gifts.[37] A twelfth-century English monastic ivory portrays the Annunciation, Visitation, Nativity, Annunciation to the Shepherds, Adoration and Baptism – Mary appears in each, and thus in more scenes than her son.[38]

Those who had chosen, or had been offered as children to, the life of religious perfection led the efflorescence of interest in Mary. The life experiences of European monks and nuns were a mixture of community living and personal meditation and prayer. Within the monastic churches they maintained an incessant flow of liturgy at the eight canonical hours which structured the day and fed the minds. Religious houses differed greatly in style and in wealth, and so too did the *opus dei* – the work of God – that they offered: their plainchant echoed sometimes in austere surroundings, and other times in ornately decorated ones. The praise of Mary became, in these early centuries of the second millennium, a frame for personal striving and for collective endeavour. It was produced in a wide range of genres and materials and ultimately influenced the devotional worlds outside monasteries too.[39]

PRAYER, PENANCE AND CONSOLATION

Monastic life offered varied opportunities for study and service. The most conscientious and the most creative religious were incessantly confronted with the reality of sin and the importance of penance. New monastic reform movements – the Cluniacs and from the late eleventh century, the Cistercians – infused renewed rigour and self-awareness into the pursuit of religious perfection. The monks of Cluny rendered

the liturgy into magnificent arrangements of sound in richly adorned edifices. The Cistercians revised the liturgy and sought inspiration in personal meditation and austere routines of prayer.[40] Even new Irish houses were turning away from their Celtic traditions: convents were now dedicated not to native saints but to Mary. An Irish poet saw in this novelty an expression of Mary's own will: 'Mary exhorts them, Mary instructs them. She desired that her Son should have large communities.'[41]

The rush of new foundations – hundreds of new houses all over Europe – offered opportunities to build for Mary. Indeed, most churches dedicated to Mary – cathedrals, as well as rural and urban churches – were founded between 1000 and 1200, a period of vast expansion in European settlement. And there was the responsibility to maintain old buildings too. The mother of the monk Guibert of Nogent (d.1124) had a vision in which Mary entered the neglected church of Nogent monastery accompanied by a young woman and knelt at its altar. Mary gestured at the ruins and pointed at Guibert. The young man's duty thus became clear: he was to join the religious house and promote the rebuilding of Mary's church, at her request. Guibert's spiritual mother conveyed a message to him through his birth mother.

All monastic houses aimed to minimize occasions for temptation through a regulated lifestyle, edifying prayer and useful work. Yet an awareness of sin was all-pervasive in these houses devoted to religious perfection. Guibert of Nogent's first little book, on virginity, shows just how obsessed was the young monk with sin, with the struggle between body and aspiring soul. He became deeply attached to Mary, who exemplified the combination of active and contemplative life and who offered help in the struggle against sin.[42] Prayer offered occasions for exploration of personal inadequacy, of human sin, but also moments of hope and support in the struggle with evil. In prayer personal sinfulness was unburdened, but trust in divine grace was mediated through age-old collective rituals. The experience and witness of prayer was part of what made them emotional communities of great intensity.[43] Prayer was one of the most expressive genres of monastic writing, and much prayer turned towards Mary.

Mary was attractive not only for her purity, but for the intimacy that linked her to the redemption promised by her son. Monks and nuns devoted to the struggle against sin, immersed in devotional work, were

particularly aware of the precarious balance between human striving and human frailty. This period saw the development of ideas and practices that offered believers avenues for penance and atonement. The idea of purgatory matured in the twelfth century; it became a place where believers suffered for minor sins after death, and for a limited period of time.[44] In all these operations hope was mixed with despair, and the figure of Mary was adopted as a particularly efficacious companion, to guide the penitent and intercede with her son at the moment of reckoning.

Mary was so effective an intercessor on behalf of sinners since she enjoyed a unique relationship with Christ. Being of a single substance, mother and son enjoyed an incomparable closeness. The son could refuse his mother nothing, as a late eleventh-century rhymed prayer from the region of Beauvais in northern France confidently claimed:

> Whatever you wish
> Your only son will give you.
> For whomever you seek
> You will have pardon and glory.[45]

Mary thus triumphs in any comparison with other meritorious figures:

> When I think of angels,
> Of prophets and apostles,
> Of victorious martyrs,
> And of the most chaste of virgins,
> No one seems more powerful,
> No one more merciful,
> With their consent I say,
> Than the mother of God.[46]

Confidence in Mary's power to intercede with her son on behalf of sinners encouraged a tone of self-abjection in the unburdening of sin. A prayer to Mary written by Anselm's associate and advisor Maurilius, archbishop of Rouen (d. 1067), expresses a sense of shame and unworthiness when facing Mary:

But what am I doing, pouring my obscenities into your purest ears? I am appalled, lady, appalled, and with my conscience arguing against me, I blush deeply, naked in front of you I pray.[47]

Mary's purity was a stark backdrop against which a vivid picture of sin was painted. Sin was ugly and repulsive in this popular prayer, known in its earliest version from a Psalter of the French Abbey of Moissac of 1075:

O blessed and most saintly Mary, always Virgin, I am thus afflicted in face of your goodness, I am greatly confused by the abominations of my sins which have made me deformed and horrible in the eyes of angels and all saints.[48]

This state of self-loathing could easily lead to despair in the protection of saints. So the supplicant turns to Mary and recounts her glories; she was, after all, born to bear a Redeemer:

You know, most merciful queen, that you were born so that of you would be born, he who is God and Man, Our Lord Jesus Christ, true God and true Man, in whom I most truly believe.[49]

In Mary were thus combined the enticing attractions of a mother – loving, and consoling – with the effective powers of an agent of redemption. A prayer of this period extols Mary's incomparable purity; she was amazed at her own body:

You, Lady, were amazed both by the integrity of your body and by the fecund conception and you delighted in bringing forth your own parent, Our Lord Jesus Christ.[50]

The sinner could turn to Mary 'dressed in black rags and half-burnt by the fire of my sins' and show himself to her 'dressed in hideous garments'. Finally, the prayer reasserts Mary's sovereignty, her superiority over all other intercessors. The supplicant trusts in Mary's power to intercede, which is more effective than any other's: 'You indeed, Lady, are better and more excellent than all these intercessors.'[51]

The turn to Mary, Mother of God, often invoked thought of family relations. The appeal to kinship takes another form in a popular short prayer to Mary and John, known in England and northern France by the late twelfth century, which offered intimacy with Jesus through two relationships: one with his mother, Mary, and the other with his favourite, John. The supplicant approaches both for the sake of their intimacy with Christ: 'Oh, two celestial gems, Mary and John! Oh, two lights which shine divinely before God! May your rays chase away the clouds of my sins.'[52] It was indeed out of depictions of Mary and John

either side of Christ in majesty – though often Christ on the cross – that the image of Mary as advocate for humanity – *Madonna Advocata* – developed. This is usually a half-length figure, where Mary in Byzantine mode looks at the viewer, her right hand pointing up and her left held to her chest. The image was loved in Rome, and its most striking and influential example is that of Santa Maria di Aracoeli. Mary was dressed there in a blue cloak trimmed in gold; she was mournful, distant and potent.[53] The imperial Mary of yore was animated with the desire for intercession and advocacy.

Anselm (1033–1109) was an Italian monk, theologian, reformer of monasticism in Normandy, and at the end of his life archbishop of Canterbury. He possessed a genius for devotional expression and more than any other of his generation affected the habits of prayer among monks and nuns and aristocrats.[54] His prayers were closely linked to his intellectual concerns, and they spread among his associates in and outside monasteries. In response to a request by his friend, Gundulf, monk of Caen (Normandy), around 1074, Anselm addressed three prayers to Mary, accompanied by a letter of guidance.[55] The prayers were to be savoured in silence, with contrition; properly used, they could lead to heavenly things.[56] During the 1090s Anselm was engaged in philosophical reflection on the necessity of the Incarnation. This resulted in his original and important *Cur deus homo* (*Why God became Man*) in 1098, a work which spread beyond monasteries to the urban centres of learning – the cathedral libraries – where copies still survive, as in Durham, Norwich, Rochester and Canterbury.[57] In it Anselm deployed logic while presenting the truth of Christianity as if it were being taught to a sceptic, or a Jew.

Anselm's prayers were sought after not only by fellow monks in Normandy and England but also by exalted women. His relationship of religious guidance with Countess Matilda of Tuscany (1046–1115) was particularly creative. In response to her request Anselm sent in 1104 a monk of Canterbury with an edition of his prayers and meditations.[58] The two themes of eucharistic devotion and attachment to Mary are closely woven in the prayers of another Anselm – of Lucca (1036–86): Mary experienced Christ's body in a unique unmediated way, inasmuch as she was his real mother, the historic nurturer of Christ.[59] Reflecting on Mary's life with Jesus was recommended in preparation for communion, the reception of Christ's body. Anselm of

Lucca's prayers envision a Christian life punctuated by sacramental experience, enhanced by reflection on biblical moments and guided by the example and unique life of Mary.[60] Anselm of Lucca's three long prayers to Mary explore her uniqueness, her incommensurability: 'For you have been elected and elevated, with your son, from among all creatures, exalted above all mortals in glory and angelic dignity.'[61] Nothing equalled Mary; nothing equalled her closeness to her son.

Lay and religious people in search of spiritual guidance were numerous, and so Anselm of Canterbury's collection became a widely used guidebook for centuries to come. The prayers sent to Matilda were such a success that many copies of them survive; one was illustrated for the use of the nuns of Admont in Styria.[62] The meditations addressed the senses and elicited memories of biblical tales and moral allegories. Monks criss-crossed Europe, serving as advisers to kings and heralds of reform, and their habits of meditation and prayerful penance were shared with the members of the European elite. The influence and suggestion of monastic culture operated on subjects well beyond the monastery's gates.

New ideas and emphases directed religious lives towards a greater awareness of Mary and her meanings. Each church and chapel was a setting for performances inspired by Mary. The twelfth-century English religious Christina of Markyate (1120s–1155) struggled hard to find her place in the world as a recluse – a religious woman living a solitary life – and she ultimately became the protégé of monks. When Mary appeared to her, it was as an imposing 'imperial' figure, her shape in contemporary representation. Christina dreamed that, during a mass, the priest summoned her:

He held out to her a branch of most beautiful leaves and flowers, saying: 'Receive this, my dear, and offer it to the lady'. At the same time he pointed out to her a lady like an empress sitting on a dais not far from the altar. Curtsying to her, she held out the branch which she had received. And the lady, taking the branch from Christina's hand, gave back to her a twig and said, 'Take care of it for me'.[63]

When Christina complained about her pain and suffering the 'Lady' offered consolation. Christina withdrew happy and content, the branch in her hand. The vision, we are told, enhanced Christina's credibility and confounded her enemies.

A mark of Christina's spiritual progress and growing reputation is the psalter which Abbot Geoffrey of Gorham commissioned, very probably for her use.[64] Mary is present throughout this sumptuous book: the calendar for August has a figure of *Virgo*, as a haloed, winged woman, rising to heaven, alongside the date of the Assumption – 15 August. The psalter is accompanied by a lively series of full-page illustrations from the life of Christ in which Mary is prominent. The Annunciation portrays a spirited, seated Mary holding a book, actively responding to the angel's message; the Visitation is a tender scene of two women embracing, faces touching; next the Nativity – a true family scene, in which Mary and Joseph are locked by gaze and gesture, and even the dumb animals join in; Pentecost has the apostles receiving the gift of tongues from the Holy Spirit in the shape of a dove, and among them – large and majestic, gazing forward – is Mary, in a gesture of benediction.[65]

Mary was deemed by Christina's spiritual patrons to be an appropriate visual companion to her prayers. In choosing Mary they were no doubt responding to Christina's own experiences of turning to Mary and being heard. In response to prayer Christina received a vision that prompted her to enact Mary's maternity:

In the guise of a small child [Jesus] came to the arms of his sorely tried spouse and remained with her a whole day . . . she took him in her hands, gave thanks, and pressed him to her bosom . . . she held Him at one moment to her virginal breast . . . at another she felt His presence within her even through the barrier of her flesh . . . From that moment the fire of lust was . . . completely extinguished.[66]

On another occasion Mary appeared with medicines as a powerful healer when Christina languished in pain. Whatever their needs, monks and nuns increasingly imagined their lives, body and mind as affected by Mary.

Within the monasteries thousands of small gestures amplified Mary in the images and sounds of religious life. Towards the end of her life the mystic Elisabeth of Schönau (*c*.1129–65) experienced visions described as the 'resurrection' of Mary, visions which led to the adjustment of her convent's calendar with the aim of enhancing the celebration of the Assumption.[67] Between 1156 and 1159 Elisabeth received visions that provided precise details about Mary's end and especially about Mary's physical rise to heaven: her age, the time which had elapsed between death and assumption, the presence of the apostles around her

tomb. Elisabeth saw Mary rise to heaven in body and in soul, and an angel confirmed this to her. The visionary would have been worried about spreading such a 'novelty' since authoritative writers, 'Pseudo-Jerome' *Cogitis me* above all, had warned against dwelling upon Mary's bodily Assumption. She reported that Mary guided her: 'It must not be divulged to the people, because this is an evil age and those who hear it will get entangled and not know how to extricate themselves.'[68] Mary encouraged her to share the privileged knowledge with others 'who especially love me'. Her guidance included the distinction between the day of her death, 15 August, and of her 'Resurrection' – like her son's forty days later – on 23 September.[69]

Elisabeth consulted her brother, Eckbert, a noted writer against perceived heresies and errors. Theirs was a relationship of kinship, religious guidance and devotional scrutiny; such relationships between religious men and women often used the figure of Mary as a model for mutual self-fashioning. Yet there was more at stake in judging Elisabeth's vision than the question of innovation and authority. The world they inhabited, the Rhineland in the twelfth century, was also a place of other types of novelty: Cathar beliefs, western offshoots of eastern dualism, taught that a chasm separated light and darkness, spirit and matter. The carefully crafted combination of humanity and divinity in Christ, the product of over a thousand years of intellectual and political efforts, was opposed by an alternative view of a world weighed down by the flesh and its desires. Eckbert himself had preached and written against Cathars; he summarized their faith in

Two creators one good and one evil . . . Everything of the flesh which lives on the earth, whether man or animal, originates from the prince of darkness, the devil, and is founded on his evil nature.[70]

Brother and sister may well have judged that the vision of Mary's bodily Assumption, one which earlier generations had shied away from imagining, was a welcome and timely gift in the struggle against error.[71]

LITURGY AND INNOVATION: THE ASSUMPTION

Penance and prayer were powerful routes to Mary, but they were not the only ones. Monks and scholars in cathedrals were drawn to learning more about Mary in liturgical offices and in biblical commentary. Fulbert of Chartres ($c.952-1028/9$), a great teacher and bishop of that city, offered a striking example of the celebration of Mary within the complex and privileged framework of a cathedral chapter. He developed in Chartres a cult of Mary's tunic, reputedly brought from the east by Charles the Bald in 876. He wrote sermons and poetry with the clarity and style for which his cathedral school was renowned.[72] He appreciated above all Mary's power and cherished the memory of her body. Chartres tradition recorded Fulbert's privileged contact with Mary's milk:

... particularly devoted to blessed Mary, [he] composed many treatises and many elegant stories about her ... The blessed Virgin visited him when he was ill, and bathed his tongue ... with an infusion of her own breast milk ... three drops of this milk remained on his face and he collected these and placed them in a precious vase appropriate for them.[73]

Fulbert's liturgical celebration of Mary marked her apart from and above all other saints. This account of his devotion, recorded for future generations, appealed to the intense attachments which cathedral canons and monks were developing towards Mary, relations that were as physical as they were emotional.

Fulbert explored the Incarnation through enthusiastic attention to God's mother. His work harnessed theological reflection to liturgical practice, and enhanced Mary's place in the life of Chartres cathedral. Fulbert reworked traditional materials that were available in most monastic libraries – like Paschasius Radbert's tract on Mary's life – and inserted into his sermons some of the oldest and best-known of Mary's miracles. Fulbert thus preserved even as he innovated. He cast an intense gaze upon Mary's life, seeing in her birth a reason to rejoice, and so the feast day of 8 September – Mary's Nativity – was solemnly celebrated just as the Nativity of Christ was. Fulbert's compositions for the feast shared some of the liturgical tropes for the Assumption, but there were

new offerings too. Most striking and influential was the responsory *Stirps Jesse* (the root, or stock, of Jesse), which provided Mary with full genealogical credentials based on Isaiah's prophecy (11:1–2):

Responsory: The stock of Jesse produced a rod, and the rod a flower, and upon that flower rests the nourishing spirit.
Versicle: The rod is the virgin mother, the flower her son. And upon this flower rests the nourishing spirit.

The responsory is full of evocations of colour and smell:

> She emits a fragrance beyond all balsams, colorings, and incense
> Purple as the violet, dewy as the rose, gleaming as the lily.[74]

Fulbert excelled in the making of litanies of praise, strings of appellations for Mary, and he created a story of Mary's birth for her feast day.[75] This responsory quickly spread through Europe and in turn influenced new compositions.

Everything that a great religious institution had to offer – music, song, vestments, decorated spaces, processions and drama – was mobilized on Mary's great feast, the summer feast of the Assumption. As we have seen, it was believed that Mary was assumed into heaven, body and soul, perfect and chaste. Everything about the feast was designed to remind participants that Mary was seated alongside her son in heaven. The Assumption set Mary apart from other saints and reassured those who sought her intercession and help as she sat alongside her son there. It presented Mary's passing as a rebirth in an abundance of sermons and hymns and in liturgical innovation. A survey of liturgical offices at the great abbey of Cluny recorded *c.*1030 the action on Assumption day, ritual set among wonderful objects:

During the Hours three tapers should be lit in front of the altar. Before the ringing for Prime, three golden chalices should be placed on the high altar and two candelabras should be lit there and burn all day long. In addition, the arm of the most blessed Maur should be placed on that altar and the gold sceptre with the vase, which is also golden, containing the milk of the blessed virgin Mary.[76]

When all were assembled the antiphon *Thou art all fair* (*Tota pulchra es*) sounded, and the procession entered the oratory of St Mary. The words are from the Song of Songs:

Thou art all fair, O my love, and there is not a spot in thee. Thy lips are as a dripping honeycomb, honey and milk are under thy tongue, the sweet smell of thy ointments is above all the aromatical spices. For winter is now past, the rain is over and gone. The flowers have appeared, the vines in flower yield their sweet smell, and the voice of the turtledove is heard in our land. Arise, make haste, my love, come from Lebanon, come thou shalt be crowned. (Song of Songs 4:7, 11; 2:11–12; 4: 8)[77]

Celebration moved from the oratory to the cloister, then to the atrium in front of the church, and then into the church to the tune of sung responsories.

All the senses were touched by the Assumption. The liturgy intoned words from that great book of love the Song of Songs, with its rich invocation of Mediterranean flora and the lushness of the Holy Land: *Emissiones tuae* spoke of the beloved's parts like a profusion of pomegranates; *Fons hortorum* – the well of living water gushed from the Lebanon; in *Veni in hortum* the lover has come into the garden of the sister/spouse, to gather myrrh; in *Comedi favum* the lover has eaten the honeycomb with the honey, wine with milk. These poetic eruptions are important in that they are new, and become ubiquitous in the liturgy for Mary's feasts: European devotion had never spoken of Mary as elaborately before. Written for an occasion when heaven and earth met, it was fitting that sermons for the Assumption used ornate language, full of pomp:

She who brought salvation to the world merits such solemnity . . . The mother of our creator is chosen. Now we are fed the vision of the spirit of God. She acted in the choirs adorned by Christ's beauty, the remarkable virgin is elevated above other blessed virgins. Now she is present, ready, to offer the prayers of those who petition God.[78]

The Assumption celebrated the enduring hope of heavenly intercession, the hope that linked heaven and earth. Mary's presence within the monastic community was offered as a beacon of efficacious practice in religious life. John, abbot of the priory of St Victor in Paris (1203–29), used the familiar verse 'Thou art Fair and Comely, daughter of Jerusalem' in his Assumption sermon, as a prompt to reflection on Mary's beauty:

Truly that beauty I would call purity of the body, which in truth adorns her whole body, clothes and dresses her whole body with loveliness, cleansing the darkness of vice; it utterly excludes all stain of corruption . . .

Since the biblical text is perfect, it harbours no redundant adjectives; so 'fair' and 'comely' each revealed a distinct quality of Mary's pulchritude:

Beautiful through virginity, lovely through humility . . . the Blessed Virgin Mary was beautiful in action, and lovely in contemplation, for she fully and appropriately displayed service of each life, in that she outwardly shone a light for men through exercise of good works, and inwardly was devoted to practice of divine contemplation . . . Note well, that she gestated our redeemer coming in the flesh in her womb, she caressed him in her lap, she nursed him with her breasts, she put the baby in the manger, and with maternal solicitude provided all the other things that necessity demands of his human fragility.[79]

The Assumption's popularity in religious houses is evident in the many and varied arrangements of sound, word and space. Old chants were adapted to the new feast, exhorting towards collective summer celebration.[80] Familiar materials were recast to serve the day: the sixth-century antiphon composed by Pope Gregory the Great for the feast of St Agatha, virgin and martyr, was made by 1165 into an introit antiphon for the Assumption:

> Today the Virgin Mary
> Begs the height of heaven;
> The heavenly host rejoices
> And we
> ALL REJOICE IN GOD
> Giving thanks to her,
> Of whom he was honoured to be born,
> Celebrating the feast day for the honour of the Virgin Mary
> Who deserved to ascend to heavenly realms.
> OF WHOSE ASSUMPTION ANGELS REJOICE
> AND EXTOL THE SON OF GOD.[81]

Religious houses delighted in placing the Assumption scene on portals, seen to great advantage during the feast's procession of monks and benefactors. Every act of decoration was a choice, and often an act of innovation too, for there was no precedent for placing Mary on the tympanum of a Romanesque doorway. At the church of St Pierre-le-Puellier in Orleans a series of reliefs depicted scenes from Mary's life: the angel's appearance to Mary, the Dormition, Mary's Funeral, her

Burial, and Mary in a mandorla held by angels.[82] An inscription explained the last scene:

THE BODY OF THE MOTHER OF GOD IS CARRIED TO HEAVEN AND JESUS MADE HIS MOTHER'S SOUL RISE TO (GOD THE) FATHER.[83]

The narrative of the Assumption depended on texts deemed 'apocryphal', and questions about Mary's passing were many: how did Mary's end affect her body? What happened to her soul? While the tympanum makers at St Pierre-le-Puellier were confident about Mary's end, some ambiguity is evident in the Romanesque tympanum of the church of Cabestany near Perpignan in Languedoc. The remaining section portrays a group with Christ at the centre, Mary on his right, and St Thomas on his left. Christ is blessing in a frontal pose, while the other two figures gesture toward him.[84] Mary stands with the palms of her hands facing outwards, as if in request or prayer. Angels surround the group, and dragons and lions rest at its margins.[85] This is an early representation in relief of Mary's Assumption, and the maker of this scene was respectful of hierarchy: Christ is the centre, even in this scene of Mary's reception in heaven. The viewer is thus reassured of Mary's intercessory powers, but it also demonstrated her subordination to her son.

The Assumption came to be closely related to the depiction of Mary's Coronation in heaven, and English artists were precocious in figuring out what such a scene should look like. The early medieval narratives which told of Mary's end imagined her reception into Christ's arms in heaven. One of the earliest examples was painted in the chapter house of Worcester cathedral – the space for communal meeting – around 1100, part of some forty scenes which no longer exist. They were, however, copied down, drawn and coloured in a manuscript of 1260, and so we know that the early Coronation was depicted as a marriage scene. The accompanying inscription makes this clear:

> Betrothed with the dowry of faith, made holy by her virtues,
> The Bride is crowned and united with God, the Bridegroom.[86]

The Coronation did not stand alone in Worcester cathedral chapter house; it was paired with another unique scene: the Unveiling of Synagogue. This scene is based on an interpretation of the Song of Songs

reworked by a theologian resident in Worcester, Honorius Augustodunensis (flourished 1106–35). Mary's Assumption formed part of the polemical narrative of Christian triumph, for the figure of Synagogue – the personification of Judaism as a young woman – was accompanied by the inscription:

Hitherto concealed in the clouded configurations of the Law; O synagogue, with the advent of Faith see the reality. Let Synagogue be made new in the refashioned cloak of the Law, let Grace adorn her in the garment of Faith.[87]

Mary's joy was the church's exultation and Synagogue's loss. The Assumption came to represent in image, gesture and song the triumph and promise of salvation through the Incarnation worked in Mary's body that never died.

MARY AND MONASTIC SONG – HILDEGARD OF BINGEN

Monastic life is often imagined as silent, lived in hushed cloisters. Although some monastic houses required abstention from speech, and all shunned idle chatter, there was nonetheless in them an abundance of sound: human voices in chant or recitation, meal-time readings, and the ringing of bells. Monks and nuns enjoyed the privilege of frequent, disciplined song. No figure was associated with musical harmony more than Mary.

Music was understood as an art that combined spirit and matter, body and soul. Using Boethius' late antique theory of music, Richard of St Victor (d.1173) described music as 'that natural amity which binds the soul to the body in non-corporeal chains'.[88] Mary similarly bound divinity to humanity in her womb. As we have seen, Luke 1:46–55 described the song of praise that marked the visit to her kinswoman Elizabeth, the epitome of musical harmony.[89] Mary's song was known by its opening Latin word 'Magnificat', and it formed part of the liturgy for vespers since at least the sixth century:

My soul doth magnify the Lord:
    And my spirit hath rejoiced in God my saviour.

Because he hath regarded the humanity of his handmaiden; for behold from
henceforth all generations shall call me blessed.

Because he that is mighty hath done great things to me: and holy is his
name.

And his mercy is from generation unto generation, to them that fear him.

He hath shewed might in his arm: he hath scattered the proud in the conceit
of their heart.

He hath put down the mighty from their seat, and hath exalted the humble.

He hath filled the hungry with good things: and the rich he hath sent empty
away.

He hath received Israel his servant, being mindful of his mercy.

As he spoke to our fathers, to Abraham and to his seed forever.

Glory be to the Father, and to the Son, and to the Holy Spirit.

As it was in the beginning, is now, and ever shall be, world without end.
Amen.

Mary's song and the Song of Songs merged in the minds of Mary's
lovers. The Cistercian abbot Bernard of Clairvaux (1090–1153)
composed homilies on the Magnificat, meditations on the miracle of the
Incarnation (homilies 1 and 2). In his third homily he reflects on Elizabeth's greeting to Mary: 'Blessed are you among women and blessed is
the fruit of your womb' (Luke 1:42) and this leads to the savouring of
Mary's son in fragrance and sweetness, like the biblical lover: 'Blessed
in his fragrance, blessed in his savour, blessed in his comeliness'.[90]

The Magnificat was Mary's defining moment. When the English
monk-scholar Alexander Nequam (1157–1217) pondered the meaning
of Song of Songs 2:12 – 'the time of pruning has come' – he chose to
use the alternative Hebrew sense of the word *zamir* – 'song', not pruning
– and thus to discover in the phrase a foretelling of Mary's song. The
Magnificat was also prefigured in Miriam's song after the miracle at the
Red Sea, and Nequam delighted in this convergence 'both of name and
of event'.[91] A religious woman from the diocese of Liège, Julianna of
Cornillon (1193–1258), described to the abbess of Salzinnes, where she
stayed for a while, how she felt while praying the Magnificat:

'It is but a little thing, Lady,' she said to the abbess, 'that I feel, but I would not
want to cede the taste of what I taste, cease feeling what I feel, not for all the
gold that this abbey in which we are could contain, the multitude that I receive
so much from the Virgin Mary because of her canticle.[92]

The worlds of cloister, cathedral and school in which Mary was being remade were sites of incessant outpourings of music. Gregorian chant – a version of the Roman liturgy – had begun to spread through continental Europe in the ninth century. It blended with local usages and was established as the prevalent musical style for the liturgy. Within its frame the new ideas about Mary were expressed and developed musically. These were inspired by the desire to express Mary afresh, often within new or refounded religious houses. The psalter structured devotions on weekdays and on feasts, but to it were added a rich array of chanted antiphons and responsories, as well as collects, special prayers for feast days. The Marian feasts – her Nativity and her Assumption – together with the feast of Christ's birth, offered occasions for invention and embellishment.

Mary's liturgy spread in Europe through prayers and sequences, which were often rhymed, metrical chants. New sequences employed biblical imagery and formulae of prayer. An appeal to nature was inspired by the Song of Songs, as in invocations such as 'Rise, sweet dove, empress and queen, medicine to the sick, pour wine on our wounds'.[93] Religious reformers frequently criticized chant for its sensuality, its ability to distract; the voices of young boys sounded disturbingly like those of women, and women's voices were seductive.[94] Yet those who loved song saw in it an expression of infinite wisdom and harmony, like Mary herself. First plainchant and later polyphony were performed in the religious houses of Europe and in leading collegiate churches and cathedrals. Many monks and canons had their first taste of polyphony in a Marian office.[95] And since music can be memorized and transmitted with ease, Marian hymns and sequences were soon reproduced in the less opulent settings of urban and even rural parishes.

The scholar Adam of St Victor (d.1192), director of music at the priory of St Victor outside Paris, combined biblical exegesis and liturgical poetry as suited a house devoted to biblical scholarship and contemplation.[96] Adam truly stood on the shoulders of giants and created elegant verses inspired by the Roman poet Horace.[97] He celebrated the Nativity as a felicitous coming together of opposites – *harmonia diversorum* – when a saviour was born of a virgin:

> At the birth of our Saviour
> Let [those of] our condition

145

Accompany the choirs of Angels.
The harmony of opposites
Yet combined in one
Is a sweet communion.

The next stanza explains the nature of the 'opposite' – it is God's birth of a Virgin:

This day is joyous,
On which the coeternal with God
Is born of a virgin!
Joyous and jocund day!
The world delights in being
lit by the true sun.[98]

With their restraint and metrical precision these elegant lines are full of joy. They render Mary as a contradiction to be savoured, a truth to be treasured. There is little appeal to Mary's many virtues, to the attributes of her person, but there is delight in her role within the founding mystery of faith, and gratitude for the gift of salvation.

Mary's feasts thus provided a generous terrain for the expression of new Marian themes, and sequences – chants for the mass, performed before the reading of the gospel – were perfect locations for innovation, easily inserted into liturgical settings.[99] The sequence *Aureo flore* (*From the Golden Flower*), known in English and French manuscripts as early as the tenth century, was a medieval composition based on late antique poetry. It celebrated the felicitous opposition of Mary and Eve that Ephrem the Syriac had cherished in his poetry as early as the fourth century. Eleventh- and twelfth-century collections of new proses demonstrate the changes in taste and desire for Marian liturgical poetry.[100] The 'old' sequence *Aureo flore* was replaced by a 'new' one: *Aurea virga – From the Golden Rod*. Everything about the new sequence is fresh and full of purpose. Written for the Assumption, it describes the meaning of Mary's rise to heaven: 'O holy mother of our God, accept our prayers on this day, on which you were assumed into the cloisters of heaven' (6b) and 'For today the host of the heavenly court meets you, they have assumed you to starry palaces' (8a).[101] The powerful link between Mary and the beauties of nature is boldly exemplified in this new offering,

146

through adjectives, descriptors and evocations. Once heard, never forgotten, new compositions such as *Aurea Virga* quickly replaced the old.

Part of a cosmic plan, equal to the rhythm of the seasons and the harmony of the movement of planets, music grew apace with the elaborated appreciations of Mary. Music and bodily awareness are pervasive in the work of the German nun Hildegard of Bingen (1098–1179). As a child Hildegard had been offered by her parents to live alongside a famous anchoress, outside the monastery of St Rupert at Disibodenberg in the Rhineland. She acquired a facility in Latin and developed insight and expertise in the natural sciences and medicine as well as a lively theological imagination. She wrote tracts of applied science, and has left accounts of the visions which troubled her mind and racked her body. These accounts were copied and illuminated in manuscripts prepared under her supervision.[102]

Hildegard expressed her understanding of the Christian story most passionately in her musical compositions. In antiphons and liturgical poetry she repeatedly worked out an original version of the Incarnation. The hymns celebrate Mary's body in which fecundity and purity coexisted. The Incarnation was like a symphony played in Mary's womb, as described in the hymn *Ave generosa*:

> For your womb held joy,
> when all the celestial harmony resounded from you
> for, virgin, you bore the Son of God
> when your chastity grew radiant in God.
>
> . . .
>
> Now let the whole Church flush with joy
> and resound in harmony
> for the sake of the most tender Virgin
> and praiseworthy Mary,
> the bearer of God.
>
> Amen.[103]

The Incarnation was a song resounding in Mary's womb; and Hildegard's music reaches a climax as the high note C is sung on the syllable *pho* of *symphonia*. More than any other poet of Mary, Hildegard realized the idea of Mary as song.[104] While most hymns used a range of ten

notes or so – to do more was considered excessive – Hildegard habitually ranged powerfully over two octaves.

In her letters Hildegard wrote about church reform, and her visions painted apocalyptic scenes, but her music was dedicated above all to Mary. The antiphon O *resplendent jewel* (O *splendidissima gemma*) tells in a single musical sentence the whole Christian history:

> O resplendent jewel
> and unclouded beauty of the sun
> which was poured into you,
> a fountain springing
> from the Father's heart,
> which is the only Word,
> through which he created
> the prime matter of the world,
> which Eve threw into confusion.[105]

Most of Hildegard's compositions dwelt on the hope-bearing opposition of Eve and Mary, as in the responsory *Ave Maria*:

> Hail Mary,
> O author of life,
> Rebuilding salvation,
> you who confounded death
> and crushed the serpent
> towards whom Eve stretched forth,
> her neck outstretched
> with the swelling of pride
> You trampled on him
> When you bore the Son of God from heaven:
> Whom the Spirit of God breathed forth.[106]

Mary is an active, dynamic woman, much like Hildegard herself. She is full of purpose, she creates and puts things to right. From the religious imagery that belittled women – associated so closely with Eve – Hildegard created a celebration of Mary and womankind:

> And O what great felicity is
> in this form,
> for malice,

which flowed from woman
woman thereafter rubbed it out,
and built
all the sweetest fragrance of the virtues,
and embellished heaven
more than she formerly troubled the earth.[107]

Within monasteries and convents Mary inspired reflection on body and nature, on love and the hope for salvation. Monastic Mary was an image of the church at its most ambitious.

THE CISTERCIANS – MARY'S SPECIAL LOVERS

Love, devotion and emotion surrounded Mary within the monastic milieu, and radiated out from it. Yet the monastic world itself was experiencing change and variation. Most monastic houses adhered to the Benedictine rule – or its Cluniac version – but a new monastic vision inspired great excitement at the end of the eleventh century. The Cistercian order was founded around 1097 by Robert of Molesmes (1029–1111) in the diocese of Langres in France. It spread to all parts of Europe in the following decades as the bearer of reform and renewal. By the year 1200 there were some 500 male abbeys and probably the same number of female houses.[108] The order promoted simplicity in religious life and required greater physical hardship than that experienced by most monks in Benedictine and Cluniac settings. The Cistercian order was bound up with Mary; its growth tracked her own rise and all its houses were dedicated to her.[109] An illustrated page in a book of biblical commentaries of the early twelfth century (c.1123) depicts Mary standing on a pedestal while two men – the third abbot of Cîteaux, Stephen Harding, on her right, and the abbot of St Vaast of Arras on her left – offer their respective monastic churches to her.[110] At the heart of Cistercian communal life was not so much the church, but the cloister, an unadorned and quiet space. Yet this space was set alight in memory of Mary on the Feast of her Purification. The whole community – monks and novices, lay brethren and servants – held candles and processed through the cloister into the church.[111] Cistercians thought about Mary

149

often and deeply; they produced new ideas about her and remade old ones.

No Cistercian came to be as closely associated with devotion to Mary as St Bernard of Clairvaux. Bernard clearly found areas of the traditions of Mary appealing and sufficient, but he suspected novelties. He drew inspiration for his thinking from the Bible, as befitted his strong sense of order and authority in Mary. A prayer found at the end of one of his sermons for Advent includes a string of titles for Mary: lady, mediator and advocate:

> Our Lady,
> Our mediatrix,
> Our advocate,
> To your Son, reconcile us,
> To your Son, commend us,
> To your Son, present us.
> Obtain,
> O blessed lady,
> By the grace found in you,
> By the privilege deserved by you,
> By the mercy born of you,
> That he who,
> By your mediation,
> Deigned to share our infirmity
> And our misery,
> May, by your intercession,
> Let us also share his glory
> And his blessedness,
> He, Jesus Christ,
> Your Son,
> Our Lord,
> Blessed above all
> For ever and ever.[112]

Bernard's contemplative immersion resulted in a vision of Mary too. Conrad of Eberbach's *Exordium magnum*, a thirteenth-century collection of Cistercian miracles, recounted Bernard's experience in front of a statue of Mary and Child: as he prayed 'show yourself to be the mother', Mary offered the milk of her breast to his prayerful lips.[113]

CHRISTMAS 2005

1. Mary is known throughout the world and is represented in many different styles. The Royal Mail's 2005 Christmas stamps featured images from Europe, Africa, Asia and the Americas.

2. Images of Mary are always affected by contemporary ideals of female beauty. This statue by David Wynne, commissioned for the medieval chapel known as the Lady Chapel at Ely Cathedral (Cambridgeshire) to mark the millennium, has a doll-like shape and texture.

3. This image of a woman breastfeeding her son in the presence of a prophet was painted on the walls of the Catacomb of Priscilla, Rome. This catacomb contains burials made as early as the second century and as late as the fourth. This may be the earliest surviving image of Mary and her son.

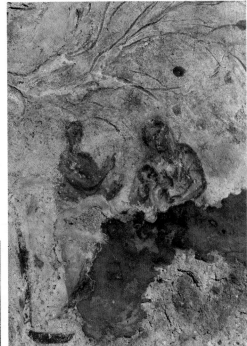

4. Mary and her son are enclosed here in a mandorla, an almond-shaped frame, which denoted majesty and sacredness. In keeping with the Egyptian Coptic tradition, Mary and her son are in a frontal pose, gazing at the viewer.

5. In Egypt, Christians appreciated Mary's maternal quality and early on represented her as a mother feeding her son at the breast, in a manner reminiscent of statues of the goddess Isis.

6. This niche from the Egyptian monastery of Bawit was decorated in the seventh century with the scene of Christ's Ascension above, and an image of Mary enthroned with her son, among the Apostles, below. Mary is majestic and solemn, and aligned with the figure of her son above.

7. This image of Mary opens the Gellone Sacramentary, made for an abbey in northern France. Mary forms the upper part of the initial letter I. She carries an incense dispenser and a cross and wears a vestment, figuring the church's liturgy function.

8. In this mosaic decoration of the church of Hagia Sofia, made c.843–67, Mary is seated on a set of cushions upon a jewelled seat, with her son in her lap. Against a gold background, her figure combines majesty with motherhood, as she gently touches her son's shoulder.

9. The Golden Madonna was made for the aristocratic women attached to Essen cathedral around the year 1000. Mary is seated, majestic and serene, with her son on her lap, an early example of the making of Mary in three dimensions.

10. This Collectary, a book of short prayers for the mass, was made at Reichenau abbey c.1010–30. It depicts the Assumption of Mary to heaven accompanied by angels, a favourite theme of the artists of the Ottonian court.

11. Rocamadour (36 kilometres north-east of Cahors) became one of the most popular medieval pilgrimage sites after the year 1100, thanks to this statue of the Virgin Mary, deemed miraculous, which is still on display at the shrine. Tales of cures at Rocamadour were widely known all over Europe.

12. In this Catalan figure, Mary is seated in a frontal position, while the son in her lap offers a blessing. The group takes the form of the trunk from which they are carved, facing forwards and static in posture. The colour, though re-touched, is a useful reminder that statues were originally painted though we usually see them as white stone or dark wood.

13. This carving was added to the Romanesque façade of Poitiers cathedral $c.1250$, and it celebrates Mary's queenship. Mary, with her son in her lap, is flanked by angels bearing crowns. Mother and son gaze at each other, and Mary's body forms a comfortable S-shape, which is characteristic of the period.

14. This brass canteen delicately inlaid with silver was made in Syria or northern Iraq *c*.1250. It depicts at its centre Mary enthroned with the Child Christ, flanked by saints. Around her are three scenes from Mary's life and Christ's infancy, separated by decorative medallions. The Near East was a home to Christian communities and attracted a constant flow of European pilgrims.

15. Much medieval religious art was made by monks and nuns. This was an act of devotion as well as craft. In this image from the Lambeth Apocalypse of *c*.1260, a monk is depicted at work making a statue of Mary and her son, in Gothic style and not unlike plate 13 in conception.

16. This decoration for the front of an altar for the church of Santa Maria de Cardet in the High Pyrenees depicts Mary and the Child Christ within a mandorla, surrounded by five scenes from her life (and her son's infancy): Annunciation, Visitation, Nativity, Adoration of the Magi and Flight into Egypt. This reflects the increased centrality of Mary and her life in the themes chosen for altarpieces and altar decorations.

17. The walls of Chalgrove parish church in Oxfordshire were decorated with lively scenes of Christ's life (north wall), and Mary's death (south wall), thanks to the gift of a local landowning family, the de Barantyn. Here is the scene of Mary's funeral: her body, covered by a cloth, is carried by the apostles, while Jews attempt to topple it but are foiled.

18. This fine glass is part of an assemblage of medieval work in the current east window of the church at Eaton Bishop, Herefordshire. It captures the Gothic image of Mary, a crowned, beautiful mother, tenderly engaged with her son. The Christ Child stands on his mother's hip, holding a bird in his left hand while his right touches his mother's face. There is an attempt at family resemblance too, and a direct gaze links the pair.

19. In the vision of the German mystic Henry Suso (c.1300–1366) the traditional roles are reversed: he holds Mary and her son in his lap, in the presence of two angels. This is an illumination accompanying a hagiographical account of Suso's life.

20. Mary as Mother of Mercy (*mater misericordia*) protects Christians of all walks of life under her mantle and holds the Trinity in her body (God the Father and the crucifix of the Son remain; the dove as Holy Spirit is now missing). The image is painted in the interior of a statue of Mary and her son, *c.*1400, in a mode known as *vierge ouvrante* or *virgen abridera*. While popular in Iberia and Germany, this type of image was also considered misleading and inappropriate.

21. This Ethiopian painted diptych represents the two interlinked themes that were also widespread in late medieval Europe: Mary and her son, and Christ's Passion, beginning and end. Made some time between 1480 and 1550, it is typical of Ethiopian religious art and of the Ethiopian image of Mary: as in the Egyptian art of early Christianity (see plates 4 and 6), here too Mary is solemn, facing the viewer with an intent gaze.

22. Based on the narrative of the Gospel of Luke, the Feast of the Visitation was created in 1389. Its themes had been adopted by the Franciscans in the thirteenth century. This altarpiece, once in the village of Csegöld in Szatmár County in eastern Hungary, dwells on the meeting of two pious kinswomen, Mary and Elizabeth, young and old. The foetuses in their wombs – Christ surrounded by rays of light, John (the future Baptist) haloed – are painted on to each mother's pregnant belly.

23. The Dutch painter David Gerard (c.1460–1523) depicts a domestic scene of Mary feeding her son some milky porridge with a wooden spoon. This panel of c.1500 expresses the devotional interest in Mary and the Holy Family as simple people performing common tasks. The child holds his own spoon, learning to eat; the apple is part of the meal but also a reminder of the sin from which the little boy has come to save humanity.

24. The emphasis in this gilded wooden sculpture made *c.*1500 in Alsace is on the relationship between the Child Christ and Joseph. The boy plays with his father's beard as his mother looks on. The fifteenth century saw an upsurge of interest in Joseph and the transformation of his figure into an exemplary Christian father and husband. His feast day was created in 1479, and his cult spread widely in the following centuries, especially in North America.

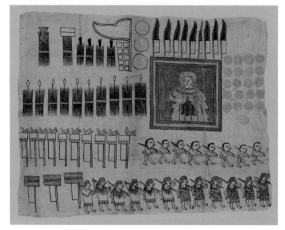

25. One of eight illustrations in the Codex Huejotzingo of 1531, this image accompanies the court case brought by the Nahua villagers of Huejotzingo against the Spanish authorities, in which they challenged the amount of tribute demanded of them. Drawn on paper made from the bark of fig trees, the image of the Virgin Mary and Child is particularly interesting: among the tribute paid by the villagers were quantities of feathers and gold for the making of a banner of the Virgin Mary in traditional Nahua featherwork.

26. *The Virgin of the Navigators* (*c.*1536), attributed to the painter Alejo Fernandez, adorns the chapel of the Casa de la Contratación, the agency in Seville that supervised exploration, commerce and administration in the Spanish holdings in the Americas. Mary is depicted as the Mother of Mercy (see plate 20), and her mantle covers and protects leading figures in the imperial enterprise: Christopher Columbus, Ferdinand of Spain, Charles I, Amerigo Vespucci and Native Americans, as well as the ships of discovery and trade.

27. This portable altar of the late sixteenth century has as its central panel an image of Mary and Child. It is set within a frame of black lacquer with gold and mother-of-pearl inlay. There was a large Christian community in Japan in the sixteenth century, which flourished under Jesuit guidance until the anti-Christian policies of the Tokugawa pushed them underground. This blend of European and Japanese style and craft is typical of the imagery of Mary that developed as Christianity was spread by European missionaries.

28. The German sculptor Käthe Kollwitz (1867–1945) made this bronze sculpture, *Mother with her Dead Son*, in 1938, almost twenty years after the death of her own son in the First World War. The peasant mother's figure – with her shawl and heavy body – echoes that of Mary in the traditional Pietà. One cannot but sense the foreboding expressed by this sculpture, which represents every bereaved mother. In 1993 it was placed in the Neue Wache in Berlin, the German national memorial for the victims of war and despotism.

29. *La Guadalupana* is an installation created by the American artist Delilah Montoya (1955–) in 1998. Our Lady of Guadalupe, the quintessential religious image of Chicano culture, is imprinted on the skin of a captive Chicano man, as a reminder of the historical context of oppression and violence within which the Christianity of the Americas was created. This work demonstrates the use of Mary to disturb and challenge the premises of religious cultures and personal devotion.

Bernard was supremely inspired by the Song of Songs. He found in it, as Origen had done before him, an account of the human soul (bride), seeking God (lover). The yearning – so sensually expressed in the Song – was the desire of those immersed in the search for God. Bernard's eighty-six sermons on the Song of Songs, written in the last eighteen years of his life, affected future generations of Cistercian writers and contemplative religious profoundly. The Song of Songs was full of associations between the carnal and the spiritual, the amalgam that was also Mary's special privilege, and this richly inspired the liturgy. This wealth of imagery also had to be made part of the quest for union with God through repentance, contemplation and the working of grace.[114]

Cistercian figures less stellar than Bernard of Clairvaux also contributed to the imaging and praise of Mary. Amadeus of Lausanne (d.1159) was born to an old aristocratic family of Clermont; his father turned to the religious life and took his baby son with him, first to the Cistercian house at Bonnevaux (near Vienne), then to Cluny. Amadeus completed his education at Clairvaux, where he became a novice under Bernard. This was a world of intellectual excellence in the service of spiritual striving and revival of religious life. Because the order was held in such reverence, its members were, paradoxically, often called to act in the world, to leave the cloister for a while and serve as bishops. And so, after serving for five years as abbot of Hautecombe Abbey in Savoy, Amadeus became bishop of Lausanne. During these years of work in pastoral care he wrote a string of eight homilies for and about Mary, reflective sermons based on scripture.[115] Writing about Mary was like spiritual nourishment for this busy monk-bishop. The homilies combine to form an epic account of Mary's place in the history of salvation: Mary as a link between both Testaments; Mary made suitable for her special role; Mary's union with the Holy Spirit and the conception of Jesus; Mary's virginal childbirth; her witness to Jesus' suffering; her joy at the Resurrection; and ultimately her Assumption into heaven in expectation of the final salvation of 'Israel', yet to come.

While Amadeus' homilies rely heavily on scripture – above all citations from the Psalms, Genesis, Isaiah, Song of Songs and the gospels – he does not follow the intricate poetic style of Song of Songs commentaries. Rather, his homilies are driven by marvel at Mary's historic role. He is more attentive than most writers to Mary's suffering at the Crucifixion;

a subject that occupies most of Homily V. Mary looked at Jesus on the cross and saw something without beauty:

She stood near the cross that she might see her son's sweet head anointed with oil above his fellows', beaten with rods, and crowned with thorns – heart-rending sight! She saw there was neither form nor beauty in him who was lovely with a beauty beyond the sons of men.[116]

The emotional turmoil of the Crucifixion was enhanced, according to Amadeus, by the knowledge that her own people – the Jews – had caused it. Yet Mary was full of love for them:

Let no one argue that the Jews were hateful to the Mother of God for their having condemned her Son to a most shameful death. For those whom she saw near to eternal death she in no way considered to deserve her hatred and insult, but to deserve great affection, many tears, and a great pity. Therefore sharing in the charity as well as in the cross of Jesus, she took of her prayer for them.[117]

Amadeus admitted the kinship of Mary and the Jews, even as he blames them for Christ's death. The result is a heightened emphasis on Mary's mercy, and the resulting awareness of the Jews' callousness.

Like all monastic writers, Amadeus had something to say about the Assumption; here too he sought a psychological insight into Mary's mind. He began Homily VII by asking why Mary stayed on earth after the death of her son. As we have seen, the earliest narratives of Mary's end attempted to answer this question and often presented Mary as continuing Jesus' work of preaching and healing, as companion to the apostles.[118] Amadeus took this even further. In keeping with his view of Mary as a mainstay of the church, he attributes to her an important role in supporting the apostles after Christ's death and consolidating Christian life. Her Assumption also separated believers from non-believers: 'Indeed for some, that is those against her, it was the odor of death into death, but for others who believed in her Son the odor of life into life'.[119] Amadeus ends by linking the Assumption to the life of every Christian:

For remembering for what purpose she was made the Mother of the Redeemer, most willingly she gathers up the sinner's prayers and pleads with her Son for all the guilt of those who are penitent. Surely she will gain what she wishes, the dear Mother through whose chaste womb the Word of God came to us, the sin

offering of the world, to wash away with his own blood the bond of original sin.[120]

Cistercian thinkers used Mary to contemplate the possibilities of virtue and the fulfilment of God's will. In his Assumption sermons the Yorkshire Cistercian Aelred of Rievaux (1110–67) celebrated Mary's reception of Christ into a safe place. Like her the Cistercian monk should build himself into a fortress, with a wall of chastity and a watchtower of charity.[121] Even more elevated and abstract was the notion of Mary as the dwelling place of the Trinity, containing the whole Christian story, beginning and end, a perfect companion for the striving monk.[122] The Assumption also called to mind the perfect end to Mary's life, when she rested alongside her perfect loved one, as captured in the phrase from the Song of Songs (3:4) 'I found him whom my soul loves'.[123]

Mary soared in these writings as the pinnacle of hopes for salvation, part of the cosmic Christian story. In his Latin *Of Jesus at the Age of Twelve* (*Expositio ... cum factus esset Iesus Annorum Duodecim*), written around 1153–7, Aelred digressed to make clear that Jesus' words in the Temple, 'And he said to them: "How is it that you sought me? did you not know, that I must be about my father's business?"' could not apply to Mary, since she was full of wisdom:

I do not think that this refers to Mary, because, since the Holy Spirit descended upon her (*supervenit*) and the power of the Highest covered her with its shadow, she could not have been ignorant of the plans for her son.

Mary was part of the grand narrative of salvation in this account of her son's life. She knew all, and she kept that knowledge in her heart:

But while the others did not comprehend what he said, Mary, knowing and understanding, *kept it all and carried it in her heart* (Luke 2:19). She kept it in her memory, ruminated over it in her contemplation, and bore with all that she had seen and heard of him.[124]

Mary understood and kept the divine design in her heart and passed this knowledge on to the disciples who preached and spread the news.

Mary was developed by another Cistercian, Adam of Perseigne (d.1222) as a companion to the striving monk. Adam began his religious life as a Benedictine monk and ended as the Cistercian abbot of

Perseigne, near Le Mans in northern France. As a valued adviser to the Count of Neuilly, one of the leaders of the Third Crusade (1189–92), his ideas and teachings reached far beyond the monastery's walls.[125] Adam developed a cogent view of Mary's powers of intercession, of her prayer on behalf of sinners. His sermons treated Mary not only as a pure and fitting vessel of the Incarnation, but as part of the plan of salvation itself: God had planned for there to be not only a judge of humans, but an intercessor too. Mary's goodness is innate, and it allows her to mediate between heaven and earth.[126] Monks in particular were guided towards Mary as the source and embodiment of wisdom because of her unrivalled closeness to God, closeness which rendered her distant from humans. To the question 'Where is Mary' he answers:

She is far away, I say, because she is our mediatrix, and singularly favourable for merciful compassion, nevertheless the incomparable privilege of her excellence exalts her above the highest angels . . . The farthest coasts are symbolic of Mary's incomparable virtues; the Prophet bears witness that he has seen in them the summit of all perfection . . . he came from the farthest coasts, that is, from the highest virtues of Mary, as the price of our redemption, in the nature he drew from the Virgin's flesh.[127]

The space carved out for Mary by Cistercian authors – of wisdom, purpose and purity – led to the emergence of an important new image: Mary as mother to all humans, *mater omnium*. An illustration to a Cistercian Legendary (book of liturgical readings) offers an elaborate image of fecundity and maternal majesty. Within a roundel made of tendrils of plants, Mary arises from the Root of Jesse and is surrounded by images of prophets who had foretold her virtue.[128] She holds her heavy bare breast to her son's mouth. Here is the blend of majestic Mary – indeed her name is written in Latin characters, THEOTOKOS – and the protective mother, whose body is truly nurturing.[129] The late twelfth century saw the mixing of the two in European words and images. In future decades it was the maternal Mary that was even more fully explored.

The love of Mary was expressed and expounded by a preacher from the diocese of Beauvais, Helinand of Froidmont (d.1229), a troubadour who had converted to the life of a Cistercian monk. He composed sermons for Marian feasts and was deeply involved in preaching against heresy, as well as against corruption among monks. Mary was a useful

ally in both campaigns. In a sermon for the Assumption he chose the biblical verse from Sirach (Ecclesiasticus) 39:17: 'Hear me, ye divine offspring, and bud forth as the rose planted by the brooks of waters'. Helinand begins with the botany of the rose: first with the structure and then the shape of the flower and its different colours. In the physical beauty of the rose he sees mystical beauty:

That delicate whiteness near the roots of the rose's leaves is the perpetual purity of the Virgin Mary's heart, I would say, caused by her birth; so that from the roots of the leaves it shields and defends the five corporal senses, an unassailable fortification from without, as well as guarding it always perfectly whole; and leads [to] a perpetual purity of sinlessness.[130]

Helinand used every occasion to magnify Mary's purity and to ground it in scripture. Moving to the book of Kings, Helinand likens Mary to the Temple: during its construction no hammer or axe was used. The allegorical meaning of the building of the Temple is Mary's time as God's dwelling place (*domus Dei*), during her pregnancy. When she was

fed by the holy spirit before the conception of the Lord, no sound was heard in her human ears, or in angelic or divine ones, hammer and axes being the sins, either of action or of thought.[131]

After exploring the allegory of God's house, Helinand returns to the rose. The rose's colour signifies three things in Mary: the redness of her shy blush, the fire of charity, the zeal of justice.[132] Just as the rose is the most beautiful flower, so Mary is the most beautiful of women. Towards the end of his sermon Helinand's rose helps him lead to admonition and exhortation against sin. Building on the verse 'Like a rose among thorns', he reminds his audience that it is good to be a rose among roses, but a rose among thorns is even better: a good thing among bad, an example among sinners.

Mary was not only beautiful, she was strong. Helinand's sermon for the Assumption takes as its theme the text from Proverbs 31:10: 'Who shall find a valiant woman?'[133] He delights in representing strength as the power to soften and mollify, which Mary possessed in abundance. She is the mother of mercy, whose strength is in her ability to

quickly soften the tears of the penitent, quickly turn the humble towards prayer, quickly turn them to beg her son the judge on their behalf. She is also the mother

of grace, and for that reason able to soften the sinner swiftly, to influence the judge quickly, also to punish the obstinate speedily, when necessary. She softens the sinner to repent, to prevail upon the judge to spare, punishes the stubborn to desist from blasphemy.[134]

Helinand identified Judith with Mary, supported by other biblical examples of feminine strength. The name Judith was understood to mean 'confessing' in Hebrew, as one biblical commentator suggested, so it fitted that greatest confessor of all, Mary, who professed her faith in the Magnificat.[135]

Strength was also seen in the ability to rise after a fall, a quality exemplified in the life of Mary Magdalene. Here Helinand quickly reminded the audience that Mary's fortitude was not of this type, since she had never stumbled: 'To be sure God's mother Mary, since she never fell in sin, she never had the need to rise in penance'. In the sermon's final words, the feast day's purpose is invoked. All that is passing and corrupt was transformed by the Assumption:

And so death and death's necessity and the corruption of weakness [are] absorbed in the resurrection of the Virgin Mary, and in her Assumption: so may in the resurrection of our bodies, if we imitate her, in the strength of so many victories. We have her, therefore, not only as an example of victory, but also as an aid in the many struggles.[136]

The thought of Mary's strength animated Helinand's sermon for the Purification too. Like many before him, he asked why Mary had to be purified at all. He set his question within a reassuring chain of appellations:

What is there to you and to purification, O Mary, most modest virgin among virgins, most innocent of girls, most beautiful of women, most fortunate of mothers, most esteemed of queens, most humble of maidens, more chaste than any turtledove, more honest than any dove?[137]

After exploring her many types of purity, Helinand hands over to Mary herself. She answers a question with a question: 'You ask what I have to do with purification?', and explains: first, in submitting to purification she acted like her son, who submitted to circumcision; second, Jesus chose to follow the laws of prophets who had foretold his coming; third, purification was an example for humility; and fourth, it was fitting that

she be purified like other women, so as to counter any doubt about her son's humanity.

Helinand's sermons cast Mary as an assertive figure, and they did more: they rallied his monks to repentance and castigated those who would not repent with the help of the many aids offered by Christ and his mother. The body is a tool for penance through purgation and purification. Mary's sanctioning of the body as a vehicle for virtue was a rebuttal of those who detested the body and rejected the church's teachings on penance – those deemed by the church to be heretics, above all Cathars. The sermon combines Helinand's two great passions: for Mary and for the fight against heresy. Helinand's Mary is the product of fruitful and creative reflection by a man-of-the-world turned monk on the qualities of nurture combined with grandeur – Lady and Loving Mother.[138] He made Mary into a preacher of sorts, one who lovingly imparted knowledge to her young, her dependents. Mary was remade as a preacher by the consummate Cistercian preacher – Helinand himself.

9

Mary of Polemic and Encounter

BIBLE COMMENTARIES AND THE SONG OF SONGS

Christian scripture was conveyed and experienced through the incessant liturgy of monastic and cathedral churches. The books used intensively in the liturgy were few – the Psalms, epistles, the gospels, the Apocalypse, Lamentations, the Acts of the Apostles. Most biblical commentary in the first Christian millennium concentrated on these books, which were familiar and necessary to monks, nuns and priests. From the late eleventh century, however, in monasteries and later in the schools maintained by bishops in their cathedrals, the project of biblical commentary was significantly expanded. The *glossa ordinaria* – the most commonly used anthology of biblical exegesis – emerged in the early twelfth century in the cathedral school of Laon. It encompassed more than a thousand years of scholarly engagement with scripture. It became essential for the understanding of liturgical texts and was heavily used by composers of sermons.[1] Scholars explored theological issues such as the Incarnation or the Trinity with the philosophical and grammatical categories of classical antiquity, which they applied to the Jewish Bible and to the gospels that announced a 'new' Christian age of grace. At the same time, Mary's place in devotional activities was growing apace; and so by the early twelfth century some of these innovative interpretations of scripture placed Mary at the heart of their enterprise.

Nowhere was the desire to explore, augment and elevate Mary more evident than in commentaries on the Song of Songs – the biblical bridal song attributed to King Solomon – of which more than a hundred were composed before the year 1200.[2] Here was a rich field for exegesis for

Jews and Christians alike. As we have seen, Origen (185–232) was the heir to the Jewish traditions of the Song of Songs, which he appropriated and transformed into a Christian manifesto. The Song of Songs was interpreted allegorically as the love-relationship between Christ and his church. Inasmuch as the church was figured in Mary, thoughts about her were never far from the minds of commentators on the Song of Songs and their readers, especially since the book was used in the liturgies for Mary's feasts.[3] The pairing bride-bridegroom of Christ and church dominated thinking within the tradition. It is manifest in the illuminated initial to Bede's commentary on the Song of Songs, in a manuscript made for St Albans abbey around 1120.[4]

The Song of Songs was the subject of a short work on Mary that dates from c.1100, the *Seal of the Blessed Mary* (*Sigillum beatae Mariae*) by the scholar Honorius of Autun (Augustodunensis). The title refers to the verse 'Put me as a seal upon thy heart, as a seal upon thy arm, for love is strong as death, jealousy as hard as hell, the lamps thereof are fire and flames' (Song of Songs 8:6) and is an exposition on God's relationship with Mary. This is a work of praise based on miracles worked by Mary, a genre which inspired much work in twelfth-century English monasteries.[5] Worcester was close to Evesham, where the monk Dominic compiled one of the earliest collections of Mary's miracles. Honorius saw in Mary remedy to the ills which beset the church of his day: as a bulwark against heresy, error and the Jews. She was also the figure through which Jews may be converted: her profound wisdom and understanding of the divine plan made her the best teacher of Christian truth.[6] When Honorius later wrote another commentary on the Song of Songs, the *Exposition on the Song of Songs* (*Expositio in Cantica Canticorum*), in Germany, some time between 1132 and the 1150s, the tenor was strikingly different. The later work is a more traditional exploration of the relationship of Christ to his church: 'a bridegroom and a bride, that is Christ and the church', and Mary is hardly ever mentioned in it at all.[7]

New ways of thinking about scripture and Mary were being created. Around the year 1125, in the monastery of Deutz near Cologne, another renowned biblical scholar created a love song to Mary in biblical commentary. Rupert of Deutz (c.1076–1129) composed the first commentary on the Song of Songs that fully engaged Mary as its allegorical key. The Song of Songs blended well with themes of monastic life: love and

longing, amity, and sublimation of human into divine embraces.[8] The idea that the Song of Songs was all about Mary was grounded in careful correlation of moments of Mary's life with Rupert's visionary imagination:

O most beautiful of women, o blessed among women, whose beauty is a blessing, whose beauty is the blessed fruit of your womb, so that you are even its cause, so that if you did not know it yourself, you would ask, saying, 'Where did you obtain such beauty, so that you are the loveliest of women?' From faith and humility or from the works of the law? Surely, from faith and humility.[9]

Rupert's work was not only a commentary on the biblical text, it also offered an unfolding dramatic relationship between Mary and Christ, whose lives were inextricably bound. The commentary was a restatement of the truth of the Incarnation; indeed, the oldest manuscript of the *Commentaria* bears the subtitle: 'On the Incarnation of the Lord' (*De incarnatione Domini*).[10] Thinking of the Incarnation was by now tantamount to reflecting upon Mary too. And more, the Incarnation was the occasion of Mary's inception as an agent of wisdom, a teacher of the gospel and an exponent of Christian truth. In the commentary on Song of Songs 5:2, 'Open to me my sister, my love, my dove, my stainless one', Rupert explains:

Open to me, that is, your mouth, to speak, so as to confirm the gospel, and in doing so display the value of the quiet for which you long; for my sake break the silence so pleasing to your singular modesty.[11]

Biblical commentators believed that no word in scripture was redundant, that apparent repetition was replete with significance. So 'my sister' means 'by faith'; 'my love', 'by hope'; 'my dove', 'in chastity'; 'my stainless one' means 'in every way incorrupt in mind and body, which is a praiseworthy thing in a mother who has both conceived and given birth'.[12]

Mary emerges from Rupert's commentary as a powerful agent of the Incarnation, an example of Christian faith and the hope for salvation. She proclaimed faith and, as Honorius had suggested in his own commentary, could call her people – the Jews – to conversion. The men who placed Mary at the heart of the work of biblical understanding also imagined a church triumphant proclaiming its truth outside the walls of monasteries and cathedral churches. They intuited Mary's growing role

not only as a companion to monks but also as a tool for confirmation of faith among Christians, and for the conversion to faith of non-Christians. Like most innovators, Rupert faced criticism, and he was forced to write in rebuttal of accusations that 'it is inappropriate to ascribe to Mary those qualities which Wisdom has ascribed to the generality of the church'.[13] Mary's precedence was an unstoppable trend.

MARY AND THE JEWS

Biblical work on Mary and her liturgy created occasions for reflection on the Jews and for engagement in polemical work. Telling the glories of Mary was linked to the work of instruction and correction of those who would not admit Mary's truth: Jews and 'bad' Christians. Fulbert of Chartres was thus remembered around 1150 as the author of 'among other things a tract against Jews and bad Christians'.[14] Indeed, in his prayer *Pia Virgo Maria, caeli regina* Fulbert had chosen to use a list of titles and invocations of Mary with tales of her miracles, including two famous miracles with Jewish protagonists: Theophilus and the Jewish Boy.[15]

Mary and the Jews met on the fertile terrains offered by discussion of the Incarnation. Anselm of Canterbury had already discussed all areas of the Incarnation and launched the powerful understanding that original sin could be vanquished only by a God born of a virgin. Anselm interpreted the Incarnation with confidence and harmony; he reformulated ideas about atonement in the language of justice and freedom. He found images to be useful aids in teaching Mary's part in the Incarnation and in answering the objections of Jews:

The conception of the Virgin Mary ... can be thought of in terms of this similitude. If someone asks how the virgin gave birth, how the virgin conceived, and how she remained a virgin *post partum*, answer by asking 'how is a crystal filled with the brightness of the sun without cracking' ... Far be it from God who is the maker of all things, not to be able to do by himself in the virgin what he brings about so often by his command through something he created in a thing of creation. So to those who ask about the intactness of the virgin giving birth and the wholeness of the crystal filled with brightness and radiating it, one and the same reply must be given, namely that it is as God has wished it.[16]

Those who wrote about the Incarnation occasionally found the use of a Jew as interlocutor to be an instructive intellectual device. Some intellectuals even engaged in real debates with Jews – on the Incarnation, the Trinity, and increasingly on Mary – and learned Hebrew from Jews. The Jewish Bible offered a treasure-trove of names and descriptions of Mary and her son, and there were the Jews in European cities, available for polemic and debate.[17] Jews were assumed to fail all Marian tests. So as Mary emerged increasingly pure, her detractors emerged ever more perverse. The abbot of Westminster, Gilbert Crispin (c.1055–1117), composed a tract on the Incarnation after discussions with a Jew of London around 1092. Gilbert answers a Jew described as objecting to the Christian interpretation of Isaiah's prophecy (Isaiah 7:14): why understand *alma* as 'virgin' and not as 'hidden one' (*abscondita*)?[18] The question of Mary's perpetual virginity was singled out too: Mary conceived as a virgin and bore as a virgin. She bore her son without knowing a man, by the coming of the highest, the holy spirit, upon her. If hidden (*abscondita*), she was hidden from the love of a man.[19] Like Anselm, debates used images from nature to surpass the natural; just as a ray of the sun passes through a glass without breaking it:

In the same way Christ, the Sun of justice, passed through the virgin by the power of his divinity; taking the flesh of the mother he passed though her while she remained intact.[20]

Odo of Tournai, bishop of Cambrai (d.1113), wrote two theological treatises, *On Original Sin* and *A Disputation with a Jew, Concerning the Advent of Christ, the Son of God* around 1106. Odo argued in his work on the Incarnation that Christ was without sin because he was born of a pure virginal body. In his disputation with Leo the Jew the polemical meaning is revealed: Mary's flesh is celebrated as a rejection of the Jew:

Odo: . . . 'Gabriel said that she is "full of grace" (Luke 1:28) . . . If full, nothing of her was in any way devoid of grace. So, nothing of hers was emptied by sin, whose whole being was filled with grace. Therefore her sex was filled with glory, her womb was filled with glory, her organs were filled with glory, the whole of her was filled with glory, because the whole of her was filled with grace. Truly that woman surpassed sense; she was wise who said: "Blessed is the womb which bore you, and the breasts which gave you suck" .' (Luke 11:27)[21]

Having established that Mary's body was utterly full of grace, Odo turns against the Jew:

Where is that which you called the uncleanliness of woman, the obscene prison, the fetid womb? Confess, you wretch, your stupidity . . . In his conception the virgin became the marriage bed of omnipotent God and the sanctuary of the Holy Spirit . . . The secret places of her blessed womb were the more holy, or rather the more divine, the more intimately divine mysteries grew there . . . What in all creation is more holy, more clean, more pure than the virgin from whom was assumed what God became? O womb, O flesh, in whom and from whom the creator was created, and God was made incarnate.[22]

The defence of Mary's purity by the bishop of Cambrai wove together all strands of the Christian story: of sin and its redemption, of incarnation through God's will to be born as a human and of a human. At the end of this triumphant peroration, all that remained for Leo the Jew was to acknowledge humbly: 'I hear what I have not heard before so fully articulated; before this, I did not know that you have the support of so many reasoned arguments.'[23] Like so many of his contemporaries, other religious men of learning, Odo attempted to blend reason and faith harmoniously. The Jew served as a cautionary reminder of what might occur if he failed: a descent into the senses, into a 'commonsense' faith which breeds aversion to the notion of a god made man, of a god born of a woman – the very rejection of God.[24]

Guibert of Nogent (c.1055–1124) began life as a monk at the Norman Abbey of St Germer of Fly and later became abbot of Nogent-sous-Coucy. Guibert expressed his practical devotion to Mary in a little book in praise of her (after 1113), which followed another work, a refutation of Jewish objections to the Incarnation *Tract on the Incarnation against the Jews*.[25] Following home education the orphan adolescent Guibert had been offered to the monastic life and to Mary. He was influenced by Anselm, whom he met during the theologian's visit to St Germer's, and whose work he referred to frequently.[26] Guibert sought to marshal reason in defence of the Incarnation, and he saw the Jew as the antithesis of that reason in faith: 'You are lacking, I claim, because you are lacking in reason'.[27] When Guibert sought to strengthen the faith of a monk of St Germer's, who had become a Christian as a child during the anti-Jewish violence of the First Crusade, he gave him a copy of his own work on the Incarnation which also served as an anti-Jewish tract.[28]

Guibert believed that Jews were unable to reason because they were hampered by an obsession with the flesh. Guibert argued against the Jewish claims that God would not assume flesh and would not dwell within a woman's womb; that Mary could not have remained a virgin after birth, and that her body was no fitting dwelling for a God.[29] Guibert the monk even mounted a defence of the female body in his polemic with the Jews: Mary's purity could not be understood by those who were impure in their own thoughts. According to him Jews were miserable beings who could not attain the reason which might lift their comprehension towards the mystery. Jews were thus invoked in the most powerful assertions of Marian sentiment within an incarnational faith.

The blend of biblical commentary, monastic liturgy, and Marian devotion was suffused with anti-Jewish themes. If Mary defended the faith and protected each monk against sin, then she was also the bulwark against heretics and Jews. The genre of miracle tale offered recurrent examples of Mary's power and mercy, which medieval Jews stubbornly rejected. The English scholar and Hebraist Alexander Nequam encompassed all the knowledge produced in the twelfth century; he was monk at St Albans but studied in Paris before returning to St Frideswide in Oxford. Men like Nequam were true encyclopedists; his life straddled many forms of religious and intellectual life, as monk, abbot and scholar.[30] His commentary on the Song of Songs is not as lyrical as that of Rupert of Deutz, rather it is full of polemical purpose and displays impressive knowledge of Hebrew and Jewish biblical exegesis, probably learned while he was a student in Paris. Nequam justified his proximity to Jews by the fact that he was acting among them as 'a spy, not a deserter'. Mary was the beloved-sister-bride of Nequam's Song of Songs, prefigured elsewhere in the Jewish Bible in the figure of Sarah. Based on a tradition of commentary as old as Jerome's, Alexander points out the felicitous congruence between the meaning of Miriam in Hebrew – lady – and that of Sarah – princess.[31]

Not all commentators on the Song of Songs chose to emphasize its affinity to Mary, but those who did were bound to confront the polemical issues arising from the use of the Jewish Bible as Christian proof-text. The Jewish Bible foretold the Virgin Birth, and if the Song of Songs was a song of Mary, then a pleasing polemical point was scored over the issue that so divided Jews and Christians – virgin birth. While Jews

claimed the antiquity of their attachment to the Bible and the immediacy of their access to its Hebrew words, Christian Hebraists claimed that 'modern Jews' suffered a moral blindness that rendered false even their literal interpretations.[32] The central proof-text, Isaiah's prophecy (7:14) 'Behold, a virgin [Hebrew: *alma*] shall conceive and bear a son and shall call his name Emmanuel' tested every biblical critic since the days of Jerome. Gilbert Crispin had argued in his *Disputation of a Jew and a Christian* of 1092/3 that the literal sense was to be rejected, for *alma* literally means *abscondita*, a hidden one. In the next century another biblical exegete, Richard of St Victor, delighted in the literal sense and followed Jerome's argument that *alma* could mean both 'young girl' and 'virgin'. He thus appropriated the biblical text in its sacred plenitude.[33]

Jewish writers in turn were highly aware of Christian ideas about Mary. Rabbi Yehudah Halevi (c.1080–1141), the poet, philosopher and polymath of Toledo, completed in 1140 the philosophical treatise the *Kuzari*, set as a religious discussion in the court of King Bulan of the Khazars, a kingdom on the Caspian Sea.[34] The king summoned a Greek philosopher, a Christian, a Muslim for discussion of their religious positions. When the king turned to the Christian for a statement of faith, Halevi cast his answer in a measured tone:

The very last of the revelations was one in which the Divinity took a physical form. This form first manifested as a foetus in the womb of a virgin. She was from a family of Jewish royalty, and she later gave birth to this entity. The child was visibly human, but secretly divine.[35]

Most Jewish writing about Mary was less measured, and Jews found it difficult to imagine a God dwelling within a woman's body. Violent confrontations, like those which swept the Rhineland in spring 1096 during the march of the People's Crusade to the Holy Land, and which resulted in massacres of hundreds of Jews in the cities of Mainz, Worms and Speyer, were commemorated by the Jewish communities in poetry of lament – *piyyutim*. Since the violence was incurred in the name of Jesus, the Christian God and his mother were singled out by Jewish poets of commemoration and lament. Here are the words of the *piyyut* attributed to Rabbi Kalonimos :

> The gentiles call their holiness which is a sin of lechery
> Your chosen ones reject the lineage of the woman of lechery

The gentiles raise an image higher than God
Your people bear witness to your lordship, God of Gods,
The gentiles have a defeated corpse as their nonsensical folly
Your cohort has you as holy seated in praise.[36]

The Jewish chroniclers who recounted the crusade massacres occasionally referred to Mary as they poured invective on Jesus. These were not extended discussions but short expletives. In the narrative of the persecutions in Mainz a group of maidens about to commit suicide as an act of martyrdom (*kiddush ha-shem*) cried out from the window of their chambers:

Look and behold, O Lord, what we are doing to sanctify Thy Great Name, in order not to exchange Your Divinity for a crucified scion who was despised, abominated, and held in contempt in his own generation, a bastard son conceived by a menstruating and wanton woman.[37]

In their tribulations the Jews of Mainz were buoyed by the extreme language of rejection, by the pleasure of defiant public speech about hitherto unspoken feelings. Late on the day of the massacre a prominent Jew, Master David, called a priest and asked him to bring the Christians to his hiding place. The chronicler reports that the priest 'rejoiced greatly' since he expected David to convert. When the crowd gathered he called out to them:

Alas, you are the children of whoredom, believing as you do in one born of whoredom. As for me – I believe in the Eternally Living God who dwells in the lofty heavens. In him I trust until my soul departs. If you slay me, my soul will abide in the Garden of Eden – in the light of life. You, however, descend to the deep pit, to eternal obloquy, condemned together with your deity – the son of promiscuity, the crucified one![38]

David and his household were, of course, immediately killed.

The Spanish Rabbi Jacob ben Reuben wrote his polemical tract *God's Wars (Sefer Milhemot Hashem)* c.1170 in order to help Jews counter the arguments of Christians who aimed to convert them. He claimed that although Jews knew Christianity to be nonsensical, an ordered set of rebuttals was nonetheless useful. He argued against Jesus' genealogy in Matthew 4:1–11:

The book of the Life of Jesus Christ son of David son of Abraham . . . Jacob bore Joseph Miriam's husband, she who bore Jesus who is called Christ. This is indeed the beginning of their new testament, and I asked him this: Why does he mention Tamar, wife of Judah, and does not mention one of the wives of Abraham, Isaac or Jacob? Why mention Rahab the Whore, the wife of Uriah, and Ruth the Moabite; not one of the wives of other men, but those women in whom there was a serious flaw? How do you attest of your God in this manner, as if recording a sin, you mention these faulty ones but forgo the perfect ones?[39]

Jews rejected above all the incongruities of a God taking flesh, a God who experienced gestation, birth and childhood. Here the full weight of the Aristotelian inheritance of medical lore – shared by Jews, Christians and Muslims – was mobilized to ridicule the notion of a God dwelling in a female body. The grammarian and exegete Rabbi David Kimhi of Provence (1160–1235) is explicit about this terrible mismatch:

[How can I believe] in a living God who is born of a woman, a child without knowledge and sense, an innocent who cannot tell his right from his left, who defecates, urinates and sucks from his mother's breast out of hunger and thirst, and cries when he is thirsty and whom his mother pities; and if she would not he would die of hunger as other people do?[40]

The culture which produced delight in a God made flesh born of a virgin was more attentive than ever in this period to those who did not share this joy. Mary's Jewish ancestry challenged commentators and inspired inventive new formulations. Around 1140 the monk Ralph, of St Germer at Fly, set to work on a commentary to the book of Leviticus.[41] Being a book of law, Leviticus was well known to Jews, but had hitherto attracted little attention from Christian exegetes. Ralph offered a Christian reading which first explained and then rejected Jewish law. Yet when he reached the laws on the purification of women after birth, he conceded that Mary had indeed been purified in the Jewish manner: 'She was not obliged by the law, but willingly submitted herself to that portion of the law.'[42] Henceforward, he argued, Christian women abstained from entering a church after childbirth out of respectful emulation of Mary.[43]

In a variety of writings and in new descriptive forms the relationship between Mary and 'her' people became a source of fascination and

dread. Jews were cast as Mary's particular enemies and imagined as the only people in Europe who openly injured her in word, thought and gesture. Mary grew in prominence as an agent of salvation and as an active participant in the Crucifixion. This was fertile ground for creative dwelling on the dangerous opposition Mary–Jew. Nowhere is this more apparent than in Mary's entry into the pair *ecclesia-synagoga*, church and synagogue. These concepts were portrayed as siblings: one sister chose the right way of Christian truth and stood erect and beautiful, the other erred, and was henceforward condemned to blindness, defeat and misery. The Lambeth Bible made for St Augustine's Canterbury around 1150 opens the book of Habakkuk with an initial O in which the crucified Christ is flanked by church and synagogue, equal in size and style, yet different in power and destiny.[44] The crowned *ecclesia* is hardly distinguishable from the evolving image of crowned Mary: virginal, majestic, erect and truthful. A silver paten made in Lower Saxony in 1170 (now at the cathedral of Gniezno) depicts these 'sisters' equal in size and in dress but with two striking differences: each holds an identical flag, one erect and the other downcast, and while one is clear-sighted, the other is blindfolded.[45] The chancel arch of the Danish parish church of Spentrup was decorated with themes of Mary's life, alongside the scene of *ecclesia* and *synagoga* – triumphant woman and blind one – above whom a Lamb of God is depicted: he is pierced by *synagoga*'s lance, but his blood is collected into the chalice held by *ecclesia*.[46] A portable altar made for the abbey of Stavelot in the diocese of Liège *c*.1160, consisted of a table top decorated in enamel. In its centre was a quatrefoil pattern with the lower and upper sections depicting *ecclesia* and *synagoga*: the former erect and crowned, with a chalice and a cross in her hand, the latter dejected and blindfolded, holding the spear and sponge of the Passion. Here too *ecclesia* resembles depictions of Mary.[47] The association operated through the powerful and long-standing habit of identifying the church as Mary.

EAST AND WEST: ICONS AND SHRINES

The eleventh and twelfth centuries saw the lives of eastern and western Christians bound together through trade, pilgrimage and crusades. The intensification of European commercial life meant the merchants – led by the enterprising men of Italian cities – sought routes to Asia through the Byzantine Empire, and then through the many Muslim principalities that existed under the Khalifate. With the loss of Christian territory to the Muslim Seldjuks the Byzantine emperors appealed to Europe for support, and this request sparked a whole series of campaigns which combined pilgrimage and warfare and which have come to be known as the Crusades. This meant that from 1096 – the launch of the First Crusade – Europeans regularly visited the Near East, and some settled in Latin kingdoms and principalities that were created there. European pilgrims now travelled the Holy Land, visiting churches and sites associated with the life of Jesus and Mary. They brought back to Europe the knowledge of eastern Christian styles in celebrating Mary's feasts and in representing her in icons.

Europeans were on the road, and thousands visited the east as warriors, settlers, merchants or pilgrims. They encountered the sites of Mary's life and death, encountering new liturgies and artefacts. Those who returned to Europe brought souvenirs and also ideas which they sought to share and adopt. Relics from the east – such as Christ's blood, thorns from the crown – were particularly precious, being so close to the site of the historic events. Memories of what was seen in the east were carved into wood and built in stone on European soil as replicas of the Holy Sepulchre were erected all over Europe.[48] In the following century stories would even be told about the translation of Mary's house to the Italian Marches, to Loreto, following the end of Christian sovereignty in the Holy Land.[49]

Eastern representations of Mary always conveyed the understanding that the matter of religion and the matter of governance were inseparable. Visual representation of Mary followed in a few authoritative and orthodox types. Around the beginning of the second millennium emerged the mother with child – the Virgin *eleousa* – Mary as merciful

169

or compassionate. This was a reserved, somewhat melancholy Mary, with her son on her arm, looking old and wise. A mantle covered Mary's head, and under it she also wore a head-cloth. Her face is depicted with elongated, almond-like eyes, her nose is long and her mouth small. Details of drapery were emphasized in such icons; gold marked folds in the garments and often dominated the background. A mosaic icon preserved at St Katherine's monastery on Mt Sinai is made of stones so small as to be hardly noticeable.[50] One such Mary icon, painted in Constantinople around 1131, reached the city of Vladimir, in the kingdom of Rus, where it became the protective icon of the Russian people, still today venerated and much restored.[51] A version in mosaic was made in the 1180s–90s for the cathedral of King William II of Sicily, in Monreale.

Although the icon of Mary and Child predominated in the Byzantine Empire, attention was also paid to the central scenes of Mary's life – the Nativity (which often included the Annunciation and the Adoration of the Magi) and the Dormition. In Dormition scenes Mary was usually prone, reclining on a bed, as in a wall painting of the church of Panhagia Phorbiotissa in Asinou, or in the Dormition painted on the beam of the icon-screen (*iconostasis*) in St Katherine's monastery.[52] The Nativity fresco in the church of Panagia tou Arkou in Lagoudera (Cyprus) sets the scene in a rocky landscape with Mary at the centre. Mourning apostles surround Mary's body, and her son stands at the centre, holding her soul. In Nativity scenes Mary is prone, as the Magi admire her swaddled son.

Mary was also portrayed in depictions of the Crucifixion, most commonly as part of the scene of Mary and John mourning the crucified Christ. An icon from St Katherine's monastery in the Sinai, dating from the late eleventh century, displays quiet expression in Mary and John: Mary gestures as if showing her son's wounded body, and John touches his head in a gesture of grief. Yet the whole scene is set against a gold background and is framed by the busts of eighteen figures: emperors, saints and fathers of the church.[53] A more animated version was displayed in a twelfth-century enamel, with angels and Roman soldiers. Mary's tearful stance and John's pained gesture are somewhat diluted by the presence of so many distracting figures and objects.[54] A silver processional cross from northern Anatolia, probably of the early twelfth century, placed Mary and her Son – the Virgin *hodegetria*, who points

at her son, literally, showing the way – at the centre, surrounded by scenes of her life at the cross's four ends. The commissioning monk, Cosmas, clearly judged – like many western artists of his time – that the story of Incarnation and Passion could be amply told through Mary's experience.[55]

All these eastern images were created during a period of encounters – some more, some less amicable – between eastern and western Christians, now more frequent and intensive than they had been for centuries. There is a great deal of mutual influence.[56] Even before the Crusades, while sites sacred to Christians were under Muslim rule, pilgrimage to the Near East continued. Southern Italy was a Byzantine province until the mid-eleventh century and several Italian cities maintained merchant communities in Byzantine ports. Dynastic marriages saw ambassadors and retinues moving between the Byzantine and the Holy Roman imperial courts. Vast regions of Europe were hybrids of east and west, such as the Balkans, Hungary and southern Italy, which contained mixed populations and followed local versions of Christianity, some Greek others Latin in emphasis. Ideas about Mary were significantly affected by all these contacts and the possibilities they engendered.

Encounters with the Holy Land could be life changing, then as now. When Bishop Lietbert (1051–76) returned from his pilgrimage to the Holy Land he was inspired to found an abbey of the Holy Sepulchre in his city of Cambrai that was dedicated to Jesus and the memory of his tomb and to 'the blessed and always virgin mother of that our God, Mary'. The liturgical books of the abbey church reflect his efforts to magnify Mary in 'memorials' – readings that extol her virtues – that were inserted into the liturgy.[57] Lietbert followed the tradition attributed to Alcuin, of linking each day of the week to a special mass; and so every Saturday was to be her special day, and the mass of the day was dedicated to her.[58] A book of lessons (Legendary) from Cambrai, of the end of the century, contains readings for the day. Among them was the Greek tale about a Jew who desecrated Mary's image in the church of the Blachernae in Constantinople, was discovered and converted to Christianity.[59] This evocation of a Greek tale reveals another possible inspiration for Cambrai's Marian focus: the image at the Blachernae chapel habitually performed a miracle on Saturdays, when the veil over the image rose as if lifted by a puff of air and the image was transformed, as if visited by the Virgin herself.[60] The east continued to feed the west

with templates for appreciation of Mary. As European monks sought new forms and occasions for Mary worship, the eastern heritage was a useful guide and inspiration.

Europeans settled in the east, built churches and commissioned manuscripts in which Mary was depicted in interesting blends of eastern and western sensibilities. The Psalter of Queen Melisende of Jerusalem (1105–61), made in the church of the Holy Sepulchre of Jerusalem between 1131 and 1134, includes a cycle of full-page depictions of the Annunciation, Visitation, Nativity, Adoration of the Magi and on to the life and ministry of Jesus, ending with the Passion, the Dormition and the Deesis.[61] This is the cycle that emerged in twelfth-century Europe, yet it is much influenced by Byzantine style and technique. Further on in the book the decoration of a prayer to Mary shows her enthroned with her son in her lap, like so many pages we have already seen in the books of monks and nuns of the early twelfth century.[62]

Eastern traditions about Mary were maintained by Christian communities under Muslim rule and these sometimes attracted the attention of European pilgrims. The fountain at al-Matariyya, near Old Cairo, was adored as a resting place of the Holy Family during the Flight to Egypt. Christians who visited Cairo – Europeans as well as Greeks and Ethiopians – habitually visited it.[63] Similarly, news of the revered miraculous image of Mary belonging to the convent of Saydnaya, some 25 kilometres north-east from Damascus, attracted European pilgrims during their sojourns in the east. This was a long-standing cult of an image procured by an abbess of the convent, from either Jerusalem or Constantinople. In 1175 the pilgrim Burchard of Strassbourg recorded the lively cultic life around the site: twelve nuns and eight monks inhabited the religious house and guarded the panel painting of Mary, which was made of flesh and exuded a constant flow of aromatic oil.[64] Muslims habitually attended the Assumption celebrations of local Christians, and western pilgrims made their way there too, beyond the areas in Christian control. So Europeans encountered there a religious diversity unknown at home. The healing oil of Saydnaya was also sent back to Europe to his home church at Altavaux, by Aymeric Brun, lord of Montbrun in 1178–9, after he procured it from a Templar who had obtained it on return from captivity.

By the late twelfth century Europeans sometimes imagined Mary through the depictions and ideas bolstered by contact with the Holy

Land. The Danish narrator of the exploits of a group of Scandinavian crusaders $c.1200$ explains the meaning of the 'land of milk and honey':

By 'milk', which is squeezed from the flesh, Christ's human nature is represented, and the word 'honey', which is formed from the dew of heaven, signifies the inner sweetness of the Godhead. Therefore the Promised Land flows with milk and honey, in other words, the Virgin Mary brings forth God and Man.[65]

In the east, shrines were to be found that told unfamiliar stories about the physical traces of Mary's life and works. The reverence paid to Mary by eastern Christians and Muslims served to reinforce her universal powers and her undeniable worth.

The influence did not only work from east to west, but also in the reverse. By the late twelfth century some Byzantine representations of Mary had incorporated the growing expressive style of the portrayal of Marian narrative scenes. An Annunciation icon from St Katherine's monastery in Sinai of the late twelfth century displays an angel who is almost dancing in front of an apprehensive Mary. Mary is seated on a throne, and the two create a pair, similar to depictions of Mary's coronation in heaven.[66] The same scene, painted in the monastery of the Syrians in Wadi al-Natrun, Egypt, after 1170 also displays aspects of western iconography, with flowing gestures between Gabriel and Mary.[67] European Mary had something affective and new to offer Christians of the east.

THE DEBATE ON MARY'S CONCEPTION

As part of the creativity around Mary some Cistercian monks became audacious innovators in thinking about her, and Mary became a subject of polemic within the order. For some Cistercian monks believed that Mary was so pure that even her own Conception in Anne had been without sin. Her intimacy with Christ required, according to some, a unique order of purity. Mary's immaculate nature was already celebrated in some eleventh-century liturgies of English cathedrals – Winchester and Canterbury – and it was an English monk, Eadmer of Canterbury ($c.1060–c.1130$), who finally gave the idea shape.[68] Mary

was born free of original sin, without the concupiscence that led to sin. In his *On the conception of saint Mary* (*De conceptione sanctae Mariae*) Eadmer proposed a number of reasons for the necessity of Mary's conception without sin. It was unfitting for the site of the greatest good to be touched by sin:

But because that conception was, as we have said, the basis of the dwelling place of the greatest good, what would we have said if any stain at all had attached to it from original sin?[69]

Nor was there any limit to such a conception, since if God willed to be born of an immaculate mother he could make it happen.[70]

In England the feast was celebrated in great abbeys and with royal support; it fitted within a framework of Marian interest that saw the blending of Anglo-Saxon custom and new monastic commitment. Osbert of Clare (active *c*.1136), monk and then prior of Westminster Abbey, corresponded with Anslem of Bury St Edmunds, another enthusiast for Mary's cause, who had laboured in collection of her miracle tales. Osbert reported the behaviour of the disapproving bishops of Salisbury and St David's during the celebration:

In God's church while we celebrated the festivity of that day, some, guided by Satan, said that it was ridiculous, because throughout all centuries until recent times, such a thing had been unheard of.[71]

The Council of London of 1139 authorized, with papal approval, the feast's reception into the English liturgical calendar.[72]

The great Cistercian abbot Bernard of Clairvaux (1091–1153) was an enthusiastic poet of Mary's praises, yet he could not accept the imputation of such purity to Mary. Here was a man full of ambition for the church and above all dedicated to the monastic ideal. He was devoted to Mary and did not doubt that she had never sinned, but her natural generation had to transmit original sin through the sexual act. His views were clearly laid out in a letter of 1139 sent to the canons of Laon cathedral, who had instituted the feast of the Conception of Mary, a feast significant only if that conception was deemed to have been immaculate. Bernard began his letter with an expression of surprise that a school renowned for sound learning (*honestis studiis*) – Laon was the foremost cathedral school – would so err as to introduce 'a new festival, a rite of which the Church knows nothing'.[73] The canons

argued that Mary should be honoured, and Bernard agreed, but with a difference:

The Virgin has many true titles to honour, many real marks of dignity, and does not need any that are false. Let us honour her for the purity of her body [and] holiness of her life. Let us marvel at her fruitful virginity, and venerate her divine Son. Let us extol her freedom from concupiscence in conceiving, and from all pain in bearing. Let us proclaim her to be reverenced by angels, desired by the nations, foretold by the patriarchs and prophets, chosen out of all and preferred before all . . . All this the Church sings in her praises and teaches me to sing too. What I have received from the Church I firmly cling to and confidently pass on to others; but, I confess, I am chary of admitting anything that I have not received from her.[74]

Bernard believed that Mary received a special dose of grace between conception and birth, a dose even larger than that received by St John the Baptist.[75] This 'sanctification' meant that Mary was not tainted by original sin and was equipped to withstand sin in her lifetime. To claim that she has been conceived without sin would have made the divine gift of 'sanctification' redundant and thus deny her a privilege which other humans had enjoyed:

We cannot for a moment suppose that a privilege which has been accorded to some, though very few, mortals, was denied to that Virgin through whom all mortals have entered life. Beyond all doubt the Mother of the Lord was holy before she was born. Holy Church is certainly not mistaken in keeping the day of her birth holy and celebrating it every year throughout the world with a glad and joyous festival. I, for my part, believe that she received a more ample blessing which not only sanctified her in the womb, but also reserved her thereafter free from sin throughout her life. This is something which we do not believe to have been accorded to any other born of woman. This unique privilege of sanctity whereby she was enabled to live her whole life without sin surely well becomes the Queen of Virgins (*decuit nimirum Regina Virginum*) who, in giving birth to him who destroyed sin and death, obtained for all of us the reward of life and righteousness.[76]

Bernard's homilies on Mary extol the purity of her life, but they were also set within the larger understanding of the Incarnation and its redemptive purpose. If original sin touched all humans, then Mary shared in it at her conception. There was another principle at work too, that of decorum

(*convenientia*);[77] it was surely fitting that Mary should become sinless because of the nature of the fruit she was destined to bear. Yet Bernard's voice did not prevail. Cistercian thinkers devoted to Mary rejected his views while protesting their admiration for his learning and sanctity.

A letter of 1180–81 from Nicholas, abbot of St Albans, to Peter of Celle (*c.*1115–83), later Bishop of Chartres, shows how alive the debate remained within this group of Anglo-Norman bishops and abbots. Nicholas adhered strongly to Augustine's dictum that 'in matters to do with sin, I want no mention to be made of the blessed and virgin Mary'.[78] Nicholas saw in the feast of the Conception a celebration not of the event, but of its fruit: God incarnate. Against him, Peter of Celle argued that there was no tradition in the church for such a celebration.[79] The monk was attracted to the devotional possibilities, while the bishop took a more institutional view. England led the way in celebration of the Conception, and the feast made its way through the Anglo-Norman realm and into the cathedrals and abbeys of France.[80]

10

Abundance and Ubiquity

A creeping 'marianization' of religious culture is evident not only in new literary genres, and visual arrangements, but also in the insertion of Mary into contexts previously occupied by other figures. A good example is the transformation of the liturgical play of the Massacre of the Innocents. In this the figure of Rachel, the mourning mother described by the prophet Jeremiah (31:18–22) and invoked in the gospel of Matthew (2:17–18), laments her dead children. The earliest of the five known versions of Rachel's Lament is in a manuscript that was in the abbey of St Martial of Limoges by the early twelfth century. Rachel is a mother in pain, consoled by an angel:

> O sweet sons, whom I have now borne,
> Once called a mother, what name have I attained now?
> Once called child-bearing on account of my children
> now I am wretched, bereaved of my sons.[1]

Rachel is treated as an historical figure, grounded in scripture, with dramatic fullness and interest. Yet throughout the twelfth century Rachel Laments in manuscripts from the monasteries of Fleury and Freising reflect a change in emphasis: Rachel becomes a prefiguration of Mary; she is even addressed as mother and virgin.[2]

In the making of Rachel of Bethlehem into a grieving virgin, indeed into a grieving Mary, we glimpse some of the devotional trends that were to animate poetry and drama in the following centuries. Liturgy, poetry and visual imagery were refigured so as to incorporate more and better Marian content. Mary 'invaded' spaces occupied for centuries by other figures and protagonists.

The practical choices of those who composed music, chose liturgical texts and trained singers offer useful indications of Mary's rise. At

Notre-Dame of Paris not only were the major feasts of Mary – Purification, Annunciation, Assumption and her Nativity – celebrated with motets, polyphonic compositions on Marian themes, but also other feasts too. For St John the Evangelist, the Nativity of St John the Baptist, for the feasts of Peter, Paul and the Apostles, the Latin tenor voice of the motet sang the liturgical text of the day, but was accompanied by a voice of Marian content sung by the other voices: the liturgy for more than half of the major feasts at Notre Dame contained Marian musical parts.[3]

Mary offered prompts towards creativity and tested theories of grammar, logic and philosophy. The work of simile is one way of exploring language and expressing praise: a book from Ripoll monastery contains the *Advocaciones de la Virgen*, a tract which lists sixty-eight names for Mary, and their meanings: Divine, Virgin, God-holder, *Theotokos*, *Christotokos*, Branch, House, Temple and more. So, for example, the name Bush is explained:

The godly Virgin is called Bush, because her virginity is designated by it. Moses the Law-giver, true witness of the Virgin Mary, saw a bush that was burning, in which there was a pyre, and God's majesty stood in the middle of the pyre, and neither the bush nor the Majesty burned. So neither Mary's blessed virginity nor the divinity of heaven was harmed in conception or in virgin birth.[4]

Such lists of praises, garlands of images, were then used by writers of devotional poetry and composers of sermons for Mary's feasts.

Mary was inserted into the learned homilies of the age, into the most technically adventurous forms of biblical commentary and into devotional poetry. An image often served as the point of departure, and Mary was then elaborated through it. A new type of sermon, the thematic sermon, usually opened with an authoritative text and developed it through the explorations of imagery. The sermon by the theologian Richard of St Victor (d.1173), begins with the text of *Hail, Star of the Sea (Ave Maris Stella)*, the author of which is unknown:[5]

This world, dearest brethren, is a sea. Because like the sea it stinks, swells, and is false and unstable . . . It is, therefore, brethren necessary that we should have a ship, and all that belongs to it, if we wish to cross the perilous sea without danger. It is necessary that we have a ship, a mast, a sail, and two masts between which the sail stretches high and low, and a crow's nest which we can call a cock, watchful over the sail. We need ropes, oars, rudders, anchor, and food as required.

We also have a net, so that we can catch some fish. See what this signifies: the ship is faith . . . This ship's planks are the sentences of the Holy Scripture . . . The mast signifies hope, by which we are raised to the heaven to seek, to know . . . The two planks, above and below, signify rationality and sensuality . . . The crow's nest signifies discretion of the spirit . . .

We must have, dearest brothers, a ship by faith, a mast by hope, a sail by charity, a crow's nest by the testing of spirits, ropes by the excitation of virtues, oars by the exhibition of good works, rudders by discretion, an anchor by humility, food by reading of scripture, a net by preaching, and an oarsman from singing the praises of God's jubilation . . . Yet in order to cross this sea safely, dear brethren, we must frequently salute, and while saluting invoke the star of the sea, that is Blessed Mary, saying *Ave Maris Stella*. Like sailors we always pour our prayers to the Blessed Mary and her son. There are many impediments on our way . . .[6]

Here Richard turns to the verses of another theologian and poet of St Victor, Adam (d.1172/92), with the appeal:

> Our carnal man
> Wastes away in these evils
> you, spiritual mother,
> free us, as we perish.

The last two stanzas appeal to Jesus, fruit of a sacred womb, to become the way, the chief, and the leader to heaven.[7] Mary's power to guide likened her to the star of the sea that helps mariners on their voyages. Mary indeed became the protector of mariners, sometimes represented as a siren, as in the church of Notre-Dame in Orcival, south-west of Clermont in the Massif Central.[8]

Richard of St Victor also wrote a short treatise *Charcoal and Ashes* (*Carbonum et cinerum*), based on the discussion of burned offerings in Leviticus (Leviticus 2:4–7 and 7:9–10). After a short introduction he discusses four types of bread: cooked in a frying pan, charred in a griddle, soaked in oil, and cold, hard bread. The work ends with an exhortation towards a search for the warm bread of the faithful soul. The predominant imagery is that of food and its preparation, so often the domain of women.[9] Perhaps that is why Richard thought Mary so useful; to each image he offers two senses, one in terms of life in the cloister, and the other in terms of Mary:

179

Leftover carbon and ashes are cleared by the baker off the oven floor; useless superstition by the rector, the simplicity of the cloister, worldly reflection and desire by the Creator at the conduct of the Virgin. The burning steam of the fire is preserved in the oven, in the fervent conduct in the cloister, the vow of chastity in the virgin's womb. Soft dough enters into the oven, the weak soul into the cloister, the suffering flesh does not enter from elsewhere, but in and of that same virginal womb, it rises in Christ. [The dough is placed in the oven] not in pieces but in the form of bread; order in the cloister must be observed jointly not individually; the Virgin of virgins did not conceive that divinity of the word in small portions or in drops. Dough is not baked in the oven shapelessly, rather it is kneaded and given shape; order cannot be established in a cloister without a rule and proper form; the Virgin conceived and put forth a human nature by the acceptance of the seven-formed grace. The oven emits a fine odour from breads; cloistered religion offers good examples of virtues to the secular; the virtues of the Virgin give off a pleasant smell onto the angelic residences. The bread of the oven nourishes flesh; the cloistered life nourishes the soul; the whole Church is nourished by the fruit of the Virgin. Poor people run to the oven for bread; the humble run to the cloister for piety; all people run to the Virgin's temple for salvation.[10]

Richard's lively style made the sermon interesting to read and enjoyable to hear when expounded aloud. It created in the listener a keen expectation for the next metaphor; it linked the cloistered life and Mary's god-bearing mission. Indeed, every monk could become Mary – and bear Christ within.

A general exaltation is apparent in the wide range of creative initiatives of this period: Mary as exegetical key, Mary as polemical ballast against the Jews, Mary as figure of the church, Mary as companion to monks and priests, depicted copiously and elegantly within the architecture that contained their lives.[11] Her emergent hegemony also took shape in hundreds of surviving, and probably thousands of once existing, statues. We have already considered the challenges posed by making Mary into sculpted form; the most striking feature of twelfth-century Mary images is her static majesty.

Mary's dominance was reflected in the most common ways of portraying her: frontal, static, serious, majestic, enthroned, in wall paintings as well as in statues and carvings.[12] By the mid-twelfth century Romanesque wall paintings also confidently portrayed scenes of Mary's life and her

life with her son: $c.1160$ the chapel of the Norman royal hunting-lodge at Petit-Quevilly was adorned with the Annunciation, Visitation and Nativity, the Adoration of the Magi, with Mary finely made. Mary in majesty is particularly striking; she is enthroned and crowned, receiving the Magi's gifts.[13] Mary and the Child enthroned in the apse of the parish church of Taüll of $c.1137$ resemble greatly the wood sculpture of Mary in red dress and blue cloak seated on a small throne in Sant Pau in Camp (Catalonia).[14] Traditional settings, like the Annunciation, solemnly emphasized Mary's unique humanity. A relief from the cloister of Santo Domingo de Silos, of $c.1180-90$ portrays Mary crowned by angels already at the moment of the Annunciation, and the Angel Gabriel not so much greeting as kneeling in front of her.[15] The emergent amalgam is one of purity, wisdom and extraordinary privilege, from which monks and lay people too could but learn and take courage and hope.[16]

The choices made by artists in the depiction of Mary reflected regional preferences and traditions, as did all other aspects of life. In the Limousin region enamel decoration was applied to statues of Mary. Some luxurious romanesque statues, like one in the treasury of Toledo cathedral of the Virgin and Child were made of gilt copper and decorated with enamel plaques.[17] Local traditions of Byzantine artistic influence are evident in the art of the Veneto and north-east Italy, in the *pala* – an altar decoration – finely incised on silver. The *pala* of Cividale cathedral of $1195-1204$ depicts Mary enthroned with the Child on her lap, flanked by ceremoniously garbed angels; similar is a Venetian *pala* of around 1200 with Mary on a throne with an elaborate back, covered in billowing drapery and looking forward.[18] A distant Byzantine heritage is even notable in the Virgin and Child painted in a niche in the Danish parish church of Måløv.[19]

The twelfth century produced in large parts of France and Iberia, along the routes of trade and pilgrimage, a powerful sense of Mary's grave majesty. She was a figure imagined above all through liturgy and prayer, most frequently and intensely by monks and priests. Mary as Seat of Wisdom encompassed the knowledge of creation – she bore a creator in her own body. She was imagined frequently in the words of Solomon – the wisest of men – author of the Song of Songs, builder of the Temple, so that her dignified person resembled a solid temple.[20] In central and southern France, in Iberia and in parts of Italy, she was

sometimes made of black, dark wood, or painted black.[21] The choice of black and the shape of these statues – above all common in the Auvergne – may be related to representations of female deities which predate the arrival of Christianity.[22]

There is also in places a new sense of closeness and bodily intimacy in some Mary and Child groups of the later twelfth century. In the tiny initial O in a late twelfth-century bible, Mary and son appear embracing flesh to flesh, sharing bodily warmth, so close that even their haloes interlock.[23] The mother is modestly clad, the son wears a light, diaphanous robe; they are secure and loving. An image of maternal love and tenderness was being born. Mary was fashioned as a mother who was also a lifelong companion in the privacy of monastic cells, in the musical work of their choirs, in the abject creativity of prayer. Mary of tender embraces challenged her makers towards greater audacity in the display of intimacy; Mary gestures towards her son in the Westminster Psalter.[24] A wooden statue carved in Italy around 1200 shows Mary as sombre yet protective of her son;[25] and a Catalan painted altar-frontal of Avià of 1170–90 shows Mary gazing tenderly at her swaddled son in his crib, while touching him with her right hand, in a Nativity scene attended by Joseph.[26] Liturgical art surrounded the monks, men who were directed towards the religious life at a very early age; they were motherless, full of longing, and so their abbots became like mothers.[27] These were the families of Mary's lovers.

MARY'S MIRACLES

Mary's power was appreciated through the miracles she worked on behalf of humans: she saved the city of Constantinople, and she saved a Jewish boy from fire and brought him into her tender embrace. The collection of Mary's miracle tales began in the early Christian centuries by eastern monks. Some of these reached Europe through the experiences of pilgrims – as in the case of Adomnan and the story of the image of Constantinople; others in histories, like the miracle of Mary's defence of Constantinople against the Avars. After the year 1000 several new shrines to Mary developed in western Europe, in which new marvels were told, fresh manifestations of her power in the contemporary world, at shrines like those of Rocamadour, Montserrat or Soissons.[28] Yet

English monks led the way in recounting her miracles around the middle of the twelfth century. With their ancient traditions of Marian feasts and poetry, English monasteries became the venue for editorial work and compilation.

The quintessential Marian story is one of transgression and return, loss and recovery of the Christian self. Protagonists in the stories ranged from monks to priests, from nuns to knights, from peasants to merchants, but their end was one and the same, a happy end: Christians returned to the Christian embrace and Jews found their way to it through conversion. So Mary's miracles offered yet another genre within which Christian truth was proven through the agency of sinners, heretics and Jews. The authors were aware of their tales' polemical power. In his collection *On the praises and miracles of St Mary* (*De laudibus et miraculis Sanctae Mariae*) William of Malmesbury (d.1143) explained why he had not included even more stories of Mary and the Jews: 'it would take a vast book to show how diligently Mary labours towards the conversion of her kindred people'.[29]

Miracles were manifestations of Mary's power: she bore her son miraculously, she remained a virgin miraculously, even her passing from the world was a miracle. Monastic office was being embellished with sequences of Mary's praise and miracle tales sometimes formed part of that praise. Dominic, monk of Evesham (d. by 1150), who compiled around 1121 a collection of fourteen miracles, explained in his preface that he did so in order to support the constant praise of Mary in his monastery.[30] The office for the feast of the Conception included readings from accounts of miracles, like that of Abbot Helsin of Ramsay (flourished 1080s) who was saved from shipwreck thanks to his appeal to Mary; in return she requested the celebration of her Conception.[31] It is not surprising that the authoritative compilation of Latin tales was probably made in an English monastery – Bury St Edmunds – and that it was made by a widely travelled, well-connected monk, who was also known for his devotion to Mary. He was Anselm the Younger, nephew of Anselm of Canterbury, who had been a monk at the Italian monastery of Chiusa and was sent as papal envoy to Normandy around 1116, where he stayed until his move to England. The miracle tales associated with him are full of details about Norman politics and are highly aware of liturgical celebration of that Marian feast.[32]

While stories about Mary were many, her relics were few. Mary's

body had been assumed to heaven and so none of it was left on earth, and the Byzantines had already secured her robe and girdle. Hagiographical writing together with diplomatic and trading efforts all combined to procure, steal or create Mary relics – like other relics – for Europeans and their shrines.[33] Mystical experiences like those of Fulbert of Chartres and Bernard of Clairvaux provided the frame for cults around drops of Mary's milk kept in precious vials. But above all images of Mary – painted and sculpted – were touched by the memory of miraculous intervention and drew the faithful in search of cure and assistance and in the offering of prayer.

The occasions and locations for encounter with Mary's miracles were growing in number and variety in this period. An interesting record is offered by a Muslim geographer from Andalusia, Bakrî (d.1094) in his *Book of routes and provinces*:

There is in Carcassonne this very important church of theirs, called *Shant Mariya Gharasha* (or *Gharâtiya)*. It includes seven columns of silver. It has a certain feast which Christians of all parts attend.[34]

Bakrî based his work on geographical materials of *c*.1000, and he probably refers in this passage to the monastery of St Mary of Lagrasse, near Carcassonne.[35] By the thirteenth century a legend linked the place to lives of seven hermits devoted to Mary.[36] France and the Iberian peninsula were linked by the route that took European pilgrims to the edge of Europe, to Santiago da Compostella, one of the greatest pilgrimage shrines, in the north-west corner of Iberia. Monks travelled in search of edifying accounts of miracles, like the monk of the Catalan Abbey of Ripoll, who included in his collection nine stories from the shrine of Rocamadour in the diocese of Cahors, in south-west France.[37] Rocamadour was the quintessential Mary shrine; its miracles were powerful and much respected. The veneration of the remains of St James the Less, Sanitago, at Compostella was followed in importance by the pilgrimage to the Black Virgin at the Benedictine abbey of Montserrat, founded in 1025. This too was a dark wooden statue of an enthroned Mary and Child, in a frontal position, covered with gilt decoration, gazing at the viewer.[38] In the Mediterranean regions and their hinterlands we find the dense concentration of 'black' statutes of Mary – some surviving and many known to have existed. The shape of Mary that emerged in the twelfth century, the enthroned Romanesque figure, may

have combined in these regions with dark figures of Roman goddesses of fertility and health, figures often worshipped in caves and trees, at wells or springs; some of the black madonnas were found in such places.[39]

The miraculous statue of Mary at Rocamadour developed mysteriously at the dramatic setting of the side of a gorge over the river Alzou. The site was famed for housing the unspoilt remains attributed to an early Christian hermit Amadour. Here medieval devotion asserted itself at the site of an early Christian hermit, around a strange dark wooden statue of Mary enthroned with her son on her lap, with traces of a crown, and a silver collar.[40] The site became renowned throughout the Christian world – and beyond – for Mary's kindness to many people of all walks of life. We are well informed about the site thanks to the composition around 1172 of a collection of 126 miracles performed there.[41] The miraculous cures involved many simple folk and relieved them of extremely common and debilitating conditions: blindness, shrivelled limbs, wounds, fevers. There were mental illnesses too: clerics seem to have been particularly prone to 'melancholy' and 'frenzy'. The miracles depict in lively detail just how important a healing shrine was to people's existence; at Rocamadour violent knights and lawless henchmen were among the social ills that the mysterious statue healed.

Mary miracles were widely told at the numerous shrines associated with her, and interest in them was great. It was possible to envisage the rebuilding of a destroyed cathedral through a fund-raising tour with relics. In 1112 a group of cathedral canons and some laymen of the city of Laon in northern France set out on such a journey. They covered some 1,000 kilometres in France and 2,000 kilometres in England, where they made accessible their relics – some threads from Mary's robe and some of her hair. There are two accounts of the journey, one by the contemporary Guibert of Nogent – Mary's great devotee, whom we have already encountered – and another by a later writer, Herman of Tournai.[42] The journey was probably organized by Anselm, head of the great school at the cathedral, and it made its way through a trail of Marian sites. The group reached Chartres cathedral on the eve of the Feast of Mary's Nativity. They then headed to England, where Mary was particularly revered – at Bury St Edmunds, at Winchester, at Bath, at St Paul's in London, each with Marian relics – and where money was readily offered to them.

Shrines like those of Laon, Rocamadour and Montserrat attracted pilgrims and supported large monastic establishments. They were embedded in local economies and often – as in Chartres – supported the emergent identities of urban centres and their people. Chartres cathedral was dedicated to Mary in the eighth century, and local tradition held that in 876 Charles the Bald gave it the gift of Mary's tunic. It was rumoured that Mary herself had made the garment and had worn it when she gave birth to Jesus (another tradition claimed she wore it at the Annunciation, too).[43] After a fire in 1134 the cathedral was rebuilt as a shrine with a vast adorned space for the reception of pilgrims. Those who came to Mary's shrine often went away with a badge that depicted the relic as a traditional linen undergarment, common in Chartres of that time, a *chemise*. Mary's garment was regarded as the city's most typical product – its wealth-making cloth, the *chartrain*.

The townsmen of Chartres, made rich by producing and selling this cloth, contributed to the decoration of the cathedral, and to the experiments in stained glass windows, most famously of the north transept: a later (1250–60) rose-shaped window, and five lancet-shaped windows below it, told the story of the Glorification of the Virgin. The first window of the aisle of the choir, on the south side, had at its centre the enthroned Mary with son in lap, frontal, crowned, majestic. It was fitting to reflect on light passing through windows since the virgin birth was often likened to the passage of light through a pane without injuring it.[44]

The church of Notre Dame of Soissons was famed for possessing another item of Mary's attire, her slipper. The canon of the church of St Jean des Vignes, Hugh of Farsit, wrote in 1143 an account of the miracles wrought at the nunnery of Our Lady of Soissons, which he began in the year 1128, a year of terrible disease and mortality, probably caused by infected rye. Sufferers saw the flesh fall off their limbs and suffered extremes of fever and chill. The afflicted of the town despaired of human help and turned to the 'pious and gracious ever-virgin mother of God, Mary'.[45] Buoyed by news of the cure of a young girl in the care of the countess of Soissons, they approached the church like the people of Nineveh, armed with humility and in a state of penance (Jonah 3). Likening their efforts to a spiritual battle, Hugh tells of the tearful cry which arose from the assembled throng. The 'imperial queen' (*imperiosa Regina*) did not disappoint them:

The cries of the sufferers were almost intolerable, before their relief. Now they express to the heavens endless voices of joy and to the people gathered around them they emit praises, and tears and the giving of thanks to her.[46]

A string of French cathedrals and abbeys boasted strong Marian connections, and their keepers collected the tales told and the miracles experienced at them. Deliverance through Mary's intervention established the link between people, cathedral and Mary's shrine, while miracles continued to happen in cures of chronic conditions. Thirty accounts of such miracles follow in the Soissons collection, among them one of a mute who began to speak, of a blind woman cured, of a deaf and dumb person made well. Occasionally the miracles illuminate areas of doubt, like that of the country bumpkin, the serf Boso, who went into Soissons with friends on a feast day. While others made offerings to the shrine of the slipper, he did not. On the way home the group discussed what they had just seen and done. Boso said: 'You must all be stupid if you think that slipper was really Saint Mary's; because surely it would have already rotted away a long time ago.'[47] At that moment his mouth was twisted and distorted violently, so that his whole face was transformed in agony. Boso asked to be taken back to the shrine, where, after suitable supplication and prostration in front of the slipper, he was relieved, his face and body restored to health. Through tales such as these Mary's power – often displayed through violent displeasure – became widely known. They spread above all orally, through the stories of pilgrims and of beneficiaries of cures, enhanced by souvenirs, such as pilgrim badges, and the songs which pilgrims learned at the shrine and brought home with them.[48]

In the many new locations where Mary's powers were celebrated old lore mixed with new. Well-known miracle stories involving even a much-loved saint could give way to Mary. This was the case some time in the late eleventh century, with the story known as the *Peril*. It told of a woman who went on pilgrimage to the island monastery of Mont Saint Michel just off the coast of Normandy some time in the early eleventh century (between 1009 and 1017). As she made her way on the causeway to the island, a storm erupted and was about to sweep her away. She then went into labour and was provided miraculously with a dry patch on which she could give birth through the intervention of the Archangel Michael. The pious pilgrim was rewarded

by the birth of a healthy son. She gratefully dedicated him to the religious life.[49]

Yet by the mid-twelfth century this story was included in collections of Marian tales. Both Dominic of Evesham and William of Malmesbury have it as a Marian miracle, and Dominic even, tellingly, comments that, although some claim that the archangel was in charge, the 'Mistress of the World' was the true miraculous protector.[50] Mary was not only a favoured protector but increasingly seemed a fitting healer and miraculous helper to women at birth and to children early in their lives. Harshly punishing an errant serf or lovingly relieving a pious mother and her new-born, Mary did what mothers always do: correct and nurture, mixing the imperative of discipline and pain with the relief of comfort and reassurance.

PART IV

Mary, Local and Familiar: 1200–1400

11

Mary in Liturgy, Song and Prayer

By the year 1200 European Christianity was varied in its features, but nonetheless broadly familiar to its peoples as well as to those who observed it, whether they be Byzantine Christians, Muslims, Jews or Mongols. Its culture – which embraced Western and Central Europe – provided the rhetorical and moral underpinnings for a Christian continent. The papacy, canon law, discussion of the sacraments in schools and universities, the politics of sacred kingship and popular preaching all combined to create a vision of a universal church. This church claimed to reach every person, everywhere, through its sacraments and liturgy, by means of a trained priesthood, in local churches that were embedded into dioceses and provinces. This world-view also saw the church as persistently confronted by its enemies – heretics, Jews, Muslims, arrogant scholars, disobedient rulers. New and renewed communities, kingdoms and city-states all enjoyed the possibilities of expressing their identities in the many media of the day. Mary was never far from these processes of self-expression.

Europe was linked up by roads and trade, ruled by ambitious royal administrations or by the councils of city-states. Religious styles were equally many and diverse. Restless Europeans were involved in conquest and conversion in North-east Europe and maintained constant traffic with North Africa. European traders had colonies on the Black Sea and trade routes through the Caliphate and into Central Asia, reaching India and China. In the Iberian peninsula Christian rulers were engaged in the enterprise known as the *reconquista*: the conquest of lands from Muslim rulers, who still governed native Iberian – Mozarab – Christian communities. The legitimation for all these projects was sought in a Christian idiom that was taught to children at their mother's knee, explained by priests and enhanced by the experience of ritual and of charismatic

191

preaching. Europeans lived their fears and dreams in association with Mary.

Mary was invoked to bless new ventures and became their protector; she was invited into the chambers of city councils and into courts as patron of cities and states. She offered a human and accessible face to projects that were complex, bureaucratic and abstract, like crusades, the extirpation of heresy, conquest and conversion of new lands. While the churches and monasteries born in the first millennium often appealed to the virtue and protection of Christian martyrs, now new villages and towns, new religious movements – like the Cistercians – appealed to Mary. She was associated not only with the struggles to spread Christianity – to pagans, to Jews – but with the whole enterprise of a Christian society made up of families, communities and religious houses. While the last section traced her rise within the monasteries and cathedrals, in this we will trace the figure of Mary as she was made accessible to lay Christians. Mary was made local and vernacular in these centuries, she was reborn out of local materials and words, in city streets, homes, parish churches and road-side shrines; she was remade by lay confraternities and in the visions of religious women.

Monks encountered figures of Mary or scenes of her life as they moved throughout their houses. The performance of Marian music is captured in fine illuminations in English psalters. Artists chose to decorate the spaces attached to Psalm 97, 'Sing to God' (*Cantate domino*), associated with themes of incarnation and redemption, with a scene of chanting clerks. The Howard Psalter, made in East Anglia around 1310–20, depicts three singers concentrating on the music and reading the anno-tated words of a well-known Marian motet, *Zelo tui/Reor nescia*.[1] The clerics are dressed in festive finery: the dalmatic worn by one of the singers is adorned with stars, as was the custom in some religious houses on the feast of the Epiphany.[2] Stars had led the kings to the new-born Jesus, and Mary was praised for her star-like qualities. This miniature depicts the professionalism of the singers who maintained the routines of Marian liturgy.

Some components of this rich world of monastic music travelled with relative ease, and music from exalted locations could reach less privileged spaces in a variety of ways. The German Cistercian monk Caesarius of Heisterbach (1199–1240) imagined in the 1220s one such trajectory in a story from his collection of edifying miracle tales, the

Dialogue of Miracles (Dialogus Miraculorum). A priest of the diocese of Trier spent some time in a Cistercian monastery and claimed that the greatest gift he took away from there was the knowledge of the antiphon *Salve regina, mater misericordie (Hail Queen, Mother of Mercy).* This hymn served him well, for when he was caught in a storm some time later and took refuge in a church, he begged Mary to calm the thunder. Mary responded and explained that she had saved him because he had sung her antiphon so often and with true devotion.[3] Sections of chanted liturgy were also internalized for personal use. Caesarius records that Daniel, instructor of the boys in a Cistercian house, developed personal and private routines: he knelt before a Marian altar in the crypt and sang the sequence *Ave praeclara maris stella (Hail Bright Star of the Sea)*; he always stood up when he reached the words 'pray to the Virgin this morning to make us worthy of heaven'.[4] While monks and canons led with the sophisticated music and the rich ornamentation of liturgy, music could also spread through the mediation of parish priests. Encounters Mary's music and devotion spread beyond monastic houses.

Mary elicited poetry, and poetry was often turned into song. Yet some contemporaries abhorred the rhythmic poetics of new prayers. St Edmund Rich, archbishop of Canterbury (?1175–1240), a contemporary of Caesarius, was distinctly opposed to the practice of praying with words 'composed in curious poetry'.[5] Just like Christ, human and divine, song was both palpably carnal and yet elusive and intangible. It is not surprising, therefore, that the German poet Heinrich von Mügeln (d.1369) saw the Incarnation as a seduction by music. In his poem *The Maiden's Crown (Das meide Kranz)* he set up twelve academic disciplines in competition for a place in Mary's crown of twelve stars. Music made a strong case for its own unique merits:

> My song was always of the maiden,
> Through whom life dawns for mankind.
> My tone struck and broke the air,
> Until I lured God into the depths of the heart,
> As was becoming for him,
> And he took on humanity from the maiden.
> For that reason I may stand in the crown,
> Since I have won the honour through song.[6]

The poetics of Mary are replete with the language of desire and amorous conquest. Lyrics about Mary drew on established rhetorical habits for the expression of longing. Clerks and monks were Mary's lovers, and they were also the poets of love. Love poetry cannot be described as being either sacred or profane. Each sphere of yearning assumed the existence of the other, and poetry engaged the tantalizing closeness of the two.

Nowhere was more energy and wit invested in Mary than in the work of that bastion of clerical culture, the cathedral of Notre Dame in Paris. Around 1200 this church was being transformed into its glorious gothic shape – a process which lasted for a number of decades – and was unrivalled as a centre for polyphonic music. Polyphony was performed in other centres too, but at Notre Dame the *musica mensurabilis* – music with clearly annotated rhythm – facilitated control of the singer's voice and thus the emergence of complex harmonies.[7] Mary's feasts, above all the Assumption, drew large crowds to the cathedral and were attended by great clergymen, rich merchants and royal officials.[8] The vespers of the Assumption in the early thirteenth century combined plainchant and polyphony. As we have seen, the Assumption liturgy was rich in antiphons based on the Song of Songs and punctuated by psalms that dramatized Israel's faith and love of God.[9] The antiphon preceding the Magnificat extols Mary's work in unmaking Eve's: 'The gate of paradise was closed to all by Eve, and was opened again by Mary, Alleluya.'[10] Mary was celebrated in music as a dynamic agent of salvation on this her greatest Feast.

The clerics of Notre Dame formed part of the large population of men – a few thousand strong – who came to Paris to seek education, patronage and careers. Most of them were in lower ecclesiastical orders, and they often combined odd jobs – as students still do today – with attendance at the lectures of famous university masters. They created a youthful, vigorous and masculine cultural milieu of great sophistication and bristling with energy. Preachers commonly complained that Paris was full of prostitutes, who served the needs of such displaced, family-less men.[11] Another aspect of their lives was the indulgence in intellectual play, in poetry and song.

The world of the canons of Notre Dame was replete with imagery, texts and sounds that aimed to explore Mary. Mary was encountered in

the liturgy and its ceremony but also in the course of daily business. At the base of the radiating chapels of the chevêt there are seven carved reliefs which once adorned the cloister: four of Mary's life, two of Christ and one of a Marian miracle. The miracle of Theophilus – the story of temptation, ambition and greed miraculously countered by Mary's grace – was a salutary reminder to the canons; so were the scenes of Mary's Dormition, Funeral and Assumption, so full of the promise of Mary's power to intercede for sinners.[12]

The world of university and cathedral produced the challenging genre of the motet (*motetus*), a composition for several voices which combined tenor voice intoning a liturgical melody with other voices, often singing love poetry or even new compositions in the vernacular. The resulting juxtapositions were often audacious: the French pastoral poem may have praised the beautiful shepherdess, while the tenor exalted Mary as Virgin and Mother of God.[13] The parts were often linked through alliterative opening lines. The cleverness of the motet was displayed in the quality of the resolution – textual as well as musical – which was reached at the end of the piece.[14] Motets became a significant part of the Parisian repertory of Mary, led by the cathedral of Notre Dame. It was a genre above all suited to the appreciation of a clerical audience steeped in liturgy and music, but also in Latin and vernacular love poetry. An example from the late thirteenth century is the motet *Plus bele que flos/ flos filius eius* (*More lovely than a flower/the flower her son*).[15] It combines the tenor part from the responsory *Stirps Jesse*, composed by Fulbert of Chartres for Mary's Nativity, with three voices in French. Here is a blend of pastoral poetry about earthly love for a woman with the Latin antiphon for the Assumption. The highest voice is that of courtly love; and the whole confection is sung in parallel to the familiar liturgical tones of the Latin antiphon. Tradition and innovation thus combined, and the creation is more exciting than comprehensible, more audacious than informative. It is a heady mixture which exemplifies in sound the inexhaustible nature of the cultural production of Mary.

These musical and poetical traditions of liturgy and of courtly song were later to blend into the fourteenth-century love poetry of Petrarch and Dante. Mary's devotees often pondered most deeply the art of love. The composer Guillaume de Machaut (*c.*1300–1377) wrote the allegorical poem *Remedy of Fortune* (*Remède de Fortune*) in 1356, a

unique blend of narrative and annotated poetry. In it Hope speaks to Lover about the ways in which his Lady might be made to know his love:

> Now I have instructed and taught you,
> And if you have retained and understood,
> How to make your lady know
> That you love her loyally . . .[16]

This lady could be Mary or another beloved; the poetical challenge was the same: how to express welling desire, how to capture eternity and totality in mere words, in ephemeral song? Moreover, when the learned cleric Machaut thought of Mary's many glories he also thought of Venus, and the long classical tradition of proclaiming beauty, desire and devotion in poetic form.[17]

One of Machaut's Latin motets – *felix virgo/inviolate genitrix/Ad te suspiramus* – uses as its tenor voice the widely intoned and familiar *Salve regina*, the Marian antiphon we have already encountered, which was known to lay people and clerics alike. This is juxtaposed with the *motetus* voice that quotes from the *Ave Maris stella* and the *triplum* voice with the words of the responsory *Gaude Maria virgo*. Machaut wove the repertory of Marian sound into new patterns, perhaps for a Marian service newly established by King Charles V in 1380.[18] The cathedral of Reims, dedicated to Mary, provided opportunities galore for inventive and ostentatious display of Marian sensibility and erudition. Late in his life, as he took up residence as canon of the cathedral of Reims, Machaut composed the earliest surviving polyphonic treatment of the weekly Mary mass, a mass already established in the cathedral's liturgy. Machaut arranged in his will for this *Messe de Notre Dame* to be celebrated after his death for the benefit of his soul.[19] The great poet of love turned his art to Mary as he contemplated the end of his days.

12

Mary, the Friars, and the Mother Tongue

The development of a robust religious culture in the thirteenth century, with Mary increasingly at its heart, was made possible thanks to the growth and wealth of European communities, especially the towns and cities. Italian cities produced new impulses in religious life, which matched the rhythms of urban work and challenged the dazzling riches of a highly commercial society. To the new forms of monastic life was now added a different path towards spiritual perfection. It was to be lived neither in monasteries nor in hermitages or rural hideaways, but at the heart of cities, in full engagement with their people: merchants, artisans and nobles. It was a path followed by men who were willing to forego the stability of monastic life for the uncertainties and hardships of itinerant living, begging and preaching.

The messenger was Francis of Assisi (1181/2–1226), who was born to a comfortable mercantile family and was imbued with all the confidence that education, wealth and status bestow. He invented a new lifestyle and mission, a new form of religious life with the purpose of converting Christians into better Christians through preaching. The friars worked in towns and cities, and their labour was akin to performance art. The mere appearance of these preachers – in a simple woollen habit, secured with a rope as belt – made them immediately identifiable. The importance of the Franciscans to the story of Mary is in their power as cultural mediators. While the parish offered for most people the main occasions for religious education, for the sacraments and the communal celebration of life, the friars added new qualities to the experience of lay people, beyond the parish. With urgency and exhortation, the friars transmitted religious ideas and images in sermons, in devotional writings, in religious drama and in theological reflection.

The desire to convert people to a more committed Christian life led

friars to creative writing in Latin, but also in all the genres available in the vernacular languages of Europe. Friars created handbooks which aimed at helping preachers prepare sermons, and they devised useful aids to personal prayer. Friars of all orders – Franciscans and Dominicans, Augustinians and Carmelites – engaged with everyday languages of work and sociability and expressed a new range of interests and emotions. They developed myths of origin in which Mary played a central role: the Dominicans claimed that she had handed St Dominic his habit, and the Carmelites grew in Mary's homeland on Mount Carmel. Christian truth became through their efforts local and idiomatic for the millions, colourful and full of possibilities for emulation. Mary did too.

Friars all over Europe were now hard at work writing sermons and dramatic pieces to match the rhythm of the liturgical year. A thirteenth-century Franciscan, known to us only by his nickname, Graeculus, offers an interesting example in his sermon on the Assumption. He chose a verse from the book of Ruth 1:22: 'So Naomi returned, and Ruth the Moabite, her daughter-in-law, with her, who returned out of the country of Moab: and they came to Bethlehem in the beginning of the barley harvest', and explains its meaning for Mary's Assumption: 'In these words the magnificence in blessed Mary, her exit from exile, and the happy door of eternal beatitude which she reaches today, are expounded to us.'[1]

Graeculus remains close to the biblical verses and finds in them great riches; the very name Naomi means beautiful (*pulchra*) like Mary. He adds other salient qualities of Mary's sweetness, propriety, and the awe (*terribilis*) she instilled in the devil. Naomi's return from exile betokens Mary's departure from this world; following Jerome, he takes this to be a reason to rejoice in Mary's removal from this worthless world. He explains the return to Bethlehem: 'By which we understand paradise. It [Bethlehem] means indeed house of bread, which clearly means eternal bliss, since bread is there, Our Lord Jesus Christ.'[2] Like the Cistercian preacher Helinand, who saw Judith as a figure of Mary just a few years earlier, this inventive preacher chose another biblical heroine, Naomi, the ancestor of King David, and thus of Jesus too. The sermon ends with an invocation of Mary's titles: brightest star, most blessed virgin Mary, more splendid than any constellation, renowned among humans, very lovely.[3]

The process by which Marian lyrics, prayers and sermons became

available to lay people in local idioms and in familiar settings was a powerful shift from Latin to the spoken languages. It had a profound and lasting impact on the ideas and practices around Mary. Friars and priests participated in it, but also men and women from an ever-wider range of social backgrounds. The growing availability of materials in the spoken languages also meant that the genres that dealt with Mary reflected an ever-wider range of social experience: works for teaching the people of the parish, poetry for the use of religious confraternities, guidebooks for pilgrims, collections of miracles in the vernacular, hymns and chanted prayers. Mary took on increasingly the features of daily life; she dwelt within surroundings familiar to most people. This is not to say that Mary was no longer represented as Queen of Heaven, but rather that thinking about Mary in the 'mother' tongue contributed greatly to the intimacy experienced in engaging with her. Just as monks created Mary in their Latin prayers and sequences, Mary's reception was now enhanced and expanded once people could encounter her more readily in the words and colours of their own lives. Mary's power in the lives of many Europeans emerged from familiarity and accessibility, not from rarity and distance.

The offering of Mary to men and women outside the strict confines of the parish and its sacramental rites led to a veritable explosion of styles. Even within the Franciscan world the variety was evident early on: the order which was aimed at creating a cadre of exemplary preachers, denuded of property and worldly ambition, soon attracted female adherents too. Letters and writings attributed to Francis' follower Clare of Assisi (1194–1253) insisted that she, like Francis, wished to imitate Christ, to be his 'footprint', that is, to live as a friar even though as a woman she could neither preach nor move about freely. Yet Clare's legacy became soon after her death associated more with the imitation of Mary than of her son.[4] An anonymous legend written soon after Clare's death described her as a 'footprint [*vestigium*] of the Mother of God' and suggested that it was fitting that a women follow another woman. No less a figure than Pope Alexander IV (1254–61), one of Clare's admirers and friends, similarly described Clare as the footprint of the Mother of Christ, in a hymn he composed in Clare's memory.[5] A tender portrayal of Christ leaning towards his mother to receive her soul adorned the north wall of the church of the Clarissas of San Sebastiano in Alatri from the 1230s. This is an unusual scene that may have fitted

particularly well the emergent sensibility of the followers of Clare, cast as followers of Mary.[6] This is a far cry from the enthroned Mary of the East, the *Theotokos*, or from the wooden statues created for so many parishes churches in the twelfth century.

While Clare was attracted to the radical imitation of Christ for which Francis had striven, those who aimed to contain her and her female followers directed them to Mary as an apt example. Mary offered a useful and reassuring companion to new forms of religious life – especially those associated with women – for which there were few precedents. Here are Clare's words of *c*.1235, from a letter of guidance which she sent to her follower, the Hungarian princess Agnes of Prague (1200–1281):

I speak of him, the Most High Son, whom the Virgin bore and after whose birth she remained a virgin. May you cling to this most sweet mother, who gave birth to a Son whom the heavens could not contain, but whom she nevertheless carried within the small enclosure of her holy womb and held on her girlish lap ... Therefore, just as the glorious Virgin of virgins [carried Christ] materially, thus you, following his footprints, especially [those] of humility and poverty, can, without any doubt, always carry [him] spiritually in a chaste and virginal body, containing him in whom you and all things are contained.[7]

Mary evolved in the role as a fitting model for chaste enclosed religious women. Even if Clare imagined herself, as Francis did, to be an imitator of Christ, the deep-seated principles that guided – and sometimes forced – female religious into enclosed lifestyles rendered that imitation problematic in practice. So Mary became the core of Clare's legacy; Clare was, like Mary, a woman of good faith and charity. In a late fourteenth-century devotional tract about Francis' experience of the stigmata – the appearance of Christ's five wounds on his body – Clare was remembered not as a follower of Francis, but as the person chosen by Mary for the renewal of her 'virginal purity and humility'. If Christ returned in every mass celebrated at the altar and in the lives of evangelically poor preachers, then Mary returned in the pure bodies of chaste, enclosed women.

THE CRIB, CHRIST THE CHILD, AND HIS FAMILY

Francis' brilliant intuition encouraged the use of modest words and actions in creating memorials to the Incarnation for lay people. These memorials were not edifices in stone and glass in the exalted spaces of cathedral naves or monastic choirs, but were located in evocative humble settings such as a cave. After a visit to Rome at Christmas 1223 Francis experimented in the hill-town of Greccio with the making of a crib with the figures of Mary, Joseph and the baby Jesus, an ass, ox and shepherds, in a scene of adoration. There he celebrated the Christmas Eve mass. Furthermore, when pilgrimage to the Holy Land was becoming increasingly dangerous, as Christians lost ground to Muslims in the east, Greccio became a 'new' Bethlehem. A rough terrain 'amid rocks and woods' provided the setting for tender scenes of family life.[8] This Nativity scene is till this day recreated all over the world.

Such scenes, inspired by the Franciscans, went further than had hitherto been the custom in portraying the physical intimacy between mother and son: the grotto sanctuary was adorned in the fourteenth century with a painting of Mary placing her breast into the swaddled Christ's mouth.[9] Franciscan churches all over Europe followed in making and displaying their own humble Nativity scenes. These, in turn, determined the imaginative world within which the Incarnation was perceived.[10] The Franciscans, who were nominated as custodians of Christian sites in the Holy Land after the fall of the Latin kingdoms of the east in 1291, invested Holy Land pilgrimages with the imagery of humble birth. The guidebook to the Holy Land written by the humanist Francesco Petrarca (1302–74) recommends that the assiduous pilgrim visit Bethlehem and find there a scene reminiscent of panels depicting Nativity scenes in parish churches: 'You will contemplate the virgin mother lying in the manger and the divine child wailing in the cradle, the angels that sing in heaven, the stunned shepherds, the stupefied foreign kings who prostrate themselves with gifts.'[11]

The Incarnation and the Crucifixion offered the two focal points for devotional experience, and these were powerfully linked in the experiences of lay people, guided by preachers, priests and artists. Mary's

own infancy was also imagined through the ancient narratives of the *Protogospel of James*; her life as a mother arose from the gospel accounts of her son's birth and infancy, and then there was the cycle of her own later life, following the Crucifixion and on to her own Dormition and Assumption.[12] All these themes were known in the monasteries of Europe from the end of the first millennium; from the thirteenth century they became increasingly accessible in vernacular words and images too.

Making Mary's life and her son's infancy available in the vernacular encouraged the absorption of local details of family life. It was also fraught with the danger of transgression and impropriety. A good example is the mid-thirteenth-century French *Evangile de l'Enfance*, which incorporated material from the gospels of John and Luke as well as from the *Infancy Gospel of Pseudo-Matthew*. In these stories Jesus is seen as a precocious boy within an adoring family. He was young but all-knowing, and he used his powers to protect his parents and outwit their enemies. He was sometimes extremely naughty, but always particularly close to his mother.[13] In the service of his family Jesus deployed his unusual gifts: on the Flight into Egypt he caused trees to bend down and offer their fruit to the hungry Mary.[14] The Flight also provided frames for the portrayal of family togetherness: Joseph leads the group with care and manfully confronts robbers who attack them en route.[15]

A thirteenth-century Italian copy of the Pseudo-Matthew *Infancy Gospel* has a powerful rendering of Mary and Joseph as patrons of Jesus' schooling: Mary leads her son, armed with his wax tablet and ink horn, to a classroom that looks disrupted and threatening.[16] In the crypt of Siena cathedral, where pilgrims congregated for instruction before their entry into church, frescoes depicted Jesus as a schoolboy writing on a diptych at school.[17] The image of Jesus going to school under Mary's tutelage meant a great deal to those engaged in training the young: Burkard of Winon, a Swiss canon of Beromünster, who held several appointments as choir master as well as priest, chose the scene of Mary leading her son to school to adorn his own personal seal.[18]

For all his love of his mother, young Jesus detested her people. Jews are presented in the *Infancy Gospel* in sharp caricature as cruel teachers, evil relatives and malign neighbours. The scene of instruction was particularly poignant; it often described an unruly Jewish classroom with swarthy children and a cruel Jewish teacher. Indeed, one of the tales in the Anglo-Norman *Les Enfaunces de Jesu Crist* was illustrated with a

scene of the teacher slapping Jesus on the cheek.[19] The Jews disliked Mary's special boy, they resented his arrogance and pride as well as his boisterous self-display. Some even felt he should be chastised, or worse:

> He should not live with us here,
> But we should crucify him
> Hang him or burn him or skin him
> Because he is destroying all our laws;
> I want him to be put on a cross.[20]

The Jews of Nazareth were clearly already plotting Jesus' end, and so he deployed his gifts against them. When Jewish neighbours refused to let their children play with him, the boy Jesus turned their children into pigs.[21] Such tales, which vary in origin and antiquity, length and moment, were assembled into the all-important collection of sacred narrative produced by the Dominican Jacobus da Voragine (1230–98), archbishop of Genoa, around 1260: the *Golden Legend* (*Legenda Aurea*). The stories of Christian saints were combined chronologically according to their feast day in the calendar. Mary's life was told from before her birth and until her unusual 'death'.

The *Golden Legend*'s influence was immense, and over a thousand manuscript copies still survive. Mary's stories appear in several locations under her feast days – winter, spring and summer – most at her Assumption.[22] The *Golden Legend* served artists particularly well. It provided a full and colourful account of Mary's life and allowed visual depictions of it to follow, like Giotto's frescoes of the Arena chapel outside Padua, or Duccio's *Maesta* in Siena, or Pietro Lorenzetti's *Nativity of the Virgin*. A book of canticles and hymns of Canterbury cathedral contains an illustrated Passion cycle with French captions: one scene shows Mary's body being prepared for burial by a number of women in the presence of the apostles, and the next a solemn procession with two Jews in disarray who had been trying to disrupt it. Similarly, the Dominicans of the priory in Thetford (Suffolk) celebrated the mass in front of an altar panel made *c.*1335 which depicted scenes of Mary's life: Nativity, Dormition, Adoration of the Magi, and the less common scene of Anne teaching Mary to read. Mary is the focus of the painting, and her own childhood learning on the right end parallels her son's childhood on the left.[23] The more modest church of Chalgrove (Oxford) was decorated by 1329 with wall paintings depicting Mary's life. The scene of Mary's

funeral shows the apostles bearing the weight of her bier and three hook-nosed men – Jews – tugging at it. The hand of one of the Jews is stuck to the bier and he dangles from it. The parishioners were expected to fill in the gaps in the tale since the next scene, right underneath, is one of jubilation as a crowd gathers around Mary, witnesses to her Assumption.[24]

Great preachers made use of the *Golden Legend*. It was disseminated systematically through all Dominican convents, but secular clergy and other preachers used it too.[25] In the fourteenth century it reached even wider audiences in translations into the vernacular. It brought Mary's life as child, wife, mother and bereft older woman to a large audience and in great detail. This style also had its detractors: a late fourteenth-century English text critical of the methods by which preachers entertained their audiences claimed that the Carmelites habitually lied in telling Mary stories:

> They pretend to be Mary's men, so they tell people,
> And lie about our Lady many a long tale . . .[26]

MOTHER AND SON

Mary gave her son life, and like all parents was understood by contemporaries to share a single substance with her offspring. The substance was the body and its many dispositions. The intimacy of mother and son was usually explored in new postures and gestures. Mary and the Christ Child seated on her lap were familiar from statues in parish churches, like those of the twelfth-century Auvergne region, or of Catalonia. These statues were trunk-like, majestic and static. They sometimes served as receptacles for relics and were meant to be seen in the round and to be carried on processional occasions.[27] Other representations, on painted panels and illuminated parchment, similarly showed Mary as a frontal, majestic and static figure of deep wisdom and purity.

These images were giving way in the thirteenth century to representations that emphasized the emotions which flowed between Mary and her son. The monastic chronicler Matthew Paris (1200–1259) had as illustration to his *Greater Chronicle* (*Chronica Majora*) a page depicting three versions of Christ's head: above, Mary and Christ as Child; below

left, the suffering face of the crucified Christ with closed eyes; and bottom right, a frontal and serene resurrected Christ.[28] In the upper image Mother and Son all but merge, depicted in the same flesh tones, adorned by similarly jewelled collars, very close and involved with each other. All this was new. In the Schernberg Psalter, made in Strasbourg in the same period, Mary and Son form the centre of an arrangement that depicts the Tree of Jesse, David, Solomon, Isaiah and Jeremiah, each within a roundel, proclaiming prophetic words about the Incarnation. The faces of mother and son touch delicately, and their expressions are schematic but full of joy.[29]

The desire to explore the bond between mother and child led artists to adjust or adapt the traditional serene pairing of the two. The new style of representation engaged with movement and hinted at a narrative. Between mother and child there are now smiles, gestures and food – rich with biblical associations – pomegranate, grape or apple. This type of representations of Mary and child deeply affected European – and later global – ideas about motherhood, beauty and affection.[30] A Mary and Child tabernacle from the Norwegian church of Dal (near Telemark) of c.1260 is made of brightly painted oak and pine. Although the pose is frontal, the Child leans to his left, his hand raised, and his mother wears an enigmatic smile.[31] The frontal Mary is still detectable in the wooden sculpture of c.1300 from Girona – the Virgin of Hope (*Verge de l'Esperança*); it shows Mary with a rounded, pregnant belly, not a lively baby son. The vibrant colours that once covered it are still in evidence.[32] Mary was reworked in distinct regional styles, but the overwhelming trend is one towards expression of emotion through movement and gesture.

Even when the frontal form was retained it could engage with the viewer, tell a story and elicit a response. Consider a group from the church of Saint-Pierre de Vivegnis in Oupeye (Belgium) of around 1270, which forms part of a tabernacle once used in the local abbey.[33] It was hollowed out in the back and so was probably visible only from the front and sides. The neatly seated group of Mary and son is majestic: Mary is dressed in gold (the original colours have recently been restored), crowned and veiled; the Child is dressed in a dark blue garment decorated with a *fleur-de-lys*, the symbol of French royalty and all those who could claim dynastic links to it.[34] Both reach out to the viewer: Mary with a red sphere (an apple or a sceptre), while the Child Jesus stretches out his hand. Both smile, their eyes directed at the viewer.

The traditional enthroned Mary and Child group was further elaborated when scenes of Mary's life were added to painted or carved altarpieces. In a Catalan altar frontal from the church of Santa Maria in Cardet (Boi valley) of the second half of the thirteenth century, Mary and Son sit with a slight inclination to their right within a *mandorla* – an almond-shaped frame – while around them scenes of Mary's life were depicted in lively colour and dramatic movement. The Nativity scene is particularly striking, with a large and dominating Joseph at the centre alongside his wife on her bed and the baby in his crib.[35] A panel painted around 1260–70 by Coppo di Marcovaldo for the church of Santa Maria Maggiore in Florence similarly surrounded an enthroned Mary and Child with attendant figures and below them included scenes of the Annunciation and Resurrection. It was an image-reliquary with remains of the cross.[36]

The greatest imaginative leap around the figure of Mary and her Child occurred in Northern Europe – especially in northern France – where it was redesigned to express abundant emotion. Mary becomes a person on the move, full of affective energy, in touch with her son. While Mary habitually held her son on her knee, artists of the thirteenth century experimented with the many ways in which mother and son might engage with each other, exploring posture and play. Curves and movement were now part of the image of Mary and her son within a story that unfolded again and again in stone and wood, on parchment and in glass.

In the Ile-de-France and Champagne regions of northern France, ideas about feminine beauty – touched by classical norms of bodily proportions and texture – merged with notions of virtue and decorum, into the epitome of Gothic grace, the S-shaped Mary and Child.[37] By the mid-thirteenth century workshops in Paris produced ivories that captured the smile and the drapery familiar from carvings in cathedral doorways.[38] These were absorbed with ease into the contiguous Anglo-Norman domain and from there spread out to the extremities of the British Isles. In these groups drapery enveloped Mary's body to hint at her fecundity; it emphasized the volume and life of her limbs, celebrated her youth and beauty and hinted at something beyond.

Regional styles determined the shape of these new representations of Mother and Son. Some retained the attachment to static presence, and in sculpture this meant that the statue retained much of its vertical

trunk-like shape. Others experimented with the possibilities of movement. A panel painting by the Master of Tressa for Siena cathedral, the *Madonna of the Large Eyes* (*Madonna dagli occhi grossi*), has Mary against a gold background facing forward, her son half-seated, half-standing in her lap, blessing and holding a parchment roll. Their faces are symmetrical and betray little emotion, though Mary's eyes are as dark and penetrating as those shown on icons since the sixth century. In fourteenth-century Wales the two types of Mary and Child co-existed: a stone carving at Grosmont church (Gwent) shows a frontal Mary and Child, while the parishioners of St Iltrud in Llantwit Major (Glamorgan) regarded a crowned and curved Mary with long tresses and the hint of a smile. Mary's smile is sometimes directed away from her son, as in the Michle Madonna made in Brno (Moravia) around 1340.[39]

By the late thirteenth century the tenderness of Mary and her son reached far and wide. A vestment from the tomb of Pope Gregory X (d.1267) is decorated with an embroidered scene showing the departed at the feet of a seated Mary carefully placing a pale breast in her son's eager mouth.[40] A window endowed by the bishop of Hereford in Eaton Bishop (Herefordshire) parish church c.1320 is a blend of colour, shape and play: Mary's body leans toward the weight of her son, who stands on her hip, supported by her left arm. They gaze at each other as the boy, with a bird in his left hand, reaches for his mother's chin with his right. Against the bright reds and greens of Mary's clothes and background, the Child in white marks the space of purity, answered by the whiteness of his mother's veil. Their eyes, with dot-like irises, are fully at play; something very intimate is happening here. A similar performance of intimacy is captured in the De Lisle Psalter, made for Robert de Lisle (1288–1344). Mary is seated, but her body takes the shape of an S, and her son plays with her veil and her dress – maybe looking for her breast – within a formal decorated archway. Another seated figure of Mary, a French ivory of 1325–50, similarly captures some of the movement that standing statues exploit so fully: Mary and the Child Jesus are engaged in placing the breast within the infant's mouth, each holding the breast, the boy's hand on his mother's as if for reassurance.[41] The wooden statue now in the Finnish parish of Raisio (near Turku) shows Mary standing with a slight movement of her body towards her left, not an elegant Gothic S, but a gesture

nonetheless. The tree-trunk has yielded to the carver and Mary smiles at her beholder.[42]

An extremely influential blending of styles and tastes – the static solemnity of Byzantine Mary and the soft tones of French painting and sculpture – was achieved in Siena, a city which defined itself as Mary's own.[43] From the early thirteenth century local artists produced a version of the highly influential Italo-Byzantine tradition: religious imagery suffused in light, with warm skin tones, with highly decorative golden backgrounds. Perched on the Via Francigena – the main artery that linked France and Italy, Northern Europe and its South – Siena was well positioned to create a vision of Mary that blended Northern European style with local artistic traditions. Thirteenth-century Sienese artists explored the possibilities of representing Mary, patron of their city and of its hinterland, since 1260, when the victory over Florence at the Battle of Montaperti was attributed to her help.[44] Duccio's *Madonna of the Franciscans* shows Mary looking forward; her body is relaxed and languid as her son blesses three kneeling friars.[45] His *Maestà* of 1308–11 is a summary of Mary's life and is inscribed with his dedication: 'Holy Mother of God, be the cause of peace to Siena, and of life to Duccio, because he has painted thee thus'.[46] The Sienese Madonnas were a brilliant blending of eastern and western tastes – golden solemnity combined with an emotional liveliness – that it was admired all over Europe. It is likely that the image revered at the Bright Mountain shrine near the town of Częstochowa – an image which drew pilgrims from all over Central and Eastern Europe – was a fourteenth-century work in that very Sienese style.[47]

The younger Sienese artist Simone Martini (active 1315–d.1344) explored Mary's expression, delighted in the shape of her limbs and placed her elegant figure against fields of gold, as the panel of Mary and Child made for the church of Lucignano d'Arbia shows.[48] The Sienese style continued to combine extraordinary serenity with adventures in mother-child play: a Mary and Child panel by Lippo Memmi (c.1290–1347) of 1330 for the church of St Augustine in San Gimignano has the Child Jesus eagerly placing his mother's nipple in his mouth; another of his panels has the Child Christ holding tight on to his mother's veil.[49] By the end of the fourteenth century Mary and Child groups have very distinctive features, detailed clothes and a family resemblance: Giovanni Fei's (c.1345–1411) panel in the great church of San Domenico in Siena,

where the local saint Catherine of Siena habitually prayed, is an example of bodily intimacy and familial closeness.[50]

Other figures were occasionally introduced into the intimate group of Mother and Child. Rich donors could realize in their commissions an imagined world of delight in Mary's maternal embrace. In a missal of c.1250 Henry of Chichester, precentor of Crediton (Devon), kneels at the feet of Mary's throne, eliciting an interest from the Child Jesus, who turns towards Henry and touches a scroll with the words 'Son of God have mercy on me'.[51] Similarly, a nun kneels to the right of Mary feeding the Child Jesus in the Amesbury Psalter of c. 1250, with the words of Gabriel's message inscribed on a scroll: 'Ave Maria full of grace the Lord is with you'.[52] The Lambeth Apocalypse of c.1260–67 has the patron, Lady Eleanor de Quincy, Countess of Winchester, outside the frame of the image of Mary – crowned and holding a bird – and her son.[53] Alice de Reymes, wife of the royal servant Sir Robert de Reydon, for whom the Reydon Book of Hours was made c.1320–24, kneels to the left of Mary and Child.[54] Mary is sumptuously dressed, crowned and seated, while Jesus stands on her left knee. The group is contained within the letter D accompanying Psalm 51:15: 'O Lord, open my lips'.

The group of Mary and Christ Child offered a focus not only for the telling of her life, but also, and increasingly, for the telling of the whole Christian story. As images of Mary grew in complexity and potential, they became sites for comprehensive telling of the Christian story. An ivory tabernacle, probably from Paris c.1300, is a good example: when opened it had in the centre a crowned Mary with a blessing Son on her left arm: either side of her were the Annunciation, the Nativity, the Adoration of the Magi and the Presentation in the Temple. Mary and her Son offered meaning and purpose to the ensemble.[55]

Mary and Son images were keenly juxtaposed with scenes of the Crucifixion, offering a beginning and end, indeed a beginning that foretold the end. A pier of St Albans abbey church was painted in the thirteenth century with the Virgin and Child enthroned below, and the Crucifixion scene, with Mary and John, above.[56] Similarly, an English ivory panel of the early fourteenth century has a frontal group of Mary and Child in deep relief at the lower register while a Crucifixion was carved above.[57] In the 1280s and 1290s two Tuscan painters – the Magdalen Master and the San Gaggio Master – created an altar panel (*dossal*) with twelve, often crowded, scenes of the Passion, but in its

209

centre a crowned Mary and Son, frontal and majestic, attended by angels.[58] Artists juxtaposed Mary's life with Christ's in a variety of combinations of elements from each: a Flemish ivory diptych of 1340–60 has Mary and Child enthroned above the Dormition on the left and the Nativity above the Passion and the Entombment on the right. At different stages of their respective lives Mary and her Son appear in each of the scenes.[59]

Mary was increasingly portrayed as equal to her son in dignity and purpose. Devotional objects reflect this relationship, like the Salting diptych, a gilt and painted ivory diptych made in England around 1310–20. When opened, the left side contained a wonderfully carved relief figure of Mary and Child, while at the right stood the figure of the adult Jesus holding an open book, and blessing with his right hand.[60] The figures are of equal size, and they share style and fineness of detail. While Jesus' open book reads 'I am the Lord thy God, Jesus Christ, who made, redeemed, and saved you', there is no doubt that he achieved all this thanks to the mother who brought him into the world. Mary and Jesus were a pair, working together.

The interweaving of Mary and Jesus' stories was arranged in interesting ways, many of which suggested parity of esteem and interest. The wall paintings made in the parish church of Croughton (Northamptonshire) reflect a carefully judged balance between Mary's life on the south aisle and Christ's ministry on the north aisle. The scenes of Jesus' childhood form part of 'Mary's' wall, while the north wall begins with the entry into Jerusalem. Further scenes were painted (some now destroyed) in the Lady chapel, like St Anne teaching Mary to read.[61]

Artists considered carefully the setting of the lives of Mary and Jesus, and Mary enters prominently into her son's life. A Parisian ivory of around 1325–35 interweaves the Mary and Jesus scenes: it progressed from the lowest register where it shows the Annunciation, the Visitation, the Annunciation to Shepherds, the Nativity and the Adoration of the Magi; to the middle tier of Christ's life: the Presentation, Jesus in the Temple, the Marriage at Cana, and the Last Supper; Mary is also portrayed in the final upper scenes of the Crucifixion, Resurrection, Ascension, Pentecost and her Coronation.[62] A later ivory diptych of 1350–75 has Mary with Child crowned by an angel, on the left, and the Crucifixion with a fainting Mary on the right. Their lives were intertwined, as were their bodies.[63] A diptych painted by Simone Martini

(d.1344) presents equal in size the Mother and Child on the left and the Man of Sorrows half-risen from his tomb, wounds bleeding, on the right.[64] Mary and Jesus emerge from these biblical scenes as equal protagonists within a hectic and dramatic Christian story.

MARY'S BREASTS AND FAMILY NURTURE

Throughout the thirteenth century Mary developed into a beautiful, feminine figure, with long locks of hair and a graceful body portrayed in movement and gesture. Her skin is smooth and her face without flaw. Her body is often explored with particular attention to her breasts, which became more visible in art and more explicitly considered in poetry. This was the body part to which Mary's son – a God – was most attached, where he sucked his food. While the lore attached to the Song of Songs offered a great number of inspiring images of the beloved's breast, poetry and imagery were catching up too. Source of food and nurture, the breast was a sign of Mary's love. Since Mary cared for all Christians she was imagined as baring her breast when she pleaded for sinners. This sentiment was captured in a prayer by the Irish bard Giolla Brighde Mac Con Midhe: 'May the breast that was laid to His lips be between me and fierce-hosted hell', or, similarly, by Donnchadh Mór Ó Dálaigh: 'May my sister's Son bring me safely to death . . . owing to the breasts whence He drank of thy substance'.[65] Mary was depicted as offering her breast as she interceded for humans at the Last Judgement, as part of the awesome scene of reward and retribution. In the Huth Psalter, which was made in England around 1280, she kneels in front of the enthroned Christ in Majesty, a queen humbling herself in front of her Lord, and revealing her breast from under an ermine-lined cloak.[66]

The breast captures everything that is good and much that is lost.[67] Smell, taste, touch, sight and even sound were lived and learned at the breast. Mary's material motherhood, as taught and shown in images and words, led poets to explore desire at its utmost: they created poetry which saw love, food and nurture combined at Mary's breast. The full meaning of such enunciations is too personal for us to appreciate fully, but the sensation they evoke is clear. The verses from the *Life of Mary*

(*Marienleben*) by the poet Werner the Swiss imagine Jesus' apprehension of his mother's breasts:

> Two noble dates, little apples,
> sweet and fair:
> God saw them
> and came thither
> in search of sustenance,
> took them at once
> in His mouth
> with joy:
> thus his love was set on fire.
> I mean, if I may praise it,
> your noble breast, full of grace,
> beautiful,
> so praiseworthy
> that God himself valued
> it above all that was ever His,
> lauds it with worthiness,
> wished to thrive and grow at it:
> for it was His desire
> to kiss it,
> he nestled against it,
> suckled it with joy
> and entered your womb:
> Wherefore your praise will always be great![68]

Here is the astonishing suggestion that God so loved being a baby at the breast, even a foetus in the womb, that he sought to re-enter Mary's body and unmake the Incarnation! The poet imagines the fulfilment of the desire for Mary's breast in Jesus' return to it and into Mary's body. Others imagined that return in fantasies of oneness with Mary. Finding that breast, that milk, was an active search. The German poet Frauenlob's (c.1250–1318) *Song of Songs* has the lovers in the cellar:

> Tell no lie, never try to deny:
> you alone were meeting
> with the king
> in his cellar –

you knew his greeting
you felt his touch. How much,
fair maid, did you dally?
We do not envy the wine of bliss
You drank there with sweet, sweet milk.[69]

The boy at the breast was part of a nurturing family with mother, father, and relatives too. Mary offered a model for good wifely conduct. A bourgeois of Paris wrote $c.1393$ a handbook for his future young wife with instructions on all her duties from kitchen to bedroom. Mary offered some useful lessons:

And, by God, it is not always the season to say to one's ruler: 'I will do naught, it is not reasonable'; greater good cometh by obeying, wherefore I take my e[x]ample from the words of the Blessed Virgin Mary, when the Angel Gabriel brought her tidings that Our Lord should be conceived in her. She did not answer, 'It is not reasonable, I am maid and virgin, I will not suffer it, I shall be defamed'; but obediently she answered, '*Fiat mihi secundum verbum tuum*', as who should say, Be it unto me according to thy word. Thus was she truly humble and obedient, and of her humility and obedience great good hath come to us, and by disobedience and pride cometh great ill and a foul end, as is aforesaid concerning her that was burnt and as ye may read in the Bible of Eve, by whose disobedience and pride she and all women that were and shall be after her, were and have been accursed by the word of God.[70]

Unlike the thrust of the *Infancy Gospel* Jesus appears here to be a good boy from a modest but loving home. Joseph provided for his family by working at 'his craft of Carpentry', Mary spun 'with the distaff and needle, cooking their food and doing all other household chores'.[71] By the fourteenth century, Tuscan panels depicted Mary knitting too: Tommaso da Modena ($1325-75$) portrayed her sharing the throne with her son, who looks at his mother's handiwork. Ambrogio Lorenzetti depicted Mary sitting on the floor knitting while her husband and son look on.[72] The knitted garment is carefully drawn in an altarpiece of $c.1410$; it is a seamless tunic which foretells the perfection of Christ.[73]

The Holy Family was busy at wholesome work and led a virtuous life. An illustration to a thirteenth-century version of the *Infancy Gospel of Pseudo-Matthew* has father and son sawing a plank of wood.[74] Jesus helped his parents by going about his chores and making the bed. The

same *Infancy Gospel* depicts Jesus fetching water from a fountain, albeit miraculously. The family worked, ate and prayed together in a house which was 'not large . . . but rather small'.[75] When Jesus was tested in the wilderness and is finally ministered to by angels, all he could ask for after his ordeals was some of his mother's home cooking 'for there is no bodily food so tasty to me as that made by her'. The angels obliged, flew home to her and returned with 'that simple food that she had made for herself and Joseph'.[76]

In Mary's acceptance of her mission, mirrored in the delicate curve of her body at the Annunciation, artists found an appealing way of celebrating Mary's femininity and offering it to their audiences. Chaste and docile, reading her book, Mary of the thirteenth and fourteenth centuries is an ideal type for young womanhood: accepting, obedient, beautiful and full of grace.[77] She increasingly served as a subject for altarpieces and especially for smaller, domestic shrines. Such is the portable altarpiece made in the late fourteenth century by Master Bertram, an Annunciation scene set against an abstract gold background.[78]

By the early fourteenth century Mary and her mother Anne were often combined to form a scene of tender motherhood similar to that of Mary and her son. English manuscripts contain some of the earliest scenes, usually within psalters, books from which mothers often taught their children to read. Such a psalter has a tiny Mary enveloped under her mother's cloak while holding a tablet with the letters 'DOMINE' ('Lord').[79] A book of the lives of saints from the same period includes an image of mother and daughter where Mary is only slightly shorter than Anne. Here too the haloed figures are engaged in a reading lesson, using Psalm 24:4, 'the clean of hand and pure of heart'.[80] There was great interest in portraying Mary with Anne in parish churches, with tens of surviving examples from fourteenth-century England alone. The gold on the draperies still can be seen on Anne's figure, in a scene of Anne teaching Mary to read in Kersey parish church in Suffolk; Anne is there the image of a respectable older woman.[81] So keen was the desire to augment Anne's place within the Holy Kindred that a wooden statue of Mary and Child that had served the parish of Urjula (Finland) was redesigned with the Mary figure becoming Anne, and the baby Jesus made into the little crowned Mary, now with an orb in her hand.[82]

Anne's steady elevation to the position of a matron who represented dynastic dignity and virtue is evident in the choices made by the com-

mune of Florence to incorporate her into civic worship. After the plague of 1348 the commune directed the Confraternity of Orsanmichele to use some of its substantial endowment – accumulated from the bequests of the members who died in the plague – towards the construction of a 'church or chapel' of St Anne and the support of a priest there.[83] The church was soon completed and was adorned with a statue, later moved into Orsanmichele, of Anne, Mary and Jesus.[84] In Tuscany the Holy Family was extended further, with the advent of the story of Ismeria, Anne's own mother.[85]

Mary entered the rich and interesting life-worlds of family and hearth, work and leisure. Biblical stories were told afresh by preachers in order to emphasize her extraordinary virtues, which were nonetheless imitable. The Visitation, for example, became more than a casual visit by a travelling woman (Mary) to an older relative (Elizabeth). In his sermon for the Annunciation the Franciscan Federico Visconti (d.1277), archbishop of Pisa, described Mary's humility in visiting but also serving her cousin Elizabeth for three months.[86] This type of creativity with the stories of Mary, their unceasing elaboration, the colouring of them with local hues, raised objections from some commentators. A sermon from late-fourteenth-century England maintained Mary's purity and used it to dismantle long traditions of stories about her:

For just as the sun comes through glass, just so the Holy Ghost caused both the conception and the birth of the blessed child, without defect of body or any disease in the worthy maiden's body, his mother. And this also proves well that she needed no midwives at that time, nor any help at that birth, as other women do. And so, those who say that Anastasia was Our Lady's midwife with withered hands at the time that her hands were healed, are dreaming.[87]

Within household images of Mary were embossed on objects for daily use. A Flemish wooden marriage casket covered with leather of the late fourteenth century was decorated with scenes of amorous chases and hunt, but when it was opened the calm figure of a seated Mary and her son beside a closed garden welcomed the female user. The wife-to-be was about to move from the sphere of the chase into that of settled motherhood, represented by Mary.

The longing and desire associated with human love contributed to the making of Mary. Here is, indeed, a contradiction, one of the 'problems' with Mary. In her was to be found a niche for every type of woman:

young maiden, chaste widows, hard-pressed housewife, leisured bookish reader, the shy as well as the outgoing, the tongue-tied and the eloquent. In her figure were already engrained the possibilities of silence as well as song, modesty as well as majesty, innocence as well as wisdom. Each and every Christian could find a place in Mary.

13

Teaching Mary in Parish and Home

The components of Christian instruction in parishes had been clearly defined throughout the thirteenth century through the efforts of popes and church councils and were disseminated to all regions of Europe by bishops and their administrations. Handbooks for the clergy, often composed by bishops and distributed in their dioceses, aimed to summarize clearly the points which parish priests then taught. Among other basic teachings the Ave Maria and the Creed were conveyed to each parishioner at a young age, and they imparted an understanding of Mary's place in the Christian story. Preaching, visual imagery and the experience of liturgy reinforced parish instruction of the laity.

MARY IN PARISH INSTRUCTION

None is more down to earth in his writings for the parish than the Kentish priest William of Shoreham, who served the parish of Chart-Sutton around the year 1320. His poem on the Five Joys of the Virgin opens with Mary's queenly stature that defies all efforts to praise her. She bore the King of Heaven, and so God was obliged to worship her just as humans did:

> When he who will judge the whole world
> is bound to worship her
> because of her motherhood.[1]

One way of approaching Mary was by considering five of her joys – four of them experienced on earth, like streams out of a well of bliss that is her son, the last in heaven. Drawing upon the rich world

217

of Marian tales, these moments are described in detail. First the Conception, foretold by Gabriel and experienced in her own body:

> So he came inside her
> To take from her flesh and blood
> As the angel had told her.[2]

The second joy was the Nativity, and in it Mary was joined by the ox and the ass, who rejoiced 'in their own way', by the Three Kings and by Simeon, to whom Jesus was presented in the Temple. The third joy was the Resurrection, the fulfilment of the angel's message, accompanied by the movement of earth ('erthe schok') and the pomp of heralding angels. Above all Mary wished to share this joy with her friends. William comments that the joy is greater for being shared with friends, especially following the great sorrow (of her son's death):

> Our Lady used this bliss herself,
> And all her friends in her time,
> So much is greater for that reason.[3]

The fourth joy was the Ascension and the fifth her own Assumption. Mary's early joys were the vicarious thrills of a mother at her son's coming and his progress in the world. In the fifth joy her son gave her what was due: respect and love. He came to take her home to his dwelling:

> And Christ himself came into her
> And took up with him body and soul
> Into his own dwelling.[4]

The poem ends with an exhortation to pray to Mary, now Queen in Heaven, for delivery from troubles.

Pastoral and devotional verses such as these conveyed a great deal of lore about Mary in accessible local idiom. In them Mary is portrayed as a mother surrounded by family and friends. Neighbourhood Mary shares her joys with kith and kin. She supports her son and delights in his unusual progress in the world, and he in turn cherishes her. The poem conveys no complex theology; it is neither polemical nor exotic in its imagery. It is biblical narrative writ small.

William of Shoreham experimented with another rhetorical mode in his *On the Virgin Mary*, with strings of titles and praise of Mary in a

mode familiar since the seventh-century *akathistos* hymn. William appeals to Mary as container (chamber) of the Trinity and asks that she listen to his song. He then mines the Hebrew Bible for images and likeness – Noah's dove, the bush at Sinai (which did not burn) – and if she was the boy David's sling, then her son – tightly packed within her – was the stone. Mary was the rod of Aaron, the Temple of Solomon and a source of wonder to Gideon and Simeon. He then moves on to female biblical figures, beginning with the violent Judith:

> You are Judith, that fair woman,
> You have abated all that strife,
> With his knife you
> Beheaded Holofernes.[5]

Mary was sweet, like Esther:

> You are Esther, that sweet thing,
> And Xerxes, the rich king,
> Has chosen you for his wife.[6]

Mary's body was closed shut like Ezekiel's Gate, she was as fair as Rachel, and – moving to the gospels – like the resting-place at Emmaus. The poem then ends with an invocation of medieval myth and Christian apocalypse: for Mary is like the pure maiden who tamed the unicorn, just as she must be the woman with a crown of twelve stars. Thanks to all these attributes, Mary is an excellent source of strength. And so the poem ends with hope for a beneficial exchange:

> Have, Lady, this little song
> That has sprung out of a sinful heart.
> Make me strong against the devil,
> And give me the knowledge
> And grant me amends for
> Any thing I have done wrong.[7]

The intimacy of family life was explored in detail in devotional writings for the spiritually expert, but also for those of more modest training and less leisure. A thirteenth-century German vernacular account of the Assumption opened by reminding its audience that Mary and Jesus were of 'one flesh and blood' ('ein fleihz vn ein blut'), hence the son granted his mother a special end.[8] The mundane home life, familiar to all, was

the milieu chosen by the author of the *Mirror of the Life of Jesus*, an alternative to secular romances. The gospel portion for each feast day was offered in translation and then explained. In the discussion of Luke 1:26–38 for the Annunciation, Mary's purity and fecundity are celebrated through the explication of the name 'Nazareth', from the Hebrew word for bloom:

Mary was in Nazareth, for all goodness flowered in her. She flowered and brought forth in such a way that her body was whole . . . When she flowered and brought forth fruit she remained a maiden here and there.

Mary was fecund but also chaste. The marriage of Mary and Joseph was similarly full of contradiction: it was chaste and yet could serve as an example for all marriages:

It is right that a virgin should marry a virgin. Also, those who have been married, if they remain together without any controversy, in chastity, doing the fleshly deed only for procreation, then they follow the example of Joseph and of Mary.[9]

Although they were chaste, William of Shoreham portrayed Mary and Joseph to his parishioners as an example for married life. Images of conjugality and joint parenting suggested that a chaste marriage was nonetheless real. Illuminations capture this intimacy with a new tenderness, like the English psalter in which Joseph holds a walking stick, wears a Jew's hat but sits erect and vigilant, guarding the space in which his son and wife peacefully sleep.[10] Yet the unusual tale could also be told in a more ambivalent fashion. An Italian devotional text even contemplated Joseph suffering when he heard the news of his young wife's pregnancy: a miniature is devoted to Joseph's distress as he contemplates leaving Mary; he sits demurely in their house and looks back at her with sadness.[11]

The vernacular vision of Mary, inspired so powerfully by Franciscan preachers and conveyed for easy reference by the *Golden Legend*, was made available through parish teaching, often illustrated by scenes of Mary's life painted on the walls of churches. Altarpieces situated in the candle-lit centres of sacramental action – the parish High Altar – occasionally told Mary's life, too. There was a coming together of the appreciation of Jesus' humanity – a child at his mother's breast – and the tenor of vernacular teaching to the laity: it was meant above all to make familiar and cherished the figure of Mary and her saving Child.

Those who could afford the luxury of private books explored the rich associations with Mary as loving mother even further.

MARY IN BOOKS OF HOURS

Liturgy and music animated the life of the religious, those who served in cathedrals and great churches. It also enriched the lives of privileged lay people who had access to such places. The desire of such people for more variety and for aids in personal participation led to the creation of special textual collections. These offered the psalms, together with prayers for special occasions, and was often accompanied by illustrations and useful instruction in prayer.

Liturgical offices were organized around the eight canonical hours – sessions of prayer – and these achieved a weekly recitation of all 150 psalms. To this monastic psalter were added in the twelfth century other necessary prayers: the office of the dead, liturgy for saints' days, prayers and hymns for Mary and her feasts.[12] By the thirteenth century a format had evolved for the use of lay people, which is often called a Book of Hours. It opened with a calendar, and included Offices of the Virgin, the Cross and the Holy Spirit, as well as well-known prayers. In some such books Mary's presence is paramount, each liturgical session marking an event in Mary life: Matins and Annunciation, Lauds and Visitation, Prime and Nativity, Terce and the Annunciation to the Shepherds, Sext and the Adoration of the Magi, None and the Presentation in the Temple, Vespers and the Flight into Egypt, and Compline with the Coronation of the Virgin. There was some variation on these themes, but the order held for most regions and tastes. In decorated prayer books miniatures represented the theme of each Hour.[13]

Books of Hours were used in homes and private chapels, with images that facilitated private meditation and prayer for those in search of consolation. In 1232 Hubert de Burgh, justiciar of England, was arrested for treason. He had all but given up hope of escaping execution and so immersed himself in his psalter for solace and begged Mary for help.[14] His psalter may have been a specifically Marian one. Such books were often made for women, often aristocratic users who taught children to read and pray from them.[15] A book made in Oxford c.1240 – the de Brailles Hours – was intended for a female user who is shown at prayer.[16]

The Latin psalms are decorated with scenes of Mary's life. The imagery accompanying Psalm 42 is particularly striking: at the bottom of the page three scenes from the story of Mary's Dormition appear in the roundels: from left to right these are Mary on her deathbed; the Jews attempting to topple Mary's bier, which we have encountered in the earliest versions of her Death; and Mary's empty tomb, evidence of her Assumption. Along the left margin there are two more scenes, placed in half-circles: at mid-page an angel carries Mary's soul, and above, Mary being crowned by her son in heaven. The psalms formed the matter of prayer, and the images reminded and reassured the user why Mary was indeed so worthy of supplication.

A great deal of thought and craft was invested in the making of Books of Hours. The Taymouth Hours of $c.1325-35$ was made for a royal woman, who is depicted in the illumination to the fifteenth psalm, being presented by Mary to Jesus, enthroned as a judge. The scenes at the bottom of this pair of pages show the rewards of the elect and the tribulations of the damned.[17] The Passion is treated in two scenes: one emphasizes the suffering of Christ's body; the other depicts Mary with John, distraught and in pain, taking little comfort from her son's words 'this is your son' which are inscribed above her head. The De Lisle Psalter was made for Robert de Lisle (1288–1344), and he bequeathed it to his two daughters, Audere and Alborou, with the expectation that it would pass after their death to Chicksands nunnery, near the family estates in Bedfordshire.[18] The book used by these provincial privileged women was a compendium of theology and moral precepts, adorned with excellent illuminations. Scenes from the Life of Christ offered occasions for portraying Mary in her nurturing maternal role. Clear moral instruction was presented in the paired images of the Tree of Vices and the Tree of Virtues, in which Mary is central too: the latter Tree grows out of the vase of the Annunciation, placed between Mary and the angel. At the bottom of the page the right corner is devoted to Mary: to a tender scene of the Visitation and to an image of Mary at the Annunciation. Mary of the Visitation has her hand on her belly, and words flow out of her mouth on a ribbon: 'Behold the handmaid of the Lord; be it unto me according to thy word' (Luke 1:38).[19]

This family psalter demonstrates how much part of the lives of privileged lay people Mary had become, people able to commission books full of Mary lore, to enjoy them and then to pass them on to their kin.

The De Lisle Psalter was made for a man who chose to end his life in a Franciscan convent: it displays the many ways in which Mary's motherhood and virginity were made immediate and relevant to the lives of engaged lay people. A full-page image portrays Mary and Child enthroned, against a gilt background. She is delicate, elegant and not too ornate.[20] Accompanied by the much-loved virgin martyrs – Catherine and Margaret – who trample under foot the lion and dragon of sin, the pair is engaged in tender play. Mary holds a flowering branch, her son reaches to her white veil and handles a goldfinch in his other hand; the two are deeply aware of each other. So when the reader's eye turns to the next page – the Crucifixion – the impact is all the more powerful: Mary still wears a brown dress and a cloak decorated with ermine, but she is now crownless, unveiled, beholding her son, the grown suffering man. In such a book owners and users were told a Christian story, which could neither be summarized nor effectively expounded without constant reference to Mary and to her maternal endorsement of the Saviour who was her son.

The space at the bottom of the pages of many such psalters and Books of Hours – the *bas-de-page* – often included narrative imagery from miracle tales. The Carew-Poyntz Book of Hours of 1350–60, made for Sir John Carew, provided a string of illuminations along the *bas-de-page*; these are new and old Mary miracle tales, several with Jewish protagonists. The well-known tale of the Jewish Boy is depicted over two pages; Mary intervenes to save the boy from his father's abuse within the Jewish home.[21] Such books included tales of sacred history with an emphasis on Mary's life and lineage. A late-thirteenth-century prayerbook for a woman of the diocese of Cambrai, 'Madame Marie', told the Christian story seamlessly from Mary's birth (with images of Anne and Joachim), through to the Nativity, and on to Christ's end. Mary is positioned centrally even in scenes of the Ascension and Pentecost. The cycle ends as it begins, with Mary's passage to the other world – her *trespassement* – and her Coronation.[22] Those who prayed from Books of Hours were also the recipients of the literature of religious guidance; they heard preaching, often from private chaplains, and recognized Marian miracle tales depicted in their prayer books. They experienced Mary in images, hymns, prayers and in the tales of her miraculous intervention in the world.

Those who used Books of Hours could also sense something of a

self-sufficiency and even develop their own ideas about Mary's power to intervene in their lives. Mary was imagined as an intercessor of great force who could determine the destiny of souls. The Parisian poet Rutebeuf ($c.1245–85$), whose poetry is earthy and irreverent, considers his end; he dreads facing it without Mary:

> Well should my heart weep,
> For never have I been able
> To serve God perfectly;
> Rather I have occupied myself
> With gambling and amusements,
> And never did I deign to read my psalms.
> If at my side on the Day of Judgement
> She in whom God took refuge is not there,
> I will have made an unwise wager.[23]

Her advocacy was a precious thing; indeed it entered the repertoire of religious drama in Normandy by the 1320s, *L'Advocacie de Nostre Dame*. A legal idiom described the terms by which she pleaded: 'She knows how to oppose and defend in order to confound our adversary.'[24] Others imagined Satan brought to trial, a genre that was highly popular with versions in Italian, Catalan, French and German, *Processus Satanae*.[25] There was a great deal at stake in the belief that Mary could act as an autonomous agent in support of humans. A chronicle account from Thuringia tells of an outburst during the performance of a religious drama, prompted by the suggestion that Mary could not pardon sinners. Count (*Landgraf*) Frederick of Thuringia was incensed as he watched the play of the Wise and Foolish Virgins in 1322: when the foolish virgins did not obtain grace he withdrew in anger, expostulating: 'What is Christian faith, if the prayers of Mary the blessed mother of God and those of all the saints cannot obtain pardon for a sinner?'[26] His death soon after inspired an edifying tale, but in his outburst the crusty nobleman expressed the abiding fear of the hereafter, and the utter centrality of Mary to beliefs in reward and retribution common among believers.

MARY — ALTERNATIVES AND REJECTION

There were, of course, those people who were not attracted to the figure of Mary as taught in the parishes and revered at home. There were Christians – and their numbers had been growing since the mid-twelfth century – who adhered to a dualist understanding of the world, and to whom the notion of mingled divinity and humanity was anathema. There were the Jews of Europe who did not believe in Jesus as a Messiah and found unreasonable the claim that his mother conceived by a Holy Spirit, gave birth and remained a virgin. Muslims, as we will see, were considered more benignly disposed towards Mary and, as we have seen, had their own respectful understanding of her. Although the numbers of all these groups are rather small, they were concentrated in particular regions and places: the Jews in cities, the Cathars in the Rhineland, southern France and northern Italy, and Muslims above all in Iberian cities. It was not the number that matters here, but the very challenge such groups raised, for the institutions of the church had the sole right to authorize beliefs and to teach them; they were also charged with identifying error and correcting it. In this work the orders of friars were particularly active, but secular rulers contributed their manpower – lawyers, bailiffs – in the effort to fight the 'disease of heresy'. Kings staged disputations, like that initiated by King Louis IX of France in 1240, in which the Jewish Law – the Talmud – was put on trial for blasphemies against Mary; some allowed the papal inquisition to operate in their domains. Mary was not the main theme, but she was part of the continuous conversations, and sometimes interrogations, which aimed to establish the prime truth of mainstream Christianity.

Cathars believed that the world was locked in a struggle between good and evil. Moderate dualists saw Christ sent among humans to take flesh from Mary, but without a human soul. Absolute dualists saw two gods in cosmic struggle, and all that was flesh and matter was the making of the evil god. Hence they removed Jesus altogether, and his mother too, from the domain of the flesh. Jesus who came to earth was a semblance alone, and his mother was an angel who took part in the enactment of his life for the sake of salvation: 'They also believe that

the Blessed Mary was a heavenly being who had not a human, but a heavenly body.'[27]

Mary was of crucial importance to the articulation of faith, of the Incarnation and its purpose, and materials composed and written about her increasingly presented her as a bulwark against heresy. A Cistercian hymn aimed against Cathars, of $c.1209$, begins with a reminder of the Jews' blind rejection of Mary, but moves on to heretics in general:

> May the heretic be confounded,
> let the mad and all misguided ones,
> come to their senses.
> The infidel will blush with shame,
> but the faithful one will be joyful
> at its deathly suffering.[28]

The hymn lists several types of errors, and it offers Mary. It invites people to come to church and get to know Mary, learn the mysteries associated with her:

> But he who wants to know Mary
> and her progeny,
> should come to church
> and learn the mysteries.[29]

The new orders of Franciscans and Dominicans were particularly mobilized towards the fight against heresy and the polemic against Jews. The Dominicans founded confraternities in those Italian cities – such as Bologna – where Cathar belief had taken root.[30] These were associations of lay people, organized around the cult of Mary and for worship under the guidance of a Dominican friar. Friars also composed polemical texts, and these contain most of what we know about the beliefs of groups deemed heretical. An early thirteenth-century description of heresy in Languedoc reports: 'They have the daring to assert that the Blessed Mary, mother of Christ, was not of the world'; and 'they believe that Christ was born in the "land of the living", of Joseph and Mary, whom they say were Adam and Eve.'[31] Although some Cathars rejected the female body as a possible home for the coming of Jesus, others clearly situated Mary and her son in the realm of angels, ethereal and bodiless.

Such a belief was never expressed by Jews, who consistently argued again virgin birth and perpetual virginity in citations from the Bible, in

contemporary medical terms and with what they presented as common sense. The French polemical text of the early thirteenth century *Sefer Nizzahon Yashan* (*The Old Book of Polemic*) said:

Ask them: how old was Mary when she gave birth to the hanged one? It says in their Scriptures that she was thirteen years of age. Now, according to your assertion that he was born without a father, why did he show his power through a thirteen-year-old, who was prepared for conception and pregnancy? He should have shown his power in a three- or four-year-old, who cannot normally conceive, and then everyone would have been able to recognize the miracle, namely, that something new has been done which has never been heard of before. The truth is that you should know with certitude that Joseph had relations with her in a normal manner and she bore his child.[32]

Another polemical text, this from southern France, may reflect knowledge of some Cathar beliefs that Jesus was born from Mary's ear:

They say too that the annunciating angel, Gabriel, said to her, 'Ave Maria, gratia plena, Dominus tecum, etc.' At that moment the Holy Spirit of the Lord entered through her ear so that she conceived. Reply to them that every intelligent person knows that the young of all creatures, whether man, animal, fowl, or beast, leave the mother's body from the place where the semen entered. Therefore, Jesus should have left though the ear through which the Holy Spirit entered her womb. Yet he did not leave from there but from the place where all others leave.[33]

We have seen the figure of Mary reach more people in more languages and shapes than ever before in the thirteenth century. She was embedded in the lives of individuals and communities as a human mother who was also a mother of God. Even those who rejected or doubted her could not let go of her. Good Christians could hope for her efficacious help throughout life: when the young mother Aude Fauré, of the occitan village of Merviel, was troubled by doubts about the eucharist, her body and life in general, she was comforted and strengthened by reflection on Mary and participation in her cult. In this complex world there were so many beliefs and conversations touching religion, it was particularly urgent to be able to argue with strong support. Nothing was so compelling as a good miracle story. So we turn to the hectic work of recording, collecting and translating the stories of Mary's miracles, a task which occupied some of the most creative minds of the period.

14

Mary's Miracles as Reward and as Punishment

MARY AND THE JEWS

Among the Christians who experienced Mary so frequently and so vividly lived the descendants of Mary's kin – the Jews. The thirteenth century was fraught with hateful and violent initiatives against Jews. The century that saw the implementation of a powerful vision for a Christian society by the institutions of the church and with support from secular rulers also saw a sustained preoccupation with the danger that Jews posed to that society. Jews were increasingly perceived as alien and dangerous to the Christian communities within which they lived. They were expelled from large parts of Europe: from England in 1290, and from France in 1306. Yet even when they were expelled the encounter with Jews was not over, for Jews were deeply embedded in imagery and biblical exegesis, in liturgy, devotional practices and popular drama.[1] Jewish rejection of Christian beliefs – the perversion that was Jewish intransigence – appeared in many and varied genres: it was invoked in the course of scholastic discussion of the Incarnation, in specialized polemical literature and in vernacular sermons.

Jews were represented in many contexts of biblical tales and miracle stories, but two settings were particularly vibrant: the juxtaposition of *ecclesia* and *synagoga* – church and synagogue – and the scene of the Passion. *Ecclesia* and *synagoga* became a theme for architectural ornamentation of cathedrals in the twelfth and thirteenth centuries. The symmetrical pair of maidens fitted neatly into the symmetry of cathedral façades, as on the south transept portal of Strasbourg cathedral carved around 1230. The image also became common in the decoration of liturgical books, often at the opening of the office of the mass, around the letter T of *Te igitur*: the letter offered a symmetrically divided space

for church and synagogue.[2] *Ecclesia* and *synagoga* figures sometimes accompanied scenes of the Passion, as in the Amesbury Psalter of *c*.1250.[3] Inasmuch as they were represented as sibling maidens – similar in appearance but fatally different in their fortunes – church and synagogue both were represented as young nubile beauties, very much like Mary herself, with long hair, lithe and elegant bodies, garbed in a cloak, and *ecclesia* often crowned.[4] If church and Mary triumphantly merged into a crowned and serene figure, their counterpart was the blind and erring synagogue, a maiden in disarray.

The symmetrical pair church-synagogue eloquently portrayed the Christian truth and triumph of which Mary was so necessary a part. After 1300 there was more elaboration and differentiation between the two figures, away from the emphasis on similarity between the sibling maidens and into a terrain of danger and pollution. A wall painting from the Bohemian parish of Dolni-Bukovsko, from the second half of the fourteenth century, has *ecclesia* holding a chalice of Christ's blood; *synagoga* holds a broken staff and a he-goat, the symbol of the devil.[5] A scene of the Coronation is painted above, and so the encounter between church and synagogue occurs within an explicit Marian context, heightened by awareness of the Passion, invoked by the chalice of Christ's blood. Mary, Jews and Passion are here blended together. The promise of conversion of the Jews that was implicit in the balanced symmetry of the sibling-virgins of the earlier depictions gave way to an image of *synagoga* as guilty, evil and lost. Such images became embedded within other cultural contexts too, like religious drama. The court of the Lords of Rozemberk – patrons of the wall painting just mentioned – staged vernacular Passion plays, while Strasbourg cathedral sponsored a play on church and synagogue, the theme of its façade.[6]

While the *ecclesia-synagoga* pair called for conversion implicitly, miracle tales expressed more explicitly the troubled terrain on which Mary and the Jews met. Latin miracle stories told of the conversion of the Jews following manifestations of Mary's power to work miracles in the world. Vernacular versions, aimed at a wider audience, transformed the tone and content of the Latin tales.[7] Rather than resolution, they now offered bloody endings. The Benedictine monk Gautier of Coinci (1177–1236) was the author of the French *Miracles de Nostre Dame* (*Miracles of Our Lady*). This work is more than a translation; it is an impassioned love-song to Mary and her work in the world. Gautier

not only rendered the Latin in French verse but also offered a running commentary on the miracles – some of them centuries old – and their place in contemporary French life. The protagonists in these tales are a diverse group of corrupt clerics, rude knights and erring nuns, a set of characters common in moralizing tales. He is much harsher in his treatment of the Jews than earlier authors had been, and he even criticizes the French royal policy towards the Jews. Gautier's complaint is familiar from modern versions of Jew-hatred: all that is wrong in the kingdom resulted from the fact that complacent rulers allowed Jews to reside there. Or worse: rulers who were financially dependent on the Jews allowed them to injure the body politic, and so Gautier exhorts rulers to purify their lands of the Jews. Worst of all Jews hated the Virgin, whom they mocked and derided in various ways.[8]

Latin Marian tales offered the prospect of Christian triumph through miracle and illumination, and the prospect of Jewish conversion without coercion. Conversely, Gautier's tone is more specifically French and highly political and proactive; he challenged the Jews' right to exist within the kingdom. His verse miracles were directed at an aristocratic audience of lords and ladies in whose courts they were performed, sometimes accompanied by music.[9] Gautier knowingly addresses them as 'Lady' or 'Sire'; he implicitly challenges the king in a stylized passage:

> God, if one day I were king,
> For the sake of Reims, of Rome, or of the Kingdom,
> I could not leave even one of them alive.
> To tolerate them is an odious thing
> Yet Holy Church does just that.[10]

Gautier's poetry was aimed at an audience attuned to courtly love, poetry and the game of chess; in all of these an all-powerful lady or queen prevails. This world rewarded refinement in chivalry and service to ladies who were also the trophies for successful players. Mary was the lady above all. Indeed, sometimes it is hard to tell apart the carved figures of enthroned chess queens and figures of Mary.[11] A fourteenth-century cleric composed a moral allegory in which the world is a chessboard and the contenders are God and the devil. In the first round Adam was the white king, and he was checkmated by the devil in three moves. In the next round:

> The white king on God's side
> And Jesus, son of God, born of the maiden.
> His mother is Queen truth be told,
> His rooks are the apostles whom he sent
> To the four parts of the world to preach his name.
> The bishops are the confessors, and we are the pawns on foot.[12]

The devotions of priests and monks – often the brothers and cousins of knights and ladies – were expressed in amorous tones far more explicit than the language of Fulbert of Chartres or Bernard of Clairvaux a century earlier. Gautier tells of a Sacristan visited by 'Nostre Dame':

> Every night by refined habit,
> He knelt before the image
> of Our Lady Saint Mary.
> For nothing did he neglect her,
> He cried many hot tears
> on bare knees and elbows.

This ardent lover was visited one night by a lady

> Who was brighter than the sun
> at noon when it is highest.
> And she wore a dress
> all made of beaten gold,
> full of precious stones
> so bright and so glorious
> that the whole monastery was
> resplendent in the light they gave.

The woman was blonde with a rosy complexion and bright eyes; she was of such perfect beauty that she struck awe into the sacristan, who asked only for the privilege of kissing her feet. Here is a courtly scene. But there is more, for an unexpected treat was in store for the sacristan, as Mary said:

> 'I do not want,
> dear sweet friend, that ever may
> your sainted mouth, which has so often hailed me,
> touch my feet.
> Rather, on my rosy [*coloree*] face,

231

> dear sweet friend, it would suit and please me,
> that your beautiful mouth kiss me.'[13]

The love of Mary is perfectly expressed, and sometimes sung, as a tale of love fulfilled in physical pleasure.

Knightly society enjoyed the telling of romance, stories of exploit and adventure in pursuit of worthy causes: grail, relics, the Holy Land, women and children. Mary miracles also directed pious anger against the Jews, who were considered to be Mary's foes and the special enemies of children. This is the age of the ritual murder accusation against Jews, and it is reflected in devotional poetry too. The best-known Marian tale of child murder is the story 'of the resuscitated boy who sang *Gaude Maria*' ('De l'enfant resuscité qui chantoit *Gaude Maria*'). In it a schoolboy passed through the Jewish quarter on his way to and from school, and he chants a hymn to Mary, the *Gaude Maria*. His song so upset a Jew that he slit the boy's throat; but Mary caused the song to rise from the severed throat. The sound led to the discovery of the crime and to the punishment of the Jew and his community:

> Then there was a great tumult
> and a hue and cry in many places.
> 'Up and at the Jews, up and at the Jews
> who have stolen our little clerk from us.'
> Clerics and lay people came together
> and quickly pushed their way into the Jews' place:
> They trip up and knock down the Jews,
> they beat them and roll them around.[14]

Gautier's Jew-hatred is the obverse of his passion for the Virgin, and his miracles develop a world of opposites: good and evil, courtly and rude (*villain*).[15] In these tales Mary is more active than ever before: she fights the devil and displays her sovereignty. The story of Theophilus is one of the best-known Marian tales. He was a man who entered into a pact with the devil in return for worldly success and goods; medieval versions often inserted a Jew as a mediator between this precursor of Dr Faustus and the devil, who is at the end of his life saved miraculously by Mary's mercy.

These miracles witness Mary hard at work not so much at miraculous cures of the body – the traditional work of saints' relics and miracles –

232

but at the liberation of souls. A worldly and violent knight had decided to mend his ways and build an abbey, but he died too soon without confession. Angels and demons fought over his soul and ultimately turned to Mary's judgement. Mary intervened in the ordered arrangements of heaven and hell and pleaded with her son:

> Son, he was indeed of evil deeds
> This knight of whom I pray to you.
> But he honoured my image and me.[16]

The world of miracle tales was a capricious one, in which Mary might choose to forgive sins even for the sake of a single good habit or deed. Listeners must have been encouraged as the teaching on sins and repentance taught in churches was countered by Mary's miracles. A greedy and crude peasant who regularly went to church on Sundays, for the love of Mary, repented on his death-bed, and angels transported him to heaven 'by the pleasure of our Lady'.[17] An illustration in a manuscript of the Miracles represents Mary, on her knees, attended by angels, as she pleads with her son.

The tone of Gautier's tales, the sense of a danger posed by Jews to the Christian body, manifested by their hatred of Mary, was expressed a few years after Gautier's death in the trial of the Jewish code of law, the Talmud. In King Louis IX's Paris in 1240 the Jews were summoned to answer to accusations that this book, the rules of which governed the lives of Jews in every detail, was full of blasphemy. The attack was led by a convert from Judaism, Nicholas Donin. The mention of a certain Miriam and her lover in the Talmud was taken to refer to Mary, and evidence offered by Jewish converts confirmed that indeed Mary was a subject of jibes and blasphemies.[18] These formed part of a long list of allegations – that the *Talmud* was full of superstition, that it had no claim to sanctity – but the discussions of the slurs against Mary seem to have raised more vitriol than any of the other complaints.[19]

Stories such as these were among the most popular told in thirteenth-century Europe, and they were widely disseminated in manuscripts, some of which were illuminated, and many of which were read and used by knightly and aristocratic owners. Marian miracle tales adorned prayer books too. The act of illumination was also interpretation: in a Parisian manuscript of around 1330 Gautier's account of the story of a Jew who abused an image of Mary – a story we have already encountered

233

in Adomnan's account of Arculf's pilgrimage to the east – presents the Jew as blind, a detail which is absent from Gautier's story but which is crucial for the portrayal of Jewish error.[20]

Miracles were thus handed down from Latin monastic collections and translated and transformed within the spoken languages of home and street. New miracles were emerging at cultic centres – Marian shrines – and these in turn entered the miracle repertoire. The Catalan Ripoll Abbey is a good example: pilgrims to Ripoll were regaled with readings of Marian miracles as part of the unfolding liturgy, above all on Saturday, Mary's special day. The Ripoll Miracle book explains the value of such stories, especially in preparation for debates with Jews, as the opening explains:

It is said that the mother of God is drawn up as a battle line, as the Holy Spirit said: Terrible as an army drawn up in battle array [Song of Songs 6:9]. Because in the sentences of the prophets and evangelists and doctors, in the assertions of all saints and divine figures, her eternal virginity is defended against Jews and heretics. She is terrible because she is to be feared by demons and heretics and Jews in God's last judgement, when the infidels will see the queen of heaven reigning above with angels and the elect, and see themselves immersed in the infernal regions. Truly then the impious will be fearful when the just will stand in great constancy against those who had oppressed them.[21]

The pilgrimages to Mary shrines offered edification, entertainment and spiritual rewards. The experience lingered even after the return home, as pilgrims told their experience, perhaps animated by new songs, and confirmed by the evidence of pilgrim badges or images bought at the shrines. Pilgrim badges represented Mary in a wide range of materials, affordable to anyone.[22]

The repertory of Mary's miracles expanded, gathering to it local concerns and experiences. Miracles were recounted on feast days and provided subject matter for emergent vernacular drama. The tale of Adam of Bristol related the killing of a Christian boy by the Jew Samuel, and it was probably performed on the Feast of the Assumption at the church of St Mary Redcliffe in Bristol.[23] A Jew, Samuel, attacked young Adam 'in insult to Christ and his mother'. Despite many types of injury and torture the dead boy's body continued to call out 'Santa Maria'. Samuel's wife and son were appalled by the deeds, and so Samuel killed them too and threw them into the latrine. He then enlisted his own sister

as an accomplice, but when she discovered that light and sweet smells emanated from around the latrine she refused to cooperate. Samuel next bribed an Irish priest, but he too was moved to repent after a while and confessed to his priest. The site of the crime was marked by the sound of angels singing 'like a monastic choir' in praise of Mary and her son.[24] The priest did penance by burying Adam properly in Ireland and then going on pilgrimage to Rome. Here is a tale of ritual murder – a narrative first told in England in the mid-twelfth century – situated locally and embellished with a great deal of detail. This tale of Mary's help to the people of Bristol confirmed her power to triumph against the Jew and to correct the ways of a sinful priest.

The usefulness of Jews as protagonists in English Marian miracle tales did not end with their expulsion. A century after the expulsion of England's Jews (1290) Mary and the Jews were dramatically combined in the story which Geoffrey Chaucer allocated to his Prioress pilgrim in the *Canterbury Tales*.[25] The genteel Prioress retells the story of child-murder in a Jewish quarter and of Mary's miraculous intervention. There was a Christian boy who habitually passed through the Jewish quarter on his way to and from school, singing sweetly a hymn to the Virgin – *Alma redemptoris mater*. He had learned it from an older boy whom he had heard singing it at school. The chanting upset the Jews so much that they gathered and decided to have the boy killed; one of their number was chosen to do the deed:

> Our first foe, the serpent Satanas,
> That hath in Jews' heart his wasps nest,
> Up swelled, and said: 'O Hebraic people, alas!
> Is this to you a thing that is honest
> That such a boy shall walken as him lest
> In your despite, and sing of such sentence,
> Which is against your law's reverence?'
> From thenceforth the Jews have conspired
> This innocent out of the world to chase.
> A homicide thereto have they hired
> That in an alley had a privy place.
> And as the child gan forby for to pace
> This cursed Jew him hent and held him fast,
> And cut his throat, and in a pit him cast. (1,748–1,761)

235

Yet the music continued to rise from the boy's severed throat, and when his distraught mother came to search for him, she discovered the body – still singing the hymn – and called Christians to take bloody vengeance. The boy's body was removed and taken to burial with great solemnity, and as the requiem progressed the child rose to heaven, like Mary and thanks to her. The old Marian miracle tale is told anew by Chaucer through the mediation of a pious and genteel figure: sentimentality and violence coincided in the experience of Marian piety.[26]

Chaucer understood that Marian practices were imparted above all at the mother's knee, at a very young age, and that they were easily acquired through songs and hymns.[27] In Chaucer's version of the old miracle tale the boy has learned the song at school from an older boy, and did not even understand its Latin meaning. We may call his act of piety – which earned Mary's miraculous intervention – a 'domestic' act, effective if unreflective. The boy enjoyed the sound of the song and learned it by heart but, singing it in a Jewish neighbourhood, he unwittingly brought Christian liturgy into the Jewish space. This violation led to violence: what the boy's mouth sang the Jew's ear could not tolerate. The worship of Mary was envisaged by Chaucer as a matter of habit, of bodily comfort. But Marian piety – repetitive, unquestioning – like that of the boy's, became a harbinger of violence.

CANTIGAS DE SANTA MARIA: MARY'S MIRACLES AND DAILY LIFE

Just a generation after Gautier de Coinci's translation of Mary's miracles into French, another exercise of compilation and translation was inspired not by a monk's passion but by the edict of a king. Alfonso X the Wise ('El Sabio') of Castile and Leon (1221–84), one of Europe's foremost rulers, initiated the enterprise. The vision of a Christian king and the organizational skills of a royal court combined to create the *Cantigas de Santa Maria* – Songs of Saint Mary – a collection of 429 tales of Mary's actions in the world, composed in the language of court poetry, in Galician-Portuguese.[28] Many of the *cantigas* were the staple Marian stories which had spread throughout Europe since the mid-twelfth century, but many were not. Hundreds of *cantigas* were clearly

of Iberian origin, full of detail and preoccupation with the realities of life in a country inhabited by Christians, Muslims and Jews in close proximity. One recurrent story-line has a Muslim present in a church, close to sacred images; another is that of armed confrontation and captivity.[29] The *cantigas* express and address the life-dramas of a society engaged in the conquest and Christianization of Iberia. Mary miracles suggested routes towards conversion through the irresistible and manifest power of Mary.[30]

As befits a book made for a king and for use in court, the most complete and sumptuous of the surviving manuscripts is illuminated, and it contains full musical notation for the verse tales. Another manuscript of 100 *cantigas* also includes partial notation: the miracles of Mary were poetry for entertainment and edification. There are miracles that originated in the Greek east, like *cantiga* 4, the story of the Jewish Boy, beginning with the boy's reception of the host from the hands of Mary on the altar; *cantiga* 34 recounts the story of the Jew of Constantinople who defiled an image of Mary. Some *cantigas* refer to events in the Iberian past, such as *cantiga* 181 about the victory over Aboyuçaf in Marrakech gained under a banner of Mary enthroned with her son on her knee. *Cantiga* 59 tells a more mundane story of Christ on the cross slapping a nun, at his mother's request, for having planned to run away with a lover. The images are particularly arresting: each tale is told in a full-page decoration divided into six scenes; image and text work closely together. Mary is repeatedly seen: the page illustrating *cantiga* 34, for example, includes an image of Mary in five of its six compartments.[31]

Most *cantigas* were heard without visual prompts. They opened with a refrain that neatly summarized the tale's moral lesson. Poetry of miracles was often created at centres of Marian pilgrimage, in compositions prompted by the expectations of pilgrims and the desire of the religious to exalt their Marian shrine. Interesting blends of Latin and vernacular poetry, music and liturgy arise from such encounters.[32] At the great pilgrimage shrine of Montserrat, outside Barcelona, a monk composed songs suitable for pilgrims; his *Cants dels Romeus* were 'decent and devout songs' (*honestas ac devotas cantilenas*) in place of the popular songs and dances with which pilgrims habitually passed the time. The Mary miracles composed by the monk Gonzalo de Berceo (*c.*1190–by 1264), the earliest poet in the Castilian language, were

probably performed in front of pilgrims on the route to Santiago de Compostella, who stopped to do homage to Mary at his monastery of San Millan de la Cogolla with its minor Marian shrine.[33]

Cantiga 227 is especially interesting as it invokes the atmosphere of a Marian shrine and the memories of pilgrims. It begins with a title: 'How Holy Mary rescued a squire from captivity in such a way that those who guarded the prison in which he lay did not see him escape'. This was followed by the refrain: 'She who guides sinners and leads them to salvation can well guide prisoners, for She frees them from bonds'. The gist of the miracle was: 'She freed from prison a captive whom the Moors, because of their beliefs, had severely mistreated and restored him to health'.[34]

The squire in captivity, who hailed from Quintanilla de Osoña in the province of Palencia, used to visit Mary's shrine at Villa-Sirga (now Villalcazar) every year on the feast of the Assumption. Having seen fighting in the region of Seville, he was taken captive, and as a prisoner he continued to pray to Mary in remembrance of the pilgrimage shrine of Villa-Sirga. On the feast of the Assumption he prayed to the Virgin but felt morose for want of a response. When a guard asked why he was so sad, the knight's answer earned him a vicious beating and isolation in the dungeon. He continued to pray to Mary, and she finally appeared, brightly illuminating the dungeon. She freed him, and, once free, the squire made his way directly to the shrine he had so lovingly remembered. As he entered he shouted the message familiar from the *cantiga*'s opening refrain: 'The Virgin who comes to the aid of the unfortunate did this'. After telling the story to the pilgrims gathered there, he joined them in prayer and was moved to copious weeping.

The liberated squire was attached to a specific Mary, from a particular shrine, set in a landscape and associated with his personal memories of pilgrimage past. Such a local setting appears in several *cantigas*, and it probably reflects the origins of many of the tales, the harvest of miracles recorded at local shrines. *Cantiga* 83 tells of a 'good man' rescued from captivity in the 'land of the Moors', Andalusia, who was aided by the Holy Mary of Sopetrán, an abbey in the province of Guadalajara (who appears in *cantiga* 318 too). His captors treated the man harshly, and he lay in chains awaiting his death. His sole consolation was the thought of

the Pure Virgin whom many worship at Sopetrán, weeping before Her, for they are soon pardoned for their sins and transgressions. Also She heals the blind and maimed and lepers and casts out many demons and cures other afflictions. Because of Her mercy, She releases many from captivity. Would that he might be among those rescued.[35]

Mary released him when his chains were miraculously broken and the guards slept so soundly that they did not notice him pass by. He then made his way directly to the site, where he told his tale and witnessed its entry into the miracle book and the praise that followed.

The *Cantigas de Santa Maria* is not only an extraordinary achievement of literary compilation and editing, it also provides important historical lessons about the ways in which people experienced Mary as a local wonder-working saint, whose memory was nurtured and enhanced at cult centres. When a farmer was attacked by an enemy of his lord, he defended himself with invocations to Mary, 'the Mother of Him Whom the Jews had killed on the cross'. The violent soldier was frustrated when he failed to pierce the farmer's body – though it was defenceless and vulnerable – and became enraged thinking that magic was at play.[36] Finally, the manifest power of Mary prompted the soldier to convert to a good Christian life and to compensate the farmer. He, in turn, joined a pilgrimage to Rocamadour, where he no doubt shared his miraculous experience of Mary. There is an ease of movement in telling of Mary from the spoken and sung to the written and recounted. The *cantigas* also demonstrate the force of pilgrimage and liturgy to console in hard times. Even though the *cantigas* are highly stylized, they nonetheless reveal the underlying raw materials with which compilers worked. All across Europe interlocking manifestations of Mary's power, past and present, were recounted and written down for posterity.

MIRACLE COLLECTIONS

Mary miracle collections tell us a great deal about their makers. Gautier de Coinci's preoccupations are manifest in his obsession with the Jews, while Alfonso X's collection is an enterprise of state aimed at securing a Christian identity within a multi-ethnic kingdom. Other types of collection characterized much intellectual work in the thirteenth century, and

encyclopedists often included Mary's miracles among the deposits of knowledge they aimed to summarize. Vincent of Beauvais (1190–1264) was a Dominican friar educated in Paris and author of an ambitious and influential summary of knowledge: the *Speculum Maius* (*Great Mirror*), in three parts. One part, the *Speculum Historiale* (*Historical Mirror*), includes some seventy stories of Mary's miracles.[37] These are a summary of the lore of centuries, told in well-structured narrative units. No compilation of knowledge was complete without Mary's might in the world, to parallel the wonders of the order of nature, to which the *Mirror's* first section was devoted. Here was a treasure trove for future preachers and writers of devotional books.

More modest, yet as telling, is the French collection known as the *Rosarius*, completed soon after 1328. It comprised some 100 tales, of which now only eighty survive, compiled by a Dominican friar, who worked in the region of Soissons. His personal spiritual quest was combined with preaching exemplary tales about Mary. He translated from a wide range of Latin sources stories with Marian content, and to these he added tales collected during his preaching journeys. The protagonists of his stories are tormented men and women: a nun whose convent was destroyed by soldiers and who returned to her father's home only to be sexually abused by him; an orphan girl raped by her uncle and forced to abort the resulting pregnancy; three young Englishmen who stole offerings from the Mary shrine at Laon and were found hanged from a tree; or pilgrims saved from shipwreck.[38] Mary is shown to have entered their lives, even very miserable lives, and to have transformed them. The friar's life was transformed too by his mission of collection and composition: he rendered tales into French verse and created reading material which was shocking and edifying, pious reading with a difference.

Miracles situated in neighbourhood settings, performed in church-yards or told as part of a parish sermon were particularly powerful in reinforcing Mary's place in domestic spheres. A telling story was inserted by the Augustinian canon John Mirk (flourished *c.*1382–*c.*1414) into a sermon for the feast of the Purification for the use of parish priests. When a sinful woman died, two fiends led her to hell, but two angels convinced them to reconsider her case. It was found that she had done no good, but Mary remembered that the woman used to light a candle in her honour, and so she received the woman, who promptly awoke,

made confession and lived a good life, serving Mary until her pious end.[39] Here Mirk subtly invokes Mary the powerful intercessor but unlike many other miracles where a single act of piety sufficed to save a soul he has the sinner repent, partaking of the sacraments, and lead a good life before her final reward. The Marian tale inserted into a sermon for use in parishes did not partake in the emotional surge of the cultic world, but rather offered teaching on proper confession and penance through regular parochial procedures and a sustained change of life.

Mary miracles offered frames within which the lust and greed, the error and violence of daily life could be discussed with the expectation of benign resolution. The vexed area of matrimony surfaced regularly in Marian miracle tales. Mary appeared to endorse the claims of women who desired the religious life rather than marriage, to the discontent of their families. In the canonization process of Delphine of Languedoc (d.1360), it was reported that, when she had been a girl of thirteen, Mary responded to her prayer and supported her.[40] Mary's and Joseph's marriage was held up as a Christian ideal of obedience and consent, a model developed by the church in the twelfth century and disseminated ever since. Yet parents and kin continued to influence and often determine the fate of young people by negotiating marital arrangements that benefited the family above all. An Icelandic Marian miracle of the fourteenth century cast in traditional verse, the *Vitnisvísur af Maríu*, tells of a young man and woman who exchanged clandestine promises of marriage in front of a carving of Mary and Child:

Then he took hold of her hand with a band of love [ring], bringing forth the most beautiful betrothal at last: 'You shall, mighty maid, be my dear wife, if Mary and the Lord deign to become witnesses for us.'

When a complex set of changes of fortune and status lead the young man to renege on the commitment, Mary appeared in court and supported the case of the distraught maiden:

As a result of this testimony, the dutiful people in the church became fired up to the utmost of their power to worship the mother of God; then the entire company together with the woman gave thanks thus: they eloquently made a pleasant hymn of praise for Mary and Christ.[41]

Here is the familiar 'happy end' of the Marian tale, as the maiden's case was vindicated and justice done to her. The ease with which an oath can

be taken by an ardent youth is tested in other Marian tales too. One is told both by Gautier de Coinci and in the *cantigas*, about a youth who put a ring on the finger of a statue of Mary.[42]

Mary maker of miracles was powerful and accessible, familiar and helpful in myriad ways; above all she gave hope and spread joy. But just as the miracle stories with happy ends became more complex in the course of the thirteenth century – and in the case of Jewish protagonists often ended with death rather than with conversion – so Mary's figure itself was increasingly touched by the intimations of sorrow. The more accessible Mary became, the more joyful did her nurturing motherhood appear. Similarly, her experience as a grieving mother at the foot of the cross gained in depth and emotional range. It ultimately became the core of thinking about and visualizing the Passion.

15

Mary at the Foot of the Cross

MATER DOLOROSA

The unique intimacy that Mary enjoyed with her son made her a powerful intercessor; it also rendered her particularly sensitive to his suffering.[1] This affinity was explored in the thirteenth century in representations of Mary and Jesus, a tender and inseparable group of mother and son that we have explored above. But that childhood portended an end that was as traumatic as it was necessary for salvation – death on the cross. Some images of Mary and Child even bear signs of the impending Passion – showing the circumcised penis, a sign of future bleeding, or placing a cross in the Child Christ's hand. The full exploration of Mary's experience of her son's death was yet to come. When it did, it overwhelmed the content and character of European devotional life.

Until the early thirteenth century, visual representations of the Crucifixion placed it against abstract, even empty, backgrounds, with John the Evangelist standing to Christ's left and Mary to his right. The sumptuous binding to a gospel book made around 1230 by the monk-goldsmith Hugh of Oignies showed John and Mary on either side of the crucified Christ against a gilt background; Mary, unusually, faces forward but raises a hand to her head in a gesture of grief.[2] Throughout the thirteenth century the tilting of the head or wringing of hands and anxious bending of fingers increasingly expressed emotions at the foot of the cross. On the whole, Mary remained a figure of controlled sorrow, delicately symmetrical to that of John. This balance was disrupted in the course of the thirteenth century as preaching and teaching of Jesus' life and death to Europeans emphasized his quite human suffering, and his mother's agony. A pair of painted panels from Umbria c.1260 combined two images of this unique compassion: Mary and Child in tender caress

alongside Jesus as the Man of Sorrows.[3] Mary and Child were linked in the embraces of his childhood, just as they shared the pain and sorrow of death.

Scenes of the Crucifixion now increasingly explored Mary's own experience. Some sequences, like the *Lignum vitae quaerimus* (*We seek the tree of life*) anticipated the moment by drawing a parallel between the cross and Mary: 'Here is the child-bearing virgin, here is the salubrious cross, two mystical trees; this one a humble hyssop, that one a noble cedar, and both life giving.' Pain is part of the love-service owed by one lover to another according to the courtly logic that sometimes informed liturgical chant.[4] By the late twelfth century Mary's lament had formed part of Passion plays.[5]

Representations increasingly considered Mary's pain, and the disruption that it caused to her mind and her body. Mary is shown recoiling, leaning away from the cross, throwing her hands into the air.[6] In carving and sculpture the possibilities of such representations were appreciated relatively early.[7] A pair of wooden statues of $c.1220$–30, once in the cathedral of Prato, formed part of a scene of the deposition of Christ: Mary and John, with delicate and sorrowful faces, each gesturing towards the crucified body.[8] Tuscan painted crucifixes were often accompanied by small figures of Mary and John on either side, level with the middle of Jesus' body. These crosses were becoming increasingly animated, like that of $c.1210$–20 by Lucchese artist Berlinghieri Berlinghiero.[9] The tendency to dramatize Mary's suffering allowed her to be seen in some alarming new positions: fainting, leaning, falling, sometimes pulling at her son's body.

The visual imagery of Mary at the foot of the cross followed a rich and growing body of exposition on the Passion, which directed readers, listeners and viewers to approach the Passion through Mary's eyes. The hymn *Stabat mater dolorosa* is a product of this period. It exemplifies the qualities of humanization, of making Mary familiar and accessible. It created a template for reflection on Mary's relation to the Passion and marked the remaking of the Passion as part of Mary's – not only Christ's – life. New materials were created to feed and form the Passion as dramatic narrative.[10]

The *Stabat mater* was reworked in over a hundred versions; one of them is *Stabat mater, rubens rosa*:

The Mother stood, a blushing rose
in tears at the foot of the cross
as she saw him undergo a criminal's fate
who was guilty of no crime.

And as she stood with full heart
grieving beside her son
the crowd shouted raucously:
'crucify him, crucify him'.

O how grievous was the pain
you suffered, Virgin full of sorrows
when you recalled former joys
now all turned to lamentation.

All the life drained from you, Mother,
while your son stood constrained there
gladly bearing his pain
that Satan might be overthrown.

By the merits, most beloved lady,
beseech your son, who takes away
all the sin that we have committed
with sweet and gracious prayer.

That, wiping away all our stain
he might plant firmly in us the gifts of grace
and might fulfil in us what they promise
In our eternal rest.

Stabat mater, rubens rosa, like the symmetrical images of the Crucifixion which we have just examined, effectively balanced pain and hope, suffering and exaltation. Alongside such hymns, images in liturgical and prayer books maintain equipoise at the foot of the cross, continuing the earlier medieval tradition of a sparse and somewhat abstract Crucifixion. Such was the crucifix which adorned the psalter of Robert de Lindsey, abbot of Peterborough (1214–22): the cross is a living thing, John and Mary, moon and sun, its witnesses.[11] Almost a century later similar decorum was maintained in the Crucifixion scene of the Gorleston Psalter, an East Anglian work of around 1310. Against the gold background Mary and John gesture in pain. The grieving Mary Magdalene

hugs the bloodied foot of the cross, but even here the sparse, traditional approach is maintained.[12] Mary is a necessary part, but she does not overwhelm. Makers of liturgical books, on the whole, tended to maintain this moderate approach to illustrations of the Crucifixion.

Mary came to encompass all the pain associated with the Crucifixion as a drama of loss and bereavement. The Passion play added around 1230 to the late twelfth-century *Carmina Burana* manuscript fully expresses the theme of pain and loss in Mary's lament, *Planctus Mariae*:

> Alas, alas, the grief is mine today and forever,
> alas, how I now look upon
> the dearest child that ever
> in this world any woman brought forth.
> Alas, my lovely child's body!
> I will look upon it forever.
> Have pity, women and men.
> Let your eyes look there
>
> Was there ever such torment
> and such terrible anguish?
> Now perceive the torment, agony and death,
> and the entire body red with blood.
>
> Let my little one live for my sake
> and let me die, his mother,
> Mary, most pitiable woman.
> What use is life and body to me?[13]

By the mid-thirteenth century the predominant trend in word and in image was toward more detailed dramatization of Mary's suffering, often with graphic details of the unmaking of Christ's body. The Crucifixion panel of Nicola Pisano's 1265 pulpit for Siena cathedral expressed this new sensibility in keeping with devotional writings and the chants of confraternities and religious drama.[14] The scene is crowded and full of agitated gesture. The chief mediator of Christ's pain was Mary, and her co-suffering was offered for the imitation of the audiences. As Jesus' pain was made more graphic so was Mary's agony in beholding it. The highly influential *Meditations on the Life of Christ*, a guidebook probably by the Tuscan Franciscan John of Caulibus, *c.*1300 (though often ascribed to St Bonaventure) offered the reader detailed descriptions

of suffering and cues for empathy.[15] The aim of such works was to leave no detail beyond description and evocation: Jesus' wounds, his tormentors' cruelty, the crowd's ferocity, the pain caused by the crown of thorns.

Mary's equipoise, her sometimes rigid grief, her gentle gestures, gave way in large parts of Europe to displays of unbearable pain. Texts like the *Meditations on the Life of Christ* helped writers and artists alike to experiment with the representation of Mary losing control. By 1304–6, when Giotto executed his remarkable scene of the Crucifixion on the wall of the Scrovegni Chapel in Padua, Mary was supported by the other Marys and by John since she was unable to remain standing.[16] A triptych from Duccio's workshop, of around 1301–15, juxtaposes Mary's loss of control, as she faints into the arms of her women friends, with the baying crowd of Jews, gesticulating and gesturing at the cross.[17] Passion scenes became crowded, full of myriad tormentors and mourners none of whom were mentioned in the gospels. Mary's warm humanity is in sharp contrast to the cold sterility of Christ's tormentors and their instruments.[18] In the Sienese Ugolino di Nerio's Crucifixion with St Francis (*c.*1317/27) Mary points to her son with her right hand while she turns her head away from the terrible sight.[19] The influence of the *Meditations on the Life of Jesus Christ* could not be more obvious here, where a Franciscan sensibility in native tongue and local colour is on full display.[20]

There is a remarkable dissenting voice to this style of representation, and it comes from across the Alps, that of the Franciscan Marquard of Lindau (d.1392), the author of devotional and pastoral works in German. Marquard's Mary was an awesome figure of dignified solemnity:

Know that the noble maiden stood under the cross, but rather stood there silently, and repressed her suffering inwardly and did not show it externally. And thus it was all the more penetrating.[21]

The preacher is then asked why it was that so many authoritative writers, like Anselm and Bernard, had described Mary behaving 'badly' (*úbel gehueb*) at the foot of the cross. Marquard explains that this was done in order to stimulate compassion. There are not many voices that dissent so obviously from the prevailing devotional style of extravagant emotional display of Mary's suffering and imitation of it.

The scenes at the foot of the cross became increasingly busy and

populous, animated and even grotesque. As she stood at the foot of the cross – most frequently with John at her side – Mary still retained a certain aloofness, which marked her apart. Although Mary was always placed just under Christ's extended right arm, which is shown bleeding from hand or wrist, she is never stained. Mary was part of the Passion narrative but she was also utterly pure, immune to the pollution of blood.

There was one striking exception to this. St Vitus' cathedral in Prague claimed to possess Mary's bloodied veil (*peplum cruentatum*), which she wore at the Crucifixion. By the mid-fourteenth century a ritual was designed for the display of this relic to pilgrims and dignitaries. This probably led Bohemian artists to dare to represent Mary in a veil stained by the blood of the Crucifixion. The Vyšší Brod Crucifixion depicts Mary and John either side of the cross, with censing angels hovering over their heads. Mary turns to her bleeding son, holding a veil in her hands which is marked by stylized stains of the blood flowing from his side wound.[22] When the same master painted a series of panels of the life of Christ and Mary, he made her prominent in the scenes of the Nativity, Adoration of the Magi and the Crucifixion; here the effect is even more dramatic as Mary swoons at the foot of the cross, her veil marked by bloodstains. The local relic of the veil encouraged the artist of Prague to think the unthinkable – a bloodied Mary – to great effect.[23]

The vehicle for participation in Mary's suffering was visual in two ways: viewing images of Mary's suffering; and by calling to mind and thus remembering and reliving – through *imitatio* – Mary's moment at the foot of the cross. English devotional poetry emphasized Mary's own gaze, in a dialogue between mother and son, as in this fourteenth-century poem:

> 'Stand well, mother, under the cross,
> Look at your child gladly,
>   You should be a happy mother.'
> 'Son, how can I stand happily?
> I see your feet, I see your hands,
>   Nailed to the hard tree.'
>
> . . .
>
> 'Mother, I can stay no longer,
> It is time for me to go to Hell,

> On the third day when I rise.'
> 'Son, I want to be with you,
> I die, you know, of your wounds.
> There was never such a bitter death.'[24]

The reader then adds his own prayer:

> Blessed be you queen of heaven
> Raise us out from hell
> Through your dear son's might.
> Mother, for that precious blood
> That he shed on the cross
> Lead us into heavenly light. Amen.[25]

The shared gaze and the shared feeling made the experience of the Crucifixion a devotional experience mediated by Mary.

MARY AND THE LAITY IN THE LIFE OF CONFRATERNITIES

The process by which Mary was made local and familiar encouraged the exploration of emotion and empathy. Medieval adherents wondered how like them Mary really was. In religious confraternities formed by lay people and guided by friars new techniques for reliving the Passion were being developed. The habits of urban consumption and display, of association and performance, enabled lay people to participate in rituals of imitation far more elaborate than those offered by the parish. Confraternities often chose a theme for their attachment: Trinity, Corpus Christi, or Mary.

Confraternities were religious associations of like-minded people who enjoyed similar social standing. They enhanced religious life among members who were bound by oaths of loyalty and the confraternity's statutes. After the Black Death that devastated European societies between 1347 and 1350 survivors were bound to commemorate the dead – a third to a half of Europe's population – and confraternities were a useful framework for securing a good funeral and related rituals. Confraternities engaged friars to lead worship that was more focused and more intense than that offered by most parishes. It was accompanied

by music, drama and frequent preaching and encouraged active participation by members.[26] Italian confraternities were above all devoted to the Crucifixion, and they engaged in penitent flagellation and in the praise of Mary.[27] The latter type came to be known as *laudesi* – singers of the lauds, or praises – since their members chanted Marian praises and focused their devotion on her. For example, the confraternity of Blessed Mary and St Francis of Parma was guided at its institution in 1295 by the Franciscan Rainerius of Genoa. The prologue to its statutes laid out its expectations and aims:

On account of human fragility all people need help in life, death and after death; and we sinners are so very unworthy of pleading for such help of God . . . that we have particularly chosen as our advocate the glorious mother of God Mary, who, as holy doctors testify, is more merciful than all others in hearing the prayers of all miserable ones; she is wiser than all others in pleading for us to the eternal judge, and is more potent than any other as a mother to obtain favours of her son on our behalf.[28]

Confraternities supported members in sickness, conducted requiem masses after death and covered the burial expenses of members who died in penury. This charitable orientation of Marian confraternities sometimes extended help beyond the group: the society devoted to Mary's praises (*laude*) at St Francis in Bologna maintained a hospital. Poverty and mercy – Francis and Mary – were the intertwined devotional foci. The 1329 hospital inventory lists beds and bedding, screens and benches, but also images of Mary:

Item, a cloth on which the image of the Virgin Mary is depicted with her only born son our lord Jesus Christ with figures of St John the Baptist and St Francis and two angels above the Virgin and with women of the said society at the feet of the said Virgin Mary.

Item a venerable gilt panel or tabernacle with the image of the Virgin Mary and her only born son Jesus Christ painted on cloth, with two angels and with a striped veil of silk.[29]

The *Stabat mater* emerged from a monastic sensibility but was adopted with enthusiasm by vernacular groupings of lay people. In Orsanmichele, the civic focus of mid- and later fourteenth-century Florence, the artist Orcagna was commissioned to produce a crucifix *c.*1360. He painted a work in which every aspect of Christ's pained body was drawn and

coloured, a tortured body on the verge of death.[30] By 1388 the image was accompanied by the inscription of the first lines of the *Stabat mater*:

> The mother stood in pain
> tearful near the cross
> as her son hung.
>
> Her suffering, her pressed
> mournful soul,
> was pierced by a sword.
>
> O how sad and how afflicted
> was this blessed one
> mother of the only born.

The drama at the foot of the cross increasingly told Mary's story. The crucifix was not complete without Mary's presence in the chanted words of this well-known and much loved hymn.

Members of the society were required to live a devout life, to avoid wine and games of chance.[31] The confraternity at Reggio Emilia provided mass and preaching, while members undertook to recite the Ave Maria and Pater Noster daily, to reflect on Mary's Joys, and to contemplate Christ's five wounds. The society promoted a Marian liturgy and benefited from indulgences for the benefit of its members.[32] It focused on the feast of the Conception, 'a feast honoured and known by few'. The confraternity of Cremona recommended that its members turn to Mary for mercy. Its 1347 statutes even cite the opening words of the *Salve regina misericordiae*:

> Hail, Queen of Mercy,
> our life, love and hope, hail!
> We, exiled sons of Eve, call to you,
> groan and cry to you
> in this vale of tears.
> So, our advocate,
> turn those two merciful eyes to us
> and show us Jesus, blessed fruit of your womb
> after this exile,
> O merciful, o pious,
> O sweet Mary.[33]

Confraternities offered a stage for the enactment of devotion through mimesis – imitation of Christ's sufferings. As Mary's suffering at the foot of the cross gained equal prestige, so the praises of Mary, *laude*, blended with the re-enactment of her grief. Members were directed towards an empathetic experience of Mary's pain through the recitation of vernacular chants that situated the devout in the position of the mother looking on at the death of her son. While the gospel and apocrypha provided some of the material for this new dramatic literature, much innovation and invention is evident too. Imitation followed Christ's suffering blow by blow and remembered Mary's pain tear by tear. *Donna de Paradiso* by the Franciscan Jacopone da Todi (1230–1306) uses rhythm and repetition to powerful dramatic effect in imagining Mary at the Passion. Jesus speaks to his mother in short, moving lines, as he recommends her to John's care:

> Mother, with the suffering heart
> I place you in the hands
> Of my elected John,
> May he be called your son.[34]

New emphasis on Mary's distress directed attention to its cause – the Jews. This period saw more elaborate reasoning and widespread preaching about Jews as knowing killers of Christ. The traditional Christian view, as articulated by Augustine in the early fifth century, argued that the Jews caused Christ's death but lacked full understanding of their deeds. Since they were to play a role in future Christian history they formed part of any Christian universe until the end of time.[35] Yet in the thirteenth century the emphasis was shifting towards the ill-intent and cruel agency of Jews. With Mary's prominence at the foot of the cross and in the mind of Christians, a powerful new link emerged, between the Jews' perceived malevolence towards Christ and Mary's sorrow. The Jew became Mary's enemy.

In the chants of confraternities this was elaborated with immediacy and colour. Vernacular poetry was passionate, graphic and highly affecting. The drama of the Passion was enacted between Mary and her son, with John looking on and in the presence of the baying *popolo* – the Jews. The friars did not shy away from using that intimate language of mothers and their children: baby-talk, which is repetitive and alliterative. Here is the version from the *laudesi* society of Urbino, copied into its book of Marian chants:

> Oh son, son, son
> oh beloved jewel
> son, who gives comfort
> to my anguished heart?
> My gracious son
> my delectable son
> my fragrant son
> why is he imprisoned?[36]

The rhythmic chants described in detail every aspect of Christ's unmaking and often emphasized the causal link between Mary's sorrows and the Jews. In Urbino the Marian confraternity viewed the drama of the Passion unfolding in stages:

> Down the white flesh
> the red blood trickled.
> Behold the bitter life
> that Mary has of her son.
> The crazed crowd
> ordained in counsel:
> death and destruction
> of the good pastor.[37]

While the *laudesi* confraternity in fourteenth-century Modena recited lines such as:

> And she cried in a loud voice: miserable Jew
> Why have you tormented my sweet son?
> You will lose power and reward because of him,
> He whom the angel had told me was the son of God.[38]

Christ's Passion was fast becoming a drama enacted over her son's body between Mary and the Jews.

The book of the *laudesi* of Urbino was organized around points for contemplation. His mother relied on their bodily closeness.[39] There were moving descriptions of intimacy and warmth, in dialogue form:

> To my glorious Son,
> Sweeter than honey,
> Were given
> Myrrh, vinegar and bile.

He was nailed to the cross,
The sweet Emmanuel,
And the cruel people
Gave him even more bitterness.[40]

In turn, Jesus himself suffers as he hears his mother's lament: 'Mamma, your lament torments me like a knife'. Mary speaks her sorrow to the assembled and thus animates their devotion: 'You who love the Creator, now listen to my pain'.[41]

In the later fourteenth century, the period after the Black Death, which saw dislocation and anxiety alongside a great deal of opportunity for survivors, penitential themes of spiritual renewal were the rallying cries of Italian preachers. Lay people were offered routes to regeneration that took them through terrains of Marian devotion and Christ-centred preoccupation, sometimes separate, other times intertwined. The habit of combining in lay groups for religious action produced in 1399 a penitential-flagellant movement of thousands in the region between Piedmont and Tuscany; they were known as the *Bianchi*, the Whites. They were prompted by a vision of Mary and her Child and conducted processional penitential marches, barefoot, while praying and chanting the *Stabat mater*.[42] The mood of excitement, prompted by the memory of the Passion, produced further showings in which Mary featured prominently. The telling of Christ's Passion was no longer complete without an equal evocation of his mother's pain.

The powerful vision of compassion with Mary that originated in Central Italy was carried and animated by friars to reach many European spheres. A devotional genre that depicted in verse Mary's lament was accessible by the second half of the thirteenth century in many languages and registers. A manuscript made by three Hungarian friars, probably Dominicans, rendered into their mother tongue something of the immediacy of the *laude* which they learned during their sojourn in Italy. Its eight stanzas are each four verses long, mostly of just two words. Christ is addressed as 'World of world/flower of flowers'; he is Mary's 'Jewish son'. There is frequent mention of sweetness and honey, of the shedding of Jesus' blood and Mary's tears. A second lament, four stanzas long, describes the details of the Crucifixion at the hands of lawless Jews, a Passion in which Mary wished to join her son. The Hungarian friars absorbed and conveyed here the mood, style and content of Italian

vernacular chants of Mary's Passion.[43] A Provencal poem on Mary's Lament offered detailed description of her attitude at every stage throughout its 905 verses; it too cries out to the Jew as a criminal and evil tormentor:

> O, Jew, cruel and criminal!
> You have killed my good and beautiful son
> Put me in the earth, we will both die.[44]

The Icelandic version was equally emphatic, in a narrative of Mary's life:

The Jewish people went up with cruelty and scorn and spat on Him for a long time; they bound, injured, beat and mocked the one who is both man and our true God; fierce men chose a multitude of all kinds of torture for the prince of glory.[45]

New ways of experiencing Mary and the Passion were evolving in the vernacular usages of confraternities. The men charged with writing, guiding, composing and directing the performance of compassion clearly judged the graphic telling of the Passion through Mary's eyes to be moving, effective and appealing. Such texts and images put Mary centre stage; they showed her suffering as only a mother can suffer over her son. They also increasingly singled out the Jews as the guilty cause for Mary's terrible pain.

16

Mary and Women, Mary and Men

Throughout these medieval encounters with Mary we have occasionally discussed creative acts by which female religious laid claim to her: Hrotsvitha in her account of Mary's early life, or Hildegard in her limpid hymns on virginity and fecundity, or Clare, who hoped to become Mary's footprint in the world. Mary was seen as an appropriate example, a suitable spiritual companion to women, be they married or chaste. Where women congregated in religious communities Mary's life formed the focus of often intense and imaginative experiences. These centuries saw the development of several new forms of religious life for women. To the many forms of monastic living were added after the year 1200 new forms of existence, within towns, alongside monasteries, or in lay orders associated with the friars. A few women even chose enclosure in cells attached to parish churches, as anchorites. Most towns offered an array of possibilities, religious lives of varying degrees of rigour, cost and social exclusivity.

MARY AND THE FEMALE RELIGIOUS: MOTHERS AND BRIDES

The Low Countries were among the most exciting regions for experimentation in religious life in these centuries. Mary was present in religious communities in many aspects of daily religious life. The local expertise in precious metalwork was employed to fashion many small objects which depicted Mary, artefacts that were seen close up and even touched in the course of worship. The priory at Oignies in the Pas-de-Calais commissioned a fine dove-shaped reliquary to contain drops of

Mary's milk, while a fine chalice made for the abbey of Saints Peter and Paul at Affligem was decorated with gilt medallions depicting Christ's life: Mary was delicately incised in the scenes of the Annunciation, Nativity and Adoration of the Magi, as well as at the foot of the cross.[1]

There was prodigious writing about religious life and often about the experience of women too. Goswin of Bossut ($c.$ 1200–1230) was monk and cantor at the Cistercian priory of Villers in the Maas valley, and he wrote three Latin accounts of the lives of people who had impressed him: two fellow monks and a woman from the neighbouring religious house of La Ramée.[2] All three were noted within their own communities for unique spiritual experiences and special merits. Mary had appeared to each in visions that supported their spiritual efforts. None of the three was particularly learned, and the sympathetic Goswin describes their lives in an engaging fashion. Mary was central to them all.

From the early decades of the thirteenth century there are many reports of the sayings and actions of religious women, sometimes in their own words. Goswin recounts an occasion on which Mary formed part of an act of friendship and charity, this time between Ida of Nivelles and a dear friend, perhaps the Cistercian Beatrice of Nazareth ($c.$ 1200–1268), from the nunnery of Bloemendaal. Beatrice was a visionary too, and she kept a spiritual journal. She recounted 'that wondrously ardent love which was the prerogative of the Virgin Mary in her ineffable loving of the supreme and indivisible Trinity'.[3] One day, while Beatrice was deep in memory of her friend Ida, Mary appeared to her in 'most ardent charity', and whispered the following request:

'I wish from now on to be as special to your heart as Ida of Nivelles has been. I wish you to take the same attitude towards me that you used to take towards Ida. And that same attitude you took those many days towards Ida, I shall take towards yourself. And thus shall we be covenanted together (*foederatae*) by a perpetual bond of indissoluble charity.'

Goswin added:

that this vision was not a matter of fantasy is made clear by several pieces of evidence given by our Lady, the Virgin Mary, both to Sister Ida and to this person.[4]

One wonders what these tokens – sign or souvenirs – may have been.

Abundus, a monk of Villers, belonged to the same Cistercian milieu.

Goswin portrays Abundus, as he did Ida, as a person whose Mary visions were widely told and who shared them with acquaintances. The liturgy features more prominently in this monk's visions of Mary. During a service on a day between Circumcision and Epiphany (1–6 January), when the Incarnation dominated the themed antiphon:

On one of those days he was standing in choir at the beginning of Terce [prayer session between 9 a.m. and noon] and it was just as if he had said to the blessed Virgin Mother: '*Show me, o sweetest one, show me your face; and let your voice sound in my ears!*' (Song of Songs 2:14). For he suddenly beheld her standing at his side, the most blessed among women (Luke 1:28, 42), mother of the King of glory, dressed in a most beautiful cowl, with her head veiled like a nun's. But the veil was finely woven and spotless in its cleanliness; also it was so arranged that it hung down a little in front of the face. And he heard her singing along with the monks, chanting that hymn composed to honour her and her most blessed Son: *A solis ortus cardine.*[5]

Goswin intuits here the liturgy's power to recreate and re-enact the biblical text, to make its truth visible and audible. On another occasion he recounts Abundus' vision of Mary 'nestling in her arms the blessed fruit of her womb and walking the circuit of both choirs, presenting her infant son to each monk in turn'.[6] What more reassuring to these professional liturgical performers, on the days which celebrated the Incarnation, than the presence of God's mother in the choir – the modest figure of a veiled woman – where no other woman had ever been?

Abundus' Mary language is different from that used by Ida. There is an unabashed eroticism in his request for Mary's intimacy, reminiscent of the words of female religious as they addressed Christ as lover.[7] On one occasion when Mary appeared to him, Abundus spoke 'not out of the boldness characteristic of presumption but out of the affection characteristic of great love':

'O most kindly Lady, the Lord knows with what yearning, if you would allow it, I yearn for your, yes, your hand, yes, to kiss it!' And how would the mother of loving-kindness reply, if not in words of loving-kindness? Lifting her right hand to her loved one's face she said: 'Draw near, dear son; be it done for you as you request!' Trustingly he drew near, and reverently and sincerely and humbly. And then he was indeed privileged to kiss that venerable hand! But the mother of fair love (Ecclesiasticus 24:24) wished to show even more aptly what

holy love she had for her servant and so, wonderful to say, she in turn drew near to him, she in turn kissed him and said: 'Be not surprised, dearly beloved, that I have bestowed on you this kiss, for it does but show afresh the bond I have shown time and again, the unbreakable bond of holy charity that glues my heart to yours. And this, all the more so in that I know how purely, how unfeignedly, the love you show me is rooted in your heart!'[8]

The stories told by the monk Goswin about fellow Cistercians, lay-brother and nun, reveal a newly affective devotional world. Mary is a vital yet perplexing part of it. She was, after all, of another time and place, and yet a regular visitor to chancel and choir, a public and eloquent participant in the lives devoted to religious perfection.[9] While Ida and Abundus were her chosen friends, Mary had a lot to say to others too. In Abundus' vision she communicated with each monk of the choir and her messages were generously shared. This is how a knowing, engaged and well-informed monk saw the working of Mary in communities he knew well: she was a companion in the hard life of religious exertion and during the terrifying passage that was death. The Flemish Dominican friar Thomas of Cantimpré (1201–72), a keen observer of monastic striving in the Low Countries, composed a life of John, abbot of Cantimpré. As John lay on his sickbed in the priory, full of the sense of approaching death, he had a vision of Mary:

As I was approaching the exit, my soul trembled, at the sight of our venerable patron the Virgin Mary, God's mother, with an admirable beautiful man, who stood in front of me, sensing my illness with pious eyes, asking where and what in my body was aching. Next, once I showed the place, she extended a phial, full of sacred medicine, which she carried in her possession in measures, and she drew it all over the middle of my stomach from side to side, and health followed its touch immediately and pardoned me from death, giving me to life . . . When I had rejoiced in great exaltation for this visitation and vision, immediately the glorious mother of Christ with her followers withdrew out of the middle of the window.[10]

Mary was a daily companion to Goswin's three visionaries, in sickness and health, and she joined them with her son. When a Cistercian abbot visited Ida and had long conversations with her, she was transfixed by the pleasure of the charity he exuded. On the third day that abbot prayed for Ida while celebrating mass elsewhere:

His prayer took wings and came before the Lord God of hosts. On that same day Ida was inwardly enlightened with an immense brightness, and within the brightness there suddenly appeared she whom all mortals must venerate, the queen of mercy, the Virgin Mary. In her motherly arms she was carrying *the blessed fruit of her womb* [from the *Salve regina*], Jesus Christ. And she now bent *those eyes of her mercy* towards Ida and, with all sweet and tender warmth, proffered her son to her, and said: 'O sweet friend of my son, receive this son of mine from my hands, sent to you by your beloved abbot, who spoke to you the day before yesterday. Receive him, I say, and set him on your lap and make festivity with him (Ps 75:11), enjoying all the embraces and kisses you have longed for.' Ida receiving the child, embraced him tightly in her bosom and began kissing him ceaselessly with insatiable desire. Meanwhile, the queen of glory sat back on the bedside chair and gazed for some time upon the delightful game they were playing together in their sweet and holy familiarity.[11]

How strange, and yet how reassuring. Goswin's story extends to Ida the benefits of the mass, which no woman could ever celebrate. It was a gift, an offering, an act of charity, which mirrored the eucharist as a gift of love. Ida enjoyed an experience even more privileged than merely observing the mass, she became Mary for a while, a mother holding and fondling her little boy. Here is charity too: Mary is a generous mother, who hands her son over for another woman's delight.

We have seen the commentaries on the Song of Songs as a conduit to Mary in twelfth-century monasteries; it was now being offered to religious women too. A verse-commentary in 318 stanzas on that all-important book was written by a woman from northern France, probably for the use of beguines like her, lay women who lived in religious communities within towns and cities. It opens with a plea for divine inspiration from Jesus and his mother:

> Very glorious God, incline
> Your ears to my prayer;
> Sweet Virgin, Mother Queen,
> To whom there is neither first nor second,
> By your holy grace illuminate
> My heart with your bright light
> So I can make Alexandrine rhymes
> Of a gracious nature.[12]

It loosely follows the Song of Songs, in images of perfection likened to natural beauty:

> Pay attention, sweet Friend, and listen
> I am the green flowering
> Of the field where the soil is not trodden
> Where man has not sown.
> It contains odour, sweetness and utter beauty
> I am the honeyed flower perfumed
> with virtue and grace,
> I am the lily of the valley.[13]

Beguines felt they knew Mary, understood her striving for purity in daily life. One, the Provençal Douceline of Digne (d.1274), even claimed that Mary had been 'the first beguine in Provence and she was the origin of all those who took that name'.[14]

Women prompted some of the specialized vernacular devotional writing that made so real both Incarnation and Passion. As we have seen, the most influential text of guidance, the *Meditations on the Life of Christ*, was written as a guidebook for a religious woman. Here was instruction and example, a prompt towards an interior life that was rich yet feasible even for lay women. The book led the reader into Christ's life through meditation at times of the day set aside for the purpose, time invested in nurturing the emergent relationship between Mary and her son. Women religious practised the relationship with the help of material aids: dolls, embroidery and paintings of their own making.[15] Women expressed their feelings towards Mary in their artwork and in their words.

A great deal of inventiveness was invested in artwork for women religious, with emphasis on figures that were considered suitable for them. Works were commissioned for women with the view of responding to their perceived needs and aspirations. *The Dream of the Virgin*, a small panel painting, was made by Simone dei Crocefissi for a female religious house in Bologna around 1365–80.[16] This is an uncommon topic: a cross/tree grows out of the centre of Mary's sleeping body, while under her bed the floor opens to reveal Adam and Eve pulled out by a helping hand. At the side sits a veiled woman reading a book.[17] The panel's shape suggests that it was the 'crowning' panel (*cimasa*) of a complex altarpiece. It is indeed all-embracing in its subject matter: the

story of sin, incarnation, sacrifice and salvation with Mary at its heart. It echoes the use of Mary as the counter-type to Eve and emphasizes the physical transaction which produced a crucified, saving God. These themes may have seemed particularly attractive for the use of women.

Within the variety of lifestyles in religion one principle seemed to prevail: Mary was associated in particular with women who guarded their virginity. In the *Bible moralisée* of the early thirteenth century – a richly illustrated book for French royals, which aimed to teach the correspondence between the Jewish Bible and Christian scripture – the scene of the three Marys at Christ's empty tomb offers the gloss: the Virgin Mary represents virgins, Mary Cleopas – Mary's half-sister – wives, and Mary Magdalene, penitents. Anchorites and nuns in particular were directed to place Mary at the centre of their self-fashioning and meditations. Mary's body helped religious women think about their own bodies, which were destined never to bear children. It is not surprising that the womb, which was understood as determining female character and bodily disposition, was often described in thinking about Mary. Mystics thought about Mary through her womb, like Gertrud the Great (1256–1301/2), of the nunnery of Helfta in Thuringia:

The spotless womb of the glorious Virgin appeared, transparent like the purest crystal; through it all her inner organs, shot through and perfused with his divine nature, shone forth just as gold wrapped in silk of varied colour is accustomed to shine through crystal. She also saw the dewy-fresh little boy, the only child of the highest Father, sucking at the heart of the Virgin Mother with hungry pleasure.[18]

Reflection on Mary's womb within the narrow space of the anchoress's dwelling included Christ too. The *Ancrene Wisse* (*Anchoress's Guide*), an early thirteenth-century English guidebook for anchoresses – women who left the world to live in enclosed solitude – imagined the anchorhold where they lived as a place in Mary's body, in her womb:

And was he not himself a recluse in Mary's womb? . . . For the womb is a narrow dwelling, where our Lord was a recluse . . . Are you imprisoned within four wide walls? And he in a narrow cradle, nailed to the cross, enclosed tight in a stone tomb. Mary's womb and this tomb were his anchorhouses.[19]

The women who lived in enclosed religious houses were sometimes able to commission the devotional imagery that surrounded them, and they often made – painted, embroidered, carved – objects too.[20] A small

triptych of Mary and son accompanied by scenes of the Nativity and the Passion stood on the transept altar of the church of Santa Chiara in Assisi, around 1265. Around 1320 Master Henry of Constance was commissioned to create an image of the Visitation for the nuns of Katharinenthal.[21] Here is a work of great simplicity and beauty: the two women face each other, and in the middle of their bodies, somewhere near the heart and above the womb, a crystal marked the place of gestation of their sons, John the Baptist and Jesus. There is a great tenderness in their gestures and a promise to nuns too: Jesus could be born in their hearts.

Mary as mother also offered privileged access to her son, and this was a rich vein for exploration. Umiliana dei Cerchi of Florence (1219–46) was a widowed mother who chose not to remarry and thus incurred the anger of her father. She was moved to pray to Mary, another mother, and was helped by the Child Christ.[22] Agnes Blannbekin (d.1315), a lay woman who lived in chastity in a community of beguines in Vienna, left an account of visions received between 1291 and 1294, which was committed to Latin by her Franciscan spiritual mentor. Agnes experienced hundreds of visions, many of them animated by Mary. Once she was allowed to witness the birth of Christ, a vision which she reported in detail:

And the Blessed Virgin Herself had a very devout face, full of grace. And while she was bright and shining before the hour of birth, during the hour of birth she appeared [to be] much brighter. She was alone when she gave birth, except that in place of midwives, a multitude of countless angels were all around her and the boy ... At the hour of birth, the Blessed [Virgin] was infused with such Divine sweetness beyond her endurance that she could not bear the tenderness of such sweetness. She collapsed and physically fainted, not because of pain, but because of the sweetness of ecstasy.[23]

Some German Dominican nuns achieved a particular intensity in reflection on the Christ Child; they became mothers for a while during contemplation and visionary experiences. Christina Ebner (1277–1356) dictated a vision to her male confessor. In it she gave birth, like Mary:

She dreamt that she was pregnant with our Lord and she was so full of grace that there was no limb of her body which did not receive special grace from it, and she came to have such tenderness for the infant, because she was his protection ... And it was in sweetness without any discontent such that no sorrow and no

sadness touched her, and after a while she dreamt how she would bear him without pain and received super-abundance of joy from the sight of him. When she had gone about for some time with this happiness she was no longer able to conceal it and took the child in her arms and carried it to the gathering of sisters in the refectory and said, 'Rejoice with me: I can no longer conceal my joy from you; I have conceived Jesus and given birth to him.'[24]

In that state of joy Christina woke up from her dream. She had sensed the delight of maternal intimacy with a child. Mary is nowhere mentioned and yet she is everywhere present: in the child, fruit of her womb, in the painless birth, in the sweetness of the encounter. Adelheide Langmann of the convent at Engelthal (1306–75) experienced not only birth but nursing during a vision which appeared to her after Christmas:

At the same time our Lady, the sweet queen Maria, came one night as she [Adelheide] lay in her bed and carried the child on her arm and gave her the child on her arm while she was in bed. And he was so beautiful that it was unspeakable and he suckled her breast and stayed with her until they sounded matins and she had such great joy.[25]

The sweetness of ecstasy was often associated with pain or with images of physical transformation. The Virgin Mary prompted visions and mystical experience, in the shapes of mother, bride and friend. Mary was above all solace, even of a very physical kind. The German religious woman Christina of Stommeln (1242–1312), whose biography was written by her spiritual advisor Peter of Dacia (1235–90), was described as feeling a snake entering her body and eating away at her inner parts, an intimation of purgatorial suffering to come. Her prayer to Mary resulted in the grant of a special drink that took the pain away:

The blessed virgin appeared and carried with her something like a chalice and put it to her mouth saying: 'take this, dearest one, and drink from this; you will receive health, and the pain which you suffered in your body, will fly away.'[26]

The mystic Elizabeth Stagel (d.1360) described the lives of her sisters in the Dominican house of Töss, near Winterthur. Among them was the beguine Adelhaid of Frauenberg, who sought above all to serve the Child Christ with her body:

she desired to remove her skin so it could be made into a skirt and imagined that her marrow be pulverized into a mash, that her blood be made into a bath, and

264

her bones be burnt in the fire, and her flesh would be consumed for all sins, and cried out from her heart that she be given a single drop of the milk of our Lady which fed our Lord.[27]

Advisors to Dominican nuns sought to guide them to correct imitation of Mary, grounded in orthodox theology. A sermon for Christmas was the obvious occasion for such advice:

Whoever wants this birth in her soul as nobly and spiritually as it occurred in Mary's she should observe the qualities which made her a mother, physically and spiritually. She was a pure maiden, a virgin, and she was betrothed, given in marriage and as separated from everything when the angel came to her. And such should a spiritual mother of God be for this birth.[28]

In the privacy of her cell the mystic Julian of Norwich (1342–c.1416) discovered why Mary was indeed the person who suffered most deeply with Christ, an understanding gained from visions:

Here I saw in part the compassion of our blessed lady Saint Mary; for Christ and she were so united in love that the greatness of her love was cause of the greatness of her pain. For in this I saw a substance of kind love continued by grace that his creatures have for him, which kind of love was most fulsomely shown in his sweet mother, and overflowing, for as much as she loved him more than all other, her pain surpassed that of all others. For ever the higher, the mightier, the sweeter a love is, the more sorrowful it is to the lover to see the body s/he loved in pain. And so all his disciples and all his true lovers suffered more pain than their own body dying, for I am sure by my own feeling that the least of them loved him so far above themselves that it is beyond all that I can say.[29]

Dorothea of Montau (1347–94) lived as a married woman in Gdansk, but strove in many ways to enhance her closeness to Mary and her son. Dorothea experimented in all forms of religious practice: while on pilgrimage with her husband to the Marian shrine of Einsiedeln she could hardy tear herself away from the place. She had particularly intense experiences on Mary's great feasts. Once she experienced hot and cold spells during prayer sessions following the Feast of Candlemas (Purification). She prayed to Mary:

Oh, most beloved virgin, honourable mother of God, blessed above all women, answer me, show and give me your most beloved son ... Behold, after much imploring and many endearments inspired by Dorothea's having been set afire

with God's love for the holy virgin, she mercifully was granted her prayer . . . and as a sign that her prayer had been granted, Mary placed into her arms a most delightful thing that Dorothea received with great reverence and delight. She was set ablaze with the fire of divine love and filled with inexpressible joy in which she remained for many days and which made her exclaim lovingly; 'o, dear rose, laugh; laugh, dear tender rose'.[30]

Dorothea begged for a share in the little boy, who was placed in her hands. This was not the sole guise in which she encountered him, for on another occasion the 'sweet bridegroom Jesus Christ' is said to have revealed himself to her and taught her spiritual love songs. Dorothea saw her own life of striving within marriage as an echo of Mary's story of chaste conjugality.[31]

Mary was easily absorbed into images of bride mysticism, since Mary herself was her son's bride. The Coronation of Mary was associated with the Assumption and its meanings, and it was represented as the coming together of Christ and his mother as equals, bride and bridegroom in heaven. This encounter could appeal to religious men as well as to women. The monk Hermann-Joseph ($c.1150-1241$) of the Premonstratensian monastery of Steinfeld near Cologne was a great devotee of Mary from an early age. His biographer, a fellow monk, described Hermann-Joseph's reception of sounds, smells and sightings of Mary. These culminated in a marriage between Mary and her devotee, in a ceremony performed by an angel attending her. In this way he became her 'second spouse', Joseph.[32] Hermann-Joseph's prayer-hymn to Jesus displays a deep immersion in the Song of Songs, which, as we have seen, offered bridal and Marian allegories. He used them to express his love to Jesus, his bridegroom:

> O Jesus sweet and beautiful!
> O rose smelling in a wondrous way!
> O my loving bridegroom,
> Magnificent beyond measure!
> O my most handsome beloved![33]

This is no simple coupling, for his hymn to Mary pleads: 'O my beloved, purify my heart so that we can live together with Jesus in an ardent and sincere love'. Hermann-Joseph seems to have experienced in turn being bride to both Mary and Jesus, child to Mary, and playmate to her son.

So the rich maternal and bridal imagery around Mary, often associated with female mystics, was explored by male religious too. A manuscript containing the Life of the German mystic Henry Suso ($c.$1295–1366) has drawings of Henry kneeling in front of Mary with her son in her arms. In another drawing the roles are reversed: Henry sits enthroned – like the traditional Mary of wisdom – and he holds Mary and her Child in his lap.[34]

Some writers of German devotional texts for the use of female religious – the John booklets, *Johannis libelli* – found in the figure of John the Evangelist, the virginal companion of Jesus, a useful model for the questing nun. At the foot of the cross Christ recommended John and Mary to each other for special love and care. While the twelfth-century commentary on the Song of Songs by Bernard of Clairvaux lamented the dismal exchange 'Behold thy mother' (John 19:27) of 'John in place of Jesus, the servant in place of the Lord', fourteenth-century mystical writers revelled in the possibilities offered by imagining such closeness to Mary. The aspiring religious might hope to occupy John's special location, to become that special friend. Some writers in this tradition suggested that John and Mary miraculously even came to share the same flesh through a 'spiritual birth on the part of the mother, and a bodily birth on the part of the child'. The *libellus* of Henry of Schaffhausen likened this transformation to the eucharist:

In the same moment the flesh and blood of St John turned into the flesh and blood of our Lady, and from the moment when God spoke the words St John was as truly the son of our Lady as if she had carried him and given birth to him.[35]

Inspired by the Song of Songs' bridal imagery, John was likened to Jesus' bride. As the lover John lay his head on the pillow – Jesus – and this pillow was elaborately described: 'The pillowcase was the delicate humanity of our Lord. The soft feathers were the sweet and lofty divinity. The pillowcase was made by the noble angel Gabriel and the Queen of Heaven and the Holy Spirit . . .'[36] The first stitch was Gabriel's *Ave*; the second was Mary's answer 'Let it be with me according to your word'. In this instance John and Christ's relationship is to the fore, but the bridal imagery's richness is the product of a century of reflection on Mary as bride in vernacular writings for and by nuns. John became Jesus' bride, but as a man he also undermined that bridal imagery. The *Johannes-libelli* are probably best understood as off-shoots from an

267

already well-established devotional interest in Mary, towards a more specialized, even esoteric, formulation of divine love between men. In the vernacular lives of Mary, like the *Marienleben* of Wernher the Swiss, Mary is mother of Christ above all, and little is made of the 'adoption' scene at the foot of the cross. Another sign of the careful balance in this relationship of three is suggested in an icon in Kiev which depicts a wild-eyed John surmounted by two roundels on either side of his head: Jesus on his right and Mary on his left.

With Mary's growth in the vernacular and with the proliferation of opportunities in religious life for women, new figures of Mary were created in words, image and gesture. While the monks of earlier centuries led the making of Mary in Latin liturgy, biblical commentary, theology and devotional poetry, Mary of religious women was available in this period through a dizzying array of vernacular poetry, devotional images and objects of daily life in religious communities. In all of these there is an immediacy in appreciating Mary's motherhood and nurture, from cradle to the foot of the cross.

MARY AND THE LEARNING OF MEN

Women related to Mary as mothers and as virgins, thereby exploring the possibilities offered by her unique combination of nurture and purity. Men explored Mary in the privacy of penance and prayer, through their duties as priests and preachers, as heads of family in charge of instruction and discipline, and as artists and makers of public works. While we rightly think about the affinities of women and Mary, we must also appreciate the privileges of education and priesthood that men could bring to their exploration of her.

Mary offered seemingly endless opportunities for display of cleverness and inventiveness. These qualities were nowhere more concentrated than in the intellectual forums of learning and writing: universities, schools and religious houses all over Europe. Cathedral schools since the eleventh century and universities since the thirteenth century had developed an intellectual method which explored and re-expressed religious and scientific truths through the disciplined dialectical debate known as scholastic method. Mary offered rich opportunities for the display of acumen in debate, of literary sensibility, and of skill in biblical

commentary. She thus became the ideal touchstone for testing and displaying those skills. Writing about Mary – like writing about the eucharist – was a challenging occasion for display, since, as we have seen repeatedly, Mary was full of contradiction. Discussion of Mary required engagement with fundamental questions of Christian history and cosmology. Since the creator dwelt within her, Mary was seen as a source of knowledge about nature, hence a fitting patron of learning: images of Mary enthroned, her son in her lap, were imprinted on the seals of the universities of Prague and Krakow.

In 1404 a German student, Anselm of Frankenstein, expressed his anxiety about his course of study by composing a letter to Mary with a request that she bless his studies. In what amounts to a rhetorical exercise, he addressed the most merciful queen of all devout people:

Therefore I ask you, empress of angels, virtuous consoler of all unhappy creatures, the well of living water, from which streams of all virtues incessantly bubble, with a prostrate body, with prayers from my whole heart humbly ... to grant me from your customary goodness the mercy to illuminate me with the dawn of beloved truth and the bright light of heavenly knowledge.[37]

Mary's answer was also imagined by the student Anselm and was copied into the letter-collection. It is a short answer to his prayer: the cleanliness of the student's heart would lead him to purity and virtue in learning:

At this time of harvest and grace cleanse yourself of all impurities, and your life will remain clean and, having rejected the impurities of your heart, you will serve your creator with all your might.[38]

Here is a playful reply from Mary, reflecting her understanding of the spiritual challenges posed by learning. The vast late medieval enterprise of university study was full of pitfalls and dangerous by-ways; it could inspire pride, despair and confusion. In the complex matters of Christian scholarship who better than Mary as guide? When understanding failed Mary was approached, sometimes with something like a tone of complaint: the Franciscan Ricoldo de Monte Croce witnessed the fall of the city of Acre, the last stronghold of Christians in the Levant, from Baghdad. He was devastated by the sight of Christian refugees and prisoners, some being sold into slavery in the city's markets, and turned his complaint into letters, the first to God and, when he did not explain, then to Mary:

And so now I am afflicted and derelict, alone in a faraway land, weak in body, sad at heart and almost totally consternated in mind, I call you, an exile, not only the son of Eve, but the son of Mary: woe, woe to miserable me, woe to me.[39]

Creative writing about Mary often involved the reorganization of knowledge, and this gave occasion for the deployment and display of skill. Competition was inherent in this world of academic exertion, in communities of men, where rivalry was intense. This tendency is playfully expressed in the fourteenth-century Netherlandish poem *The Praise of Mary* (*Den lof van Maria*). The Dutch poet Jacob van Maerlant sets the scene for a competitive conversation with two famous philosophers – Albert the Great (*c.*1206–80) and Henry of Ghent (*c.*1217–93) – on the subject of Mary's praise. Albert claimed that even if all the flowers, animals, stars and plants tried to speak as wisely as scholars they could not tell her praises fully. Henry claimed further that even if all grains of sand, drops of water, rain and hale tried to do so, they would fail. Jacob followed his colleagues and added all creatures in sky and on land, all angels, apostles and confessors to his list, and this won him praise as the philosophers concluded: 'Master Jacob, we offer you the mastery because you have spoken the praise of Mary better than we did. This we admit.'[40] Mary tested scholars' ingenuity, and here allowed the Netherlandish poet to elevate the effect of his vernacular effort above the Latin learning of university scholars.

Scholars attended not only to theological questions and legal disputations – very few of which touched the subject of Mary – they heard sermons tailored to their interests in college and university churches. A sermon from mid-thirteenth-century Oxford University offers insight into the technique of similitude (*similitudo*), a device commonly used in preaching. In one of his fifteen sermons about her the Dominican friar Richard Fishacre (d.1248), likened Mary to an olive tree.[41] The sermon is based on Psalm 52:10: 'But I, like an olive tree in the house of God, trust in God's faithful love forever'. It proceeds by addressing three questions: 'Why is Mary to be compared to a tree?', 'Why is Mary to be compared to a fruit-bearing tree rather than to a sterile one?', and 'Why is Mary to be compared to a garden tree, not one of the forest?' The answers are simple yet compelling, told in a language that avoids technical terms even when it uses Aristotle's categories. Mary is excellent, just like trees that are 'singularly eminent' earthly adornments. Like Mary

the tree is both useful and sublime; the tree offers shelter from heat and storm, so does Mary from the feverish desires of the flesh. Like the tree Mary is generative and fecund; just as trees fertilize themselves – so people believed, following Aristotle – she gave birth without the intrusion of a man. Trees bear fruit without losing their integrity or feeling pain, just as Mary did. Why compare Mary to an olive tree? Because it is the sign of peace: like the olive-branch that brought hope after the Flood, so did Mary after a long flood which had distanced humans from God. Furthermore, the olive tree combines a bitter root with sweet fruit; likewise Mary suffered bitterly with her son, while remaining sweet. The olive tree requires little cultivation; Mary too grew and developed without the guidance of her parents, alone in the Temple. Finally, like garden fruit which is less abundant than that of the forest but is better and matures more quickly, so Mary made fruit superior to that of any other woman, one sole perfect fruit – Jesus.

Fishacre inhabited a Latin sphere of experimentation with biblical reference and botanical insight all in the service of understanding Mary and explaining her. Some of those who heard him may have become priests in parishes or preachers in the English language. Men like William of Shoreham, the priest of Kent whose pastoral verse we have already encountered, conveyed insights from the schools to parishioners in a language they could appreciate. In the second stanza of Shoreham's poem *Mary Maiden Mild and Generous* (*Marye mayde milde and fre*) the imagery of the olive tree seems close to that expounded by Fishacre:

> You are the dove of Noah
> That brought the branch of olive tree,
> As a sign of peace to come
> Between God and humans.
> Sweet Lady, help me,
> When I shall journey to heaven.[42]

Richard Fishacre displayed his skill and influenced future preachers by turning to the Bible. The Franciscan Servosanctus of Faenza (d.1300) used the Bible in a different way. His *Mariale* likened each of the 150 psalms to an image of Mary: eighteen psalms are linked with biblical images (light, sun, moon), twenty-four with earthly elements (land, gold, gem), thirty-three with biblical trees and plants (like the olive tree), eight with animals (as does the bestiary), thirty-seven with products of arts and

crafts (book, mirror), and in the final thirty psalms Mary's praise was told through a spiritual relationship (queen, sister). Here are some examples:

c. 19
Ave, you who relieve pain,
sweet, gentle, light breeze,
sapphire-like and serene
always full of celestial manna.

c. 22
Ave, gate of delights,
you, heart of joy,
to you aspire all those shipwrecked
all those who love you find joy in you.

c. 26
Ave, pre-elected virgin
you are the chosen arrow
you run like a swift tiger
and always aid your people.

c. 34
Ave, cause of our laughter
paradise of pleasures,
a garden which God planted
and in which he dwelt.

c. 39
Ave, haven for sinners,
solid rock, hope of the guilty,
you give drink to the thirsty,
you give salvation to the suffering.

c. 42
Ave, precious jewel
beautiful, shiny, worthy
you are truly the gem of gems,
the fullness of all grace.[43]

The Franciscan author mediates knowledge at several levels. He adopts from the liturgy of votive masses for Saturdays the eulogy of Wisdom and turns it Mary's way. He produces easily memorable epithets, for use in prayer, in processions or for the enrichment of sermons. He demonstrates God's desire to unite Mary with the whole of creation.

In schools and universities all students engaged with those parts of the curriculum that taught the arts of writing and argument. Mary's complexities elicited attempts at virtuosity. The bestiary and the lapidary, as well as cycles of myths and ancient poetry – Christian spoils from antiquity – were moralized afresh in a Marian key. Guillaume le Clerc composed a bestiary – a moralizing allegorical exposition on the qualities of animals – in England around 1265–70, with an allegorical interpretation for every beast. The elephant's well-known quality of chastity made it an image of monastic purity, but also an image of Mary.[44] A fourteenth-century Dominican also adapted the bestiary to Mary, in his *Rosarius*. Here is his entry on the panther (meaning a leopard):

> The panther is a temperate beast
> Adorned with many markings
>
> . . .
>
> The panther is very courteous
> And bears offspring only once.

He then reveals the moralizing Marian meaning of the panther:

> The panther is Mary
> Full of moderation
>
> . . .
>
> the variety of colours
> is her plurality of virtues.
> which are adornment to the soul.[45]

The salamander does not burn in fire, and so it too was like Mary:

> By salamander Mary is meant
> Every wise person is amazed
> to see how neat and harmonious she is
> Conscience in this life
>
> . . .

> purify your conscience
> pour copious tears,
> and you will get to see Mary.[46]

The world of university learning, a world of many young men and a few seasoned ones, offered transferable skills for the making of careers in church, state, civic or aristocratic service. A Christian version of the ancient liberal arts – dialectic, grammar, rhetoric, music, geometry, astronomy and arithmetic – was the foundation, a set of skills that was used in compositions about Mary. Heinrich von Mügeln's *Meide Kranz* has twelve academic disciplines compete for a place in Mary's crown, the crown of twelve stars, like that of the Woman of the Apocalypse, an image that often merged with Mary. Each art boasted its suitability to dwell in Mary's crown, and the contest was to be adjudicated by no less than Emperor Charles IV (1316–78), to whom the poem was dedicated. It was only appropriate that all wisdom should dwell in this crown since Mary herself was the embodiment of knowledge. Mary bore not only Jesus, but a vision of nature, replete with wisdom: 'through the narrow passage of your heart/nature emerged in the proper way'.[47] These intellectual projects manifest the journey towards knowledge as a journey of exploration with the mother, of her body and its secrets, and of seeking her approving embrace.

Poets tested their skills in the arduous transformation of Latin poetry into verse suitable for Christians. The poetry of Ovid (43BCE–17CE) was translated by the French Benedictine monk Pierre Bersuire (*c.*1290–1362), with Christian moralizing interpretations, in the vast poem – 70,000 lines long – the *Ovide moralisé (Moralized Ovid).*[48] A Marian connection now gave meaning to the lives of gods and goddesses: so Daphne represents Mary since she became a laurel, the sign of constancy. A competitive dialogue, which pitted the qualities of Ajax against those of Ulysses, was turned into a dispute over the relative importance of John the Baptist and Christ. John had foreknowledge of the Incarnation within

> The Virgin Lady
> who carried her son and father
> and was purely [both] virgin and mother.

But Christ triumphs since he *is* the Incarnation. He is the possessor of divine knowledge through a mother pure and fecund:

> Mary
> fecund virginity
> and virginal fecundity.[49]

The *Ovide moralisé* revealed Christian truths inherent even in the most outrageous pre-Christian stories about gods and goddesses.

Other forms of knowledge challenged Christian truths: the esoteric sciences of astrology and alchemy, as well as Jewish lore. These did not cohabit comfortably with the curriculum of Christian schools, yet they often attracted men who sang Mary's praises. Mary was sometimes invoked to ease the tension, lessen the danger of the intellectual encounters with covert knowledge. The late thirteenth-century French *Le livre de Sydrac* (*The Book of Sydrac*), is a dialogue between King Boctus and the sage Sydrac, 'a fountain of all knowledge'. The 1,227 questions posed by the king covered all areas of knowledge, beginning with original sin and salvation through the Incarnation. He even asked the most fundamental question: 'Why would he want to be born of a virgin and how could she be a virgin if he was born of her?' Sydrac answers that God became man in four ways, of which two were:

The first manner: when Adam was created he had neither father nor mother besides God, and so the Son of God was born of the Virgin; he is his own son and the father of the daughter who was to be his mother.

The second manner: of man alone; just as Eve who was born from the rib of a man became woman, so the Son of God born of a Virgin and the Spirit of the Father, and it was the same, he became man.[50]

The king continues to explore the virgin-mother's origins and asks who the virgin's people were (*De quel gent sera cele Virge de qui naitra le Fis de Dieu?*).

Sydrac answers: from the beginning of the world God cherished (*garda*) those who loved him best. And from that people the Virgin was chosen, who was clean and pure of all sin and blooming (*florissant*) in all dignities, and bore the Saviour without any sin nor with any dirt or pain. And the Saviour entered her womb, and the door was closed, just as when the sun penetrates through and exits glass without damaging it. And in her womb he took on human nature, and remained

nine months so as to complete the nine orders of angels just like those born in the world.[51]

For all these qualities the Virgin was awarded a special end, to be assumed into heaven in the flesh (*en char*) and there to sit, crowned beside her son, above the angels and the heavenly host.[52] Here is an inventive exercise, in the didactic pattern of question and answer, in pursuit of truth through the interrogation of a non-Christian sage.

Mary became counsellor and balm to the fevered and tormented intellect of the monk Jean of Morigny, who was troubled by a different type of knowledge. Born late in the thirteenth century in a village near Blois, Jean studied theology and canon law at the University of Orléans in the first decade of the fourteenth century and returned to his monastery at Morigny, near Chartres, in 1308, where he began a career of writing. He produced *The Book of Thirty Simple Prayers* between 1304 and 1307, *The Book of Visions* (*Livre des visions*) in 1313, and two years later *The Book of Figures of the Virgin Mary* (*Livre des figures de la Vierge Marie*).[53] His dabbling in magic and alchemy took him away from religious certainty. In his confusion and despair, he turned to Mary and composed prayers for consolation through her praise. These sometimes sounded like the conjuring of a spirit: 'rise, rise, rise, sweetest Virgin Mary ... I invoke you, come, come, come to me'.[54]

Universities offered occasions for intellectual sparring and display, for competitive invention around the figure of Mary. Unlike so many areas of speculation which scholars were accused of pursuing out of sheer curiosity, Mary was always a worthy subject and an intriguing one too. Conventional schemes of knowledge attempted to encompass Mary in mnemonic schemes and categories of organization. The alphabet offered the pattern for the most exhaustive collections, which aimed to present total scientific grasp, linguistic control and pious intention. The Londoner James Le Palmer, clerk of the Exchequer (before 1327–75), compiled an encyclopedia, *Omne Bonum* (*All that is Good*) in the third quarter of the fourteenth century. The two volumes are spectacular artefacts, a symphony of knowledge in word and image.[55] Each entry opens with an illustrative initial. The entry for 'Virgin Mary Mother of God' (*Maria Mater Dei Virgo*) was accompanied by four illustrations. Le Palmer even provided instructions for the illustrator as to the scene

he wanted for each of the four initials: Mary in Glory, Mary Learning to Read, the Assumption, and the Annunciation.

The lengthy entry uses material from an earlier encyclopedia, the *Manipulus florum*. To this were added extracts from formative and popular texts about Mary, all of which we have already encountered: the Gospel of Pseudo-Matthew, Elizabeth of Schönau's vision of Mary, Bernard of Clairvaux's sermons on the Annunciation and the Adoration of the Magi, readings for Marian feasts, and even an academic theological *quaestio* on the Immaculate Conception. This was a compendium of knowledge useful for composers of sermons, for writers of pastoral tracts, even for those who habitually wrote in Middle English. Wisdom about Mary by this late point in the fourteenth century was closely linked to imagery, and so opens with an illustration of Mary clothed in rays of gold, standing on a crescent moon. There is also a more homely scene of Mary learning to read alongside the celestial Assumption. The *Omne bonum* offered access to all knowledge for good use in teaching and preaching, yet there was an underlying sense of mystery too. The Annunciation shows Mary receiving the news with good faith and acceptance:

Mary, Blessed mother of Jesus, is to be commended for the faith. What even all the priests of the world could not prove, a maiden believed. If the angel had said that, knowing a man, she would conceive, it would have been believed easily, but that a virgin should conceive, that would be most difficult.[56]

All the learning of priests paled in comparison with the mystery of Mary's faith.

Mary was not only an approved subject worthy of intellectual efforts, likely to earn sympathetic reception by patrons or peers. In her also resided the very essence of creativity and equipoise. Medieval pedagogy, based on much physical pain, directed its pupils towards the warm maternal embrace of a gentler teacher, Mary. Mary was the consoling mother from whom such men were removed early in life, and so students dreamed about her and presented their best work to her as offerings. Unlike *grammatica*, the exacting teacher with a rod in her hand, Mary accepted and forgave, appreciated and consoled. By the mid-fourteenth century the two seem to have merged: *grammatica* was maternalized – or 'marianized' – into a gentler nurturing figure.[57] Mary was an ally, as well as a worthy subject, in the competitive worlds of intellectual work.

The ABC epitomizes the acquisition of the formal properties of language, that learning which removes the child from the breast where it first learns to speak into the world of grammar. ABC is innocence and its loss; from it children learned to read and pray. Jesus was habitually shown with Mary, learning to read, sometimes from an ABC in his primer.[58] The visionary poem by Guillaume de Deguileville c.1330–35, *The Pilgrimage of Human Life* (*Le Pèlerinage de la vie humaine*) imagines the tribulations of the soul as it travels the world by land and sea, assailed by demons and temptations. At a dramatic turning point in the poem the Pilgrim invokes Mary through an ABC poem, each stanza beginning with a letter of the alphabet.[59] Geoffrey Chaucer translated this poem into Middle English in a display of linguistic as well as devotional ingenuity within the seemingly restrictive and simpleminded rhythm of the childish ABC. It begins with A: 'Almighty and all-merciable Queen!'[60]

Writing about Mary was turned by poets into an occasion for display, as in the mid-thirteenth-century macaronic poem, which combines Latin and Middle English:

> Of one that is so fair and bright,
> *Velud maris stella,* [or star of the sea]
> Brighter than the daylight,
> *Parens et puella:*[parent and maiden]
> I cry to thee, thou say to me,
> Lady pray thy Son for me,
> *Tam pia,* [so pious]
> That I may come to thee
> *Maria.*[61]

Lyrics about spring seemed particularly suitable for praises of Mary and form a vehicle for poetical pleasure, display and edification, as inserted into a fourteenth-century sermon:

The dew of Averil, *id est gracia et bonitas Spiritus Sancti;* Haveth y-maked the grene lef to spryng, *id est Beatam Virginem;* My sorrow is gon, *id est pena pro meritis;* My joye is comen, *scilicet per Dei Filium vita beata;* Ich herde a foul synge, *id est angelum, scilicet, Ave Maria.*[62]

Breaking into the mother tongue sometimes marked the poet's move into a register of greater intimacy. The devotional work by Archbishop

(and later Saint) Edmund of Abingdon (1175–1240), *Merure de Seinte Eglise* (*Mirror of Holy Church*), was written in French as edifying reading material for monks. In the section which dwells on Mary's sorrow:

> At this point you must think upon sweet Mary,
> upon what anguish she was filled with
> when she was at his right side
> and received the disciple [John] instead of the Master
>
> . . .
>
> And about this an Englishman says in the following pitying manner:
> 'Now the son goes under the wood
> It saddens me, Mary, your fair cross.
> Now the son goes under the tree
> It saddens me, Mary, your son and thee.'[63]

Laymen privileged with learning, wealth and social status also experimented with writing in search of Mary's consolation for sinful lives. Henry of Grosmont, First Duke of Lancaster, and war hero, indulged his interests and skill in a devotional text in French, *The book of holy medicines* of *c.*1354. Men of the world, like the author, were essentially sick beings, wounded in ears and eyes, nose and mouth, hands and heart, through the sins that come so easily to a man of his station. Henry sought a cure, a healthy lifestyle (*regimen*), won through Christ's bleeding body and ministered by Mary. Each of her joys was imagined as matching perfectly one of his wounds. Mary's milk was to be his nourishment, his wounds were to be cleansed with Mary's tears, as sweet as rose-water:

My most sweet lady Saint Mary, I recommend myself to you, and now beseech you piteously, for the love of your blessed son, that it would please you to look upon me with a kind eye. Most sweet lady, I pray that you see my great need of your help in wrapping my sores with your lovely, clean white cloths, after the application of the above-mentioned precious medicines . . .

And now, most sweet lady, just as I have boldly asked you for your precious milk to drink and for your holy tears to wash my filthy sores, and then asked your most dear son for the precious blood of his blessed body as an ointment . . . I would in no way wish to lose those good medicines entirely for lack of a bandage.

279

Now it is time to identity this fine and beautiful white bandage, and to wrap my dangerous sores in it before they fester. Most sweet lady, this bandage is – as is perfectly right – your greatest joys, which are white, clean, and fair.

Each of Mary's cures touched one of Henry's senses, those conduits to sin. The bandage for the nose is linked to Mary's joy in her son's birth, for while her son was born in a poor house, it was nonetheless

full of a good and noble odor, since it held the flower of flowers . . . and all things that have good odors and sweet fragrances, such as roses, violets, and many other flowers, and also many plants that smell so very sweet, and trees like cypress and leaves of laurel.[64]

This fine odour was to combat the stench of gluttony and lechery.

MARY: THE POETIC IMPOSSIBLE

For all these attempts, for all that we have seen in image and song, in drama and liturgy, for all that Mary was expressed in the dialects and idioms of daily life and was present frequently and readily, poets still protested the impossibility of ever getting Mary quite right. Gautier de Coinci, who made Mary's miracles accessible to French knights and ladies in the early thirteenth century, saw Mary as inexhaustible. While the poet's knowledge may be finite, Mary is not:

> My poor knowledge I can very soon
> Exhaust and extinguish
> If I do not dip in her deep well,
> that no well-digger can exhaust
> no matter how well the well-digger draws:
> It is a sea that no one ever exhausted.
> See her name: M and then A,
> R and then I, then A, and then
> a sea you will find, not a well at all;
> Mary is the sea that no one exhausts;
> The more one draws from it the more he finds.[65]

The impossibility of capturing the fullness of Mary, of doing justice to her plenitude even in the exalted language of poetry, challenged one

of the greatest of poets of the Christian tradition, the Florentine Dante Alighieri (1265–1321). Dante was formed in the world we have just explored – of *laudesi* confraternities, of Duccio's solemn Madonnas – a world in which Mary of gilt majesty blended with the figure of the tender mother offering her breast.[66] After walking through the Inferno with the poet Virgil as his guide, then guided by his loved one, Beatrice, Dante was led by Bernard of Clairvaux, the model Christian and contemplator of the divine. Bernard takes charge in canto 31, gazing at Dante 'as only a loving father can' (line 63). He encourages his charge to approach Mary:

> '. . . but look upon the circles, even the most remote
> until you see upon her seat the Queen
> to whom this realm is subject and devoted'.[67]

Dante does just that, and Mary is, as he had expected, a fusion of all the beauty that poetry and art, liturgy and song had explored and invented over centuries. When he protests the poverty of his words to describe her, this is a declaration of love and of frustration too:

> And at the midpoint, with outstretched wings,
> I saw more than a thousand Angels making festival,
> each one distinct in effulgence and in ministry.
> I saw there, smiling to their sports and to their songs,
> a beauty which was gladness
> in the eyes of all the other saints.
> And had I equal wealth in speech
> as in conception, yet would I not dare
> to attempt the least of her delightfulness.[68]

Mary was the inspiration of poets and their frustration too. There was an abundance of genres and ways of approaching her, yet none seemed quite adequate.

The years between 1200 and 1400 saw the creation of two enduring images of Mary – the ubiquitous group of Mary and her Child and the moving figure of Mary at the foot of the cross. Ideas and practices which were developed in monasteries and cathedrals in earlier centuries were transmitted into homes and streets, parish churches and confraternity chapels of European cities and their hinterlands. This dissemination was

also a process of translation, of movement in words and sounds, from indoor Latin to often outdoor Tuscan and English, French and German, Danish and Icelandic, Hungarian and Czech. As Mary entered homes, inspired family life, visited religious in their cells and habitually greeted people from church façades, she acquired local colour and relevance. Some of this quality in turn fed back into the spheres of Latin clerical writing too. The styles of representing Mary, of thinking and relating to her, were as diverse as were her users: men and women, young and old, learned and simple, townspeople and rustic folk. There were Christians of all walks of life, and there were Jews and Muslims too, whose relationship to her was a source of fascination and dread.

The consequences of Mary's increased familiarity were far from banal. The process was accompanied by an elevation of Mary to an importance equal to that of her son in European devotional life: she gained a Coronation of great dignity, was associated with the Trinity, and some even claimed that she had never been touched by original sin. In Mary was thus to be found not only the key for domestic devotion, but a marker of civic and dynastic dignity. In the fifteenth century – with its Renaissance of great creativity in word, sound and image – Mary was mobilized by the politics of reform, in efforts to correct, discipline and inspire Europeans, and to move them to defend European lands assailed by the Turks.

PART V

Mary as Queen and Reformer: 1400–1500

17

Mary the Sublime

MARY OF COURT AND RULE

One of the most stunning images made in late medieval Europe is the Wilton Diptych, a pair of panels which links Mary and majesty in new and interesting ways. On the left panel are three male figures: King Edmund of East Anglia, King Edward the Confessor, St John the Baptist and, at their feet, kneeling, King Richard II (1367–1400). This group regards the second panel, and its gaze leads the viewer to the scene on the right: Mary and Child, surrounded by a court of eleven angels, set in a flowering meadow. Like Mary, the angels are dressed in blue; they wear garlands of pink roses and carry the badge of the white hart, Richard's personal emblem. The naked Christ Child leans towards the praying king, as if to receive him into Mary's exalted court. King Richard in turn appeals to Mary, supported by England's special patrons: two devout kings, St Edmund and St Edward, in rich royal attire, and Richard II's favourite saint, John the Baptist. Royalty, dynasty and sanctity combine and connect across the hinges that link the panels with Mary's celestial court.

The Wilton Diptych was made for a king who cherished ideas of sacred kingship. He may have learned how rich such notions could be from his wife, Anne of Bohemia, daughter of the Holy Roman Emperor Charles IV, who had chosen Mary as patron of his dynasty. Richard II's adoption of the idiom which his grandfather Edward III had already identified and explored – Mary as patron of sacred monarchy – demonstrates some of the possibilities which European rulers were discovering in Mary. Imperial Mary was the creation of Byzantine Christianity; as Mother of God (*Theotokos*) she offered a focus for the emergent Christian world of the fifth century. Almost a thousand years later European

polities – kingdoms, principalities, duchies, city states – were invoking Mary in support of their own claims to rule. Moreover, Mary's fecundity endorsed the aspirations for healthy lineage, which all dynasts desired. Her power to protect people of all conditions – as Mother of Mercy (*Mater misericordiae*) – was a reminder of the duties of those whose privilege it was to wield power.

Each European region produced its own favourite interpretations of Mary, and these coalesced into local visual traditions. Images from churches of the Tirol region, for example, represent Mary crowned by the persons of the Trinity. Mary is sometimes seated and approached by all three, or kneels in front of God the Father to receive her crown in their presence.[1] An unusual variation on the Coronation appears in a Book of Hours made in Rouen around 1470–80: Mary kneels in front of God the Father, who wears a pope's tiara, while an angel plunges from above with a crown for Mary's head.[2]

For her quality of queenliness Mary attracted the special devotion of kings and princes. Henry V (1387–1422), king of England, approached Mary not only as a penitent, as his great-grandfather, Henry of Grosmont, had done some sixty years earlier, he claimed her as a model of majesty and priesthood, of sacred kingship embodied in his own person. For the victorious return to England following the Battle of Agincourt in 1415, Henry's uncle, Henry Beaufort, bishop of Winchester, designed a grand royal entry into London. The theme was more virginity than chivalry, more celestial than martial. Sung verses welcomed the victor as if he were Christ at his birth:

> Virgins out of the castle did glide
> For joy of him they were dancing.
> They kneeled down all at once,
> 'Nowell,' 'Nowell', they all sang.[3]

Mary was a dynastic patron, and she merged with the well-being and safety of England.[4] Henry V's son was crowned as a baby to become Henry VI. Though much different in character to his father, Henry VI shared Henry V's devotion to Mary. He enjoyed visions of Mary, and as he matured into a serious-minded young man he wore a blue cloak like Mary's. When he founded the educational institutions at Eton and Cambridge, he dedicated them to Mary, too. After his death Henry VI was acclaimed as a saint, and although he was never officially

canonized he was widely believed to have worked miracles with Mary.[5]

For this English court, oriented towards conquest and colonization, Henry V commissioned a poem about Mary's life from the monk-poet John Lydgate (c.1370–1451). *The Life of Mary*, in almost 6000 lines, tells the story of Mary, a girl born of a good lineage, 'daughter of David', 'heavenly queen', 'of so high estate'. Lydgate's tone is neither penitential nor humble; he celebrates above all Mary's fecundity, her breast and milk, by combining devotional language with medical and pharmacological terms:

> For in the licour was full remedye,
> Holy refute, and pleynly medycyne
> Ayayne the venyme brought in by envye,
> Thorugh fals engyne and malyce serpentine,
> Whan the snake made Adam to dyne ·
> Of the Appull that was intoxicate,
> Falsely with god to make hym at debate.
>
> . . .
>
> Of mayden mylke spryng as a Ryuer,
> To yefe hym drynke that is kyng of alle.
> O goode lady, o hevenly boteler,
> When we in myscheve to clepe and calle,
> Some drope of grace lat vpon vs falle;
> And to that seler make a Redy waye,
> Wher thou alone of mercy beryste the keye.[6]

Like other poets of Mary, Lydgate was inspired by his subject to produce some of his best poetry.[7] Lydgate's telling of Mary's life encompasses classical antiquity, Old Testament prophecy, scripture and apocrypha; the traditions of centuries were elegantly combined in rhyme for the pleasure of the English king and his court.

Earlier in his life, as Prince of Wales, Henry had been reminded of Mary's power to protect and inspire. *The Regiment of Princes* was a poem for princely guidance, composed by a bureaucrat and poet of his court, Thomas Hoccleve. Hoccleve advised and directed the prince to take good counsel from young and old, a common trope in books for princes. While advising Prince Henry, Hoccleve was reminded of his own intellectual master – Chaucer – and turns to Mary for advocacy on behalf of that great poet. Hoccleve recommends Chaucer to Mary:

287

> As you well know, o blessed virgin,
> With loving heart, and high devotion
> In your honour he wrote full many a line;
> Oh now your help and your assistance,
> To God your son offers a prayer
> How he your servant was, maiden Mary,
> And let love of him flower and fructify. (Lines 4,985–91)[8]

Hoccleve sought intercession from Mary for the sake of both men – poet and king, dead and alive.

The poetry of Mary's excellent queenship was expressed by a multitude of vernacular renderings of earlier Latin chants. Some were inspired by the *Regina coeli* (*Queen of Heaven*), the twelfth-century prayer which is sung throughout the Easter week at Compline, the final service of the day:

> Queen of Heaven rejoice, alleluia: for He whom you merited to bear, alleluia, Has risen as He said, alleluia. Pray for us to God, alleluia.[9]

The fifteenth-century poem *Regina coeli, Queen of the South* offers a string of appellations to Mary as the Queen of Sheba, who was thought to have inspired Solomon's Song of Songs. The English and Latin blend into a heady address to a woman full of wisdom:

> Regina Coeli, queen of the south
> Created by Solomon in his sapience,
> Full sweet are the words that come out of your mouth,
> You blissful maiden, with great prudence,
> *Quo progredieris* [where are you going] from your presence?
> Most highest *in montibus* [in the mountains], most salient,
> *Maria Virga Assumpta est* [Mary the Virgin is assumed].
> Harvest is come, I come to shear,
> The mirror of immortality,
> *Vox dilecta* [the voice of the beloved] is in her ear,
> Thus she said, *Transite ad me* [come to me].[10]

Mary was inspiration to poets, Mary was a companion of kings, Mary was a companion of the Trinity. These themes evolved side by side over the medieval centuries. Nor were these associations unique to England. The Catalan painter Lluís Dalmau articulated in 1443 Mary's power to

inspire good rule in the altarpiece *The Virgin and the Councillors*: Mary and God are seated on an elaborate throne in the company of the kneeling Council of One Hundred, Barcelona's ruling group, together with saints and martyrs.[11] Dalmau had spent time in the Netherlands, and his altarpiece situates Mary within courtly order and grandeur typical of that region, especially under the rule of the Burgundian dynasty.

MARY IN BURGUNDY

The Burgundian dukes ruled a vast agglomeration of territories in the Low Countries and on the borderlands of France and Germany, extending as far as Switzerland. They tapped the resources of some of the robust urbanized zones of late medieval Europe and perfected rituals of rule through which they displayed might and honoured loyal followers. They created an order of chivalry at the court in Dijon to whose membership they invited the sons of great nobles, aristocrats and foreign dynasts. Philip the Good (1396–1467), duke of Burgundy, summoned the Order of the Golden Fleece, with the aim of reviving crusades. The Order's knightly display was steeped in Marian themes: it celebrated a choral Marian Office which was composed for it in 1454 and approved by the University of Louvain. The image of the golden fleece invoked the biblical story of Gideon, who was marked as God's favoured warrior, first by a wet fleece that did not moisten the ground under it, and then by a dry fleece, untouched by dew. This was also the symbol of Mary: the dew which moistened it figures the Holy Spirit descending on Mary.[12]

While the dukes of Burgundy invoked Mary as a patron of chivalry, their mothers and wives combined interest in Mary with the patronage of the fashionable Bridgettine religious order. These women, foreign princesses who moved at their marriage into this sophisticated court, used the devotion to Mary actively. Mary of Burgundy, duchess of Cleves, chose the site of a Marian shrine – Marienbaum in the Duchy of Cleves in the Rhineland – for the foundation of a Bridgettine convent in 1460. A few years later, in 1469, she persuaded her sister-in-law, Isabella of Portugal, duchess of Burgundy, to found a Bridgettine house, Mariatroon (Mary's Throne), at Dendermonde near Ghent.[13]

Mary was explored in the many arts fostered by the Burgundian court, and so tens of artisans were involved in minute daily judgements about

the style, colours and materials of making Mary for use by nobles and courtiers. The libraries of the dukes of Burgundy contained numerous Books of Hours with Marian emphases and collections of Marian prayers. A typical manuscript of this kind contains translations into French of Anselm's eleventh-century Latin prayers, with commentary for the use of Duke Philip the Good. The two miniatures which adorn the book depict the two acts of homage which prompted its making: the translator's offering of the book to his patron the duke and the duke's homage to Mary.[14] The duke's relation to Mary was an active commitment; his favourite pilgrimage site was the church of Our Lady of Boulogne, which he visited more than a dozen times.[15]

The Burgundian court in Flanders created a European courtly style which was then adopted by other courts and emulated more widely. The finest tapestries were made in Flanders, the most famous of which is the series of the Lady and the Unicorn. Mary is ever present within this courtly fable: the fabulous beast which yearned to lay its head in the lap of a virgin; and as the triumphant lady holding a banner aloft within a stylized garden; the lady merges with the figure of Mary.[16] Mary's life and the life of the court blended even more explicitly in the Tapestry of the Three Kings, made in Tournai around 1440. Here the Magi approach the sumptuously garbed Mary and her son with all the splendour of gift-bearing diplomats of the fifteenth century.[17]

Mary's association with court life led to a vast production of new devotional and musical compositions. The œuvre of the court's man of letters, Georges Chastellain (1403–75), scholarly soldier and chronicler, included poetry that displayed an enchantment and attraction to Mary, like his *Praise to the Very-Glorious Virgin* (*Louenge à la Très-Glorieuse Vierge*). This courtly effusion uses all the imagery of splendour and majesty:

> O saintly splendour in a seraphic court
> Elevated subject of august knowledge
> Repository of joy for all saints and prophets
> In which is clasped all grace divine,
> Every celestial virtue rests,
> Each is there shadowed and accepted
> Each explores its secret riches.

The tone then changes to one of private supplication:

> O holy mirror of wondrous glory,
> Of whom we read of prodigious humility
> You have risen so high, queen,
> Yet all humble, your meritorious sweetness,
> Turn to me in my oratory,
> And allow me to tell a solemn story
> Speaking to you as well as I can.[18]

These poems were made into a booklet of twenty-five folios, which was offered as a gift to Duke Charles the Bold (1433–77); it still remains as part of the Burgundian library.[19]

Mary had long been associated with song, intimately linked to the liturgies of monastery and church and to the chants of confraternities. Fifteenth-century courts were active centres for new musical commissions, for experimentation in composition and performance.[20] All the great composers of the century – many of whom were trained in Burgundy – toured the courts of Europe: England, Burgundy, France, Savoy, Milan and the papal court. John Dunstable ($c.$1390–1453) worked in England and France, Guillaume Dufay (1397–1474) in Cambrai and Rome, Johannes Ockeghem ($c.$1410–97) in Paris and Tours. Ockeghem composed an elegant motet *Nuper rosarum flores* for the consecration of the cathedral of Florence in 1436, of which Mary was the patron; it combined the established liturgy for the dedication of a church and the traditional themes of the church as Temple of Solomon with a new sequence written for the occasion. Here is a blend of old and new, northern and southern, all around the theme of Mary as supreme patron of the church.[21]

Music for Mary's feasts and masses on Marian themes were commissioned by courtiers and celebrated in their chapels. A late fifteenth-century illuminated manuscript made for Philippe Bouton (1418–1515), who served both Philip the Good and Philip the Fair, opens with a prayer, that Mary look down on the human 'exiles' who sing to her. The same manuscript includes Ockeghem's motet for five voices *O intemerata dei mater* and Loyset Compère's ($c.$1445–1518) motet *Sile fragor*.[22] The Burgundian experience was adopted elsewhere too: from the 1470s the Sforza dukes of Milan lured Europe's finest musicians and

composers to a court in which the Milanese Ambrosian tradition yielded new fruit in the form of Marian motet cycles.

Patricians imitated princes and aristocrats and invested prodigiously in the cultural production which drew its inspiration from the figure of Mary. The van Gleijmes family of Bergen founded a family chapel of Our Lady in the church of St Gertrude, which from the 1470s developed into a powerhouse of musical creativity around Mary. Patricians combined in confraternities, some of which were dedicated to themes associated with Mary. The confraternity of the Dry Tree (*Den Droghene Boome*) in Bruges assembled in the Franciscan church, where its members – merchants, craftsmen and aristocrats – supported choral music by the hefty annual membership fee.[23] The Dry Tree invoked the phrase in Ezekiel 17:24: 'And all the trees of the field shall know that I the Lord have brought down the high tree, have exalted the low tree, have dried up the green tree, and have made the dry tree to flourish', which was interpreted as referring to the miracle of a virgin giving birth. The confraternity also generated devotional panels. The artist Petrus Christus created a haunting image of Mary as just such a Dry Tree. The tree's dry branches are arranged in a circle within which Mary and Child are placed, and the letter a (for 'ave') hangs from fifteen of the branches. The atmosphere of the painting is one of mystery. Experiments with Mary's majesty were led by privileged courts but travelled widely through European regions and informed emulation and interpretation within wider social circles.

MARY IN ETHIOPIA

The force of Mary as a figurehead for dynasty and kingdom was also appreciated by Christian rulers outside Europe, as the case of Ethiopia demonstrates in a striking manner. The Ethiopian Emperor Zär'a Ya'eqob (1434–68) consolidated a Christian empire following his father Dawit's territorial gains. He consecrated a new capital city, Däbrä Berhan (Mountain or Monastery of Light), and from his court the worship of Mary was disseminated throughout his lands.[24] As with Henry V, military ambition, religious enthusiasm and an appreciation of the power of patronage combined around the figure of Mary. Zär'a Ya'eqob also confronted unrest and division within the church. In

Ethiopia this was exacerbated by the incorporation into the realm of non-Christian people, among whom polygamy and animistic religion prevailed. He confronted them with the power of Mary: he wore a Marian amulet against attacks by enemy magic and promoted the cult of Mary as a national theme for unification and the incorporation of diverse peoples.

Zär'a Ya'eqob's devotion to Mary had been learned in childhood; his mother believed that Mary had aided her by averting a miscarriage.[25] Like Alfonso the Wise in the mid-thirteenth century, Dawit had commissioned the translation of the Miracles of Mary from Coptic into an official collection, *Tä'ammerä Maryam*. These tales included miraculous interventions in the lives of people in many walks of life. Above all, Mary demonstrated her support to the emperor in struggles against his foes:

Listen, my brothers, to what Our Lady Mary has done. In the middle of the night while I was asleep, (just) at that time, I heard a voice (of a shining man) . . . 'Look, and fear not' . . . He ushered me to the inner side of the gate. There I saw the awe-inspiring ones of the tribe of Israel. A royal crown, whiter than snow, was placed on the head of (each) of them. I asked him saying, 'Who are these whose stature(s) are (so) beautiful, whose countenance(s) (so) comely, and (who) are vested in bright clothes?' He said to me, 'These are the kings of Israel' . . .

Then the ground where I stood brightened like broad daylight. I was startled. I lifted up my eyes into the atmosphere. There I saw a decorated crown which had the color of the star(s) . . . It was held in the hand of Our Lady Mary. With her were two angels vested in fire, one on her right and one on her left side. Beneath her was a circle like a rainbow. And above her was (a spot) like a palace. As for her, she stood in the inner side of this picture and spoke in the direction of the voice that spoke from the atmosphere, 'Give me (this) kingdom which I want.' He said to her, 'I have given (it) to you, a tithe for you in accordance with the previous covenant.' He delivered the kingdom to her . . . She, on her part, called him [ZY] and brought him up into the atmosphere to stand where she was. She put the royal crown on the head of Zär'a Ya'eqob with her (own) hands. She blessed him and said to him, 'Keep this kingdom.' When the kings who were standing under him saw the man arrayed with great honor, they sang (praise) . . .

There are (some) people (who), not understanding the counsel of the Most High, destroyed themselves. (These are) those who conspired in violation of the law. For they have become enemies of God and his Mother Mary . . . He makes

a king reign over his people till (the end of) the period he ordained. No one shall do evil against what he has made good.

O our Lady Mary, who delivered the (kingdom) to Zär'a Ya'eqob, keep his kingdom and root out his enemies and foes, amen and amen.[26]

Zär'a Ya'eqob's authority was also proclaimed through a vision of Mary, revealed to a holy man, Abbot Mälkä Şedeq. In it Mary led the abbot to a mountain top on which Zär'a Ya'eqob was seated on a throne. Mary explained:

This mountain is the throne of the kingdom of Zär'a Ya'eqob. No one can shake it because he is an executor of the will of my son. His kingdom is (greater) than (those of) his fathers . . . Follow him in good conduct.[27]

The *Tä'ammerä Maryam* was disseminated as part of the official liturgy and reached every corner of the Empire, as did images of Mary. Zär'a Ya'eqob promoted the making of icons that were to be treated like emanations of Mary. The artists were monks, like Fré Şeyon, whose work was supported by Zär'a Ya'eqob's patronage.[28] Ethiopian ascetics built a world of emotion and devotion around the contemplation of icons of Mary, such as the portable panel of mother and son the mid-fifteenth century, from Shawa in the centre of the kingdom.[29] Such images were meant to inspire religious illumination in their beholders. As a young man seeking direction in life Marha-Krestos (1408–98), abbot of Dabra Libanos, had prayed to an image of Mary while wearing a Marian prayer-amulet on the nape of his neck. The image came alive and directed him 'Go' and then 'Go toward the north', and so he found his destiny as a holy man.[30] Like his European counterparts, Zär'a Ya'eqob made great gestures of endowment and patronage: when news of the destruction of an important Coptic Marian shrine by Muslim ascetics reached Ethiopia, he hastened to replace it and in 1441 founded the Däbrä Meṭmak (Monastery of the Baptistery).

Zär'a Ya'eqob's political vision was of an empire unified in Christian devotion and political loyalty. Devotion to Mary, and to the cross, was disseminated from his court. In such a way his subjects could pray, process and chant in a similar manner. The Marian programme was promoted by the state. Its reception, however, was bound to be personal and local, just as it was in the many European regions. Mary's power to forgive resonated throughout the *Tä'ammerä Maryam* as it did for

Europeans in the miracle tales of Gautier de Coinci. The miracle of the sinful knight forgiven for a single act of Marian piety – one we have seen in several European versions – has its parallel in the story of the cannibal and Mary in the *Tä'ammerä Maryam*. In this account a cannibal was prompted to give his victim some respite when he said: 'Take, drink for the sake of the name of the holy Virgin Mary; the God-bearer.' After his death,

The Angels of Darkness came in a fear- and awe-inspiring state and surrounded him. They took out his soul, rending (it) away forcibly. Our Lady Mary . . . Mary, the God-bearer, came in search of any good deed in him. Our Lady . . . saw on his side the handful of water which he gave the poor (man) to drink (as) almsgiving for the sake of her name. At that time she rejoiced.[31]

Zär'a Ya'eqob aimed to embed Mary in the chants and images, processions and prayers of monasteries and the communities they served. Mary mediated between parts, peoples and regions in the making of a political whole. Her figure helped define dynastic and national identity for a Christian kingdom in Africa. The materials forged in the fifteenth century still lie at the heart of Ethiopian Christianity today.

MARY AND THE EUROPEAN ORDER

Mary's association with majesty, order, and Christian cosmic fulfilment inspired the use of her figure as an emblem of European renewal. This was a mobilization of efforts on the part of some churchmen, kings and aristocrats to turn the political tide of Turkish ascendency in the Mediterranean. Political and religious themes were, as ever in medieval Europe, closely intertwined. Those who had visited the east were particularly inspired to act through diplomacy to raise the awareness of European leaders. Such efforts were often accompanied by a devotional tone, and Mary – so evidently cherished in both east and west – offered a theme around which cooperation might be envisaged. A French soldier and diplomat, Philippe de Mezières (d.1405), marshalled devotion to Mary in this manner: on a diplomatic mission to the papal court in Avignon on behalf of the king of Cyprus in 1372 Philippe presented a petition for the creation of a feast of the Presentation of Mary in the Temple. He had learned of this feast, celebrated by Greek Christians

since the seventh century, and suggested that Pope Gregory XI institute it in Europe. He wrote a liturgical office for the day and composed a liturgical drama and a sermon. Here was Mary in her infantile purity; here was a symbol of what Europeans could lose if they did not address the pressing military challenges of the day.[32] The play was performed at the papal court at Avignon and in the French court, where Mary was played by a young girl.[33] The feast was promoted with some zeal by the Carmelite friars whose order was devoted to Mary and who cherished links with the Holy Land since their very foundation.[34]

Mary was also invoked as part of efforts to pacify strife within Europe. In 1386 Archbishop John of Jenstein, famed also as a prolific writer of hymns, approached Pope Urban VI in Rome, while a rival pope – Clement VII – presided in Avignon over those parts of Europe which recognized him. He requested that a feast of the Visitation be created following a message from Mary received by him in a dream.[35] Jenstein composed a liturgical office for the feast, which he had already introduced to his own cathedral in Prague. Urban VI agreed to the request and established the new Marian feast in a bull that professed peaceful and conciliatory intent towards his opponents. Over the following decades liturgical books were made to incorporate the feast of the Visitation and often allocated space for its decoration. The scene of two holy women greeting each other with kiss or embrace appeared more frequently, above all in the decoration of books of liturgy and prayer.[36] Yet much opposition in Bohemia meant that his efforts were never truly realized.

Mary's new feasts did not heal the papal schism nor did they calm struggles over European hegemony. Christian polities were forced to think hard about their efforts at cooperation and mutual help as Turkish might delivered a fatal blow to the Byzantine Empire in 1453 and threatened Eastern and Southern Europe. European policy-makers met in Church councils, where plans for internal reform and external crusade were discussed and determined. If Christian Europe was to act as one and support eastern Christians then it had first to settle its dynastic struggles.

When the Christian story was offered to new and recent converts, it had to encompass Mary too. The Teutonic order, which conquered and converted North-east Europe, named its castles in Prussia and Livonia after Mary: Marienwerder, Frauenberg, Marienburg.[37] The churches they founded in conquered and Christianized lands often sported trium-

phant statues of Mary within which were enfolded Father, Son and Holy Spirit. One such *Vierge ouvrante*, from the Lithuanian monastery of Sejny, reveals when opened God the Father holding the crucifix, while on either side are exalted people painted against a gold background, led by a pope and Teutonic Knights.[38] This form was particularly well known in German-speaking lands, but there are some examples from Iberia too.[39] Mary appeared as a capacious and capable mother, a protector powerful for her closeness to the Trinity.

The geopolitical arrangements of the Mediterranean were in flux. Following the fall of what had remained of the Byzantine Empire, with the taking of Constantinople by the Ottomans in 1453, Rome had effectively become the political centre of Christianity. The Christian communities of the Middle East and Africa now turned to Rome for fellowship and support. Europe was inundated with the arrival of Greek religious dignitaries and holy objects that circulated together with exiles from the Christian east. The church of Santa Maria Maggiore in Rome, for example, received in 1453 a belt of Mary, claimed to be the very one kept in the church of the Blachernae for centuries.[40] To the variety of European images of Mary were now added the creations of Ethiopian and Greek, Bulgarian and Armenian artists.

Greek images of Mary were, of course, already known. We have seen how Byzantine narratives – above all the Dormition – were made into Latin stories and how religious artefacts – above all ivories – affected the making of European Mary around the millennium. In Italy Byzantine models gave inspiration to so much of the religious imagery beloved of Tuscan painters. In Northern Europe Greek icons of Mary seemed even more exotic, archaic and potent. Some eastern images were believed to have been painted by the apostle Luke himself. When in 1450 a canon of Cambrai cathedral bestowed upon it an image of Mary that he had purchased in Italy, this created a stir. The image, which came to be known locally as Notre-Dame de Grace, drew many admirers; even the duke of Burgundy came to glimpse the foreign image.[41] The icon was in fact a fourteenth-century work – a smallish image – in a typical Byzantine-Italian pose of the Virgin *Eleousa*, showing Mary tenderly holding her son.

After the shock of the fall of Constantinople to the Turks in 1453 – the city long identified with Mary, where the churches of the *Theotokos* were now being turned into mosques – the duke of Burgundy began to

rally a crusade against the Turks, as did other European rulers. Philip the Good used the festive gathering of the Order of the Golden Fleece in 1454 as an occasion for recruitment of potential crusaders. He announced with bravura:

I vow to God my creator and to the most glorious Virgin his mother and to the ladies . . . that if the most Christian and victorious prince my lord king [of France] takes the cross and exposes his body in defence of the Christian faith and in resisting the damnable enterprises of the Grand Turk and the infidels, and if I am not physically incapacitated, I shall serve him on the crusade in person and with an army.[42]

At the same time his trusted adviser, the count of Etampes, commissioned fifteen copies of the beloved painting of Notre-Dame de Grace: three from the famous master Petrus Christus and twelve from the less-renowned Hayne de Bruxelles. The count made this preference clear: the fifteen copies were to be made 'in the Greek manner' – 'de la façon de Grèce'.[43] These commissioned images may have been intended as standards for a forthcoming crusade: it was fitting that an image which looked so eastern should lead the crusading armies in battles to save the fallen Eastern Empire. Indeed, the circulation of revered Byzantine icons in Europe – especially after the fall of Constantinople – inspired some Northern artists to create their own hybrid forms of 'icons'.[44]

Mary's solace was appreciated by the men who mounted programmes for collective renewal, by those who wielded the power to confront the many dilemmas which faced European institutions in the centuries between Dante and Luther, such as: who was the real pope? What was his authority? How was the Turkish threat to be countered? Such questions were discussed in council chambers, in local and national representative assemblies, in universities, at church councils and in school-rooms. Mary appears along the trails of reform led by some of the most powerful rulers and bureaucrats of Europe. In their attempts to instil a revitalized Christian order – of Christian marriage, Christian polity, sound belief – they called for the excision of groups and individuals who threatened that order: Jews and witches, heretics and incontinent priests, usurers and corrupt rulers. Charismatic preachers and activist churchmen criss-crossed Europe with the message of reform: they preached to thousands with fiery oratory and with a great awareness of spectacle and imagery. They were Marian devotees to a man.

Much of the mobilization of European politics by the mid-fifteenth century was facilitated by the work of charismatic preachers, men hired by town councils or by enthusiastic princes. Polities came to be known by the brand of religious enthusiasm they favoured: the duke of Bavaria bore the title Reformer of the Church (*reformator ecclesiae*), while the duke of Austria was styled Prince of the Church (*princeps in ecclesia*).[45] Such titles tell us little of the personal inclinations of rulers – the sincerity of political gestures is always hard to gauge – but it is clear that some cities and states engaged powerful disseminators to spread messages of religious renewal. Programmes of reform addressed clusters of inter-related concerns: female chastity and the values of the Christian family; crusades against unbelievers; modesty in consumption and the abolition of luxurious public display; Jews as money-lenders in the midst of Christian communities; heresy and public irreverence. In preaching all these – chastity, humility, modesty, orthodoxy and a Christian Europe – Mary was adopted as the preacher's emblem.

One of the most exciting preachers of fifteenth-century Europe was Bernardino of Siena (1380–1444). He belonged to the Observant branch of the Franciscan order, which emphasized enclosure and simplicity for its members and promoted correction in houses deemed to be less rigorous. Bernardino preached in several Italian cities in the 1420s; in 1425 he preached intensively in Siena against vanity, luxury and immodesty. His sermons attracted large crowds; they were long and highly dramatic performances. Bernardino did not shy away from dis-cussing the sexual duties of wives or from chastising fathers who endowed their daughters with large trousseaux and squandered wealth on sumptuous wedding feasts. Against all such manner of sin and vanity he presented Mary, yet nothing about his language was familiar. Mary was a wild, even violent Jewess, who 'wounded' God's heart:

A Hebrew woman invaded the house of the eternal king; a girl, I know not with what allurements, with what enticements, with what violations, she seduced, deceived and, may I say, wounded and raped the divine heart, and assailed God's wisdom. Therefore, the Lord complained bitterly about the Blessed Virgin Mary, as in Cant. 4.9: 'You have wounded my heart, sister my wife, you have wounded my heart.'[46]

Mary ravished her lover, she overwhelmed him with her passion for him.

Bernardino did not reiterate the common images of Mary but invented new ones. His Mary was not so much meek as powerful and all-knowing. She radiated four types of knowledge: corporal, rational, spiritual and divine. Among her corporal insights was her knowledge of the universe:

Similarly, all the orbits of the Moon, of Mercury, Venus, the Sun, Mars, Jupiter, Saturn. There is not a star of the starry sky whose course Mary would not know; and the same is true of the Crystalline Heaven.[47]

Mary's rational knowledge endowed her with understanding of all rational souls, damned and saved, those in Abraham's bosom, or in limbo, or in purgatory. Her divine knowledge was of the glory of eternal life.[48] Above all, Mary was the city's protector, 'advocate of our city' – *avvocata di nostra città* – and this relationship was mediated and facilitated by Bernardino's support.[49] She rewarded loyal virtue not cultic excesses. Bernardino was explicit, if not shocking, as he expressed his view on the fascination with relics, like Mary's milk, in his usual command of image and rhetoric:

And, oh, oh, by the way, the milk of the Virgin Mary! Ladies, where are your heads? And you, fine sirs, have you seen any of it? You know, they're passing it off as a relic. It's all over the place. Don't you believe in it for a moment. It's not real. Don't you believe in it! Do you think that the Virgin Mary was a cow, that she would give away her milk in this way – just like an animal that lets itself be milked?[50]

Charismatic preachers like Bernardino had the power to move crowds towards extravagant gestures of conversion and commitment. His campaigns against finery and vanities were not just inscribed in town statutes or delivered from the pulpit, they were performed in mass rallies that culminated in bonfires of cards, combs, dice, cosmetics, ornaments and magical amulets. In their place he recommended the emblem of Christ's monogram – IHS – emblazoned on a sun, a constant and pure reminder of Jesus. But Bernardino's emblem had a strong Marian connection: Mary had given Jesus his name as instructed by Gabriel at the Annunciation; the name 'Jesus' was Mary's gift, and she spoke it before any other. Bernardino thus placed Mary at the heart of his programme for Christian renewal: in Modena in 1423 he preached and led to the burning of hundreds of game boards, dice and pamphlets and a bag of women's hair. In their place he encouraged the Modenese to adorn their

houses with the IHS. He even granted the confraternity devoted to the Annunciation the gift of a gold monogram mounted on a blue board.[51] The monogram can still be seen on the wall of many Sienese houses.

Preachers drew crowds of thousands and involved them in the performance of sermons, events that often lasted for hours. They offered Mary as an alternative to lives of mundane sinfulness and as a source of hope. This enthusiasm and reforming fervour was sometimes inspired by invocation of an imagined Jewish enmity towards Mary. Following expulsions of Jews from German cities and the destruction of their quarters, the vacated spaces were sometimes turned into chapels for Mary, or were adorned with statues of Mary and son.[52] Revivalist preachers created a habit of mind that linked the danger posed by Jews within the Christian polity to the solace and succour offered by Mary. In his tract on the *Magnificat*, the German physician Johannes Lange von Wetzlar (c.1365–c.1427) described a massacre of the Jews of Prague in 1389, following an alleged utterance of a eucharistic blasphemy, as just punishment for an offence against Mary. The destruction of the Jewish community was followed by the construction of a Marian chapel on the site of the synagogue, fitting retribution in Mary's name.[53]

The coupling of Mary with the triumph over Jews and Judaism also operated in more private, less monumental, spheres. In a book of commentary on the psalms, composed by a parish priest from Württemburg in the 1460s, Mary was assimilated into a complex representation of church-synagogue. Four painted pages adorn the book, and one shows Mary as the Woman of the Apocalypse. Mary was also present in the figure of *ecclesia* who vanquishes sad *synagoga*.[54] Reflection on the Crucifixion – the *locus classicus* for reflection on Jews – had become so imbued with Mary that a triangular drama emerged: between Mary and the Jews over her dead son's body. A new and rich visual image – the Living Cross – explored the operation of the cross in the contemporary world. The cross was not dead wood but a still-growing tree, alive and able to dispense truth and justice. The arms of the cross were shown as sword and hand, grasping and punishing. This image of revival and reform invoked a world in which Christ was still an active judge. The Living Cross sought out its enemies: sinners, heretics and Jews. Mary was present wherever the cross was, and so the Living Cross was home to other binary pairs: church and synagogue, Mary and Eve.[55] A Westphalian panel from the early fifteenth century elaborated just such

oppositions against a gold background: blind Jewish man as synagogue/ upright female church; broken Jewish banner/erect Christian standard; a skull/the building of a church; Eve's sin/a virgin receiving the host; the golden calf of idolatry/the Lamb of God. The figure of Church is a haloed woman in a red dress and blue cloak – Mary in all her details. Into this Christian allegory Mary is woven as enemy of the old Jew, under the protective arms of a blessing but also avenging Living Cross.[56] Visions for European renewal habitually coupled Mary with the triumph of Christianity – Mary as church, Mary as herald of the apocalypse, in a world of sin and disorder.

18

Mary: Unlike Any Other

Like the kings and emperors who welcomed her into their courts, Mary was considered a unique person. The purity and powers attributed to her made her a patron apart, above humans, saints or angels. Her unparalleled order of purity led over the centuries to repeated attempts at defining her moral qualities. Early discussions suggested that Mary was the recipient of special grace that erased the stain of original sin and left her sinless to become the pure Mother of God. In the twelfth century a belief developed that Mary had not been conceived like other humans, hence she did not carry the stain (*macula*) of original sin. God dwelt in Mary and so she had to be spotless, perfect.[1] An important formulation was offered by the Catalan preacher and theologian the Franciscan Ramon Lull (*c.*1235–1315), who linked Immaculate Mary to the very message of redemption. In Jesus, God broke the hold of sin upon humanity, first and foremost by liberating Mary of original sin. The Franciscan theologian Duns Scotus (*c.*1266–1308) elaborated most clearly the necessity of Mary's Conception without sin: God prepared Mary as a fitting mother of God.[2] Mary's *natural* humanity, which Franciscans valued so greatly, required an infusion of grace to make her worthy of the motherhood of Christ.[3]

Ideas about Mary's immaculate purity were cherished in the theology and devotional practices of the Franciscan order. By the fifteenth century the claim of Mary's Immaculate Conception had become highly divisive. It grew into a controversy between Franciscans (supported by Carmelites) and Dominicans, which erupted in university discussions, Church councils, and even during processions in city streets. The Immaculate Conception generated debates and brawls, polemical tracts and mutual accusations of heresy. A Dominican scholar of the University of Paris

was reported to have claimed in the 1380s: 'Those who claim the Virgin Mary was not conceived in sin hold against the teaching of St Paul.'[4]

For these sentiments this scholar was tried by his peers in the university court; we do not, alas, know how his peers ultimately judged him. It is not surprising, therefore, to find in the preface to a collection of sermons delivered by Bernardino of Siena (1380–1444) advice against preaching the Immaculate Conception in the company of Dominicans.[5]

This debate divided Europe's intellectuals, above all the members of the Franciscan and the Dominican orders. It involved kings too: King Joao I of Aragon promulgated the feast of the Conception of Mary in his kingdom in 1394 and acted against the Dominican Nicholas Eymerich, who opposed it.[6] In 1417 the king of Aragon approached the Holy Roman Emperor with a request that the Immaculate Conception be endorsed at the ecumenical church council at Constance (1415–1418). The next series of ecclesiastical gatherings, the Council of Basle (1431–1449), began celebrating the feast of Mary's Conception in 1435; in the following year it deposed the pope, Eugenius IV, replacing him by Felix V. Opponents of the Immaculate Conception were now able to rally and claim that the council that had deposed the pope was not a legitimate one. The Dominican Juan de Torquemada (1388–1468) published a dossier that summarized all possible objections to the Immaculate Conception and also declared that the gathering at Basle was a 'congregation of Satan', a schismatic gathering. Franciscan initiatives continued to promote the belief and its related liturgy and images. The Franciscan pope, Sixtus IV (1414–84), once minister general of the Franciscan order, reasserted the Immaculate Conception. He headed discussions in Rome in 1477 and in 1480 established the feast of the Conception in the papal chapel. Five years later his bull *Grave Nimis* proclaimed that, since the church had never found against the Immaculate Conception, it could not be condemned.[7]

The representation of Mary as immaculate situated her beyond the domestic and the mundane and drew her into spaces replete with majestic and celestial imagery.[8] A gilt and painted wood Annunciation tabernacle from the southern Netherlands shows Mary robed in gold at a lectern and under a canopy the curtains of which are lifted by a pair of angels.[9] All is golden, nothing mundane. Even when she was depicted in less fanciful spaces, majestic Mary was carefully set apart. Canopies were useful devices to mark her separately; an Eyckian panel of Mary

and Child with Saints and Donors, $c.1440/60$, places Mary under a sumptuous canopy of red tapestry in her bold blue cloak.[10]

MARY AMONG ANGELS

As Mary soared she was joined by her heavenly companions, the angels. Angels were active agents in the unfolding drama of Mary's life: an angel announced her arrival to Joachim and Anna, another heralded the arrival of her son, and yet another revealed her purity to the doubting Joseph. Angels attended the Nativity and generally marked Mary's purity and privilege. They served as a courtly entourage in the Wilton Diptych and were imaginatively mobilized into her service as musicians or as playmates for the Child Jesus. Angels often attended the tender scene of breast-feeding: a Catalan artist painted angels playing music around the throne of the crowned Mary as she offered her breast to an eager son.[11] The central panel of a Sienese triptych of the 1430s depicts four elegant angels in gestures of awe and prayer against a gilt background behind Mary and Child resting on a cushioned seat.[12] Angels are the main figurative decoration of a blue silken vestment, a chasuble, made in the Rhineland $c.1400$: gold and red angels are arranged so as to face the vertical panel of vegetal embroidery punctuated by the words *ave praeclara* (beautiful or bright) *ihesus maria* *ave praeclara*.[13]

Angels reminded viewers that Mary was not just of the world, but of heaven, a place of light and music. They accompanied Mary on her final journey, when she was assumed into heaven and received by her son; they welcomed her there with their song.[14] The angels depicted in the magnificent choir-book of Siena cathedral resembled the boys who sang on her Assumption.[15] Like the choir they produced perfect speech and harmonious sound. Angelic music formed part of the vision seen by the English mystic Margery Kempe ($c.1373-1438$), of Mary's Assumption foretold by Christ: 'Therefore fear not, daughter, for with my own hands, which were nailed to the cross, I shall take your soul from your body with great joy and melody, with sweet smells and good odours.'[16]

Angels reinforced the sense of Mary's celestial connections, even while she acted on earth among other humans. To separate her further from the earthliness which is tantamount to sin, Mary was surrounded by a frame of golden rays emanating from her and separating her from

others. This was the Immaculate Mary, portrayed most frequently at her Assumption. This image, which epitomized Mary's difference from other humans, was captured by the wooden panel painted by Andrea del Castagno ($c.$1421–57) in 1449/50 of the *Assumption Attended by Saints Julian and Minas*. Mary is seated surrounded by rays of sun, with the sun behind her head.[17] The book of the London Confraternity of the Assumption of $c.$1441 represents Mary in a blue gown flecked with gold stars, encased within golden rays as she rose into the Trinity's outstretched hands.[18] A wall-painting in Århus cathedral of the 1490s is accompanied by the inscription 'Alma redemptoris mater, quae pervia caeli, porta manes, et stella maris' (mother of the redeemer, who are the gate of heaven and the star of the sea), telling Mary's uniqueness.[19]

MARY CROWNED, MARY WITH THE TRINITY

Mary was herself a ruler, a queen. By the twelfth century it was clear to all that Mary's extraordinary end was followed by Assumption into heaven and Coronation by her son. So two formative strands met in Mary: bridehood and queenship; Mary, like all brides, was treated as a queen who was crowned, heralded and preciously adorned on her wedding day. Mary's queenship was captured most commonly in scenes of Coronation. By the fourteenth century, Mary and Jesus – bride and bridegroom – were often shown sitting companionably, equal in size, while Jesus crowns his mother's slightly bent head.[20] This tradition of parity is evident in the altarpiece made by Neri di Bicci (1419–91) and Benedetto da Maiano in 1471 for the Calmaldolese Abbey of San Piero at Ruoti near Arezzo. The Coronation pair is placed within a garland of angels above a tiny crucifixion scene and attended by monks and saints.[21] Intimate settings were developed for the Coronation: a northern French master carved a pendant in ivory around 1410, painted it and then set it under rock crystal within a gilt frame, to be worn on the chest.[22] Even a simple household could view the Coronation on a moulded oven tile while its members ate together.[23] The parishioners of the Danish village of Nødebo enjoyed the Coronation painted on a whitewashed chancel vault: Mary and Jesus were seated on a fine

cushioned bench, as the scene of the Adoration of the Magi was depicted below.[24] Most images of Mary and Child of this period show Mary crowned – some statues were even dressed with a real, precious crown.[25] An Italian wave of classicizing simplification later in the fifteenth century led to the removal of that crown and to perfection centred on Mary's nubile facial beauty.

The Coronation was the climax of Mary's life story, and an occasion to tell the Christian story too. In 1453 Jean de Montagnac, canon of the church of St Agricol in Avignon, approached the artist Enguerrand Quarton with a commission for a panel painting. The contract spelled out the patron's wish:

There should be the form of Paradise, and in the Paradise should be the Holy Trinity, and there should not be any difference between the Father and the Son; and the Holy Ghost in the form of a dove; and Our Lady in front as it will seem best to Master Enguerrand; the Holy Trinity will place the crown on the head of Our Lady.[26]

The artist followed the directions clearly and produced a work full of fascination.

The magnificence and potency of the crowned Mary became an attractive adjunct to priestly power.[27] The association was sometimes symbolic: in Botticelli's Madonna of the Eucharist, Mary fingers a sheaf of wheat with her right hand, while her left holds her son. Wheat and child both signify the crucified Body of Christ, which is renewed, in the form of bread, at every celebration of the Eucharist.[28] An ivory pax – the object circulated among the congregation for kissing during mass – from Utrecht has the Virgin and Child in the centre, flanked by St Catherine and St John the Baptist.[29] References to Mary were sometimes overwhelmingly direct, as in a panel from an altarpiece made for a confraternity in Amiens in 1437, of Mary as priest of the Temple within a church: the kneeling donor exclaims: 'Fitting vestment for a sovereign priest' (*Digne vesture au prestre souverain*).[30] Mary is magnificently vested, situated in a church – she is the church – as priest of the sort in Jan van Eyck's small (31×14 cm) but exquisite panel painting of $c.1425$.

It is not surprising, therefore, that Mary was a popular choice for the decoration of priestly garments: above all the chasubles worn by priests during the mass. Some priests wore this scene on the back of their vestments instead of the Crucifixion.[31] A red tunic from Nuremberg

dating from around 1465 had a scene of the Annunciation at the nape and of Mary's Coronation lower down, referring in this way to Mary's beginning and end.[32] The red velvet Cope at Skenfrith (Monmouthshire) is strewn with royal symbols of eagles, *fleur-de-lys* and pomegranates, but the central image is of Mary's Assumption.[33] The enthroned Mary and Child group was worked into the top of the cross and flanked below by figures of saints on a green chasuble embroidered in Italy in the late fifteenth century. Mary and Child have here displaced the Crucifixion.[34] In many different ways Mary was intimately linked with priesthood and its privileges.

The immaculate and crowned representations of Mary offered an alternative to the highly domesticated images of her as an ordinary woman, which we have seen develop since the thirteenth century. The desire to reflect upon Mary in more symbolic ways is also evident in the choices of several northern artists. Robert Campin's *Madonna of the Firescreen* has Mary seated holding her son, her elbow leaning on a finely carved altar-like table, upon which stands a chalice. On Mary's right a book is open. No trivial pots and pans or looms are anywhere to be seen. Drops of Mary's milk drip from her bare breast on to the circumcised infantile penis, a symbol of the bodily suffering of the Crucifixion to come.[35] Even the fire screen – woven from straw – brings to mind the bread of the eucharist and the fire of sacrifice. Mary is set here in an austere and priestly situation. The altar frontal (*paliotto*) made for the Corpus Domini nunnery in Venice depicts twelve arcaded scenes from the life of Christ, and at its centre a large scene of the Presentation. Here Mary stands at an altar – that of the Temple – alongside the priest. We have at the heart of the work, then, a Mary scene, not a Mary and Child as was so often the case, but a more muted depiction which is subservient to the overarching theme of Christ's offering at the altar – the eucharist.[36] The Crowned Mary was an empowered Mary, one who possessed wisdom, prophecy, who read scripture and composed sacred texts. Botticelli's *Madonna del Magnificat* (1480–81), combines all the themes of Mary's majesty and autonomy; she was the author of the *Magnificat*, the writer of holy words. Two youthful angels hold a crown over the head of an extraordinarily beautiful Mary.[37]

As Mary rose – crowned and powerful – she was increasingly associated with spheres and shapes of divinity, and thus with the Trinity. This

absorption of the Trinity into Mary, or the creation of something new – a quaternity – delighted the creative minds of poets too, above all those who wrote in German. Mary became a fourth part, like the fourth light imagined by the fourteenth-century poet Konrad of Würzburg. More commonly the dialectic of three-in-one is preserved, as in the images we have just seen: the poet Frauenlob imagined the Trinity as three suitors wooing Mary, or in Mary picking three roses of a single branch.[38] Mary may have inspired the making of the Holy Ghost feminine, in mystical visions, and by the very late fourteenth century even in the depiction which adorned the walls of the parish church of Urschalling in Bavaria.[39] These attempts express a fascination with Mary's relevance, the appropriateness of linking her to all-important manifestations of Christian logic. They also bespoke a sheer desire to see her everywhere.

The alignment of the Trinity within Mary's body was a rich late medieval symbolic possibility, yet its connotations were troubling. Jean Gerson (1363–1429) censored images with the Trinity in Mary's womb:

I say it in part about an image in the Carmelite church and about others which have a Trinity in the womb, as if the whole Trinity had taken flesh in the Virgin Mary . . . And I do not see why it should be put that way, because in my humble opinion there is neither beauty nor devotion in such an opening, and it can be cause of error and impiety.[40]

What pleased viewers in one region, or even in a single church, could displease viewers with different sensibilities. The possibilities of Mary were many, but some manifestations inspired discomfort rather than awe.

PRECIOUS OBJECTS, RAREFIED SETTINGS – MARY AND LUXURY

Mary's pure body had contained for a while the body of God. It was thus seen as a special type of receptacle, and was sometimes used as one. Reliquaries took the shape of Mary, especially in Northern Europe, like the gilt silver statuette of Mary and Child in the church of St Martin, in Emmerich (Lower Rhine) of $c.1480$.[41] When the church of Notre-Dame-en-Vaux in Châlons-sur-Marne (Champagne) was left a bequest for the

making of a shrine, queenly Mary was seen as fitting to contain the parish's consecrated hosts, morsels of her son's eucharistic body.[42] When a reliquary contained remains from several saints – each separately packed and labelled – the image of Mary and Child could offer overall cohesion, as in a reliquary at Krakow cathedral.[43] A silver gilt statue of Mary enthroned, with the Child in her lap, a sumptuous gem-encrusted work, was made for Osnabrück cathedral in 1483. The craftsmanship in silver, gold and precious stones reflected the value of the relics contained therein and enhanced them too.[44] Less sumptuous but equally elegant is a gilt silver statuette of Mary and Child, where the Child holds the transparent (now reproduction) container of a relic of the umbilical cord that had fed him in his mother's womb.[45]

The emergence of spheres in which Mary was majestic and bejewelled, surrounded by angels – Mary away from home and hearth – turned her into an object *de luxe:* made in gold and silver, covered by canopies, announced by angels, dressed in silk and velvet and situated in private niches unlike any inhabited by ordinary humans. Within these spaces Mary was imagined as removed from the propriety of home, village and parish church. This is how we may understand a panel painting of *c*.1450, the Melun Diptych, by the French court painter Jean Fouquet (1415–80), whose right wing depicted the Virgin and Child surrounded by angels.[46] This is a fashionable Mary, with a high (shaven) forehead, smooth skin, dainty veil, sumptuous crown, tight bodice and bulging bare left breast. It has been claimed that she was modelled after King Charles VII's mistress, Agnes Sorel, whose executors commissioned the altarpiece in her memory. Although her eye is downcast, the whole effect is courtly, celestial and other-worldly in an unusual field created in contrasting red, white and blues, which is none the less personal and enticing.

MARY'S GARDENS

Mary was habitually situated in elaborate imaginary spaces that were courtly or celestial, or both. It seemed fitting to situate Mary, so often likened to a lily or a rose, within a garden. The name of her birthplace, Nazareth, stemmed from the Hebrew word *netzer* – bloom. Mary's purity was associated with the lily, but her persona was one of the

sweet-smelling flowers of the Song of Songs (2:1–2). A Middle English carol on Mary's Joys used the refrain 'Of a rose, a lovely rose, / Of a rose, I sing a song', after each stanza. Mary's Joys were likened to five branches of the fairest rose: the Annunciation, Nativity, Adoration of the Magi, Descent into Hell, and Ascension. These are not the Five Joys we have already encountered: the Descent into Hell is not a Joy, and it replaces here the definite joy of the Assumption. The poet chose to incorporate Descent into Hell, a scene from the life of Jesus, into his mother's cycle of joy. The rose had five branches, and in them were mingled her life and her son's.[47]

So Mary was situated away from family and kin – who were celebrated so powerfully in homiletic and devotional texts – in closed gardens and arbours.[48] The garden encloses Mary just as her womb had enclosed Christ. The sweet-smelling rose garden was the painters' favourite. A Sienese panel has Mary in a rose garden against a hilly landscape: she sits on a plush cushion and plays with her son tenderly.[49] Seclusion and majesty are combined in a winged altarpiece, the central panel of which depicts Mary in a rose garden, dressed in lustrous red, against a backdrop of roses, where she is seated on a bench planted with wallflowers while two angels hold a crown over her head.[50] The garden is sometimes situated in the grounds of a castle, as in the Flemish panel where Mary sits on a raised bed picking a flower for the son on her knee.[51] Mary's enclosure and chastity are thus related to her noble birth and standing. Alone and undisturbed, she passed her time in reading and handling flowers: in a Swiss altarpiece of c.1420 the crowned Mary hands a rose to her son while the donor looks on.[52] Nobility and seclusion within a garden combine as Mary is assisted by dainty maidens who read or play with the Child Jesus.[53] The garden turns into a flowered forest floor in Filippo Lippi's *Mary Adoring the Child Christ* of c.1459, with the Trinity hovering over them.[54]

Reflection on Mary in gardens sometimes brought to mind the primal scene of Eve's sin. Mary's mission was defined early on as the reversal of Eve's legacy, and thinking of Mary and Eve in a single frame amounted to telling the whole Christian story: of Incarnation and promise of salvation. The *Virgin and Child Enthroned with Angels* by the Master of the Straus Madonna (flourished 1385–1415) does just that: Mary at the centre, modestly yet richly dressed, is seated with her son at her breast, adored by saints, while beneath lies Eve, whose naked body is

visible through a transparent gown. A vase of roses stands at Mary's feet, while Eve holds the telltale branch of a fruit tree.[55] Both Eve and Mary dwelt in gardens, but very different ones. With Mary the tree of 'death' turned into a veritable tree of life, as *Eva* became *Ave*. The Salzburg Missal was decorated by Berthold Furtmeyer in 1481 with a finely dressed Mary and a naked Eve either side of a tree: Eve's side bears death – a skull – while Mary bears a fruitful Crucifixion and a multitude of eucharistic hosts, which she hands to kneeling, grateful believers.[56] Mary's life made the death of sin more visible and offered the hope that it was not invincible.

19

Mary of Parish Practice and Family Life

MATER DOLOROSA – PIETÀ

Mary was a cure against the deadliness of sin. She earned that power through her role in Christ's birth, but also through her sorrow at his death. We have seen how central Mary had become to depictions of the Passion: without her the Crucifixion seemed to be incomplete. So important was Mary to the appreciation of the Passion that by the fourteenth century a new way of representing that sorrow emerged, the Pietà: Mary lamenting her son, his dead body limps in her lap. This is not the rendering of a moment told in scripture, but a condensation of Mary's pain and her son's sacrifice – his beginning in her lap, and his end there, with an invitation to the compassionate viewer to join. Scenes of the Crucifixion rich in detail existed alongside the simple Pietà favoured by contemplatives and mystics. The Pietà was starker in style than the Crucifixion, and in Germany it was perfected in the medium of wood and stone sculpture.[1] A good example from the middle-Rhine region, of c.1420, has a young, plump Mary holding an emaciated and wounded boy-son.[2] Carved in alabaster, and thus somewhat more plastic, is the Lorsch Pietà from the same region, of 1420–30, which offers an isolated moment of the mother's contemplation of her dead, wounded son. This quintessentially German subject affected artistic practice and devotional taste in Bohemia: a workshop in Prague created around 1400 a painted limestone sculpture of young mother with the body of her son.[3]

The Pietà was created for the use of northern religious women in the late thirteenth century; it captured an arresting and static moment for contemplation.[4] The Pietà was often used in private spaces, framed within enclosures suited for the implied intimacy of the moment. A gilt

tabernacle, probably from Paris, has an angel hold Christ's body as Mary and John lament on either side-wing. Rogier van der Weyden's Pietà of 1450 portrays John and Mary Magdalen either side, but Jesus' body – with its bleeding head and wounds – is enfolded in the arms of Mary alone.[5] A panel painting of the Pietà with John and the Holy Women was made for Jeanne de Laval, wife of King René of Anjou, and an inventory of 1457 describes its location in her 'new' chamber in the castle of Tarascon (Vaucluse).[6] By the fifteenth century it was a common image in parish churches too, carved in wood or stone, by workmen of varying degrees of skill. In England alabaster Pietàs of modest size existed in many parishes.[7] In the Pietà in Leeuw church (Brabant), Christ's body is painted white with red gashes at the wounds and it lies in Mary's lap, while Mary sits looking forward, her hands joined in prayer.[8] The Pietà was also combined with the devotional image of the Man of Sorrows around the bleeding body after the Crucifixion. A small panel made in Ulm $c.1410-12$ has Mary and two angels hold and behold the upper body of Jesus standing in his tomb. His body is marked by stylized wounds, and blood trickles from his forehead. Mary is tormented in the presence of such suffering, but she is also, as ever, pure.[9]

The suffering mother Mary was also appreciated in the more animated and less private scenes of the Crucifixion offered in European altarpieces. Crucifixions of the fifteenth century show Mary in pain, even fainting. The Crucifixion painted $c.1430$ for the church of St John on the Flattnitz (Carinthia) has John and another woman supporting Mary with Longinus and a group of Jews on the right.[10] In Northern Europe a whole tradition of the 'Secret Passion' filled in the details provided by devotional texts and biblical commentary: Christ beset by dogs, mocked by ugly and deranged individuals, with Jews of ill intent and every possible instrument of torture.[11] Mary witnessed it all.

After the Crucifixion came the Deposition of Christ's body and the Lamentation over it. One of a pair of panels made by a Rhenish Master, $c.1420$, has Jesus' body removed from the cross, lifeless and wounded, above a crowd of ugly Jews, with the holy women at the foot of the cross: Mary in a blue cloak swoons into the arms of her companion in red, and Mary Magdalen, in green, clasps her hands in sorrow as scheming Jews surround them. Mary's swooning is not as yet spectacular, but it is dramatized by the menacing atmosphere surrounding it.[12] Her swooning – *spasimo* – drew some attention away from Christ's body.

Nowhere is this more evident than in the highly influential *Descent from the Cross* altarpiece by Rogier van der Weyden (1399/1400–1464) of c.1435–40. Ten figures, a cross and crucifixion paraphernalia create a surreal scene against a background of carved wood. The Crucifixion has been turned into a tableau of rich colour and strong emotion. Christ's body is lowered, marble-white, in a lifeless diagonal across the canvas. Mary's figure in blue answers it, large, voluminous, yet lifeless with pain.[13]

A few years later, in 1463–4, van der Weyden conceived another composition: his diptych of the Crucifixion has Christ on the right hanging on the cross against a red cloth; on the left, his mother, in white, swoons, supported by John the Evangelist. The terrain is rocky, moon-like, with no vestige of place or season. Mother and son each inhabit a panel, but the viewer's eyes are drawn powerfully to the mother, away from the smooth body of the son.[14] A delicate *Lamentation* painted by van der Weyden has Mary in a bare landscape at the foot of the cross, with Mary Magdalen and John: Mary dressed in blue, all but touches the wound on the side; she embraces the head, with eyes closed, just like those of her son.[15] This stark image only hints at Mary's grief rather than portraying a collective scene. Some scenes of the deposition of Christ's body combined the Crucifixion with elements of the Pietà. A winged altarpiece from Kalkar (North Westphalia) of around 1483 has six scenes of the Passion on its outer wings, while the centre offers an agitated scene of Mary holding her son's body at the foot of the cross, surrounded by John and the holy women as well as the patron, a Carthusian monk.[16]

While some artists dwelt on the wounded body and others chose not to, all reflected on Mary's pain, the focus of so much devotional writing, so many prayers and hymns. Mary's suffering was already stylized in schemes of her Joys and Sorrows, which dominated the structure of many prayer books. Mary's pain was likened to the piercing of swords and was turned into a devotion that became particularly popular in the Low Countries. It elaborated the biblical verse Luke 2:34–5, the prophecy to Mary at the Presentation in the Temple: 'Behold this child is set for the fall and rising again of many in Israel; and for a sign which shall be spoken against; yea, a sword shall pierce through thy own soul too.'[17] She was often depicted pierced by a sword, or by seven swords. This devotion imagined the piercing of Mary's breast, and the theme

gained currency with the dissemination of printed images from the mid-century.[18] A nun-artist from St Walburg's in Eichstätt elaborated on paper a unique symbolic Crucifixion: in this the crucified Christ is flanked by images of his younger self – as baby and as young man. His mother too sits upon the top-bar of the cross, above her son's head, her heart pierced by five swords.[19]

MARY IN THE PARISH

The complex imagery of reforming sermons and the eloquence of articulate preachers coexisted with the teaching that was provided in parishes, instruction aimed above all at clarity of exposition and correctness of content. Parish communities all over Europe were audiences to Sunday and feast-day sermons and users of painted, carved and sculpted images. While the parishes in big cities benefited from the presence of many professional image-makers – in words, wood, glass, metal and stone – rural communities depended on the initiatives of their church-wardens for providing such backdrops to the liturgy; local worthies occasionally supplied expensive gifts of liturgical books, vessels or furnishings. When we assess parish art we must bear in mind that people worshipped among images that were sometimes centuries old, or which reflected the personal taste of a specific donor. Mary emerged not only from the decoration of walls and furnishings, altars and windows but also from the performance of outdoor processions, and in some regions religious drama too. Mary was situated within daily routines recommended by the parish: in Long Stretton, Norfolk, a mechanical device on the church wall reminded parishoners of the weekly fast in honour of Mary.[20]

Mary was ever-present in Crucifixion altarpieces. While priests and their helpers busied themselves at the altar during the celebration of the mass the congregation dwelt in the nave. At the meeting of the two spaces – in the crossing – a screen often marked the boundary and above it a crucifix was frequently mounted. In some regions the lofty space above the crossing became the home for elaborate scenes of Mary and John alongside the cross. The screen itself could tell the story of the Crucifixion: the Welsh parish of St Mary at Betws Gwerful Goch (Merioneth) had wooden panels depicting Mary and John either

side of Jesus, with panels devoted to the instruments of the Passion: nails, the crown of thorns, pincers, lance and more.[21] The wall above the crossing offered a space for scenes of the Last Judgement ('Doom'), where Mary had a role to play. The still brightly coloured wooden 'doom' painting at Wenhaston (Suffolk) offered around 1480 a graphic depiction of the weighing of souls at the mouth of hell; above sat Christ, blessing, and his mother on the right, with John the Baptist, offering prayers.[22]

While the main (high) altar was frequently adorned with an altarpiece the central panel of which depicted the Crucifixion, side chapels offered an opportunity for more specifically Marian emphases. Great cathedrals acquired Lady Chapels and Mary altars, especially in England, and in them were celebrated masses which were often accompanied with music. The Lady Chapel was usually north of the chancel or in the transept. That of Winchester cathedral was decorated with scenes of the Miracle of the Virgin; an inventory from the Lady Chapel of Worcester records vestments and ivory carvings.[23] Some smaller churches developed variations too; spaces for Mary were dedicated in small side chapels. A number of statues of Mary and Child enthroned survive in Danish churches and were probably made for such chapels, like that in St Mary's church at Båstad.[24] In the church of Saint Olaf (Scania) there is a Mary shrine in a corner with an enthroned Mary and Child flanked by female saints in the double wings.[25] Soft furnishings added to the Marian emphasis too: in 1449 Theobald of Vitry, canon of Notre Dame cathedral and councillor to the king, donated five sections of tapestry for the adornment of the choir-stalls: altogether they depicted fifteenth scenes, from the Annunciation to the Assumption and Coronation, as they hung between the stalls.[26]

Alabaster was worked into a wide range of devotional objects in fifteenth-century England, and these adorned parish churches as well as homes. The statuettes were sometimes housed in painted wooden cases, like the Mary and Child still at Worcester cathedral. Some of these carvings still retain their colouring, like the Annunciation of the later fifteenth century, where Mary reads at an altar as she receives the news, and God the father blows upon her and makes Mary conceive.[27] The alabaster Swansea altarpiece of c.1460–90 offers a comprehensive Marian backdrop to the liturgy with scenes of the Joys of Mary: the Annunciation, the Adoration of the Magi, the Ascension of her Son, the

Assumption, and the Trinity in the centre; figures of the two Johns flank the piece.[28] Mary was, after all, widely understood as part of the Trinity itself.

Although popular all over Europe, Mary images were also highly regional. The Mother of Mercy – the figure of Mary protecting Christians of all stations of life under her ample mantle – brought much comfort with its promise of Mary's intercession for people of all estates and conditions. It showed her guarding believers under a cloak, like a hen with chicks under her wings. A version from mid-fifteenth-century Krems portrays Mary as protector of people of all estates and ages, with special emphasis on privileged figures with marks of priesthood and civic office. Yet the Mother of Mercy common in fifteenth-century Finnish churches, like Lohja and Hattula, is quite different: against the common whitewashed background of the vault she is drawn, in the sole colour of reddish-brown, save for her blue cloak. Here are no pope and emperors, but naked souls, androgynous, undifferentiated, sheer humanity under Mary's mantle.[29] Parish churches in the Dauphiné were also habitually decorated with scenes of Mary, her unusually long arms stretched at her sides so that her mantle covers and shields groups of men and women.[30]

The Mother of Mercy is sometimes associated with the Man of Sorrows, the suffering body to whose bleeding wounds Mary turns in intercession, as in the Finnish churches of Kalanti and Parainen.[31] So many churches had Marian altars or statues in separate Mary Chapels, and against this backdrop pastoral knowledge of Mary was conveyed. The parish also disseminated mnemonic ditties, like this, about Mary's age, entered into the commonplace book of Robert Reynes of Acle (Norfolk):

> The virgin parent Mary lived sixty-three years.
> She was fourteen at the blessed birth,
> She lived thirty-three [years] with her son,
> And sixteen, she suffered alone, like the stars.[32]

Religious understanding was produced from the mutual efforts of home teaching and parish instruction. The Ave Maria was the most widely taught and readily available prayer for personal as well as collective use. It was taught at home, by parents and nurturing relatives – usually women – and it could be used on many occasions, private and public,

at home and away, in hardship and as an expression of gratitude and joy. Many elaborations of the Ave Maria were offered to European parishioners in the fifteenth century.[33] While it was known in Latin,

Ave Maria, Gratia Plena, Dominus tecum, benedicta tu in mulieribus er benedictus fructus ventris tui Jesus. Santa Maria, mater Dei, ora pro nobis peccatoribus nunc et in hora mortis nostrae. Amen.

the Ave Maria was also offered in vernacular versions and explained in them too. An Austrian version of 1458 presents each of the Latin phrases in translation – only Ave Maria appears in its original form – with further comment:

Vol genaden You do most powerful things, Empress, who will disperse my sins . . . Come as my warranty so I shall not fear your enemy but have your company.[34]

Instruction to parishioners was at its most intensive during the days leading up to Easter Communion, and so a Polish Ave Maria hymn was copied into a book of sermons of 1408 above the Good Friday sermon.[35] An exposition was offered, which progresses phrase by phrase:

You are full of grace, he loved you, sent Gabriel to you to announce to you the great joy that the Son of God wished to be born.
  You are Aaron's flower, Moses' burning bush.
  In you blossomed the branch of Jesse, she who gave birth to her creator.[36]

The Ave Maria – the child's first prayer, the dying person's last – was offered in many different and familiar forms. As we will see later, it became the building block of a new and exciting devotion, the Rosary.

MARY IN RELIGIOUS PLAYS

Urban folk benefitted from religious drama that was performed in city streets, and often under the auspices of town councils. These took the form of single plays – like a play of the Assumption – or in cycles of plays that aimed to tell the whole Christian story, or large parts of it, a form particularly common in the cities of northern England. The resources of city churches, the organizational skills of guilds and religious writers were combined in producing the dramas. So from the mid-fifteenth century a string of plays on the *Seven Joys of Mary* (*Seven*

Bliscappen van Maria) was performed in the Great Square of Brussels. From the Annunciation – the First Joy – to the Assumption – the Seventh Joy – Mary's life is told with the purpose of informing as well as entertaining. At the opening of the Annunciation play, the prologue explains that 'Even though the message [of the Annunciation] is the main point, it is necessary that we explain why God, for our salvation, wished to take on human form.'[37] Indeed, the play provides ample background to the Fall of Adam and Eve, in the actions of envious Satan. Adam and Eve are banished; a debate in heaven then follows as to God's action in the world for humankind. Once it is determined, God sends an angel to Joachim, and so the story of Mary's birth begins, her early life, and the Annunciation. The stories of Mary's early life, which we have traced from their beginnings in the *Protogospel of James*, are set alongside a debate about the necessity of the Incarnation. The familiar is offered with the less familiar, and together they set Mary at the heart of the story of redemption.

Mary's life and death were a challenge to those who set and staged them. The *Mystery of the Assumption* (*Mystère de l'Assomption*) enacted in Rodez in the fifteenth century evokes Mary's life after the death of her son and her desire to join him in heaven. She opens the play, while praying to her son:

> O dearest son, sitting
> On God's right so high,
> You who came down here
> To be born from my womb so virginally,
> Without departing at all
> From that elevated deity.
> When will it please you kindly
> That I sit close by you?[38]

Mary continues and asks for her death to come:

> Dearest son, when will the hour come
> When I die
> And be in your company?
> It is late for me, it has been a while,
> When I cry
> From my heart and tearful eyes.[39]

320

Mary takes her leave from her closest ones, Joseph and the virgins who accompany her. She tells them not to mourn for her; she wishes to die because the world holds only hardship and vanity:

> For you will see clearly
> That the world is nothing but vanity,
> Domination and honours.

A similar disdain for life on earth is expressed in Mary's presence by the Evangelist John in the Catalan *Assumption Play* of Elx. The play, which is still performed every year, was enacted on the eve of the Assumption in the Basilica of Santa Maria, upon a temporary stage. John intones his lament:

> Ay, sad corporal life!
> Oh, world cruel and unjust![40]

The *Assumption Play* likens Mary's death-bed acts and rituals to those of fifteenth-century folk. Mary expresses some trepidation as her last hour approaches. She gives away her belongings:

> To you my son perfectly
> And to Joseph similarly
> And also to my sisters
> An equal share
> Of all my clothing,
> Gowns and other garments
> Which according to their value
> Should be kept properly
> And my houses and property
> be guarded with holy intent.[41]

Mary is welcomed by her son to heaven:

> My mother in whom all good things reside
> This is your royal seat
> And the imperial crown
> Above all groups of Angels
> Dominations, and Archangels.

The play ends with mention of miracles worked by the girdle, dropped to earth by Mary to prove the truth of her Assumption.[42]

By the fifteenth century Mary was associated with preparation for death, a journey which she could make smoother and less frightening. The portrayal of Mary's own passing offered a model for a good Christian death. The *Death of the Virgin* play which formed part of the York dramatic cycle has Mary pleading with her son to ease her death by removing any demonic temptation from her last hours. Her request was not granted, and her son explains why:

> But mother, the fiend must be at your end
> In a figure that is foul and frightening.
> My angels will be around you,
> And therefore, dear dame, you need not suffer any doubt,
> Because without doubt your deeds will not be injurious to you.[43]

The *Assumption Play* from the dramatic sequence known as the *N-Town Play* – probably written for East Anglian towns and villages – has Jewish priests and a bishop attempting to disrupt Mary's funeral:

> But be that sister, Mary, that stench,
> We shall burn her body and hide her ashes
> And do to her all the harm we can devise.
> And then slay the disciples that walk everywhere.[44]

Those producing the plays faced the challenge of staging Mary's Assumption, a challenge which confronts modern productions too.[45] The York *Assumption Play* was staged on a wagon able to accommodate heaven and earth. When this wagon was used as part of the greeting ceremony mounted for Henry VII it was reported as having a working lift.[46]

In religious drama we find combined so many of the genres through which Mary was explored: vernacular biblical tales from gospel and apocrypha, miracle tales, the visual imagery of Mary in the many scenes of her life, and the music – hymns, lullabies, and liturgical pieces for her many feasts. The *Assumption* of the *N-Town Play* indeed comments on the music which follows Mary's elevation: 'Now blessed be your name we cry! / for on this holy Assumption all heaven makes melody.'[47] Mary is addressed in the plays of the *Annunciation Play* of York with the familiar words that each viewer could recite with Gabriel: 'Hail Mary, full of grace and blysse'.

Viewing, joining in song and even acting on stage offered occasions

for participation. Composers and producers of plays aimed at achieving a sense of immediacy and relevance. The Augustinian priory of Bordesholm in Holstein turned its drama of Mary's lament into action unfolding, not memory. The play lasted two and a half hours 'easily', and the instructions also directed that a priest be used as Jesus, but a youth as Mary. Mary is to be seen sometimes 'flinging her arms to the out, sometimes raising her hands and eyes towards her Son and everything is to happen in a measured fashion'.[48]

THE EUROPEAN FAMILY AND THE HOLY ONE

Mary was found in home and parish, the very places which reformers sought to turn into workshops for good Christian living. One such innovative thinker and church reformer was Jean Gerson (1363–1429), chancellor of the University of Paris.[49] Gerson was a theologian, mystic, preacher and ecclesiastical activist, and a prolific writer of devotional tracts. Although he was deeply involved in church politics, Gerson was particularly committed to the renewal of the Christian family and, within it, of simple Christian lives.

Gerson offered an understanding of Christian marriage and order based on his interpretation of Mary's and Joseph's exemplary conjugality. Gerson saw the virtue of their life together in Mary's obedience and Joseph's faith. And so by 1410 he composed a public letter which encouraged churches to celebrate Joseph and Mary's marriage as a feast day.[50] The Holy Family was central to his vision, and within it Joseph attracted particular attention in the tract *Reflections on St Joseph (Considérations sur St Joseph)* of 1413.[51] Here Joseph is an active, chaste and energetic man, who provided for his family and maintained a happy home. As a leading member of the ecumenical church council that assembled in Constance, Gerson was invited to preach in front of Europe's most influential churchmen, and he chose the subject of the marriage of Joseph, on the feast of Mary's Nativity 1416.[52] The sermon began with Matthew 1:16: 'Moreover, Jacob begat Joseph, the husband of Mary, from whom was born Jesus, who is called Christ'. Joseph's genealogy inspired in Gerson reflection on the unique

relationship between Mary and her spouse, on the feast of her birth.

Gerson appreciated Joseph's roles as husband to Mary and father to Jesus. He attributed to Joseph qualities of nobility that made him suitable for these tasks and praised him as a caring husband and father. The desire to represent Mary as an exemplary devout woman, reading her book, sometimes meant that Joseph was assigned a leading role in nurture. In a French Book of Hours, the serene scene of the Nativity has Mary relaxing with her book, under a fine red blanket, while Joseph tends to the swaddled baby.[53] More commonly, though, labour is divided between them: in a scene carved in wood in Roskilde cathedral, Mary breastfeeds the swaddled baby, while Joseph fills the animals' trough with feed.[54]

Gerson thought of their marriage as pure and companionate: how fitting it was for Mary to have a mate with whom she might share her own great secret, and that of her kinswoman Elizabeth's pregnancy. Joseph was also a good father to Jesus: he taught him to walk and marvelled at his progress and growth. Gerson's Mary was beautiful, but she did not inspire lust; his Joseph was immune to 'womanly touch'.[55] This theme of the faithful household was to be developed in the following century by Martin Luther: Mary not as queen of heaven, not resplendent bride or queen, but as a simple housewife of great resilience and perfect faith and obedience. Gerson emphasized the companionate conjugality of the holy household. It was only fitting that Mary have support through the extraordinary events which were unfolding in her life; Joseph was that helpmate. The Holy Family shared embraces and warm feelings. The poem *Jospehina*, written by Gerson while travelling in Central Europe in 1418, imagined the exertions of the Flight to Egypt; yet even there the family is close:

> He rushes into their embrace when called
> Lifting his little arms he wants to hang on the necks of his parents
> With tender embrace to give chaste kisses
> He places his hands in yours, Mary and Joseph
> And with his uneven step
> He follows you all over the house.[56]

There is a great deal of nostalgia in imaging the family romance, the perfect families that men like Gerson were obliged to foreswear early in life.

324

Gerson worked hard and creatively to help the 'new' Joseph emerge as a substantial figure in the drama of salvation. We have seen the Holy Family become familiar and rich in colour. Yet questions still attached to the figure of Joseph: he was not Jesus' biological father, but he was the family's provider and protector; he was a hard-working Jew, so could he be made into a convincing Christian? Earlier medieval representations included Joseph in scenes of the Nativity and sometimes at the Circumcision and Presentation, but he was often placed in marginal positions: asleep, on the edge, turning away from the action. Placing a medieval Jewish hat on his head was an act of labelling – as if to say 'here is a Jewish man' – but it also conveyed deeper ambivalence rooted in Jesus' Jewish human parentage.[57] Even the imagery that depicted the pair in pleasant companionship nonetheless often had Mary at prayer, reading or in adoration of the Christ Child, while Joseph cooked the birth-soup or mended his hoses.[58]

Gerson both expressed and led the emergence of new emphases in the figure of Joseph; these run in two seemingly contrary directions. On the one hand, Joseph was bolstered by attempts to place him at the heart of a rigorous vision of Christian marriage, and so his figure gained in stature and dignity.[59] On the other hand, vernacular drama explored the ambiguity of Joseph's position, often for comical effect. Mary and Joseph offered a classic case of suggestive cuckoldry, for the humorous exploration of a May and December marriage. These scenes were enclosed within a narrative of faith, since Joseph ultimately came to trust his pregnant virgin wife. But the body of vernacular drama was bold in exploring the possibilities of betrayal and mistrust too. The delicate issue of Joseph's doubt of Mary, so prominent in the comedy of vernacular drama, could be treated with greater decorum too: a stained-glass window in the choir of St Leonhard's church in Frankfurt, of $c.1450$, has Mary and Joseph facing each other, equal in size, while an angel hovers over Joseph, touching his shoulder, as if saying at the moment: 'Joseph, son of David, fear not to take unto thee Mary thy wife, for that which is conceived in her, is of the Holy Ghost' (Matthew 1:20).[60]

Visual representations of Joseph and Mary express the parity which prevailed between them by making them equal or close in size, and by placing them symmetrically; Joseph also looks younger on occasion, a significant change from earlier medieval practice. A panel by the Constance Master depicted the Betrothal of Mary and Joseph; both kneel in

front of the priest, equal in size, in gesture and in the haloes around their heads.[61] The vault bosses of Norwich cathedral, carved $c.1468$, depict a Nativity scene with Mary and Joseph either side of the manger, each in a golden gown, gesturing with their hands and gazing forward.[62] Joseph makes himself useful; he is present at the Nativity with a candle in hand in a panel by Dieric Bouts ($c.1420-75$). The wings of a south Swabian altarpiece of $c.1515$ copy the schemes of famous engravings with Joseph holding a lamp at the scene of the Nativity and Mary kneeling in front of the infant, who is adored by angels.[63] A panel painted in 1475 by Lienhard Heischer for Strasbourg cathedral similarly has Mary kneeling and Joseph standing, but he is present and involved and piously looking on. A different type of complementarity is offered in a French Book of Hours; the Nativity scene has Mary reading after birth while Joseph holds the swaddled baby at her feet and the ox and ass are neatly corralled away in their enclosure.[64] A diptych of the Nativity shows the quiet moments after the birth as a time for Mary to rest, while the midwife tends to the baby, and Joseph diligently sews swaddling clothes from his hose, hence his bare feet. Mary's bed, the midwife's dress and even the little tray with food and drink indicate not a poor and humble family, but a well-appointed and ordered one.[65]

Scenes from Jesus' infancy depicted Joseph's involvement in the boy's life. A panel painting by the Sienese artist Giovanni di Paolo (1400–1482) of the *Presentation of Jesus in the Temple* puts the couple and relatives either side of the altar, and the haloed Joseph holds the baby Jesus in his arms, as was the Jewish custom during the Circumcision ceremony.[66] A different emphasis appears in a choral book of Siena cathedral: Mary leads the family group towards the priest, followed by Joseph and Anne – all of equal size.[67] A terracotta panel by Lucca della Robbia the Younger (1475–1548) places Mary and Joseph, equally sized and both with haloes, at either side of the priest Simeon at the scene of the Circumcision: Mary wears a blue cloak over a red dress, and Joseph wears a blue garment under a yellow cloak.[68]

Scenes of the Flight into Egypt provided possibilities for exploration of Joseph's care and nurture: many artists portray Joseph leading the donkey on which Mother and Child travel, and gazing back tenderly to them.[69] Another scene is that of Mary and Joseph taking Jesus to school, while Mary leads the way holding her son's hand as he carries his writing tablet inscribed with the words 'I am Jesus' (*Ich bin Jesus*); Joseph

326

follows, prayer beads in his hand.[70] The booklet *On the childhood of our lord Jesus Christ called Vita Christi*, printed in 1491, is adorned with a woodcut showing Joseph leading the haloed mother and son to school, a scene traditionally led by Mary alone.[71]

The Holy Family's home was a fascinating space and northern artists so interested in the depiction of domestic interiors, rose to the challenge of painting it. The Holy Household was a place of work; in it the carpenter's family dwelt and laboured, rested, and nurtured its son. An illuminated page of the Book of Hours of Catherine of Cleves of *c.*1440 shows Mary spinning and Joseph filing down a plank of wood while their son practises his steps in a baby-walker, all within a modest but well-appointed interior.[72] The *Mérode Altarpiece* of *c.*1425, painted by Robert Campin, celebrates Joseph's labour by allocating a whole wing to his work-space. While his wife receives the Annunciation in the family room – the triptych's central panel – Joseph is hard at work, providing for his family, absorbed in the careful use of the tools of his craft.[73] In *The Holy Family at a Meal* by Jan Mostaert of *c.*1495–1500, Joseph cuts a loaf of dark brown bread while Jesus sits on his mother's knee, where he is fed some baby-food from a bowl.[74]

Some writers and artists sought to explore the relationship between Joseph and Jesus even further, by creating scenes of play between father and son. A group sculpted in wood in Alsace *c.*1500 has Mary sitting on the left with a book in her hand while Jesus reaches from her lap towards Joseph's beard and forehead in a familiar infantile gesture of curiosity and fascination.[75] A complex and rich scene of parental play is shown in a print made in the Upper Rhine *c.*1475–1500, of the Holy Family by the Rose Bush.[76] In the background appear many of Mary's most common attributes: citadel, tower, rose-bush and a haven, while the front is a scene of tender play. At first sight Joseph seems marginal, even menacing, but a closer look shows him to be at play, and in the best manner: on his knees, an apple in his hand to attract his son's attention. Joseph is perhaps playing a game of making the apple appear and disappear.[77] Europeans became familiar with the Holy Family's life and could see some of their own reflected in it.

ST ANNE – FAVOURITE GRANDMOTHER

Christian families were encouraged to respect the order of gender, of paternal authority and maternal nurture. The amplification of Mary's family life extended beyond her marriage to Joseph and saw the prominent rise of other relatives. Mary's purity and its extension to the moment of her conception – the Immaculate Conception – also elevated the status of her own mother.[78] Like Mary and Jesus, Anne and Mary enjoyed a powerful affinity of body and feeling. The popular German *Life of Mary* (*Marienleben*) by Henry of St Gallen (flourished 1371–97) described that intimacy:

And so the beloved dwelt in the beloved Anna for nine months. Then she was born into this world with great joy for our consolation and for all those who call out to her with good intent.[79]

Anne was bolstered by the theology of Mary's purity, but her popularity shows just how great was the interest in an older female member of the Holy Family. Anne was Jesus' grandmother. She helped amplify the Holy Kindred into three generations. While maidenly decorum attached to Mary, matronly presence characterized Anne; even her face was shown to be careworn, as her daughter's never was. While Mary was maidenly and decorous, Anne was a woman of a certain age and experience in the world. She was popular with women who had remarried and with widows. Though she began as an associate to Mary she came to occupy a significant position of her own.

The apocrypha on Mary's life and those dedicated to Anne alone provided a family saga with her three marriages – the *trinubium* – to Cleophas, to Salomas and to Joachim, Mary's father. Anne's story was represented with a circle of respectable and supportive family ties, cemented by her as matriarch. A common iconography portrayed the 'trinity' of Anne, Mary and Jesus, with Anne as the apex of the triangle formed by them.[80] Sometimes Anne is a large, nurturing figure who holds and supports the other two: in a statue-reliquary the seated Anne holds two doll-like creatures, Mary and Jesus.[81] At other times Anne was seated with her daughter, each beside the infant, as in a gilt statue from

the Polish Carmelite house at Sąsiadowice.[82] One rare depiction even considered the sadness of her earlier life as a barren woman: a wing of the altarpiece in the St Anne chapel of Tettnang church (near Hamburg) has Anne seated tearful in her house, as the angel announced the arrival of their child; through a window, Joachim is shown with his flock, receiving his own Annunciation.[83]

As Anne grew in prominence her daughter was represented ever younger, and smaller too. The mystic Julian of Norwich saw her as 'a simple maiden and meek, young of age, a little waxen [grown] above a chylde'.[84] In a Netherlandish Book of Hours of the 1490s there are seven Hours devoted to Anne. Each begins with a decorated initial in which Anne is the large central figure dressed in red, with a small Mary in her lap, and baby Jesus in hers. Mary looks child-like, as her mother is situated central and authoritative, nurturing and respectable.[85]

Anne became a popular choice as patron of patrician confraternities in the fifteenth century, above all in Northern Europe. Just as Mary's life emerged in the fourteenth century as a subject worthy of the detail and focus of an elaborate altarpiece, Anne received such attention in the later fifteenth century. Anne is depicted in the central panel of an altarpiece surrounded by scenes from her life.[86] The confraternity of St Anne in Louvain commissioned the artist Quentin Metsys to paint a triptych; in the centre of the panel all generations combined: Anne, Mary and Jesus in the centre, cousins either side, children learning to read, and the four men behind, divided by a low wall.[87] An altarpiece made in 1515 in Lower Saxony presented Anne and Mary with all their men: women in the front with the Child Jesus, and the four men on a gallery above them, well-dressed bourgeois figures gesturing in wonder at the group below.[88] The outer wings of this altarpiece depicted scenes of mature motherhood: Anne on the right and Elizabeth on the left, each nurturing her child and each with spouse (and other children) behind. Those who cherished lineage found in Anne a responsible spouse: stained glass from St Peter Mancroft church in Norwich (now in the Great Hall of Felbrigg Hall, Norfolk) depicts the scene of Anne and Cleophas, her second husband. Anne provided occasions for the portrayal of fecund multi-generational families: the Holy Kinship was blessed with plenty in an altarpiece by a Swabian artist of c.1500 where a dove hovers above the comfortable domestic scene.[89]

Patron of marriage and families, protector of dynasties, Anne was

sometimes dismissed by purists who found her apocryphal origins and her serial nuptials to be embarrassing.[90] This was true of austere women who espoused virginity, like the religious reformer St Colette, who operated for the renewal of religious life under the auspices of the Burgundian court. Her brand of female religion combined poverty and virginity; her biographer claimed that, accordingly, Colette prayed to saints who had kept their own bodies chaste. Yet Anne came to her in a vision, surrounded by her ample progeny, and this persuaded Colette to change her mind. The encounter with Anne meant that Colette's mission could be reoriented to attract once-married women too. Even the thrice-married Duke Charles the Bold became a patron and turned to the new devotion to Mary's mother with enthusiasm.[91]

Anne offered a matronly presence in a devotional world full of virgin saints and martyrs. She thus appealed to a different sensibility of dynastic aspirations and bourgeois values. She is usually dressed in sumptuous though dignified apparel, her hair covered, and sometimes her face and neck too. Elizabeth, mother of St John the Baptist, is another older woman who shared Mary's world. Anne is occasionally presented with this other older woman of Mary's kin. Lucas Cranach the Elder combined these two matrons with a pair of patrician donors in a painting of around 1514. The abbot of a Premonstratensian monastery near Ulm was depicted kneeling in prayer at the foot of St Anne, on the wing of an altarpiece; the other wing depicted St Elizabeth.[92] Mary's relationship with Elizabeth, sealed during their pregnancies, was interpreted as a quintessential image of female friendship, with glimpses of a young woman's gesture as she greeted an older one. They sometimes kiss, as in an Austrian panel for the Scottish Cloister in Vienna of around 1469/80, at other times just hold hands or embrace.[93] Particular joy is conveyed in the depictions of the quickening babies in their wombs, represented as flashes of light, or as little creatures who gesture towards each other.[94] Their relationship was further elaborated in scenes of Mary attending Elizabeth at the birth of John the Baptist; the young woman's charity is manifest in her assistance to her older kinswoman.[95]

We enter even more deeply into Mary's home with scenes of Jesus and John the Baptist as playful toddlers depicted in this period for the first time. A German panel that once formed part of an altarpiece painted around the year 1400 shows the boys at play at their mothers' feet. The women are at work: Mary juggles her reading and her spinning, while

Elizabeth turns the handle of a rotating wool-winder. Jesus holds a spoon, and John a pan, but what seems like a peaceful scene soon emerges as one of conflict. Jesus is up to his tricks, as inscribed on a ribbon containing the words of complaint: 'Look, mum, Jesus is hurting me!' ('Sich in muter: Ihesus tut mier').[96] An early woodcut in a book of prayer has the two naked haloed boys mock-jousting, armed respectively with spoon and pan.[97] There is in these themes something of the infantile aggression which early infancy stories about Jesus expressed in tales and images, part of the myriad attempts to imagine the earthly life of God. In a Book of Hours from the north of France the scene is much more serene. The group of mothers and sons is seated on the flowering grass of a walled garden, where all eat with spoons out of a bowl of milky porridge. There is a lamb at their feet – emblem of each boy – and Jesus holds a parrot and wears a coral necklace, symbol of the passion.[98]

These children were attractive figures, and their stories served in the education of children. One can imagine the attraction felt by youngsters towards the doll-like statues or the colourfully painted figures of the child Jesus and his kin encountered in churches and at street corners. An illumination in a Flemish *Miracles de la Vierge* depicts a little boy in church with his mother: he runs up to a relief of Mary and Child leaning against a wall and touches the holy baby.[99] The *Salve regina*, Mary's foremost antiphon, was worked in fifteenth-century England into a poem in fourteen stanzas, to teach children their table manners. Mary as mother and as domestic goddess helped mothers teach their children the basic lessons of a good life. Even before priests weighed in with their authority, or tutors with their books, children were alive with Mary lore taught by women among caresses and chidings. Mary was a member of the late medieval family.

20

Mary: a World of Devotional Possibilities

THE ROSARY – MARY'S PRAYER AND THE MEMORY OF THE PASSION

While Mary and Anne ruled serenely over the Holy Family, Mary also dominated scenes of the Passion. Towards the end of the fifteenth century a new devotion was created, and it combined the daily prayer to Mary – Ave Maria – with meditation on the Passion. This is the rosary, a devotional practice of 150 Ave Marias divided into groups of ten by meditations on the Passion. It thus integrated fully prayer to Mary and the narrative of the Passion. The image used to describe the rosary is that of a chain, or a garland, and later a crown: it contained sequences of prayers marked in groups of ten, like a necklace of pearls, punctuated by gems.

Marian psalters had already developed for the use of monks and nuns, and these often adhered to the number 150, the number of psalms, with meditative recitations, each opening with *Ave Maria*.[1] Such recitation was open even to the least literate and was favoured by many. The rosary was patterned in a new and exciting way: it linked the Ave Maria prayer with the Pater Noster, and both to meditations on the Passion.[2]

Like so many late medieval devotional practices, the rosary has its origins in monastic routines of prayer. One early text, of around 1300, was a Life of Christ for the use of the Cistercian nuns of St Thomas of Kyll, in the diocese of Trier, patterned as a rosary. While Mary was 'intruding' into the space of the Passion, Marian psalters, for the use of women, introduced Jesus into prayerful meditations on Mary's life. By the early fourteenth century a rhymed Mary psalter dedicated the last

332

fifty invocations to the life of Christ. Over the next hundred years many vernacular 'rosaries' were written, psalters of Mary's names and strings of her praise. One is titled 'rôsenkrenzlein' – a little garland of roses – and in it the Latin Ave Maria salutation was given in German 'ich grûze dich'.[3]

A devotion designed for religious women in German-speaking lands formed the basis for a new form: the rosary designed by a Carthusian monk, Dominic of Prussia (1384–1460), of the Charterhouse of Trier. In his rosary Mary's and Jesus' lives were intertwined. This new monastic devotion spread quickly to other houses of the Carthusian order throughout Europe. It took a Dominican, however, Alan of Rupa (1428–75), to introduce the new devotion to large groups of lay people. He did so by founding a confraternity in the city of Douai around 1468. Members were required to recite the rosary/psalter daily. He provided instruction in prayer as well as edifying *exempla*, short instructive tales about the power of the rosary. Other Dominicans followed his lead.[4] In 1475 the Dominican dean of the Theology Faculty at the University of Cologne, Jakob Sprenger, founded a rosary confraternity in the city. The confraternity grew rapidly and by the end of the century it numbered over 100,000 members from Cologne and beyond. Little was required of the brethren and sisters – just weekly recitation of the rosary. The confraternity received the approval of the Dominican order, and of popes, and was showered with indulgences for the benefit of its members.

The confraternity's statute book of 1477 portrays Mary enthroned on a raised platform with Jesus on her right knee, while two angels hold a crown over her haloed head. Mary receives from the kneeling Emperor Frederick III a rose garland in her left hand, while her son receives a rose garland from a kneeling cardinal, behind whom stands the Dominican founder, Jakob Sprenger. In the foreground two men and two women kneel, members of the confraternity, with garlands in their hands.[5] The pattern was soon adopted all over Northern Europe. The Colmar confraternity was based on a revised version of Alan of Rupa's model. Members were obliged to recite the rosary weekly, each ten Ave Marias followed by a Pater Noster associated with a specific mediation:

And then ten more Ave Maria in praise of our beloved lady as she received the greeting from the angel Gabriel. Then say the first Pater Noster to Christ's sorrow on the Mount of Olives where he sweated bloody sweat.[6]

The rosary resulted from a benign combination of Marian prayer of the simplest kind with mental images of Christ's life, above all the Crucifixion. Those who worried about the 'marianization' of devotional life found balance in the rosary. Those who wished to acknowledge Mary's place in the Crucifixion were similarly satisfied. Jakob Sprenger's original scheme was sound, he was after all an expert on orthodoxy. He was the author of the theological section – perhaps a third – of the *Hammer of Witches* (*Malleus maleficarum*) the handbook for inquisitors in the identification of error.[7] The rosary similarly disciplined 'feminine' Mary worship with a frame of meditation on Christ's suffering.

The rosary was a quintessentially northern creation, and from Cologne its influence radiated out throughout German-speaking and Netherlandish regions. The first known Italian rosary confraternity was in Venice; the rosary confraternity of 1480 emerged there from an older Marian one, of San Domenico, in Castello. The rosary reached other Italian cities only some twenty years later. It probably arrived in Venice early thanks to the city's strong trading links with Cologne (there was a thriving trade in rich brocades between the cities) and Venice's influential community of German merchants. The German confraternity of the rosary met in St Bartholomew's church, and in 1506 it commissioned no less a master than Albrecht Dürer to paint an altar piece for the German merchants of Venice, the *Rosenkrantzfesten*.[8] The quintessentially northern devotion gradually made its way southwards too.

The rosary spread among working people. It appears in the scrapbook of Robert Reynes of Acle in Norfolk (after 1430–1505), a local reeve and alderman, which included instruction on prayer with rosary beads:

> Man, do not stand idle in the church
> but take your beads in your hands
> and if you do not have any
> I ask you to take these for the moment
> and say a psalter cheerfully
> in worship of our dear Lady.
> She will give (*aqwyte*) you grace (well)
> and present your earthly prayer to her son.
> And for a single psalter you will have 23 years,
> 11 score days and 14,

334

[indulgences] granted by two popes
in remission of your sin,
when your soul will flame and burn.
And therefore pray with heart and mind,
and make the Queen of Heaven your friend,
so that you may stand in her grace so much
that she will be your shield when you die.
And when you wish to stand no longer,
leave the beads where you found them.[9]

The rosary's spread was facilitated by the development of print. Rosary woodcuts travelled with the promise of salvation, indulgences related to their use as aids in rosary prayer. Erhard Schön (c.1491–1542) of Nuremberg created a hand-painted woodcut in 1515 – the Great Rosary. At the centre hung Christ from the cross, surrounded by a garland (chaplet) of fifty roses, a third of the whole rosary. Each group of ten roses was marked by a cross-signed medallion, a contemplation of the Crucifixion. The circle was full of figures of saints, martyrs and angels of every type. Below the chaplet, on earth, stood hopeful humans led by pope and emperor, and under them, below the crust of the earth, the suffering dwellers of hell. The serene circle of roses was laid over this hectic Christian story.[10] At the very bottom the indulgence was offered: 'To those who pray the heavenly rosary will be given all the indulgences of our lady of the rosary thereto 107 years, 100 Lents, and 1780 days.'

While cheaper print disseminated rosary possibilities widely, the more exclusive painted rosary panels were still produced. Hans Suess of Kulmbach made by 1510 a triptych of the Heavenly Rosary, probably for a church in Nuremberg. The rosary occupies the larger central panel, with Christ on the cross, surrounded by a chaplet of fifty-five roses, each ten silver roses punctuated by a larger golden rose bearing a cross. Above the cross are Mary with God the Father and the Holy Ghost as a dove, and under the arms of the cross are prophets and saints, including a group of Mary, Anne and the Child Jesus. Beneath the chaplet are scenes of heaven and hell. The wings of the triptych show scenes of Mary's early life: the kiss at the Golden Gate at which Mary was conceived (right), and her entry to the Temple. Despite attempts to make the rosary a balanced memorial of incarnation and death on the cross, the qualities

that emerge repeatedly and strongly are the appreciation and attachment to Mary's life.[11]

The plenitude and multitude that was the rosary tested existing conventions of representation. New combinations were prompted by the rose garland that was also a crown; like other brides Mary wore a crown, but unlike them it was her son who placed it on her head in heaven. It is not surprising that a branch of the Observant Franciscans devoted to the legacy of Bernardino of Siena – the Bernardines – commissioned a fascinating visual display. Around 1500 a panel entitled *The Crown of the Most Blessed Virgin* (*Corona beatissimae virginis*) was made for the Bernardine church of Wrocław (it now hangs in the National Museum in Warsaw). At the foot of the image Mary and Child stand surrounded by the familiar rays of chastity and virtue, flanked by friars in prayers. Two angels grasp an enormous crown – some ten times the appropriate size for a crown. But this was no ordinary queenly ornament: it was an all-embracing crown adorned with seven layers of seven scenes, producing forty-nine medallions of

Mary's seven joys

Mary's seven sorrows

The seven heavenly choirs (angels, apostles, martyrs, bishops, widows, virgins and saints)

The seven deadly sins

The seven virtues

The seven gifts of the Holy Spirit

The seven human groups protected by Mary: parents, clergy, lay, friars, needy, sinners and the dead.

This elaborate scheme was a pictorial rendering of some of the numerical patterns of a rosary tract by a brother of the order, Władisław of Gielniow.[12] The order, following the leanings of Bernardino and of its founder Giovanni da Capistrano, emphasized Marian prayer, and the substantial crown could have served as an enticing object for the friars' prayers. It may also have served as a pastoral tool; the illustrated rows of vices and virtues were the stuff of pastoral and catechism, just as the joys and sorrows of Mary told the whole Christian story from the Incarnation, through Christ's Passion and Resurrection.

The didactic tone of the rosary was never far from view. When the Hungarian Observant Franciscan Palbert of Temesvar (d.1504)

recovered from the plague he fulfilled the vow taken on his death-bed and wrote a series of sermons on Mary, who had saved him. This was the *Stellarium coronae beatae Mariae virginis* (*The Stellarium of the Blessed Virgin Mary*), which was published in 1496. It described Mary's mysteries as the twelve stars – hence *Stellarium* – in the crown of the Woman of the Apocalypse, a figure with whom we have seen Mary merge on occasion: Annunciation and Incarnation, Visitation, Purification, Immaculate Conception, Nativity, Naming of Jesus, Virtuous Life, Virginity, Charity, Assumption and the cult of Mary. This was an inexpensive book which was to be used by less educated friars, who would communicate the contents to their audiences.[13]

Like other areas of interest in Mary, the rosary offered niche devotions for exclusive groups of professional religious. But it also created occasions for participation which were collective and communal, including even some outdoor events. The rosary was underpinned by an inclusive rhetoric that presented it as cheap, easy and accessible to all. Anyone could pray the rosary, if not the full rosary psalter then the Ave Maria and Pater Noster prayers. Nothing could be easier. Cornelis Everaert, a textile worker from Bruges, who also wrote religious plays, composed in 1509 the *Play of Mary's Chaplet*. This allegorical piece recorded the adventures of a youth, Good Company (Goet Gheselscip), who made a chaplet for Mary every day. Deserted, seduced and inveigled, he was advised by the figure of Virtuous Instruction on how simple it could be:

> If you wish to make a crown for Mary
> Of flowers sweet
>
> . . .
>
> You should read
> Fifty Ave Marias, and add to them
> There should be between each ten
> A Pater Noster.[14]

Here is the perfect recipe for a rosary: a string of Ave Marias, punctuated by the memory of Christ through the recitation of his unique prayer. The materials are simple, imparted at the mother's knee and in parish instruction. Cornelis Everaert's story blended traditional miracles, in which those who aim to paint, sculpt or adorn Mary are rewarded, with the awareness of the recent creation of confraternities of the rosary all

over Europe. Everaert may even have written his play at the request of the Bruges Confraternity of the Rosary.[15]

The rosary exposed anxiety about the prominence of Mary in contemporary devotional practices. By the fifteenth century it had become all but impossible to tell the Passion fully and movingly without also addressing Mary's pain. Following the reform of the Cistercian nunnery at Weinhausen in Saxony in 1469 a devotional tract on the crown of thorns, the *Dornenkron*, became the house's preferred devotional text, and it has survived in Middle German and Latin versions. It told Christ's Passion in its final, painful, bloody stages, by imagining the crown of thorns that pierced Christ's head. The nun-scribes who copied the booklet stamped their interests upon their handiwork, and 'marianized' them. Some versions punctuated the devotion with recitations of the Ave Maria; others instructed nuns to recite the *Dornenkron* before an image of Mary or of the Crucifixion and Mary. A Latin version directed readers towards the Ave Maria and the ten virtues after the recitation: the crown of thorns was offered to Mary with the expectation that she would pray for the nun and her relatives.[16] Mary's relatives were invoked too; one scribe addressed Mary's own teacher in prayer, her mother Anne. The pristine, impeccably correct meditation on the crown of thorns, on Christ's suffering on the cross, was bedecked and elaborated with Marian prayers and salutations by the female copiers; they turned meditation on Christ's bleeding head into a passionate encounter with his suffering mother. Perhaps the two were inseparable. The Crucifixion seemed incomplete without Mary, and only Mary was sufficiently compelling to make the Crucifixion real. The rosary aimed to balance the devotional energy directed at mother and son – sufferers both.

MARY – PICTURE OF MOTHERHOOD

With new feasts and schemes for devotion, with altarpieces that told the story of her life – sometimes queen of heaven, sometimes simple maiden – Mary was encountered throughout Europe more frequently than ever before. Not only were materials and representations of Mary diverse, but there was a constant stream of new artefacts, alongside the constant flow of the liturgy. The claims about Mary – as intercessor and protector, as redeemer and sufferer with Christ – were reinforced by the ubiquity

of her images in churches and on street corners, in prayer books and on clothing. The desire to possess Mary was facilitated by the middle of the century thanks to technologies and patterns of work which encouraged cheap reproduction of images: alabaster carvings were produced in fifteenth-century England in the thousands; clay figurines of Mary and Child were produced by the potters of Cologne and Utrecht; and pilgrim badges were cast cheaply in dies, like the image of the Virgin and Child from St Michael's church at Chibury Priory (Shropshire).[17] Books of Hours were also being produced increasingly efficiently – and thus more cheaply – with the use of techniques of stencilling.[18]

Artists in all traditions were experimenting with the rendering of Mary's motherhood, her pregnancy above all. A wooden statue of Mary, made around 1430 in Bohemia, has her seated with a hand just above her pregnant belly, covered by a maternity garment. Tuscan artists worked with the classical aesthetic that had already intrigued and inspired fourteenth-century artists like Giotto. In the case of Mary the term classical denotes a fullness of body, a roundness of face, a statuesque presence, a sense of depth in space.[19] Where sinuous lines made a French Mary elegant and regal in earlier centuries, Mary was now more symmetrical in form, as if drawn with a compass. Consider Piero della Francesca's *Madonna del Prato*, painted in 1467 for the cemetery chapel of Monterchi near Arezzo. Mary is revealed by the pulling aside of brocaded curtains, as if within a tent, in a spectacular epiphany, large with child. Mary wears a sky-blue dress, a pregnancy garment, which opens comfortably over her ample stomach to reveal an undergarment. The classical illusion of physical presence situates Mary in the present, yet she is also a distant figure gazing beyond, never meeting the eye.

New technologies of engraving and print allowed traditional and emergent images to spread widely as single sheets or in cheap books. Shrines gained wider fame through the circulation of engravings and woodcuts: the black statue of Mary at Einsiedeln was immortalized by Master ES, who produced two engravings in 1466: a sumptuous large tinted image of the consecration of Einsiedeln church, and a cut-price, smaller one with fewer figures arranged more modestly.[20] Images of Mary were now available for sewing or pasting into existing prayerbooks.

The scenes of Mary's life and associations were cast from the traditions of manuscript illumination into print: single page scenes of the

Pietà were widely available in late fifteenth-century Europe, and the new devotion to the rosary benefited greatly from the circulation of replicated images, like the copper engraving of 1488 by the Catalan friar Francese Doménech. With Mary in a mandorla – an almond-shaped frame – at the centre bottom, it told in fifteen scenes above an integrated version of the lives of Mary and Jesus, as did the rosary.[21] The circulation of prints by innovative artists readily inspired others. A German ivory roundel of the Annunciation owes much to an engraving by Master ES of around 1450–60.[22] An anonymous Swabian painter executed an altarpiece with an Adoration/Nativity scene around 1515; it was inspired by an engraving by the artist Martin Schongauer (c.1448–91) and a Presentation that followed a woodcut by Albrecht Dürer.[23]

In this hectic world of writing, printing, copying and illumination the role of the artist ranged from that of the modest artisan to the innovative and appreciated *auteur*. Mary challenged minds and offered interesting fields for intellectual expression by poets and exegetes; by the fifteenth century artists also reflected self-consciously on what making an image of Mary really meant. Just how meaningful the portrayal of the epitome of purity and beauty could be to an artist was captured well by Rogier van der Weyden in his *St Luke Drawing the Virgin* of c.1435–40.[24] The artist chose to portray himself as the Evangelist, hard at work making a fine silverpoint drawing.[25] St Luke, not surprisingly, became the patron of artists. The scene of Luke drawing Mary was also adopted as a devotional image for contemplation of Mary's modesty and beauty, as in a Book of Hours decorated by Jean Colombe.[26]

Poets and artists pondered the alchemy of imitation and invention – of old and new – which inspired affective art. In making Mary for devotional use artists struggled with the desire to innovate on the one hand and the lure of tradition on the other. The illustrations to two luxurious manuscripts of Boccaccio's *Of Illustrious Women* (*De mulieribus claris*), made in 1402 and 1403 for French aristocrats, depict women famed for their art: two worthy women from classical myth, Thamarys and Irene, were shown at work, making images of Mary and Child in painting and sculpture. They worked not from a model but from memory. Here is a clue to one contemporary understanding of the artistic process authorized by the thousands of Mary figures: that it was the work of imagination through memory, rather than the application of skill alone. Thamarys and Irene were virtuous women with a rich

inner life, and so they produced perfect images.[27] Having Mary on the mind assisted the making of good Mary images.

Images and statues of Mary in churches, on the outer walls of houses and at street corners all contributed to a reassuring sense of her presence. Around 1450 Italian cities began to decree that images of Mary be installed in street corners, to ensure better behaviour by citizens in the public domain.[28] People were obliged to behave accordingly, as they were taught from childhood that the mother figure *par excellence* was always near by. The house and the street blended in dangerous ways since images on houses participated in this public sacred economy. When the Jewish banker Daniele da Norsa bought a house in Mantua he received permission to remove the image of Mary and Child on it, in keeping with an established procedure by which he applied and paid for the right to do so. When he attempted to have the image removed, violence broke out in the streets. When he sought protection from the duke of Mantua, he found his request rebuffed and a punishment heaped on: the banker was obliged to commission a new image by the Mantuan painter Andrea Mantegna (1431–1506); this became the famous *Virgin and Child Surrounded by Six Saints and Gianfrancesco II Gonzaga*, better known as the *Madonna of Victory*. The house was turned into a Mary Chapel.[29]

The ubiquitous, outdoor Mary could seem exposed and vulnerable to the effect of the elements, to derisive taunts, to the dirt and disorder generated by urban life. Not only Jews were in danger of being seen as breakers of the codes of propriety around Mary. When in 1501 the Florentine Antonio Rinaldeschi left the Fig Tree tavern after losing some money at a game of chance, he cursed Mary for his bad luck. He passed by a church dedicated to her – Santa Maria degli Alberghi – picked up a handful of dry horse dung and flung it at a tabernacle with her image situated on the church's outer wall. Some of the dung stuck to the image and formed – so some people claimed – the shape of a rosette. The image of the Annunciation, which bespoke Mary's purity, innocence and faith, was defiled by dung, and it fought back. Here was a wonder that soon drew the attention of the archbishop and the city magistrates, and to it were also added other miracles. A shrine was born, while Rinaldeschi was caught and hanged.[30]

And so a careless blasphemy cost Rinaldeschi his life.[31] The new cult inspired more images in turn. For the adornment of the chapel built on

341

the site the painter Filippo Dolciati adopted a format commonly used for the report of contemporary miraculous narratives: the story unfolded scene by scene from top left to bottom right in nine stages.[32] The dung rosette was painted gold and formed part of a new, miraculous image.

While patricians hoped that Mary's vigilant presence would bring out the best in people, the intimate links with Mary also allowed otherwise humble persons to define themselves in more interesting and adventurous ways than their daily life might suggest. The peasant girl Jeanne d'Arc was inspired to seek out the prince of France following a vision of the Virgin Mary; such conversations were clearly no longer the privilege of monks, nuns and priests. In spring 1476 the young drummer and shepherd Hans Behem received a vision of Mary which explained recent turbulent weather on Christ's anger with human sin. She recommended a cleansing mass penitential pilgrimage to Niklashausen in expiation of sin. Hans spread the word, and thousands began to congregate on the little town in the Tauber valley in Franconia.[33] Hans was emboldened to call the people to himself since neither secular rulers nor bishops cared about their well-being. Here was a political message from Mary's mouth, and it was treated as political subversion: the pilgrims to Niklashausen, who had become a veritable movement over the summer with its slogans and songs, were attacked by the forces of the prince-bishop of Würzburg and dispersed after the arrest of their leader. There was clearly some limit to Mary's power to protect her charges on earth.

ANNUNCIATION – THE COMMONEST MARY-SCENE?

In Europe awash with images a single scene marked the beginning of Mary's extraordinary career as mother of God: the Annunciation. Early Christian writers developed a manner of thinking about the conception of Jesus in Mary as an act of hearing. This was developed in Syriac poetry and absorbed into Latin thought through the writings of Bernard of Clairvaux. Those who favoured the ear made words the agents of conception, and so the common device of presenting Gabriel's words as a scroll between him and Mary with the words: 'Ave Maria gratia plena', as in a Book of Hours once owned by King Richard III, and in the

depiction which adorned one of Bernard's homilies in a book made for the nuns of Unterlinden in Alsace.[34]

Yet the artists and their patrons sought to visualize something more compelling, the quickening of Mary's womb. They were called to do so in altarpieces which told the story of Mary's life, and even more frequently in the decoration of Books of Hours, where the scene of the Annunciation usually accompanied the beginning of the cycle of the Hours of the Virgin. Mary's body had to be shown at the precise moment of penetration, but artists devised strategies that made that entry pure. Filippo Lippi's *Annunciation* shows a somewhat reluctant Mary turning away from the angel but has a ray of light issue from the beak of a dove – the Holy Spirit – to Mary's womb.[35] Reference to the womb strained propriety; it was the most private feminine part, perceived as the site of disorder and habitually associated with pollution. So a variation was devised, the substitution of chest – or even head – for womb. An initial in an antiphonary used in Siena cathedral depicts a dove directing a ray of light on to the reluctant Mary's chest.[36] And lest any viewer doubt the truth of the Conception, the artist who decorated a Book of Hours for the duke of Warwick in the 1430s, has a little Christ figure dive towards his mother on the rays.[37]

Mary's position at the Annunciation spawned a great deal of speculation and interpretation: was Mary reluctant, fearful, accepting of her mission? Most representations attempt to convey a sense of gentle modesty and to steer away from reluctance or resistance. Mary is habitually shown in a gesture – with one hand or both folded against her breast – that denotes self-effacing humility. She kneels, bows her head and folds her hands in Carlo Crivelli's (1430/35–by 1500) Annunciation of *c.*1482, while she turns her back altogether and half-faces the lectern in an embroidered processional banner.[38]

Many artists enjoyed exploring the interior space of the Annunciation, setting it within comfortable urban households, like those in which the painting might be displayed: Peter Christus' (*c.*1410–72/3) *Annunciation* takes place, suggestively, in a bed chamber and an *Annunciation* in the style of the Master of Flemalle, within a well-appointed parlour.[39] A tapestry made in Mantua around 1506–19 created an enclosed space for Mary: a curtain is pulled back to reveal her while the angel is placed out of doors.[40] A variation on the distinction between exterior and interior is offered by the Sienese Giovanni di Paolo (*c.*1403–82) in his

Annunciation scene of $c.1435$: while Gabriel offers the news within an open gazebo, Adam and Eve are expelled from the Garden of Eden, outdoors.[41] This tradition was conceived anew by the Dominican friar Fra Angelico ($c.1395-1455$) in his wall painting of $c.1441$ for cell 3 of the Dominican monastery of San Marco in Florence. He set the scene within an elaborate portico, which frames the scene and creates a sense of closure and protection so meaningful in the portrayal of Mary's chaste body.[42] Mary clasps a prayer book and folds both hands to her chest, a gesture mirrored by the angel, who kneels and thus comes down to Mary's height. Eye into eye they gaze, golden-haired and haloed, observed by a Dominican saint. The building with a portico is set alongside a garden surrounded by a high, well-made fence. A similar preoccupation with framing is evident in the Annunciation by Domenico Veneziano painted for the church of S. Lucia de'Magnoli in Florence: Mary kneels under a portico, while the angel kneels within the courtyard on to which it opens.[43] Mary's enclosure is further reinforced by the presence of a closed door – one of Mary's oldest attributes – at the centre of the composition.

Be it indoors or out, in elegant porticos or domestic settings, one of Mary's attributes – the white lily – was rarely absent from the scene. Here too there is much interesting variation. The Master of Flémalle ($c.1375-1444$) placed an ordinary vase with lilies on the table between Gabriel and Mary; Peter Christus put it at Gabriel's feet, in between the two. If the approaching angel seemed to threaten Mary's pristine isolation, the vase stood as a barrier, securing Mary's aloof chastity. The mass-produced English alabasters displayed in their supple carving a trend we have already encountered – the merging of Christ and Mary through the lily. A Welsh version linked the Annunciation and Crucifixion in the image of the Lily Crucifixion used in the Annunciation scene in the Llanbeblig Book of Hours of $c.1400$, where the crucifix arises from the vase at Mary's feet.[44] A Welsh alabaster tomb in St Mary's church, Abergavenny, depicts a similar scene, with Mary under a canopy, a kneeling angel, and the hovering figure of Christ, crucified upon the lily.[45]

Mary of the Annunciation was situated in many different settings, which ranged from mundane domestic interiors to grand spaces reminiscent of temples or palaces. Even at the moment of modest acceptance, Mary was made to assume the majesty of clerical dignity. In these

decades she was seated at lecterns, or even placed in structures that resemble pulpits. The view of Mary as a sacramental vessel, which produced the powerful image of the *Vierge ouvrante*, and which placed Mary in clerical vestments, also inspired portrayals of the Annunciation that were laden with sacramental meaning. Robert Campin embedded eucharistic clues in his *Madonna of the Firescreen*, where he set a parlour table as an altar with open book, candles and lilies. A portable altarpiece carved in walnut and oak depicts the Annunciation with a canopy held open by angels, Mary at a lectern and alongside a table set like an altar, wearing golden garments which recall liturgical vestments.[46] An illuminated page of a German Book of Hours situates the Annunciation in a church-like space, adorned with holy images, and has Gabriel dressed as a deacon and Mary reading at a lectern.[47] Mary reads at a lectern in a scene from a Polish antiphonary; and here an interesting reversal occurs, for at her feet kneels an angel/deacon, his hands folded across his chest, in deference to the expounding Mary.[48] This book, for the use of a male clerical choir, opened its vespers with Psalm 43:2: 'We have heard, O God, with our ears: our fathers have declared to us, The work thou hast wrought in their days, and in the days of old [*antiquis*].' The initial A of *antiquis* has Mary as a poignant, ever-present teacher.

MARY AND THE STRIVING RELIGIOUS SUBJECT

In home, street and parish Mary was widely available to many. For the few, Mary was embedded within a religious vocation that lived away from 'the world'. In the religious houses of Europe whole lives were devoted to testing and experiencing the meaning of a life with Mary as companion. Mary appealed to women religious through the many roles she endorsed and amplified: daughter, mother, bride and kinswoman; she attracted male religious as comforting companion, the mother lost, the hope for inner perfection. Insofar as the lives of male and female religious were different in several ways, we witness differing practices. Women often imagined religious encounters through their breasts and enacted scenes related to birth and motherhood, while men imagined being at the breast or being Mary at the altar as they consecrated bread

and brought forth Christ's body. Men frequently produced devotional works for the use of women, decorated with edifying images deemed particularly suited to women's mental and spiritual capacities. And since the requirement of enclosure was applied more strictly to women, much of the art produced by them or for them has a particularly intimate, private quality.[49]

Awareness of Mary was stark in the spirituality that spread throughout Europe in the fifteenth century by way of the Bridgettine order. Birgitta of Sweden (1303–73) was a noblewoman, a widow who left her family to found a new religious order and preach reform of the church in Rome. She was not only an effective reformer and organizer of religious life but a recipient of Marian revelations. Through these she expressed identification and identity with Mary: just as Birgitta was a mother to children, so was Mary to all Christians; like Mary and the apostles, Birgitta received the Holy Spirit.[50] Mary appeared in a third of Birgitta's revelations, and the theme of pregnancy pervaded this affinity. Birgitta experienced a mystical sense of pregnancy one Christmas Eve: a movement as if 'a living child were in her heart turning itself around and around'. Those who saw her perceived this pregnancy too.[51] Just as Mary felt at the Annunciation, so did Birgitta: 'For when I assented to the angel who announced the conception of the Son of God to me, immediately I felt a certain marvellous and living thing in me.'[52] The Bridgettine order absorbed men and women, and appealed to privileged patrons, among them kings and princes. In England it received a boost from Henry V with the creation of a house at Syon (Middlesex) in 1415. The order required that its members celebrate a daily office of Our Lady. The days of the week offered a frame for celebration of the Christian story: Sunday's emphasis was the Trinity; Monday – the angels; Tuesday – the prophecies of Mary's birth; Wednesday – Mary's parentage and birth; Thursday – the Annunciation and Jesus' birth; Friday – Mary's suffering at the Crucifixion; and Saturday commemorated Mary's end. The Swedish houses celebrated a feast of Mary's Compassion at the Crucifixion.[53] Bridgettine spirituality emphasized Mary's redemptive power and urged both male and female members to see themselves in Mary. Their Mary of choice was the co-suffering Mary, who played so important a role in salvation.

Birgitta's charisma worked through Marian materials, and so it was fitting that the Brigittine liturgical office incorporated her words, the

angel-speak (*sermo angelicus*) revealed to her. In this the Brigittine women differed from the men affiliated to their houses, who followed the customary liturgy of each diocese. The sisters' chant was composed by Peter of Skänninge (d.1378), Birgitta's close associate, and was based on her revelations. It spread throughout Europe to Italy and Bavaria, northern Germany, the Netherlands and England. For other parts of the liturgy Peter turned to antiphons used on the Marian feasts of the Assumption and Conception, for which he composed new melodies.[54]

The new religious order, founded by a woman, ruled by abbesses and to which men could be associated, defined itself through Mary and her appearance to a contemporary woman. Bridgettine Mary was an agent of redemption, a public actor in Christian history. She was also a private sufferer with her son. Like Mary, whose heart was pierced by the pain of the Crucifixion, Birgitta felt through her heart, where her spiritual child was born.[55] Jesus had been born from the heart, and in her heart Mary suffered with him:

His members were to me as if [they were] my members and as if [they were] my heart. For as other children are accustomed to be in the wombs of their mothers, so was he in me . . . He obviously was to me as if [he was] my heart. For that reason, when he was born from me, I felt that as if half my heart was being born and was going out from me. And when he was suffering, felt that as if my heart was suffering . . . When my son was being whipped and pierced, I [felt] as if my heart was beaten and pierced . . .[56]

Birgitta introduced a powerful script for imitation: through Mary's compassion and in the work of redemption that began with a marvellous birth. This is clear in the words which Birgitta scripted for Mary: 'For as Adam and Eve sold the world with one apple, so my son and I redeemed the world as if with one heart.'[57]

Birgitta was not the only religious innovator to whom Mary was an inspiration. Beatriz de Silva (1424–91) was a young Portuguese noblewoman who accompanied her kinswoman, Princess Isabella of Portugal, when she married Juan II, king of Castile. Her sixteenth-century hagiographer claimed that the princess came to resent Beatriz because of her beauty. When Beatriz was locked in a trunk by the jealous princess, she prayed to Mary, who brought about her deliverance without harm after three days. Beatriz abandoned the court and made her way to Toledo, where she entered the convent of San

Domingo el Real. She lived there as a devout lay woman, immersed in prayer. The next queen, Isabella of Castile, supported Beatriz's religious programme.[58]

Beatriz nurtured a devotion to Mary's Conception that was closely linked to the Immaculate Conception. In buildings handed over by the queen in 1484, she and eleven sisters realized their dream. Their habit imitated the clothes worn by Mary when she appeared to the young Beatriz: a white tunic and blue cloak. In 1489 the house was recognized by Pope Innocent VIII as the kernel for a new order, the order of the Immaculate Conception. Its women were to live according to the strict enclosure demanded by the Cistercian rule, and the sisters wore a rope belt – a symbol of poverty and physical endurance – as Franciscan friars did.[59]

Women's religious houses offered an institutional setting for interests within the vast creative world around Mary. While a new order like the Bridgettines made a spectacular splash, traditional institutions were also engaged in important decisions about the scope and the form of their interest in Mary. The heads of convents in Florence, for example, were almost all members of leading patrician families, women who had grown up in households that supported religious art, music and literature. The Bridgettine house of the Paradiso in Pian di Ripoli had Lorenzo de' Medici as a member of its building committee. It commissioned in 1439 an altarpiece with Mary and Child, St Bridget and St Michael. Nuns of Paradiso were free to commission devotional art for private use: one commissioned Neri di Bicci in 1461 to make a small and costly tabernacle of the *Assumption of the Virgin with the Gift of the Girdle*. This included scenes of the Annunciation, the Nativity, the Assumption and of St John in the Desert. The Benedictine nuns of Santa Apollonia in Via S. Gallo commissioned of Paolo Schiavo in 1448 a wall painting of *The Crucified Christ adored by Benedictine Nuns*: here is the most central of devotional images – the Crucifixion – accompanied by the nuns, all acting as Mary, contemplating compassionately Christ's suffering.[60]

The contracts between convents and artists make it clear that the women chose their own artwork and negotiated directly over its execution. The high-born Venetian canonesses of Le Vergini expressed their interest in Mary's lineage in the making of a genealogical tree for their house, one which led from Adam and Eve to Mary and Jesus. Some work was executed jointly: Paolo Schiavo designed an altar frontal with

fifteen scenes of Mary's life, which the nuns of Paradiso embroidered.[61]

Whether made at their request, or by their own hands, a certain style emerges in the works used by women, so many of which include Mary. The nuns of St Walburg in Eichstätt painted small pictures for contemplation. In one a crowned Mary and Child receive seven virgins as they are consecrated to the religious life.[62] The virgins kneel with hands clasped as if in prayer. Their long locks, like Mary's, fell down their backs – Mary is crowned, as is their leader, and a scroll announces, based on Exodus 2:9, 'Accept this boy and suckle me', 'I shall give you your reward' ('Accipe puerum istum et nutre michi', 'Ego dabo tibi mercedem tuam'). Another drawing has Mary with Jesus facing Barbara, who carries a branch of palm, the symbol of her martyrdom. The Child Jesus beckons to a chalice held by the saint with a host hovering above, as if to his own body; a nun kneels at the feet of each saint. The art of convents emphasized the powerful figures of female patron saints, of abbesses and founders, and like all convents it favoured Mary greatly.[63]

The rare occasions when we can link contemplation and works of art are particularly revealing. Saint Catherine of Bologna (1413–1463) was the recipient of a vision on Christmas Eve, when most devotional energy was directed towards the birth of Jesus. She was inspired to execute paintings of Mary and Child. Her devotional work *The Seven Spiritual Weapons* (*Le sette armi spirituali*) described the experience as if it had happened to an unnamed religious:

The glorious Virgin appeared immediately before her, holding her beloved Son in her arms, swaddled in just the same manner used for other little ones when they are born . . . The Virgin graciously put him in her arms; and, knowing by divine grace that this was the true Son of the Eternal Father, she drew him tightly between her arms placing her face over that of the sweet infant Jesus . . .[64]

Female religious houses were homes not only to nuns and those who served them, but also to lay residents and benefactors. Dame Eleanor Hull (*c.*1394–1460) was well married and had served the English queen, Joan of Navarre. In widowhood she chose an intensive religious life, lived under the tutelage of a confessor and enjoyed a strong association with a number of nunneries. Toward the end of her life she became resident at the Benedictine house at Cannington (Somerset), where she translated devotional works from French. It is significant that this able

woman also produced what seems like an original meditation on the Name of Mary. While the Name of Jesus was a contemporary devotion which was growing in popularity, Eleanor made her Marian version of it, based in part on sermons by Bernard of Clairvaux. Here is another moment of 'marianization':

All this world is a great sea, full of clouds and of tempests. There is in it no stability, nor security, no more than in the wild sea. For now we are whole, now sick, now glad, now sorry, now angry, or well pleased, upon this sea that is so full of perils. Almighty God has supplied us with a bright star, fair and radiant, sitting very close to him, that is Our Lady Saint Mary, by whose example we should guide all the course of our life . . .

If you are tempted, that you may fall, too much for your own resources, behold the star and call 'Mary'. If you are troubled by avarice, with envy and slander, behold the star and call 'Mary'. If anger or sloth assails the ship of your courage, behold the star and call 'Mary'.[65]

The subjects yearning for Mary were not only women like her, but men too, and these often yearned for her breast, as a child. The visual depiction of Bernard's own favoured experience of Mary's milk came into wider circulation in this period. This came to be known as the 'lactation' of St Bernard, who had prayed to God to come down to be touched. Instead, Christ appeared in his mother's arms. Visual representations of this amazing scene refrained from showing Bernard at Mary's breast. Instead, he kneels as Mary directs the flow of milk at his mouth, and her baby son looks on, sometimes gesturing towards the breast. A Catalan mural in the Cistercian monastery of Santa Maria de Casbas near Huseca places the scene outdoors, within a rocky landscape, and catches Bernard with his prayer book still open.[66] An engraving made in the Netherlands by the Master of Zwolle in the 1480s depicted the encounter within the side-chapel of a church: Mary is seated enthroned with the Christ Child in her lap, with Bernard dressed as abbot and holding his crosier at prayer. Three lines indicate the milk squirted from the breast on to Bernard's eyes, through which he apprehended the vision. In a pastiche of the common Annunciation scene we have just studied, Bernard's words, seeking God's appearance to him, are directed at Mary, while Mary addresses him in fitting reversal: *Ave Barnarde!* Hail Bernard![67] A Flemish painting of *c.*1480 situates Bernard very close to the Christ Child and to Mary's body. His face seems like

350

an older version of the Christ Child's, as if he aimed to enter Mary's arms and replace the recumbent babe.[68]

By the year 1500 Mary had become embedded in private and public worlds of great variety. Mary-language expressed fear and desire, power as well as abjection. Mary was the quintessence of European culture in which the most intimate feelings were drawn out in public – a world of images and of emotions on display. This culture was about to reach all continents and many peoples all over the world. Mary was about to become a global icon.

PART VI

Mary Reformed, Mary Global: 1500 and Beyond

21

Mary of Reform and Reformation

MARY'S GLOBAL REACH

Mary was a familiar companion to sixteenth-century Europeans in an age of great strife and of unparalleled opportunity. In these decades Mary achieved the highest levels of visibility and availability, her images not only sculpted and painted and carved, but also reproduced in prints, engravings and woodcuts that were cheap and soon ubiquitous too.[1] But these many and varied faces of Mary also attracted criticism. The heaping of contradictory images from different quarters provoked a sharp reaction. Some reformers sought to change Christian life within the framework of existing institutions; others proposed reform through a dramatic break with the sacramental religion administered by priests. At the same time European armies, rulers and diplomats attempted to contain and counter the Ottomans, who replaced the Christian Byzantine Empire as Europe's neighbour to the east and subjected Christian populations to their rule.

Over the long sixteenth century Mary was imagined through many shapes and sounds in homes, in parishes, in vernacular preaching throughout the busy calendar year. Mary emerged afresh in Protestant spheres: Martin Luther's (1483–1546) Mary was no longer a queenly advocate, but a woman full of faith and scriptural certitude. In response, a new, triumphant Mary was born from the efforts of Catholics to counter that challenge.

European institutions, the patterns of governance and social relations, were imbued with the language of Christian religion. The parishes and dioceses through which the legacy of grace was mediated to every parishioner experienced greater stimulus than ever before. Every genre – motets and Books of Hours, antiphons and altarpieces, alabaster figures

and stained glass windows, poems and prayers – was used in daily routines as well as on the special occasions. To Mary's new feasts – the Presentation, the Visitation – was added by the late fifteenth century the feast of St Joseph. These feasts combined with the age-old rhythms of the calendar year from Christmas, to Purification, to Annunciation, to Holy Week and on to the summer feast of the Assumption, followed by the autumn with Mary's birth. There was an abundance of opportunities to craft and shape, to consume and access experiences and knowledge about Mary. This abundance also offered innumerable occasions for criticism, objection, satire and derision of the shapes and sounds of Mary's many manifestations.

By the end of the sixteenth century the medieval European Mary – with her family background, her sometimes majestic poise, her promise of protection and nurture, her accessible familiarity – had reached all parts of the world then known to Europeans. At the very same time Europeans were experiencing the most dramatic onslaught on Christian life – the Protestant Reformation – which resulted in the tearing of Europe asunder for centuries to come. The 1520s and 1530s, the years that saw large parts of the Holy Roman Empire, England and Scandinavia turn away from traditional religion, also saw Christianity's arrival and spread in the Americas, Africa and Asia. Missionaries, usually friars, at home and abroad, used the tools of European Christian instruction – pastoral care in parishes, inquisitorial investigation and campaigns of preaching, imagery in propagation of faith – wherever they aimed to introduce Christianity.

These decades witnessed Mary's extension all over the globe.[2] When Vasco da Gama arrived in Calicut on the coast of northern Kerala, after he sailed around the southern tip of Africa, the Cape of Good Hope, he entered a temple and offered his thanks in front of a carved figure of an imposing woman. This was the Hindu goddess Kali. Since the Temple did not resemble a mosque, he must have assumed it was a church. In another temple he may have encountered an even more familiar figure, that of the God Krishna at the breast of his foster mother, Yashoda.[3] The Kali figure must have had many arms, but then Mary was represented in so many different ways by her European adherents, perhaps da Gama, keen to offer his thanks, assumed this was an Asian version of Mary Mother of God.

By the 1520s European friars were introducing Mary to the conquered

people of the Caribbean and Mexico. Missionaries and merchants had already reached northwest Africa, southern India, and China. Mary soon became the experience – new and startling, attractive as well as puzzling – of people whose lives were affected by Europeans in many ways. Their perceptions of her blended and merged: Ethiopian Mary was sometimes given elongated oriental eyes; Mexican artists similarly explored the possibilities suggested by Asian artefacts globally traded by Portuguese and Spanish merchants.[4] In southern India, European traders met the communities of Christians who held St Thomas as their apostle, and whose sacred language was Syriac, the language of some of the earliest Mary-poetry. Along the coasts of Africa and Asia contacts between Christians and non-Christians were centuries old and Mary fitted into fragile patterns of coexistence.[5]

European clergy understood the southern India liturgy, prayers and hymns in Syriac – the genres within which Mary was explored and expressed for these eastern Christians over more than a thousand years – as an obstacle to a Christian life. Tools of discipline which had developed in medieval Europe – inquisition and forced preaching aimed at conversion – were now applied in Asian lands.[6] Mary was exported as *Stella Maris* – Star of the Sea – patron of Europe's seafarers and fishermen. In Macao she blended with the Buddhist cult of Kwan-yin. The cathedral there was dedicated to Mary, in her Portuguese form of *Nossa Senhora da Conceição* – Our Lady of the Conception.[7] In Japan Kwan-yin became Kwannon, a goddess of virtue, who came to look increasingly like Mary in those areas touched by Christianity.[8] When Japanese Christians were forced to pursue their religion in secrecy after the banning of Christianity by the Tokugawa dynasty, they worshipped Mary as Kwannon, and placed a cross in the folds of her statue's garments.[9]

Europe's private and public spaces were awash with images of Mary, and these regularly prompted people to think about her. The home imparted Mary-knowledge at a young age through family routines of nurture and education. The development of print now meant that even modest homes might be adorned with devotional images. This familiarity was the essence of the encounter with Mary, a figure that seemed obvious and necessary, which required little explanation or emphasis. Conversely, in areas affected by the Lutheran challenge, or in those lands where Mary was being encountered for the first time, she had to be

presented in a more emphatic manner: she had to be explained and defended, offered with supportive teaching, represented in dense assemblages, like the image of the Immaculate Mary, unique and unlike any other.

MARY OF HEARTH AND HOME

Much of Mary's life was embedded in scenes of the Holy Family, and these fitted comfortably within the life experiences of most people. Artists derived a great deal of pleasure from placing Mary within domestic settings. The painter Joos van Cleve (1480–1540) worked in Antwerp from around 1511 as a prolific producer of paintings of Mary for prosperous merchants, for city councils and for parish churches. He brought a remarkable freshness to them through attention to the details of vibrant, shimmering things: a breast, a lily, an orange, or cherries, as can be seen in *The Holy Family*.[10] In another painting of the Holy Family the baby Jesus plays with the rosary around his neck while his father reads. Joseph is older and somewhat smaller than Mary in these scenes but within the calm domesticity he seems dignified.[11] Jesus displays all the roundness and mischief of a child: in one scene he is suckled by his mother; in another he is asleep in her arms, still fondling her breast. This sleepy boy elicits from Mary one of her very rare smiles and a glimpse of her orderly teeth.[12]

Mary's daily life was depicted in these years with more detail and imagination than ever before, and in it we may see the genesis of genre painting. Joos van Cleve sets the Annunciation in a well-appointed chamber: on the right is a bed with its suggestions of comfortable domesticity and conventional conjugality; there are lilies in a ceramic vase, a prie-dieu at which Mary reads her devotions, a cupboard on which a family altarpiece is set; there is even a coloured print of Moses with the tablets of the Law nailed to the wall, as well as fine details of flooring, windows and lighting.[13] Gerard David (1460–1523), who worked in Bruges, painted Mary and Child with a bowl of porridge and the Child holding a spoon in his hand; an apple, a knife and bread are placed on a cutting-board, invoking the intimations of sin, death and eucharistic return.[14] This scene was also treated in the panel of the Nativity painted by Albrecht Altdorfer of *c*.1513; the Holy Parents

behold their son within a tumbledown barn, open to the elements, with two attendant child-angels. They are all situated away from the centre and are small in size; here is neither majesty, nor luxury, just simple faith and awesome mystery.[15] Hans Burgkmaier's Holy Family with little John the Baptist of 1525 depicts an elderly yet robust Joseph alongside Mary in the centre with the two playful boys; both parents wear haloes, yet they are simply dressed.[16] The emphasis on the poverty of the Holy Family is even more starkly expressed in a Polish Nativity play of this period. The penury is described by a witness who

> sees no candlewood
> Nor fire, where you could be warmed,
> So you have to stay here so frozen.[17]

The 'new' figure of Joseph was increasingly shown in scenes of family life that rendered him active and important.[18] A wooden statue made in Alsace $c.1500$ has the Child Jesus straddling his parents' knees; the chief object of his playful interest is Joseph's head, especially his ample beard, which the Child grabs vigorously.[19] Even where Mary is presented as the more prominent figure, as in a panel painting by Albrecht Dürer of 1495–7, Joseph is nonetheless shown to be of pious and respectable demeanour.[20] Artists devised subtle ways of distinguishing between Mary and Joseph: Dürer did so by placing a curtain between them, while in the Danish church of Elmelunde (by 1507) they were placed back to back in separate spaces.[21] A Nativity scene assembled in the church of Kezmarok, in the Spis region of Slovakia, has both parents kneeling, but Joseph – a well-dressed man in his prime – kneels a bit lower than Mary.[22] Situating Joseph in this way, at once part of and apart from the Mother and Child group, was a prompt towards creative devotional thinking. Joseph was, after all, not Jesus' biological parent; though he enjoyed the privilege of nurturing the God-boy, he was different from the mother who gave him life.

The scenes of the Crucifixion, in which we have seen his mother become so very prominent, were familiar in their graphic detail. The variety of influences which animated sixteenth-century art – travel, print, pilgrimage – contributed detail and colour to the making of an exotic Mary. An unusual arrangement is shown in a panel painted by Ulrich Apt the Elder ($c.1460–1532$) $c.1510$: in a rugged rocky terrain the four mourners enact extravagant gestures, with the luxuriously dressed Mary

Magdalene to the fore.[23] A Polish manuscript of Dominican origins tells the Passion in minute detail. Mary is recognizable in her blue cloak, and she appears in scenes never before connected with her: Mary at the time of the Last Supper, Mary during Christ's imprisonment, Mary with John while Christ appears before Pilate; Mary and the Holy Women as the bleeding Christ is nailed to the cross, as well as the more familiar Mary at the Tomb.[24] In 1511 a tract entitled *A Little Bundle of Myrrhe (Fasciculus Myrrhe)* by a Franciscan of Castile offered a set of meditations on the Passion in which Mary plays the central role: she repeatedly intervenes in the action by speaking to soldiers, Jews, and even to Pilate.[25] Mary's centrality to the Passion story is not new, we have seen it develop from the thirteenth century, and its dissemination through works such as the *Meditations on the Life of Christ*. Yet in this work Mary's presence is multiplied: even her swooning occurs on several occasions. While the work was printed in several editions, it was also condemned later in the century and placed on the index of prohibited books.

LESS IS MORE — THE CRITIQUE OF MARY'S WORLD

Such multiplication and ubiquity of Mary, her displacement of Christ's centrality in the story of the Passion and the hope for salvation, created unease, even among those most devoted to her. Hints of a critique of this late medieval devotional world are to be found in Netherlandish cities, with their own 'new devotion': *devotio moderna*.[26] Most adherents lived in families and homes, but some joined communities. Their schools were renowned for discipline and intellectual excellence, and their engagement with scripture was sharp and invigorating. The young Luther (at fourteen, in 1497) had been educated in the house of Brethren of the Common Life in Magdeburg where biblical learning and communal observance were central life practices.[27]

A Christmas carol composed around the year 1500, probably in the diocese of Utrecht, is heavily scriptural, based on the gospels of Luke and Matthew. This carol on the Incarnation is set as a wedding song (*epithalamium*):

> Let them sing a nuptial song,
> Asaph, Heman, and Jeduthun,
> Before the Virgin's couch.[28]

The poet next recounts the prophecies in the Jewish Bible which foretold the Virgin Birth. The bulk of the carol, stanzas 10 to 71, unfolds the mystery of the birth. Mary is ever-present in the carol, but in a language of praise that is purely biblical:

> As the bush stands on fire
> But does not endure harm,
> So shall you bear the Lord.
>
> Through you at the end of time
> The star of Jacob in full view
> Will arise, the rescue of peoples.
>
> Have you not read of the wondrous
> Fleece moistened by dew,
> And all the ground remaining dry?[29]

Here are no appellations, no prolific lauds of Mary, but a pristine recounting of scripture's Mary as a bride, in the language of the Song of Songs, not as a lady of miracles and legend.

Another strand of northern devotion, which aimed to inform and discipline routines of meditation and prayer, is expressed in the sermons of the preacher Johannes Geiler von Kaysersberg (1445–1510). This theologian-turned-preacher at St Lawrence's cathedral in Strasbourg developed a weekly devotional scheme for the use of the Dominican nuns at the house of St Margaret and St Agnes. To each day he allocated a subject for meditation, a sin and a virtue for contemplation and a station of Christ's Passion. The scheme recommends only the most authoritative and well-established saints, the sacraments, vices and virtues, gifts of the Holy Spirit, and helps recall the stages of the Passion; it is scripturally based and uses the cues provided for parish instruction. It is striking to see just how little Mary appears in the programme: she is the subject for prayer on Sunday, together with the Trinity. After turning in prayer to the members of the Trinity, the devotee is directed to offer praise to her: 'Have pity for us O holy Mary pray for us O holy bearer of God pray for us O you holy virgin among all virgins.'[30] Here

is another gesture, around the year 1500, towards a rosary-like ordering of devotional energy. Here too is a subtle critique of the 'marianized world' so widely on offer.

Disagreement over the representation of Mary emerged in a number of public controversies. Pope Julius II (1443–1513) was lobbied with a request for a feast of the *spasimo*, Mary's swooning at the foot of the cross. This moment had already captured the imagination of artists, who sought ways to represent it powerfully since the fourteenth century. By the fifteenth century it was a familiar theme, shown so memorably by Rogier van der Weyden in his *Descent from the Cross* and *Crucifixion with Mary and John*.[31] Julius II consulted theologians, as was the custom when liturgical innovations were being considered, and charged one of his advisors, the Dominican theologian Thomas de Vio (the future Cardinal Cajetan), with the task of assessing the merits of the proposed feast.[32] De Vio's report of 1506 emphatically opposed it: firstly, the swooning had no basis in the gospel story; secondly, attributing such a swooning to Mary was improper. De Vio was loath to accept that Mary might have lost her faculties at the all-important moment of her son's Passion:

It was more pleasing to God that Mary should have shared in the passion of her Son not only in her feelings but also in her mind since that is the nobler part . . . Therefore, it was necessary that if the suffering of the Blessed Virgin should be most intense, then her whole lower affectivity should be governed and controlled by her fully conscious mind.[33]

Mary was able to observe the Passion intelligently and with decorum; even as she suffered she saw its place within salvation history with the eyes of faith.

The art and artifice which contributed to so many representations of Mary – the play of perspective, the use of jewels to adorn statues – together with miraculous accounts of images that cried or bled prompted suspicion of spectacular displays in Mary's spheres. A *cause célèbre* occurred in Bern, in 1507, when a Dominican novice Hans Jetzer received visions of Mary while praying in front of a Pietà: Mary cried tears of blood in response to his prayers. Jetzer, in turn, was marked with stigmata – marks of Christ's wounds on his body. Suspicion was raised a few months later, and under torture Jetzer confessed to being part of a conspiracy involving four Dominican friars: while one man

caused the red tears to trickle down Mary's cheek, others drew crowds to view the miracle. A detailed account of the trial published in 1509 was accompanied by a woodcut that illustrated the working of the fraud, and spread the news widely in German-speaking lands.[34]

The men who contributed to the making of Mary – theologians, polemicists, mystical writers, commissioners of great works for monasteries and for cathedrals – had left their own mothers at a young age. They had left the home and the hearth, the local idiom, mother and sisters and carers, and entered the world of Latin pedagogy, a world of discipline and pain, among boys and men.[35] Their yearnings for Mary echo that loss, the nostalgia for the sounds of childhood, the warmth of kindred bodies, for the incomparable acceptance of the maternal embrace. The diptych made in 1523 for the abbot of a Carthusian house in the diocese of Utrecht, Willem Bibaut (c.1484–1535), captures the intimacy that could infuse the relation between a religious and Mary. When closed, the diptych displayed the five wounds around a cross, the Crown of Thorns and a chalice of saving blood. Here is highly orthodox Passion-related imagery for meditation. Yet the open diptych has the abbot on the right, in his white habit, in prayer, gazing at Mary and her Child, on the left part. The Child Christ is held in Mary's hands in a white cloth and the Child touches his mother's breast. A white hood covers the ageing abbot's childlike face; he longs for Mary and her Child, to become that Child dressed in white, too. There is a great deal of intimacy in this family of three.[36]

MARY – CLASSICAL BEAUTY AND HUMANIST SCRUTINY

In Italy the immersion in classical ideas and imagery produced distinctive effects on the representation of Mary. The classical aesthetic was not only a philological and literary experience; it influenced the work of sculptors, painters, engravers, and thus their favourite subject – Mary – too. Italian paintings were somewhat more sombre in their care for aesthetic perfection and distant refinement. Palma the Elder (c.1480–1528) painted a scene of the Holy Family against a rocky terrain: the plump baby is adored by his mother while his elderly father looks on,

walking stick in hand. There is no attribute of sanctity, just faith and love.[37] Galeazzo Campi's (1477–1536) *Virgin and Child* shows the pair seated against a fine velvet curtain; Mary wears red under a blue shawl and is adorned with jewels; the Child wears a necklace and holds an apple and a three-leaved branch. This static group is placed against a sombre, brown-green landscape of trees; there is little movement, just stillness.[38] Fanciful scenes within mythological landscapes became backdrops for Mary's majesty, like the *Adoration of the Shepherds* by the Emilian artist Francesco di Marco Marmitta, of Parma (1462/6–1505), a scene of around 1492–5, with Pan-like shepherds outside a classical ruin overgrown with ivy.

This Italian, above all Tuscan, taste affected northern artists who travelled and worked in Italy. A northern conifer wood is the setting for Lucas Cranach's *Rest on the Flight to Egypt* of 1504: at the centre of the composition is Joseph, who stands above the group of Mary and Child and the eight angels as playmates.[39] Albrecht Dürer's *Madonna with a Siskin* of 1506 blends the traditional Mary and the Christ Child scene with the joyful treatment of the Christ Child's body, of the angels with which he plays, and of the *putti* who crown Mary's head. Mary's body is solid, and it fills the panel so fully as to leave just a little space, above her shoulders, for a glimpse of a wooded landscape strewn with classical remains.[40]

The classical antiquities so abundant in Italy suggested new settings for the image of Mary. The *tondo*, the circular image framing a figure, became a favourite frame for a bust of Mary and Child. The humanist values of stoical conduct affected the representation of Mary, now sometimes a figure of stoic solidity. The regal Mary of the fifteenth century evolved in the sixteenth into a figure surrounded by plump children/angels, and situated within symmetrical compositions.

The desire to represent the human body in the round, even when it was painted on wood or as a fresco, meant that Mary's elongated and elegant shape gave way in the work of many artists to a more rounded, plump Mary. Mary emerges from her garments with an oval face, rounded shoulders and perfect proportions, seated within interiors that resembled patrician urban homes. Less well-known madonnas, like that of Sebastiano Mainardi (c.1460–1513), the *Virgin with the Child Christ and St John and Two Angels*, of c.1500, or of Cima da Conegliano (c.1459–1517), *Madonna and Child*, were produced alongside more

overtly classicizing experiments which inspired the madonnas of Perugino (1446–1524) and Raphael (1483–1520) that are so familiar to us.[41] This Italian style in turn affected French imagery and ultimately touched all European art. The Book of Hours made for Henry VII, king of England, around 1500 in Tours places Mary of the Annunciation within an arched alcove, in an elegant room; she is a classical beauty at home.[42]

The humanist engagement with classical imagery was accompanied by the scrutiny of texts and practices too. Biblical scholars like Desiderius Erasmus (1466–1536) brought to scripture philological scrutiny that aimed to distil an authoritative text. This move 'back to scripture' often raised or intensified questions about the authority of religious practices that lacked a biblical basis. During his time in England in 1512 (and again in 1515) Erasmus went on pilgrimage to the famous shrines of Our Lady of Walsingham in Norfolk and St Thomas of Canterbury. These inspired his colloquy *A Pilgrimage for Religion's Sake,* first printed in 1526. This is a satire of the world of pilgrimage that lampooned the greed of the keepers of relics and the credulity of pilgrims.[43] It is cast as a dialogue between two 'philosophers': Ogygyus was bound by his mother-in-law's vow, made in the hope of the safe delivery of her grandson. The shrine-keeper shared some of the site's marvels with the pilgrim:

He offered me from his bag a piece of wood, cut from a beam on which the Virgin Mother was seen to stand. A marvellous fragrance proved at once that the object was an extremely sacred one! [44]

Erasmus scorned the belief that Mary's house in Nazareth could be known in detail and rebuilt in Walsingham, and that the vessel of breast-milk held there contained anything that was sacred. Like those medieval doubters who claimed that all the consecrated hosts in the world far outstripped the size of Christ's body, so Erasmus derided the belief that a mother who bore only one child might have produced milk sufficient to fill all the holy bottles revered at shrines like Walsingham. Erasmus' vision was one of correction and reform; he hoped that errors might be removed from Christian practice without violence or rancour by enlightened men, guided by Christian scholars.[45]

Ideas such as these were common fare in late medieval Europe. The shrine at Walsingham was often mocked as Our Lady of 'Falsingam'.[46] Yet the comments produced by Erasmus' pen – and which spread widely

in print among Europe's educated and bookish folk – were particularly witty, sharp, and authoritative.[47] The work of historical reassessment that so many humanists undertook in these decades occasionally contributed, even somewhat obliquely, to the further undermining of aspects of Mary's worlds. The scholar and papal diplomat Polydore Vergil ($c.1470$-$c.1555$), native of Urbino, worked for decades in England, and his *On Discovery* (*De inventoribus rerum*) is an erudite consideration of the origins of religious practices.[48] He provided a developmental account of the use of images and statues within Christianity, a religion that began by rejecting idolatry. First, he claimed, Christians desired to have images of Christ, and slowly more and more were made and used.[49] Vergil was led by his investigations to believe that this process had gone too far by his own time. Although his critique of images did not focus on Mary, writings such as his contributed to a 'disenchantment' of the world of image cults and pilgrimage. They offered arguments for use in the current polemics against images, debates which multiplied with the coming of Martin Luther and his followers. Mary's figure was vulnerable to criticism that sought biblical grounding for devotional practices; she was so much the product of tradition, memory and of experience prompted by image and sound.

Humanistic scholarship on the genealogies of Christian practices was undertaken not only by secular scholars but by monks too. One of the most prolific was John Trithemius (1462-1516), abbot of the Benedictine house of Sponheim in the Rhineland-Palatinate. His prodigious literary output is often characterized by a forensic and even polemical orientation, and his bibliophilia aimed at shoring up traditional religion by making it encompass all areas of knowledge. Trithemius's scholarship led him to innovative contributions to the growing cult of St Anne, about whom he wrote a treatise *In Praise of the Holy Mother Anne* (*De laudibus sanctissimae matris Anne tractatus*).[50] He admired the inspiration of feminine prophets such as Hildegard of Bingen and sought renewal and reform within the Christian traditions of devotion to Mary and her family.

Figures like Anne and Joseph were promoted by reformers as sober examples for Christian lives, and as worthy companions to Mary. Turning to Anne for consolation and help was a common act; she was favoured not only by older women and maidens but by men too. One of the most dramatic events in Martin Luther's (1483-1546) life took

place during a journey in July 1505. When he was caught in a thunderstorm near Stotternheim, and was fearful for his life, he vowed to dedicate himself to St Anne if he were saved. His desire to enter the religious life was already maturing, but the dramatic events that led him to plead for Anne's succour may have brought him to the final decision; a fortnight later he approached the Augustinian Hermits of Erfurt, asking to be taken in.[51] Later Luther was to excoriate mercilessly this world of late medieval religion, of which Mary and her family formed so central a part.

LUTHER AND THE PROTESTANT CRITIQUE OF MARY

The marianization, the perceived feminization, of Christian religion, with the proliferation of feasts, miracles and images, pilgrimages and devotions, seemed to overwhelm Mary's slim scriptural persona. Individuals and communities attempted to forge ways out of, or even more deeply into, Marian traditions. Martin Luther's critique of devotions to Mary paralleled his onslaught on the 'judaizing sacrifice' of the medieval eucharist: neither Mary's many attributes nor the sacrament of the altar were based on scripture.[52] The sole guide in faith was to be God's Word. All else was the invention of fallible, sinful humans. Apocrypha polluted scriptural Christianity, and even the fathers of the church were sometimes misguided in using such materials. Since the bulk of the stories of Mary's life were apocryphal, Luther insisted most of the traditions of Mary had to be excised. Like other scholars of his day, he examined every word of scripture as against the Greek of the Old Testament. Even the basic prayer – *Ave Maria* – was not immune from examination. Gabriel's words rendered 'full of grace' (*gratia plena*, or in German *voll gnade*) was found lacking, since it suggested too active a role for Mary in generating or containing that grace; Mary was gracious, but she needed God's grace for her own salvation.[53]

The emergent debate over the future of the Christian Church saw groups of reformers break away from the church led by Rome, and develop within polities, kingdoms like England and Demark, or republics like Geneva. The landscape and the fabric of towns and villages were

full of imagery, and much of it was related to Mary. The fundamental beliefs about Mary – that she bore Jesus in a Virgin Birth, that she interceded for Christians, that she worked miracles – were now the subject of debate and polemic.

Luther and his followers rejected most of the beliefs and practices attached to Mary; they espoused those that possessed scriptural grounding. The Protestant music-master of the recently founded town of Joachimsthal in Bohemia – a town founded when silver was discovered there earlier in the century – commented on the musical religious heritage of its populace, miners and townsmen:

I will speak only of the songs, from which the state of religion may readily be understood. These were for the most part intended for the invocation of the highly-praised Virgin Mary and the dead saints. No one knew how to sing or speak about the Lord Christ. He was regarded and set forth only as a strict judge, from whom no grace could be expected, but only wrath and punishment . . . The elderly will still remember some of the songs: 'O Mary, mild, maid undefiled'; 'Thee, Queen of Heaven, I invoke' . . . and similar songs, which were then very popular in the German language.[54]

Luther objected to just such forms of Mary worship. They had no basis in scripture and distracted Christians from listening to the unsullied Word of God. In his sermon for Sunday after Epiphany 1523 Luther imagined the message to the shepherds, who were led by an angel to Bethlehem: 'Why is it not Mother Mary and Joseph that are used as signs but rather the cloth or the crib?'[55] Luther was letting go of the feasts of Mary's Conception, Birth and Assumption. About the Conception, Luther had opined wryly as early as 1516/17 that those who wished to celebrate and offer indulgences for the feast will be remembered by posterity:

This I say of those who wish the Feast of the Conception of the Virgin Mary to be the first and foremost, and who fill new feasts with privileges, indulgences and ample sermons. Posterity will not judge [see] our lives to have been lived in vain, for we made new feasts and made old ones grow older; that alone is worthy of eternal memory . . .[56]

Luther's sarcasm is cutting: should Christian achievement indeed be judged by the sheer profusion of feasts? The answer he elicits here is a resounding 'no'.

Some of the religious heritage associated with Mary was preserved in the feasts of the Annunciation, the Visitation and the Purification. Thanks to their biblical foundation they were appreciated by Lutherans and enjoyed the attention of preachers, artists and composers of church music. These feasts demonstrated Mary's virtues: at the Annunciation her humility was manifest, her openness to God's word; at the Visitation she praised God fulsomely; her modesty shone forth at the Purification.[57] In his sermon on the Visitation of 1516 Luther made her merits clear:

The Blessed Virgin saw God in everything ... and this happens only to those who are in God's vision, all other things all but disappear ... A soul cannot be both intent on magnifying the creature and the creator.[58]

Mary's privilege was not one of birth without sin, for she was born in sin, like all humans, and was granted the gift of the Holy Spirit that descended upon her. Luther applied a stringent scriptural test: scripture did not tell of an immaculate conception, but it did offer much that was beautiful and sustaining. So he promoted the Marian texts in scripture. He translated the Magnificat (Luke 1:45–77) into German and offered a commentary too. While he rejected many of the claims about Mary's perfection – for these would suggest Mary did not need God's saving grace – he exalted her example 'of the grace of God':

What are they doing but contrasting us with her instead of her with God? Thus they make us timid and afraid and hide the Virgin's comfortable picture ... For they deprive us of her example, from which we might take comfort; they make an exception of her and set her above all examples. But she should be, and herself gladly would be, the foremost example of the grace of God, to incite all the world to trust in this grace and to love and praise it.

Mary's mundane activities only reinforced her value as an example:

She seeks not any glory, but goes about her meals and her usual household duties, milking the cows, cooking the meals, washing pots and kettles, sweeping out the rooms, and performing the work of a maidservant or housemother in lowly and despised tasks.[59]

Martin Luther reformed the mass and removed altogether those parts that were claimed to enact transubstantiation, the change of bread and wine into Christ's body and blood. Reformers associated transubstantiation with another error, the worship of images. Neither belief had a

basis in scripture – indeed the use of images in worship seemed to break the second commandment. The Swiss reformer Ulrich Zwingli (1484–1531) coupled Mary and the Eucharist when he likened the notion that Christ was present in the bread and wine at the altar to the prevalent belief that Mary was present in her statues.[60] Since both were wrong, he concluded, the mass required reform and statues of the Virgin should be removed from churches.

While the liturgy was reformed it was not utterly remade, and certain continuities with Mary's past were still maintained by Protestants. The general shape of the mass survived. The short sung prayers, the sequences, which had developed since the twelfth century, remained in place, since Luther favoured them as occasions for congregational singing in German. Most of Luther's thirty-six hymns were composed by him over a few months in 1523–4 while he was detained at Wartburg Castle under the protection of Duke Frederick the Wise. He envisaged the reformed mass as being full of song and helped make it so:

I also wish that we had as many songs as possible in the vernacular which the people could sing during mass . . . For who doubts that everybody sang these songs originally, which the choir now sings or responds to while the bishop is consecrating?[61]

Music was a gift of God and it could drive away the devil. Like all God's gifts it could be used well, or otherwise. Even in the Catholic past good musical practice was discerned and praised. Luther's friend Johannes Aurifaber rephrased one of Luther's comments on music as a manifestation of joy in the gospel, with reference to the music of Josquin de Prez (*c.*1450–1521):

what is Gospel, that comes out successfully, delightfully and willingly. In this way, God has preached the Gospel also through music, as one sees in Josquin's music, that all his composition gladly, willingly, mildly, and lovingly flows and goes forth, is not forced and compelled and tightly and directly bound to the rules.[62]

Frau Musica – Lady Music – had a place in the reformed order.

And so it was. The 1529 Lutheran hymnal included ten hymns composed by Luther and sung to traditional melodies. There was 'With Peace and Joy' (*Mit Fried und Freud ich fahr dahin*) for the feast of the Purification, based on the biblical text of the priest Simeon's song (Luke

2:29–32).[63] In his preface to a songbook with Latin and German songs of 1542, Luther explained the value of retaining old melodies, despite his distaste for traditional devotional hymns: 'The melodies and notes are precious. It would be a pity to let them perish. But the texts and words are non-Christian and absurd. They deserve to perish.'[64]

In the course of the sixteenth century Lutheran song developed apace with strong local traditions. The increasing popularity of complex polyphony amongst Lutheran congregations evolved in the following century into new genres such as the cantata.[65] Songs for Mary's feasts were few, but they regularly formed part of such collections. The powerful medieval link between Mary and song was not totally severed by Protestants. It was transformed, as the new tone was biblical rather than devotional or mystical. This shift is true in other areas of religious life too. Death had traditionally been accompanied by advice from preachers and from guidebooks, and Mary loomed large in such lore. Those languishing on their sickbed were encouraged to pray to her and draw hope from her intercession. Lutheran guidebooks to the dying did not dispense with Mary altogether but significantly diminished her place. The *Evangelical Teaching and Exhortation of the Dying Man*, published in Leipzig in 1523, contains twelve sections aimed at preparation for the reception of the final sacrament and for dying well. The section 'Prayer to the mother Mary' offers a prayer to her, and others to angels, to the wounds of Christ, and to the holy church. Through sacrament and prayer the Christian was made part of the universal church in faith based on scripture. Mary's part was small indeed, yet for some Lutherans even this was too much. When Johannes Oecolampadius (1482–1531), pastor of St Martin in Basel, revised the city's worship, he acknowledged the use of the Ave Maria, which was based on scripture, but removed all other mention of Mary from the manual used by pastors when visiting the sick and dying.[66]

While Lutherans diminished, and Calvinists later banished, Mary altogether from their world of affect and thought, this was neither a simple process, nor one whose contours were at all clear at the time.[67] Initially images were not a central issue in Protestant programmes, but polemic became ubiquitous as the Word replaced external and communal aspects of religious life. Reform involved the 'relocation' of holiness, the redistribution of access to the holy so that it was equally and widely available, rather than monopolized by certain places, artefacts or

people.[68] In the 1520s, when several German cities appointed reforming preachers and considered ways of transforming themselves into reformed communities, the issue of images was vigorously present. So much of civic life was bound up with the worship of patron saints, often Mary herself. Luther stated clearly in a report to his confidant Nikolaus Hausmann in 1522, 'I condemn images' (damno imagines), but this did not mean that all images had to be dismantled, demoted or removed. There were types of images, pervasive in most parish churches, cathedrals and monastic foundations, that misled and distracted believers away from the Gospel. But images could also have a benign and instructive effect.

Luther was not unlike Erasmus, who hoped that through education and de-mystification communities of believers would turn away from the obsession with images and prefer sacred text and ethical reflection.[69] People absorbed the Gospel when read or heard by making mental images:

Of this I am certain, that God desires to have his works heard and read, especially the passion of our Lord. But it is impossible for me to hear and bear it in mind without forming mental images of it in my heart. For whether I like it or not, when I hear of Christ, an image of a man hanging on a cross takes form in my heart.[70]

Arguing against those who broke images (Bildstürmer) Luther argued that they used images too when they

read out of my German Bible. I know that they have it and read out of it, as one can easily determine from the words they use. Now there are a great many pictures in those books . . . So now we would kindly beg them to permit us to do what they themselves do. Pictures contained in these books we would paint on the walls for the remembrance and better understanding, since they do not more harm on walls than in books.[71]

Luther's attitude was practical, and it allowed a Protestant art to flourish. The publisher and artist Sigismund Feyerabend (1528–90), who produced Luther's works, celebrated the arrival of printed texts, after decades in which print was used to produce the much-desired mass-produced pious images:

Now, however, we cannot give sufficient thanks to the Lord God that the honorable art of printing has come to light . . . After that, still other marvellous

and praiseworthy arts were invented such as the copying and cutting of pictures and other illustrations.[72]

Lutherans spoke of images in many different voices, and one of the most conservative was Luther's own. It pained him to see the violence of iconoclasm – the breaking of images – of which he said in 1525 that 'no one who sees the iconoclasts raging thus against wood and stone should doubt that there is a spirit hidden in them that is death-dealing, not life-giving'.[73] Breaking images could easily lead to the killing of Christians. He wished for most cult images to be removed from churches, but for 'a crucifix or saints' image' to be retained for the purpose of witness and memorial.[74]

The generation of artists, priests and believers that experienced the emergence of Lutheran Christianity was acting out a vast social experiment for which there were few models beyond stark apocalyptic visions of reward and retribution. In large parts of Europe the materials of Marian experience were being scrutinized by individuals and communities. While some images were destroyed, others were retained as they received new interpretations. An altarpiece painted by Lucas Cranach the Elder in 1516, which adorned the *Spitalkirche* in Joachimthal, depicted the scene *of Mary and the Child with St Catherine* in which the Christ Child offered the saint the ring of mystical union. In Lutheran Joachimthal this image was kept intact; a Lutheran hymn sung to a folk melody explained that the ring now represented baptism.[75] Cranach revisited his own work with new scrutiny, and so a woodcut of the Annunciation made in 1511, with an indulgence-bearing prayer, was produced in 1524, without that now offensive prayer.[76]

Other reformers of this first generation were more outspoken, and so images – now considered 'idols' – were removed from Wittenberg and Zurich in 1525. Yet what to do with the old and cherished images? Churches were full of images of Mary, images that were precious, venerated and much loved.[77] In 1525 the reform-minded townsmen of Strasbourg followed Lutheran principles requesting that the mass be abolished, but also went further in demanding to 'have the Marian idol in the chapel, with its cage and birds, put away efficiently' and that the silver statue behind the altar be put in the alms box. Indeed, on 1 April 1525 a crucifix replaced the image of Mary, a wooden statue made in Prague and noted for its quality.[78] Later in the decade, in 1529, Heinrich

373

Bullinger explained in his *Concerning the Origins and Errors in the Veneration of Saints and Images* that images should not be worshipped since they were mere representations of the holy, and not holy in themselves. John Calvin's (1509–64) understanding of the mass – no longer as re-enactment of Christ's sacrifice at the altar, but a memorial of that sacrifice – implied a view of images too: not sacred, but a memorial of sanctity. This position undercut image cults, and the rich overlap between the materiality of images and their meaning to believers.

The personal vitriol exchanged by reformers sometimes brought to the fore an invective which linked Mary and the Jews. The Swiss reformer Ulrich Zwingli attacked Balthasar Hubmaier, an opponent of child baptism, by reminding him of events in Regensburg in the not-so-distant past. In 1519 Hubmaier had taken part in the anti-Jewish agitation around an alleged host desecration, which led to the expulsion of the Jews ('idle, lecherous and greedy') and the destruction of their quarter. During the clearing work a mason was badly injured but was miraculously saved thanks to his wife's prayers to Mary. News of the miracle attracted pilgrims, and soon a chapel was built, a miracle book was composed, and a cardinal issued an indulgence for the benefit of all comers. A statue of Mary and Child was made, in the guise most expressive of purity and innocence – the *schöne Maria* – an emphatic statement of the triumph of Mary over the Jews who rejected her.[79] This shrine was included in the list of sites singled out for destruction by Luther in 1520, so harmful did he judge their influence to be.[80] Zwingli cites the cult poem associated with the pilgrimage, *The Song of the Schöne Maria of Regensburg*, a product of those trends in late medieval religion most reviled by reformers: pilgrimage, miracles, images and rabble-rousing by preachers.[81] Lingering attachment to Mary was repeatedly used as a sign of attachment to the enchanted and misleading universe that reformers were working to transform.

Through such reflection by the makers of images, and the polemical guidance of preachers, Protestant art was born. It was an art which had Christ at its centre, and which also created space for biblical personages, cut down to size – human and virtuous – Mary, Joseph, John. The Colditz Altarpiece, attributed to Lucas Cranach the Younger, of 1584 was made for Duke August of Saxony for use in that castle's chapel, and it offers a good example of Protestant practice: when closed, this heart-shaped triptych depicted Adam and Eve with the Apple (left) and

the Annunciation (right), the events which made redemption necessary and possible. When open, the central scene of the Crucifixion emerged flanked by the Nativity (left) and the Resurrection (right).[82] Even in Lutheran lands the reformation of images was a long process, and it depended on the vigilance of the new religious leaders. During his visitation of 1589 Jacob Madsen, bishop of the Danish diocese of Funen, recorded that the parish of Kværndrop possessed a gilt altarpiece depicting the Coronation of the Virgin; he opined that 'if there had been a cross in its place, then it would have been a lovely altarpiece'.[83] In the parish of Tanderup an altarpiece of 'A Young God crowning the Virgin'; by 1601 the parish owned a new altarpiece 'with the words of the Catechism'.[84] Bishop Madsen patiently but insistently oversaw the change, the remaking of altarpieces and the replacement of Coronations with crucifixes.

Mary was being redrawn in a world of reform in which the sole source of salvation was Christ, and the sole vehicle towards him was faith in his Word. In Protestant communities much traditional Mary worship was no longer permitted; her images were removed, replaced or reassigned. Artists rose to the challenge of imagining Mary anew. Since it was important to display the scriptural basis of religious scenes, text now accompanied images more often than before. From 1520 Danish churchwardens were obliged to seek consultation before decorating the churches in their care. The walls of the parish church of Sulsted, in Jylland, were painted in 1548, and the Nativity scene has a haloed Mary and Joseph with their newborn son in a modest manger, accompanied by the explanatory inscription: 'Here is the birth of the Lord in Bethlehem'.[85] The central theme of the Passion was reoriented from the emphasis on Mary to a more scriptural and Christ-centred experience. Over time old altarpieces were replaced with new ones, painted catechisms. Philipp Melanchthon (1497–1560) composed the *Passional Christi und Antichristi* and it was accompanied by thirteen pairs of woodcuts from the workshop of the leading Protestant artist Lucas Cranach the Elder (1472–1553). Mary and Joseph appear as a modest couple at the Nativity, a scene accompanied by a citation from Matthew 8:20 in the words of Luther's German Bible: 'Foxes have holes, and birds of the air have nests; but the Son of man hath not where to lay his head.'[86] In Lutheran areas an integrated aesthetic of preaching, singing and architectural spaces created a new sensibility within which Mary had only a modest place.

A different type of Mary was emerging among Protestants. The ex-Capuchin monk and theologian turned Protestant, Bernardino Ochino (1487–1564), presented his faith as centred on Christ alone. Yet Mary was important too, not as a heavenly figure but as an example of humility and good belief:

Notice the great humility of Mary who did not offer herself to accept the dignity and honour of being the mother of God, but said 'I am the maid and the servant'. In plain form, we have to suppose that she would have said: 'My Lord, I am happy to be your servant, and your son's too, whom I shall nourish, and am happy to clasp and hold Him in my arms, and to suffer every privation and pain in order to nourish and nurse Him, for the benefit of the elect.[87]

In Ochino's words Mary also declared her willingness to see her son crucified, to hold his deposed body, to accompany it to its tomb. All Christians could strive to be a Mary, situated on earth, not in heaven.

PROTESTANT ENGLAND'S MARY

In England the disengagement from Mary was part of a policy of state that saw the dissolution of monasteries – the last monastery was dissolved in 1541 – and the introduction of new orders of service and books of prayer. In 1535, royal officials were sent by Henry VIII to the counties of England to report on 'any relics or feigned miracles for increase of lucre [profit]'.[88] Investigation into miracles and relics, so many of them related to Mary, was part of the campaign that presented monasteries as centres of harmful and deceitful superstition. State officials surveyed the country, and their reports reveal just how widely spread Marian materials were. The Abbey of Bury St Edmunds, where the corpus of Mary miracles was compiled under Anselm the Younger in the 1140s, had 'vain and fictitious relics'; at the Walsingham shrine relics of Mary's milk were 'vane and fictitious' too, and the milk revered at St Paul's cathedral was nothing but a piece of chalk.[89] Christ Church cathedral in Dublin also possessed precious relics – Mary's girdle, milk and a piece of her tomb – and these attracted the attention of Reformers as early as the 1530s.[90] Such worthless remains could be demystified, destroyed.

The presence of Mary's relics was a ubiquitous local affair. Since her

body had been assumed into heaven, there were no bodily parts to venerate. Yet the milk of Mary's breast – sometimes lavished upon those most devoted to her, like Fulbert of Chartres and Bernard of Clairvaux – remained for a while within reach of most English folk. The 'false milk' of Mary became emblematic of the type of relics that the reforming king was about to sweep away. The royal commissioners, who listed their findings in the course of the Visitation of the Monasteries, ordered by Henry VIII in 1536, recorded most frequently two types of relics: Mary's girdle – which she dropped to earth as proof of her ascent into heaven – and Mary's milk. Of 199 entries in the list from the diocese of Coventry and Lichfield, eight mention Mary-girdles for the help of women at childbirth, four note the presence of Mary's milk, and one records an image of Mary. Mary relics were part of the diverse treasury of grace: in Shelford 'They venerate the girdle and milk of St Mary, and part of a candle which it is believed she carried at the time of her purification; they have also the oil of the Holy Cross and the oil of St Katharine', while at Dale 'They reverence part of the girdle and the milk of St Mary, and the wheel of St Katharine in silver'; the girdle of Mary at Haltemprise was 'thought to be helpful in childbirth', and the belief at Calder, that 'a girdle of St Mary [was] good for lying-in women', was deemed to be superstitious. Similar distaste is manifested in the entry for Kirkeham where 'also they have (as it pretended) the belt of the Blessed Mary, good for lying in women'.[91] Few people in the diocese lived far from a pain-relieving girdle or a life-giving drop of Mary's milk. In turn, Protestants clung to the drops of Mary's breast-milk as an epitome of the worst medieval beliefs. A poem by the Yorkshire Protestant, Wilfrid Holme, of the 1530s derided 'papist' belief in

> Girdles invented, and their fair hairs dyed,
> With the chalk old for the milk of Our Lady.[92]

The story of Mary's presence and her subsequent removal from sacred spaces is a story of local sentiment and local change.[93] Protestant religion was established by the state, yet as late as the 1540s the people of York habitually opened their testaments by commending themselves to God, his mother and the saints.[94] The advent of a committed Protestant king, Edward VI, in 1547 marked a new dispensation. The rood screens of parish churches, with their carved figures of Mary and John at the foot of the cross, were dismantled. When the York City Council mounted its

famous Corpus Christi cycle of plays during the reign of Edward VI, it omitted the 'Deying of our Lady / assumpcion of our Lady / and Coronacion of our Lady'.[95] These were much loved plays of the medieval repertoire based on apocryphal gospels and early Christian legend. Even the 'scriptural' plays of the Annunciation and the Visitation were subject to substantial revision.[96] Despite the brief attempt after Edward VI's premature death to re-establish Catholicism under Mary I (1553–58), a broad Protestantism reversed this permanently under Elizabeth I (1558–1603). Protestants in England and elsewhere were not isolated from the signs of Mary worship, from statues deemed idols, from relics deemed false, and from the sound of liturgies and processions abolished within the Protestants' sphere.[97]

Despite the attempts to erase the Virgin Mary from the memory of the English the symbolic deposits were too great to be ignored. The Protestant queen of England, Elizabeth I, who succeed her Catholic half-sister Mary in 1559, was never loath to demonstrate her solid Protestant faith. On occasion events seem to have been staged so as to allow Elizabeth to emerge as such. In 1578, while she toured Norfolk and lodged with a Catholic gentleman near Thetford, it is told that a search for a piece of royal silver led to the discovery of an image of 'Our Lady', 'an idol' which Elizabeth promptly had burned.[98] By the 1590s, as she remained unmarried, Elizabeth's use of the imagery of pure virginity was more pointed. Elizabethan writers celebrated her as a closed garden, like the Virgin Mary a *hortus conclusus*, at once a chaste body and a kingdom safe and on its own.[99] Her person was bedecked in silk and pearls – as majestic Mary so often was – and the poetry that praised her did so with all the combination of biblical imagery and classical allusion that we have seen the figure of Mary attract.[100] So when Elizabeth died it did not seem too fanciful to write these lines:

> She was, She is (what can here more be said?)
> In earth the first, in heaven second Maid.[101]

22

From Europe to the Rest of the World

IBERIAN MARY, TRIUMPHANT MARY

While all this change in attitudes and practices around Mary was taking place in Northern Europe, in the southern kingdoms of Iberia Mary was triumphant. The Iberian religious heritage was infused with crusade, conquest and a symbolic preponderance of Mary as patron of the state's enterprises in a world which saw Christians, Muslims and Jews living side by side.

Since the late fifteenth century Mary had offered themes for Iberian national unification. Ferdinand of Aragon (1452–1516) and Isabella of Castile (1451–1504) were joined by marriage in 1469, and subsequently ruled their kingdoms jointly. Mary was the personal mentor to the young Isabella; she was depicted on banners as the last Muslim stronghold, Granada, fell in 1492. Mary is ever-present in the altarpiece made for Queen Isabella in the 1490s, a collection of twenty panels. Tender scenes of Jesus' life link subtly the life of mother and son. An unusual scene shows Mary beside her son at the Marriage at Cana; there is one in which Jesus appears to his mother alone after his death; Mary assists at the Transfiguration and is present at Pentecost, a leader among apostles.[1] Mary is associated here with her adult son as he embarks on his ministry. This affinity differs greatly from the popular image of Mary suckling her son, for Mary is portrayed as a partner of Christ, accepting his inevitable end. The scene of Mary's greatest privilege, so closely linked to her special purity – her Assumption – was there too; she was raised by angels, who crowned her as she rose into the clouds bathed in sunlight. Mary of Isabella's altarpiece is an agent alongside her son, a figure worthy of the powerful queen's devotional attention.

For their efforts in Iberia Isabella and Ferdinand gained the titles of

'Catholic Monarchs'. They introduced the Spanish Inquisition as an arm of the state with the task of addressing the challenge of its multi-ethnic religious heritage. There were hundreds of thousands of 'new' Christians, Jewish and Muslim converts and their families, the legacy of the decades of religious violence experienced in Iberia since the 1390s. The Spanish Inquisition was meant to 'purify' Iberian society by identifying those 'new' Christians who secretly adhered to Jewish or Muslim practices and beliefs. The Christian polity was geared towards purification, and its ruler legislated laws to promote purity of blood (*limpieza de sangre*).

Queen Isabella was attached to another vision of purity, too, to the Immaculate Conception, which she adopted as a national theme of unity in faith.[2] Marian themes facilitated the unending work of conversion, and so converts to Christianity sometimes adopted them as badges of conformity and belonging. The Confraternity of San Pedro Mártir in Toledo was the association of the city's silk weavers, most of whom were converts from Judaism. The confraternity's chant-books are richly illustrated and adorned with a profusion of Marian images. Among them was the story of the miracle of the Knight of Cologne, a Rosary miracle, based on an older tale from the *Cantigas de Santa Maria*. Here is a tale of Marian devotion, of personal dedication to Mary, through the offering up of simple prayer, the equivalent of a garland of roses, a rosary.[3] Subtle variation may have been introduced into the devotional imagery of the Passion in this world full of recent converts: the narratives – visual and literary – offered in the 1490s were far less centred on Mary's physical pain and presented her as a figure of deep faith and prophetic knowledge, a power in the unfolding story of salvation.[4]

Marian themes were, in turn, used to describe Isabella herself. After she delivered her second child, her first male offspring, she was likened to the Virgin Mary, who bore a single son and remained chaste for the rest of her life.[5] Like Mary, Isabella nurtured her people, and Christians in general, through her pursuit of purity. This was the purity of Christian zeal combined with ethnic purity which resulted in fierce measures that scrutinized the lives of 'new' Christians.

Where the queen led, others followed. Ecclesiastical and aristocratic patrons celebrated the orthodoxy of national religion. The sense of Christian purpose and national mobilization was tantamount to a personal devotional exercise offered by the Catholic Monarchs to their

courtiers. The Aragonese aristocrat Martín Martínez de Ampiés was a soldier and writer, warrior and devout Christian. Mary was at the heart of his devotion, an endorsement of the different spheres of his life. Ampiés translated the most innovative pieces of devotional writing, like contemporary descriptions of the Holy Land, and composed a Marian work entitled *The Triumph of Mary* (*Triumpho de Maria*) as well as an apocalyptic tract on the Antichrist. The *Triumph of the Mother of God* was the theme of a series of tapestries made in Brussels c.1500, given to Isabella by her daughter, Juana. The series includes the unusual scene of God's sending of the Angel to Mary, followed by the Annunciation, Nativity and Coronation. The highlights of Mary's life as part of a providential plan were made into a tapestry whose predominant colour was gold.[6]

Polyphony seemed a particularly suitable expression of the ambition of Iberian religion. In 1499 Pedro of Toledo, bishop of Malaga, offered an endowment to his cathedral for the maintenance of polyphonic adornment of the Saturday Marian mass.[7] Another gift was made by Juan Rodriguez de Fonseca, bishop of Palencia, in 1514 to support the Saturday service. Fonseca was not only a bishop but an experienced courtier and ambassador; he had supervised the provisioning of Columbus' first voyages to the Atlantic and spent months on missions to the Low Countries. While in Brussels, Fonseca joined a confraternity devoted to Mary's Seven Sorrows – a devotion characteristic of the region – and he commissioned in 1505 from a local artist an altarpiece on this theme.[8]

Fonseca's Marian vocabulary had been extended by his northern sojourn. His provision for enhanced polyphony in Palencia supported liturgical music within a space unlike any other in Spain at the time, one created by him. In 1514 he endowed choral music to be sung in the crypt of St Antolin within the cathedral in front of the imported altarpiece of the Seven Sorrows. Flemish and Iberian styles, private devotion and public liturgy all met in Fonseca's creation. The tradition of Mary masses of Saturday, with the much-loved singing of the *Salve Regina*, offered powerful patrons all over Europe occasion for display and for experimentation with the many possibilities of Mary.

Marian music was the cornerstone of successful musical careers. Given the richness of endowment in Spain, it is not surprising to find Iberian composers rising to prominence in early sixteenth-century Europe, where Flemish and English composers had dominated before. Francisco

de Peñalosa (*c*.1470–1528) was the most famous Spanish composer of his day, and was promoted to positions in the Spanish and the papal courts. His Mary compositions were made for use in the liturgy, but also as offerings for insertion at will, like his setting of the traditional 'Hail, Queen of Heaven' (*Ave Regina Coelorum*). Rich Marian themes in these Iberian compositions were offered for the pleasure and insight of informed priests, diplomats and musicians at court. Peñalosa's mass *Ave Maria Peregrina* ('Hail, Mary, Pilgrim') is an excellent example. The *agnus dei* – often the occasion for creative display – has the familiar *Salve Regina* alongside the well-known 'De tous biens plaine', a secular song which was often used to extol Mary 'full of all good things'. But this song is sung *backwards*, a reversal which brings to mind the great reversal operated by Mary: she unmade Eve's guilt and brought the *Agnus dei* into the world. We have already encountered the thirteenth-century Parisian motets that tantalized singers and listeners alike with combinations of Latin and French, the sacred and the seemingly profane. Peñalosa's *Ave Maria Peregrina* is such a motet, but it does more. The reversal of Mary's music does not result in confusion but rather in affirmation of Mary's role in salvation. Mary, like all Christians, was a pilgrim, a traveller in this world.[9] The sacred music of courts combined the display of secular power by divine grace with praise of Immaculate Mary.

Mary spread with the many types of Iberian – Spanish and Portuguese – extensions and influences in the Mediterranean and the Atlantic. There was a heady mixture of cultures and ethnicities in the cities of North Africa which came under Iberian domination – Ceuta in 1415, Tangier in 1471, Oran in 1509. In these cities there were indigenous Muslim, Christian and Jewish populations living in proximity. To these were added the Moriscos, Muslim converts, who were ultimately expelled from Spain in 1614.[10] Mary was a fitting figure for shared Muslim-Christian practices. A sixteenth-century Arabic manuscript contains a Muslim prayer to Mary with a remarkable Christian tone:

> In the name of God the Compassionate and the Merciful
> O God, our Lord, we believe in the truth of your Word
> by which you sent our lord Jesus your spirit
> and in the truth of the sublime Gospel . . .
> revealed on the holy mountain,

382

written by the hand of our Lady Mary (*Maryama*),

one of the Scriptures written about the Magnificence

and that you have caused to descend on her and which you ordered her to
send on to earth.

We invoke you for your powerful name . . .

and for your majesty and beauty and power

and for your blessing and grandeur and compassion,

which you have caused your servants to enjoy.

Strengthen through Her and Him your favour for those of your religion
who follow the right path

and consolidate through Her and Him the community of pious believers.

And grant salvation to the great community and allow your your servants
the believers to enter under your shield, your compassion,

and disperse through Her and Him the infidelity of the ignorant, of
unbelievers and of renegades,

because, You, you are the Merciful who is omnipotent.[11]

This interesting prayer opens with a statement of faith, goes on to beg
for favour and protection and ends with a call for the support of true
believers and protection against enemies of the faith. In it Jesus is not so
much an incarnation of the divine but as a Holy Spirit. Mary and Jesus
are equal in the invocations of the body of the text, though Mary occurs
first; Mary is also the instrument through which scripture was written
and transmitted to earth. Encounters in the Muslim Maghreb made
Mary a particularly popular figure in these westernmost regions of Islam.
Verse 37 of *sura* 3, where Mary explains the miracle of her pregnancy
to the priest in the Temple, was often inscribed in the interior of the
mihrab, the mosque sanctuary.[12]

The Iberian enterprise of crusade, conversion and conquest created
real challenges to the process of integration. 'New' Christians were
suspected of religious insincerity, and their presence added another
dimension to neighbourhood conflicts. Some of the social exchanges
find their way into narratives extracted by the Inquisition. While these
tell us nothing credible about Jewish converts and their beliefs, they tell
us much of ideas harboured by some Christians. In August 1520 the
pig-breeder Gonçalo Martin, of Gran Canaria, sent a shepherd to report
to the Holy Office that he had seen Alonso Nunez weeping and chanting
in his house; the man was distressed since the Inquisition in Seville was

holding his mother prisoner. When Martin commented that if she is a Jew they would burn her, the distraught son answered 'with violent and ugly blasphemies', saying: 'Leave me, god's mercy, my mother is a better woman than holy Mary.'[13]

Testimonies from servants, employees and slaves exposed intimate domestic scenes to the court's gaze. Some magical formulae for the production of love amulets included among the invocations the holy names of Abraham, Isaac and Jacob, and 'Abe Marya'.[14] Touch the desired woman with such an amulet on a Wednesday, and she is yours! In 1520 the black slave Beatriz bore witness that her owner, Francisco del Castillo, had warned her against revealing the happenings she saw in his house. Not only did members of the household refrain from habitual signs of piety such as kneeling when the *angelus* bell was rung, they also chided her when she knelt: 'Listen, don't kneel when I ask you to bring me a jug of water, I am not your God or your Holy Mary who can save you.'[15] Moreover, when Fernando found Beatriz praying, he took away her rosary, beat her and beat her even worse when he heard her cry 'Ave Maria', saying to her, 'Take this for the love of Holy Mary, and for the love of God.'

Converted Muslims were also reported in connection with utterances that belittled Mary. A *morisco* labourer joined his employer after dinner one evening to chat about religious matters with his friend. The *morisco* was asked by his friend whether he believed in God and Saint Mary and in that article of faith which asserts that Mary was virgin during, before and after giving birth. The *morisco* answered, 'we believe indeed in God, but do not believe that the Virgin Mary gave birth as a virgin'. Many other converted Muslims held the same view: they denied Mary's virginity.[16] This is a particularly interesting attitude, since the Koran asserts, as we have seen, that Mary was a virgin and remained so. This may be a legacy of generations, whereby Muslims – like Jews – opposed and engaged polemically with the Christian claims of Virgin Birth.[17]

Yet the shared terrain suggested that Mary might be a meeting point for Christians and Muslims, in a way that was not possible between Muslims and Jews. During construction work between 1558 and 1595 on Granada cathedral, which was being built on the site of the city's old mosque, 'ancient' remains were discovered by workmen: a cloth belonging to Mary, some bones attributed to martyrs and a series of

inscribed lead tablets. Upon these tablets were written a variety of Arabic prophecies and arcane truths. The message was that Arabs has been the region's earliest settlers, that Mary had spoken Arabic and was indeed immaculately pure.[18] One of the tablets even attributed to Mary the following words:

I tell you that the Arabs are one of the finest nations and their language one of the good languages. God chose them to exalt his holy law and his sacred gospel and his holy church at the end of Time and I am sent to work with it what was worked by the Tablet of Moses.[19]

Through Mary – not Christ or the Trinity – a vision of belonging for *moriscos* was imagined.[20] The Iberian Christian programme was as violent and unwieldy as it was potentially capacious and embracing of all comers. Mary was the symbol of such authoritarian inclusion; and she was soon on offer within the Spanish Empire to people who had never heard her name.

MARY IN THE AMERICAS, MARY IN ASIA

Mary was the patron of the Christianization of Iberia, which was completed with the fall of Muslim Granada in 1492. The Iberian enterprise also aimed at traversing the Atlantic, and that is how the momentous encounter between the Iberian politics of religious aggression and the adventures motivated by the desire for trade and prosperity brought Christianity to the Caribbean Islands and America. Mary travelled from Iberia with conquerors, missionaries and merchants to all parts of the world.

Iberia was poised against Muslims and Jews; it was fascinated with crusade, and thus with the Holy Land, Mary's Land. It was drawn into North Africa, the Canaries and ultimately into the Atlantic and beyond.[21] The territories were called New Spain by their rulers, and in them military control, settlement, economic exploitation and missionary work went hand in hand. The introduction of Mary to these lands was the state-sponsored enterprise of the kingdom of Spain (and in other regions, of Portugal). In New Spain cities and dioceses, schools and convents,

parishes and printing houses were soon established.[22] For the indigenous peoples of these parts Mary's arrival coincided with the traumatic transformation of a whole way of life.

The figure of Mary was central to the sense of purpose that animated these grand projects. She was the patron not only of the religious, but of those laymen – mariners, merchants, soldiers – who were sailing into the unknown. Indeed, when the Casa de la Contratación, the agency in Seville that handled the business of the Spanish Empire, commissioned a painting in 1531–5 to adorn its chapel, the subject was The Virgin of Navigators (*Virgen de los Mareantes*). It was painted by an artist of German origin and took the form of the Mother of Mercy.[23] Mary's ample cloak protected not only the ships, but also some of the leading figures in the drama of expansion: King Ferdinand, the archbishop of Fonseca, Christopher Columbus, Amerigo Vespucci. Lower down she shelters less illustrious folk, the indigenous people of the Americas.

Something of the enormity of the encounter between Europeans and the people of the Caribbean and Central America is captured in the account of the Franciscan Ramon Pané, who was commissioned by Christopher Columbus on his second journey to the Caribbean to record the ceremonies and customs of the people of Hispaniola. The friar resided among soldiers and administrators, in the fortress of Magdalena, and there he witnessed the first conversions to Christianity: those of the lord of Macorís and his extended household of sixteen.[24] One young man, Juan, now a Christian, joined Pané in his work of conversion offering invaluable linguistic skills and cultural insight.

Some of Pané's efforts bore results. For he also recounts that some of the people he was forced to leave behind built a house next to the chapel he had erected, and in it they housed 'some images before which the catechumens might kneel; and pray and find comfort'. These were the first Christians of Hispaniola, and they guarded the place, as well as the patrimony of fields that Pané had tilled.[25] Kinship, work and worship were closely woven in their lives and set them apart from the community around them. In the absence of the friar, they maintained a religion of images and prayer.

It is highly likely that some of the earliest Christian images offered to people of the Americas portrayed Mary and her son. Such images may have seemed quite familiar: Columbus reported in the diary of his first voyage that he found 'many statues of female figures and many head-

386

shaped masks, very well carved'.[26] He wondered whether they were kept for their beauty or for worship, though we know the two can coincide. Half a century later, in his account of the conquest and conversion, *History of the Indies*, which is sometimes sympathetic to local culture, the Dominican Bartolomeo de las Casas (1484–1566) described the beliefs of the people of Hispaniola, working with Pané's account. Las Casas considered Pané to be 'a simple man of good intention who knew something of the language of the Indians', but his own observations and insights are sharper and more nuanced. He observed a process whereby local religion blended with the new Christian world of ideas and practices:

Into this true and catholic knowledge of the true God these errors intruded, to wit: that God had a mother, whose name was Atabex, and a brother Guaca and other relatives in like fashion.[27]

By the time of writing in 1561 a vast establishment of religious orders and ecclesiastical administration, armed with books and images, linguistic skills and indigenous clergy, was at work to make New Spain a Christian polity and its people Christian subjects.

Here is a new chapter in the history of Mary. She was carried across the Atlantic – in books and images, in liturgies and statues – to places where she was utterly unknown. Mary was chosen by those engaged in conquest and conversion to be a token for communication with the indigenous people who seemed so different and unknowable. As Iberian involvement in America took shape with the conquest of Mexico by Cortés in 1521, Christianization of people and landscape followed, supported by vast resources and energy. Cortés' troops were led by the banner of Mary, as the oldest American account of the conquest shows.[28] Two years after the conquest, in the summer of 1523, three highly educated and well-connected missionaries intent on engaging with the native people set foot on Mexican soil. These were a Frenchman, a Fleming and a Scot, all trained in the Franciscan house of Ghent, all licensed by Emperor Charles V to convert native people. These men were formed in the milieu of *devotio moderna*, which emphasized education and preaching. Once they learned the local language, Nahuatl, they began to teach local boys, in schools modelled on the Northern European type, the sort of school where Martin Luther had been educated just a few decades earlier.[29] In a report to the emperor, friar

Pedro of Ghent described the quality of preaching and the application of music; the quality of the music produced by the Mexican choristers was as good, he claimed, as any sung in the imperial chapel.

A barrage of conflicting influences assailed the men who were charged with the task of bringing Christianity to the people of New Spain.[30] A dozen Franciscans arrived in Vera Cruz in 1524, an apostolic group geared towards mission.[31] These friars possessed a developed Marian sensibility of their own, linked with themes of Passion and compassion in words and in images. Their habits of thought, prayer and contemplation were deeply touched by association with Mary. They sought out bridging concepts and practices by which to make Christianity tangible, comprehensible and above all useful.[32] In New Spain they used some of the skills honed in Old Europe: accommodation to local idioms, provision of useful examples in texts and images and preaching in the language of the people they sought to convert. The great difference was that in New Spain the friars were very few indeed, and the people they aimed to convert were many. New models for pastoral care were developed: churches were built to accommodate the multitudes coerced and enticed into the new religion. These were open churches in walled courtyards with a large cross in the middle and a central chapel facing the courtyard. While people assembled in the courtyard they heard and watched the services conducted in the central church. This is where most Mexicans first saw Mary displayed and celebrated.[33]

The indigenous people of New Spain were offered a Mother of God in Iberian form, but also in local colour. The cloister of the Augustinian convent of San Agustin in Acolman, founded in 1539, was decorated with scenes of Christ's life, traditional in content, though with animated greenery typical of indigenous art. The cloister of the Epazoyucan Augustinian convent, decorated in 1556, was similarly traditional, with scenes of Christ's life – including a Passion with Mary at the foot of the cross – and the scene of Mary's passing in the suitable location of the cloister portal.[34] These were religious houses founded and led by Europeans, the members of which included local recruits, and which offered education to local boys.

Interactions between Franciscans and local people within urban centres occurred in the realm of religious drama too. By 1538 a whole series of productions were made in Tlaxcala with Mexican performers. In June they offered the Annunciation of St John the Baptist's birth, the

Annunciation to Mary, the Visitation and the Birth of St John the Baptist. In his description of the region's religious drama, Bartolomeo de las Casas noted that 'he who represented Our Lady was an Indian, and all those who participated were Indians'.[35] Mary took the form of the Mother Church, as she did in Europe, in a play attributed to the Franciscan Andrés de Olmos (c.1485–1571), who had her speak authoritatively as Mary and church:

I am the ever-merciful mother. My beloved son Jesus Christ has established me here for the people of the earth. I am always weeping for them, especially when some of them die. For when I shed tears I pray to my beloved Mother, the sacred fountain of Joy, to have pity on her creatures and to give light to them.

The play ended with a priest's exhortation:

The day of Judgement is coming soon. Pray to our Lord Jesus Christ and to the Virgin Mary, that she may entreat Her beloved Son Jesus Christ that you merit and deserve the joy of Heaven – that eternal glory! Amen.[36]

Nurture and fertility were the themes which the newly converted attached to Mary as they associated her with goddesses of protection and nurture. The female deities of the Mexican people were powerful symbols of staple foods, fertility and sexuality.[37] Mary came to be identified with the fruit of the maguey plant – a large cactus – the fermented juice of which produced the alcoholic drink *pulque*. *Pulque* was drunk at festivals, was offered to the gods and was associated with fertility and plenty, the domain of the goddess Mayahuel.[38]

The Franciscan missionaries who converted the first generations of Mexicans feared the very Christians they were creating. They adhered ardently to Mary in her immaculate purity but could not easily trust the indigenous priests, who served the vast majority of new parishes throughout the land, to do so. It was easy to merge Mary with indigenous deities, and this is what the bearers of Christianity feared most. While in the cities Hispanic priests set the tone of public worship in churches and religious houses, the rural hinterland of villages and small towns was too vast to transform in this way. Official ambivalence prevailed when initiatives for Mary worship took place without close supervision. An episcopal visitation of Chiapas as late as 1584 deemed the rituals of a local confraternity to be diabolical rather than pious, as they involved the confusion of Mary and female members:

There is a confraternity of twelve Indians entitled Twelve Apostles, and they come out at night and go forth from hill to hill, cave to cave, and have their meetings, gathering below, and under the pretext of religion they enact their rites, and the cult of the demon, against our Christian religion, and they carried on with two women – one they call Saint Mary, the other Magdalena – with whom they commit much turpitude . . . And they communicated spiritually (*espiritualizaban*) with them and they turn into Gods and the women into Goddesses . . .[39]

There were imaginative attempts to organize Christian life for indigenous people in ways that made Mary a focus for mutual help within a community. The Chancery judge Vasco de Quiroga (*c.*1470–1565) used his own wealth to create the utopian community of Santa Fe in Mexico City. This is how it was shaped:

the visitation of the hospital had the Virgin Mary's . . . cult as its justification, and the whole community was organized around this cult; it is a brotherhood in which all participated; it was the most important source of social aid.[40]

This was a privileged community guided by a lawyer-priest at the heart of a bustling city. Most new Christians were living more contradictory lives suspended between traditional belief and the new order associated with Christianity and Hispanic rule.

Mary was remade in parishes as a goddess of fertility and protection. She was much more prominent in expressions of indigenous religious sentiment – when we can fathom it from this distance – than was the figure of Christ. Just as she was in Europe Mary was celebrated not only in universal liturgies, but in myriad local manifestations of her power through images deemed holy.[41] In the diocese of Chiapas there was Our Lady of the Rosary in Copanahuastla, guarded and served by a confraternity since its foundation on the feast of the Purification 1561. The image was famed for its powers to cure the sick and dying. Like its European – French, Iberian, Bavarian – counterparts, this rural cult attracted pilgrims and dispensed solace.[42] Like so many apparitions of Mary in Europe, colonial America produced visionaries who imagined justice and comfort through encounters with Mary.[43]

Within this pained and vital world of resistant imagination, the most popular devotion to Mary in the Americas was born: the Virgin of Guadalupe.[44] We know of it from an account of 1648 by Miguel Sánchez, a native Franciscan, the *Image of the Virgin Mary, Mother of Guadal-*

upe.[45] This first printed version was decorated with engravings and gave shape to myriad tales that had developed over the previous 100 years. The cult's origins were situated by Sánchez in December 1531 when the Christian Juan Diego – once the Indian Quauhtlatoatzin – on his way to Mexico City saw a beautiful woman on a hillside, at Tepeyac. This was a *huaca* – an indigenous holy place, a pilgrimage site – and Mary chose to appear there and convey her wondrous message: she requested that the bishop be informed that she wished a chapel to be built for her there, at Tepeyac.[46] We have already encountered several cases in which modest folk were privileged with a vision of Mary and a message only to be rejected by the established church. In this case, too, Juan was sent away by the bishop, who requested that he return with some tangible proof. Mary instructed the visionary to climb the hill of Tepeyac and collect roses, a true wonder in the month of December. Diego gathered these in his cape and brought them to the bishop, only to find that his cloak had become imprinted with an image of Mary. The bishop preserved the image in the cathedral, but ultimately lent it to Mary's chosen site at Tepeyac.

Sánchez's vision of the Guadalupe gave shape to a cult the beginnings of which we will never be able to fathom. The Virgin venerated at Tepeyac was transformed by him into the image of the triumphant immaculate Mary, the Woman of the Apocalypse.[47] Yet in its inception the cult at Tepeyac was treated with suspicion by the Franciscans; it was, after all, the product of the imagination of a recent convert, a modest man of no learning.[48] It was an Indian devotion tolerated by the Hispanic church.

Further south, in the territories conquered and managed as part of the Viceroyalty of Peru, the Andean cosmology challenged missionaries in the wake of conquest. Central to the Andean conception of the sacred were the mountains: Titicaca, Pachamama, Chimborazo, each with its powers and history of supernatural action. In 1533 the whole array of man-made artefacts – buildings, decorations and vessels of gold and silver – offered to Pachcamac, 'Maker of the World', were destroyed, dismantled or taken away to offer as ransom to Francisco Pizarro.[49]

For decades after the conquest it was still widely believed that the mountain-gods might yet oust the Spaniards as they had done other conquerors before them.[50] Such hopes were dashed by powerful counter-myths, like that of Mary's apparition at Cuzco. Following the conquest

Pizarro and his men left the capital of the Inca Manco Capac, who in turn raised a rebellion in the absence of the Spanish cohort. The Spanish settlers were forced out of their houses by fire and congregated anxiously in the city-square around a chapel. They were soon saved by Mary, who blinded the rebels with dust (some said hail) and put out the fire. Mary acted in Cuzco as she had done so often during the reconquest of Iberia, as aid to Christians against infidel enemies during sieges and battles.[51] A number of influential accounts within local histories spread the fame of the miraculous apparition; it was told in a mural painted on the outer wall of Cuzco cathedral in the 1560s. By the late seventeenth century local artists had developed an iconography based on the Immaculate Mary and the Assumption to tell the miracle: Mary inhabits the upper register of the canvas, in full control and protection of her people, while Inca warriors in colourful clothing tumble down in confusion.

Friars learned the Andean languages – Quechua and Aymara – and taught the rudiments of Christianity in them: Adam and Eve had offended God and were punished for it, just as they would have been in an Andean morality tale. Yet the Andean cosmology endured, embedded in the landscape and in all aspects of nature, reinforced by relations among living and dead kindred, and it inspired in friars and administrators suspicion towards indigenous Christianity. Not only were peasant converts of little learning suspected of lapses, sophisticated 'new' Christians were kept at arm's length too. In 1554 the son of an Inca noble became a Christian in Cuzco. The Peruvian writer and soldier (of mixed Inca/Spanish parentage) Garcilaso de la Vega (c.1539–1616) described with disapproval the convert at prayer. As he prayed in the Dominican church, which had once been the imperial sanctuary of the Inca sun god, the Inca addressed the sacrament 'Pachacamac', and the image of Mary 'Mother of God'.[52] Within a space so redolent of rich memories of old religion any gesture of devotion was bound to appear as an amalgam of old and new.

In the Peruvian capital Cuzco important dates in the local dynastic calendar were incorporated into the new Christian one. Cuzco had been a centre for the production of luxury goods, and it became a powerhouse for the making of Christian art of Mary.[53] A distinctive artistic style developed there, which blended local artistic skills of work in silver with the panel-painting traditions of Hispanic friars who trained local artists. The Castilian Jeronomite monk Diego de Ocaña (c.1570–1608)

developed an Andean version of the now widespread Virgin of Guadalupe, and in his wide travels throughout the southern Andes commented on and encouraged indigenous attachment to miraculous images. As was the case in Europe, and above all in Iberia, local versions of Mary became widely recognized, cult images like the Virgin of Copacabana on Lake Titicaca, who drew pilgrims along an ancient Inca pilgrimage route.[54]

In the highlands, like the silver town of Potosí in what is now Bolivia, public religious rituals celebrated the wealth-giving power of mountains. An eighteenth-century painting has Mary as the silver mountain: local people and their animals walk on her body, plants grow on it, and an Inca king supervises his people as they mined the precious metal.[55] At the foot of the mountain stand, from left to right, Pope Paul III, a cardinal, a bishop and on the far right Emperor Charles V, dressed in the habit of the prestigious military order of Alcantara. The extraction of wealth was linked with the mountain's sanctity through its association with the Andean female deity Pachamama. This *huaca* was identified with Mary, with a chapel at its summit. A century later legend embraced the mountain's identity with Mary: like a virgin guards her chastity, the mountain kept secret its silver treasure until the coming of the Christians.[56]

Women seem to have been particularly receptive to Christianity. Jesuit missionaries approached women and girls with the cult of Mary and the female saints. These were sometimes reinforced by the presence of nuns on some missions.[57] When the Jesuit José de Acosta (1540–1600) described the social and natural environment of Peru in the 1580s, he noted with disgust the attitude of indigenous people to virginity:

Virginity, which is admired with esteem and honour amongst all people, these barbarians despise as vile and offensive. Except for the virgins consecrated to the Sun or to the Inca, who are guarded in holy enclosures, while all other virgins are despised.[58]

Men resisted the suggestion that they marry women who were still virgins.[59]

The Christian model of female virginity, personified in Mary's unique perpetual virginity, disrupted social arrangements in other regions of encounter and mission too. The Christian view of sexuality and gender provided women with some new opportunities within the prevailing

systems of kinship. In North America Huron women responded to the possibility of choosing a European husband; alternatively, they now valued virginity – so unfamiliar – which could offer some areas of autonomy to young women. In the Illinois communities addressed by the French Jesuit father Marquette in the 1670s a pattern was emerging: Mary was the special friend of older girls and young women. Onto the Algonquin understanding that maidens were 'masters of their own body' was grafted the Christian teaching of chastity, to the dismay of young men – prospective sexual partners – and elders, whose teachings and control of conjugality were challenged in this way.[60]

Virginity seized the imagination of women as a new and exciting lifestyle in other continents too. When the Carmelite missionaries entered into Kongo in 1569, then a Christian kingdom under Portuguese tutelage, they approached the capital city with an impressive procession heralded by a statue of Mary, dressed in white, as a Carmelite. One of the princesses, daughter of Alvaro I, king of Kongo, was attracted by the figure of Mary. She listened to sermons and was moved to join the order. Attempts by the Carmelite prior to ascertain whether she could do so through the offices of the prioress of the Carmelite of Lisbon foundered. There was no model, nor any desire to see a black princess in Mary's white garb.[61]

Mary's diverse images offered opportunities for expression to the many groups which made up the complex societies of conquest where disease and dislocation were rife. Further south, in New Portugal – northern Brazil of today – the Jesuit mission was under way from the 1540s, and by the 1560s Jesuit 'reductions' (reducciones) – congregations of Christianized indigenous people – were established under the management and care of Jesuits. Encounter with the locals was best achieved, according to the Jesuit father José de Anchieta, by teaching the Indians to pray the Ave Maria with the aid of the rosary. Such simple practices led inexorably to an appreciation of Mary and, through her, of the Christian universe.[62] In Brazil the sugar plantations were worked by enslaved Africans. The whole colonial economy depended on extracting their labour, and so the missionaries who sought to make them Christians had to accept the reality of servitude and wretchedness. Plantation owners appreciated the power of religious mobilization, as did the viceroys who protected the colony. In 1586 the Jesuits were encouraged to create rosary confraternities of Africans and Indians, all

recent converts.[63] Religion, with Mary's consoling figure at its heart, was used in the efforts to control and pacify the oppressed. It also marked the beginning of the association of Mary with the oppressed people – prisoners, the poor – still a powerful force in contemporary Brazil.

Some preachers developed in their sermons the theme of Mary's humility; Mary was, after all, God's handmaiden. Themes of nurture and kinship, so prominent in descriptions of Mary, encouraged among members of Marian confraternities the creation of ties of solidarity and friendship. Such groups offered affinities which could fill some of the gaps caused by dispossession, dislocation and enslavement. The preaching of the Jesuit Antonio Vieira, Portuguese-born and reared in the Brazilian capital Salvador, shows just how far dispossession and new devotion could be bound. In a sermon of 1633 he offered African members of a rosary confraternity a unique perspective on their identity as Christians. Slaves should give thanks to Mary for having brought them from Africa, and for having given them the chance to become Christian. Mary was their protector, and her son was one of them: for 'there is no work or type of life on earth more like the cross and passion of Christ than your work in one of these sugar mills'.[64]

Mary reached the northern parts of America through the work of French Jesuits – in New France, today's Quebec – and in the region of the Great Lakes. Such men often worked alone, or in very small groups, in harsh snowy terrains, and they led with Mary. They followed the routes created by fur traders and reached peoples whose contact with Europeans had been slight and haphazard. English settlers along the Atlantic coast were primarily Protestant, mostly Puritan. They did not represent a state, and they were less oriented towards mission than the colonizers of Central and Southern America. Protestants lacked the specialized personnel, members of religious orders, committed to mission.

Mary marked the beginning of encounter with Christianity.[65] The account of Marquette's journey to the Illinois – an edited version of his own journal – describes his staging of Mary. Father Marquette had been gravely ill during his journey; he suffered flux of blood and constant pain. Accompanied by a single servant, he arrived at the Illinois village in March 1674:

It was a beautiful prairie, close to a village, which was Selected for the great Council; this was adorned, after the fashion of the country, by Covering it with

mats and bearskins. Then the father, having directed them to stretch out upon Lines several pieces of chinese taffeta, attached to these four large Pictures of the blessed Virgin, which were visible on all Sides. The audience was Composed of 500 chiefs and elders, seated in a circle around the father, and of all the Young men, who remained standing.[66]

The man who carried Mary's images through the snow was not just a dutiful exponent of Christian teaching but a fervent enthusiast. Father Marquette was devoted to the Immaculate Conception: 'It was a pleasure to hear him speak or preach on the subject.'[67] The devotion was part of his youthful formation; at the age of nine he had begun a regime of Saturday fasts. As an adult, isolated on his trails of mission, he devised a scheme of recitation and prayer, a rosary-like sequence:

he said every Day with his two men a little corona (*une petite couronne*) of the immaculate conception which he had devised as follows: After the Credo, there is said once the *pater* and *ave*, and then 4 times these words: *Ave daughter of God the Father, Ave mother of God the son, Ave spouse of the holy spirit, Ave temple of the whole trinity: cleanse my heart and flesh, purest virgin, by your holy virginity and your immaculate conception: in the name of the father, and the son, and the holy spirit* – concluding with the *Gloria patri*, the whole repeated three times.[68]

At the frontiers of Christian endeavour Mary sustained the Jesuit missionary and bemused the people he sought out. Mary was related with nostalgia for home and homeland. The Jesuit Matteo Ricci (1552–1610), who spent his life as a missionary in China, and whose diary is so intimate and revealing, frequently wrote about his memory of childhood in the town of Macerata near the Marian shrine of Loreto. He recalls the green and lovely land but also the elaborate processions with images of Mary. Nature and cult sustained him in the work of mission, a world away.[69]

The Iberian realm of influence was characterized by a great diversity of peoples and cultures, but throughout it operated a concerted desire to make power palpable and ubiquitous. The Iberian empires developed great urban centres – Mexico City, Goa, Manila – and an imperial system of weights and measures, liturgy and ceremony thus came to encompass the globe. Since the Spanish conquest of Muslim Maynilad and the building of Manila on its ashes in 1571, that city became a rich

and diverse global trading centre. Asian goods – silk, porcelain, spices, objets d'art – were transported from Manila to Mexico, and from there to Europe. The Philippines were administered from Mexico City as a province of New Spain. It is, therefore, not surprising that one of Mary's local guises was Virgin of Peace and Good Voyage (Virgen de Paz y buen Viaje). She was patron of the galleons which traded between Manila and Acapulco and was later called the Virgin of Antipolo.[70] Mary became part of public civic celebration of great events in the life of the Spanish commonwealth: the arrival of governors, coronations, the birth of princes, great religious festivals. Indigenous forms of theatre, music and dance were prefaced by the distinctive loa (a word derived from the Spanish loar, to praise). Strings of appellations were lavished on the honoured person of the occasion, like those traditionally offered to Mary. Sometimes Mary herself was the subject of praise, as on celebrations of new statues.[71] Throughout the Spanish and Portuguese Empires Mary was available not only for mission but as a force towards conversion of Christians to a more committed life: the merchant João de Eiro was drawn by the example of the Jesuit Francis Xavier but could not easily leave his prosperous and adventurous life. Mary appeared to him during his contemplation, and guided his decision to join the order.[72]

A single Christian calendar framed administration and festivities here as in the rest of the Empire, and Mary's ritual year was central to its rhythms. The Iberian calendar inspired elaborate celebrations: it culminated in Manila in 1619 on the feast of the Immaculate Conception, which was celebrated over nineteen days with 'bullfights, masquerades, nightly illuminations and fireworks'.[73] Every religious order offered its praise: the Franciscans first, followed by archers and musketeers; next 'came a rich standard bearing the image of the conception of the Virgin and at her feet Escoto [Duns Scotus (1265/1275–1308), the theologian who had formulated so forcefully the understanding of the Immaculate Conception]'; next the Augustinians, the Jesuits, and the seminarians. On Saturday – Mary's special day – a chariot processed with an enthroned figure of Mary, heralded by clarion-players and children dressed in silk, who recited Mary's praises. On the following day another celebration saw some sixty Japanese people sing and dance 'according to their custom'.[74] After the celebrations in Manila there were eight days of Franciscan festivities outside the city. Everything that Asia

and Europe could offer in praise, spectacle and music, song and drama (including a play of the 'Prince of Transylvania' by the Augustinians), was offered to Mary on her feast day.

The experience of Mary in the rest of Asia was utterly different. In China, India and Japan trading companies and religious orders acted not as confident agents of a conquering empire, but as a tolerated presence dependent on the fluctuating approval of rulers. Mary arrived not with the transformation of the local world, not as balm to follow conquest and dislocation, but as part of a cosmology that competed with other, traditional, local ones of immense power and range. While the surviving members of Aztec and Inca elites were expected to conform to Hispanic religion with Mary at its heart, in China and Japan converts still lived within established hegemonic non-Christian worlds. In these parts converts chose Christianity knowingly and willingly, and there were some half a million Christians in Asia by the end of the sixteenth century.[75] Their confidence is manifest in a great deal of writing and cultural production: like the holy biographies of exemplary Chinese Christians, or translations of devotional poetry 'according to the versification of China'.[76]

The Jesuits were particularly proud of their achievements in Japan, with perhaps 100,000 converts. They founded in 1583 a painting academy in Arima, where European members of the order trained Asian artists. Local materials received the imprint of Mary in an art that blended traditions of Mary with new materials and sensibilities: a Madonna of the Snows was depicted around 1600 on a paper scroll, embossed with textile that formed a frame for a delicate Mary, whose eyes were drawn in gentle sweeps of the pen, her orientalized head crowned with roses.[77] Even when artists copied European models they made something new of Mary and helped her figure blend with local aesthetics. When a Chinese artist copied the Madonna of St Luke – the famous image from Santa Maria Maggiore in Rome – he worked in watercolours on a long silk scroll: Mary and Child have delicate Chinese features, the Child Christ is a little bookish Chinese boy in a dress, the drapery is billowing, and Mary's bare feet gently protrude from under her garment.[78]

When Japan entered a period of national seclusion (*sakoku*) in the early Edo period (1615–1868) under the Tokugawa Shogunate and Christianity was banned from 1639, the Spanish and Portuguese were

expelled. The Protestant Dutch succeeded in convincing the Shoguns that, unlike their Iberian rivals, they were not driven by missionary zeal, and so they gained the monopoly of foreign trade in Nagasaki. Crews of incoming ships were sometimes obliged to prove their religious 'coolness' by trampling on images of Mary and Child in front of Japanese officials.[79] Indeed the images came to be known as *fumie* – trampled-on pictures – and became the test by which individuals, and sometimes whole villages, demonstrated their renunciation of Christianity.

The same and yet new – Mary was remade with the skill, sensibility and confidence of an often beleaguered little group of Asian artists, poets and thinkers; the Mary of Japan and China was for the few, not the many.

23
Mary in a World of Neighbouring Diversity

Far from the conquests of the Americas and the conversion of Asia, the daily, seasonal and annual routines of life in Europe were lived within a religious landscape of polemical awareness. By the mid-sixteenth century European Christians thought of themselves as either Catholics or Protestants. Within each denomination there was an array of possibilities, particularly within the Protestant world, which recognized no single leading figure. Protestant identity was anchored in a perceived return to true Christian values, above all to the Bible. Among Protestants Mary lost much of her devotional adornment and visual glamour, but she gained an embedded quality as a symbol of good faith and Christian family values. Conversely, the Catholic world was embroiled in attempts to assert, defend and often reform practices and beliefs.

The confrontation with Protestantism did not occur everywhere, and it was often experienced as a local, communal debate within a town council, or among neighbours, within a family. The official response of the Catholic world to the Protestant challenge was debated and formulated at the meetings of the Council of Trent between 1545 and 1563. World Catholicism – its bishops, abbots, theologians and heads of religious orders – rebutted the Protestant 'heretics' and offered guidelines for life in a world where a variety of Christian world views coexisted. Many of their deliberations affected the image and understanding of Mary.

The statement on the use of images and the veneration of relics, offered at the session of Christmas 1563 under Pope Pius IV, is a good example of the Council's aims and orientations. It asserted the utility of images as sources for instruction, memorials of the idea they represented and as inspiration towards devotion. The Council endorsed images but also warned against the representation of 'false doctrines' and prohibited the making of images 'painted and adorned with a seductive charm'.[1]

The figure of Mary and her Child had become seductively charming since the Gothic transformation of the later twelfth century. Such images were not to be removed, as many Protestants and all Calvinists had it, but rather new ones were to be produced with greater care. A new theory of art and a new style of painting were being born.

Mary's place in Catholic material culture had been secured and enhanced by emphatic statements pronounced in one of the early sessions of the Council in 1546.[2] The Catholic world was animated for decades to come by the intellectual challenge of shoring up local saints, pilgrimage sites, liturgies and images. Practices of recent creation were particularly vulnerable to criticism. By the later sixteenth century these were scrutinized not only by Protestants but by the probing eye of Catholics too. There was never any doubt that Mary deserved the highest praise, as did the eucharist. Indeed, the Catholic historian and apologist Cesare Baronius (1538–1607) argued the case for honouring both in his revision of the *Martyrologium Romanum* (*The Roman Martyrology*) of 1598, the official hagiographical compendium of the Roman church.[3] He did so in the entry on the feast of the Assumption, Mary's greatest feast, yet one with no scriptural support.

The Catholic world was not only challenged by the successes of Protestantism in large parts of Europe, it was also locked in struggle with the Ottoman Empire. First fifteenth-century reformers and later Protestants interpreted the progress of Islam in Europe as punishment for Christian sinfulness. When the combined navies of Spain, Venice and Genoa, under the command of Don John of Austria and the aegis of Pope Pius V, crushed the Ottoman fleet at Lepanto (off the coast of Epirus in modern Greece) on 7 October 1571, a dramatic shift occurred in Catholic self-belief. Catholic art and literature expressed a renewed sense of purpose on all fronts: mission in Europe and the rest of the world, and zeal for further crusading against 'infidels' and 'heretics' alike. The victory was celebrated as Mary's feat: she had been the patron of the enterprise and harbinger of its success. Paolo Veronese's painting *The Allegory of the Battle of Lepanto* was made just a year after the battle for the Doge's Palace in Venice. He had been present at the momentous event, and his panel conveys the immediacy of confusion and drama in battle. Mary emerges from heavenly clouds, answering the call of the Venetian patron saints Peter, Roch, Justine and Mark. Unlike the ubiquitous representation of Mary as intercessor for humans,

here Mary receives the intercession of saints who turn to her for help. Mary's courtiers, the angels, direct fiery darts at the enemy ships. With Mary on their side, the Christians achieved a famous victory.[4]

MARY: PILGRIMAGE AND MIRACLES

The defence of Catholic traditions was necessary and timely work, and it was not only a project of conservation, but one of innovation and aggressive restatement of values. By the late sixteenth century, Catholic renewal was evident in the emergence of new miracles and shrines like the Netherlandish Marian shrines of Halle and of Montaigu (Scherpenheuvel). The account of these miracles was particularly effective, since it was written by the humanist and legal scholar Justus Lipsius (1547–1606), a man often sceptical about miracles, who had taught for thirteen years at the Calvinist University of Leiden.[5] The dossier on the shrines assembled by the archbishop of Malines was compiled and translated by the English priest, Robert Chambers, resident in Brussels, and was printed in Antwerp (with a dedication to King James I) in 1606. The book's structure is telling: it contains not only a customary preface to the king, but a lengthy preface to the 'Christian Reader' (thirty-nine pages long) which offers support for belief in miracles (from biblical as well as patristic sources), followed by a preface to the Marian miracles which surveys medieval discussions and precedents.[6]

Finally, after this lengthy preamble, the story begins. It recounts the medieval tradition at Montaigu, where an image of Mary, normally fastened to an oak tree, was found by a shepherd boy some 'hundreth yeares and more ago' lying on the ground.[7] The boy was immobilized by the image, and it later became a subject of devotion to the local people. Some time in the 1570s it had been removed 'by heretikes'. The new miraculous eruption happened through the agency of a 'good old man', a townsman of Sichen who in 1587 approached a widow who owned an image of 'our lady made of wood, placed in a litle frame or tabernacle'. He carried it to the denuded oak at Montaigu and set it where the old image had once been. In 1602 a priest of Sichen had a small ('six foot long and five broad') wooden chapel built there, and soon people came there for cure of 'vehement head-ache'. Healing miracles attracted the multitudes, and on the Feast of the Nativity of Mary 1603

20,000 pilgrims were in attendance. People of all estates and regions visited the shrine, 'Princes, Earles, Lordes, Gentlemen and Ladies, the rehearsal of whose names would here be too tedious'.[8] The rest of the book comprises stories of miraculous healings. The miraculous image cured cankers, leprosy, falling sickness, incurable wounds, palsy and much more.

Sichen and the whole region of Brabant thus became famous throughout the Catholic world for its contemporary miracles after decades of destruction. In Protestant countries, like England, such news brought consolation to Catholics but also formed part of the continuous religious polemic against them. Mary was clearly at work as she manifested herself in landscapes, reclaiming her place after years of rude and violent disruption. The merest ruin could be made to bear new Marian meaning, especially in relatively isolated locations. The abandoned chapel at the top of the Skirrid just outside Abergavenny became the site of Catholic preaching.[9] New reformed houses were established in places redolent with memories of the cults of 'old' Catholicism: Las Nievas and Las Batuecas near Salamanca were new houses founded near old Marian shrines.[10]

Europe with its diverse competing religious confessions saw a revitalized identification of dynasts with religious programmes. Even before the Reformation, the Catholic monarchs of Iberia had forged a national programme around orthodoxy and crusade; throughout their global empire Catholic culture was spread and tested. The Bavarian Wittelsbach dynasty embraced new shrines and revived old ones. The favourite Bavarian Mary shrine at Altötting was revived, and Mary was entitled *patrona Bavariae*.[11] When Bavarian troops marched into Protestant Prague in 1620, they hoisted flags with Mary's image and rallied to the battle cry 'Maria'.[12] Dynasts and their armies marked territory by avid pilgrimage too. They claimed lands by travelling through them in the extravagant pose of the humble pilgrim. In the throes of invasion by Sweden in 1655, King Jan II Casimir (1609–72) dedicated his kingdom of Poland-Lithuania to Mary in her emanation as Our Lady of Grace.[13]

Miracles and shrines – so many of them related to images of Mary – were at the heart of polemical exchanges. Just like many medieval people before them Catholic bishops and ecclesiastical visitors aimed to secure the dignity and authenticity of shrines. Like those before them, pilgrims

sought an immediacy of contact with the miraculous that mere parish religion could not offer: a pilgrim to our Lady of Fuensanta (La Roda) reported of Mary that she 'seemed that she was flesh and blood'.[14] The habit of pilgrimage was thus hard to extirpate; Protestant preachers, pamphleteers as well as town councils made repeated and energetic efforts to dispel the attraction of shrines. As early as 1518 the council of the Swiss city of Bern ordered that the image of Mary in the pilgrimage shrine of Oberbüren be 'hacked and burned' in front of a crowd and to the sound of bells. The shrine was noted for miraculous revivals of stillborn babies, long enough for them to be baptised.[15] The city also commissioned a play in 1531 with the ominous title *Abgötterei – Idolatry* – in which naive women displayed misguided trust in miracles of Mary. Catholic women were considered to be especially avid pilgrims. The Franciscan Bernardino d'Amico, who spent the years between 1593 and 1597 in the Holy Land, taking notes and making drawing of landscape and buildings, describes the church of the Nativity in Bethlehem, and the cave where Mary fed her son. The shrine attracted Christians as well as infidels, and its rocks, when powdered were called 'milk of the Madonna'. Innumerable ladies of France, Italy and Spain were his witness.[16]

The very polemical nature of miracles made such shrines centres not only for cures, but also for conversion away from the 'heretical' error of Protestantism. In 1597 the Venetian Francesco Barbaro, patriarch of Aquilea, told his nephew Cardinal Pietro Aldobrandini about a Carinthian pilgrimage site, Our Lady of Luggau. The shrine had been founded some seventy years earlier:

by a heretic [Protestant], who was journeying on horseback, and fell into a deep chasm and came out of it unharmed, while his horse was crushed to death. The recipient of the miracle built the aforementioned sanctuary at his own expense, and dedicated it to the Holy Virgin and called it Our Lady of Luggau. And so this sanctuary became an attraction to a great number of pilgrims who came from all neighbouring regions; it became the object of extreme devotion, which grew daily, and which led to the conversion of many heretics. In fact, several villages near Luggau, previously infected by heresy, are becoming cured quite miraculously.[17]

The power of this Marian shrine was demonstrated through a specific miraculous act: the revival of those babies who had died without

baptism. Placed upon the altar, they came back to life long enough for baptism to take place. To further support the shrine the patriarch requested that the cardinal issue an indulgence to all Luggau pilgrims.

Here is an unauthorized shrine, one created by popular initiative, without the scrutiny required by the Council of Trent. Here too was, quite clearly, a case of resistance to the Catholic theology of salvation, according to which only the baptized could be saved.[18] Only Mary could reverse the injustice of innocents dying without baptism; nothing in Protestant lore offered anything like it, and so the revival of babes led to the birth of Catholic yearnings in the hearts of Protestants. The patriarch was moved to support the shrine, and it enjoyed the admiration of Carinthian aristocrats and Catholic apologists.[19] While theologians and prelates demurred, those engaged in polemical guerrilla warfare appreciated the contribution made by the miracle-working Mary.

In Carinthia Mary moved whole villages towards the Catholic faith; elsewhere in Europe a new, communal character of Marian pilgrimage was also apparent. The Portuguese sanctuary of Our Lady de Nazaré (on the Sitio promontory) was known from the fourteenth century, but it gained new notoriety as a shrine under royal patronage.[20] Its miracles were effectively disseminated in the sixteenth century by the Cistercian writer Bernardo de Brito (1586–1617). Bernardo combined history and hagiography in support of the shrine, the miraculous image of which he claimed to have been the work of Saint Joseph himself. The shrine was renowned for its protective power against shipwreck, disease and accidents. From around 1600 it attracted not only individuals, but communal pilgrimages; parishes and neighbourhoods sought assurance and succour in collective journeys to it.[21] This pragmatic engagement with favoured sanctuaries also meant that disappointing shrines were abandoned in favour of more satisfying ones. Several of those miraculously cured by the body of the saint-in-the-making Mary of the Incarnation (1566–1618) reported that they had previously been let down by the Marian shrine of Notre-Dame de Liesse, near Soissons.[22] Modest people deliberated and took advice on which shrine or image would be most efficacious. When Maria Caroens' breasts produced no milk with which to feed her fourteenth baby, she consulted female friends and finally decided that she should visit the statue of Mary sheltering in the Franciscan church of Ghent. She all but despaired when her prayers

were not answered, but after her third pious appeal she felt her breast fill up with milk.[23]

Such expression of hope and expectation, such knowing engagement with the promise of Mary's power, clashed with official ecclesiastical attempts to design and control Marian devotion. A visitation made by the archbishop of Cracow at the great shrine of the Black Madonna of Czestochowa in 1593 prohibited the practice by which the miraculous image was removed from the high altar and processed around the church. Yet accounts of subsequent miracles describe the image being held or seen in a variety of positions away from the safety of the high altar.[24] Visions of Mary were often experienced by modest folk such as shepherds and farmers; a religious order usually intervened and turned the sites of such visions into shrines.[25] Confraternities encouraged communal worship, guarded and promoted images and their cult. The city of Zamora was dedicated to the Virgin of Los Remedios; its image was carried in procession through the city streets in 1589 in order to benefit the whole community during a drought: 'by means of Our Lady, God Our Lord would be induced to send water from the heavens and bread and fruit of the land'.[26]

Mary's Catholic geography emerged as a combination of exciting pilgrimage destinations and the routines of parish living. Many of the medieval forms of worship and enthusiasm – in confraternities, in processional festivity – were retained, though bursts of official scrutiny occasionally intruded on much-loved and familiar images and rituals. The worship of confraternities offered occasions for a heightened musical experience in the singing of psalms, hymns and *laude*, all of which were primarily Marian. Novel compositions were noted in the records of the seventeenth-century confraternity of San Raffaele Archangelo in Florence:

And on the day the usual Vespers was sung, with the organ to accompany all the psalms, and the Magnificat and the Salve Regina all in music, with a truly beautiful motet, and this novelty was unexpected and brought the greatest satisfaction.[27]

Marian themes intersected with the promotion of new devotions. In 1593 the confraternity of San Raffaele observed the Forty Hour eucharistic exercise (*Quaranta Hore*) and enacted scenes of Mary's visit to Christ's sepulchre.[28] The desire to perform biblical scenes in the parish

and to embellish worship beyond the core liturgy led to the hiring of professional performers. Out of such display of sacred drama the oratorio was born. Opera was soon to follow.

The world of Catholic revival cherished the late medieval theme of the Christian family, which merged so forcefully in the cult of the Holy Family, St Joseph and St Anne. These were dramatized in new and lavish ways in Baroque art and devotional writing. With its image of dynastic stability and order the Holy Family attracted men as well as women to it.[29] The Jesuit bishop and later saint Francis de Sales (1567–1622) offered guidance in his *Introduction to the Devout Life*. Mary was presented above all as a mother of each Christian:

She is the Mother of our sovereign Father and consequently she is our own Mother in an especial way. Let us run to her and like little children place ourselves into her arms with perfect confidence. At every moment and on every occasion let us call on this dear Mother. Let us invoke her maternal love and by trying to imitate her virtues let us have true filial affection for her.[30]

He recommended to Christians the example of those 'who owed care for the exterior house to that of the interior, that is the love of their earthly spouse with that of the heavenly Spouse'. The examples to follow are 'the Blessed Virgin together with St Joseph, St Louis, St Monica, and a hundred thousand others in the ranks of those living in the world invite you and encourage you'.[31] A good Catholic life was not impossible if one followed the guidance of Mary and Joseph. Artists rediscovered the subject of the Holy Family and infused it with emotional intensity. The *Montalto Madonna*, painted by Annibale Caracci (1560–1609) around the year 1600, situated a young and lively Mary and her wriggling son between John the Baptist and Joseph. While Mary turns to the viewer, Joseph and John intently examine the Child.[32]

Reform of Catholicism thus involved the embrace of doctrinal truth with some attention to legitimacy and propriety. There was no dilution of the Christian promise of salvation through a God made flesh, born of a virgin, but a renewed and uncompromising statement of this incomparable truth. Like their medieval antecedent these beliefs had Mary at their heart; not Mary of the hearth and home, but Mary of lofty magnificence.

THE IMMACULATE CONCEPTION AND THE ART OF THE COUNTER REFORMATION

Nothing emphasized Catholic triumph in the face of Protestant derision more than affirmation of the Immaculate Conception. We have already seen how attractive this belief was for dynasts and rulers, to those who embodied sacral kingship. Yet the polemical thrust of the sixteenth century seems to have inspired new emphasis on the Immaculate Conception, a belief that no Protestant should entertain. This led to a vindication of the belief as never before; the French Jesuit Nicolas Caussin (1583–1651) preached that the creation of Mary was even greater than the creation of the world, since she was the beginning of all happiness in the world.[33] This is evident in the art of Rome. Rome offered leadership to the global Catholic world as home to the pope and headquarters to the religious orders charged with mission and reform. Mary was central to the spirituality and visual experience of the men trained to accomplish this work. Alongside the martyrs of the missionary orders – like the Jesuit Francis Xavier – Mary inspired and consoled men intent on mission and its challenges, in Europe and in the rest of the world. Mary's life was an example for the young Jesuits trained in the Novitiate of S. Andrea al Quirinale in Rome, founded in 1565. One room had an altarpiece of the Presentation of Mary in the Temple: in it Mary contemplates the future awe-inspiring birth of her son and serves as an example to the novice as he prepared for the great tasks ahead.[34] The communal space of the dormitory was adorned with images of Mary and Child with distinct groups of exemplary Christians: patriarchs and prophets, apostles, martyrs, virgins, confessors and blessed Jesuits.[35] The order of these scenes follows that of the Litany of the Saints and the weekly cycle of devotions. The example of confessors and martyrs was a poignant reminder of future challenges, as the young missionaries left the Novitiate to face the world.

The elite of Catholic priests and scholars was trained in Rome. These were men who would assume high ecclesiastical office, design the shape of the faith, train priests in their work. The Collegio Romano trained

laymen and priests whose studies were accompanied by a rich devotional routine embellished by music and art. The Collegio's four oratories, in which students assembled according to class, were dedicated to Mary: to the Immaculate Conception, the Nativity and two to the Visitation.[36]

Those scholars who went on to higher degrees displayed a desire to nestle under Mary's protection too. Just as we have seen in the later medieval universities, so in Catholic Rome of the early seventeenth century scholars displayed cleverness and skill by exploring the many paths to Mary. The doctoral candidates of the Collegio Romano associated as a fraternity known as the *Accademia Parthenia* – the Virgin's Academy – and they performed complex rituals at the defence and celebration of their doctorates. They devised intricate frontispieces for the pamphlets distributed at these events, encoded with Marian messages among a profusion of ostentatious references to classical myths. In one designed in 1635 by Pietro da Cortona, Mary was likened to a magnetic stone, which attracted to it iron rings which formed a chain: Mary's magnetism was the love which linked the young members to her, and to each other, as links in a family of love.[37]

Mary was a constant presence in the life of priests, scholars and missionaries, in the life of men charged with the care of Catholic souls and with making the Catholic faith a universal presence. Traditional Marian themes were rethought, enhanced and redeployed. Rome celebrated Mary as never before in innovative decoration of the Quirinal Palace, the popes' summer residence. Construction began in 1573, and Pope Paul V commissioned from the artist Guido Reni frescoes for the Chapel of the Annunciation in 1610. Five narrative scenes told Mary's story: the Annunciation to Joachim, the Nativity of the Virgin, the Presentation of the Virgin in the Temple, the Annunciation to Mary, and the Virgin Sewing in the Temple. In the cupola, outside the narrative sequence, is the Conception of the Virgin Immaculate by God the Father.

The frescoes of the Quirinal Chapel demonstrate several interesting points about the role that Mary came to play in Catholic elite culture in the century of the Protestant and Catholic Reformations. In this world, claims about Mary were not diminished, but held firm; narratives based in apocrypha, and beliefs crystallized in medieval theology and devotion – such as the Immaculate Conception – were reasserted and embedded within a compelling story of salvation. Moreover, Mary's hegemony,

rejected by Luther and Calvin, was celebrated in this papal chapel: into the five scenes of Mary's life the whole promise of salvation was enfolded. The scene of The Virgin Sewing added a pastoral vision too: that of virtue and good works, exemplified in Mary for all Christians.[38] The art of triumphant Catholicism may have been affected here by the domestic refashioning of Mary prompted by Protestant art: Mary as a faithful woman, busy at her chores. If so, it only affected the five scenes of Mary's life. Their economy is contrasted by an exuberant burst of fantasy overhead in the scene of the Immaculate Conception of Mary by God. Here is a heroic scene of creation and an artistic display of all the pent-up illusionism that Reni kept under check when painting the other frescoes.

The Immaculate Conception guided communication with religious men and women alike. In his painting for the Carmelite nuns of Seville, Diego Velasquez (1599–1660) depicted Mary as a young girl, an image of each Carmelite nun as she entered her novitiate. Mary is unique – young, and set apart among clouds, crowned with tiny stars – as the Immaculate Conception so powerfully claimed. Yet another, of St John the Evangelist, accompanies the panel as he receives the vision of the Woman of the Apocalypse, a theme so closely associated with the Immaculate Mary.[39] A distinct iconography of the Immaculate Mary embodied the Apocalyptic image and the fruit of visions too. Velasquez's father-in-law, Francisco Pacheco (d.1654), recommended in his manual *The Art of Painting* (*Arte de la Pintura*) of 1649 that the Immaculate Mary should be painted

with a white dress and a blue mantel, as this lady appeared to Dona Beatriz de Silva, the Portuguese woman, who later was taken into (*recogió después*) the royal nunnery of Santo Domingo in Toledo, to found the religious order of the Immaculate Conception, which was confirmed by Pope Julius II in 1511.[40]

The Immaculate Conception was the symbol of world Catholicism. Bernardo Bitti (1548–1610), for example, worked in Rome and later in Spanish America. His Virgin and Child of c.1603 in the Jesuit church of Arequipa (southern Peru) has Mary standing in a dark void, with her naked, long-limbed son in her arms; her dress pale, almost white, and her mantle blue.[41] There is little adornment, no crown, no distraction, and she arises impressive and majestic, utterly unique. The Assumption also offered opportunities for display of talent and ingenuity, and some

410

artists specialized in tricking the eye of the beholder. Guido Reni's Assumption of 1631/42 has Mary borne aloft by angels, received into a golden heavenly sphere. Everything about this painting lifts the eye.[42] In Mexico the scene adorned the cathedral of Mexico City, in the painting by Juan Correa, which tells the whole Christian story, with the Resurrection at the bottom, leading on to Christ's reception of Mary into heaven as God the Father looks on.[43]

The art of Catholic Europe was being transported in shiploads to the Americas and beyond. Italy and the Low Countries, the artistic powerhouses of Europe in which Mary was imagined and represented in a multitude of styles, genres and materials, influenced artistic work in Iberia and thus throughout the Hispanic Empire.[44] Spanish artists acted as mediators who bought and collected, and then exported, European art. The Flemish gift for situating Mary within intimate household interiors helped create a whole visual universe for Mary: people of European extraction regarded these with some nostalgia, and for indigenous people they underpinned narratives which were still unfamiliar.

As the religious map of Europe was redrawn some Catholics became minority groups within Protestant regions and polities. This was the case in England after the reign of Mary, who had re-established Catholic practice during her reign. A Catholic gentleman like Thomas Maynell nurtured some of his most cherished devotions in a private prayer book. It is full of invocations which no longer had a place in the practice of his Anglican parish: to Mary, saints, martyrs and to the Name of Jesus. Maynell practised with great self-awareness what had been mundane to English parishioners just a century earlier; when his daughter Ann, a mother of four, died he wrote a prayer seeking mercy from God and his mother.[45] Jesuits worked hard to adapt traditional materials for the clandestine life of Catholics in Protestant lands. The rosary was re-worked into a compendium of material for instruction and a token of loyalty to the faith. A rosary rewritten by Henry Garnett and printed secretly in England c.1593 proclaimed the rosary's inclusive nature; it was for 'simpler sorte they which most please our Lady'.[46]

Conversely, around the same time the Catholic priest turned Puritan William Harrison wrote a polemical *Description of Britain*. Under the year 1389 he reports a debate over the Immaculate Conception among medieval scholars:

The friars preachers in France revive their old error as it is called whereby they affirm that the virgin Mary was conceived in sin . . . Jean Mautzor, a Dominican of Paris, was the chief maintainer of this doctrine, who at length was so handled that he was compelled before pope Innocent to recant his sayings which made very well for the minors who held that the virgin Mary was conceived without sin . . . But by a kiss only which Joachim gave unto her mother.[47]

The Immaculate Conception in particular, and Mary more generally, epitomized for those intent on polemic the worst errors and excesses of Catholic Christianity.

A millennium and a half after her emergence in the Holy Land, the figure of Mary was a global carrier of Christian meaning, in her seductive accessibility, in her hope-giving and consoling person. Mary was known all over the world, and nowhere was she ignored.

After Mary: A Conclusion

Tracing Mary's history has led us to reflect on the uses of the feminine in private yearnings and public supplications. It has shown us how the image of the mother – nurturing, suffering and bereaved – became the emblem of European and then world Christian cultures: an image of solace and of exhortation, looking over to admonish, looking on to comfort. Artists of all traditions, Catholics, Protestants and others, continued to reproduce Mary and her son in their making of images of both a loving and a suffering humanity.

Mary has not disappeared from the modern world of secular politics and personal liberation or from sometimes oppressive religious regimes. Her figure has not been lost, but transformed. Mary is present to visionaries in Rwanda, to modern pilgrims at Lourdes, in the feminist aspirations of American Catholics, and is ever-present in conversations aimed at ecumenical coming together. Those who proclaimed the death of God and the end of religion in the wake of the French Revolution and the liberal transformations of nineteenth-century states pronounced it prematurely.[1] Even the French Republic came to be captured by the female allegory of Liberty, which by 1792/3 was named Marianne; like the Virgin Mary this figure was to be seen everywhere – in villages and on street corners, on coins and, as a goddess, at the heart of rituals of the Religion of Reason. In dialectical rhythm, each affront to religious sensibilities seems only to have spurred believers into more elaborate attachments and aggressive assertions of their devotional habits.

Despite the presence of the feminine in symbols of statehood which echo the powerful figure of Mary, the nineteenth-century public world in Europe and America was very largely a world of men. States with secular constitutions, with modern economies, armies, bureaucracies,

cities and industry, imagined the citizen – soldier, peasant, professional or merchant – as a man among men. They were tax-paying, arms-bearing men, endowed with freedom of movement and of conscience. Such men played dramatic roles as players in imperial enterprises based upon the industrial transformations, and the exploitation of labour and the natural resources of subjugated people on a global scale. The modern world began as a world of men, propelled by science and technology. In its wake Christianity reached deeper and further into Africa and the Americas, but it was based on a separation of religion from the political sphere: in France, England, parts of Germany, Belgium, the Netherlands and in the US.

This separation led to a complex set of reactions from groups who were not fully drawn into the circle of politics and civic life, those marginalized by it. Women, priests and peasants led movements of Catholic and Protestant revival throughout the nineteenth century.[2] Some of the most arresting revelations and mass mystical experience since the medieval period were experienced in the middle decades of that century and produced Marian shrines to rival Rocamadour, Chartres and Loreto. The papacy affirmed the Immaculate Conception – a belief we have encountered throughout this book – as doctrine in 1854. In doing so it inspired clerical participation in new orders such as the Assumptionists, who originated in southern France, but also forged links with a popular folk Catholicism.[3]

One of the most spectacular signs of the Immaculist energy was the series of visions experienced by young Bernadette Soubirous in 1858 at Lourdes, in the foothills of the Pyrenees. A girl from a poor family, in a marginal region of France, encountered Mary and was urged by her in the local dialect to promote a new heavenly order of purity. At Lourdes feeling for Mary among the feminine and the abject, in marginal places, in terms alien to the official language of politics forced men – priests, doctors and scientists – to take heed. The village thereby became one of the world's greatest Mary shrines. This movement was led by Catholic aristocratic women and their clerical supporters, friars in religious orders, Mary's traditional devotees. Everything about Lourdes was a challenge to the state, to the science and the law on which it was based; it was also a challenge to the established church in France, which had reached a precarious coexistence within the republic. Enthusiasm and Mary cults authorized by popular dictate were not part of their scheme.[4]

The same phenomenon was happening all over Europe: Mary visions appeared to simple people, often to children – as they did in Marpingen in the Saarland in 1876 – exacerbating the conflict of church and state, upsetting the social order and the hierarchy of church authority.[5] For all that cities were centres for liberal and cosmopolitan cultures of commercial societies, large parts of Catholic Europe were enthralled by the excitement, reassurance and consolation of Mary visions in their midst.

In the age of machinery and industry artists and poets sometimes dwelt on Mary as they reflected on the locations of spirit in the new world of technology. The American man of letters Henry Adams (1838–1918) visited the World Exposition in Paris 1900 and was mesmerized by the new technology: the harnessing of electricity in dynamos. The vast Hall of the Dynamos inspired his admiration, but also unsettled him. While fathoming the dynamo it occurred to Adams that this invention resembled another force for which great architectural spaces were built and which had the power to move people across lands and continents, a force the operations of which he had seen on his visits to Chartres and to Lourdes – and that force was the Virgin Mary.[6] Adams was poised between the past he admired and the promise of the new. In his native Protestant Boston Mary was nothing but a rumoured superstition. That is why, he remarked, America did not celebrate femininity and fecundity as France did. This decent, learned man believed that 'An American virgin would never dare command'. How wrong he was in imagining the unfolding role of women and femininity in the coming century.

Another talented American, the Philadelphia painter Mary Cassatt, studied women and children of her family circle in Philadelphia. She was inspired by Italian Renaissance art, by the Madonnas of Correggio (1489–1534) and Parmigianino (1503–40), which she studied closely in Italy; by the magical flesh tones developed by Peter Paul Rubens (1577–1640) contemplated in Madrid and then in Antwerp.[7] Her *Baby's First Caress* of c.1891 captures the intimacy but also the inner worlds of mother and child, just as medieval artists so often dwelt on the interiority and subjectivity of Mary at scenes such as the Annunciation (without her son) and the Nativity.[8] Mary is a conduit towards the exploration of female subjectivity, far beyond the areas touched by traditions of affective Mary piety. These Protestant Americans saw in the rich traces of Mary – in Europe's architecture and panel painting – an

inspiration in reflecting on science, knowledge, family and subjectivity, within the modernity they observed so consciously all around them.

Women in this modern world were domestic creatures who nurtured the family, helped socialize the young and make of them citizens. They also provided religious education – their domains were *Küche und Kirche*. This powerful vision meant that women were relegated into the religious backwater, together with ministers and priests. Bourgeois women, who enjoyed leisure and economic wherewithal in Victorian Britain, the US or France inhabited a domain of sentimental exploration. They wrote diaries and poetry and adorned homes with elevating spiritual imagery.[9] They were the consumers of Mary; and as they taught their sons and daughters they explained her, conveying the image of unique pure maternity, through the linguistic and emotional tools of a real mother, flesh and blood.

Relegated to domestic spheres, Mary became refeminized, associated with the subaltern business of women: mothers, sisters, aunts, grandmothers. She also interested those who imagined the world beyond states: poets and revolutionaries, apocalyptic visionaries and, later, feminists. That domestic sphere of sentiment and habitual piety was ready to come alive in periods of crisis and trauma. The Franco-Prussian war and its enormities was the setting for the vision in the Northern French town of Pontmain in January 1871, where the fear of invasion was real. The two boys of the Barnadette family were working with their father in the barn when the eldest, twelve years old, saw against the night sky a vision of Mary in her black robe, crowned in gold and wearing a black veil. She carried a crucifix, her suffering son, and encouraged the children to pray for his compassion.[10] The village and its men in uniform were all spared. News of these eruptions of the holy in old Catholic regions travelled quickly and widely, especially through the new forms of communication and travel – telegraph, photography, steam boats crisscrossing the Atlantic – and inspired the mass production of mementos for the vast and growing American Catholic market. American homes – from gracious mansions to modest tenements – were decorated with prints and statuary, as they still are.[11]

The next great trauma of all was that of the Great War (1914–18), a war which devastated Europe's families, demography and landscape. With husbands, fathers, brothers and sons at the front, Europe's women used every sacred medal, prayer and ritual they could muster. Mary

was the most important intercessor from whom protection and consolation were sought by those at the front. Soldiers left messages on the altars of churches near the battlefields, in the hope that these would reach Mary. The Virgin of Lourdes was the most common addressee of those soldiers in the French trenches. Many asked for deliverance, and to see their 'little family' again, like the soldier whose letter was found in 1915 on the altar of the sanctuary at Noulette, at the foot of the Lorette hill:

Our Lady of Lourdes I turn to you so you can give me the grace of coming home some day to my little home with my whole little family how far away I am. Preserve me against the disasters I see every day, and I beg you, stop at last this terrible carnage that makes so many corpses.[12]

Practically every parish in France has its own war memorial, so often a carved image of the Pietà: Mary holds her dead son, sometimes a soldier in uniform.[13] Mary emerged as a necessary link with the dead, and an effective consoler of the living. The French poet Paul Claudel (1868–1955) even saw in the War a struggle between 'sombre Germany', a Protestant nation that detested Mary, and Mary's devotees, the French, like himself.[14]

Protestant cultures too exhibited a new openness to forms of intercession and lament associated with Catholic practice. European cultures since the First World War have been marked by Catholic iconography and rituals of death, with Mary at their heart. The German artist Käthe Kollwitz (1867–1945) explored her own loss – her son died in the Great War – in a series of statues and prints made in the 1930s, as she contemplated her country's descent into violence. These are Pietàs revisited, and her mourners are peasant women, quintessential European mothers. Kollwitz's *Mother with her Dead Son* serves as a focus for remembrance in the *Neue Wache* in Berlin – the central memorial of the Federal Republic of Germany for the victims of war and tyranny, rededicated in 1993.

To the cause of Mary rallied disaffected French citizens, whose world had collapsed in the liberal order of the French Republic, as well as German Catholics within the new united Germany after 1870. Mary expressed the grief of the indigenous peoples of Colombia and Peru who lived and still live in poverty and powerlessness in states where church and state maintained fear-inducing pacts of mutual interest. The

attachment to Mary was not even then wrested away. As the people of Central and Latin America trod the routes of migration they brought with them the magic of Mary to California and Texas and New Mexico.[15]

In Catholic countries artists continue to use traditional forms to probe the location of femininity and the holy in the nation state. The Colombian Fernando Botero's (b. 1932) whimsical paintings cast life in modern Colombia as interactions between rotund people – just as Giacometti preferred the elongated shape before him – at play, at table and in intimate social interactions. His *Our Lady of Colombia* of 1967 draws on the rich Andean painting traditions by placing a large Mary between minute figures of priest and state official, against the background of four Colombian flags. The image is tender, but it is an open question not a devotional statement.[16] Based on the iconography of the *Virgin of Pachamama*, this satirical portrayal of 'order' in a state so devoid of order makes us think again about those older formal portrayals of the order of Pachamama, the mountain poised between viceregal authority and native ownership of the silver mountain cast as Mary.

The habits developed in the nineteenth century, of apocalyptic devotional mobilization around shrines, in reaction to perceived attacks by liberal and democratic movements, served some Catholics well during the 'Godless' twentieth.[17] The Russian Revolution and the world order which emerged after the Second World War found Catholics in Ireland, the United States and France full of renewed purpose.[18] Sodalities – voluntary organizations focused on a devotional theme – aimed to redress the deficit caused by state atheism in Poland, Hungary, Romania and East Germany. New orders such as *Opus dei* in 1928 were developed in the fight against 'communism'. The Marian revelations to children at Fatima in Portugal in 1917 sought to mobilize and console communities of faith in a world threatened again – as it was after 1789 – by the politics of modernity, in which the church was an organ of the body politic, not its head.[19] In those political movements, where fascism and Catholicism worked hand in hand – Salazar's Portugal, Franco's Spain – Mary was disseminated again as a model for women as mothers and wives.[20] The paintings of the Portuguese artist Paula Rego (b. 1935), who works in London, contest the images of women that fascist regimes had sought to imprint on Portuguese people throughout the twentieth century: her images of women's solitary pleasure, and pain, the suggestion of sexual desire and fulfilment, the violence of childbirth all question

and defy the wholesome continuity between mother and son which Catholic devotional practice – in word and image – offered Portuguese women.[21]

The portrayal of Mary as national symbol in Catholic states is particularly intriguing since she was experienced as so domestic a figure in Catholic cultures. The Irish poet Seamus Heaney (b. 1939) describes that world of mother's devotions, imparted to him, the eldest, and his eight siblings. He comments on this early influence:

My sensibility was formed by the dolorous murmurings of the rosary, and the generally Marian quality of devotion. The reality that was addressed was maternal, and the posture was one of supplication . . . The attitude to life that was inculcated into me – not by priests, but by the active, lived thing of prayers and so on, in my house through my mother – was really patience . . . In practice, the shrines, the rosary beads, all the devotions, were centred towards a feminine presence, which I think was terrific for the sensibility. I think that 'Hail Mary' is more of a poem than the 'Our Father'. 'Our Father' is between chaps, but there is something faintly amorous about the 'Hail Mary'.[22]

Twenty-first-century artists continue to engage with the world of affect and emotion, the perplexing spirituality of the late medieval Mary. Bill Viola restages the bodies of contemporary men and women who enact scenes of love and lament inspired by the religious art of late medieval Europe. His *The Greeting*, a twenty-five-minute-long video installation, first exhibited in the Venice Biennale in 1995, restages the meeting of Mary and her kinswoman Elizabeth as an encounter between young and old. These are figures of warmth and colour in a mundane street, an eruption of recognition and friendship. It reminds us of the medieval art we know, and it offers a wholly different level of intimacy with the encounter.[23] The American novelist David Guterson (b. 1956) imagined in *Our Lady of the Forest* (2003) how an experience in a forest clearing could offer dignity and purpose to the sixteen-year-old homeless Ann Holmes. Sexually abused and dependent on drugs, this runaway victim travels the Pacific Northwest and supports herself by selling magic mushrooms. On one picking foray into the forest she experiences a vision of Mary and receives the command that a chapel be built on that spot in the forest.[24]

Similarly secluded is the chapel indeed built in a clearing on the hillside above the village of Larrivière in the Adour Valley in south-west France.

It is dedicated to Notre Dame de Rugby: the stained glass window has Mary and her son holding a rugby ball, as six men in colourful sports gear strive to reach the ball. Artists and writers still find in Mary a subject that defies genre and tests new formats and technologies. Such creativity exists alongside the continuous lived experience of devotional culture – expressed and documented in film, graffiti, street art, in venerable marble, but even more commonly in plastic and paper.

Mary is now probably most vibrantly present in the lives of Catholics in Africa and the Americas. As we have seen in this book – in Egypt and Ethiopia and West Africa – Mary's presence there was long-standing. When colonial powers scrambled for Africa in the nineteenth century they often met the traces of earlier encounters with Mary. In Nyasaland the Barure called the ancestress to whom first fruits were offered 'Maria'; 'Mother Maria' was also invoked in devotional chants. The regal Mary fitted in well with local matrilineal sensibilities. When missionaries introduced the disciplines of the rosary and membership in the cohorts of the Slaves of Mary (*Les esclaves de Marie*), daughters of respected families – of village headmen – were particularly drawn to the challenge and distinction of such association.[25]

Colonial powers ceded to African nation states a subtle reworking of Christianity. Mary was not a public symbol, but within Catholic communities – like those of the Bemba-speaking people of Zambia – habits of devotional association were sometimes put to political use. The Legion of Mary, a system of local women's groups that adhered to the litany of Mary, resembled the rosary confraternities of fifteenth-century Germany or seventeenth-century Brazil. Rosary prayer required no reading, and it mobilized an aggressive, even martial, language that appealed to the Bemba. Mary waged war against evil, and she was greeted in traditional manner:

> Who is she!
> Who comes forth
> As the morning light
> Beautiful as the moon
> Bright as the sun
> Terrible as an army
> Set in battle array.[26]

The words of the Revelation (12:1) combined with the Bemba reverence for female ancestors. The *Legion of Mary* confronted physically as well as legally the practitioners of traditional ancestor worship and refused to contribute financially to the support of rituals of expiation, what Catholics considered to be 'divine tribute' offered to mere humans.[27] Most members of the Legion were women, and its groupings became the core of evolving parishes in cities too. Women – devotees of Mary – became and remain central to the life of the Zambian church.

African visions of Mary exist within that continent and without in the post-colonial world. The British artist Chris Ofili (*b.* 1968) imagined the *Holy Virgin Mary* in 1996: Mary is black, her lips are thick and sensuous, her hair is dark. Her breast shows through the blue dress, and it is made of elephant dung, a material sometimes used in African ritual. Like so many icons of Mary, the background is gold, textured with enamel and glitter. Against it Mary is surrounded by tens of images of female genitalia, attached in collage, like the angels of traditional iconography. Ofili uses well the European traditions of Mary and tests them – as so many artists did before him – through the use of unusual materials, by making Mary African. He forces the question: when does an image of Mary stop being an image of Mary?[28]

Mary's diverse qualities – mother and virgin, chaste and fertile, chosen and modest – made her an effective symbol for diverse communities of Christianity. In May 2005 a Working Party of the Anglican–Roman Catholic International Commission published its report, *Mary: Grace and Hope in Christ*; Mary is identified as a shared symbol suggestive of the possibilities for greater closeness between Catholics and Anglicans.[29]

As in most areas of life the US offers a cornucopia of images and experiences of Mary. Its vast Catholic population (some 24 million adults, and 50 million overall) spans the most traditional to the most eclectic. Hispanic Americans have made the Lady of Guadalupe central to the religious culture of the west and south-west, but also beyond. Following a call by Pope John Paul II in 1979, that the image of Mary will 'illuminate the entire world', 220 replicas of the Guadalupe image were consecrated at the basilica in Mexico City and spread to every country. The relic went on tour in the United States, visiting Catholic communities old and new. Catholic parishes founded by missionaries in the seventeenth century among Native Americans of the Great Lakes – like La Crosse, Wisconsin – were on its trail.[30] Hispanic Americans now

set the tone in the American west and south-west: festivals of religious chalk paintings – *I Madonnari* – take pace in Santa Barbara and San Luis Obispo in California and in Tucson in Arizona. The most common figure is, as it was, the Virgin Mary.[31]

Such an embrace of Mary is countered by the powerful voices of Catholic women. Scholars and activists see the Mary tradition so closely linked with a history of subjugation and subordination as to make it unfit as a vehicle for the successful integration of women into contemporary Catholicism.[32] As this book has shown, Mary was made in important ways by men and is thus rejected by some as a route to the exploration of femininity and spirituality. The rise of mass feminism in the second half of the twentieth century forced reflection on the nature of femininity in all its forms, and often through the visuals of film, of demonstrations, of defiant gestures, of logos and emblems. Like all cultural processes feminist public gestures draw upon the old, subverting or rededicating existing words, shapes and sounds. And so Mary has been truly rediscovered through a feminist sensibility: sometimes by writers and artists familiar with the Catholic heritage – Germaine Greer, Marina Warner – but in the US and Europe by Protestant, Jewish and agnostic women who continue to interrogate the feminine through her ample possibilities. In the churches some feminists see in Mary a barrier to liberation, but others seek to seize Mary as a powerful example for women and for the churches: of love and faith, of charity and nurture.

Mary is discovered and rediscovered by Catholics and other Christians, but also outside those faith traditions. Just as we have seen in the earlier centuries, poets marvelled and imagined her as a key to understanding mysteries of creativity and love, captured so powerfully in maternity. Male poets were often attached to the image of her continuous and unfailing acts of giving and tried to imagine how it must have felt. Rainer-Marie Rilke (1875–1926) composed a poetic cycle of the life of Mary, begun in 1900 and inspired by sketches by Heinrich Vögler. Mary's body is a wonder in the landscape, physically present, formally introduced, respectfully, by the beholder, the third person poet-narrator, who describes the Visitation as a landscape within which Mary sensed the heaviness of her pregnant body as 'panting then she stood upon the lofty/Judean hills'. Her condition also inspires amity towards Elizabeth, whose body was 'still more ripe than hers. / And they both

tottered toward one another / and touched each other's garments and hair'.[33] The Irish poet W. B. Yeats (1865–1939) imagined some of the inner turmoil of Mary at the Annunciation, in his 'Mother of God' of 1933:

> The threefold terror of love, a fallen flare
> Through the hollow of an ear;
> Wings beating about the room;
> The terror of all terrors that I bore
> The Heavens in my womb.

Like so many paintings of this moment, Gabriel's message is often depicted as a ray of sunshine entering Mary's womb, or indeed her ear: that is enough to terrify! Then there is the noisy appearance of an angel; and finally the unexpected pregnancy, and what a pregnancy! Yeats' Mary is alarmed by her historic tasks and wonders why she was chosen for it. Wasn't she happy enough with the routines of women's work?

> Had I not found content among the shows
> Every common woman knows,
> Chimney corner, garden walk,
> Or rocky cistern where we tread the clothes
> And gather all the talk?

She then turns to the son whom she bore and nurtured and loves:

> What is this flesh I purchased with my pains,
> This fallen star my milk sustains,
> This love that makes my heart's blood stop
> Or strikes a sudden chill into my bones
> And bids my hair stand up?[34]

We move closer to Mary's inner life in this twentieth-century poetry, a maternal life marked by a love that 'strikes a sudden chill' and makes her 'hair stand up'. The American poet Sylvia Plath (1932–63) expresses this sense in her poem 'Love Letter' (1960), dedicated to her daughter. It opens:

> Not easy to state the change you made.
> If I'm alive now, then I was dead.

And it ends:

> Now I resemble a sort of god
> Floating through the air in my soul-shift
> Pure as a pane of ice. It's a gift.[35]

The mother as a god, in Plath's words, is one of the potent realizations in the figure of Mary. The Christian story allowed this unuttered sense to unfold and could not deny it. The woman who bore God was exalted; and so might every woman who bears a child become a maker of life – a god.

In Christianity was created 'the most refined construct in which femininity . . . is focussed on *Maternality*'.[36] Mary was made into daughter and sister and bride, but these were ultimately subordinate to the mother – life-giver and mourner. For in woman's capacity to act as generous host, to contain a body in her body, there is an act of tremendous hospitality: the act is so great that it often threatens to destroy the mother herself. This is a truth which so many myths and rituals act to deny as they establish the authority of fathers.[37] It is one which the infinite meanings of Mary, the many voices and shapes which she has taken in different historical contexts, make abundantly clear.

A Few Comments on Scholarship and Reading

In an essay of 1977 Janet Nelson opined that when 'one day some bold historian takes up the challenge' of writing a 'definitive' history of the Virgin's cult this enterprise will require attention to a long period and will rely on a few seminal books.[1] One such book is Marina Warner's much-loved *Alone of All Her Sex*, an imaginative exploration on the meaning of Mary to the lives of women over the centuries, based on a wide range of literary, artistic and theological sources. Never out of print, this book has introduced Catholic women to ways of thinking about their heritage and their feminism.[2] In subsequent work Marina Warner has continued to explore the ways in which narrative and image capture and convey the operations of gender and human anxiety about the unknown and the unknowable. Jiri Pelikan's *Mary through the Centuries* explores the traditions of theological reflection on Mary over twenty centuries. He interprets theology in a capacious way and includes hymns and religions poetry, some drama and imagery too. Klaus Schreiner has similarly offered a sensitive survey of the theological ideas and devotional practices which the Virgin Mary inspired among medieval Europeans.[3]

Caroline Walker Bynum has exemplified and taught new ways of considering medieval religious cultures. Her historical writing about the inner lives of medieval women has uncovered their deep attachment to Christ of the Passion and the Eucharist; it has also sympathetically shown the Virgin Mary to be model and companion to women, religious as well as lay.[4] Rachel Fulton's reflection of the intellectual-religious cultures of the high medieval centuries, *From Judgement of Compassion*, offers a subtle analysis of the move from a Christ-centred sensibility to one in which Christ is perceived through the compassionate gaze of his mother.[5] I have chosen to mention these books among many others with admiration and thanks, for they helped plot this book's terrain. I also wish to mention Susan Boynton and Christopher Page, whose generosity and example have helped me understand Mary as song.

The following list of books and articles is a preliminary orientation towards the scholarship that addresses the historical understanding of the figure of Mary.

HISTORICAL STUDIES, BEFORE 1000

Clayton, Mary, *The Cult of the Virgin Mary in Anglo-Saxon England*, Cambridge, 1990.

Clayton, Mary, *The Apocryphal Gospels of Mary in Anglo-Saxon England*, Cambridge 1998.

Shoemaker, Stephen, *The Ancient Traditions of the Virgin Mary's Dormition and Assumption*, Oxford, 2002; repr. 2005.

HISTORICAL STUDIES, AFTER 1000

Burkhart, Louise M., *Before Guadalupe: The Virgin Mary in Early Colonial Nahuatl Literature*, Albany, 2001.

Ellington, Donna Spivey, *From Sacred Body to Angelic Soul: Understanding Mary in Late Medieval and Early Modern Europe*, Washington, DC, 2001.

Gold, Penny Schine, *The Lady and the Virgin: Image, Attitude, and Experience in Twelfth-Century France*, Chicago, 1985.

Heal, Bridget, *The Cult of the Virgin Mary in Early Modern Germany: Protestant and Catholic Piety, 1500–1648*, Cambridge, 2007.

Kreitzer, Beth, *Reforming Mary: Changing Images of the Virgin Mary in Lutheran Sermons of the Sixteenth Century*, New York, 2004.

COLLECTED ESSAYS

Abbild oder Vorbild? Zur Sozialgeschichte mittelalterlicher Marienverehrung, eds. Hedwig Röckelein, Claudia Opitz, Dieter R. Bauer, Tübingen, 1990.

The Church and Mary, ed. R. N. Swanson, Woodbridge, 2006.

Maria in der Welt: Marienverehrung im Kontext der Sozialgeschichte, 10–18. Jahrhundert, ed. Claudia Opitz, Zurich, 1993.

Marie: Le Culte de la vierge dans la société médiévale, eds. Dominique Iogna-Prat, Eric Palazzo and Danile Russo, Paris, 1996.

POETRY

Flory, David A., *Marian Representation in the Miracle Tales of Thirteenth-Century Spain and France*, Washington, DC, 2000.

Goering, Joseph, *The Virgin and the Grail: Origins of a Legend*, New Haven, 2005.

Newman, Barbara, *Frauenlob's Song of Songs: A Medieval German Poet and His Masterpiece*, Philadelphia, 2006.

O'Sullivan, Daniel, *Marian Devotion in Thirteenth-Century French Lyric*, Toronto, 2005.

MUSIC

Fassler, Margot, 'Mary's Nativity, Fulbert of Chartres, and the Stirps Jesse: Liturgical Innovation circa 1000 and Its Afterlife', *Speculum* 75 (2000), pp. 389–434.

Huot, Sylvia, *Allegorical Play in the Old French Motet: The Sacred and the Profane in Thirteenth-Century Polyphony*, Stanford, 1997.

Rothenberg, David J., 'The Marian Symbolism of Spring, ca. 1200–ca. 1500: Two Case Studies', *Journal of the American Musicological Society* 59 (2006), pp. 319–98.

ART

Damian, Carol, *The Virgin of the Andes: Art and Ritual in Colonial Cuzco*, Grassfield, 1995.

Forsyth, Irene H., *The Throne of Wisdom: Wood Sculptures of the Madonna in Romanesque France*, Princeton, 1972.

Mother of God: Representations of the Virgin in Byzantine Art, ed. Maria Vassilaki, Milan, 2000.

Murray, Stephen, *A Gothic Sermon: Making a Contract with the Mother of God, Saint Mary of Amiens*, Berkeley, 2004.

Purtle, Carol J., *The Marian Paintings of Jan van Eyck*, Princeton, 1982.

Stratton, Suzanne L., The *Immaculate Conception in Spanish Art*, New York, 1994.

Wright, Rosemary Muir, *Sacred Distance: Representing the Virgin in Italian Altarpieces, c.1300–c.1630*, Manchester, 2006.

Notes

Writing about Mary: An Introduction

1. For a few ideas on the artist and Catholic culture see John Fiske, 'Madonna', in *Reception Studies: From Literary Theory to Cultural Studies*, eds. James L. Machor and Philip Goldstein, New York and London, 2001, esp. pp. 250–205.
2. *Guardian*, 29 October 2005, p. 6. A Holy Toast bread press, which reproduced the image, soon followed, at £5.99.

PART I: FROM TEMPLE MAIDEN TO THE BEARER OF GOD: TO THE YEAR 431

Chapter 1: The Earliest Glimpses of Mary

1. Daniel Boyarin, 'Semantic Differences; or, "Judaism" / "Christianity"', in *The Ways That Never Parted: Jews and Christians in Late Antiquity and the Early Middle Ages*, eds. Adam H. Becker and Annette Yoshiko Reed, Texts and Studies in Ancient Judaism 95, Tübingen, 2003, pp. 65–86.
2. Amnon Linder, '*Ecclesia* and *Synagoga* in the Medieval Myth of Constantine the Great', *Revue Belge d'Histoire et de Philosophie* 54 (1976), pp. 1,019–1,060, at pp. 1,022–7.
3. On Jewish-Christian communities see Simon Claude Mimouni, *Les Chrétiens d'origine juive dans l'antiquité*, Paris, 2004; on the aftermath of the Revolt see Martin Goodman, *Rome and Jerusalem: The Clash of Ancient Civilizations*, London, 2007, pp. 11–29.
4. Peter Brown, *Authority and the Sacred*, Cambridge, 1995, p. 3.
5. On Jewish identity and Romanness see Goodman, *Rome and Jerusalem*, pp. 163–94.
6. M. D. Goulder, *Midrash and Lection in Matthew*, Speaker's Lectures in Biblical Studies, University of Oxford, Faculty of Theology, 1969–71, London, 1974, pp. 54–7.
7. James D. G. Dunn, *Jesus Remembered*, Grand Rapids and Cambridge, 2003, pp. 339–44.
8. Maarten J. J. Menken, 'Fulfillment of Scripture as a Propaganda Tool in Early Christianity', in *Persuasion and Dissuasion in Early Christianity, Ancient Judaism, and Hellenism*, eds. Pieter W. van der Horst et al., Louvain, 2003, pp. 178–98, at pp. 180, 186.
9. Larry W. Hurtado, *Lord Jesus Christ: Devotion to Jesus in Earliest Christianity*, Grand Rapids, 2003, p. 328.
10. On eyewitness accounts and the making of the gospels see Richard Bauckham, *Jesus and the Eyewitnesses: The Gospels as Eyewitness Testimony*, Grand Rapids and Cambridge, 2006; on the heritage of Sarah, see Joshua Levinson, 'Bodies and Bo(a)rders: Emerging Fictions of Identity in Late Antiquity', *Harvard Theological Review* 93 (2000), pp. 343–72, at pp. 352–65.
11. Nicholas de Lange, 'A Woman in Israel', in *Mary's Place in Christian Dialogue:*

Occasional Papers of the Ecumenical Society of the Blessed Virgin Mary, ed. Alberic Stacpoole, Slough, 1982, pp. 192–201, at p. 199.

12. Hurtado, *Lord Jesus Christ*, p. 191.

13. Martin Morard, '*L'Instruction sur le ministère des hymnes et de la louange* de Nicétas de Rémésiana (†vers 414)', in *La Prière en latin, de l'antiquité au XVIe siècle: Formes, évolutions, significations*, ed. Jean-François Cottier, Turnhout, 2006, pp. 393–417, at pp. 396–7.

14. In a letter to the community of Smyrna in Asia Minor, the Syrian bishop Ignatius of Antioch (d.107) led back to the House of David, David Flusser (in collaboration with R. Steven Notley), *Jesus*, Jerusalem, 1997, p. 25.

15. The traditions about Paul's preaching were crystallized in the second century in the *Acts of Paul*, which commends 'Mary the Galilean' for her acceptance of the Holy Spirit: *New Testament Apocrypha* II, ed. Wilhelm Schneemelcher and trans. R. McL. Wilson, London, 1965, p. 382; Judith M. Lieu, *Image and Reality: The Jews in the World of the Christians in the Second Century*, Edinburgh, 1996, p. 173.

16. On hints about the contents of Jewish-Christian gospels that no longer survive see A. F. J. Klijn, *Jewish-Christian Gospel Tradition*, Leiden, 1992, esp. chapter 1.

17. Guy G. Stroumsa, 'Christ's Laughter: Docetic Origins Reconsidered', *Journal of Early Christian Studies* 12 (2004), pp. 267–88. The literal meaning of Isaac in Hebrew is 'he who will laugh'.

18. Peter Brown, *The Body and Society: Men, Women and Sexual Renunciation in Early Christianity*, New York, 1988, p. 40.

19. Averil Cameron, *Christianity and the Rhetoric of Empire: The Development of Christian Discourse*, Berkeley, 1991, pp. 98–100.

20. 'The Protoevangelium of James', ed. O. Cullmann, in *New Testament Apocrypha*, I, ed. W. Schneemelcher and trans. R. McL. Wilson, Louisville, 1991, pp. 370–88; on the place of composition see Emile de Strycker, *La forme la plus ancienne du protévangile de Jacques*, Brussels, 1961, pp. 419–23. On the *Protoevangelium* see Bart D. Ehrman, *Lost Christianities: the Battle for Scripture and the Faiths we Never Knew*, Oxford, 2003, pp. 207–210.

21. For discussion of apocrypha see Simon C. Mimouni, 'Le Concept d'apocryphité dans le christianisme ancien et médiéval: Réflexions en guise d'introduction', in *Apocryphité: Histoire d'un concept transversal aux religions du livre: en hommage à Pierre Geoltrain*, ed. Simon Claude Mimouni, Turnhout, 2002, pp. 1–21, esp. pp. 4–6. I have benefited greatly from illuminating conversation with György Geréby, of the Central European University, who is preparing a critical edition of the *Protoevangelium of James*.

22. 'The Protoevangelium of James', 1:1–2, p. 374; B. Dehandschutter, 'Anti-Judaism in the Apocrypha', in *Studia Patristica* 19, ed. Elizabeth Livingstone, Leuven, 1985, pp. 345–50, at p. 346.

23. 'The Protoevangelium of James', 4:1; and 5:2, pp. 376 and 377.

24. Ibid., 6:1, p. 377.

25. Edouard Cothenet, 'Le Protévangile de Jacques: Origine, genre et signification d'un premier midrash chrétien sur la Nativité de Marie', in *Aufstieg und Niedergang der römischen Welt: Geschichte und Kultur Roms im Spiegel der neueren Forschung*, ed. W. Haase, Berlin and New York, 1988, II 25.6, pp. 4,252–69.

26. 'The Protoevangelium of James' 8:2–3, pp. 378–9; Daniel Stökl Ben Ezra, *The Impact of Yom Kippur on Early Christianity: The Day of Atonement from Second Temple Judaism to the Fifth Century*, Tübingen, 2003, p. 251.

27. 'The Protoevangelium of James', 9.1, p. 379.

28. Ibid., 10.1, pp. 379–80.

29. On Mary's work in the Temple see Frédéric Manns, 'Une ancienne tradition sur la Jeunesse de Marie', in Frédéric Manns, *Essais sur le Judéo-Christianisme*, Analecta studium biblicum franciscanum 12, Jerusalem, 1977, pp. 106–14. A similar tradition, from another

contemporary culture, was the weaving of Athene's garments by 120 girls aged between seven and eleven, *Etymologium magnum*, mxlix, 91.

30. *Tosephta Moed, Masekhet Shekalim*, ed. Saul Liebermann, New York, 1962, 3.13, pp. 215–16.

31. I am indebted here to my colleague Dr Aharon Oppenheimer of Tel Aviv University.

32. *Die Geschichte von Joseph dem Zimmermann*, ed. S. Morenz, Berlin, 1951. See the Arabic translation in *Edizione critica del testo arabo della Historia Iosephi Fabri Lignarii e ricerche sulla sua origine*, eds. A. Battista and B. Bagatti, Studium biblicum franciscanum collectio minor 20, Jerusalem, 1978; see also Frédéric Manns, 'Le Portrait de Joseph dans L'Histoire de Joseph le Charpentier', in *Essais sur le Judéo-Christianisme*, Jerusalem, 1977, pp. 94–105.

33. *Die Geschichte*, c. ix, line 2, p. 4.

34. Ibid., c. xvi, lines 1–4, p. 8.

35. Ibid., c. xxvi, line 1, p. 22.

36. Majella Franzmann, *Jesus in the Nag Hammadi Writings*, Edinburgh, 1996, pp. 48–9.

37. Aristide di Atene, *Apologia*, ed. Carlotta Alpigiano, Florence, 1988; see, for example, cs. 15–17, pp. 114–27.

38. *An Early Christian Philosopher: Justin Martyr's Dialogue with Trypho, Chapters One to Nine*, ed. J. C. M. van Winden, Leiden, 1971, see introduction, pp. 1–5, and esp. pp. 118–25; on Justin see Peter Brown, *The Body and Society*, pp. 33–4.

39. Joseph Vogt, *Ancient Slavery and the Ideal of Man*, trans. Thomas Wiedemann, Oxford, 1974, pp. 154–5. Michael Frede, 'Origen's Treatise *Against Celsus*', in *Apologetics in the Roman Empire: Pagans, Jews and Christians*, eds. Mark Edwards, Martin Goodman and Simon Price, Oxford, 1999, pp. 131–55.

40. Augustine, 'De carne Christi' 17, *Patrologia Latina* (hereafter *PL*) 2, cols. 751–92, at cols. 781–2.

41. Origen, *Contra Celsum*, trans. with an introduction Henry Chadwick, Cambridge, 1980, I, c. 28; I, c. 32; Michael Frede, 'Origen's Treatise *Against Celsus*', *Apologetics in the Roman Empire: Pagans, Jews and Christians*, ed. Mark Edwards, Martin Goodman and Simon Price with Christopher Rowland, Oxford, 1995, pp. 131–55; Paula Fredriksen and Oded Irshai, 'Christian Anti-Judaism: Polemics and Policies', in *The Cambridge History of Judaism*, IV, ed. Steven T. Katz, Cambridge, 2006, pp. 977–1,035.

42. Peter Shäffer, *Jesus in the Talmud*, Princeton, 2007, pp. 15–24.

43. Origen, *Contra Celsum*, I, cs. 37, 39.

44. By Rufinus *c.*410 in Sicily, and Jerome, see Origen, *The Song of Songs Commentary and Homilies*, trans. and annotated. R. P. Lawson, Ancient Christian Writers 26, Westminster, MD, 1957, p. 4; Origen, *Homiliae in Canticum canticorum*, in *Origenes Werke*, VIII, ed. W. A. Baehrens, Leipzig, 1925, pp. 26–60.

45. Andrew Carriker, *The Library of Euesebius of Caesarea*, Leiden, 2003, p. 126.

46. Ephraim E. Urbach, 'The Homiletical Interpretation of the Sages and the Expositions of Origen on Canticles, and the Jewish-Christian Disputation', *Scripta hierosolymitana* 22, Jerusalem, 1971, pp. 247–75, at pp. 249–52.

47. Reuven Kimelman, 'Rabbi Yohanan and Origen on the Song of Songs: A Third-Century Jewish-Christian Disputation', *Harvard Theological Review* 73 (1980), pp. 567–95, at p. 580.

48. Origen, *The Song of Songs*, p. 293.

49. Ibid., pp. 302–3.

50. Ann Matter, *The Voice of My Beloved: The Song of Songs in Western Medieval Christianity*, Philadelphia, 1990, pp. 20–34.

51. Mark Edwards, 'The Flowering of Latin Apologetics: Lactantius and Arnobius', in *Apologetics in the Roman Empire: Pagans, Jews and Christians*, eds. Mark Edwards, Martin Goodman and Simon Price, Oxford, 1999, pp. 179–221, at pp. 202–3.

52. On competition over the magical power of Judaism and Christianity see Elhanan Reiner,

'The Seal of Christos and the Potion that Failed', in *Continuity and Renewal: Jews and Judaism in Byzantine-Christian Palestine*, ed. Israel L. Levine, Jerusalem, 2004, pp. 355–86.

Chapter 2: Mary in a Christian Empire

1. On policies towards Christianity leading up to Constantine see J. H. W. G. Liebeschutz, *Continuity and Change in Roman Religion*, Oxford, 1979, pp. 232–52; see also Goodman, *Rome and Jerusalem*, pp. 539–48.

2. On emperor worship and Christianity see R. MacMullen, *Christianity and Paganism in the Fourth to Eighth Centuries*, New Haven, 1997, pp. 34–5.

3. Rowan Williams, *Arius. Heresy and Tradition*, 2nd edn, London, 2001.

4. J. N. D. Kelly, *Early Christian Creeds*, 2nd edn, London, 1960, p. 210.

5. *Aithallae episcopi edesseni epistola ad Christianos in persarum regione de fide*, ed. Johannes Thorossian, Venice, 1942, p. 75.

6. J. N. D. Kelly, *Early Christian Creeds*, 3rd edn, London, 1972, chapter 7, pp. 205–16.

7. Oded Irshai, 'Confronting a Christian Empire: Jewish Culture in the World of Byzantium', in *Cultures of the Jews: A New History*, ed. David Biale, New York, 2002, pp. 181–202, esp. pp. 193–204; see in that volume also Eric M. Meyers, 'Jewish Culture in Greco-Roman Palestine', pp. 166–74.

8. E. Leigh Gibson, 'Jewish Antagonism or Christian Polemic: The Case of *The Martyrdom of Pionius*', *Journal of Early Christian Studies* 9 (2001), pp. 339–58, at p. 349; see also E. D. Hunt, *Holy Land Pilgrimage in the Later Roman Empire AD 312–460*, Oxford, 1982, p. 101.

9. Jane Taylor, *Christians and the Holy Places*, Oxford, 1993, pp. 95–112 (Bethlehem), pp. 113–42 (Golgotha). On the Jews in the Christian Empire see Guy G. Stroumsa, 'Religious Dynamics between Christianity and Jews in Late Antiquity (312–640)', in *The Cambridge History of Christianity*, II, ed. Augustine Casiday and Frederick W. Norris, Cambridge, 2007, pp. 151–72. On the polemical contest in Jerusalem see Linder, '*Ecclesia* and *Synagoga*', pp. 1033–60.

10. *Egeria's Travels*, trans. John Wilkinson, 3rd edn, Warminster, 1999.

11. David Brakke, *Athanasius and the Politics of Asceticism*, Oxford, 1995, Appendix B, Second Letter to Virgins, pp. 292–302, at p. 292.

12. Georgia Frank, *The Memory of the Eyes: Pilgrims to Living Saints in Christian Late Antiquity*, Berkeley, 2000, p. 106.

13. G. G. Stroumsa, ' "Vetus Israel": Les juifs dans la littérature hiérosolymitaine d'époque byzantine', *Revue de l'histoire des religions* 205 (1988), pp. 115–31, at p. 127.

14. Antoine Paulin, *Saint Cyrille de Jérusalem catéchète*, Paris, 1959, pp. 80–81; P. W. L. Walker, *Holy City, Holy Places: Christian Attitudes to Jerusalem and the Holy Land in the Fourth Century*, Oxford, 1990, pp. 116–22.

15. Averil Cameron, 'The Virgin in Late Antiquity', *Studies in Church History* 39 (2004), pp. 1–21, at pp. 5–6; Benedicta Ward, *Harlots of the Desert: A Study of Repentance in Early Monastic Sources*, Kalamazoo, 1987; for Perpetua see *The Acts of the Christian Martyrs*, ed. Herbert Musurillo, Oxford, 1972, pp. 106–31.

16. *The Panarion of St Epiphanius of Salamis* I, ed. and trans. Frank Williams, Leiden, 1994, pp. 112–19, esp. pp. 112–15.

17. Ibid., pp. 270–71.

18. Ibid., p. 601.

19. Ibid., p. 621.

20. Ibid.

21. Robin Lane Fox, *Pagans and Christians*, Harmondsworth, 1986, pp. 311–12.

22. V. E. F. Harrison, 'Gender, Generation and Virginity in Cappadocian Theology', *Journal of Theological Studies* new series 47 (1996), pp. 38–68.

23. Brouria Bitton-Ashkelony and Aryeh Kofsky, 'Monasticism in the Holy Land', in *Christians and Christianity in the Holy Land: From the Origins to the Latin Kingdoms*, ed. Ora Limor and Guy Stroumsa, Turnhout, 2006, pp. 253–87, at pp. 260–70.

24. Fox, *Pagans and Christians*, pp. 359–60.

25. *Athanasius and the Politics of Asceticism*, ed. David Brakke, Oxford, 1995, Appendix A, First Letter to Virgins, pp. 274–91, at pp. 277–8; George E. Demacopoulos, *Five Models of Spiritual Direction in the Early Church*, Notre Dame, 2007, pp. 40–42; Susanna Elm, '*Virgins of God': The Making of Asceticism in Late Antiquity*, Oxford, 1994, pp. 336–7.

26. J. Lebon, 'Athanasiaca syriaca', *Le Muséon* 40 (1927), pp. 205–48, at p. 226.

27. L. Th. Lefort, 'S. Athanase: sur la virginité', *Le Muséon* 42 (1929), pp. 197–275, at pp. 243, 244, 245, 246.

28. Ibid., p. 248.

29. For some such figures see the collection of the Musée de la Normandie in Caen.

30. Antonio Ferrua, *The Unknown Catacomb: A Unique Discovery of Early Christian Art*, trans. Iain Inglis, New Lanark, 1990, p. 22. Image in Jaroslav Pelikan, *Mary through the Centuries, Her Place in the History of Culture*, New Haven, 1996. See the Adoration of the Magi scene leading to the seated, though very hard to see, figure of a statuesque, seated Mary and Child, Neil MacGregor and Erika Langmuir, *Seeing Salvation: Images of Christ in Art*, London, 2000, figure 3, p. 26.

31. Fabrizio Mancinelli, *The Catacombs of Rome and the Origins of Christianity*, with introduction by Umberto M. Fasola, Florence, 1981, pp. 39–43.

32. Ibid., figure 28, p. 61. In the fourth-century Coemeterium Maius in Rome, a figure which may be Mary is shown at prayer, her hands raised at her sides in the position known as *orans*; her Son sits in her lap.

33. 'Nihil torvum in oculis, nihil in verbis procax, nihil in actu inverecundum; non gestus fractior, non incessus solutior; ut ipsa corporis species simulacrum fuerit mentis, figura probitatis', *Ambrose, De virginibus* II, 2,7; *PL* 16, col. 209.

34. Ambrose, *De virginibus*, I,11,63, in *Opera omnia, PL* 16, cols. 187–234, at col. 206: 'si vincis domum, vincis et saeculum'; John R. Curran, *Pagan City and Christian Capital: Rome in the Fourth Century*, Oxford, 2000, pp. 273–4.

35. Ambrose, *De virginibus*, II, c. 15; *PL* 16, col. 210D.

36. 'Is not Mary the gate through which the Redeemer entered this world?', from a letter to Siricus, bishop of Rome, of *c.* 389, Saint Ambrose, *Letters*, ed. Mary Melchior Beyenka, New York, 1954, letter 44, pp. 225–30, at p. 227.

37. Brown, *The Body and Society*, pp. 352–6.

38. 'Non enim virilis coitus vulvae virginalis secreta reseravit', Ambrose, *Expositio evangelii secundum Lucam*, ed. M. Adriaen, Turnhout, 1957, p. 55.

39. Ambrose, 'The Mysteries', in *Theological and Dogmatic Works*, trans. Roy J. Deferrari, Washington, 1963, c. 53, pp. 25–6, at p. 25.

40. Ambrose, 'The Sacraments of the Incarnation of Our Lord', in *Theological and Dogmatic Works*, c. 104, pp. 257–8, at p. 257.

41. Jan Willem Drijvers, *Helena Augusta: The Mother of Constantine the Great and the Legend of Her Finding of the True Cross*, Leiden, 1992, p. 110.

42. Barbara Baert, *A Heritage of Holy Wood: The Legend of the True Cross in Text and Image*, trans. Lee Preedy, Leiden, 2004, pp. 26–9.

43. Diliana Angelova, 'The Ivories of Ariadne and Ideas about Female Imperial Authority in Rome and Early Byzantium', *Gesta* 43 (2004), pp. 1–15, at pp. 8–9.

44. 'Visitata est Maria, ut Euam liberaret, visitata est Helena, ut redimerentur imperatores', Ambrose, *De obitu Theodosii*, in *Orationes funebres/Discorsi e letterre 1: Le orazione funebri*, ed. Otto Faller, trans. Gabriele Banterle, Milan, 1985, pp. 244–5.

45. Drijvers, *Helena Augusta*, pp. 109–113.

46. 'Haec, haec profecto vera pulchritudo est, cui nichil deest, quae sola meretur audire a domino: *tota es formosa, proxima mea, et reprehensio non est in te. Veni huc a Libano,*

432

sponsa, veni huc a Libano: transibis et pertransibis a principio fidei, a capite Sanir et Hermon, a latibulis leonum, a montibus pardorum (Cant 4:7–8)', in Franca Ela Consolino, '*Veni huc a Libano:* la *sponsa* del Cantico dei Cantici come modello per le vergini negli scritti esortativi di Ambrogio', *Athenaeum* new series 62 (1984), pp. 399–415, esp. pp. 400, 410–11.

47. On Helvidius see J. N. D. Kelly, *Jerome: His Life, Writings and Controversies*, London, 1975, pp. 104–7.

48. Jerome's answers are structured as a dialogue, 'De perpetua virginitate B. Marie adversus Helvidium', *PL* 23, cols. 182–206; 'Adversus Jovinianum libri due', *PL* 23, cols. 211–338.

49. Kate Cooper, *The Virgin and the Bride: Idealized Womanhood in Late Antiquity*, Cambridge, MA, 1996, pp. 96–7.

50. *Adversus Helvidium* 4,19; *PL* 23, cols. 201–12.

51. Jerome, 'Epistolae', *PL* 22, cols. 483–92, at col. 490.

52. Curran, *Pagan City and Christian Capital*, pp. 275–80.

53. On Augustine's relation to Ambrose's mystical language see F. B. A. Asiedu, 'The Song of Songs and the Ascent of the Soul: Ambrose, Augustine and the Language of Mysticism', *Vigiliae Christianae* 55 (2001), pp. 299–317.

54. On Mary in Augustine's thought see Philipp Friedrich, *Die Mariologie des hl. Augustinus*, Cologne, 1907.

55. 'Excepta itaque sancta virgine Maria, de qua propter honorem domini nullam prorsus, cum de peccatis agitur, haberi volo questionem – unde enim scimus quid ei plus gratie conlatum fuerit ad vincendum omni ex parte peccatum?', Augustine, *De natura et gratia*, eds. K. F. Urba and J. Zycha, Vienna and Leipzig, 1913, 36, 42, pp. 263–4.

56. 'Christus solus nullum umquam peccatum habuit nec de carne peccati quamvis de materna carne peccati', *PL* 44, col. 267.

57. See, for example, on the singular circumstances of Christ's parentage Augustine, *Tractatus in Johannem*, viii. 8, ed. Radboldus Willens, Turnhout, 1954, pp. 86–7.

58. Augustine, Sermon 291 for the Nativity of St John the Baptist, in *PL* 38, cols 1316–19, at col. 1319: 'Dic mihi, angele, unde Mariae hoc? Iam dixi, cum salutavi: Ave, gratia plena.'

59. Augustine, *De fide et symbolo*, ed. J. Zycha, Prague and Vienna, 1900, pp. 187–231; Dyan Elliott, *Spiritual Marriage: Sexual Abstinence in Medieval Wedlock*, Princeton, 1993, esp. pp. 43–5.

60. See of *c*.390–410, *Contra Secundinum* 23, ed. J. Zycha, Vienna, Prague and Leipzig, 1892, p. 940. Elizabeth A. Clark, ' "Adam's Only Companion": Augustine and the Early Christian Debate on Marriage', in *The Olde Daunce: Love, Friendship, Sex, and Marriage in the Medieval World*, eds. Robert R. Edwards and Stephen Spector, Albany, 1991, pp. 15–31, at p. 22.

61. Augustine, *De genesi as litteram* X, 19–20, ed. J. Zycha, Vienna, 1894, 321–4; Philip Lyndon Reynolds, *Food and the Body: Some Peculiar Questions in High Medieval Theology*, Leiden, 1999, pp. 26–8.

Chapter 3: Versions of Mary

1. Sebastian Brock, 'Mary in the Syriac Tradition', *Mary's Place in Christian Dialogue: Occasional Papers of the Ecumenical Society of the Blessed Virgin Mary*, ed. Alberic Stacpoole, Slough, 1982, pp. 182–91. Sebastian Brock has been most kind in providing me with copies of several articles and in answering queries.

2. John Anthony McGuckin, *The Transfiguration of Christ in Scripture and Tradition*, Lewiston, 1986, pp. 62–9; Arthur Green, 'Shekhinah, the Virgin Mary, and the Song of Songs: Reflections on a Kabbalistic Symbol in its Historical Context', *AJS Review* 26 (2002), pp. 1–52. On Syriac Christianity and Judaism see L. W. Barnard, 'The Origins and Emergence of the Church in Edessa during the First Two Centuries', *Vox Christiana* 22 (1968), pp. 167–75.

433

3. *The Odes of Solomon*, ed. and trans. James Hamilton Charlesworth, Oxford, 1973, Ode 19, pp. 81–4, at verses 2, 6–9, p. 82; Hans J. W. Drijvers, 'The 19th Ode of Solomon: Its Interpretation and Place in Syriac Christianity', in *East of Antioch: Studies in Early Syriac Christianity*, London, 1984, IX, pp. 339–55.

4. James H. Charlesworth, *Critical Reflections on the Odes of Solomon*, Journal for the Study of Pseudoepigrapha supplement series 22, Sheffield, 1998, pp. 35–9.

5. Hannah Hunt, *Joy-bearing Grief: Tears of Contrition in the Writings of the Early Syrian and Byzantine Fathers*, Leiden, 2004, p. 101.

6. James Leslie Houlden, *Jesus in History, Thought and Culture*, Oxford, 2003, p. 825.

7. *Saint Ephrem's Commentary on Tatian's Diatesseron: An English Translation of Chester Beatty Syriac MS 709*, trans. Carmel McCarthy, Journal of Semitic Studies supplement 2, Oxford, 1993, pp. 1–2.

8. *The Diatessaron of Tatian*, ed. Samuel Hemphill, London and Dublin, 1888, c. 3, p. 4.

9. Jacob Neusner, *Aphrahat and Judaism: The Christian-Jewish Argument in Fourth-Century Iran*, Leiden, 1971, chapter 1.

10. *Ascensio Isaiae*, ed. Paolo Bettiolo et al., Turnhout, 1995, c. 11, 2–11, pp. 119–24, at pp. 118–20.

11. Ian Gillman and Hans-Joachim Klimekeit, *Christians in Asia before 1500*, Richmond, 1999, p. 37.

12. On Theodore see P. F. M. Fontaine, *The Light and the Dark: A Cultural History of Dualism*, Amsterdam, 2000, pp. 34–5.

13. Sebastian Brock, 'Passover, Annunciation and Epiclesis: Some Remarks on the Term *aggen* in the Syriac Versions of Lk 1:35', *Novum Testamentum* 24 (1982), pp. 222–33.

14. J. Bugge, *Virginitas: An Essay in the History of a Medieval Ideal*, The Hague, 1975, pp. 14–54.

15. Sebastian P. Brock, 'Ephrem and the Syriac Tradition', in *The Cambridge History of Early Christian Literature*, eds. Frances M. Young, Lewis Ayres and Andrew Louth, Cambridge, 2004, pp. 362–72; on Ephrem and Jewish exegetical traditions see Lucas Van Rompay, 'The Christian Syriac Tradition of Interpretation', in *Hebrew Bible/Old Testament: The History of its Interpretation*, I, ed. Magne Saebø, Göttingen, 1996, pp. 622–8; on fourth-century Antioch and the interchange with Jews see Isabella Sandwell, *Religious Identity in Late Antiquity: Greeks, Jews and Christians in Antioch*, Cambridge, 2007, esp. pp. 46–7.

16. 'Hymn on the Unleavened Bread 6', in Sebastian Brock, *The Luminous Eye: The Spiritual World Vision of Saint Ephrem*, Kalamazoo, 1992, p. 110.

17. Ephrem the Syrian, *Hymns*, trans. Kathleen E. McVey, Mahweh, 1989, hymn 24, pp. 366–8, at p. 368.

18. Ephrem, *Hymns of Faith*, 81,1, 82,1. http://www.uoregon.edu/~sshoemak/324/texts/ephrem_hymns_faith.htm.

19. St Ephrem the Syriac, *Hymns on Paradise*, trans. Sebastian Brock, Crestwood, 1990, p. 99.

20. Sebastian Brock, 'Some Aspects of Greek Words in Syriac', in Sebastian Brock, *Syriac Perspectives on Late Antiquity*, London, 1984, IV, pp. 80–108, at p. 100; on such metaphors see Sebastian Brock, 'Clothing Metaphors as a Means of Theological Expression in Syriac Tradition', *Typus, Symbol, Allegorie bei den östlichen Vätern und ihren Parallelen im Mittelalter*, ed. Margot Schmidt, Regensburg, 1982, pp. 11–38, esp. p. 12.

21. Henry Chadwick, *East and West: The Making of a Rift in the Church: From Apostolic Times until the Council of Florence*, Oxford, 2003, esp. chapters 1–6.

22. *Saint Ephrem's Commentary*, trans. McCarthy, II, c. 6, p. 63; McCarthy, ibid., pp. 1–2.

23. 'Something flowed down from the Father of Life/And the Mother became pregnant with the mystery/Of the fish and bore him,/And he was called Son of Life', Nicola Denzey, 'Bardaisn of Edessa', in *A Companion to Second-Century Christian 'Heretics'*, ed. Antti Marjanen and Petri Luomanen, Cambridge, 2005, p. 172.

24. Sebastian Brock, 'Syriac Dispute Poems: The Various Types', in *Dispute Poems and*

Dialogues in the Ancient and Mediaeval Near East: Forms and Types of Literary Debates in Semitic and Related Literatures, eds. G. J. Reinink and H. L. J. Vanstiphout, Louvain, 1991, pp. 109–19, esp. 111–14.

25. Sebastian Brock, 'A Dispute of the Month and Some Related Syriac Texts', in Sebastian Brock, *From Ephrem to Romanos: Interactions between Syriac and Greek in Late Antiquity*, Variorum Collected Studies, Aldershot, 1999, IV, pp. 181–211, at p. 194, stanzas 6–8, and commentary on pp. 197–8.

26. Robert Eric Frykenberg, 'Christians in India: An Historical Overview of their Complex Origins', in *Christians and Missionaries in India: Cross-cultural Communication since 1500*, ed. Robert Eric Frykenberg, London, 2003, pp. 33–61, at pp. 33–9.

27. Jean Leclant, 'Prefazione', in *Iside: il mito, il mistero, la magia*, eds. Ermanno A. Arslan et al., Milan, 1997, pp. 19–27; see, for example, figure II.5, p. 47. I am indebted to Dr Racheli Hen-Shalomi for illuminating discussions of all things Egyptian.

28. R. E. Witt, *Isis in the Graeco-Roman World*, London, 1971, p. 238.

29. Stephen Benko, *The Virgin Goddess: Studies in the Pagan and Christian Roots of Mariology*, Leiden, 1993, pp. 44–53. See an example in *Iside*, p. 446, figure V.75 (first century CE), or p. 521, figure V.219 (second century CE); Arnaldo Momigliano, *On Pagans, Jews and Christians*, Middletown, 1987, p. 188.

30. Hans Wolfgang Müller, 'Isis mit dem Horuskinde: Ein Beitrag zur Ikonographie der stillenden Gottesmutter im hellenistischen und römischen Äegypten', *Münchner Jahrbuch der bildenden Kunst* 14 (1963), pp. 7–38, at pp. 31–2, and image 29 on p. 31.

31. Alan K. Bowman, *Egypt after the Pharaohs 332BC–AD642 from Alexander to the Arab Conquest*, Oxford, 1990, pp. 171–2; Witt, *Isis in the Greco-Roman World*, p. 178.

32. Bowman, *Egypt after the Pharaohs*, p. 148; Thomas F. Mathews and Norman Muller, 'Isis and Mary in Early Icons', in *Images of the Mother of God: Perceptions of the Theotokos in Byzantium*, ed. Maria Vassilaki, Aldershot, 2005, pp. 3–11, at pp. 5–6.

33. *Diodorus of Sicily in Twelve Volumes*, trans. C. H. Oldfather, London, 1968, pp. 79–83, at p. 81.

34. *The Four Greek Hymns of Isidorus and the Cult of Isis*, ed. and trans. Vera F. Vanderlip, Toronto, 1972, lines 3–6 and 17–20, pp. 35–6.

35. J. Gwyn Griffiths, *Triads and Trinity*, Cardiff, 1996, pp. 292–4. See also Jan den Boeft, 'Propaganda in the Cult of Isis', in *Persuasion and Dissuasion in Early Christianity, Ancient Judaism, and Hellenism*, ed. Pieter W. van der Horst et al., Louvain: Peeters, 2003, pp. 9–23, esp. 14–18.

36. V. Tam Tinh Tram, *Isis lactans: Corpus des monuments gréco-romains d'Isis allaitant Harpocrate*, Leiden, 1973, figure 48, pp. 72–3.

37. Ibid., figure 202, p. 45.

38. For an inscription from the first century BCE, Siegfried G. Richter, *Studien zur Christianisierung Nubiens*, Wiesbaden, 2002, n. 87, p. 134.

39. *Lexikon der Ägyptischen Götter und Götterbezeichnungen* III, ed. Christian Leitz, Louvain, 2002, pp. 261–2.

40. Mathews and Muller, 'Isis and Mary', pp. 8–9.

Chapter 4: Mary of the Imperial State

1. D. F. Wright, 'From "God-Bearer" to "Mother of God" in the Later Fathers', *Studies in Church History* 39 (2004), pp. 22–30, at p. 26.

2. Timothy E. Gregory, *Vox Populi: Popular Opinion and Violence in the Religious Controversies of the Fifth Century*, Columbus, 1979, p. 84.

3. Gregory, *Vox Populi*, pp. 88–9. Fergus Millar, *A Greek Roman Empire: Power and Belief under Theodosius II (408–450)*, Berkeley, 2006, pp. 158–61.

4. Nicholas Constas, *Proclus of Constantinople and the Cult of the Virgin in Late Antiquity*, Leiden, 2003, Homily I, p. 137, lines 15–31, and on it, pp. 56–7; Margot Fassler, 'The First Marian Feast in Constantinople and Jerusalem: Chant Texts, Readings, and Homiletic

Literature', in *The Study of Medieval Chant: Paths and Bridged, East and West: In Honor of Kenneth Levy*, ed. Peter Jeffery, Woodbridge, 2001, pp. 25–87, at pp. 34–41.

5. Constas, *Proclus of Constantinople*, Homily 2, p. 171, lines 130–34.

6. On the Egyptian contribution to early Christianity see Colin H. Roberts, *Manuscript, Society and Belief in Early Christian Egypt*, London, 1979, esp. pp. 53–73.

7. Gregory, *Vox Populi*, p. 31.

8. Ramsay MacMullen, *Voting about God in Early Church Councils*, New Haven, 2006, pp. 68–9, 89.

9. David N. Bell, 'Shenoute the Great and the Passion of Christ', *Cistercian Studies* 22 (1987), pp. 291–303, at pp. 292–3.

10. From the Council canons; Gregory, *Vox Populi*, p. 105.

11. Constas, *Proclus of Constantinople*, pp. 136–47, at p. 145.

12. On contradiction in Byzantine rhetoric, with special reference to Mary, see H. Maguire, *Art and Eloquence*, Princeton, 1981, pp. 59–68.

13. Cyril of Alexandria, *Letters 1–110 / St Cyril of Alexandria*, trans. John I. McEnerney, Washington, 1987, pp. 151–2.

14. From Kate Cooper, 'Empress and *Theotokos*: Gender and Patronage in the Christological Controversy', in *The Church and Mary: Papers Read at the 2001 Summer Meeting and the 2002 Winter Meeting of the Ecclesiastical History Society*, ed. R. N. Swanson, Woodbridge, 2004, pp. 39–51, at p. 45. On Pulcheria see also Fassler, 'The First Marian feast in Constantinople and Jerusalem', pp. 32–4.

15. *The Bazaar of Heraklides*, 1.3. On this affair see Kate Cooper, 'Contesting the Nativity: Wives, Virgins, and Pulcheria's *Imitatio Mariae*', *Scottish Journal of Religious Studies* 19 (1998), pp. 31–43.

16. Cameron, 'The Virgin in Late Antiquity', pp. 9–11.

17. *Decrees of the Ecumenical Councils*, ed. Norman P. Tanner, Washington, DC, 1990, pp. 86–*86.

18. Cooper, 'Empress and *Theotokos*', *Studies in Church History* 39 (2004), pp. 39–51.

19. Eznik of Kołb, *A Treatise on God Written in Armenian*, ed. Monica J. Blanchard and Robin Darling Young, Louvain, 1998, p. 11. Armenian Christian art concentrated on themes from the Old Testament and on scenes from Jesus' life: Lynn Jones, *Between Islam and Byzantium: Aght'amar and the Visual Construction of Armenian Rulership*, Aldershot, 2007.

PART II: FROM THE EASTERN MEDITERRANEAN TO THE IRISH SEA: TO THE YEAR 1000

Chapter 5: Mary of the Christian Empire

1. Peter Brown, *Power and Persuasion in Late Antiquity: Towards a Christian Empire*, Madison, 1992, p. 155.

2. Oded Irshai, 'Confronting a Christian Empire: Jewish Culture in the World of Byzantium', in *Cultures of the Jews: A New History*, ed. David Biale, New York, 2002, pp. 180–221.

3. L. Gładyszewski, 'Die Marienhomilien des Hesychius von Jerusalem', *Studia patristica* 17 (1982), pp. 93–6.

4. A. Wenger, 'Note sur les discours inédits et sur le texte grec du commentaire "In Leviticum"', *Revue des Etudes Augustiniennes* 2 (1956), pp. 457–70, at p. 460.

5. Built by Babah Rabah. For the sources on this episode and the archaeological remains see Y. Magen, 'The Church of Mary Theotokos on Mount Gerizim', in *Christian Archaeology in the Holy Land, New Discoveries: Essays in Honour of Virgilio C. Corbo, OFM*, eds. G. C. Bottini, L. D. Segni and E. Alliata, Jerusalem, 1990, pp. 333–42.

6. Procopius of Caesaria, *Buildings*, trans. H. B. Dewing with Glanville Downey, London, 1961, V.vii, pp. 349–55, at pp. 351–3.

7. It is attributed to a fifth-century abbot: *Pseudo-Shenoute on Christian Behaviour*, ed. and trans. K. H. Kuhn, Louvain, 1960, p. 16.

8. In this section I rely heavily on Stephen J. Shoemaker's excellent book *Ancient Traditions of the Virgin Mary's Dormition and Assumption*, Oxford, 2002, pp. 290–414. See also Antoine Wenger, *L'Assomption de la T. S. Vierge dans la tradition byzantine du VIe au Xe siècle: Etudes et documents*, Paris, 1955, and Simon Claude Minouni, *Dormition et assomption de Marie: Histoire des traditions anciennes*, Paris, 1995.

9. Andrew Louth, 'St John Damascene: Preacher and Poet', in *Preacher and Audience: Studies in Early Christian and Byzantine Homiletics*, eds. Mary B. Cunningham and Pauline Allen, Leiden, 1998, pp. 247–66, at p. 264.

10. *Apocrypha Syriaca: The Protoevangelium Jacobi and Transitus Mariae*, ed. and trans. Agnes S. Lewis, London, 1902, p. 52; Stephen Shoemaker, ' "Let Us Go and Burn Her Body": The Image of the Jews in the Early Dormition Tradition', *Church History* 68 (1999), pp. 775–823.

11. Stephen J. Shoemaker, 'The Sahidic Coptic Homily of the Virgin Attributed to Evdoius of Rome: An Edition from Morgan MSS 596 & 598 with Translation', *Analecta Bollandiana* 117 (1999), pp. 241–83, at c. 7, p. 263.

12. Shoemaker, 'The Sahidic', c. 17, pp. 271–3.

13. Susan Ashbrook Harvey, 'Incense Offerings in the Syriac *Transitus Mariae*: Ritual and Knowledge in Ancient Christianity', in *The Early Church in its Context: Essays in Honor of Everett Ferguson*, eds. Abraham J. Malherbe, Frederick W. Norris and James W. Thompson, Leiden, 1988, pp. 175–91, at pp. 183–5.

14. Shoemaker, ' "Let Us Go and Burn" ', pp. 789–90; see also Ora Limor, 'Mary and the Jews: Story, Controversy, and Testimony', *Historein* 6 (2006), pp. 55–71.

15. *On the Dormition of Mary: Early Patristic Homilies*, trans. Brian E. Daley, Crestwood, 1998, p. 78.

16. See, for example, the suggestion in Burton L. Visotzky, 'Anti-Christian Polemic in Leviticus Rabbah', *American Academy for Jewish Research* 56 (1990), pp. 83–100, at pp. 98–9. I am grateful to my learned friends Oded Irshai and Joshua Levinson for their comments on this article.

17. William Horbury, 'Christ as Brigard in Ancient Anti-Christian Polemic', in *Jesus and the Politics of His Day*, eds. E. Bammel and C. F. D. Moule, Cambridge, 1984, pp. 183–95, at p. 189.

18. David Biale, 'Counter-history and Jewish Polemics against Christianity: The *Sefer toldot yeshu* and the *Sefer zerubavel*', *Jewish Social Studies* new series 6 (1999), pp. 130–45, at pp. 134–7; Daniel Lasker, *Jewish Philosophical Polemics against Christianity in the Middle Ages*, New York, 1977, pp. 4–5.

19. My translation is from Yaakov Deutsch, 'New Evidence of Early Versions of *Toldot Yeshu*', *Tarbiz* 69 (2000), pp. 177–97 (in Hebrew), at p. 183; on it Peter Schäfer, *Jesus in the Talmud*, Princeton, 2007, pp. 2–7.

20. Samuel Krauss, *Das Leben Jesu nach jüdsichen Quellen: Herausgegeben und erläutert von S. Krauss*, Berlin, 1902, pp. 38–9; on *niddah* in the Jewish tradition and its use in *Toledoth Yeshu* see Evyatar Marienberg, *Niddah: Lorsque les Juifs conceptualisent la menstruation*, Paris, 2003, pp. 172–6.

21. On the usage see below p. 166.

22. Joan E. Taylor, *Christians and the Holy Places: The Myth of Jewish-Christian Origins*, Oxford, 1993, pp. 202–5.

23. There were two churches at the location of the *kathisma*: see Stephen J. Shoemaker, 'Christmas in the Qur'an: The Qur'anic Account of Jesus' Nativity and Palestinian Local Tradition', *Jerusalem Studies in Arabic and Islam* 28 (2003), pp. 11–39, at pp. 31–4. Once the Nativity was securely fixed in Bethlehem, the *kathisma* came to be associated with the Holy Family's rest during their Flight to Egypt.

24. Rina Avner, 'The Recovery of the Kathisma Church and its Influence on Octagonal Buildings', *One Land – Many Cultures: Archaeological Studies in Honour of Stanislao Loffreda OFM*, eds. G. Claudio Bottini, Leah Di Segni and L. Daniel Chrupcala, Jerusalem, 2003, pp. 173–86; for a short report with a drawing of the site see http://www.hadashot-esi.org.il/report_detail_eng.asp?id=106&mag_id=110.

25. Joseph Patrich, 'Early Christian Churches in the Holy Land', in *Christians and Christianity in the Holy Land: From the Origins to the Latin Kingdoms*, eds. Ora Limor and Guy G. Stroumsa, Turnhout, 2006, pp. 355–99, at p. 386.

26. Michel van Esbroeck, 'Nouveaux apocryphes de la Dormition conservés en Grégorien', *Analecta Bollandiana* 90 (1972), pp. 363–9, at pp. 364–5.

27. *Jerusalem Pilgrims before the Crusades*, trans. John Wilkinson, rev. edn, Warminster, 2002, pp. 166 and 212.

28. Ora Limor, ' "Holy Journey": Pilgrimage and Christian Sacred Landscape', in *Christians and Christianity in the Holy Land*, pp. 321–53, at p. 352. Mary was mentioned by Antoninus, the pilgrim of Piacenza, who was impressed by the sight of the 'flagon and the breadbasket of Saint Mary' in Diocaesarea, and of the site of the Marriage at Cana, in *Jerusalem Pilgrims before the Crusades*, p. 131.

29. *The Cambridge Companion to the Age of Justinian*, ed. Michael Maas, Cambridge, 2005, plate V.

30. *Adomnan's De locis sanctis*, ed. Denis Mechan, Scriptores Latini Hiberniae 3, Dublin, 1958, c. 10, p. 57.

31. Gary Vikan, ' "Guided by Land and Sea": Pilgrim Art and Pilgrim Travel in Early Byzantium', in *Sacred Images and Sacred Power in Byzantium*, Aldershot, 2003, VIII, pp. 74–92, at pp. 76–7.

32. B. Gary Vikan, 'Byzantine Pilgrims's Art', in *Sacred Images and Sacred Power in Byzantium*, Aldershot, 2003, V, pp. 229–66, figure 8.29, p. 251; Bianca Kühnel, 'The Holy Land as a Factor in Christian Art', in *Christians and Christianity in the Holy Land: From the Origins to the Latin Kingdoms*, eds. Ora Limor and Guy G. Stroumsa, Turnhout, 2006, pp. 463–504, at pp. 478, 482–3.

33. Vikan, ' "Guided by Land and Sea" ', p. 85.

34. Baynes, 'The Finding of the Virgin's Robe', in *Byzantine Studies and Other Essays*, London, 1955, pp. 240–47, at p. 242; Annemarie Weyl Carr, 'Threads of Authority: The Virgin Mary's Veil in the Middle Ages', in *Robes and Honour: The Medieval World of Investiture*, ed. Stewart Gordon, Basingstoke, 2001, pp. 59–93, at pp. 62–3.

35. One tradition claims that the old woman died of heartbreak, Ora Limor, 'Mary and the Jews: Three Witness Stories' (in Hebrew), *Alpaïm* 28 (2005), pp. 129–51 (= 'Mary and the Jews: Story, Controversy and Testimony', *Historein* 6 (2006), pp. 55–71), at p. 142.

36. Baynes, 'The Finding of the Virgin's Robe'; Averil Cameron, 'The Cult of the Virgin in Late Antiquity: Religious Developments and Myth-making', *Studies in Church History* 39 (2004), pp. 1–21. For a nuanced comparative analysis of narratives about Mary's relics see Limor, 'Mary and the Jews'.

37. Baynes, 'The Finding of the Virgin's Robe', p. 245.

38. Michael Avi-Yonah, *The Jews of Palestine: A Political History from the Bar Kokhba War to the Arab Conquest*, Oxford, 1976, pp. 395–415.

39. Biale, 'Counter-history and Jewish Polemics', pp. 137–42. See also Guy G. Stroumsa, 'False Prophet, False Messiah and the Religious Scene in Sixth-Century Jerusalem', in *Redemption and Resistance*, eds. M. Bockmuehl and James Carleton Paget, London and New York, 2007, pp. 285–96.

40. Martha Himmelfarb, 'Sefer Zerubbabel', in *Rabbinic Fantasies: Imaginative Narratives from Classical Hebrew Literature*, eds. David Stern and Mark J. Mirsky, Philadelphia: Jewish Publication Society, 1990, pp. 67–90, at p. 74. Katja Vehlow spoke interestingly about this work on 8 April 2005 at the 'Mary: Mediterranean, European, Global' conference at New York University.

41. Himmelfarb, 'Sefer Zerubbabel', p. 75.

42. Averil Cameron, 'The Jews in Seventh-century Palestine', *Scripta Classica Israelitica* 13 (1994), pp. 75–93, at pp. 80–81; Shoemaker, ' "Let Us Go and Burn" ', pp. 818–23.

43. Leslie Brubaker, 'Introduction: The Sacred Image', in *The Sacred Image East and West*, eds. Robert Ousterhout and Leslie Brubaker, Urbana and Chicago, 1995, pp. 1–24, esp. at p. 9.

44. Gilbert Dagron, *Naissance d'une capital: Constantinople et ses institutions*, Paris, 1974, p. 293.

45. Robin Cormack, 'The Eyes of the Mother of God', in *Images of the Mother of God: Perceptions of the Theotokos in Byzantium*, ed. Maria Vassilaki, Aldershot, 2005, pp. 167–75. The surviving icons are discussed by the contributors to the catalogue *Masterpieces of Early Christian Art and Icons*, eds. Richard Temple et al., London, 2005.

46. Robin Cormack, in *Masterpieces of Early Christian Art and Icons*, ed. Richard Temple et al., London, 2005, pp. 22–9.

47. Kurt Weitzmann, *The Icon: Holy Images, Sixth to Fourteenth Century*, London, 1978, plate 3, pp. 44–5.

48. Ibid., plate 4, pp. 46–7; see also a fragile linen with the scene of the Annunciation from the same period, P. M. du Bourguet, *Coptic Art*, trans. Caryll Hay-Shaw, London, 1971, pp. 132–3.

49. Paris Bibliothèque nationale de France (hereafter BNF) Cod. Syr. 341, fol. 118r; on it see Reiner Sörries, *Die Syrische Bibel von Paris: Paris, Bibliothèque Nationale, syr. 341: eine frühchristliche Bilderhandschrift aus dem 6. Jahrhundert*, Wiesbaden, 1991, pp. 33–6, figure 8, p. 84; and Hans Belting and Guglielmo Cavallo, *Die Bibel des Niketas: Ein Werk der höfischen Buchkunst in Byzanz und sein antikes Vorbild*, Wiesbaden, 1979, p. 36.

50. P. P. V. van Moorsel, 'Die stillende Gottesmutter und die Monophysiten', in *Kunst und Geschichte Nubiens in christlicher Zeit: Ergebnisse und Probleme auf Grund der jüngsten Ausgrabungen*, ed. Erich Dinkler, Recklinghausen, 1970, pp. 281–90; and du Bourguet, *Coptic Art*, pp. 46–7 and image on p. 53.

51. See image in Johann Konrad Eberlein, *Apparitio regis – revelatio veritatis: Studien zur Darstellung des Vorhangs in der bildenden Kunst von der Spätantike bis zum Ende des Mittelalters*, Wiesbaden, 1982, figure 15, p. 225.

52. Vittorio Bartoletti, 'La Madonna con il bambino in un papiro copto di Antinoe', *Studi in onore di Luisa Banti*, Rome, 1953, pp. 29–31; Astrid Pesarino, 'Contributo allo studio del tipo della *Virgo lactans*: il papiro PSI XV 1574 dell'Istituto Papirologico G. Vitelli di Firenze', *Latomus* 59 (2000), pp. 640–46. I am deeply indebted to Professor Bastianini, Director of the Istituto Papirologico G. Vitelli in Florence, who has kindly provided me with advice and with a high-quality reproduction of the papyrus.

53. Siegfried G. Richter, *Studien zur Christianisierung Nubiens*, Wiesbaden, 2002, pp. 158–9.

54. Ps. Cyril of Jerusalem, *Omelie Copte sulla passione, sulla croce e sulla Vergine*, ed. Antonella Campagnano, Milan, 1980, p. 153.

55. Ibid., p. 159.

56. Ibid., p. 169.

57. *Miscellaneous Coptic Texts in the Dialect of Upper Egypt*, ed. and trans. E. A. W. Budge, London, 1915; the text is cited and discussed in Brown, *The Body and Society*, p. 445.

58. For some variations within the Egyptian Christian sphere see Kazimierz Michałowski, 'Open Problems of Nubian Art and Culture in the Light of the Discoveries at Farous', in *Kunst und Geschichte Nubiens in christlicher Zeit: Ergebnisse und Probleme auf Grund der jüngsten Ausgrabungen*, ed. E. Dinkler, Recklinghausen, 1970, pp. 11–28, at pp. 11–20.

59. Averil Cameron, *Christianity and the Rhetoric of Empire: The Development of Christian Discourse*, Berkeley, pp. 211–12. On the nature of interaction with the icon within their spatial contexts see the suggestive insights in Bissera V. Pentcheva, 'The Performative Icon', *Art Bulletin* 88 (2006), pp. 631–55.

60. Pauline Allen, 'The Sixth-century Greek Homily: A Re-assessment', in *Preacher and*

Audience: Studies in Early Christian and Byzantine Homiletics, ed. Mary B. Cunningham and Pauline Allen, Leiden, 1998, pp. 201–25, at pp. 207–8.

61. J. F. Haldon, *Byzantium in the Seventh Century: The Transformation of a Culture*, Cambridge, 1990, pp. 37, 423; for a map of Marian churches in Constantinople see Cyril Mango, 'Constantinople as Theotokoupolis', in *Mother of God: Representations of the Virgin in Byzantine Art*, ed. Maria Vassilaki, Athens, 2000, p. 18; on Constantinople as Mary's city see Françoise Jeanlin, 'Konstantinopel, die Stadt der Theotokos', in *Maria: Abbild oder Vorbild? Zur Sozialgeschichte mittelalterlicher Marienverehrung*, ed. Hedwig Röckelein, Claudia Opitz and Dieter R. Bauer, Tübingen, 1990, pp. 48–57.

62. Brown, *The Body and Society*, p. 445.

63. George of Pisidia, *Poemi. I. Panegirici epici*, ed. and trans. Agostino Pertusio, Ettal, 1959, pp. 142–3.

64. *The Seventh Century in the West-Syrian Chronicles: Including Two Seventh-Century Syriac Apocalyptic Texts*, trans. and annot. Andrew Palmer and Sebastian Brock, Liverpool, 1993, p. 117.

65. See for example in the later poetry of Joseph the Hymnographer ($c.$810–86), Richard Hillier, 'Joseph the Hymnographer and Mary the Gate', *Journal of Theological Studies* new series 36 (1985), pp. 311–20, at p. 314.

66. For a seminal study of the poem and its context see Averil Cameron, 'The Theotokos in Sixth-century Constantinople', *Journal of Theological Studies* new series 29 (1978), pp. 79–108.

67. Cameron, 'The Theotokos', p. 95.

68. Ibid.

69. Robert G. Hoyland, *Arabia and the Arabs: From the Bronze Age to the Coming of Islam*, London, 2001, pp. 49–57.

70. *Maximus the Confessor and his Companions: Documents from Exile*, eds. and trans. Pauline Allen and Bronwen Neil, Oxford, 2002, pp. 11–12.

71. Robert Louis Wilken, *The Spirit of Early Christian Thought: Seeking the Face of God*, New Haven and London, 2003, pp. 113–18.

72. *Maximus the Confessor*, c. 14, pp. 115–16.

73. Ibid., p. 101.

74. Ibid., p. 117.

75. On Mary's kinship with Jesus see Peter Brown, *The Rise of Western Christendom: Triumph and Diversity AD 200–1000*, Oxford, 2003, pp. 120, 389.

76. The text has survived in Georgian and is edited (with French translation) in *Maximus the Confessor, Vie de la Vierge*, ed. Michel van Esbroeck, 2 vols., Leuven, 1986. For an appreciation of the *Life* and its later influence see Stephen J. Shoemaker, 'The Virgin Mary in the Ministry of Jesus in the Early Church according to the Earliest *Life of the Virgin*', *Harvard Theological Review* 98 (2005), pp. 441–67. On *Lives* of Mary see also Simon C. Mimouni, 'Les *Vies de la Vierge*: Etat de la question', *Apocrypha* 5 (1994), pp. 211–48.

77. *Maximus the Confessor, Vie de la Vièrge* II, p. 63, lines 5–7.

78. Derek Krueger, 'Christian Piety and Practice in the Sixth Century', in *The Cambridge Companion to the Age of Justinian*, ed. Michael Maas, Cambridge, 2005, pp. 291–315, at pp. 297–300.

79. R. J. Schork, *Sacred Song from the Byzantine Pulpit: Romanos the Melodist*, Gainesville, 1995, c. 15, p. 113.

80. Ibid., c. 16, p. 113.

81. Ibid., p. 107. I have benefited greatly from Margaret Alexiou, *The Ritual Lament in Greek Tradition*, Cambridge, 1974, pp. 62–78; and Gregory W. Dobrov, 'A Dialogue with Death: Ritual Lament and the θρῆνος Θεοτόκου of Romanos Melodos', *Greek, Roman and Byzantine Studies* 35 (1994), pp. 385–405.

82. Averil Cameron, 'The Virgin's Robe: An Episode in the History of Seventh-century Constantinople', *Byzantion* 49 (1979), pp. 42–56, esp. pp. 48–56.

83. Ibid., pp. 53–4.

84. Leena Mari Peltomaa, *Image of the Virgin Mary in the Akathistos Hymn*, Leiden, 2001, Proemium II, p. 3.

85. Ibid., c. 24, p. 19.

86. Mary B. Cunningham, 'Andrew of Crete: A High Style Preacher of the Eighth Century', in *Preacher and Audience: Studies in Early Christian and Byzantine Homiletics*, eds. Mary B. Cunningham and Pauline Allen, Leiden, 1998, pp. 267–93, at p. 281.

87. Henry Maguire, *Art and Eloquence in Byzantium*, Princeton, 1981, esp. pp. 44–5.

88. Ibid., p. 46.

89. Fourth sermon, Cunningham, 'Andrew of Crete', p. 275.

90. Ibid., p. 280.

91. He relayed an account of his travels to Adomnan (d.704), abbot of Iona, who committed it to writing: Adomnan, *De locis sanctis*, ed. L. Bieler, in *Itineraria et alia geographica*, Corpus Christianorum Series Latina (hereafter CCSL) 175, Turnhout, 1965, pp. 175–234, at book III, 5, pp. 233–4. On his testimony see Ora Limor, 'Pilgrims and Authors: Adomnán's *De locis sanctis* and Hugeburc's *Hodoeporicon Sancti Willibaldi*', *Revue Bénédictine* 114 (2004), pp. 273–5; 'Introduction' in Adomnan of Iona, *Life of ST Columba*, trans. Richard Sharpe, London, 1995, pp. 54–5. See above p. 61.

92. See Miri Rubin, *Gentile Tales: The Narrative Assault on Late Medieval Jews*, London and New Haven, 1999, chapter 2.

93. John Moschus, *The Spiritual Meadow (Pratum Spirituale)*, trans. and intro. John Wortley, Kalamazoo, 1992, pp. 227–8.

94. Ibid., pp. 228–9.

95. *The Polemic of Nestor the Priest*, eds. Daniel J. Lasker and Sarah Stroumsa, Jerusalem, 1996, c. 81, p. 68.

96. Ibid., c. 82, p. 115; another variant is less graphic (ibid., n. 2). On this work see also Ora Limor, 'Judaism Examines Christianity: The Polemic of Nestor the Priest and Sefer Toledot Yeshu' (in Hebrew), *Pe'amim* 75 (1998), pp. 109–28.

97. Henry Chadwick, *East and West: The Making of a Rift in the Church: From Apostolic Times until the Council of Florence*, Oxford, 2003, p. 66; see also Judith Herrin, ' "Femina byzantina": The Council in Trullo on Women', *Dumbarton Oaks Papers* 46 (1992), pp. 97–105; J. M. Hussey, *The Orthodox Church in the Byzantine Empire*, Oxford, 1986, pp. 24–5. See also Leslie Brubaker, 'Gender and Society', in *The Cambridge Companion to the Age of Justinian*, pp. 427–47, at p. 444.

98. Andrew Louth, 'St John Damascene: Preacher and Poet', in *Preacher and Audience: Studies in Early Christian and Byzantine Homiletics*, eds. Mary B. Cunningham and Pauline Allen, Leiden, 1998, pp. 247–66, at p. 255; Bissera Pentcheva, 'The Performative Icon', *The Art Bulletin* 88 (2006), pp. 631–55, at p. 632.

99. Gilbert Dagron, 'Le Culte des images dans le monde byzantin', in *Histoire vécue du peuple chrétien*, I, ed. Jean Delumeau, Toulouse, 1979, pp. 133–60, at pp. 142–3 (=*La Romanité chrétienne en Orient: Héritages et mutations*, London, 1984, article XI).

100. Chadwick, *East and West*, p. 79.

101. For discussion of the council of Hiereia (754) see Stephen Gero, *Byzantine Iconoclasm during the Reign of Constantine V with Particular Attention to the Oriental Sources*, Louvain, 1997, and quote on p. 79.

102. Louth, 'St John Damascene', p. 255.

103. Cyril Mango, *The Art of the Byzantine Empire, 312–1453*, Englewood Cliffs, 1972, pp. 156–7.

104. Translation from Ann Freeman, 'Scripture and Images in the *Libri Carolini*', in *Theodulf of Orleans: Charlemagne's Spokesman against the Second Council of Nicaea*, Aldershot: Ashgate, 2003, VII, pp. 163–88, at p. 164; the Greek 'venerate' was translated as 'adore', pp. 166–7.

105. *Libri Carolini – Opus Caroli regis contra synodum (Libri Carolini)*, ed. Ann Freeman with Paul Meyvaert, Monumentae Germaniae Historica (hereafter MGH), *Concilia* II, supp. I, Hanover, 1998, c. IV 2, p. 492.

106. Ibid., c. II 25, p. 457, lines 2–6.

107. Ibid., c. II 27, pp. 290–96.

108. Ibid., c. IV 21, p. 540, esp. lines 15–36; translation from Ann Freeman, 'Scripture and Images in the *Libri Carolini*', pp. 163–88, at p. 165. See also the comments in Leslie Brubaker, *Vision and Meaning in Ninth-century Byzantium: Image as Exegesis in the Homilies of Gregory of Nazianzus*, Cambridge, 1999, pp. 35–9.

109. William D. Wixom, 'Medieval Sculpture at the Metropolitan, 800 to 1400', *The Metropolitan Museum of Art Bulletin* (spring 2005), p. 7.

110. Bernice M. Kaczynski, *Greek in the Carolingian Age: The St Gall Manuscripts*, Speculum Anniversary Monographs 13, Cambridge, MA, 1988, pp. 107–8, 135.

111. Rico Franses, 'When All That Is Gold Does not Glitter: On the Strange History of Looking at Byzantine Art', in *Icon and Word: The Power of Images in Byzantium: Studies Presented to Robin Cormack*, eds. Anthony Eastmond and Liz James, Aldershot, 2003, pp. 13–24, plate III and pp. 16–17. On the directions explored in the making of images of the *Theotokos* see Ioli Kalavrezou, 'Images of the Mother: When the Virgin Mary became *Meter Theou*', *Dumbarton Oaks Papers* 44 (1990), pp. 165–72.

112. John Lowden, *Early Christian and Byzantine Art*, London, 1997, figure 99, p. 176. Gilbert Dagron, *Constantinople imaginaire. Etudes sur le receuil des 'patria'*, Paris, 1984, plate 8 and p. 273.

113. Johann Konrad Eberlein, *Apparitio regis – revelatio veritatis: Studien zur Darstellung des Vorhangs in der bildenden Kunst von der Spätantike bis zum Ende des Mittelalters*, Wiesbaden, 1982, figures 14 and 23. On Armenia and images see Norman H. Baynes, 'The Icons before Iconoclasm', in *Byzantine Studies and Other Essays*, London, 1955, pp. 226–39, at pp. 238–9.

114. John Fennell, *A History of the Russian Church to 1448*, London and New York, 1995, pp. 42, 55.

115. Leslie Brubaker *Vision and Meaning in Ninth-century Byzantium: Image as Exegesis in the Homilies of Gregory of Nazianzus*, Cambridge, 1999.

116. Ibid., figure 6.

117. Kathleen Corrigan, *Visual Polemics in the Ninth-Century Byzantine Psalters*, Cambridge, 1992, pp. 76–7; on this image see also Brubaker, *Vision and Meaning*, p. 350.

118. Corrigan, *Visual Polemics*, p. 76.

119. Karin M. Skawran, 'Peripheral Byzantine Frescoes in Greece: The Problem of their Connections', in *Mosaic: Festschrift for A. H. S. Megaw*, eds. Judith Herrin, Margaret Mullett and Catherine Otten-Froux, British School at Athens Studies 8, London, 2001, pp. 75–83, at pp. 76–7.

120. *Ivories in Liverpool Museums*, plate XVIIIa, no. 17, p. 48; see also *deesis* there on p. 52.

121. Weitzmann, *The Icon*, plate 12, pp. 62–3.

122. Henry Maguire, 'A Murderer among the Angels: The Frontispiece Miniatures of Paris Gr.510 and the Iconography of the Archangels in Byzantine Art', in *The Sacred Image East and West*, ed. Robert Ousterhout and Leslie Brubaker, Chicago and Urbana, 1995, pp. 63–71, at p. 66 (and figure 25).

123. Lowden, *Early Christian and Byzantine Art*, figures 96–7, pp. 170–71 and discussion on p. 172.

124. Carolyn L. Connor, *The Colour of Ivory: Polychromy on Byzantine Ivories*, Princeton, 1998, pp. 19–22, figure 7 and plates IX–X.

125. Kurt Weitzmann, *The Monastery of St Catherine at Mount Sinai: the Icons* I, Princeton, 1976, plate B51.

126. Jane Baun, *Tales from Another Byzantium: Celestial Journey and Local Community in the Medieval Greek Apocrypha*, Cambridge, 2007, throughout and esp. pp. 4–22, 39, 59.

Chapter 6: Beyond the Greek World

1. For a masterly description of this world see James Montgomery, 'The Empty Hijaz', in *Arabic Theology, Arabic Philosophy: From the Many to the One: Essays in Celebration of Richard M. Frank*, ed. J. E. Montgomery, Leuven, 2006, pp. 37–97; Glen W. Bowersock, *Hellenism in Late Antiquity*, Ann Arbor, 1990, esp. p. 75 and figures 12 and 13. See also Hugh Kennedy, 'Islam', in *Interpreting Late Antiquity: Essays on the Postclassical World*, eds. G. W. Bowersock, Peter Brown and Oleg Grabar, Cambridge, MA, 2001, pp. 219–37.

2. P. F. M. Fontaine, *The Light and the Dark: A Cultural History of Dualism*, Amsterdam, 2000, pp. 299–302; Hoyland, *Arabia and the Arabs*, pp. 146–50.

3. Marston Speight, 'Christians in the *Hadīth* Literature', in *Islamic Interpretations of Christianity*, ed. Lloyd Ridgeon, Richmond, 2001, pp. 30–53, at p. 37. On the appellation 'son of Maryam' see Tarif Khalidi, *The Muslim Jesus. Sayings and Stories in Islamic Literature*, Cambridge, MA, and London, 2002, p. 14.

4. Averil Cameron, 'The Eastern Provinces in the 7th Century A. D.: Hellenism and the Emergence of Islam', in '*ΕΛΛΗΝΙΣΜΟΣ: Quelques jalons pour une histoire de l'identité grecque*, ed. S. Said, Leiden, 1991, pp. 287–313, at pp. 297–8.

5. Jane I. Smith and Yvonne Y. Haddad, 'The Virgin Mary in Islamic Tradition and Commentary', *The Muslim World* 79 (1989), pp. 161–87, at p. 162; Suleiman Mourad, 'The Origin of the Palm-Tree Story in the Gospel of Pseudo Matthew', *Oriens Christianus* 86 (2002), pp. 206–16, esp. pp. 15–22.

6. David Marshall, 'Christianity in the Qur'ān', in *Islamic Interpretations of Christianity*, ed. Lloyd Ridgeon, Richmond, 2001, pp. 3–29, at pp. 10–18.

7. Ibid., pp. 14–18. Mary was highly respected alongside Fatima, the Prophet's daughter: J. D. McAuliffe, 'Chosen of All Women: Mary and Fatima in Quranic Exegesis', *Islamochristiana* 6 (1981), pp. 19–28.

8. Amikam Elad, *Medieval Jerusalem and Islamic Worship: Holy Places, Ceremonies, Pilgrimage*, Islamic History and Civilization, Studies and Texts 8, Leiden, 1995, pp. 138–40.

9. David E. Sklare, *Samuel ben Hofni Gaon and his Cultural World: Texts and Studies*, Leiden, 1996, pp. 100–101. On Baghdad see Dmitri Gutas, *Greek Thought, Arabic Culture: The Graeco-Arabic Translation Movement in Baghdad and Early 'Abbāsid Society (2nd–4th/8th–10th centuries)*, London and New York, 1998.

10. Adolph Jelineck, *Beit Hamidrash*, Jerusalem, 1967, Rooms VI, XI–XIII. On the literary richness of this milieu and the following material see Eli Yassif, *Ke-margalit ba-mishbetset: kovets ha-sipurim ha-Ivri bi-Yeme ha-benayim*, Bene Berak, 2000, pp. 76–83; see also Cameron, 'The Jews in Seventh-century Palestine', p. 86 and Cameron, 'The Eastern Provinces in the 7th Century A.D.', p. 305.

11. *The Zend-Avesta*, ed. James Darmesteter, Oxford, 1883, II, p. 195, n. 2.

12. Commonly known as the Mausoleum of Galla Placidia, Yitzhak Hen, *Roman Barbarians: The Royal Court and Culture in the Early Medieval West*, Basingstoke, 2007, pp. 33–5, and for a map of Ravenna, p. 34, map 3.

13. Gillian Mackie, *Early Christian Chapels in the West: Decoration, Function, and Patronage*, Toronto, 2003, pp. 25–7.

14. I have been inspired by conversation with Professor Thomas Head on relics and saints in early medieval Europe.

15. Vincent Déroche, *Etudes sur Léontios de Néapolis*, Uppsala, 1995, pp. 146–53.

16. Gregory of Tours wore reliquary with remains of saints Mary and Martin, see Raymond Van Dam, *Saints and their Miracles in Late Antique Gaul*, Princeton, 1993, pp. 33–4; Gregory of Tours, *Glory of Martyrs*, trans. Raymond Van Dam, Liverpool, 1988, no. 9, pp. 29–32; Averil Cameron, 'The Byzantine Sources of Gregory of Tours', *Journal of Theological Studies* new series 26 (1975), pp. 421–6, at p. 422. On Gregory and the cult of saints in his time see Ian Wood, 'Topographies of Holy Power in Sixth-century Gaul', in *Topographies of Power in the Early Middle Ages*, eds. Mayke de Jong and Frans Theuws with Carine van Rhijn, Leiden, 2001, pp. 137–54.

17. 'Cui luna, sol et omnia/Deserviunt per tempora,/Perfusa coeli gratia,/gestant puellae viscera', Venantius Fortunatus, 'Miscellanea', *PL* 88, col. 265A, lines 5–8.

18. 'O gloriosa domina,/Excelsa super sidera,/Qui te creavit provide,/Lactasti sacro ubere./Quod Eva tristis abstulit/Tu reddis almo gremine;/Intrent ut astra flebiles,/Coeli fenestra facta est', ibid., col. 265B.

19. Venance Fortunat, *Poèmes, Tome 2, Livres V–VIII*, ed. and trans. Marc Reydellet, Collection des universités de France, Paris, 1998, Book 8.III, p. 130.

20. Venantius Fortunatus, 'Miscellanea', col. 277, lines 11–12.

21. 'In deitate Patris aequalis, vel corpore matri,/Et sine peccato de genitrice caro', ibid., col. 282A.

22. 'Pulchra super gemmas, splendorem solis obumbrans,/Alta super coelos, et super astra nitens./Vellere candidior niveo, rutilantior aura,/Fulgidior radio, dulcior ore favo . . ./ Chara, benigna, micans, pia, sancta, verenda, venusta,/Flos, decus, ara, nitor, palma, corona, pudor', ibid., col. 284A.

23. *Venantius Fortunatus: Personal and Political Poems*, trans. Judith George, Translated Texts for Historians 23, Liverpool, 1995, Poem 4.26, at p. 12.

24. Hen, *Roman Barbarians*, pp. 132–3.

25. 'Domina mea, dominatrix mea, dominans mihi, mater Domini mei, ancilla Filii tui, genetrix factoris mundi, te rogo, te oro, te quaeso', San Ildefonso de Toledo, *La virginidad perpetua de Santa Maria*, ed. Julio Campos Ruiz, Madrid, 1971, p. 49, lines 83–4.

26. 'Sit amabile tantae gloriae virginem in tuo genere invenisse. Sit laetum in tuo traduce tantae pudicitiae visum insigne. Sit iocundum in stirpe tantundem tua patefacum tale miraculum', ibid., p. 68, lines 360–62. Ildefonsus was much copied in the Middle Ages, with twenty-five surviving manuscripts: David Raizman, 'A Rediscovered Illuminated Manuscript of St Ildefionsus's *De Virginitate Beatae Mariae* in the Bibliotexa Nacional in Madrid', *Gesta* 26 (1987), pp. 37–46, at pp. 38–9.

27. Christian Sapin, *La Bourgogne préromane: Construction, décor et fonction des édifices réligieux*, Paris, 1986, pp. 24–5.

28. Jean-Claude Hélas and Pierre-André Sigal, 'Hagiotoponymes et dédicaces d'églises en Bas Languedoc du Moyen Age à nos jours', in *Faire mémoire: Souvenir et commémoration au Moyen Age*, eds. Claude Carozzi and Huguette Taviani-Carozzi, Aix-en-Provence, 1999, pp. 163–91. Lists of relics owned by abbeys or cathedral churches show what a small proportion were linked to Mary: three out of 94 relics held at Sens cathedral in the eighth century: *Chartae Latinae Antiquiores*, XIX, ed. Albert Bruckner (†) and Robert Marichal, Dietikon-Zurich, 1987, no. 682, pp. 40–59.

29. Thomas Deswarte, *De la destruction à la restauration: L'Idéologie de la royaume d'Oviedo-Léon (VIIIe–XIe siècles)*, Turnhout, 2003, pp. 89, 152.

30. Jean-François Goudesenne, *Les Offices historiques ou historiae composés pour les fêtes des saints dans la province ecclésiastique de Reims (775–1030)*, Turnhout, 2002.

31. Alison Binns, *Dedications of Monastic Houses in England and Wales, 1066–1216*, Woodbridge, 1989, pp. 19–20.

32. Arnold Angenendt, 'Die liturgische Zeit: zyklisch und linear', in *Hochmittelalterliches Geschichtsbewusstsein im Spiegel nichthistoriographischer Quellen*, ed. Hans-Werner Goetz, Berlin, 1998, pp. 101–15, at p. 105; Hen, *Roman Barbarians*, pp. 111–23.

33. José Janini, 'El oficio mozárabe de la Asunción', *Hispania sacra* 28 (1975), pp. 1–31, at p. 4; Christophe Picard, 'Le Culte marial en al-Andalus au Moyen Age', in *Autour du culte marial en Forez: Coutumes. Art. Histoire*, Saint-Étienne, 1999, pp. 47–54, at pp. 48–9.

34. G. G. Willis, *History of Early Roman Liturgy: To the Death of Pope Gregory the Great*, London, 1994, pp. 68–9; Brown, *Body and Society*, pp. 444–5.

35. It was near the old market of foodstuffs named after Livia, wife of Augustus, Aldo Nestori, 'La basilica di santa Maria Maggiore sull'Esquilino', in *I mosaici paleocristiani di Santa Maria Maggiore negli acquarelli della collezione Wilpert*, eds. Aldo Nestori and Fabrizio Bisconti, Vatican City, 2000, pp. 7–12; Hugo Brandenburg, 'Kirchenbau und Liturgie: Überlegungen zum Verhältnis von architektonischer Gestalt und Zweckbestim-

mung des frühchristlichen Kultbaues im 4. und 5. Jh.', in *Divitiae Aegypti: Koptologische und verwandte Studien zu Ehren von Martin Krause*, eds. Cäcilia Fluck et al., Wiesbaden, 1995, pp. 36–61, at pp. 49–51, 55–6.

36. Weitzmann, *The Icon*, plate 5, p. 48; Gerhard Wolf, *Salus Populi Romani: Die Geschichte römischer Kultbilder im Mittelalter*, Weinheim, 1990, pp. 161–70.

37. Outside Rome a similar representation in the apse mosaic of the Basilica of Parenzo in Istria has Mary in black, enthroned and flanked by saints.

38. Bruno Judic, 'Grégoire le Grand, un maître de la parole', in *La Parole du prédicateur, Ve–XVe siècle*, eds. Rosa Maria Dessì and Michel Lauwers, Nice, 1997, pp. 49–107; Willis, *A History of the Early Roman Liturgy*, p. 107.

39. *The Book of Pontiffs (Liber pontificalis)*, trans. Raymond Davis, 1989, p. 64.

40. Gerhard Wolf, *Salus Populi Romani: Die Geschichte römischer Kultbilder in Mittelalter*, Weinheim, 1990, figure 4, p. 276.

41. On the ceremony and icon see Charles Barber, *Figure and Likeness: On the Limits of Representation in Byzantine Iconoclasm*, Princeton, 2002, figure 9, pp. 31–2; *The Book of Pontiffs (Liber pontificalis): The Ancient Biographies of the First Ninety Roman Bishops to AD 715*, trans. Raymond Davis, rev. 2nd edn, Liverpool, 2000.

42. For text and analysis see Louis Brou, 'Marie "Destructrice de toutes les hérésies" et la belle légende du répons *Gaude Maria Virgo*', *Ephemerides liturgicae* 62 (1948), pp. 321–53, cited from pp. 321–2.

43. *The Book of Pontiffs*, 1989, p. 87; Mary Stroll, 'Maria *Regina*: Papal Symbol', in *Queens and Queenship in Medieval Europe: Proceedings of a Conference held at King's College London, April 1995*, ed. Anne J. Duggan, Woodbridge, 1997, pp. 173–203.

44. *La basilica romana di Santa Maria Maggiore*, ed. Carlo Pietrangeli, Florence, 1987.

45. Christa Ihm, *Die Programme der christlichen Apsismalerei vom vierten Jahrhundert bis zur Mitte des achten Jahrhunderts*, Wiesbaden, 1960, pp. 52–68.

46. Liz James, *Empresses and Power in Early Byzantium*, London, 2001, p. 143. See also Mary with John at the crucifixion scene, in the Chapel of Theodotus, Santa Maria Antiqua, Celia Chazelle, *The Crucified God in the Carolingian Era: Theology and Art of Christ's Passion*, Cambridge, 2001, figure 8, p. 90.

47. On the blending of Byzantine and Roman rites, exemplified through the Feast on the Presentation, see Bert Groen, 'The Festival of the Presentation of the Lord: Its Origin, Structure and Theology in the Byzantine and Roman Rites', in *Christian Feast and Festival: The Dynamics of Western Liturgy and Culture*, eds. P. Post et al., Leuven, Paris and Sterling, 2001, pp. 345–81.

48. See the letter of Hadrian c. 791, *Epistolae* V, MGH V, Berlin, 1899, pp. 6–57, at p.19.

49. Weitzmann, *The Icon*, plate 6, pp. 50–51, and on it Wolf, *Salus Populi Romani*, p. 121.

50. *The Lives of the Ninth-Century Popes (Liber pontificalis): The Ancient Biographies of Ten Popes from AD 817–891*, trans. Raymond Davis, Liverpool, 1995, pp. 13–14.

51. Charles B. McClendon, *The Origins of Medieval Architecture: Building in Europe, A.D. 600–900*, New Haven and London, 2005, pp. 146–7.

52. Michele Trimarchi, 'Per una revisione iconografica del ciclo di affreschi nel Tempio della "Fortuna Virile"', *Studi medievali* 19 (1978), pp. 653–79, esp. pp. 666–7 and plate VIII.

53. Barber, *Figure and Likeness*, pp. 27–30.

54. Thomas F. X. Noble, 'Topography, Celebration and Power: The Making of Papal Rome in the Eighth and Ninth Centuries', in *Places of Power in the Early Middle Ages*, ed. Frans Theuws and Mayke de Jong, Leiden, 2001, pp. 45–91, at pp. 87–9.

Chapter 7: The Emergence of European Mary

1. MGH, *Legum Sectio II, Capitularia Regum Francorum*, I, no. 22, c. 82, p. 61.

2. Yitzhak Hen, *The Royal Patronage of Liturgy in Frankish Gaul to the Death of Charles the Bald (877)*, London and Woodbridge, 2001, pp. 31, 49, 79, 289.

3. MGH, *Concilia*, II, 2, ed. A. Werminghoff, Hanover, 1906, no. 36, c. 36, p. 270; MGH,

Concilia, I, ed. A. Boretius, Hanover, 1883, no. 81, c. 19, p. 179. These rulings were then enforced by bishops, as in MGH, *Capitula Episcoporum*, I, ed. P. Brommer, Hanover, 1994, c. 8, p. 212. On the spread of Marian feasts see also *The Feasts of the Blessed Virgin Mary*, ed. Ann-Katrin Andrews Johansson, Stockholm, 1998, pp. 11–20. I am grateful to Christina Possel for help with this material.

4. Louis Van Tongeren, 'Transformations of the Calendar in the Early Middle Ages', in *Christian Feast and Festival: The Dynamics of Western Liturgy and Culture*, eds. P. Post et al., Louvain and Sterling, 2001, pp. 287–318.

5. Hen, *The Royal Patronage of Liturgy*, pp. 128–9.

6. *The Annals of St Bertin*, trans. J. Nelson, Manchester, 1991, p. 101.

7. Janet L. Nelson, *Charles the Bald*, London, 1992, pp. 246–8, at p. 247.

8. Paris, BNF, Lat. 12048, fol. 1v. On this image see also Chazelle, *The Crucified God*, pp. 82–5.

9. David Ganz, 'Le *De Laude Dei* d'Alcuin', *Annales de Bretagne et des Pays de l'Ouest* 111 (2004), pp. 387–91, at pp. 389–90; Chazelle, *The Crucified God*, p. 84.

10. Donald A. Bullough, *Alcuin: Achievement and Reputation*, Education and Society in the Middle Ages and Renaissance 16, Leiden, 2004, pp. 199 and 250–51.

11. Ibid. pp. 405–6. For the Mary mass associated with Alcuin see Jean Deshusses, 'Les Messes d'Alcuin', *Archiv für Liturgiewissenschaft* 14 (1972), pp. 7–41, at pp. 19–20.

12. Cullen J. Chandler, 'Heresy and Empire: The Role of the Adoptionist Controversy in Charlemagne's Conquest of the Spanish March', *International History Review* 24 (2002), pp. 505–27, at pp. 517–24; John C. Cavadini, *The Last Christology of the West*, Philadelphia, 1993, pp. 107–29.

13. At fol. 32v; Franz Unterkircher, *Zur Ikonographie und Liturgie des Drogo-Sakramentars (Paris, Bibliothèque Nationale. Ms.Lat.9428)*, Graz, 1977, p. 35.

14. Celia Chazelle, 'An "Exemplum" of Humility: The Crucifixion Image in the Drogo Sacramentary', in *Reading Medieval Images: The Art Historian and the Object*, eds. Elizabeth Sears and Thelma K. Thomas, Ann Arbor, 2002, pp. 27–35, at p. 27, and figure 2.1, p. 28.

15. Chazelle, *The Crucified God*, pp. 246–51.

16. Rachel Fulton, ' "Quae est ista quae ascendit sicut aurora consurgens?" The Song of Songs as the Historia for the Office of the Assumption', *Mediaeval Studies* 69 (1998), pp. 55–122, at pp. 91–101; Paschasius Radbert, 'De partu virginis', ed. E. Ann Matter, Turnhout, 1985, p. 10, n. 8.

17. Paschasius Radbert, *Expositio in Matheo* II, ed. Beda Paulus, Turnhout, 1984, 1, 19–20, pp. 122 and 125.

18. 'Et hoc quod conficitur in verbo Christi per Spiritum sanctum corpus ipsius esse ex virgine', Paschasius Radbert, *De corpore et sanguine Domini*, ed. Beda Paulus, Turnhout, 1969, p. 30; see Patrick Henriet, '*Invocatio sanctificatorum nominum*: Efficacité de la prière et société chrétienne (IXe–XIIe siècle)', in *La Prière en latin de l'antiquité au XVIe siècle: formes, évolutions, significations*, ed. Jean-François Cottier, Turnhout, 2006, pp. 229–44, at pp. 232–3.

19. 'Hanc oram Domini genetricis honorem dicatam,/Cultor ubique suus decoravit episcopus Hincmar/Muneribus sacris, functus hac sede sacerdos/Jam bene completis centenis octies annis,/Quadraginta simul quinto volvente sub ipsis,/Cum juvenis Carolus regeret diademata regni,/Hunc sibi pastorem poscentibus urbis alumnis', 'Hincmari carmina aliquot', *PL* 125, Paris, 1852, cols. 1201–2.

20. 'Sancta Dei genitrix, et semper virgo Maria,/Hincmarus praesul defero dona tibi./Haec pia quae gessit, docuit nos Christus Iesus/Editus ex utero, casta puella, tuo', ibid., col. 1202.

21. See also Chazelle, *The Crucified God*, pp. 252–4, and on Hincmar and the eucharist see p. 155.

22. Y. Hen, 'Rome, Anglo-Saxon England and the Formation of Frankish Liturgy', *Revue Bénédictine* 112 (2002), pp. 301–22.

23. On the antiquity of the cults see Mary Clayton, *The Cult of the Virgin Mary in Anglo-Saxon England*, Cambridge, 1990; for a summary on feasts see Mary Clayton, 'Feasts of the Virgin in the Liturgy of the Anglo-Saxon Church', *Anglo-Saxon England* 13 (1984), pp. 209–33.

24. 'The Dream of the Rood', in *The Vercelli Book*, ed. George Philip Krapp, New York, 1932, lines 90–94, p. 64.

25. Ross Trench-Jellicot, 'A Missing Figure on Slab Fragment No. 2 from Monifieth, Angus, the a'Chill Cross, Canna, and Some Implications of the Development of a Variant Form of the Virgin's Hairstyle and Dress in Early Medieval Scotland', *Proceedings of the Society of Antiquaries of Scotland* 129 (1999), pp. 597–647.

26. Maria, mater miranda,/patrem suum edidit,/per quem aqua late lotus,/totus mundus credidit', *Analecta hymnica medii aevi* LI, eds. Guido Maria Dreves and Clemens Blume, Leipzig, 1908, p. 305, stanza 8; on this theme see Andrew Breeze, 'The Virgin Mary, Daughter to her Son', *Etudes celtiques* 27 (1990), pp. 267–83, at p. 269.

27. James Bradley, 'St Joseph's Trade and Old English *Smiþ*', *Leeds Studies in English* new series 22 (1991), pp. 21–42, at p. 37.

28. James Lang, *Anglo-Saxon Sculpture*, Shire Archaeology 52, Aylesbury, 1988, p. 34; David M. Wilson, *Anglo-Saxon Art: From the Seventh Century to the Norman Conquest*, London 1984, pp. 80–81, figure 88.

29. *The Poems of Blathmac, Son of Cú Brettan*, ed. James Carney, Dublin, 1964, p. 3, no. 1.

30. Ibid., p. 15, no. 41.

31. Ibid. p. 37, no. 105.

32. Ibid., pp. 47–9, nos. 138–40.

33. Ibid., pp. 49–51, nos. 144–5, 149.

34. *Treasures of Early Irish Art, 1500 B.C. to 1500 A.D., from the Collections of the National Museum of Ireland, Royal Irish Academy, Trinity College, Dublin, Exhibited at the Metropolitan Museum of Art*, ed. Polly Cone, New York, 1977, figure 29, p. 84 and description on pp. 91–2.

35. *The Poems of Blathmac*, p. 59, no. 173, p. 63, no. 185.

36. *Early Irish Lyrics: Eighth to Twelfth Century*, ed. and trans. Gerard Murphy, Dublin, 1998, no. 16, pp. 36–9.

37. On this, the Genoels-Elderen diptych, see John Beckwith, *Ivory Carvings in Early Medieval England*, London, 1972, no. 3, p. 118, images 14 and 15, pp. 20–21; and *The Making of England: Anglo-Saxon Art and Culture, AD 600–900*, eds. Leslie Webster and Janet Backhouse, London, 1991, no. 141, pp. 180–83. I am very grateful to Jinty Nelson for pointing the diptych out to me, and appreciating its beauty.

38. Elizabeth Coatsworth, 'Cloth-making and the Virgin Mary in Anglo-Saxon Literature and Art', in *Medieval Art: Recent Perspectives: A Memorial Tribute to C. R. Dodwell*, eds. Gale R. Owen-Crocker and Timothy Graham, Manchester and New York, 1998, pp. 8–25, at pp. 16–20.

39. Beckwith, *Ivory Carvings*, p. 45, fig. 54.

40. *The Liverpool Ivories: Late Antique and Medieval Ivory and Bone Carving in Liverpool Museum and the Walker Art Gallery*, ed. Margaret Gibson, London, 1994, no. 15, plate XVa, p. 41.

41. *The Advent Lyrics of the Exeter Book*, ed. Jackson J. Campbell, Princeton, 1959, lyric VII, pp. 58–61, at p. 58.

42. 'ne ic culpan in þe/incan ænigne æfre onfunde,/womma geworhtra ond þu þa word spricest/swa þu sylfa sie synna gehwylcre/firena gefylled". "Ic to fela hæbbe/þæs byrdscypes bealwa onfongen/Hu mæg ic ladigan laþan spræce', Ibid., p. 59. On Joseph's speech see Judith N. Grade, '*Christ* I (164–95a): The Mary-Joseph Dialogue in Medieval Christian Perspective', *Neophilologus* 74 (1990), pp. 122–30.

43. Peter Lord, *The Visual Culture of Wales: Medieval Vision*, Cardiff, 2003, figure 35, p. 40.

44. It is of the late ninth or early tenth century: Lord, *The Visual Culture of Wales*, figure. 34, p. 39.

447

45. Beckwith, *Ivory Carvings*, no. 17a, pp. 121, 144, and figure 6, p. 15.

46. Ibid., no. 46, p. 42.

47. *The Golden Age of Anglo-Saxon Art 966–1066*, eds. Janet Backhouse, F. H. Turner and Leslie Webster, London, 1984, plate XXIV, figure 115.

48. Robert Deshman, *The Benedictional of Æthelwold*, Princeton, 1995, list of plates on p. ix. See also the facsimile edition, *The Benedictional of Saint Æthelwold: A Masterpiece of Anglo-Saxon Art: A Facsimile*, introduced by Andrew Prescott, London, 2002.

49. Ibid., pp. 121–4, plate 28. See the equally impressive New Minster Charter of 966 with the image of King Edgar offering the Church at Winchester to Christ with Mary at his side: Janet Backhouse, D. H. Turner and Leslie Webster, *The Golden Age of Anglo-Saxon Art, 966–1066*, Bloomington, 1984, plate IV.

50. On this feast see Mary Clayton, 'Feasts of the Virgin in the Liturgy of the Anglo-Saxon Church', *Anglo-Saxon England* 13 (1984), pp. 209–33.

51. Ælfric, *Aelfric's Catholic Homilies: The Second Series Text*, ed. M. Godden, London, 1979, p. 271, lines 1–10; on this issue see Mary Clayton, 'Ælfric and the Nativity of the Blessed Virgin Mary', *Anglia* 104 (1986), pp. 286–315, esp. p. 298. I am extremely grateful to Mr Conan Doyle of the University of Cambridge who assisted me with the translation.

52. Clayton, 'Ælfric and the Nativity', p. 290.

53. Emile De Struker and Jean Gribomont, 'Une anciènne version latine du protoévangile de Jacques', *Analecta Bollandiana* 83 (1965), pp. 365–410.

54. *The Missal of New Minster, Winchester (Le Havre, Bibliothèque Municipale, MS 330)*, ed. D. H. Turner, London, 1962, p. 190.

55. I am most grateful to my friend Gabor Klaniczay for an edifying conversation and to Professor Marianne Saghy for a well-posed question. On Hungary and Mary see Gabor Klaniczay, *Holy Rulers and Blessed Princesses: Dynastic Cults in Medieval Central Europe*, trans. Éva Pálami, Cambridge, 2000, pp. 140–42.

56. Peter Dronke, *Women Writers of the Middle Ages: A Critical Study of Texts from Perpetua (d. 203) to Marguerite Porete (d. 1310)*, Cambridge, 1984, pp. 56–7.

57. On style see Dronke, *Women Writers*, pp. 35–47. She also dramatized the Marian tale of Theophilus; see Patricia Silber, 'Hrotsvit and the Devil', in *Hrotsvit of Gandersheim: Contexts, Identities, Affinities, and Performances*, eds. Phyllis R. Brown, Linda A. McMillin and Katharina M. Wilson, Toronto, 2004, pp. 177–92, esp. at pp. 182–91.

58. Translation is from Gonsalva Wiegand, *The Non-dramatic Works of Hrotsvitha: Text, Translation, and Commentary*, Saint Louis, 1936, pp. 28–9, lines 267–77. On Hrotsvitha see Dronke, *Women Writers*, chapter 3.

59. On the milieu of Ottonian aristocratic women see Karl J. Leyser, *Rule and Conflict in an Early Medieval Society: Ottonian Saxony*, Bloomington, 1979, pp. 49–74.

60. Wiegand, *The Non-dramatic Works*, pp. 32–3, lines 330–35.

61. Ibid., pp. 42–3, lines 513–17.

62. Ibid., pp. 62–5, lines 863–5, 870–72, 880–81, 902–3.

63. On Otto III's devotion to Mary see Henry Mayr-Harting, *Ottonian Manuscript Illumination: An Historical Study*, London, 1991, II, pp. 90–95.

64. 'Princeps naturae regnans simul omnis ubique contentus gremio terris dominatur et alto', Berlin, Staatsbibliothek Preussischer Kulturbesitz, ms theol. lat. qu 199, 67r; see Bianca Kühnel, *The End of Time in the Order of Things: Science and Eschatology in Early Medieval Art*, Regensburg, 2003, p. 259, and figure 173, p. 383. On representations of Mary by the Ottonians, as a royal palace, for example, see Daniel Russo, 'Les Représentations mariales dans l'art d'Occident du Moyen Age: Essai sur la formation d'une tradition iconographique', in *Marie: Le Culte de la Vierge dans la société médiévale*, Etudes réunies par Dominique Iogna-Prat, Eric Palazzo, Daniel Russo, Paris, 1996, pp. 173–291.

65. Jean-Claude Schmitt, *La Raison des Gestes dans l'Occident médiévale*, Paris, 1990, pp. 118–19.

66. Mayr-Harting, *Ottonian Manuscript Illumination*, II, colour plate XIV; see also, plate

XV for a slightly younger sacramentary. The tradition of imperial self-presentation in the presence of Mary was adopted already by Otto I – see the gilt relief panel made in Milan around 970: Mary is enthroned, Otto, his wife Adelheid and their son young Otto kneel at her feet, while the patron saints Maurice and Vitus pray either side of Mary: Géza Jászai, *Werke des frühen und hohen Mittelalters*, Münster, 1989, figure 1, p. 7, and on it see pp. 5–7.

67. Mayr-Harting, *Ottonian Manuscript Illumination*, II, colour plate II.

68. Ibid., I, figure 85, p. 146; see for example Corrigan, *Visual Polemics*, figures 1, 42 and 50 on pp. 225, 255 and 263.

69. Mayr-Harting, *Ottonian Manuscript Illumination*, II, colour plate XV.

70. On Bernward's patronage see Francis J. Tschan, *Saint Bernward of Hildesheim, II: His Works of Art*, Notre Dame, 1951. I am extremely grateful to Dr Christine Wulf for sharing with me some of her unpublished work on the artistic patronage of Bishop Bernward.

71. On the *Goldene Madonna*'s history in Essen see Birgitta Falk, ' "Ein Mutter gottesbild mit gold plattirt . . .": Zum Erhaltungszustand der Goldenen Madonna des Essener Doms', in *Alfred Pothmann–Hüter and Bewahrer – Forscher und Erzähler – Gedenkschrift*, eds. Reimund Haas and Gabriele Beudel, Essen, 2003, pp. 159–74.

PART III: THE EMERGENCE OF MARY'S HEGEMONY: 1000–1200

Chapter 8: Mary of the Cloister

1. Robert Bartlett, *The Making of the Middle Ages: Conquest, Colonization and Cultural Change, 950–1350*, London, 1994.

2. On the Gorze reform movement and its expression in art see Adam S. Cohen, 'The Art of Reform in a Bavarian Nunnery', *Speculum* 74 (1999), pp. 992–1020.

3. Rodulfus Glaber, *The Five Books of the Histories*, ed. and trans. John France, and *The Life of St William*, ed. Neithard Bulst, trans. John France and Paul Reynolds, Oxford, 1990, pp. 114–17. On the church which may have inspired Rodulphus see Carolyn Malone, 'Saint-Bénigne in Dijon as Exemplum of Rodulfus Glaber's Metaphoric "White Mantle" ', in *The White Mantle of Churches*, ed. Nigel Hiscock, Turnhout, 2003, pp. 160–79.

4. Jacqueline Caille, 'Urban Expansion in the Region of Languedoc from the Eleventh to the Fourteenth Centuries: The Examples of Narbonne and Montpellier', in *Urban and Rural Communities in Medieval France: Provence and Languedoc, 1000–1500*, eds. Kathryn Reyerson and John Drendel, Leiden, 1998, pp. 51–72, at pp. 55–6. On the naming of churches of London, with a preponderance of dedications to Mary in the eleventh and twelfth centuries, see Caroline M. Barron, 'The Saints of London', in *Medieval Religious Cultures*, ed. Miri Rubin, *Historical Research*, Special Issue, London 2008, pp. 131–47.

5. Imad Madonna, Diocesan Museum Paderborn; New York Metropolitan Museum, see William D. Wixom, *Medieval Sculpture at the Metropolitan: 800–1400*, New York: Metropolitan Museum of Modern Art, 2005, pp. 12–13.

6. Irene H. Forsyth, *Throne of Wisdom: Wood Sculptures of the Madonna in Romanesque France*, Princeton, 1972, pp. 40–60.

7. Julia M. H. Smith, *Europe after Rome: A New Cultural History 500–1000*, Oxford: Oxford University Press, 2005, pp. 290–91.

8. Stéphane Boisselier, 'Organisation sociale et altérité culturelle dans l'hagionymie médiévale du midi portugais', *Lusitania sacra* 17 (2005), pp. 255–98.

9. André Vauchez, 'La Paix dans les mouvements religieux populaires (XIe–XVe siècles)', in *Pace e guerra nel basso medioevo: Atti del XV Convegno Storico Internazionale*, ed.

Enrico Menestò, Spoleto, 2004, pp. 313–33, at pp. 320–21; George Duby, *The Three Orders: Feudal Society Imagined*, trans. Arthur Goldhammer, Chicago, 1980, pp. 327–36.

10. Margaret Cormack, *The Saints in Iceland: Their Veneration from the Conversion to 1400*, Brussels, 1994, p. 126.

11. *900 Jahre Heilig-Blut-Verehrung in Weingarten 1094–1994*, ed. Norbert Kruse and Hans Ulrich Rudolf, Sigmaringen, 1994, figure 209, p. 270.

12. Indeed, it has been called 'the Byzantine diptych', see discussion in Francis Wormald, *The Winchester Psalter*, London, 1973, pp. 87–92; also Kristine Edmondson Haney, *The Winchester Psalter: An Iconographic Study*, Leicester, 1986, pp. 36–46. G. Zarnecki, *Later English Romanesque Sculpture, 1140–1210*, London, 1953, p. 30.

13. Beckwith, *Ivory Carvings*, figure 161, p. 91 and discussion on p. 91.

14. Fiona J. Griffiths, 'Brides and *Dominae*: Abelard's *cura monialium* at the Augustinian Monastery of Marbach', *Viator* 34 (2003), pp. 57–88, esp. pp. 57–60.

15. Ibid., note 4 (my translation) and note 5, pp. 57–8.

16. Donors to religious houses increasingly named the recipients as Mary and the monastery. See, for example, the case of Farfa: Susan Boynton, *Shaping a Monastic Identity: Liturgy and History at the Imperial Abbey of Farfa, 1000–1125*, Ithaca, 2006, pp. 31–2; Dominique Iogna-Prat, 'Politische Aspekte der Marienverehrung in Cluny um das Jahr 1000', in *Maria in der Welt: Marienverehrung im Kontext der Sozialgeschicte, 10.–18. Jahrhundert*, eds. Claudia Opitz, Hedwig Röckelein, Gabriela Signori and G. P. Marchal, Zurich, 1993, pp. 243–51. For a map of Cluniac houses see Christopher Brooke, *The Rise and Fall of the Medieval Monastery*, London, 2006, figure 4, p. 41.

17. Monique-Cécile Garand, 'Une collection de saint Odilon de Cluny et ses compléments', *Scriptorium* 33 (1979), pp. 163–80; description on pp. 165–6.

18. Barbara H. Rosenwein, *Negotiating Space: Power, Restraint, and Privileges in Early Medieval Europe*, Manchester, 1999, pp. 173–83.

19. ' "Scias," inquit, "O Heriberte, exauditas esse orationes tuas; nam ecce venio ad te, ut indicem tibi, votum, quod mente geris, quo in loci perficias. Ego, enim, sum Maria, mater Domini. Surge ergo et Tuitiense castrum petens locum in eodem mundari precipe, ibique monasterium Deo michique et omnium sanctis constitue, ut ubi quondam *habundavit peccatum* et cultus demonum, ibi *iustitia regnet* in multitudine sanctorum" ', *Rupert von Deutz, Vita Heriberti: Kritische Edition mit Kommentar und Untersuchungen*, ed. Peter Dinter, Bonn, 1976, p. 54.

20. ' "Benedictus domino vir iste, qui nos hodie bene consolatus est. Sed estne soror eius", inquiunt, "domina illa praeclara, que in tam commode radios ad manum dat et docet, quid faciat?" ', Ekkehard IV, *Casus sancti Galli*, ed. and trans. H. F. Häfele, Darmstadt, 1980, p. 102, c. 45.

21. On this tale see Jean-Marie Sansterre, 'Le Moine ciseleur, la Vierge Marie et son image: un récit d'Ekkehard IV de Saint-Gall', *Revue bénédictine* 106 (1996), pp. 185–91.

22. Schmitt, *La Raison des gestes dans l'Occident médiéval*, pp. 243–4. Manuals with instruction on the appropriate correlation in imagery between Old Testament and New Testament scenes emerge in this period. See M. R. James, '*Pictor in carmine*', *Archeologia* 94 (1951), pp. 141–66.

23. Diana Webb, 'The Holy Face of Lucca', *Anglo-Norman Studies* 9 (1987), pp. 227–37.

24. 'Orderic Vitalis, *The Ecclesiastical History of Orderic Vitalis* III, ed. and trans. Marjorie Chibnall, Oxford, 1972, p. 201. I first came across this case in Karl Morrison, *History as a Visual Art in the Twelfth-century Renaissance*, Princeton, 1990, p. 96, n. 14.

25. Jean-Claude Schmitt, *La Raison des gestes*, Paris, 2003, p. 270.

26. Henry Mayr-Harting, *Ottonian Book Illumination: An Historical Study* I, 2nd edn, London, 1999, pp. 139–56.

27. This drawing, at the very beginning of the psalter, may have been inspired by a bronze crucifix owned by that religious house, *Das Jahrtausend der Mönche: Kloster Welt Werden 799–1803*, ed. Jan Gerchow, Cologne, 1999, p. 364 and reproduction no. 65, p. 366.

28. Fulda Collectory before 1130, fol. 81r; *900 Jahre Heilig-Blut-Verehrung*, figure 139, p. 189.

29. On the Byzantine iconography see Christa Schaffer, *Aufgenommen ist Maria in den Himmel*, Regensburg, 1985.

30. Manchester, John Rylands Library, lat. 110, fol. 17r; Bernd Michael, 'Liudger und Probianus: Zur Geschichte der illuminierten Liudgervita und des spätantiken Konsulardip-tychons', in *Das Jahrtausend der Mönche: Kloster Welt Werden 799–1803*, ed. Jan Gerchow, Cologne, 1999, pp. 223–31; illustration no. 86, p. 225.

31. Frankfurt, Stadt- und Universitätsbibliothek, Ms. Barth. 42, fol. 169r; Jeffrey Hamburger, 'To Make Women Weep: Ugly Art as "Feminine" and the Origins of Modern Aesthetics', *Res* 31 (1997), pp. 9–34; p. 29, figure 16.

32. T. A. Heslop, 'The Virgin Mary's Regalia and 12th-century English Seals', in *The Vanishing Past: Studies of Medieval Art, Liturgy and Metrology presented to Christopher Hohler*, eds. Alan Borg and Andrew Martindale, British Archaeological Research International Series 111, Oxford, 1981, pp. 53–62, at pp. 53, 55.

33. For insightful comments on this image and a reproduction see Sara Lipton, ' "The Sweet Lean of his Head": Writing about Looking at the Crucifix in the High Middle Ages', *Speculum* 80 (2005), pp. 1172–208, at pp. 1186–7, and figure 3 on p. 1187.

34. Cambridge Corpus Christi College 422, p. 53.

35. Beckwith, *Ivory Carvings*, figure 130, p. 78 and no. 74, p. 133.

36. 'Victima mactatur qua nostra ruina levatur', *Autour de Hugo d'Oignies*, eds. Robert Dicker and Jacques Toussaint, Namur, 2003, colour plate on p. 62.

37. Neil MacGregor and Erika Langmuir, *Seeing Salvation: Images of Christ in Art*, London, 2000, no. 9 colour plate, p. 38.

38. Berlin, Staatliche Museen; Beckwith, *Ivory Carvings*, figure 131, p. 78, no. 76, pp. 133–4.

39. On the relations between monasteries and the laity through fraternities see Arnoud-Jan A. Bijsterveld, 'Looking for Common Ground: From Monastic Fraternitas to Lay Confraternity in the Southern Low Countries in the Tenth to Twelfth Centuries', in *Religious and Laity in Western Europe, 1000–1400: Interaction, Negotiation, and Power*, eds. Emilia Jamroziak and Janet E. Burton, Turnhout, 2006, pp. 287–314.

40. Christopher Page, *The Owl and the Nightingale*, pp. 135–6.

41. Dianne Hall, *Women and the Church in Medieval Ireland, c.1140–1540*, Dublin, 2003, p. 73.

42. Jay Rubenstein, *Guibert of Nogent: Portrait of a Medieval Mind*, New York and London, 2002, pp. 23, 178.

43. On emotional communities see Barbara H. Rosenwein, *Emotional Communities in the Early Middle Ages*, Ithaca, 2006; on prayer and emotion see Rachel Fulton, 'Praying with Anselm at Admont: A Meditation on Practice', *Speculum* 81 (2006), pp. 700–33, and Rachel Fulton, *From Judgment to Passion: Devotion to Christ and the Virgin Mary, 800–1200*, New York, 2002, pp. 218–43.

44. Jacques Le Goff, *The Birth of Purgatory*, trans. Arthur Goldhammer, Aldershot, 1990.

45. 'Quod uoles, unigenitus,/Donabit tibi Filius;/Pro quibus uoles veniam/Impetrabis et gloriam', *Anima mea: prières privées et textes de dévotion du moyen âge latin*, ed. Jean-François Cottier, Turnhout, 2001, p. 144, lines 13–16.

46. 'Cum mente tracto Angelos,/Prophetas et Apostolos,/victoriosos Martyres, et perpudicas Virgines, Nullus michi potentior,/nullus misericordior,/Illorum pace dixerim, Videtur Matre Domini', ibid., p. 146, lines 33–40.

47. 'Sed quis ago, obscenitates meas referens auribus illibatis? Horresco, Domina, horresco, et arguente me conscientia, male nudus coram te erubesco', ibid., p. 114, lines 7–9. The prayer is often attributed to St Anselm (1033–1109).

48. 'O beatissima et sanctissima Virgo semper Maria, ecce asto maerens ante faciem pietatis tuae, et confundor nimis pro abominationibus peccatorum meorum quibus deformis factus

sum et horribilis angelis et omnibus sanctis', ibid., p. 230, lines 1–3. See an Irish monastic prayer of this period: *Early Irish Lyrics: Eighth to Twelfth Century*, ed. and trans. Gerard Murphy, Dublin, 1998, no. 20, pp. 46–51.

49. 'Tu enim nosti, misericordissima Regina, quia ad hoc nata es ut per te nasceretur idem Deus et homo, Dominus noster Ihesus Christus, uerus Deus et uerus homo, in quem veracissime credo', *Anima mea*, p. 230, lines 12–14.

50. 'Tu, Domina, mirabiris et corporis integritatem et conceptus fecunditatem, et gaudebas tuum paritura parentem, Dominus nostrum Ihesus Christum', ibid., p. 232, lines 22–3.

51. 'Tu, vero, Domina, omnibus his adiutoribus melior et excellentior es', Ibid., p. 234, lines 61–2.

52. 'O duae gemmae caelestes, Maria et Iohannes! O duo luminaria divinitus ante Deum lucentia! uestris radiis scelerum meorum effugate nubila', ibid., PsOr 12, p. 204, lines 9–10.

53. Herbert L. Kessler, *Spiritual Seeing: Picturing God's Invisibility in Medieval Art*, Middle Ages Series, Philadelphia, 2000, pp. 16–17. Mary drove people to penance through chastisement, as she did a group of crusaders during the siege of Antioch in 1097: see Thomas Asbridge, 'The Holy Lance of Antioch: Power, Devotion and Memory on the First Crusade', *Reading Medieval Studies* 33 (2007), pp. 3–36, at p. 7.

54. Richard W. Southern, *Saint Anselm: A Portrait in a Landscape*, Cambridge, 1990.

55. Fulton, 'Praying with Anselm at Admont'.

56. 'Et utinam ita sint longae ut, antequam ad finem cuiuslibet earum legendo vel potius meditando perveniatur, id ad quod factae sunt, compunctio scilicet contritionis vel dilectionis, in eis per supernum respectum inveniatur', Letter 28, Anselm, *Opera omnia* III, ed. F. S. Schmitt, Edinburgh, 1946, lines 15–18. On these writings see *Anima mea*, pp. cviii–cx.

57. Anselm of Canterbury, *Sancti Anselmi Cantuariensis archiepiscopi opera omnia*, ed. F. S. Schmitt, II, pp. 39–133 (*Cur Deus Homo*) and I, pp. 137–73 (*De conceptu virginali*); on circulation see Joan Greatrex, 'Marian Studies and Devotion in the Benedictine Cathedral Priories in Later Medieval England', *Studies in Church History* 39 (2004), pp. 157–67.

58. Fulton, 'Praying with Anselm at Admont'; Fulton, *From Judgement to Compassion*, pp. 194–5; Otto Pächt, 'The Illustrations of Saint Anselm's Prayers and Meditations', *Journal of the Warburg and Courtauld Institutes* 19 (1956), pp. 68–83. In seeking these prayers Matilda was following the advice given her by Pope Gregory VII: 'I am, therefore, directing you to entrust yourself wholly to the unfailing protection of the Mother of God . . . But now concerning the Mother of God, to whom above all I have committed you, do now commit, and shall never cease to commit you until, as we hope, we shall meet her face to face, what can I say of her whom earth and heaven cease not to praise, though never as her merits deserve', *The Correspondence of Pope Gregory VII: Selected Letters from the Registrum*, trans. Ephraim Emerton, New York, 1932, pp. 23–4.

59. 'Corporaliter te [Christum] prima tetigit atque tractavit', André Wilmart, 'Cinq textes de prières composés par Anselme de Lucque pour la Comtesse Mathilde', *Revue d'Ascétique et de mystique* 19 (1938), pp. 23–72, at p. 70.

60. Wilmart, 'Cinq textes', p. 54. See Silvia Cantelli, 'Le preghiere a Maria di Anselmo da Lucca', in *Sant'Anselmo, Mantova e la lotta per le investiture: atti del convegno internazionale di Studi (Mantova 23–24–25 maggio 1986)*, ed. Paolo Golinelli, Bologna, 1987, pp. 291–9.

61. 'Sed, quia ad hec electa es et universis creatures cum filio tuo prelata, super omnium mortalium gloriam et angelicam dignitatem exaltata', Wilmart, 'Cinq textes', p. 51, lines 39–41.

62. Otto Pächt, 'The Illustrations of Saint Anselm's Prayers', pp. 70–71; Fulton, 'Praying with Anselm at Admont', p. 706, n. 26.

63. *The Life of Christina of Markyate a Twelfth Century Recluse*, ed. and trans. C. H. Talbot, Oxford, 1959, repr. 1987, pp. 74–7, at p. 74.

64. Jane Geddes, *The St Albans Psalter: A Book for Christina of Markyate*, London, 2005, on Abbot Geoffrey, pp. 12–14; Morgan Powell, 'Making the Psalter of Christina of Markyate (The St Albans Psalter)', *Viator* 36 (2005), pp. 293–335. The Psalter is available electronically at http://www.abdn.ac.uk/stalbanspsalter/.

65. Geddes, *The St Albans Psalter: A Book for Christina of Markyate*, plates 5, p. 17; 10, p. 23; 11, p. 24; 12, p.25; and Pentecost plate 46, p. 59.

66. *Life of Christina*, p. 119.

67. Anne L. Clark, 'Holy Woman or Unworthy Vessel? The Representations of Elisabeth of Schönau', in *Gendered Voices: Medieval Saints and their Interpreters*, ed. Catherine M. Mooney, Philadelphia, 1999, pp. 35–51, 202–7, at pp. 38, 47.

68. Elisabeth of Schönau. *The Complete Works*, ed. and trans. Anne L. Clark, New York and Mahwah, 2000, p. 208; Anne L. Clark, 'Why All the Fuss about the Mind? A Medievalist's Perspective on Cognitive Theory', in *History in the Comic Mode: Medieval Communities and the Matter of Person*, eds. Rachel Fulton and Bruce W. Holsinger, New York, 2007, pp. 170–81, at pp. 178–80.

69. Elisabeth of Schönau. *The Complete Works*, p. 24; Anne L. Clark, *Elisabeth of Schönau: A Twelfth-Century Visionary*, Philadelphia, 1992, pp. 40, 59, 109–110.

70. R. I. Moore, *The Birth of Popular Heresy*, London, 1975, p. 93.

71. Henry Mayr-Harting, 'The Idea of the Assumption of Mary in the West, 800–1200', *Studies in Church History* 39 (2004), pp. 86–111, at pp. 109–10; on their relationship see John W. Coakley, *Women, Men, and Spiritual Power: Female Saints and Their Male Collaborators*, New York, 2006, pp. 30–32.

72. Legend linked the Chartres tunic to victory in battle; Antelm, bishop of Chartres (*c.*898–*c.*911), defended the city against Rollo, duke of Normandy, with the tunic, and rebuffed the attack, *The Gesta Normannorum ducum of William of Jumièges, Orderic Vitalis, and Robert of Torigni* II, ed. and trans. Elisabeth M. C. Van Houts, Oxford, 1992, pp. 62–3.

73. William of Malmesbury, *El libro De laudibus et miraculis Sanctae Mariae*, ed. José M. Canal, 2nd edn, Rome, 1968.

74. Margot Fassler, 'Mary's Nativity: Fulbert of Chartres, and the *Stirps Jesse*: Liturgical Innovation circa 1000 and its Afterlife', *Speculum* 75 (2000), pp. 389–434. '*R*: Stirps Iesse virgam produxit, virgaque florem, et super hunc florem requiescat Spiritus almus. *V*: Virga dei genitrix virgo est, flos filius eius. Et super hunc florem requiescat Spiritus almus. *R*: Flegrescit ultra omnia balsama pigmenta et timiamata. *V*: Purpurea ut viola roscida ut rosa candens ut lilia', p. 421 with notes.

75. See Fulbert's sermons for the feast, *PL* 141 cols. 320–24; at cols. 324–5.

76. 'In horis tres candele ante altare illuminentur. Priusque sonetur Prima, ponantur in altare maius tres calices aurei, et duo candelabra in eodem loco accendantur totaque die ardeant. Insuper et in ipsa ara ponant brachium beatissimi Mauri et sceptrum aureum cum vaso similiter aureo in quo lac beatissimae Mariae virginis', in Ruth Steiner, 'Marian Antiphons at Cluny and Lewes', in *Music in the Medieval English Liturgy*, eds. Susan Rankin and David Hiley, Oxford, 1993, pp. 175–204, at p. 199; *Liber Tramitis Aevi Odilonis Abbatis*, ed. P. Dinter, Siegburg, 1980, pp. 148–52, at p. 150; Susan Boynton, 'Les Coutumes clunisiennes au temps d'Odilon', in *Odilon de Mercoeur: L'Auvergne et Cluny, La 'Paix de Dieu' et l'Europe de l'an mil*, ed. Marcel Pacaut, Nonette, 2002, pp. 193–203.

77. On the use of the Song of Songs in the Assumption liturgy see Rachel Fulton, ' "Quae est ista quae ascendit sicut aurora consurgens?": The Song of Songs as the *historia* for the Office of the Assumption', *Mediaeval Studies* 60 (1998), pp. 55–122, and E. Ann Matter, *The Voice of My Beloved: The Song of Songs in Western Medieval Christianity*, Philadelphia, 1992, pp. 151–77.

75. 'Talem pompam promeruit quae mundo salutem protulit … Electa est genitrix sui creatoris. Nunc visionem pascitur almae deitatis. Primatum gerit illa in choris quos pulchritude Christi ornavit, gloriatur virgo insignis, beatis praelata virginum cateris. Adest parata igitur, supplicantibus deo supplex offerre preces'. François Leroy, 'Un fragment de sermon

nouveau ou peu connu sur l'Assomption (Bibliothèque des Bollandistes, cod. 293, f. 1ra)', *Analecta bollandiana* 118 (2000), pp. 325–8, at p. 327.

79. Paris, BNF Ms. 14525, fols. 77r–80r, at fols. 77v–78r. I am most grateful to my friend Dr Sara Lipton, who introduced me to this sermon, which she discusses in her forthcoming book *The Vulgate Experience: Preaching, Art and Piety in the High Middle Ages*.

80. See, for example, in Farfa, Boynton, *Shaping a Monastic Identity*, p. 11.

81. 'Hodie virgo Maria/Caelorum peciit alta;/Gaudet celestis caterva/Et nos/GAUDE-AMUS OMNES IN DOMINO/Agentes gratias ili,/Qui ex ea nasci dignatus est, atque/DIEM FESTUM CELEBRANTES SUB HONORE MARIE VIRGINIS,/Quo there<a> ascendere meruit regna/DE CUIUS ASSUMPTIONE GAUDENT ANGELI/ET COLLAUDANT FILIUM DEI', Brian Møller Jensen, '*Beata Maria semper virgo* in Piacenza, Biblioteca Capitolare, c. 65', in *Liturgy and the Arts in the Middle Ages: Studies in Honour of C. Clifford Flanigan*, eds. Eva Louise Lillie and Nils Holger Petersen, Copenhagen, 1996, pp. 134–67, at p. 143; *Tropes of the Proper of the Mass IV: The Feasts of the Blessed Virgin Mary*, ed. Ann-Katrin Andrews Johansson, Stockholm, 1998, no. 44, pp. 97–9.

82. Philippe Verdier, *Le Couronnement de la Vierge: Les Origines et les premiers développements d'un thème iconographique*, Paris, 1980, pp. 115–16, figure 8; Teresa Vicens Soler, 'Possibles bases textuales per a representacions assumpcionistes a Catalunya: el Timpà de Cabestany i el Frontal de Mosoll', *Acta historica et archaeologica mediaevalia* 19 (1998), pp. 273–93, at p. 277.

83. 'CORPUS MATRIS DEI FERTUR AD COELUM ET IESUS AD PATREM PECIT ALMAM SCANDERE MATREM'. The early-twelfth-century tympanum of the south doorway of St Swithin's church, Quenington (Gloucestershire), is carved with an early scene of the Coronation in heaven. Mary is seated, crowned, beside a somewhat damaged figure of her son, surrounded by the symbols of the evangelists: T. A. Heslop, 'The English Origins of the Coronation of the Virgin', *The Burlington Magazine* 147 (2005), pp. 790–97.

84. Barcelona, Museum of Catalan Art.

85. Simon Claude Mimouni, *Dormition et Assomption de Marie: Histoire des traditions anciennes*, Paris, 1995, pp. 213–17.

86. 'Dote subarrata fidei meritisque sacrata/Sponsa coronatur sponsoque deo sociatur', Heslop, 'The English Origins', p. 791, n. 11.

87. Ibid., p. 790, n. 7.

88. 'Musica in conexu utriusque "est illa naturalis amicitia qua anima corpori non corporeis vinculis" alligata tenetur', Richard of St Victor, *Liber exceptionum*, I, i, c. 10, ed. J. Châtillon, Paris, 1958, p. 108.

89. There is a touching representation of the Visitation on the façade of Notre-Dame-la-Grande, in Poitiers, a church consecrated in 1086.

90. Bernard of Clairvaux and Amadeus of Lausanne, *Magnificat: Homilies in Praise of the Blessed Virgin Mary*, trans. Marie-Bernard Saïd and Grace Perigo, Kalamazoo, 1979, pp. 36–7.

91. Avrom Saltman, 'The Exegetical Material in Alexander Nequam's Commentary on the Song of Songs' (in Hebrew), p. 429, Appendix A, 21. On Nequam see Richard W. Hunt, *The Schools and the Cloister: The Life and Writings of Alexander Nequam (1157–1217)*, ed. and revised Margaret Gibson, Oxford, 1984; on his Hebrew, pp.108–110. See the twelfth-century English guide to biblical typology, M. R. James, '*Pictor in carmine*', *Archaeologia* 94 (1951), pp. 141–66.

92. On this see Jean-Pierre Delville, 'Julienne de Cornillon à la lumière de son biographie', in *Fête -Dieu (1246–1996): Actes du colloque de Liège, 12–14 Septembre 1996*, ed. André Haquin, Louvain-la-Neuve, 1999, pp. 27–53, at p. 46.

93. Margot Fassler, *Gothic Song: Victorine Sequences and Augustinian Reform in Twelfth-century Paris*, Cambridge, 1993, p. 184.

94. Bruce W. Holsinger. *Music, Body, and Desire in Medieval Culture: Hildegard of Bingen to Chaucer*, Stanford, 2001, esp. chapter 4.

95. Fassler, *Gothic Song*, pp. 103–4.

96. Ibid., pp. 206–10; also Margot Fassler, 'Who was Adam of St Victor? The Evidence of the Sequence Manuscripts', *Journal of the American Musicological Society* 37 (1984), pp. 233–69.

97. Jean-Yves Tilliette, 'La Musique des mots: Douceur et plaisir dans la poésie latine au Moyen Age', in *Rhétorique et poétique au Moyen Age*, ed. Alain Michel, Turnhout, 2002, pp. 121–36, at pp. 134–6.

98. 'In natale Salvatoris / Angelorum nostra choris / Succinat conditio. / Harmonia diversorum, / Sed in unum redactorum, / Dulcis est connexio. // Felix dies hodiernus, / In quo Patri coaeternus / Nascitur ex virgine. / Felix dies et iocundus. / Illustrari gaudet mundus / Veri solis lumine', *Oeuvres poétiques d'Adam de Saint-Victor*, ed. L. Gautier, Paris, 1881, p. 4.

99. James Grier, 'A New Voice in the Monastery: Tropes and *Versus* from Eleventh- and Twelfth-Century Aquitaine', *Speculum* 69 (1994), pp. 1023–69, esp. pp. 1034–47; Gunilla Iversen, 'A la louange de la vierge mère: sequences du XIIe siècle', in *Chanter avec les anges: Poésie dans la messe médiévale, interpretations et commentaries*, Paris, 2001, pp. 177–89.

100. Susan Boynton, 'Rewriting the Early Sequence: *Aureo flore* and *Aurea virga*', *Comitatus* 25 (1994), pp. 21–42, at p. 22.

101. 'O dei nostri genitrixque pia suscipe nostra hac die peccata in qua es assumpta ad caeli claustra / Hodie namque curiae caelestis tibi hobviat agmina te adsumpserunt ad palacia stellata'. For another example of the remaking of an old chant into *Radix Iesse*, for greater Mary content, see Susan Boynton, *Shaping a Monastic Identity: Liturgy and History at the Imperial Abbey of Farfa 1000–1125*, Ithaca, 2006, pp. 51–62.

102. On Hildegard's life see Sabina Flanagan, *Hildegard of Bingen, 1098–1179: A Visionary Life*, London, 2nd edn, 1998; and Marianne Richert Pfau and Stefan Johannes Morent, *Hildegard von Bingen: Der Klang des Himmels*, Cologne, 2005.

103. Hildegard of Bingen, *Symphonia: A Critical Edition of the Symphonia Armonie Celestium Revelationum*, 2nd edn, Ithaca, 1998, pp. 122–3, see also p. 275.

104. Bruce W. Holsinger offers an insightful analysis of the music in *Music, Body, and Desire in Medieval Culture, 1150–1400: Hildegard of Bingen to Chaucer*, Stanford, 2001, pp. 105–13, esp. p. 107 and musical example 1, and on music and the Incarnation pp. 91–4; Margot Fassler, 'Music for the Love Feast: Hildegard of Bingen and the Song of Songs', in *Women's Voices across Musical Worlds*, ed. Jane A. Bernstein, Boston, 2004, pp. 92–117. I have benefited greatly from conversations with Christopher Page, who conducted the recording of *Ave generosa* with Gothic Voices in HYP66039 Hildegard of Bingen, *Feather on the Breath of God*, HYPERION, Emma Kirkby / Page / Gothic Voices. On Hildegard's music and the feminine see also María Eugenia Góngora, '*Feminea Forma* and *Virga*: Two Images of Incarnation in Hildegard of Bingen's *Symphonia*', in *The Voice of Silence: Women's Literacy in a Men's Church*, eds. Thérèse de Hemptinne and María Eugenia Góngora, Turnhout, 2004, pp. 23–36.

105. Hildegard of Bingen, *Symphonia*, pp. 114–15, see also p. 272. See also Pascale Bourgain, 'Formes et figures de l'esthétique poétique au XIIe siècle', in *Rhétorique et poétique au moyenâge*, ed. Alain Michel, Turnhout, 2002, pp. 103–19, esp. at pp. 113–14.

106. Hildegard of Bingen, *Symphonia*, pp. 110–11 and 271; on it Gunilla Iversen, *Chanter avec les anges: Poésie dans la messe médiévale: Interprétations et commentaires*, Paris, 2001, pp. 255–6. On the opposition and comparison between Mary and Eve in Hildegard's musical, as well as mystical works, see María Isabel Flisfisch, 'The Eve-Mary Dichotomy in the *Symphonia* of Hildegard of Bingen', in *the Voices of Silence: Women's Literacy in a Men's Church*, eds. Thérèse de Hemptinne and María Eugenia Góngora, Turnhout, 2004, pp. 37–46.

107. Hildegard of Bingen, *Symphonia*, pp. 120–21 and 271.

108. R. W. Southern, *Western Society and the Church in the Middle Ages*, Harmondsworth, 1970, p. 254 and Frédéric van der Meer, *Atlas de l'Ordre Cistercien*, Paris and Brussels, 1965. I am most grateful to Professor Connie Berman, who advised me on the number of houses.

109. Gabriela Signori, ' "Totius ordinis nostri patrona et advocata": Maria als Haus- und Ordensheilige des Zisterzienser', in *Maria in der Welt: Marienverehrung im Kontext der Sozialgeschichte, 10.–18. Jahrhundert,* eds. Claudia Opitz, Hedwig Röckelein, Gabriela Signori and G. P. Marchal, Zurich, 1993, pp. 253–77.

110. See the image in *Mönchtum in Ost und West: Historischer Atlas*, ed. J. M. Laboa, Regensburg, 2003, figure 401.

111. Terry N. Kinder, *Cistercian Europe: Architecture of Contemplation*, Cistercian Studies Series 191, Kalamazoo, 2002, pp. 131, 217. On Cistercian architecture generally see Peter Fergusson, *Architecture of Solitude: Abbeys in Twelfth Century England*, Princeton, 1984. For evidence of Mary's entry into the Cistercian calendar see *Fiant festa per ordinem universum*, eds. Kateřína Charvátová and Zuzana Silagiová, Prague, 2003. See a Cistercian sermon on the Purification: Alered of Rievaulx, *The Liturgical Sermons*, trans. Theodore Berkeley and M. Basil Penignton, Kalamazoo, 2001, pp. 119–28.

112. Domina nostra,/mediatrix nostra,/advocate nostra,/tuo Filio nos reconcilia,/tuo Filio nos recommenda,/tuo filio nos representa./Fac,/o benedicta,/per gratiam quam invenisti,/per praerogativam quam meruisti,/per misericordiam quam peperisti,/ut qui, e mediante,/fieri dignatus est particeps infirmitatis/et miseriae nostrae,/te quoque intercedente/participes faciat nos gloriae/et beatitudinis suae,/Iesus Christus/Filius tuus,/Dominus noster'. For the translation and discussion of the prayer see Jean Leclercq, *Women and Saint Bernard of Clairvaux*, trans. Marie-Bernard Saïd, Kalamazoo, 1989, pp. 92–109, for text see p. 93; see Fulton, *From Judgement to Passion*, pp. 303–9.

113. Brian Patrick McGuire, 'Bernard and Mary's Milk: A Northern Contribution', in *The Difficult Saint: Bernard of Clairvaux and His Tradition*, Kalamazoo, 1991, pp. 189–225, esp. 196–202.

114. Denis Renevey, *Language, Self and Love: Hermeneutics in the Writings of Richard Rolle and the Commentaries on the Song of Songs*, Cardiff, 2001, pp. 26–32.

115. On Amadeus' life see *Magnificat: Homilies in Praise of the Blessed Virgin Mary*, eds. Marie-Bernard Saïd and Grace Perigo, Kalamazoo, 1979, pp. xxiii–xxvi.

116. *Magnificat*, p. 101.

117. *Magnificat*, p. xxxv.

118. Above, pp. 53–7.

119. *Magnificat*, p. 121.

120. Ibid., pp. 127–8.

121. 'Nisi enim hoc fossatim primo fuerit in corde nostro, id est vera humilitas, non poterimus aedificare nisi ruinam super proprium caput', Aelred of Rievaulx, *Sermones*, ed. Gaetano Raciti, Turnhout, 1989, Sermon XIX, c. 8, p. 148. On the imagery of fortification and Mary see Paul Binksi, 'The Imagery of the High Altar Piscine of Saint-Urban at Troyes', forthcoming.

122. Aelred of Rievaulx, *Sermones*, p. 149.

123. Ibid., p. 156.

124. Aelred of Rievaulx, 'De Iesu puero duodenni', *Opera Omnia. I. Opera ascetica*, eds. A. Hoste and C. H. Talbot, Turnhout, 1971, pp. 245–78, at p. 257.

125. Kazimierz Romaniuk, 'Mary, Mediatrix of All Graces, in the Works of Adam of Perseigne', *Cistercian Studies* 33 (1988), pp. 185–90, at p. 185.

126. 'Ipsa media est inter coelum et terram, media et mediatrix inter Deum et hominem', Adam of Perseigne, *Fragmenta Mariana*, *PL* 211, Paris, 1855, cols. 743–54; col. 752.

127. Adam of Perseigne, 'Sermon Five, On the Assumption, by Adam of Perseigne', trans. Philip F. O'Mara, *Cistercian Studies* 33 (1998), pp. 151–63, at pp. 157–8.

128. Dijon, Bibliothèque municipale, 641, fol. 40; see also Katrin Kogman-Appel, 'The Tree of Life and the Tree of Death: The Hanging of Haman in Medieval Jewish Manuscript

Painting', in *Between the Picture and the Word: Manuscript Studies from the Index of Christian Art*, ed. Colum Hourihane, University Park, 2005, pp. 187–208, at pp. 189–190.

129. For another example of Mary as Tree of Life see Dominique Paris-Poulain, 'A Representation of the Arbor-Ecclesia: Contribution to the Study of the Murals of Petit-Quevilly', in *The Role of Ornament in the Mural from the Middle Ages*, Poitiers, 1997, pp. 121–37; plate XXXIV, figure 8.

130. Helinand of Froidmont, 'Sermones', *PL* 212, Paris, 1855, cols. 636–46, sermon 19, at col. 636.

131. 'Nutrita est a Spiritu sancto ante conceptionem Domini, non sunt audita in ea humanibus auribus vel angelicis vel divinis, malleus et secures, peccata scilicet actionis et cogitationis', Helinand of Froidmont, 'Sermones', col. 638, quote from col. 639.

132. Ibid., col. 642.

133. Ibid., Sermon 20, cols. 646–52.

134. Ibid., col. 648.

135. Anne T. Thayer, 'Judith and Mary: Hélinand's Sermon for the Assumption', in *Medieval Sermons and Society: Cloister, City, University*, eds. Jacqueline Hamesse et al., Louvain-La-Neuve, 1998, pp. 63–75. I am most grateful to Professor Thayer for discussing this sermon with me and providing me with an offprint of her article.

136. Helinand of Froidmont, 'Sermones', col. 652; and earlier quote at col. 651.

137. 'Quid tibi et purgacioni, O Maria, virgo virginum pudicissima, puellarum innocentissima, mulierum pulcherrima, matrum felicissima, reginarum dignissima, ancillarum humillima, turutrum castissima, simplicissima columbarum', Beverly Mayne Kienzle, 'Mary Speaks against Heresy: An Unedited Sermon of Hélinand for the Purification, Paris BNF Ms. Lat. 14591', *Sacris erudiri* 32 (1991), pp. 291–308, at p. 300.

138. Beverly Mayne Kienzle, 'Maternal Imagery in the Sermons of Hélinand of Froidmont', in *De Ore Domini: Preacher and Word in the Middle Ages*, eds. Thomas L. Amos, Eugene A. Green and Beverly Mayne Kienzle, Kalamazoo, 1989, pp. 93–103, esp. at pp. 93–6.

Chapter 9: Mary of Polemic and Encounter

1. Beryl Smalley, *The Study of the Bible in the Middle Ages*, 3rd edn, Oxford, 1983, pp. 64–6.

2. E. Anne Matter, *The Voice of My Beloved: The Song of Songs in Western Medieval Christianity*, Middle Ages Series, Philadelphia, 1990, pp. 151–77. See also Rachel Fulton, 'Mimetic Devotion, Marian Exegesis, and the Historical Sense of the Song of Songs', *Viator* 27 (1996), pp. 85–116, esp. at pp. 85–9.

3. Valerie I. J. Flint, 'The Commentaries of Honorius Augustodunensis on the Song of Songs', *Revue Bénédictine* 84 (1974), pp. 197–211, at pp. 198-200; Rachel Fulton, *From Judgment to Passion: Devotion to Christ and the Virgin 800–1200*, New York, 2002, pp. 247–58.

4. C. M. Kauffmann, *Biblical Imagery in Medieval England 100–1500*, London, 2003, no. 57, p. 78.

5. Richard W. Southern, 'The English Origins of the Miracles of the Virgin', *Mediaeval and Renaissance Studies* 4 (1958), pp. 176–216.

6. Honorius Augustodunensis, *The Seal of the Blessed Mary*, trans. Amelia Carr, Toronto, 1991, pp. 23–7; Fulton, *From Judgment to Passion*, pp. 279–85.

7. See on this world Jeremy Cohen, '*Synagoga conversa*: Honorius Augustodunensis, the Song of Songs, and Christianity's "Eschatological Jew" ', *Speculum* 79 (2004), pp. 309–40.

8. On monks and the Song of Songs see Jean Leclercq, *Monks and Love in the Twelfth Century: Psycho-historical Essays*, Oxford, 1979, pp. 29–40; and Fulton, *From Judgment to Passion*, pp. 297–303, 318–23.

9. 'O pulcherrima mulierum, o benedicta inter mulieres, cuius pulchritudo benedictio est, cuius pulchritudo ipse benedictus fructus uentris tui est, talis ac tanta causa tua est, ut si teipsam non ignores, statim scias illud quod quaeris, dicens: . . . Vnde pulchritudinem

istam acquisisti, ut sis pulcherrima mulierum? Ex fide et humilitate an ex operibus legis? Nonne ex fide et humilitate', Rupert of Deutz, *Commentaria in Canticum Canticorum*, ed. H. Haacke, Turnhout, 1974, p. 25, lines 542–4, 552–4. Fulton, *From Judgment to Passion*, pp. 317–44.

10. Fulton, 'Mimetic Devotion', p. 93.

11. 'Aperi mihi, scilicet os tuum, loquere, prout ad confirmandum pertinet euangelium, et in hoc optatae tibi quietis patere dispendium; ut gratum singulari pudicitiae tuae propter me rumpas silentium', Rupert of Deutz, *Commentaria in canticum canticorum*, ed. Hrabanus Haacke, Turnhout, 1974, pp. 107–8. On this see also Fulton, 'Mimetic Devotion', pp. 103–4.

12. Rupert of Deutz, *Commentaria*, pp. 107–8, lines 102–10.

13. See Lajos Csóka, 'Ein unbekannter Brief des Abtes Rupert von Deutz', *Studien und Mitteilungen zur Geschichte des Benediktinerordens* 84 (1973), pp. 383–93, at p. 383.

14. Anonymous of Melk, 'De scriptoribus ecclesiasticis', *PL* 213, Paris, 1855, cols. 959–84, col. 979C, c. 113.

15. Paris, BNF Lat. 15045, fols. 59–60.

16. *Memorials of St Anselm*, ed. R. W. Southern and F. S. Schmitt, London, 1969, pp. 302–3; Anna Sapir Abulafia, 'Jewish-Christian Disputations and the Twelfth-Century Renaissance', in *Christians and Jews in Dispute: Disputational Literature and the Rise of Anti-Judaism in the West (c. 1000–1150)*, Aldershot, 1998, IX, pp. 105–25, at pp. 115–16.

17. On relations between Jews and Christians see Jonathan Elukin, *Living Together, Living Apart: Rethinking Jewish-Christian Relations in the Middle Ages*, Princeton, 2007.

18. Gilbert Crispin, 'Disputatio iudei et Christiani', in *The Works of Gilbert Crispin Abbot of Westminster*, eds. Anna Sapir Abulafia and G. R. Evans, London, 1986, c. 132, p. 44.

19. Ibid., c. 134, p. 45.

20. 'Dialogue between a Christian and a Jew', *PL* 163, col. 1055A–B; Abulafia, 'Jewish-Christian Disputations'.

21. Odo of Tournai, *On Original Sin; and, A Disputation with the Jew, Leo, concerning the Advent of Christ, the Son of God: Two Theological Treatises*, trans. Irven M. Resnick, Middle Ages Series, Philadelphia, 1994, p. 97.

22. Ibid., p. 97.

23. Ibid., pp. 96–7.

24. Anna Sapir Abulafia, 'Christian Imagery of Jews in the Twelfth Century: A Look at Odo of Cambrai and Guibert of Nogent', in Anna Sapir Abulafia, *Christians and Jews in Dispute: Disputational Literature and the Rise of Anti-Judaism in the West (c.1000–1150)*, Aldershot, 1998, X, pp. 383–91.

25. *Tractatus de incarnatione contra iudaeos*; Dominique Iogna-Prat, 'Éverard de Breteuil et son double: morphologie de la conversion en milieu aristocratique (v.1070–v.1120)', in *Guerriers et moines: Conversion et sainteté aristocratiques dans l'Occident médiéval, IXe–XIIe siècle*, ed. Michel Lauwers, Antibes, 2002, pp. 537–57, at pp. 538–41.

26. Jay Rubenstein, *Guibert of Nogent: Portrait of a Medieval Mind*, New York and London, 2002, pp. 39–44; above p. 131.

27. 'Deficite, quaeso, quia ratio vobis deficit', 'Tractatus de incarnatione contra Judaeos', *PL* 156, cols. 489–528, at col. 514.

28. Guibert of Nogent, *Autobiographie*, ed. and trans. Edmond-René Labande, Paris, 1981, p. 252; *A Monk's Confession: The Memoirs of Guibert of Nogent*, trans. Paul J. Archambault, University Park, 1996, p. 113. On this see Jan M. Ziolkowski, 'Put in No-man's-land: Guibert of Nogent's Accusations against the Judaizing and Jew-supporting Christian', in *Jews and Christians in Twelfth-century Europe*, eds. Michael A. Signer and John Van Engen, Notre Dame, 2001, pp. 110–22, at pp. 114–15; Rubenstein, *Guibert of Nogent*, pp. 116–24.

29. Anselm had argued clearly that it was not simply necessary but indeed fitting that Jesus be born of a virgin, Anselm, 'De conceptu virginali er de originali peccato', in *S. Anselmi cantuareinses Archiepiscopi Opera Omnia* III, ed. F. S. Schmitt, Edinburgh, 1946,

pp.135–73; c. 18, p. 159; for English translation 'On the Virginal Conception and Original Sin', in Anselm, *The Major Works*, eds. Brian Davies and G. R. Evans, Oxford, 1998, pp. 357–89, at c. 18, p. 376.; see also Irven M. Resnick, 'Anselm of Canterbury and Odo of Tournai on the Miraculous Birth of the God-Man', *Mediaeval Studies* 58 (1996), pp. 67–86, at pp. 71–9.

30. Hunt, *The Schools and the Cloister*, pp. 1–18.

31. Avrom Saltman, 'Alexander Nequam – His Commentary on the Song of Songs' [in Hebrew], in *Sefer Zikkaron le-Sara Kammin*, Jerusalem, 1994, Appendix, ss. nos. 34, 423, 428.

32. See, for example, ibid., cs. 30, 34, 42, 48.

33. I am most grateful to Dr Ineke van t'Spijker, who shared with me her work on Richard of St Victor's *De Emmanuele*, soon to be published as 'The Literal and the Spiritual. Richard of Saint-Victor and the Multiple Meaning of Scripture' in *The Role of Exegesis in Medieval Culture*, forthcoming, Leiden, 2009.

34. Rabbi Yehuda Halevi, *The Kuzari: In Defense of the Despised Faith*, trans. N. Daniel Korobkin, Northvale and Jerusalem, 1998.

35. Ibid., c. 7, p. 8.

36. *Sefer Gezerot Ashkenaz ve-Zarefat*, ed. Abraham Habermann, Jerusalem, 1945; this *piyyut*, chanted on Yom Kippur, was included in the Latin translation of Jewish texts associated with the burning of the Talmud in 1240, in BNF, Ms. Lat. 16658, fol. 230; Evyatar Marienberg, *Niddah: lorsque les juifs conceptualisent la menstruation*, Paris, 2003, p. 177.

37. 'The Narrative of the Old Persecutions or Mainz Anonymous', in *The Jews and the Crusaders: The Hebrew Chronicles of the First and Second Crusades*, ed. and trans. Shlomo Eidelberg, Madison, 1977, pp. 95–115, at p. 110.

38. Ibid., p. 114.

39. Jacob ben Reuben, *Milhamot Has-shem*, ed. Y. Rosenthal, Jerusalem, 1963.

40. *Sefer Ha-brit u-vikuchei Radak im Ha Natzrut*, ed. Ephraim Talmage, Jerusalem, 1984.

41. John Van Engen, 'Ralph of Flaix: The Book of Leviticus Interpreted as Christian Community', in *Jews and Christians in Twelfth-Century Europe*, eds. Michael A. Singer and John Van Engen, Notre Dame, 2001, pp. 150–70.

42. 'Que nichil debens sponte in hac parte legi se subdidit', Ralph of Flaix, 'Super Leviticum', in *Maxima bibliotheca veterum patrum, et antiquorum scriptorum ecclesiasticorum*, 17, ed. Marguerin de La Bigne, Lyons, 1677, pp. 47–246, at p. 127.

43. On churching in Scandinavia see Margrete Syrstad Andås, 'Art and Ritual in the Liminal Zone', in *The Medieval Cathedral of Trondheim*, pp. 47–126, at pp. 62–4.

44. Kauffmann, *Biblical Imagery in Medieval England*, figure 61, p. 86.

45. Barbara Baert, *Heritage of Holy Wood: The Legend of the True Cross in Text and Image*, trans. Lee Preedy, Leiden, 2004, figure 20, p. 117. On Mary as a figure of *ecclesia* in Romanesque wall-painting see Dominique Paris-Poulain, 'Une Représentation de *l'Arbor*-ecclesia: Contribution à l'étude des peintures murales du Petit-Quevilly', in *Le Rôle de l'ornement dans la peinture murale du Moyen Age*, Poitiers, 1997, pp. 121–37.

46. *Danske Kalkmalerier: Senromansk Tid 1175–1275*, eds. Ulla Haastrup and Robert Egevang, Copenhagen, 1987, pp. 110–11.

47. Beda Kleinschmidt, 'Der mittelalterliche Tragaltar. V', *Zeitschrift für christliche Kunst* 17 (1904), cols. 65–80, at col. 70, figure 7. Fulton, *From Judgment to Passion*, pp. 248–51.

48. Colin Morris, *The Sepulchre of Christ and the Medieval West: From the Beginning to 1600*, Oxford, 2005, pp. 153–65; Martin Biddle, *The Tomb of Christ*, Stroud, 1999, pp. 28–31.

49. *Loreto: crocevia religioso tra Italia, Europa ed Oriente*, eds. Ferdinando Citterio and Luciano Vaccaro, Brescia, 1997.

50. Of *c.*1200: Weitzmann, *The Icon*, plate 32, pp. 102–3.

51. Sergej S. Averintsev, 'The Image of the Virgin Mary in Russian Piety', *Gregorianum* 75

(1994), pp. 611–22, at p. 613. On the Byzantine influence in the Finnish Karelian sphere see Senni Timonen, 'The Cult of the Virgin Mary in Karelian Popular Tradition', in *Byzantium and the North*, Helsinki, 1987, pp. 101–19.

52. Herbert L. Kessler, *Spiritual Seing: Picturing God's Invisibility in Medieval Art*, Philadelphia, 2000, p. 47 and figure 2.15, p. 50.

53. Weitzmann, *The Icon*, plate 26, pp. 90–91.

54. Ibid., plate 16, pp. 70–71.

55. *Musée national du moyen âge: Thermes de Cluny*, ed. Elisabeth Antoine *et al.*, Paris, 2003, pp. 58–9.

56. For a discussion of these encounters see Annemarie Weyl Carr, 'Thoughts on Mary East and West', in *Images of the Mother of God: Perceptions of the Theotokos in Byzantium*, ed. Maria Vassilaki, Aldershot, 2005, pp. 277–92.

57. H. Barré, 'Un plaidoyer monastique pour le Samedi marial', *Revue bénédictine* 77 (1967), pp. 375–99, at pp. 375–77.

58. Alcuin, 'Liber sacramentorum', *PL* 101, Paris, 1851, cols. 445–66, at c. 7, cols. 445–6.

59. See above pp. 73–4.

60. Barré, 'Un plaidoyer', p. 381.

61. Hugo Buchthal, *Miniature Painting in the Latin Kingdom of Jerusalem*, London, 1986, no. 1, pp. 139–40, plates 1–12.

62. Ibid. plate 17 (fol. 22v), and above pp. 126–9.

63. Benjamin Z. Kedar, 'Convergences of Oriental Christian, Muslim, and Frankish Worshippers: The Case of Saydnaya', *De Sion exibit lex et verbum de Hierusalem: Essays in Medieval Law, Liturgy, and Literature in Honour of Amnon Linder*, ed. Yitzhak Hen, Turnhout, 2001, pp. 59–69, at p. 59; Bernard Hamilton, 'Our Lady of Saidnaiya: an Orthodox Shrine Revered by Muslims and Knight Templar at the Time of the Crusades', *Studies in Church History* 36 (2000), pp. 207–15, and Ugo Zanetti, 'Matarieh, la Sainte Famille et les baumiers', *Analecta Bollandiana* 111 (1993), pp. 21–68.

64. See translation in Kedar, 'Convergences of Oriental', p. 64.

65. 'Terra ista Virgo Maria fuit, generans Jesus Christum, Deum et hominem; per "lac", quod exprimitur de carne, humanitas Christi figuratur, nomine vero "mellis", quod de rore celi pervenit divinitatis eius interna dulcedo signature. Manat ergo terra promissionis lac et mel, id est: Virgo Maria generat deum et hominem,' Karen Skovgaard-Petersen, *A Journey to the Promised Land: Crusading Theology in the Historia de profectione Danorum in Hierosolymam (c. 1200)*, Copenhagen, 2001, p. 53.

66. Weitzmann, *The Icon*, plate 27, pp. 92–3.

67. Lucy-Anne Hunt, 'The Fine Incense of Virginity: A Late Twelfth-century Wallpainting of the Annunciation at the Monastery of the Syrians, Egypt', *Bulletin of Modern Greek Studies* 19 (1995), pp. 182–232.

68. Mary Clayton, 'Feasts of the Virgin in the Liturgy of the Anglo-Saxon Church', *Anglo-Saxon England* 13 (1984), pp. 209–33.

69. 'Sed cum ipsa conceptione fundamentum, ut diximus, fuerit habitaculi summi boni, si peccati alicuius ex prima praevaricationis origine maculuam traxit, quid diximus,' Eadmer of Canterbury, *Tractatus de conceptione sanctae Mariae*, eds. Herbert Thurston and P. T. Slater, Freiburg im Breisgau, 1904, p. 8; Marielle Lamy, *L'Imaculée Conception: étapes et enjeux d'une controverse au Moyen-Age (XIIe–XVe siècles)*, Paris, 2000, pp. 38–42.

70. 'Voluit enim te fieri matrem suam, et quia voluit, fecit esse,' Eadmer of Canterbury, *Tractatus de conceptione*, p. 11.

71. 'Unde in ecclesia dei cum a nobis celebris ageretur illius diei festivitas, quidem post Sathan abeuntes dixerunt esse ridiculum, quod usque ad haec tempora omnibus fuisset saeculis inauditum', Osbert of Clare, *The Letters of Osbert of Clare, prior of Westminster*, ed. E. W. Williamson, London, 1929, letter 7, pp. 65–8, at p. 65. I am grateful to Julie Barrau for bringing this letter to my attention.

72. Edmund Bishop, 'On the Origins of the Feast of the Conception of the Virgin Mary', *Downside Review* 5 (1886), pp. 107–19, at p. 112.

73. Bernard of Clairvaux, *Letters of St Bernard of Clairvaux*, trans. Bruno Scott James, London, 1953, letter 215, pp. 289–93, at p. 289. See the Latin original in *Sancti Bernardi opera*, VII, eds. Jean Leclercq, C. H. Talbot and H. Rochais, Rome, 1974, pp. 388–92, at p. 388, line 6.

74. Bernard of Clairvaux, *Letters*, p. 290; *Sancti Bernardi opera*, VII, p. 388 line 19 to p. 389 line 4.

75. Lamy, *L'Imaculée Conception*, pp. 42–3.

76. Bernard of Clairvaux, *Letters*, pp. 291–2; *Sancti Bernardi opera*, VII, p. 390, lines 13–24.

77. On this concept see Ferrucio Gastaldelli, 'San Bernardo e l'immacolata concezione: Le ragioni teologiche della lettera 174', *Analecta Cisterciensia* 44 (1988), pp. 190–200, esp. at pp. 197–200.

78. Frances M. Mildner, 'The Immaculate Conception I: The Writings of Nicholas of St Albans', *Marianum* 29 (1940), pp. 173–93.

79. Peter of Celle, *The Letters of Peter of Celle*, ed. Julian Haseldine, Oxford, 2001, pp. 157–60.

80. By 1196 Notre Dame cathedral in Paris celebrated the feast, Jean Vezin, 'L'Evolution du culte des saints à Paris aux XIIIe et XIV siècles', in *Rituels: Mélanges offerts à Pierre-Marie Gy, o.p.*, eds. Paul de Clerck and Eric Palazzo, Paris, 1990, pp. 473–9, at p. 478.

Chapter 10: Abundance and Ubiquity

1. 'O dulces filii, quos nunc progenui/Olim dicta mater, quod nomen tenui?/Olim per pignora vocor puerpera,/Modo sum misera, natorum vidua', Susan Boynton, 'From the Lament of Rachel to the Lament of Mary: A Transformation in the History of Drama and Spirituality', in *Signs of Change: Transformations of Christian Traditions and their Representation in the Arts, 1000–1200*, eds. Nils Holger Petersen, Claus Clüver and Nicolas Bell, Amsterdam and New York, 2004, pp. 319–40, at p. 320.

2. The Fleury Playbook has three exchanges between Rachel and her (female) consolers: one as a mother of Bethlehem, the next as a figure of the church, who is preferred over her sister Leah, representing Synagogue. The third and last exchange realizes Rachel's Marian potential.

3. Rebecca A. Baltzer, 'Why Marian Motets on Non-Marian Tenors? An Answer', *Music in Medieval Europe: Studies in Honour of Bryan Gillingham*, eds. Terence Bailey and Alma Santosuosso, Aldershot and Burlington, 2007, pp. 112–28.

4. A. Sinues Ruis, 'Advocaciones de la Virgen en un códice del siglo XII', *Analecta Sacra Tarraconensia* 21 (1948), pp. 1–34, at p. 25. I am very grateful to Dr Kathleen Stewart and Ms Jennifer K. Nelson of the Robbins Collection at University of California, Berkeley, for their assistance in obtaining the article.

5. One manuscript has the title 'Of the Blessed Virgin Mary and of the Faith', Richard of St Victor, *Liber exceptionum*, p. 381; Smalley, *Study of the Bible*, pp. 83–97, 106–111.

6. Richard of St Victor, *Liber exceptionum*, pp. 381–4.

7. 'Contabescit in his malis, homo noster animalis, tu nos, mater spiritualis, pereuntes libera', ibid., p. 385, lines 32–5, and 36–9.

8. I am most grateful to Dr Avital Heyman of Ben-Gurion University, who first informed me of this connection and helped me to follow it up.

9. Caroline Walker Bynum, *Holy Feast and Holy Fast: The Religious Significance of Food for Medieval Women*, Berkeley, 1988, pp. 220–27.

10. Richard of St Victor, *Trois opuscules spirituels de Richard de Saint-Victor: Textes inédits accompagnés d'études critiques et de notes*, ed. Jean Châtillon, Paris, 1986, pp. 253–4.

11. On Mary in early Gothic monuments see Penny Schine Gold, *The Lady and the Virgin: Image, Attitude, and Experience in Twelfth-Century France*, Women in Culture and Society, Chicago, 1985, chapter 2, esp. at pp. 51–61.

12. Mary and female saints fill the spaces of a Romanesque window as shown in Marcia

Kupfer, *Romanesque Wall Painting in Central France: The Politics of Narrative*, Yale Publications in the History of Art, New Haven and London, 1993, p. 170 and figure 107.

13. Paris-Poulain, 'Une représentation de *l'Arbor*-ecclesia'.

14. Barcelona, Catalan Museum of Art. See also the Virgin and Child of the Mosan region, now in the abbey church of St Peter, Remiremont, *Figures de madones: vierges sculptées des Vosges XIIe–XVIe siècle*, Épinal, 2005, no. 1, pp. 24–5.

15. *Year 1200*, II: *A Background Survey*, ed. Florence Deuchler, New York, 1970, figure 43.

16. Elizabeth Saxon, *The Eucharist in Romanesque France: Iconography and Theology*, Woodbridge, 2006, p. 290.

17. *The Year 1200*, I, no. 132, p. 128.

18. For the two *palas* see *The Year 1200*, II, nos. 213 and 218, pp. 164 and 167.

19. *Danske Kalkmalerier: Romansk tid*, ed. Ulla Haastrup and Robert Egevang, Copenhagen, 1986, no. 46, pp. 166–7.

20. For an elegant and authoritative discussion see Ilene H. Forsyth, *The Throne of Wisdom: Wood Sculptures of the Madonna in Romanesque France*, Princeton, 1972.

21. On Italian spread see Lucia Chiavola Birnbaum, *Black Madonnas: Feminism, Religion, and Politics in Italy*, Boston, 1993, p. xiii. I am grateful to Professor Liz McGrath of the Warburg Institute, London for an illuminating conversation on Mary and blackness.

22. Sophie Cassagnes-Brouquet with Jean-Pierre Cassagnes, *Vierges noires*, Rodez, 2000; René Germain, 'Les Représentations de la vierge, expression de la foi au Moyen Age en France', *Autour du culte marial en Forez*, pp. 75–83, at pp. 75–9. Some figures of Mary were described as 'white' (*alba*) or dressed in white; I am grateful to Richard Marks for letting me read his work in progress 'Alba Maria: Uncoloured Medieval Images of the Virgin'.

23. Lyons Bibliothèque municipale 410, fol. 207v.

24. London British Library Royal 1.A.XXII, fol. 13v.

25. *The Year 1200*, II, no. 59.

26. Catalan National Museum of Art. On the figure of Joseph in the twelfth century see Paul Payan, *Joseph: Une image de la paternité dans l'Occident médiéval*, Paris, 2006, pp. 50–58.

27. As shown so memorably by Caroline Walker Bynum, 'Jesus as Mother and Abbot as Mother: Some Themes in Twelfth-Century Cistercian Writing', in *Jesus as Mother: Studies in the Spirituality of the High Middle Ages*, Berkeley, 1982, pp. 110–68.

28. Benedicta Ward, *Miracles and the Medieval Mind*, London, 1982, pp. 132–65.

29. 'Ingens documentum futurum, quantum in cognatae gentis conuersione laboret industria Mariae', in William of Malmesbury, *El libro De laudibus et miraculis Sanctae Mariae de Guillermo de Malmesbury, OSB (+c. 1143)*, Estudio y texto, ed. José M. Canal, Rome, 1968, no. 32, pp. 132–6, at p. 136.

30. R. W. Southern, 'The English Origins of the "Miracles of the Virgin"', *Mediaeval and Renaissance Studies* 4 (1958), pp. 176–216, at pp. 181–2; J. C. Jennings, 'The Origins of the *Elements Series* of the Miracles of the Virgin', *Mediaeval and Renaissance Studies* 6 (1968), pp. 84–93.

31. Solange Corbin, 'Miracula beatae Mariae semper virginis', *Cahiers de civilisation médiévale* 10 (1967), pp. 409–33, at p. 409.

32. Anselm the Younger was, indeed, a committed promoter of the feast of Mary's Conception, the English feast which was being introduced to the Normans of England: he even introduced it to the abbey of which he was the abbot: Edmund Bishop, 'On the Origins of the Feast of the Conception of the Blessed Virgin Mary', in *Liturgica historica*, Oxford, 1918, pp. 238–60, at p. 247.

33. On the trade in relics see Patrick J. Geary, *Furta sacra: Thefts of Relics in the Central Middle Ages*, Princeton, 1978.

34. François Clément, 'Le Pèlerinage à Lagrasse, d'après un source arabe du XIe siècle', *Annales du Midi* 100 (1988), pp. 489–95, at p. 489.

35. Ibid., pp. 494–5.
36. Amy Remensnyder, *Remembering Kings Past: Monastic Foundation Legends in Medieval Southern France*, Ithaca, 1995, p. 1.
37. I am most grateful to Dr Kathleen Stewart, who shared with me some of her original work on Ripoll before publication.
38. Sophie Cassagnes-Brouquet (with Jean-Pierre Cassagnes), *Vierges noires*, Rodez, 2000, p. 31.
39. Ibid., pp. 140–50; Monique Scheer, 'From Majesty to Mystery: Change in the Meaning of Black Madonnas from the Sixteenth to Nineteenth Centuries', *American Historical Review* 107 (2002), pp. 1,412–40, at pp. 1,421–2.
40. Cassagnes-Brouquet, *Vierges noires*, p. 66.
41. For an exemplary treatment of the collection in its full social context see Marcus Bull, *The Miracles of Our Lady of Rocamadour*, Woodbridge, 1999.
42. For an insightful and multi-faceted discussion see Simon Yarrow, *Saints and their Communities: Miracle Stories in Twelfth Century England*, Oxford, 2006, chapter 3, pp. 63–99.
43. E. Jane Burns, 'Saracen Silk and the Virgin's *Chemise*: Cultural Crossings in Cloth', *Speculum* 81 (2006), pp. 365–97, esp. at p. 366.
44. Milard Meiss, 'Light as Form and Symbol in Some Fifteenth-Century Paintings', *Art Bulletin* 27 (1945), pp. 175–81. On the thirteenth-century collection of Chartres miracles see Dawn Marie Hayes, *Body and Sacred Place in Medieval Europe, 1100–1389: Interpreting the Case of Chartres Cathedral*, New York, 2003, pp. 25–49.
45. Ward, *Miracles and the Medieval Mind*, pp. 142–4.
46. 'Quorum ergo gemitus dolentium intolerabiles modo erant, prae subita liberatione nunc emittunt infinitas voces laetitiae ad coelum, et cunctis sibi exsultantibus populis laudes et lacrymae et gratiarum actiones', Hugh of Frachet, 'Libellus de miraculis B. Mariae Virginis in urbe Suessionensi', in *PL* 179, Paris, 1855, cols. 1777–1800, at col. 1779.
47. Ibid., no. 12, col. 1786.
48. In the thirteenth century a collection of Chartres miracles was composed in French: Jean le Marchant, *Miracles de Notre-Dame de Chartres*, ed. Pierre Kunstmann, Ottawa, 1973; for a fascinating exploration of the insertion of Marian themes within the Grail narratives, see Joseph Goering, *The Virgin and the Grail: Origins of a Legend*, New Haven, 2005.
49. I am indebted here to Katherine Allen Smith, 'Mary or Michael? Saint-switching, Gender, and Sanctity in a Medieval Miracle of Childbirth', *Church History* 74 (2005), pp. 758–83, and to a most enjoyable conversation with Professor Smith.
50. William of Malmesbury, *El libro De laudibus*, p. 268.

PART IV: MARY, LOCAL AND FAMILIAR: 1200–1400

Chapter 11: Mary in Liturgy, Song and Prayer

1. This discussion is indebted to Christopher Page, 'An English Motet of the 14th Century in Performance: Two Contemporary Images', *Early Music* 25 (1997), pp. 7–32, and to illuminating conversations with its author.
2. Ibid., pp. 18–20. On Mary and stars see Nigel Morgan, 'Texts and Images of Marian Devotion in English Twelfth Century Monasticism', in *Monasticism and Society*, Proceedings of the 1994 Harlaxton Symposium, ed. B. Thompson, Stamford, 1999, pp. 117–36.
3. Caesarius of Heisterbach, *Dialogue of Miracles* I, trans. H. von E. Scott and C. C. Swinton Bland, London, 1929, c. 29, pp. 497–8.
4. Ibid., pp. 38–9; and see Christopher Page, *The Owl and the Nightingale: Musical Life and Ideas in France 1100–1300*, London, 1989, pp. 167–8.

5. On the penetration of music into religious practice in this period I am influenced by several conversations with Christopher Page and by his *The Owl and the Nightingale*, esp. pp. 165–9.

6. The original and translation are Annette Volfing, *Heinrich von Mügeln, Der meide Kranz: A Commentary*, Tübingen, 1997, p. 122, lines 461–8, and on this passage see pp. 128–9.

7. Olivier Cullin, 'La Musique à Notre-Dame: Un manifeste artistique et son paradoxe', in *Notre Dame de Paris: Un manifeste chrétien (1160–1230)*, Turnhout, 2004, pp. 93–105.

8. On contacts in Paris between scholars, officials and merchants see John Baldwin, *Masters, Princes and Merchants: The Social Views of Peter the Chanter and his Circle*, 2 vols., Princeton, 1970. For the layout of the chapels at Notre Dame see Craig Wright, *Music and Ceremony at Notre Dame of Paris*, Cambridge, 1989, p. 8.

9. Rachel Fulton, ' "Quae est ista quae ascendit sicut aurora consurgens?": The Song of Songs as the *Historia* for the Office of the Assumption', *Mediaeval Studies* 60 (1998), pp. 55–122.

10. 'Paradisi porta per Evam cunctis clausa, et per Mariam virginem iterum patefacta est, alleluya'.

11. See the miracle tale in which Mary intervenes to save a student at Paris who prayed to Mary at Notre Dame cathedral on most days, but was tempted to go to a brothel: *Miracles de Notre-Dame: tirés du Rosarius, Paris, ms. B. N.fr. 12483*, Ottawa, 1991, miracle 3, p. ix.

12. Michael T. Davis, 'Canonical Views: The Theophilus Story and the Choir Reliefs at Notre-Dame, Paris', in *Reading Medieval Images: The Art Historian and the Object*, Ann Arbor, 2002, pp. 102–16. The Parisian poet Rutebeuf put the tale to verse: Daniel E O'Sullivan, *Marian Devotion in Thirteenth-Century French Lyric*, Toronto, 2005, pp. 98–108.

13. Christopher Page, *Discarding Images: Reflections on Music and Culture in Medieval France*, Oxford, 1993, pp. 43–59.

14. Oliver Cullin, *Laborintus: Essai sur la musique au Moyen-Age*, Paris, 2004, chapter 4, pp. 91–110.

15. Sylvia Huot, *Allegorical Play in the Old French Motet*, Palo Alto, 1997, pp. 90–99.

16. Lines 1,935–8; Jody Enders, 'Music, Delivery, and the Rhetoric of Memory in Guillaume de Machaut's *Remède de Fortune*', *Publications of the Modern Languages Association* 107 (1992), pp. 450–64, at p. 454.

17. Jacqueline Cerquiglini-Toulet and Alain Michel, 'Le *Voir Dir* de Guillaume de Machaut: entre Dante et Pétrarque l'amour et la poésie au XIVe siècle', in *Rhétorique et poétique au Moyen Age*, Turnhout, 2002, pp. 137–49.

18. Anne Walters Robertson, *Guillaume de Machaut and Reims: Context and Meaning in his Musical Works*, Cambridge, 2002, pp. 215–21.

19. Roger Bowers, 'Guillaume de Machaut and his Canonry of Reims, 1338–1377', *Early Music History* 23 (2004), pp. 1–48.

Chapter 12: Mary, the Friars, and the Mother Tongue

1. 'In istis uerbis proponitur nobis magnificencitia sanctitatis in beata Maria, exitus huius exilii, felix porta ad quem hodie peruenit eterne beatitudinis', Gérard de Martel, 'Le Sermon de Graeculus sur Ruth 1,22 pour la fête de l'Assomption de la Vierge Marie', *Archivum franciscanum historicum* 90 (1997), pp. 487–503, at p. 495.

2. 'Per quam intelligitur paradysus. Interpretatur enim domus panis, quod bene conuenit eterne beautudini, ubi est panis Dominus noster Ihesus Christi', ibid., pp. 500–501.

3. Ibid., p. 503. On Helinand see above, pp. 154–7.

4. Catherine M. Mooney, '*Imitatio Christi* or *Imitatio Mariae*? Clare of Assisi and her Interpreters', in *Gendered Voices: Medieval Saints and the Interpreters*, Philadelphia, 1999, pp. 52–77, esp. at pp. 58–67. On the friars and Mary see Kaspar Elm, 'Devozione

alla Madonna e vita religiosa femminile', in *Loreto: crocevia religioso tra Italia, Europa ed Oriente*, ed. Ferdinando Citterio and Luciano Vaccaro, Brescia, 1997, pp. 33–50, at pp. 44–5.

5. Mooney, '*Imitatio Christi* or *Imitatio Mariae?*', p. 60.

6. Serena Romano, 'The Frescoes of the Church and Oratory', in *Walls and Memory: The Abbey of San Sebastiano at Alatri (Lazio), from Late Roman Monastery to Renaissance Villa and Beyond*, Turnhout, 2005, pp. 114–40, colour plates 9–10.

7. Mooney, '*Imitatio Christi* or *Imitatio Mariae?*', pp. 65–6; Clare of Assisi, *Ecrits: Claire d'Assise*, eds. M.-F. Becker, J.-F. Godet and T. Mattura, Paris, 1985, pp. 104, 106.

8. Thomas of Celano, *The First Life of St Francis of Assisi*, trans. Christopher Stace, London, 2000, cs. 20, 84–7, pp. 81–5; 1296 Assisi, St Francis, Upper Basilica, fresco 230 × 270 cms.

9. Neil MacGregor (with Erika Langmuir), *Seeing Salvation: Images of Christ in Art*, London, 2000, figure 13, p. 50.

10. Beth Williamson, 'The Virgin *Lactans* as Second Eve: Image of the Salvatrix', *Studies in Iconography* 19 (1998), pp. 105–38.

11. *Petrarch's Guide to the Holy Land: Itinerary to the Sepulchre of Our Lord Jesus Christ: Itinerarium ad sepulchrum domini nostri Yehsu Christi*, ed. Theodore J. Cachey Jr, Notre Dame, 2002, 17.1–2, at 17.2.

12. On manuscripts of the *Protogospel* in the thirteenth century see F. Vattioni, 'Frammento latino del Vangelo di Giacomo', *Augustinianum* 17 (1977), pp. 505–9.

13. Julie Nelson Couch, 'Misbehaving God: The Case of the Christ Child in MS Laud Misc. 108 "Infancy of Jesus Christ" ', in *Mindful Spirit in Late Medieval Literature: Essays in Honor of Elizabeth D. Kirk*, ed. Bonnie Wheeler, Basingstoke, 2006, pp. 31–43.

14. For example, on Holkham and Tring, see C. M. Kauffmann, *Biblical Imagery in Medieval England 700–1550*, London, 2003, pp. 232–7. On the Holkham Bible see C. M. Kauffmann, 'Art and Popular Culture: New Themes in the Holkham Bible Picture Book', in *Studies in Medieval Art and Architecture Presented to Peter Lasko*, eds. David Buckton and T. A. Heslop, Stroud, 1994, pp. 46–69.

15. In a manuscript of the *Speculum Humanae Salvationis* made in the second half of the fourteenth century, Vienna ONB s.n.2612, fol. 13v, see Gerhard Jaritz, 'The Destruction of Things in the Late Middle Ages: Outburst versus Control of Emotions', *Emotions and Material Culture: International Round-table Discussion, Krems an der Donau, October 7 and 8, 2002*, Vienna, 2003, pp. 51–76, at figure 1, p. 70; Holkham Bible, *c*.1320–30 BL 47682 fol. 14. Mary often seems anxious en route and clings to her swaddled son, as in the frontal of Santa Maria de Lluçà; Episcopal Museum of Vic.

16. BNF, Lat. 2688 fol. 40v, 38; Pierre Riché and Danièle Alexandre-Bidon, *L'Enfance au Moyen Age*, Paris, 1994, p. 121 More commonly it is Mary alone with her son; see the embossed chalice which served the Swiss house of Wettingen: Mary holding a flowering branch pulling hard at the hand of the little boy carrying a basket.

17. *Sotto il duomo di Siena: Scoperte archeologiche, architettoniche e figurative*, Milan, 2003, figure 30, p. 127.

18. Luzern, Staasarchiv, seal; Hans Wentzel, 'Das Jesuskind an der Hand Mariae auf dem Siegel des Burkhard von Winon, 1277', in *Festschrift Hans R. Hahnloser zum 60. Geburtstag*, eds. Ellen J. Beer, Paul Hofer and Luc Mojon, Basel and Stuttgart, 1961, pp. 251–70.

19. Oxford Bodleian Library ms. Selden Supra 38, fol. 18r.

20. 'Vivre ne devroit o nous chi, / Ains le doit on crucifier / Pendre ou ardoir en escorchier, / Car il confront toutes nos loys; / Je veul que il soit mis en crois', *The Old French Evangile de l'Enfance: An Edition with Introduction and Notes*, ed. Maureen Barry McCann Boulton, Toronto, 1984, lines 1,232–6, p. 60; translation from Evelyn Birge Vitz, 'The Apocryphal and the Biblical, the Oral and the Written, in Medieval Legends of Christ's Childhood: The Old French *Evangile de l'Enfance*', in *Satura: Studies in Medieval Literature in Honour of Robert R. Raymo*, ed. Nancy M. Reale and Ruth E. Sternglanz, Donington, 2001, pp. 124–49, at p. 128.

21. Holkham Bible fol. 16, see Kauffmann, *Biblical Imagery in Medieval England*, figure 173, p. 232.

22. *The Golden Legend: Reading on the Saints*, trans. William Granger Ryan, 2 vols., Princeton, 1992, Assumption, II, no. 119, pp. 77–99; Purification, I, no. 37, pp. 143–51; Nativity of the Virgin Mary, II, no. 131, pp. 149–58.

23. 0.75 × 2.85m; Christopher Norton, David Park and Paul Binski, *Dominican Painting in East Anglia: The Thornton Parva Retable and the Musée de Cluny Frontal*, Woodbridge, 1987, with a reproduction as frontispiece.

24. Kauffmann, *Biblical Imagery in Medieval England*, figure XIVb; see also Ellen Ross, *The Grief of God: Images of the Suffering Jesus in Late Medieval England*, Oxford, 1997, figures 2.28–30, pp. 47–8.

25. Barbara Fleith, *Studien zur Überlieferungsgeschichte der lateinischen Legenda aurea*, Subsidia hagiographica 72, Brussels, 1991, esp. pp. 404–30.

26. 'Thei maketh hem Maries men (so thei men tellen), and lieth on our Ladie many a longe tale', John Scattergood, '*Pierce the Ploughman's Crede*: Lollardy and Texts', in *Lollardy and the Gentry in the Later Middle Ages*, eds. Margaret Aston and Colin Richmond, Stroud, 1997, pp. 77–94, at p. 86.

27. See, for example, the Virgin of Walcourt, *c.* 1260, Notre Dame Basilica, Walcourt, *Autour de Hugo d'Oignies*, eds. Robert Didier and Jacques Toussaint, Namur, 2003, p. 320.

28. Suzanne Lewis, *The Art of Matthew Paris in the Chronica majora*, California Studies in the History of Art 21, Aldershot, 1987, frontispiece. On these images see Paul Binski, 'The Faces of Christ in Matthew Paris's Chronica Majora', in *Tributes in Honour of James H Marrow. Studies in Painting and Manuscript Illumination of the Late Middle Ages*, eds. J. F. Hamburger and A. S. Korteweg, London, 2006, pp. 85–92. In his description of meditative imagery Alexander Nequam makes reference to an image of Mother and Child much like that painted by Matthew Paris, 'We create in our mind's eye the mother of sweetness and sweet son embracing each other sweetly. I see shown to me now the mother of joy holding her son gently in her motherly arms', from R. W. Hunt (revised by Margaret Gibson), *The Schools and the Cloister: The Life and Writings of Alexander Nequam (1157–1217)*, Oxford, 1984, p. 107.

29. Karlsruhe, Landesbibliothek St Peter perg. 139, fol. 7v; Riché and Alexandre-Bidon, *L'Enfance au Moyen Age*, p. 19.

30. An ivory statuette of *c.*1220 from the area of Liège displays a transitional stage: Mary enthroned gazing forward, but her son's head is turned towards her, touching her veil, seeking her response: *Autour de Hugo d'Oignies*, p. 69.

31. *Wonder: Painted Sculpture from Medieval England*, Leeds, 2002, p. 43 and catalogue no. 3, pp. 62–3.

32. Girona, Museu d'Art.

33. For a description see, *Wonder*, catalogue no. 35, pp. 101–2.

34. On fashion in the making of statues of Mary see Max Hasse, 'Studien zur Skulptur des ausgehenden 14. Jahrhunderts', *Städel-Jahrbuch* new series 6 (1977), pp. 99–127.

35. Barcelona Museu Nacional de Catalunya, tempera on wood with stucco relief 96 × 160 cms.

36. 250 × 123 cms; *The Art of Devotion in the Late Middle Ages in Europe, 1300–1500*, ed. Henk van Os with Eugène Honée, Hans Nieuwdorp and Bernhard Ridderbos, trans. Michael Hoyle, London, 1994, plate 37, p. 121, on it see p. 120; Herbert L Kessler, *Seeing Medieval Art*, Peterborough, Ontario, 2004, pp. 76–8.

37. On the Gothic aesthetic see Paul Binski, *Becket's Crown: Art and Imagination in Gothic England, 1170–1350*, London and New Haven, 2004, esp. chapters 9–10.

38. *Musée national du moyen âge*, pp. 76–7.

39. Peter Lord, *The Visual Culture of Wales: Medieval Vision*, Cardiff, 2003, p. 157, figures 239 and 240; Prague National Gallery 701. See the standing Mary and Child of the Vexin of *c.*1300, and Catalonia, of *c.*1350, sculpted by Guillem Sequer, *Medieval Sculpture at*

the Metropolitan: 800–1400 = *The Metropolitan Museum of Art Bulletin*, 62 (spring 2005), pp. 32–3.

40. Julian Gardiner, *The Tomb and the Tiara: Curial Tomb Sculpture in Rome and Avignon in the Later Middle Ages*, Oxford, 1992, figure 1.

41. *The Liverpool Ivories: Late Antique and Medieval Ivory and Bone Carving in Liverpool Museum and the Walker Art Gallery*, Liverpool, 1994, plate XXIX, p. 76, and on it p. 77.

42. Helsinki, National Museum, *c.*1480–1550.

43. Bram Kempers, 'Icons, Altarpieces, and Civic Ritual in Siena Cathedral, 1100–1530', in *City and Spectacle in Medieval Europe*, eds. Barbara A. Hanawalt and Kathryn L. Reyerson, Minneapolis, 1994, pp. 89–136. On devotional imagery in Siena see Victor M. Schmidt, *Painted Piety: Panel Paintings for Personal Devotion in Tuscany, 1250–1400*, Florence, 2005.

44. Siena, Pinacoteca Nazionale, Maestà of the Badia d'Isola; Kempers, 'Icons, Altarpieces and Civic Ritual', pp. 89–110.

45. Siena, Museo del'Opera del Duomo; *Duccio: Alle origini della pinture senese*, eds. Alessandro Bagnoli, Roberto Bartalini, Luciano Bellosi and Michel Lacotte, Milan, 2003, no. 24, pp. 158–61.

46. Ibid., no. 32, pp. 208–31.

47. For a detailed and compelling account of the cult at Częstochowa, still going strong, see Robert Maniura, *Pilgrimage to Images in the Fifteenth Century: The Origins of the Cult of Our Lady of Częstochowa*, Woodbridge, 2004, on the image esp. pp. 10–45.

48. Pierlugi Leone de Castris, *Simone Martini*, Milan, 2003, p. 211, 357–8.

49. San Gimignano, St Augustine's Church.

50. New York Metropolitan Museum, Madonna del Latte. On this image see Williamson, 'The Virgin *Lactans*', pp. 116–18. On representations of breastfeeding see Max Seidel, '*Ubera matris*: Die vielschichtige Bedeutung eines Symbols in der Mittelalterlichen Kunst', *Städel-Jahrbuch* new series 6 (1977), pp. 41–98; see also the same effect in Naddo Ceccarelli's *Madonna and Child* of 1347. Mary's kinship and lineage posed challenges to artists as they considered the appropriate 'Jewishness' of Mary's appearance: Diane Owen Hughes, 'Distinguishing Signs: Ear-Rings, Jews and Franciscan Rhetoric in the Italian Renaissance City', *Past and Present* 112 (1986), pp. 3–59.

51. Richard Marks and Nigel Morgan, *The Golden age of English Manuscript Painting 1200–1500*, London, 1981, plate 8, and p. 54. A rather abject Abbot Conrad von Scheyer inserted himself, prostrate, at the feet of a traditionally cast image of Mary and Jesus: *Liber matutinalis*, Munich, Bayerische Staatsbibliothek, Cod. Lat. 17401, fol. 25r; *The Year 1200: A Centennial Exhibition at the Metropolitan Museum of Art*, New York, 1970, p. 205.

52. Kauffmann, *Biblical Imagery in Medieval England*, figure 119, p. 168; Gee, *Women, Art and Patronage*, p. 56 and plate 13.

53. Nigel Morgan, *The Lambeth Apocalypse: Manuscript 209 in Lambeth Palace Library: A critical Study*, London, 1990, p. 254.

54. Cambridge University Library, Dd.4.17, fol. 19; on it see Loveday Lewes Gee, *Women, Art and Patronage from Henry III to Edward III, 1216–1377*, Woodbridge, 2002, figure 3 and pp. 41–4.

55. Berlin Gemäldegalerie; Van Os (ed.), *Art of Devotion*, p. 77.

56. Ross, *The Grief of God*, figure 2.37, pp. 52–3.

57. *The Liverpool Ivories: Late Antique and Medieval Ivory and Bone Carving in Liverpool Museum and the Walker Art Gallery*, ed. Margaret Gibson, London, 1994, no. 27, pp. 71–2.

58. Timken Museum of Art, San Diego; on it see Anne Derbes, *Picturing the Passion in Late Medieval Italy: Narrative Painting, Franciscan Ideologies, and the Levant*, Cambridge, 1996, pp. 162–5; Anne Derbes, 'Siena and the Levant in the Later Duecento', *Gesta* 28 (1989), pp. 190–204.

59. *The Liverpool Ivories*, no. 30, plate XIX, p. 78 and on it p. 79.

60. *Images in Ivory: Precious Objects of the Gothic Age*, Detroit, 1997, no. 37, pp. 186–7.

61. For a description see Ernest William Tristram, *English Wall Painting of the Fourteenth Century*, London, 1955, pp. 162–5.

62. *Images in Ivory*, no. 25, pp. 159–60.

63. Ibid., no. 43, pp. 202–3; see also *The Liverpool Ivories*, plate XXXIa, pp. 81–2.

64. Florence, Collection of the Fondazione Horne.

65. Salvador Ryan, 'The Persuasive Power of a Mother's Breast: The Most Desperate Act of the Virgin Mary's Advocacy', *Studia hibernica* 32 (2002–3), pp. 59–74, at pp. 60, 62. See also Susan Marti and Daniela Mondini, ' "Ich manen dich der brüsten min, Das du dem sünder wellest milte sin!": Marienbrüste und Marienmilch im Heilsgeschehen', in *Himmel, Hölle, Fegefeuer: Das Jenseits im Mittelalter*, ed. Peter Jezler, Zurich, 1994, pp. 79–90.

66. London, British Library, Add. 38116, fol. 13v; Kauffmann, *Biblical Imagery in Medieval England*, pp. 169–70; see also figure 154, at p. 209, where Mary kneels and bears her breast in front of the Risen Christ.

67. Marilyn Yalom, *A History of the Breast*, London, 1997, pp. 31–49.

68. *Das Marienleben des Schweizers Wernher*, eds. Max Päpke and Arthur Hübner, Dublin and Zurich, 1967, pp. 18–19, lines, 1038–60; translation from Timothy R. Jackson, 'Erotic Imagery in Medieval Spiritual Poetry and the Hermeneutics of Metaphor', in *Metaphor and Rational Discourse*, eds. Max Bernhard Debatin, Timothy R. Jackson and Daniel Steuer, Tübingen, 1997, pp. 113–24, at p. 121, n. 20.

69. *Frauenlob's Song of Songs: A Medieval German Poet and his Masterpiece*, trans. Barbara Newman, University Park, 2007, no. 4, pp. 8–9. I am most grateful to Barbara Newman who kindly shared her inspired translations with me even before their publication.

70. *The Goodman of Paris (Le Ménagier de Paris): A Treatise on Moral and Domestic Economy by a Citizen of Paris c.1393*, trans. Eileen Power, London, 1992, pp. 93–4.

71. Nicholas Love, *Mirror of the Blessed Life of Jesus Christ: A Critical Edition*, ed. Michael G. Sargent, New York, 1992, p. 63.

72. Richard Rutt, *A History of Hand Knitting*, London, 1987, pp. 44–50, figures 44 and 42.

73. Gail M. Gibson, *The Theater of Devotion: East Anglian Drama and Society in the Late Middle Ages*, Chicago, 1989, figure 6.8, p. 158.

74. BNF, Lat. 2688, fol. 52v; Riché and Alexandre-Bidon, *L'Enfance au Moyen-Age*, p. 162.

75. Love, *Mirror*, pp. 63–4.

76. Ibid., pp. 75–6

77. Kim M. Phillips, *Medieval Maidens: Young Women and Gender in England, 1270–1540*, Manchester, 2003, esp. at pp. 48–51.

78. By Master Bertram (c.1330/40–1414), see *Early German Painting, 1350–1550*, ed. Isolde Lübbeke, trans. Margaret Thomas Will, London, 1991, pp. 302, 304, 306. See also the closed wooden altarpiece of later in the century made by Master Bertram, where Mary and angel each stand on a grassy rock, against a red background.

79. Oxford, Bodleian Library, Douce 231, fol. 3.

80. Michael Clanchy has led the way in identifying and interpreting these rich images which bear testimony to ideas about Mary and some evidence of the practices of teaching girls to read: Michael Clanchy, 'Images of Ladies with Prayer Books: What Do They Signify?', *Studies in Church History* 38 (2004), pp. 106–22. See also Wendy Scase, 'St Anne and the Education of the Virgin: Literary and Artistic Traditions and Their Implications', in *England in the Fourteenth Century: Proceedings of the 1991 Harlaxton Symposium*, ed. Nicholas Rogers, Stamford, 1993, pp. 81–96.

81. Made between 1350 and 1375, *Wonder: Painted Sculpture from Medieval England*, Leeds, 2002, no. 12, pp. 79–80.

82. Helsinki, National Museum, Master of Sääksmäki.

83. Diane Finiello Zervas, 'Niccolò Gerini's *Entombment and Resurrection of Christ*, S.

Anna/S. Michele/S. Carlo and Orsanmichele in Florence: Clarifications and New Documentation', *Zeitschrift für Kunstgeschichte* 66 (2003), pp. 33–64.

84. Florence, Santa Maria della Carmine, Brancacci Chapel, 175 × 303 cm.

85. *Storia di Santa Ismeria avola della Vergine Maria: testo inedito del buon secolo di nostra lingua*, Imola, 1869. For another legend on Anne's lineage see Barbara Baert, *A Heritage of Holy Wood: The Legend of the True Cross in Text and Image*, trans. Lee Preedy, Leiden, 2004, p. 297; see also Pamela Sheingorn, ' "The Wise Mother": The Image of St Anne Teaching the Virgin Mary', *Gesta* 32 (1993), pp. 69–80.

86. *Les Sermons et la visite pastorale de Federico Visconti, archevêque de Pise (1253–77)*, eds. Nicole Bériou and Isabelle le Masne de Chermont, Rome, 2001, sermon 299 on the Annunciation, pp. 562–70, at cs. 14–15, p. 568.

87. *Lollard Sermons: British Library MS Additional 41321, Bodleian Library MS Rawlinson C 751, John Rylands MS Eng 412*, Oxford, 1989, p. 59. This is based on the *Protogospel of James* and is recounted in the *Legenda Aurea*.

Chapter 13: Teaching Mary in Parish and Home

1. William of Shoreham, *The Poems of William of Shoreham, ab. 1320 Vicar of Chart-Sutton*, ed. M. Konrath, London, 1902, p. 115, lines 22–4.

2. Ibid., p. 117, lines 79–81.

3. Ibid., p. 122, lines 217–19.

4. Ibid., p. 126, pp. 334–6.

5. Ibid., pp. 127–9, lines 37–40.

6. Ibid., p. 128, lines 43–6.

7. Ibid., p. 129, lines 79–84.

8. Karl L. Weigand, ed. 'Rheinfränkische Himmelfahrt Mariae', *Zeitschrift für deutsches Alterthum* 5 (1845), pp. 515–64, at p. 555, line 1,492; Bettina Bildhauer, *Medieval Blood*, Cardiff, 2006, p. 90.

9. 'Marie was in Nazareth, for al goodnesse flurist in hire. Sche flurist & brou3t forþ fruyt so þat hire body was al hol . . . When sche florist & forþ brou3t fruyt, sche dwelled mayden here & þere'; 'Ri3t it was þat mayden was wedded to mayden. Also, þei þat ben wedded togidere, 3if þei kepen hem togidere wiþouten ony contrariouste, in chaste oþer in doynge þe fleschliche dede onliche for the bi3eten children, þan þei taken ensaumple of Ioseph & of Marye', *The Middle English 'Mirror': An Edition Based on Bodleian Library MS Holkham misc. 40*, Tempe, 2002, pp. 445–6.

10. Oxford, Bodleian Library, Auct D 4 2, fol. 11v; on this marriage see Christopher Brooke, *The Medieval Idea of Marriage*, Oxford, 1989, pp. 53–4. For a tender image of the Nativity see the fourteenth-century roof-boss in the basilica dedicated to Mary of the Sea (*Santa Maria del Mar*) in Barcelona, which contains within a circle Mary in a blue cloak and Joseph in red, either side of a carved figure of Jesus, adored by an ox and an ass. At the same time the mid-fourteenth-century painting of the Nativity on the vaulting of the Danish parish church of Skibby has Joseph with a white beard and a Jew's hat, while Mary handles the Child.

11. Dianne Phillips, '*The Meditations on the Life of Christ*: An Illustrated Fourteenth-century Italian Manuscript at the University of Notre Dame', in *The Text in the Community: Essays on Medieval Works, Manuscripts, Authors, and Readers*, Notre Dame, 2006, pp. 237–81; figure 8.5, at p. 249.

12. Edmund Bishop, 'The Origin of the Primer', in *Liturgica historica: Papers on the Liturgy and Religious life of the Western Church*, Oxford, 1918, pp. 211–37.

13. Roger S. Wieck, 'Hours of the Virgin', in *The Book of Hours in Medieval Art and Life*, London, 1988, pp. 60–88; Eamon Duffy, *Marking the Hours: English People and their Prayers 1240–1570*, London, 2006, pp. 3–22. Books became highly personalized and complex with the addition of prayers for several occasions: see, for example, Kathryn A.

Smith, *Art, Identity and Devotion in Fourteenth-century England: Three Women and Their Books of Hours*, London and Toronto, 2003; and Virginia Reinburg, 'Prayer and the Book of Horus', in *The Book of Hours in Medieval Art and Life*, London, 1988, pp. 39–44.

14. Marvin L. Coker, 'The "Margam Chronicle" in a Dublin Manuscript', *Haskins Society Journal* 4 (1992), pp. 123–48, at p. 135: 'Et cum iam nulla ei foret spes exeundi nisi forte ad iudicium mortis ... psalmos tamen Daviticos ruminabat in psalterio, quod secum habebat ad solatium, et spem beate virginis devote implorabat.' I am most grateful to David Carpenter for bringing this example to my attention.

15. Michael Clanchy, 'Images of Ladies with Prayer Books: What Do They Mean?', *Studies in Church History* 38 (2004), 106–22, esp. pp. 121–2.

16. Claire Donovan, *The De Brailes Hours: Shaping the Book of Hours in Thirteenth-Century Oxford*, London, 1991, see colour plates there 2, 15 and 16a.

17. BL, Yates Thompson 13, fols. 138v, 138v–139 opening.

18. On the book and its patron see Lucy Freeman Sandler, *The Psalter of Robert De Lisle in the British Library*, London, 1999, pp. 11–13.

19. Ibid., figure, fol. 124, plate 11, p. 55 (on it p. 54); fol. 129, plate 9, p. 51 (on it p. 50). On the Franciscan influence evident in this image see Lawrence M. Clopper, 'Inscribing Mentalities: Alan of Lille, the De Lisle Psalter Cherub, and Franciscan Meditation', in *Mindful Spirit in Late Medieval Literature: Essays in Honor of Elizabeth D. Kirk*, Basingstoke, 2006, pp. 57–79, at pp. 64–5.

20. Sandler, *The Psalter of Robert De Lisle*, fol. 131v, plate 16 on p. 65 (on it p. 64).

21. Fitzwilliam Museum Ms. 48, fols. 188v–189r; on the tale see above p. 74; for further discussion see Miri Rubin, *Gentile Tales: The Narrative Assault on Late Medieval Jews*, London and New Haven, 1999, figure 3, pp. 18–19, and Denise Despres, 'Immaculate Flesh and the Social Body: Mary and the Jews in Cambridge Fitzwilliam Ms. 48, The Carew-Poyntz Hours', *Jewish History* 12 (1998), pp. 47–69.

22. See the images and discussion in Andreas Bräm, *Das Andachtsbuch der Marie de Gavre: Paris, Bibliothèque nationale, Ms. nouv. acq. fr. 16251: Buchmalerei in der Diözese Cambrai im letzten Viertel des 13. Jahrhunderts*, Wiesbaden, 1997.

23. 'La Repentence/Mort Rutebeuf', in O'Sullivan, *Marian Devotion*, pp. 202–5; lines 4–12, p. 202.

24. Jody Enders, *Rhetoric and the Origins of Medieval Drama*, Ithaca, 1992, pp. 222–33; 'El sçeit opposer et responder/Pour nostre adversaire confondre', p. 223.

25. Carmen Cardelle de Hartmann, 'Die *Processus Sathanae* und die Tradition der Satansprozesse', *Mittellateinisches Jahrbuch* 40 (2005), pp. 417–30.

26. I am grateful to Dr Mark Chinca for discussion of this episode and am indebted to his article '*Tout exemple cloche*: erzählen vom Tode Friedrichs des Friedigen in Mittelalter und früher Neuzeit', *Zeitschrift für deutsche Philologie* 123 (2004), pp. 341–64, at p. 343.

27. *Heresies of the High Middle Ages*, trans. Walter L. Wakefield and Austin O. Evans, New York, 1969, p. 311; Sarah Hamilton, 'The Virgin Mary in Cathar Thought', *Journal of Ecclesiastical History* 56 (2005), pp. 24–47, at pp. 26–7.

28. 'Confundatur haereticus,/Resipiscat phreneticus/Et omnis erroneous;/Infidelis erubescat,/Sed fidelis hilarescat,/Ferali durita', Joseph Szövérffy, 'Maria und die Häretiker: Ein Zisterzienserhymnus zum Albigenserkrieg', *Analecta Cisterciensia* 43(1987), pp. 223–32; 7a–b, p. 226.

29. 'Sed qui nosse vult Mariam/Et ipsius prolem diam,/Veniat ad ecclesiam/Discere mysteria', ibid., 12b, p. 227.

30. Hamilton, 'The Virgin Mary in Cathar Thought', pp. 29–31.

31. *Heresies of the High Middle Ages*, eds. Austin P. Evans and Walter L. Wakefield, New York, 1969, pp. 232–3.

32. *The Jewish Christian Debate in the High Middle Ages: A Critical Edition of the NIZZAHON VETUS with an Introduction, Translation and Commentary*, ed. David Berger, Philadelphia, 1979, no. 220, pp. 214–15.

33. Frank Talmage, 'An Hebrew Polemical Treatise: Anti-Cathar and Anti-Orthodox', *Harvard Theological Review* 60 (1967), pp. 323–48, p. at 341.

Chapter 14: Mary's Miracles as Reward and as Punishment

1. Anthony Bale, *The Jew in the Medieval Book: English Antisemitisms, 1350–1500*, Cambridge, 2006, chapters 3–5.
2. Robert Branner, *Manuscript Painting in Paris during the Reign of Saint Louis*, Berkeley, 1977, figure 391. On the complex rhetorical strategies realized in Gothic Façades, see Stephen Murray, *A Gothic Sermon: Making a Contract with the Mother of God, Saint Mary of Amiens*, Berkeley, 2004.
3. C. M. Kauffmann, *Biblical Imagery in Medieval England 700–1500*, London, 2003, figure 127, p. 178.
4. Sara Lipton, *Images of Intolerance: The Representation of Jews and Judaism in Bible moralisée*, Berkeley, 1999, pp. 24–5, 43, 59, 60, 68, 84–5. On Mary as *ecclesia* see Helga Sciurie, 'Maria-ecclesia als Mitherrscherin Christi: Zur Funktion des *Sponsus-Sponsa*-Modells in der Bildkunst des 13. Jahrhunderts', in *Maria: Abbild oder Vorbild? Zur Sozialgeschichte mittelalterlicher Marienverehrung*, eds. Hedwig Röckelein, Claudia Opitz and Dieter R. Bauer, Tübingen, 1990, pp. 110–46.
5. Pavel Kroupa and Jaroslava Kroupova, 'K Ikonografii nástěnných maleb v kostele Narozeni P. Marie v Dolnim Bukovsku [On the Iconography of Fresco Painting in the Church of the Nativity of the Virgin Mary at Dolni-Bukovsko]', *Umĕni* 36 (1988), pp. 558–60. I am most grateful to my friend Professor Petr Charvat for translating this article for me from the Czech.
6. Ibid., p. 559.
7. Sarah Kay, *Courtly Contradictions: The Emergence of the Literary Object in the Twelfth Century*, Stanford, 2001, pp. 178–215.
8. William Chester Jordan, 'Marian Devotion and the Talmud Trial of 1240', in *Ideology and Royal Power in Medieval France: Kingship, Crusades and the Jews*, Aldershot, 2001, XI, pp. 61–76.
9. On the performative aspects of these tales see Adrian P. Tudor, 'Preaching, Storytelling, and the Performance of Short Pious Narratives', in *Performing Medieval Narrative*, Woodbridge, 2005, pp. 141–53; and Kathryn A. Duys, 'Performing Song in Monastic Culture: The *Lectio Divina* in Gautier de Coinci's *Miracles de Nostre Dame*', in *Cultural Performances in Medieval France: Essays in Honor of Nancy Freeman Regalado*, Woodbridge, 2007, pp. 123–33. For songs and music see Daniel O'Sullivan, *Marian Devotion in the Thirteenth-Century Lyric*, Toronto, 2005, pp. 11–32, 118, 120–33.
10. 'Diex! s'un jor ere en liu de roy,/Por Rains, por Rome ne por Roye/Laissier un vivre n'en porroie./D'aus endurer est grans laidure,/Mais Sainte Eglyse les endure/Por la sainte mort ramenbrer/Dont il nos doit toz tanz menbrer:/Li crucefis et li Ebriu/Nos renovelent la mort Dieu./Les laies gens n'ont autre escrit;/Ce leur mostre, ce leur descrit/De Jhesu Crist la paissïon', *Miracles de Nostre Dame*, II, ed. V. F. Koenig, Geneva and Paris, 1961, p. 22, lines 436–47. See also Jennifer Shea, 'Adgar's Gracial and Christian Images of Jews in Twelfth-century Vernacular Literature', *Journal of Medieval History* 33 (2007), pp. 181–96. I am grateful to Jane Gilbert for her help with translation from the Old French.
11. Marilyn Yalom, *Birth of the Chess Queen: A History*, London, 2004, pp. 107–15; see plates 13–14 and figure on p. 108. On chess in courts see Remi O. Constable, 'Chess and Courtly Culture in Medieval Castile: The *Libro de ajedrez* of Alfonso X, el Sabio', *Speculum* 82 (2007), pp. 301–47.
12. Östen Södegård, 'Petit poème allégorique sur les échecs', *Studia neophilologica* 23 (1950/51), pp. 127–36, at p. 133, lines 20–25. I am most grateful to my friend Jean-Michael Vinet for considering this poem with me.
13. Gautier de Coinci, *Les Miracles de Nostre Dame*, Geneva and Paris, 1960, III, pp. 19–24,

471

83–90, 162–8. See discussion in David A. Flory, *Marian Representations in the Miracle Tales of Thirteenth-century Spain and France*, Washington, 2000, pp. 59–62.

14. 'Adont i ot tumulte grant/Et escrïee en mout de liuz:/'Or as gïuz! Or as gïuz,/Qui no clerçon noz ont emblé!'/Et clerc et lai sont assamblé,/Chiez les gïus mout tost s'enbatent;/ Gïuz trebuchent et abatent,/Gïuz batent et gïus roillent', Gautier de Coinci, *Les Miracles de Nostre Dame* IV, ed. V. F. Koenig, Geneva, 1970, pp. 42–75, at p. 58, lines 406–13.

15. Jennifer A. Shea, 'The Influence of the Cult of the Virgin Mary on Christian Perceptions of Jews, with Particular Reference to the Role of Marian Miracle Stories in England and France, c. 1050–c.1300', unpublished Ph.D. thesis, University of Cambridge, 2004, chapters 3–4.

16. 'Fius, encor fust de males meurs/Cis chevaliers dont je te proi,/S'oneroit il m'image et moi', Gautier de Coinci, *Les Miracles de Nostre Dame*, II, ed. Koenig, p. 267, lines 144–6; A. Garnier, 'Autour de la mort: Temps de la dilation et Purgatoire dans les "Miracles de Nostre Dame" de Gautier de Coinci', *Le Moyen Age* 94 (1988), pp. 183–202, at pp. 190–93.

17. 'Par le plaisir de Nostre Dame', Gautier de Coinci, *Les Miracles de Nostre Dame*, IV, p. 167, line 332.

18. *Judaism on Trial: Jewish-Christian Disputations in the Middle Ages*, trans. Hyam Maccoby, London, 1993, pp. 156–7.

19. Robert Chazan, *Barcelona and Beyond: The Disputation of 1267 and its Aftermath*, Berkeley, 1992, pp. 26–7, 58.

20. Anna D. Russakoff, ' "Marian Image Insulted": Jews, Iconoclasm, and Miraculous Images in the Illustrated Gautier de Coinci Manuscripts', a paper delivered at the 'Mary: Mediterranean, European, Global' Conference, New York University, 8 April 2005. That manuscript opens the tale on fol. 234 with an image of the owner, kneeling before Mary and Child, while an inscription reads 'gratia plena' – full of grace. I am most grateful to Dr Russakoff for allowing me to cite this material from her doctoral dissertation, 'Imaging the Miraculous: *Les Miracles de Notre Dame* (Paris, BnF, n.acq.fr 24541)', Ph.D. dissertation, Institute of Fine Arts, New York University, January 2006, soon to be published as a book.

21. 'Acies ordinata Dei Mater dicitur, ut Spiritus Sanctus ait: Terribilis ut castrorum acies ordinate. Quia prophetarum et euangelistarum doctorumque sentenciis, omniumque sanctorum diuinis figuris et assercionibus, eterna eius uirginitas, contra iudeos et hereticos, munita habetur. Terribilis est, quia demonibus et hereticis et iudeos in dei ultimo timenda erit, dum ipsi infideles celorum reginam cum angelis et electis in celo regnantem videbunt et se ipsos in orco mersos. Vere tunc timebunt impii, dum stabunt iusti in magna constantia aduersus eos qui se angustiauerunt.' I am extremely grateful to Dr Kathleen Stewart of University of California, Berkeley, for sharing with me this unpublished material, which she has transcribed from Ripoll ms. 193.

22. See for examples Brian Spencer, *Medieval Pilgrim Badges from Norfolk*, Hunstanton, 1980, pp. 10–12; *Medieval Pilgrim and Secular Badges*, ed. Mitchell Mitchener, London, 1986.

23. Robert Stacey, 'From Ritual Crucifixion to Host Desecration: Jews and the Body of Christ', *Jewish History* 12 (1998), pp. 11–28.

24. For the text see Christoph Cluse, ' "Fabula ineptissima": Die Ritualmordlegende um Adam von Bristol nach der Handschrift London, British Library, Harley 957', *Aschkenas* 5 (1995), pp. 293–330; see Harvey J. Hames, 'The Limits of Conversion: Ritual Murder and the Virgin Mary in the Account of Adam of Bristol', *Journal of Medieval History* 33 (2007), pp. 43–59.

25. Bale, *The Jew in the Medieval Book*, pp. 55–103.

26. Christopher N. L. Brooke, *Churches and Churchmen in Medieval Europe*, London, 1999, p. 302. Attraction to practices associated with Mary, especially of healing, on the part of Jewish women, has been suggested by some scholars and offers an interesting

subject for study: see Israel M. Ta-Shma, *Early Franco-German Ritual and Custom* (in Hebrew), Jerusalem, 1992, pp. 215–16.

27. Beverly Boyd, *The Middle English Miracles of the Virgin*, San Marino: Huntingdon Library, 1964, pp. 33–7, 116–17; Roger Dahood, 'The Punishment of the Jews, Hugh of Lincoln, and the Question of Satire in Chaucer's Prioress's Tale, *Viator* 26 (2005), pp. 465–91. For a discussion attentive to music and song see Bruce W. Holsinger, *Music, Body, and Desire in Medieval Culture: Hildegard of Bingen to Chaucer*, Stanford, 2001, chapter 6, pp. 259–92.

28. David A. Flory, *Marian Representations in the Miracle Tales of Thirteenth-century Spain and France*, Washington, DC, 2000, pp. 110–29.

29. See on the theme of Mary and captivity in Iberian narratives Amy G. Remensnyder, 'Christian Captives, Muslim Maidens, and Mary', *Speculum* 82 (2007), pp. 642–77. On Jews in the *Cantigas de Santa Maria* see Paulino Rodriguez Barrel, 'La dialéctica Testo-Imagen a propósito de la representación del Judío en las *Cantigas de Santa Maria*', *Anuario de Estudios Medievales* 37 (2007), pp. 213–43.

30. A digital *cantigas* project offers easy access to information on the diverse sources of the *cantigas* and more at http://csm.mml.ox.ac.uk.

31. On the illustration of the *cantigas* John E. Keller, 'The Art of Illumination in the Books of Alfonso X (Primarily in the *Canticles of Holy Mary*)', *Thought* 60 (1985), pp. 388–406; for representation of the faith of non-Christians, see Francisco Prado-Vilar, 'The Gothic Anamorphic Gaze: Regarding the Worth of Others', in *Under the Influence: Questioning the Comparative in Medieval Castile*, Leiden, 2005, pp. 67–100.

32. For a wide range of disciplinary approaches see *Studies on the Cantigas de Santa Maria: Art, Music, and Poetry*, Madison, 1987. The *Cantigas de Santa Maria* is linked to other activities in court, such as writing on the Immaculate Conception: see James W. Marchand and Spurgeon W. Baldwin, 'A Maculist at the Court of Alfonso el Sabio: Gil de Zamora's Lost Treatise on the Immaculate Conception', *Franciscan Studies* 47 (1988), pp. 171–80.

33. Gonzalo de Berceo, *Miracles of Our Lady*, trans. Richard Terry Mount and Annette Grant Cash, Lexington, 1997, pp. 13–14; Gonzalo de Berceo, *Milagros de Nuestra Señora*, ed. Vicente Beltrán, Madrid, 1985, p. 23.

34. 'Como santa Maris sacou un escudeiro de cativo de guisa que eo non viron os que guardavan o carcer en que jazia'; 'Quen os peccadored guia e aduz a salvaçon, ben pode guiar os presos, pois os saca de prijon'; '. . . e que sacou un cativo de prijon e de suade, a que muito mal fezeran os muoros por sa razon', *Songs of Holy Mary of Alfonso X, the Wise: A Translation of the Cantigas de Santa María*, trans. Kathleen Kulp-Hill, Medieval and Renaissance Texts and Studies 173, Tempe, 2000, no. 227, pp. 272–3; Alfonso X. el Sabio, *Cantigas de Santa María (cantigas 101 a 260)*, ed. Walter Mettmann, Madrid, 1988, II, pp. 297–9, at p. 297.

35. *Songs of Holy Mary*, p. 107; see on intercession Spurgeon W. Baldwin and James W. Marchand, 'The Virgin Mary as Advocate before the Heavenly Court', *Medievalia et humanistica* new series 18 (1992), pp. 79–93. On the local in understanding saints see John H. Arnold, *Belief and Unbelief in Medieval Europe*, London, 2005, pp. 86–7.

36. *Songs of Holy Mary*, Cantiga 22, p. 31.

37. Michel Tarayre, *La Vierge et le miracle: Le Speculum Historiale de Vincent de Beauvais*, Paris, 1999.

38. *Miracles de Nostre-Dame, tirés du Rosarius (Paris, ms. B.N.fr. 12438)*, ed. Pierre Kunstmann, Ottawa and Paris, 1991, miracle nos. iv, x, xvii, on pp. x, xii, xiv–v.

39. 'And seruet our lady deuotly all hur lyue-dayes aftyr, and had þe blysse of Heuen', *Mirk's Festial: A Collection of Homiliès by Johannes Mirkus (John Mirk)*, ed. Theodor Erbe, London, 1905, sermon 14, pp. 56–62, at p. 62; for another example see p. 302.

40. Michael E. Goodich, *Miracles and Wonders: The Development of the Concept of Miracle, 1150–1350*, London, 2007, p. 107.

41. Flory, *Marian Representations in the Miracle Tales of Thirteenth-century Spain and*

France, pp. 63–5. I am very grateful to Andrew Pfrenger for introducing me to this interesting material. The translation is his, from 'Secular vs. Canon Law: Consent in the Icelandic Miracle of the Virgin, Vitnisvísur af Maríu', pp. 15, 24. On the spread of Mary miracles in Scandinavia see Helena Edgren, *Mercy and Justice: Miracles of the Virgin Mary in Finnish Medieval Wall-Paintings*, Helsinki, 1993, and Margaret Cormack, *The Saints in Iceland: Their Veneration from the Conversion to 1400*, Brussels, 1994, pp. 127–9.

42. As a youth St Edmund of Abingdon (d.1240) placed a ring on a statue of Mary as a sign of his commitment to celibacy. On Mary's interventions for those struggling with lust see Cynthia Powell Jayne, 'The Virgin's Cures for Lust', in *Estudios alfonsinos y otros escritos: en homenaje a John Esten Keller y a Anibal A. Biglieri*, New York, 1991, pp. 118–24.

Chapter 15: Mary at the Foot of the Cross

1. For a discussion of the emphasis on Mary's compassion see Fulton, *From Judgment to Passion*, pp. 405–70.

2. *Autour de Hugo d'Oignies*, p. 47; see also p. 63 for an example from Cologne.

3. Neil MacGregor with Erika Langmuir, *Seeing Salvation: Images of Christ in Art*, London, 2000, plate 40, pp. 130–31.

4. Huot, *Allegorical Play in the Old French Motet*, pp. 160–88.

5. *Nine Medieval Latin Plays*, ed. Peter Dronke, Cambridge, 1994.

6. Oxford Rawlinson C821; Lord, *The Visual Culture of Wales*, no. 268, p. 173.

7. See the statue of the weeping Mary from Halberstadt cathedral of around 1220, Berlin, Bode-Museum, and from Naumburg cathedral of around 1230.

8. *Musée national du moyen âge*, pp. 66–7.

9. Lucca Museo Civico; *Year 1200*, II, no. 91, p.87. Mary gestures dramatically towards her son's side-wound, and John's face is highly expressive on a cross by Rinaldo da Siena: see *Sotto il Duomo di Siena: Scoperte archeologiche, architettoniche e figurative*, ed. Roberto Guerrini with Max Seidel, Siena, 2003, plate 35, p. 132.

10. On the process in Northern Europe see James H. Marrow, *Passion Iconography in Northern European Art of the Late Middle Ages and Early Renaissance: A Study of the Transformation of Sacred Metaphor into Descriptive Narrative*, Kortrijk, 1979.

11. London Society of Antiquaries, 59, fol. 35v.

12. London, British Library, Add. 49622, fol. 7r.

13. Susan Boynton, 'From the Lament of Rachel to the Lament of Mary: A Transformation in the History of Drama and Spirituality', in *Signs of Change: Transformations of Christian Traditions and their Representation in the Arts, 1000–1200*, Amsterdam and New York, 2004, pp. 319–40, at pp. 328–30.

14. Michael Ayrton, *Giovanni Pisano: Sculptor*, London, 1969, pp. 37–8.

15. *Iohannis de Caulibus Meditaciones Vite Christi*, ed. M. Stallings Taney, Turnhout, 1997; on authorship see pp. ix–xi. See also *Meditations on the Life of Christ: An Illustrated Manuscript of the Fourteenth Century, Paris, Bibliothèque Nationale Ms.Ital.115*, trans. Isa Ragusa and eds. Isa Ragusa and Rosalie B. Green, Princeton, 1977; on Franciscan Passion poetry see F. J. E. Raby, *History of Christian-Latin Poetry from the Beginnings to the Close of the Middle Ages*, Oxford, 1953, pp. 421–42.

16. On Giotto and the spirituality of the friars see Joanna Cannon, 'Giotto and Art for the Friars: Revolutions Spiritual and Artistic', in *The Cambridge Companion to Giotto*, Cambridge, 2004, pp. 103–34. On the representation of emotion by Giotto see Michael Schwartz, 'Bodies of Self-Transcendence: The Spirit of Affect in Giotto and Piero', in *Representing Emotions: New Connections in the Histories of Art, Music and Medicine*, Aldershot, 2005, pp. 69–87, esp. pp. 72–7.

17. *Duccio: Alle origini della pittura senese*, Milan, 2003, no. 28, pp. 188–91.

18. Boston Museum of Fine Arts, Grant Walker and Charles Potter Kling Funds. On this theme see Anne Derbes and Mark Sandona, 'Barren Metal and the Fruitful Womb: The Program of Giotto's Arena Chapel in Padua', *Art Bulletin* 80 (1998), pp. 274–91.

474

19. The left wing has the Nativity (below) and the Crucifixion of Peter; the right wing, Mary enthroned (below) and the miracle of St Nicholas. The central panel depicts the Crucifixion (with a small medallion of Christ as the Word in its gable) and it is dominated by the depiction of Mary swooning at the foot of the cross. Siena, Pinacoteca Nazionale.

20. *The Art of Devotion in the Late Middle Ages in Europe*, pp. 22–5. A similar panel by Daddi still stands in the Bigallo Chapel in Florence.

21. Marquard of Lindau, *Deutsche Predigten*, ed. Rüdiger Blumrich, Tübingen, 1994, sermon 21, pp. 137–42, at pp. 141–2. I am grateful to Dr Stephen Mossman, whose research on Marquard I first encountered at a seminar and then read thanks to his generosity.

22. This argument is developed in Olga Pujmanová, 'The Vyšší Brod Crucifixion', *Bulletin of the National Gallery in Prague* 5–6 (1995–6), pp. 105–12. I am most grateful to Professor Viktor Schmidt of the University of Groningen for having discussed Mary and blood with me and having sent me a copy of this article.

23. Prague National Gallery; see the whole cycle in *Medieval Painting in Bohemia*, ed. Jan Royt, Prague, 2003. I am grateful to the Yandell family for their insightful comments during our visit to the gallery.

24. 'Stonde wel, moder, under rode, / Bihold thi child wyth glade mode, / Blythe moder might thou be.' / 'Sone, how may I blithe stonden? / I se thin feet, I se thin honden, / Naylëd to the harde tre'. / 'Moder, I may no lenger dwelle / The time is come I fare to helle, / The thridde day I rise upon'. / 'Sone, I willë with thee founden, / I deye, y-wis, of thine wounden, / So rewful deth was never non', *Medieval English Lyrics, 1200–1400*, ed. Thomas G. Duncan, London, 1995, no. 91, pp. 124–6, lines 1–6, 49–54.

25. 'Blissed be thou quen of hevene, / Bring us out of helle levene / Thurgh thi dere sones might. / Moder, for that heighe blode / That He shadde upon the rode / Led us into hevene light. Amen', *Medieval English Lyrics*, p. 126, lines 61–6. See also Sarah Stanbury, 'The Virgin's Gaze: Spectacle and Transgression in Middle English Lyrics of the Passion', *Publications of the Modern Languages Association* 106 (1991), pp. 1,083–93; see also Barbara Newman, *From Virile Woman to WomanChrist: Studies in Medieval Religion and Literature*, Philadelphia, 1995, pp. 82–3.

26. On the art of confraternities see *Confraternities and the Visual Arts in Renaissance Italy: Ritual, Spectacle, Image*, eds. Barbara Wisch and Diane Cole Ahl, Cambridge, 2000. The Franciscans' support of Mary's Immaculate Conception was reflected in the devotional choice of some Italian confraternities: Barbara Sella, 'Northern Italian Confraternities and the Immaculate Conception in the Fourteenth Century', *Journal of Ecclesiastical History* 49 (1998), pp. 599–619.

27. On the types of confraternities in late medieval Italian cities see Giovanna Casagrande, 'Confraternities and Indulgences in Italy in the Later Middle Ages', in *Promissory Notes on the Treasury of Merits: Indulgences in Late Medieval Europe*, ed. R. N. Swanson, Leiden, pp. 37–63. On themes in the art of confraternities, especially banners and panels depicting Mary as Mother of Mercy, see Daniel Arasse, 'Entre devotion et culture: Fonctions de l'image religieuse au Xve siècle', in *Faire croire: Modalités de la diffusion et de la reception des messages religieux du XIIe au XVe siècles*, Rome, 1981, pp. 131–46.

28. Bonaventura Giordani, 'Statuta consortii B. Mariae Virginis et S. Francisci Parmae saec. XIV', *Archivum franciscanum historicum* 16 (1923), pp. 356–68, at pp. 358–9.

29. Candido Mesini, 'La Compagnia di S. Maria delle Laudi e di San Francesco di Bologna', *Archivum franciscanum historicum* 52 (1959), pp. 361–89, at p. 385. I am grateful to Kate Lowe for helping me with the translation of some words in this passage.

30. Zervas, 'Niccolò Gerini's *Entombment and Resurrection of Christ*', pp. 54–5.

31. Giordani, 'Statuta', c. 1, p. 360.

32. For an example of an indulgence (in favour of a St George in Immeldorf, Würzburg diocese) illustrated by a figure of Mary and Child looking on see Alexander Seibold, *Sammelindulgenzen: Ablassurkunden des Spätmittelalters und der Frühneuzeit*, Cologne, 2001, p. 289.

33. For an edition of the statutes see Barbara Sella, 'Northern Italian Confraternities and

the Immaculate Conception in the Fourteenth Century', *Journal of Ecclesiastical History* 49 (1998), pp. 599–619, at pp. 612–19. For the *Salve regina* reference see c. 9, p. 615.

34. 'Mamma, col cor afflitto/entro 'n le man' te metto/de Ioanne meo eletto,/sia tuo figlio appellato', 'Donna de Paradiso', in *Laude*, ed. Ferdinando Pappalardo, Bari, 2006, no. 70, pp. 222–7, at lines 104–7, p. 226. On the performance of *laude* see Cyrilla Barr, *The Monophonic Lauda and the Lay Religious Confraternities of Tuscany and Umbria in the Late Middle Ages*, Kalamazoo, 1988.

35. On Jewish guilt see Jeremy Cohen, *Living Letters of the Law: Ideas of the Jew in Medieval Christianity*, Berkeley, 1999, pp. 23–65; Jeremy Cohen, 'The Jews as Killers of Christ in the Latin Tradition, from Augustine to the Friars', *Traditio* 39 (1983), pp. 1–27. See also Nigel Morgan, *The Lambeth Apocalypse: Manuscript 209 in Lambeth Palace Library: A Critical Study*, London, 1990, fol. 51v.

36. 'O fillo, fillo, fillo/oi amoroso gillo/fillo ki da consillo/Al cormio angustiato . . ./Fillo mio gratioso/fillo mio delectoso/fillo mio saporoso/oue si inpresonato?', Giulio Grimaldi, 'Il laudario di Urbino', *Studj Romanzi* 12 (1915), pp. 1–96, at no. 16, pp. 22–4, stanzas 7 and 10, at p. 22.

37. 'Per la carne polita/currea sangue uermillo/Orecco amara uita/kavera maria del fillo./ Lagente desmentita/ordenaro consillo:/la morte elo dessillo/Delo bono pastore', ibid., no. 7, pp. 9–10, stanza 10, p. 9.

38. 'E crida ad alte voxe: o povel çudeo/Perchè me turmentavu' lo dolce fiolo meo?/To perdera per lue la segnoria e 'l pheo/che l'angello m'a dicto ch' el è fiolo de deo', Bertoni, 'Il Laudario', p. 63.

39. 'Leplage kelo mio corpo a de fore/tullai in core o mamma pietosa/pero se po estimar lo to dolore/assai maiore ke plu uiua cosa/et amme ne resulta la inçendore/per lardore kenno me da posa/conoscendo kettu mammi assai', ibid., no. 2, pp. 4–5, stanza 3, p. 5.

40. 'Almio fillo beato/dulçe plu ke lo mele./Abreuar li fo dato mirra aceto effele./Era incroce clauato/lo dulçe emanuele/ela gente crudele/lidaua plu amarore', ibid., no. 7, pp. 9–10, stanza 11, p. 9.

41. 'Mamma lo planto keffai/simme uno coltello/kettucto me ua tormentando', ibid., no. 17, pp. 21–2, stanza 1, p. 21. On the qualities associated with vernacular writing, with an emphasis on unease, see Jane Gilbert, 'Men Behaving Badly: Linguistic Purity and Sexual Perversity in Derrida's *Le Monologuisme de l'autre* and Gower's *Traitié pour essampler les amantz marietz*', *Romance Studies* 24 (2006), pp. 77–89; esp. p. 88.

42. Daniel E. Bornstein, *The Bianchi of 1399: Popular Devotion in Late Medieval Italy*, Ithaca, 1993, pp. 38–9, 114, 120–21.

43. Robert Gragger, 'Eine altungarische Marienklage', in *Ungarische Bibliothek* 7 (1923), pp. 1–21, at pp. 18–19.

44. 'O, Juzieu cruzel e felo!/Mon filh m'avetz tout bel e bo./Metetz m'en totz sols, moiram abdui', *Altprovenzalische Marienklage des XIII. Jahrhunderts*, ed. W. Muschake Romanische Bibliothek 3, Halle, 1890, at p. 16, lines 389–91.

45. 'Drápa af Mariugrát', in *Fourteenth-Century Icelandic Verse on the Virgin Mary*, ed. Kellinde Wrightson, London, 2001, lines 1–6, p. 7.

Chapter 16: Mary and Women, Mary and Men

1. C.1225; *Autour de Hugo d'Oignies*, pp. 361–3.

2. Goswin of Bossut, *Send Me God: The Lives of Ida the Compassionate of Nivelles, Nun of La Ramée, Arnulf, Lay Brother of Villers, and Abundus, Monk of Villers*, trans. Martinus Cawley, preface by Barbara Newman, Turnhout, 2003.

3. Ibid., pp. 70–71.

4. Ibid., pp. 71–2.

5. Ibid., pp. 221–2; this is a hymn by the fifth-century Roman poet Caelius Sedulius.

6. Ibid., p. 227.

7. Caroline Walker Bynum, *Holy Feast and Holy Fast: The Religious Significance of Food to Medieval Women*, Berkeley, 1987.
8. Goswin of Bossut, *Send Me God*, pp. 224–5.
9. I invoke here the insights expressed by Claire M. Waters, *Angels and Earthly Creatures: Preaching, Performance, and Gender in the Later Middle Ages*, Philadelphia, 2004, p. 119.
10. 'Cumque iam ad exitum appropinquarem, formidaretque anima mea, ecce uenerabilis patrona nostra Dei genitrix Virgo Maria, cum quodam admirabilis uenustatis uiro, coram me astitit, egrumque me piis oculis intuens, ubi uel quid dolorem corpore requisivit. Mox, cum designassem locum, illa, phialam extendens, quam sacro medicamine plenam penes se gestabat in minibus, per uentris medium traxit a latere usque ad latus, cuius tactum salus insecuta continuo morti me condonauit et uite . . . Cumque talium uisitatione et uisione in multa exultatione gauderem, subito gloriosa Christi mater cum comitibus suis per fenestre huius medium ablati sunt', in Robert Godding, 'Une oeuvre inédite de Thomas de Cantimpré: *La Vita Iohannis Cantipratensis*', *Revue d'histoire ecclésiastique* 76 (1981), pp. 241–316, at III, 2, pp. 309–10.
11. Goswin of Bossut, *Send Me God*, pp. 67–8.
12. 'Tres glorïeus Diex, or encline,/Tes oreilles a ma priiere;/Douce Vierge, Mere, Roÿne,/ Qui n'as seconde ne premiere,/Par ta sainte grace enlumine/Mon cuer de ta clere lumiere,/ Pour faire rime alexandrine/D'une gracïeuse matiere', *Les Cantiques Salemon: The Song of Songs in MS Paris BNF fr. 14966*, Turnhout, 2006, p. 105, lines 1–8.
13. 'Enten, douce Amie, et escoute,/Je sui la florette esmeree/Dou chan ou la terre n'est route/ Aree d'omme ne semee./Odeur, douceur et biauté toute/Contieng, je sui fleurs emmiellee/ Dont vertus et grace degoute,/Je sui li lys de la valee', ibid., p. 141, lines 1,049–56.
14. *The Life of Saint Douceline, a Beguine of Provence*, trans. Kathleen Garay and Madeleine Jeay, Woodbridge, 2002, c. 2.11, p. 31. On Beguines and Mary see Martina Wehrli-Johns, 'Haushälterin Gottes: Zur Mariennachfolge der Beginen', in *Maria: Abbild oder Vorbild? Zur Sozialgeschichte mittelalterlicher Marienverehrung*, eds. Hedwig Röckelein, Claudia Opitz and Dieter R. Bauer, Tübingen, 1990, pp. 147–67.
15. On art and female religious see Jeffrey F. Hamburger, ' "To Make Women Weep": Ugly Art as "Feminine" and the Origins of Modern Aesthetics', *Res* 31 (1997), pp. 9–33.
16. 56 × 42 cm; Caroline Villers, Robert Gibbs, Rebecca Hellen and Annette King, 'Simone dei Crocefissi's "Dream of the Virgin" ', *Burlington Magazine* 142 (2000), pp. 481–6.
17. Ibid., p. 482.
18. Alexandra Barratt, 'Context: Some Reflections on Wombs and Tombs and Inclusive Language', in *Anchorites, Wombs and Tombs: Intersections of Gender and Enclosure in the Middle Ages*, Cardiff, 2005, pp. 27–38, at p. 31, her translation – from '*Sanctae Gertrudis magnae virginis ordinis sancti benedicti legatus divinae pietatis* 4,3' in *Revelationes Gertrudianae ac Mechtildianae*, I, Poitiers, 1875, p. 300.
19. *Anchoritic Spirituality: Ancrene Wisse and Associated Works*, trans. Anne Savage and Nicholas Watson, New York, 1991, p. 186.
20. Judith H. Oliver, *Singing with Angels: Liturgy, Music, and Art in the Gradual of Gisela von Kerssenbrock*, Turnhout, 2007.
21. New York Metropolitan Museum of Art; Jacqueline E. Jung, 'Crystalline Wombs and Pregnant Hearts: The Exuberant Bodies of the Katharinenthal Visitation Group', in *History in the Comic Mode: Medieval Communities and the Matter of Person*, eds. Rachel Fulton and Bruce W. Holsinger, New York, 2007, pp. 223–37.
22. Newman, *From Virile Woman to WomanChrist*, p. 87.
23. *Agnes Blannbekin, Viennese Beguine: Life and Revelations*, trans. with introduction Ulrike Wiethaus, Cambridge, 2002, cs. 193–4, pp. 132–4, at p. 132.
24. Rosemary Drage Hale, '*Imitatio Mariae*: Motherhood Motifs in Devotional Memoires', *Mystics Quarterly* 16 (1990), pp. 193–203, at p. 194.
25. Hale, '*Imitatio Mariae*', p. 192; Religious women related to Mary's maternity as much as they did to her chastity, Elliott, *Spiritual Marriage*, 178–9.

26. Petrus de Dacia, *Vita Christinae Stumbelensis*, ed. Johannes Paulson, Frankfurt, 1985, p. 131. On Christina see John Coakley, 'A Marriage and Its Observer: Christine of Stommeln, the Heavenly Bridegroom, and Friar Peter of Dacia', in *Gendered Voices: Medieval Saints and Their Interpreters*, Philadelphia, 1999, pp. 99–117, 229–35, at pp. 104–5; Aviad M. Kleinberg, *Prophets in Their Own Country: Living Saints and the Making of Sainthood in the Later Middle Ages*, Chicago, 1992, pp. 71–98.

27. *Das Leben der Schwestern zu Töss beschrieben von Elsbet Stagel*, ed. Ferdinand Vetter Berlin, 1906, p. 52.

28. *Die Predigten Taulers aus der Engelberger und der Freiburger Handschriften sowie aus Schmidts Abschriften der ehemaligen Strassburger Handschriften*, ed. Ferdinand Vetter, Berlin, 1910, p. 7; Newman, *From Virile Woman to WomanChrist*, p. 83.

29. From *A Book of Showings to the Anchoress Julian of Norwich*, Toronto, 1978, II, pp. 366–7.

30. Johannes von Marienwerder, *The Life of Dorothea von Montau, a Fourteenth-century Recluse*, trans. Ute Stargardt, Lewiston, 1997, c. 3, pp. 82–3.

31. Ibid., p. 83; Elliott, *Spiritual Marriage*, pp. 224–38.

32. Carolyn Diskant Muir, 'Bride or Bridegroom? Masculine Identity in Mystic Marriages', in *Holiness and Masculinity in the Middle Ages*, Cardiff, 2004, pp. 58–78, esp. at pp. 69–73.

33. Ibid., p. 71 and also Josef Brosch, *Hymnen und Gebete des seligen Hermann Josef*, Aachen ,1950, pp. 11–15.

34. Strasbourg, Bibliothèque nationale et universitaire de Strasbourg ms. 2929, fols. 62r and 8v; the manuscript is of around 1360: Gérard Cames, *Dix siècles d'enluminaire en Alsace*, Strasbourg, 1989, figures 139 and 140, p. 90.

35. Annette Volfing, *John the Evangelist and Medieval German Writing: Imitating the Inimitable*, Oxford, 2001, p. 144.

36. Ibid., n. 47, p. 153.

37. *Schlesisch-böhmische Briefmuster aus der Wende des vierzehnten Jahrhunderts*, ed. Konrad Burdach, Berlin, 1926, no. 68, pp. 99–100; on this letter see Michael Stolz, 'Maria und die Artes liberales: Aspekte einer mittelalterlichen Zuordnung', in *Maria in der Welt: Marienverehrung im Kontext der Sozialgeschichte, 10.–18. Jahrhundert*, Zurich, 1993, pp. 95–120, at pp. 107–12.

38. *Schlesisch-böhmische Briefmuster*, no. 69, p. 101.

39. 'Et ecce nunc afflictus et derelictus solus in terra longiqua, debilis in corpore, tristis in corde et quasi totaliter consternates in mente, ad te clamo exsul non solum filius Eve, set filius multorum; ve, ve michi misero, ve michi.', in Reinhold Röhricht, 'Lettres de Ricoldo de Monte-Croce', *Archives de l'Orient latin* 2 (1884), pp. 258–96, letter to Mary on pp. 271–6, p. at 272; on it also see Stephen Mossman, 'The Western Understanding of Islamic Theology in the Later Middle Ages', *Recherches de Théologie et Philosophie Médiévales*, 74 (2007), pp. 169–224, at p. 206, n. 110. I am most grateful to Iris Shagrir for introducing me to this fascinating writer.

40. I am grateful to my colleague Dr Geert Warnar of the University of Leiden for sharing with me his article 'Men of Letters: Medieval Dutch Literature and Learning' before its publication.

41. R. James Long, 'The Virgin Mary as Olive-tree: A Marian Sermon of Richard Fishacre and Science in Oxford', *Archivum fratrum praedicatorum* 55 (1982), pp. 77–87, text on pp. 83–7.

42. 'þou ert þe coluere of noe,/þat broute þe braunche of olyue tre,/In tokne þat pays scholde be/By-tuexte god and manne;/Suete leuedy, help þou me,/Wanne ich schal wende hanne', *The Poems of William of Shoreham*, lines 13–18, p. 127.

43. Théodor W. Koehler, 'Une liste d'*Ave* en l'honneur de la Vierge Marie: 24 titres empruntés à l'éloge de la Sagesse', *Revue française d'histoire du livre* new series 61(1992), pp. 5–22, at pp. 15–19.

44. Debra Hassig, *Medieval Bestiaries: Text, Image, Ideology*, Cambridge, 1995, pp. 133, 143.

45. 'Panthere est beste atrempee / De diverses couleurs coulouree; / . . . / Mout est le panthere courtois / Et ne fait enfans c'une fois. / . . . / La panthere si est Marie / Qui d'atrempance fu garnie. / . . . / De couleurs la diversite / Sont de vertus pluralité / Qui sont le parement de l'ame', *Le Bestiaire et le lapidaire du Rosarius (B.N.F.fr. 12483)*, ed. Sven Sandqvist, Lund, 1996, lines 1–4, 8–9, 17–18, 29–31, pp. 7–8.

46. 'Par salemandre enten Marie. / Chascuns preudons ne la voit mie, / Combien qu'ait nete et serie / La conscïence en ceste vie . . . / Ta conscïence purefie / Et gete larmes a copie, / Veoir pourras dame Marie', ibid., lines 42–5, 69–71, pp. 64–5.

47. 'Durch dines herzen klamme drank / naturen art in rechter sass', Annette Volfing, *Heinrich von Mügeln: 'Der Meide Kranz': A Commentary*, Tübingen, 1997, pp. 13–14, prologue lines 34–5.

48. On the *Ovide moralisé* see Rita Copeland, *Rhetoric, Hermeneutics and Translation in the Middle Ages: Academic Traditions and Vernacular Texts*, Cambridge, 1991, pp. 107–30. I am most grateful to Sarah Kay who generously shared with me her research materials on the *Ovide moralisé*.

49. 'Fors li filz de la Vierge Dame / Qui porta son fil et son pere / Et purement fu vierge et mere', *Ovide moralisé: Poème du commencement du quatorzième siècle publié d'après les manuscrits connus*, ed. C. de Boer with Martina G. de Boer and Jeannette T. M. van 's Sant, Amsterdam, 1936, Book XIII, lines 1022–4, pp. 390–91; 'Volt prendre en la Vierge Marie / Plenteïve virginitez / Et virge plenteïvitez', lines 1101–3, pp. 392–3.

50. *Sydrac le philosophe: Le Livre de la fontaine de toutes sciences*, ed. Ernstpeter Ruhe, Wiesbaden, 2000, q. 27, pp. 54–5.

51. *Sydrac le philosophe*, q. 28, p. 55. At a later stage (question 402) the king inquires about the relative value of the term maiden (*pucel*) and virgin (*virge*), and Sydrac answers: 'Virgin is more meritorious, more worthy than maiden. Virgin means pure and clean and worthy in both her heart and her body and in her members and in her thoughts and in her wishes and in her mouth and her ears and her eyes and her feet and her hands and in the whole of her body inside and out', ibid. q. 402, p. 167.

52. Ibid., q. 1,222, p. 420.

53. Sylvie Barnay, 'La Mariophanie au regard de Jean de Morigny: Magie ou miracle de la vision mariale?', in *Miracles, prodiges et merveilles au moyen âge: Actes du XXVe congrès de la Société des Historiens Médiévistes de l'Enseignement Supérieur Public, Orléans, juin 1994*, Paris, 1995, pp. 173–90.

54. 'Surge, surge, surge dulcissima Virgo Maria . . . invoco te, veni, veni, veni ad me', Barnay, 'La Mariophanie', p. 183.

55. Lucy Freeman Sandler, *Omne bonum: A Fourteenth-century Encyclopedia of Universal Knowledge: British Library MSS Royal 6E VI-6E VII*, 2 vols. London, 1996, I, pp. 124–5; II, pp. 241–2.

56. Ibid., p. 241.

57. Gary P. Cestaro, *Dante and the Grammar of the Nursing Body*, Notre Dame, 2003, figure 8, p. 38.

58. Ayers Bagley, 'Jesus at School', *Journal of Psychohistory* 13 (1985), pp. 13–31 and Ayers Bagley, 'Grammar as Teacher', *Studies in Medieval and Renaissance Teaching* new series 1 (1990), pp. 17–48; Michael Clanchy, 'An Icon of Literacy: The Depiction at Tuse of Jesus Going to School', in *Literacy in Medieval and Early Modern Scandinavian Culture*, ed. Pernille Hermann, Copenhagen, 2005, pp. 47–73.

59. Guillaume de Deguileville, *Le Pelerinaige de vie humaine*, ed. Alfred W. Pollard, London, 1912; for the poem's influence on Chaucer's ABC, see Helen Phillips, 'Chaucer and Deguileville: The ABC in Context', *Medium Aevum* 62 (1993), pp. 1–19.

60. On the ABC and Chaucer's poem see Georgia Ronan Crampton, 'Chaucer's Singular Prayer', *Medium Ævum* 59 (1990), pp. 191–213, esp. at pp. 193–4.

61. *One Hundred Middle English Lyrics*, Indianapolis, 1964, p. 15.

62. Worcester Cathedral Library F 126, fol. 248, as in Alan J. Fletcher, 'The Lyric in the Sermon', in *A Companion to the Middle English Lyric*, Cambridge, 2005, pp. 189–202, at pp. 198–9 (Latin in italics my emphasis). On the theme of spring in poetry and song see the excellent David J. Rothenburg, 'The Marian Symbolism of Spring, ca.1200–ca.1500: Two Case Studies', *Journal of the American Musicological Society* 59 (2006), pp. 319–98. The macaronic tradition probably inspired a fifteenth-century poem by a Welsh student at Oxford, who transcribed into Welsh orthography a Middle English hymn to Mary, *The Hymn to the Virgin Attributed to Iewan ap Hywel Swrdwal*, ed. Raymond Garlick, Newtown, 1985.

63. 'Ci doit tu penser de la duce Marie / De quel angusse ele estoit replenie / Quant estut a son destre / E receust le disciple pur le mestre; . . . / E pur ceo dit un Engelis en teu manere de pite: / 'Now goth sonne under wode / Me reweth, Marie, thi fare rode. / Now goth son under tre / Me reweth, Marie, thy sone and thee'. On the poem see Fletcher, 'The Lyric in the Sermon', pp. 200–202, and W. A. Pantin, *The English Church in the Fourteenth Century*, Cambridge, 1955, pp. 222–4.

64. English translation from M. Teresa Tavormina (trans.), 'Henry of Lancaster, *The Book of Holy Medicines* (*Le Livre des Seyntz Medicines*)', in *Cultures of Piety: Medieval English Devotional Literature in Translation*, Ithaca, 1999, pp. 19–40, at pp. 29–30 and 31.

65. Translation, together with instructive comments, is offered in Michelle Bolduc, 'The Poetics of Authorship and Vernacular Religious Devotion', in *Varieties of Devotion in the Middle Ages and Renaissance*, Turnhout, 2003, pp. 125–43, at pp. 131–5, citation from pp. 133–4, I Pr 1, lines 40–50. On the challenges of performing the *Miracles de Nostre Dame* see Anne Azéma, ' "Une aventure vous dirai": Performing Medieval Narrative', in *Performing Medieval Narrative*, eds. Evelyn Birge Vitz, Nancy Freeman Regalado and Marilyn Lawrence, Woodbridge, 2005, pp. 209–19.

66. On Dante's Mary see Jaroslav Pelikan, 'Mary as *Nostra Regina*', in *Eternal Feminines: Three Theological Allegories in Dante's Paradiso*, New Brunswick, 1990, chapter 5, pp. 101–19.

67. Dante Alighieri, *The Divine Comedy III: Paradise*, I, trans. Charles S. Singleton, Princeton, 1975, canto XXXI, pp. 354–5; lines 115–17; 'ma guarda i cerchi infino al più remoto, / tanto che veggi seder la regina / cui questo regno è suddito e devoto.'

68. 'e a quell mezzo, con le penne sparte / vid'io più di mille angeli festanti, / ciascun distinto di fulgore e d'arte. / Vidi ai lor giochi quivi e a lor canti / ridere una bellezza, che letizia / era ne li occhi a tutti gli altri santi; / e s'io avessi in dir tanta divizia / quanta ad imaginar, non ardirei / lo minimo tentar di sua delizia', ibid., lines 130–38, pp. 354–7

PART V: MARY AS QUEEN AND REFORMER: 1400–1500

Chapter 17: Mary the Sublime

1. Veronica B. Plesch, 'Innovazione Iconografica e Unità Alpina: La Vergine Incoronata dalla Trinità', *Lo Spazio Alpino: Area di Civiltà, Regione Cerniera*, Quaderni di Europa Mediterranea 5, Naples, 1991, pp. 263–79, see figure 4 (Roletto, Piedmont) and figure 6 (Murau, Stiria).

2. Manuscript Einsiedeln 290/1236, fol. 96r; see, with description, Miriam Milman, *Les Heures de la Prière: Catalogue des Livres d'Heures de la Bibliothèque de l'Abbaye d'Einsiedeln*, Turnhout, 2003, pp. 111–24, at p. 119.

3. On this theme see Nancy Bradley Warren, 'Kings, Saints, and Nuns: Gender, Religion, and Authority in the Reign of Henry V', *Viator* 30 (1999), pp. 307–22, at pp. 309–13.

4. The Valencia Altarpiece of c.1415 (London Victoria and Albert Museum) includes Mary in the scene of the arming of St George: her hand lies on his sword as angels place his helmet and attach his spurs, all under the guidance of Christ in heaven. It was made by the German painter Marzal de Sas for the confraternity of St George in Valenica: Samantha Riches, *St George: Hero, Martyr and Myth*, Stroud, 2000, figure 2.2, p. 41.

5. Ronald Knox, *Miracles of Henry VI*, Cambridge, 1923.

6. *A Critical Edition of John Lydgate's Life of Our Lady*, Pittsburgh, 1961, pp. 549–51, lines 1695–701, 1709–15.

7. *The Minor Poems of John Lydgate*, I, London, 1911, repr. 1961, II, p. 344; IV, p. 381; V, p. 663. See also Phillipa Hardman, 'Lydgate's Uneasy Syntax', in *John Lydgate: Poetry, Culture, and Lancastrian England*, Notre Dame, 2006, pp. 12–35; and in the same collection Robert J. Meyer-Lee, 'Lydgate's Laureate Pose', pp. 36–60, esp. at pp. 43–5.

8. *The Regiment of Princes*, ed. Charles R. Blyth, Kalamazoo, 1999, lines 41985–91, p. 186.

9. Regina coeli, laetare, alleluia: Quia quem meruisti portare, alleluia. / Resurrexit sicut dixit, alleluia. Ora pro nobis Deum, alleluia.

10. H. N. MacCracken, 'Lydgatiana V: Fourteen Short Religious Poems', *Archiv für das Studium der neueren Sprachen und Literaturen* 131 (1913), pp. 40–59, at pp. 50–51. On this poem see Helen Phillips, ' "Almighty and Al Merciable Queene": Marian Titles and Marian Lyrics', in *Medieval Women: Texts and Contexts in Late Medieval Britain: Essays for Felicity Riddy*, Turnhout, 2000, pp. 83–99, at pp. 88–93.

11. Marina Belozerskaya, *Rethinking the Renaissance: Burgundian Arts across Europe*, Cambridge, 2002, pp. 179–80, and figure 41, p. 181.

12. Ibid., pp. 65–7; Barbara Haggh, 'The Virgin Mary and the Order of the Golden Fleece', in *Le Banquet du faisan, 1454: L'Occident face au défi de l'Empire ottoman*, eds. Marie-Thérèse Caron and Denis Clauzel, Arras, 1997, pp. 273–87.

13. Virginia R. Bainbridge, 'Women and the Transmission of Religious Culture: Benefactresses of Three Bridgettine Convents c.1400–1600', *Birgittiana* 3 (1997), pp. 55–76, at pp. 66–7; and Virginia R. Bainbridge, 'The Bridgettines and Major Trends in Religious Devotion c.1400–1600: With Reference to Syon Abbey, Mariatron and Marienbaum', *Birgittiana* 19 (2005), pp. 225–40.

14. *La librairie des ducs de Bourgogne: Manuscrits conservés à la Bibliothèque royale de Belgique*, I, Turnhout, 2000, pp. 280–82, on fols. 1r and 3r.

15. Harry Schnitker, 'Margaret of York on Pilgrimage: The Exercise of Devotion and the Religious Traditions of the House of York', in *Reputation and Representation in Fifteenth-century Europe*, The Northern World 8, Leiden, 2004, pp. 87–122, at p. 116.

16. See for example, the series of tapestries described in Elisabeth Delehaye, *La Dame à la Licorne*, Paris, 2007.

17. Bern, Historisches Museum.

18. 'O splendour sainte en la court séraphine. / Subject haultain de sciences augustine, / Puisoir de joye à tous saints et prophètes, / En qui fermoir toute grâce divine, / Toute vertu céleste se recline, / Tout y obombre et tout s'y atermine, / Tout y respant ses richesses secrètes; / O saint miroir d'esmerveillable gloire, / De qui on lit que humilité notoire / T'a fait monter si excelse royne, / Tout humble donc, ta doulceur méritoire, / Tourne envers moi dedens mon oratoire, / Et me permets faire une sobre histoire, / Parlant à toi du mesmes de ma mine', *Œuvres de Georges Chastellain*, VIII, Brussels, 1866, pp. 269–92, at p. 272. Chastellain also wrote a poem dedicated to Notre-Dame of Boulogne, ibid., pp. 294–7.

19. *La librairie des ducs de Bourgogne* I, pp. 50–52.

20. Mary's garden is full of music and flowers in an engraving by the Master of the Berlin Passion, Ursula Weekes, *Early Engravers and their Public: The Master of the Berlin Passion and Manuscripts from Convents in the Rhine-Maas Region, ca.1450–1500*, Turnhout, 2004, pp. 44–5 (figure 37 on p. 44).

21. On the dedication ceremony see *Building the Kingdom: Giannozzo Manetti on the Material and Spiritual Edifice*, eds. Christine Smith and Joseph O'Connor, Turnhout, 2006, pp. 46–9 and 344–55.

22. *Vatican City, Biblioteca Apostolica Vaticana, MS Chigi C VIII 234*, New York and London, 1987, introduction, esp. p. vi. On endowments for performance of the popular motets see Julie E. Cumming, *The Motet in the Age of Dufay*, Cambridge, 1999, pp. 46–51. It is important to remember that Marian motets could also be coded messages about contemporary events, as demonstrated in Paula Higgins, 'Love and Death in the Fifteenth-Century Motet' in *Hearing the Motet: Essays on the Motet of the Middle Ages and Renaissance*, ed. Dolores Pesce, New York, 1997, pp. 142–68.

23. Reinhard Strohm, *Music in Late Medieval Bruges*, Oxford, 1990, pp. 71–3; Janet van der Meulen, 'Onze Lieve Vrouwe van de Droge Boom in Brugge: Devotiebeeld en literaire traditie', in *Aan de vruchten kent men de boom: De boom in tekst en beeld in de middeleeuwse Nederlanden*, Leuven, 2001, pp. 209–37.

24. For much that follows I am indebted to Steven Kaplan's scholarship and many kindnesses. Steven Kaplan, 'Seeing Is Believing: The Power of Visual Culture in the Religious World of Aşe Zär'a Ya'eqob of Ethiopia (1434–1468)', *Journal of Religion in Africa* 32 (2002), pp. 403–21. See also Daniel Baraz, 'The Incarnated Icon of Saidnaya Goes West: A Re-Examination of the Motif in the Light of New Manuscript Evidence', *Le Muséon* 108 (1995), pp. 181–91, at pp. 187–9.

25. Kaplan, 'Seeing Is Believing', p. 407.

26. Getatchew Haile, *The Mariology of Emperor Zär'a Ya'eqob of Ethiopia: Texts and Translations*, Orientalia Christiana Analecta 242, Rome, 1992, pp. 153–7.

27. Ibid., pp. 161–3.

28. See image in Daga Stiphanos, Gojjam; Jacques Mercier, *Art That Heals: The Image as Medicine in Ethiopia*, New York, 1997, figure 76, p. 77; Marilyn E. Heldman, *The Marian Icons of Painter Fre Seyon: A Study in Fifteenth-century Ethiopian Art*, Wiesbaden, 1994.

29. Mercier, *Art That Heals*, figure 73, p. 75.

30. Ibid., p. 74.

31. Haile, *Mariology*, pp. 4–10, esp. pp. 8–9.

32. *Philippe de Mézières' Campaign for the Feast of Mary's Presentation Edited from Bibliothèque Nationale MSS. Latin 17330 and 14454*, ed. William E. Coleman, Toronto, 1981. On attitudes to Mary in Cyprus see Sophia Kalopissi-Verti, 'Representations of the Virgin in Lusignan Cyprus', in *Images of the Mother of God: Perceptions of the Theotokos in Byzantium*, Aldershot, 2005, pp. 305–19. On the cult of Mary in Cyprus, where European and Byzantine religious practices met, see Jean Richard, 'Un but de pèlerinage: Notre-Dame de Nicosie', in *Mosaic. Festschrift for A. H. S. Megaw*, eds. Judith Herrin, Margaret Mullett and Catherine Otten-Froux, Athens, 2001, pp. 135–8.

33. Susan Udry, ' "Putting on the Girls": Mary's Girlhood and the Performance of Monarchical Authority in Philippe de Mézières's Dramatic Office for the *Presentation of the Virgin in the Temple*', *European Medieval Drama* 8 (2004), pp. 1–17. On the feast's liturgy see Andrew Hughes, '*Fons hortorum*: The Office of the Presentation: Origins and Authorship', *Dichtung und Musik*, eds. Walter Berschin and David Hiley, Tutzing, 1999, pp. 153–77.

34. James Boyce, 'The Office of the Presentation of Mary in the Carmelite Liturgy', in *The Land of Carmel: Essays in Honour of Joachim Smet, O.Carm.*, eds. Paul Chandler and Keith J. Egan, Rome, 1991, pp. 231–45.

35. Ruben Ernest Weltsch, *Archbishop John of Jenstein (1348–1400): Papalism, Humanism and Reform in Pre-Hussite Prague*, The Hague, 1968, pp. 87–91, 127–30.

36. Choral book from Siena, decorated by Liberale da Verona (1445–1526), Siena, Duomo, Piccolomini Library; see also Kristin Vincke, *Die Heimsuchung: Marienikonographie in der italienischen Kunst bis 1600*, Cologne, 1997.

37. Eric Christiansen, *The Northern Crusades*, new edn, London, 1997, p. 221.

38. Marian Dygo, 'The Political Role of the Cult of the Virgin Mary in Teutonic Prussia in the Fourteenth and Fifteenth Centuries', *Journal of Medieval History* 15 (1989), pp. 63–80, figure 5, p. 73; see also the example from the Teutonic Order's castle of Rogenhausen, Polish Olsztyn, Nuremberg, Germanisches Nationalmuseum. For other examples Manfred Tripps, 'Hans Multschers Frankfurter Gnadenstuhl – ehemaliges Herz-

stück einer *Vierge Ouvrante?'*, *Zeitschrift für Württemburgische Landesgeschichte* 58 (1999), pp. 99–111.

39. Irene Gonzálvez Hernando, 'La Virgen de San Blas de Buriñondo en Bergara: Ejemplo y excepción de Virgen abridera trinitaria', *Anales de Historia del Arte* 16 (2006), pp. 59–78. I am grateful to the author for sending me a copy of this article.

40. Annemarie Weyl Carr, 'Threads of Authority: The Virgin Mary's Veil in the Middle Ages', in *Robes and Honor: The Medieval World of Investiture*, ed. Stewart Gordon, Basingstoke, 2001, pp. 59–93, at p. 68.

41. For this whole interesting episode see Jean C. Wilson, 'Reflections on St Luke's Hand: Icons and the Nature of Aura in the Burgundian Low Countries during the Fifteenth Century', in *The Sacred Image East and West*, Champaign, 1995, pp. 132–46.

42. Richard Vaughan, *Philip the Good: The Apogee of Burgundy*, New York, 1970, p. 297.

43. Wilson, 'Reflections', p. 141. For Byzantine influence on Renaissance art see Maryan W. Ainsworth, ' "A la façon grèce": The Encounter of Northern Renaissance Artists with Byzantine Icons', in *Byzantium: Faith and Power (1261–1557)*, ed. Helen C. Evans, New York, 2004, pp. 545–93; see also the image of Mary and child painted in Cologne around 1470 by the Master of the Life of Mary, Berlin, Gemäldegalerie, catalogue no. 1235 B.

44. Maryan W. Ainsworth, ' "A la façon grèce": The Encounter of Northern Renaissance Artists with Byzantine Icons', pp. 545–5, esp. at catalogue numbers 331, 337–8, 340–42, 345–7, 349–53.

45. Miri Rubin, 'Europe Remade: Purity and Danger in Late Medieval Europe', *Transactions of the Royal Historical Society* 11 (2001), pp. 101–24, at pp. 121–3.

46. 'Una mulier hebraea fecit invasionem in domo Regis aeterni; una puella, nescio quibus blanditiis, nescio quibus cautelis, nescio quibus violentiis, seduxit, decepit et, ut ita dicam, vulneravit et rapuit divinum cor, et Dei sapientiam circumvenit. Propterea conqueritur Dominus de beata Virgine dicens, Cant. 4.9: Vulnerasti cor meum, soror mea sponsa, vulnerasti cor meum', Sermon for Thursday after the Resurrection, Bernardino da Siena, *Opera omnia*, II, Quaracchi, 1950, pp. 371–97, at p. 376.

47. 'Simile tutti e corsi de la Luna, di Mercurio, di Venus, del Sole, di Marte, di Giove, di Saturno. Del cielo stellato non è niuna stella che Maria non sapesse e non conoscesse l'uffizio suo; e simile del cielo cristallino', Bernardino of Siena, *Prediche volgari*, I, Florence, 1958, sermon on the Blessed Virgin Mary, pp. 159–72, at p. 163.

48. Ibid., pp. 163–4.

49. See Siena, Pinacoteca, Sano di Pietro, Mary pleading for Siena; Cynthia L. Polecritti, *Preaching Peace in Renaissance Italy: Bernardino of Siena and his Audience*, Washington, DC, 2000, p. 189; see also Bram Kempers, 'Icons, Altarpieces, and Civic Ritual in Siena Cathedral, 1100–1530', in *City and Spectacle in Medieval Europe*, Minneapolis, 1994, pp. 89–136, esp. at pp. 113–25. On the use of Mary on city seals in general see Przemysław Wiszewski, 'The Effigies of the Blessed Virgin Mary or Saints on the Medieval Seals of Silesian Cities and Towns (since the 13th to the Middle of the 16th Century)', in *Fonctions sociales et politiques du culte des saints dans les sociétés de rite grec et latin au Moyen Age et à l'époque moderne: Approche comparative*, eds. M Derwich and M. Dimitriev, Wrocław, 1999, pp.183–208.

50. 'O, o, del latte de la Vergine Maria; o donne, dove sete voi? E anco voi, valenti uomini, vedestene mai? Sapete che si va mostrando per reliquie; non v'aviate fede, ché elli non è vero: elli se ne trouva in tanti luoghi! Tenete che non è vero. Forse che ella fu una vacca la Vergine Maria, che ella avesse lassato il latte suo, come si lassa de le bestie, che si lassano mugniare?', Franco Mormando, *The Preachers' Demons: Bernardino of Siena and the Social Underworld of Early Renaissance Italy*, Chicago, 1999, p. 102 and n. 214, p. 283.

51. Emily Michelson, 'Bernardino of Siena Visualises the Name of God', in *Speculum sermonis: Interdisciplinary Reflections on the Medieval Sermon*, eds. Georgina Donavin, Cary J. Nederman and Richard Utz, Turnhout, 2004, pp. 157–79, esp. at pp. 171–5.

52. Hedwig Röckelein, 'Marie, l'église et la synagogue: Culte de la Vierge et lutte contre les

Juifs en Allemagne à la fin du Moyen-Age', in *Marie: Le culte de la vierge dans la société médiévale*, Paris, 1996, pp. 512–32; see also Mary Minty, '*Judengasse* to Christian Quarter: The Phenomenon of the Converted Synagogue in the Late Medieval and Early Modern Holy Roman Empire', in *Popular Religion in Germany and Central Europe, 1400–1800*, eds. Bob Scribner and Trevor Johnson, Basingstoke, 1996, pp. 58–86.

53. Rubin, *Gentile Tales*, pp. 138–9.

54. Michael Stolz, 'Maria und die Artes liberales: Aspekte einer mittelalterlichen Zuordnung', *Maria in der Welt: Marienverehrung im Kontext des Sozialgeschichte 10.–18. Jahrhundert*, Zurich, 1993, pp. 95–120.

55. Achim Timmermann, 'The Avenging Crucifix: Some Observations on the Iconography of the Living Cross', *Gesta* 40 (2001), pp. 141–60.

56. *Early German Painting, 1350–1550*, trans. Margaret Thomas Will, London, 1991, pp. 110–15.

Chapter 18: Mary Unlike Any Other

1. Above, pp. 173–6.

2. George H. Tavard, 'John Duns Scotus and the Immaculate Conception', in *One Mediator, the Saints, and Mary*, eds. H. George Anderson, J. Francis Stafford and Joseph A. Burgess, Minneapolis, 1992, pp. 209–17. For the impact of Scotus' formulations see Alexander A. Di Lella, 'The Immaculate Conception in the Writings of Peter Aureoli', *Francicsan Studies* new series 15(1955), pp. 146–74, and Ignatius Brady, 'The Development of the Doctrine of the Immaculate Conception in the Fourteenth Century after Aureoli', *Franciscan Studies* new series 15 (1955), pp. 175–202.

3. Alejandro de Villalmonte, 'Duns Escoto, la Immaculada y el Pecado Original', *Collectanea Franciscana* 60 (1990), pp. 137–53, esp. at pp. 145–6.

4. *Chartularium universitatis parisiensis* III, ed. Henri Denifle, Paris, 1897, pp. 518–19; Lamy, *L'Immaculée conception*, pp. 562–75.

5. Vatican Library, Ms. Lat. 13097, fol. 1r. On this see Celestino Piana, 'San Bernardino da Siena Teologo', in *San Bernardino da Siena: Saggi e Ricerche Pubblicati nel Qunito Centenatio della Morte (1444–1944)*, Milan, 1945, pp. 139–201, at p. 149 n. 9. I am most grateful to Franco Mormando for introducing me to this manuscript.

6. Fernando Domínguez Reboiras, 'Els Apòrcifs Lullians sobre la Immaculada: La Seva Importància en la Història del Lullisme', *Randa* 27 (1990), pp. 11–43, esp. at pp. 25–7. On the Immaculate Conception in Iberian court life see also Peggy K. Liss, *Isabel the Queen: Life and Times*, New York and Oxford, 1992, pp. 156–9. On literary and liturgical activity around the Immaculate Conception in Aragon see Isaac Vázquez Janeiro, 'El encomio mariano "cunctas haereses sola intermisti": Origen de su sentido immaculista', *Antonianum* 66 (1991), pp. 499–531.

7. On these events see Thomas M. Izbicki, 'The Immaculate Conception and Ecclesiastical Politics from the Council of Basel to the Council of Trent: The Dominicans and their Foes', *Archiv für Reformationsgeschichte* 96 (2005), pp. 145–70, esp. pp. 150–54; Sixtus IV proceeded to offer indulgences, or have indulgences associated with his name; for prayer to images of Our Lady of the Sun, the apocalyptic Mary of the Immaculate Conception, see Robert N. Swanson, 'Praying for Pardon: Devotional Indulgences in Late Medieval England', in *Promissory Notes on the Treasury of Merits: Indulgences in Late Medieval Europe*, ed. R. N. Swanson, Leiden, 2006, pp. 215–40, esp. pp. 225–30, and for an example of such an image see the engraving by Israhel van Meckenem, of *c.*1490, reproduced in Jeffrey Chipps Smith, *The Art of the Goldsmith in Late Fifteenth-Century Germany: The Kimball Virgin and Her Bishop*, Fort Worth, 2006, figure 70, p. 63; on the spread of the cult see Rosa Maria Dessi, 'La controversia sull'Immacolata Concezione e la "propaganda" per il culto in Italie nel XV secolo', *Cristianesimo nella storia* 12 (1991), pp. 265–93. Only in 1854 did the Immaculate Conception become dogma in the Roman Catholic Church.

8. On the iconography of the Immaculate Conception in the Renaissance see Rosemary Muir Wright, *Sacred Distance: Representing the Virgin*, Manchester, 2006, esp. pp. 116–45.

9. Van Os, *Art of Devotion*, p. 19.

10. New York, The Frick Collection. Mary, in the company of the humble Francis and Jerome, painted by Petrus Christus (1415–1472/3), is enthroned beneath a canopy and surrounded by hangings in a space of her own: Frankfurt, Städelsches Kunstinstitut.

11. Ramon de Mur, *c.*1415–25, Barcelona Catalan Museum of Art. Angels witness a similar scene in a Sienese panel with a dove hovering over the assembly. Virgin of Humility with Angels and Saints, Gregorio di Cecco (d.1423), Siena, Museo del'Opera del Duomo. See also an example from the crypt of St Katherine's church, Bad Kleinkirchheim (Carinthia), Janez Höfler, *Die Tafelmalerei der Gotik in Kärnten (1420–1500)*, Klagenfurt, 1987, no. 12, pp. 47–8, figure 37.

12. Master of Veronica *c.*1410, Kreuzlingen, Heinz Kisters Collection; see van Os, *Art of Devotion*, no. 26, pp. 88–91; Master of the Osservanza, Siena, Galleria Chigi Saracini.

13. Karen Stolleis, *Messgewänder aus deutschen Kirchenschätzen vom Mittelalter bis zur Gegenwart: Geschichte, Form und Material*, Regensburg, 2001, pp. 96–8. On angels see Maurice B. McNamee, *Vested Angels: Eucharistic Allusions in Early Netherlandish Painting*, Louvain, 1998, chapters VII–VIII.

14. Johann Korbecke (by 1420–1490), *Early German Painting*, no. 56, pp. 266–73.

15. Siena, Duomo, Piccolomini Library.

16. Siena, Duomo, Piccolomini Library, codex 23.8; Assumption initial by Girolamo da Cremona (1431–83).

17. Berlin, Gemäldegalerie, 131 × 150.7 cm. This is a version of the Woman of the Apocalypse, more fully realized in a Finnish figure of around 1420, Helsinki, National Museum.

18. *Gothic: Art for England 1400–1547*, eds. Richard Marks and Paul Williamson, London, 2003, no. 133, p. 271, and figure 32, p. 58.

19. *The Birth of Identities: Denmark and Europe in the Middle Ages*, Copenhagen, 1996, p. 250.

20. See for example the Venetian Triptych of *c.*1360–70 in *Images in Ivory*, no. 49, pp. 213–14.

21. Anabel Thomas, 'A New Date for Neri di Bicci's San Giovannino dei Cavalieri "Coronation of the Virgin",' *Burlington Magazine* 139 (1997), pp. 103–6, figure 24, p. 105.

22. *Images in Ivory*, no. 67, pp. 254–5.

23. See tile from oven at Hohensalzburg castle, Rosemarie Franz, *Der Kachelofen*, Graz, 1969, nos. 134–5. On images in mundane spaces, like chimneys, see Danièle Alexandre-Bidon, 'Une foi en deux ou trois dimensions? Images et objets du faire croire à l'usage des laïcs', *Annales HSS* 53 (1998), pp. 1155–90, esp. at pp. 1166–8.

24. Made some time after 1425.

25. The crown of Margaret of York, Duchess of Burgundy, made *c.*1461–74 and later used for the statue of Mary at Aachen cathedral: *Gothic: Art for England*, no. 11, pp. 54–5.

26. Véronique B. Plesch, 'Enguerrand Quarton's *Coronation of the Virgin*: This World and the Next, the Dogma and the Devotion, the Individual and the Community', *Historical Reflections* 26 (2000), pp. 189–221, at pp. 190–92. On sculpture of the Coronation in the Avignon area see Françoise Baron, 'Collèges apostoliques et Couronnement de la Vierge dans la sculpture avignonnaise des XIVe et XVe siècles', *La Revue du Louvre et des Musées de France* 3 (1999), pp. 169–86.

27. Paul Y. Cardile, 'Mary as Priest: Mary's Sacerdotal Position in the Visual Arts', *Arte cristiana* new series 72: 703 (1984), pp. 199–208.

28. Boston, Isabella Stewart Gardner Museum.

29. *Images in Ivory*, no. 72, p. 265.

30. Paris, Louvre; Susie Nash, *Between France and Flanders: Manuscript Illumination in Amiens*, Toronto, 1999, p. 42, figure 3.

31. For a colour reproduction see Stolleis, *Messgewänder*, pp. 78–9.

32. Stolleis, *Messgewänder*, pp. 70, 72; see colour plates 8 and 13.

33. K. Buckland, 'The Skenfrith Cope and Its Companions', *Textile History* 14 (1983), pp. 125–39.

34. Stolleis, *Messgewänder*, no. 22, pp. 126–8.

35. Beth Williamson, 'Liturgical Image or Devotional Image? The London *Madonna of the Firescreen*', in *Objects, Images and the Word: Art in the Service of the Liturgy*, Princeton, 2003, pp. 298–318.

36. I am grateful to Professor Paul Kaplan who kindly sent me an offprint of his interesting article on the frontal, Paul H. D. Kaplan, 'The Paliotto of the Corpus Domini: A Eucharistic Sculpture for a Venetian Nunnery', *Studies in Iconography* 26 (2005), pp. 121–74, esp. at pp. 129–32.

37. http://www.wga.hu/frames-e.html?/html/b/botticel/22/30magnif.html. On this image see Susan Schibanoff, 'Botticelli's *Madonna del Magnificat*: Constructing the Woman Writer in Early Humanist Italy', *Publications of the Modern Languages Association* 109 (1994), pp. 190–206.

38. Annette Volfing, *Heinrich von Mügeln, Der Meide Kranz: A Commentary*, Tübingen, 1997, pp. 206–7.

39. Barbara Newman, *From Virile Woman to WomanChrist*, pp. 198–209.

40. 'Je le dy en partie pour une ymaige qui est aux Carmes et semblables qui ont dedans leur ventre une Trinité comme se toute la Trinité eus prins cher humainne en la Vierge Marie ... Et ne vois pas pour quelle chose on le mire ainsy, car a mon petit jugement il n'y a beauté ne devocion en telle ouverture, et puet estre cause d'erreur et d'indevocion', Jean Gerson, *Oeuvres complètes* VII/2, Paris, 1968, p. 963. On the critique of Trinitarian image-making see Robert Mills, 'Jesus as Monster', in *The Monstrous Middle Ages*, Cardiff, 2003, pp. 28–54, at pp. 45–6.

41. Henk van Os, *The Way to Heaven: Relic Veneration in the Middle Ages*, Baarn, 2000, no. 156, p. 129.

42. See an example from *c*.1400, with a multitude of people of all estates on the open 'mantle', and the Trinity against Mary's body, for St Mary's church at Elbing, Luneburg, Landesmuseum.

43. *Treasures of the Cracow Monasteries*, p. 29.

44. Van Os, *The Way to Heaven*, pp. 123–4 and colour image on p. 125.

45. *Musée national du moyen âge*, pp. 106–7; also van Os, *The Way to Heaven*, p. 40, and figure 33, p. 39; Jacqueline Tasioulas, ' "Heaven and earth in a little space": The foetal existence of Christ in medieval literature and thought', *Medium Aevum* 76 (2007), pp. 24–48.

46. The second wing portrays Etienne Chevalier, Treasurer of France, with St Peter Martyr, Berlin, Staatliche Museen. See also Higgins, 'Love and Death'.

47. Thomas D. Hill, ' "Mary, the Rose-bush" and the Leaps of Christ', *English Studies* 67 (1986), pp. 478–82, esp. at p. 480.

48. A German painter who placed two angels as musicians around Mary and her chubby son imagined a garden of paradise: Master of St Lawrence, Cologne, Wallraf-Richartz Museum, Dep. 361; on it see Brigitta Corley, 'A Plausible Provenance for Stefan Lochner?', *Zeitschrift für Kunstgeschichte* 59 (1996), pp. 78–96, figure 10, p. 87.

49. Siena, Pinacoteca Nazionale, Giovanni di Paolo, *c*.1399–1482.

50. *The Virgin in a Rose Bush* of 1473, St Martin's cathedral, Colmar.

51. Sylvia Landesberg, *The Medieval Garden*, London, 1995, p. 54, School of Dieric Bouts, late fifteenth century.

52. Solothurn, Museum der Stadt.

53. Landesberg, *The Medieval Garden*, p. 14. The panel is of *c*.1490.

54. *Filippo Lippi Catalogo completo*, p. 74, no. 52.

55. Stalybridge, Astley Cheetham Art Gallery, of *c*.1410; see Williamson, 'The Virgin *lactans*', figure 5, and pp. 122–3.

56. Berthold Furtmeyer, *Tree of Life and Death c*.1479–89; Roger Cook, *The Tree of Life: Image for the Cosmos*, New York, 1974, p. 44.

Chapter 19: Mary of Parish Practice and Family Life

1. On the late medieval wood carvings and statues, including many depicting the Deposition and Lamentation, see Michael Baxandall, *The Linewood Sculptors of Renaissance Germany*, New Haven and London, 1980.

2. Frankfurt, Liebighaus Museum. For a painted example see the fifteenth-century Pietà at Leau.

3. Lorsch Pietà, van Os, *The Art of Devotion*, plate 31, pp. 104–5; from the Parler workshop, see *Musée national du moyen âge*, pp. 104–5.

4. Joanna E. Ziegler, *Sculpture of Compassion: The Pietà and the Beguines in the Southern Low Countries c.1300–c.1600*, Brussels, 1992.

5. For a similar arrangement in a manuscript illumination see Oxford, Bodleian Library, Lat. Lit. f.2, fol. 10.

6. *Musée national du moyen âge*, p. 108.

7. See an example which measures 70.5 × 37.2 cm, Margaret Aston, *England's Iconoclasts*, I: *Laws against Images*, Oxford, 1988 figure 6b, p. 108.

8. I am grateful to my friend the historian of drama Dr Elsa Strietman for bringing this statue to my attention.

9. Jan Assmann, 'Text und Ritus: Die Bedeutung der Medien für die Religionsgeschichte', in *Audiovisualität vor und nach Gutenberg: Zur Kulturgeschichte der medialen Umbrüche*, eds. Horst Wenzel, Wilfried Seipel and Gotthart Wunberg, Vienna, 2001, pp. 97–117, at p. 111.

10. Klagenfurt, Diocesan Museum; Höfler, *Die Tafelmalerei der Gotik in Kärnten*, no. 3, pp. 36–7, figure 13.

11. James A. Marrow, 'Inventing the Passion in the Late Middle Ages', in *The Passion Story: From Visual Representation to Social Drama*, ed. Marcia Kupfer, University Park, 2008, pp. 23–52.

12. *Early German Painting*, no. 12, pp. 72–7.

13. Dirk De Vos, *Rogier van der Weyden: The Complete Works*, Antwerp, 1999, pp. 10–41 (including several plates).

14. Ibid., no. 36, pp. 335–8. For a discussion of the affinity between meditative practice and devotional art see Anne D. Hedeman, 'Roger van de Weyden's *Crucifixion* and the Carthusian Devotional Practices', in *The Sacred Image East and West*, eds. Robert Ousterhout and Leslie Brubaker, Urbana and Chicago, 1995, pp. 191–203.

15. De Vos, *Rogier von der Weyden*, no. 24, pp. 295–7.

16. *Musée national du moyen âge*, pp. 112–13.

17. On the devotion see Carol M. Schuler, 'The Seven Sorrows of the Virgin: Popular Culture and Cultic Imagery in Pre-Reformation Europe', *Simiolus* 21 (1992), pp. 5–28.

18. 'Ein seltzame kouffmanschatz', Stadtarchiv Freiburg; Ronnie Po-chia Hsia, *The Myth of Ritual Murder: Jews and Magic in Reformation Germany*, New Haven, 1988, figure 6, p. 59.

19. On this image see Jeffrey F. Hamburger, *Nuns as Artists: The Visual Culture of a Medieval Convent*, Berkeley, 1997, plate 9 (colour reproduction), and pp. 101–36.

20. Gail McMurray Gibson, *The Theater of Devotion: East Anglian Drama and Society in the Late Middle Ages*, Chicago, 1989, figure 6.7, p. 153.

21. Peter Lord, *The Visual Culture of Wales: Medieval Vision*, Cardiff, 2003, figure 252, p. 164, and detail of Mary in the left margin; for another carved representation of the Crucifixion see figure 262, p. 169, from the Priory church of St John the Evangelist in Brecon. And see also the carved pews of Fressingfield church, Suffolk.

22. See images at http://www.paintedchurch.org/wenhast.htm.

23. Julian M. Luxford, *The Art and Architecture of English Benedictine Monasteries, 1300–1540: A Patronage History*, Woodbridge, 2005, pp. 24–5, at p. 19.

24. On English Lady Chapels and their liturgy see Roger Bowers, 'The Musicians and Liturgy of the Lady Chapels of the Monastery Church, c.1235–1540', in *Westminster*

Abbey: The Lady Chapel of Henry VII, eds. Tim Tatton-Brown and Richard Mortimer, Woodbridge, 2003, pp. 33–57; Lena Liepe, 'On the Connection between Medieval Wooden Sculpture and Murals in Scanian Churches', in *Liturgy and the Arts in the Middle Ages: Studies in Honour of C. Clifford Flanigan*, Copenhagen, 1996, pp. 221–49, at p. 227; *Wonder: Painted Sculpture from Medieval England*, Leeds, 2002, pp. 42–3.

25. Liepe, 'On the Connection', p. 244.

26. Craig Wright, *Music and Ceremony at Notre Dame of Paris*, Cambridge, 1989, p. 15.

27. London Victoria and Albert Museum 91–1946; *Wonder: Painted Sculpture from Medieval England*, pp. 68–9.

28. Francis Cheetham, *English Medieval Alabasters; with a Catalogue of the Collection of the Victoria and Albert Museum*, Oxford, 1984, pp. 70–71 and plate 1.

29. Helena Edgren, *Mercy and Justice: Miracles of the Virgin Mary in Finnish Medieval Wall-Paintings*, Helsinki, 1993, figures 89–90, p. 226.

30. Pierrette Paravy, *De la Chrétienté romaine à la Réforme en Dauphiné: Évêques, fidèles et deviants (vers 1340-vers 1530)*, II, Rome, 1993, plate 2.

31. Edgren, *Mercy and Justice*, pp. 68–70, figures 11–14.

32. 'Virgo parens Maria vixit lxiii annis,/Quatuor atque decem [fuit] in partu benedicto,/Triginta tribus vixit cum filio suo,/Sexdecim solo, simul astra subiuit', *The Commonplace Book of Robert Reynes of Acle: An Edition of Tanner MS 407*, New York and London, 1980, p. 153.

33. The *Ave Maria* accompanied the monks of the German Cistercian Abbey of Zinna in Brandenburg in the form of floor tiles which spelt out the salutation, Christian Klamt, 'Letters van baksteen in een cisterciënzerklooster: Het *Ave Maria* te Zinna', in *Meer dan muziek aleen: In memoriam Kees Vellekoop*, ed. R. E. V. Stuip, Hilversum, 2004, pp. 195–210.

34. Joseph Kehrein, *Pater Noster und Ave Maria in deutschen Uebersetzungen*, Frankfurt am Main, 1865, p. 72.

35. Krystyna Gorska-Golaska, 'Glosa historyka do Modlitwy Maryjnej', *Slavia Occidentalis* 52 (1995), pp. 129–30.

36. I am most grateful to Mr Jerzy Mazur of Brandeis University, who kindly translated this hymn for me from medieval Polish; Wojciech Rebowski, Wojciech Ryszard Rzepka and Wiesław Wydra, 'Najdawniejsza Polska *Modlitwa Maryjna*', *Slavia Occidentalis* 52 (1995), pp. 121–7, text at pp. 123–4.

37. *De Eerste Blisacap van Maria en Die Sevenste Blisacap can Onser Vrouwen*, ed. W. H. Beuken, 1973, lines 45–8. For an analysis of the play see John Cartwright, 'From the Old Law to the New: The Brussels *Eerste Blisacap van Maria*', *Medieval English Theatre* 20 (1998), pp. 118–26; Penny Granger, 'Devotion to Drama: The N-Town Play and Religious Observance in Fifteenth-Century East Anglia', in *Medieval East Anglia*, ed., Christopher Harper-Bill, Woodbridge, 2005, pp. 302–17. On the portrayal of Mary see J. A. Tasioulas, 'Between Doctrine and Domesticity: The Portrayal of Mary in the N-Town Plays', *Medieval Women in their Communities*, ed. Diane Watt, Cardiff, 1997, pp. 222–45.

38. My translation from Aurélie Mazingue, 'Paroles et présence de Marie dans le *Mystère de l'Assomption* de Rodez', *European Medieval Drama* 8 (2004), pp. 173–83, at p. 175.

39. Ibid., p. 176,

40. *La Festa o Misteri d'Elx*, fifth edn, Alicante, 1999, p. 41.

41. Ibid., p. 179.

42. Ibid., pp. 182, 183.

43. John D. Cox, *The Devil and the Sacred in English Drama, 1350–1642*, Cambridge, 2000, p. 25 fn. 18.

44. My modern version from *The N-Town Play* I, ed. Stephen Spector, Oxford, 1991, lines 83–7, p. 390.

45. Cox, *The Devil*, p. 50; John McKinnell, 'Producing the York Mary Plays', *Medieval English Theatre* 12 (1990), pp. 101–23, see esp. p. 104, figure 1.

46. Ibid., p. 103.

47. *The N-Town Play* I, play 41, lines 527–8, at p. 409; see Richard Rastall, *The Heaven Signing: Music in Early English Religious Drama*, Cambridge, 1996, pp. 176–7. Other scenes attracted music too, like the lullabies sung to the Christ in scenes of *The Adoration of the Shepherds*, pp. 69–71.

48. 'Aliquando beata virgo expandit brachia sua, aliquando levat manus suas ad filium cum oculis; omnia cum moderamine', G. Kühl, 'Die Bordesholmer Marienklage, herausgegeben und eingeleitet', *Niederdeutsches Jahrbuch* 24 (1898), pp. 1–75, at p. 40. A recording is available, by the group *Sequentia*, on CD Harmonia Mundi 05472 77280 2. I am most grateful to Nils Holger Petersen, from whom I first heard of this play.

49. Brian Patrick McGuire, *Jean Gerson and the Last Medieval Reformation*, University Park, 2005.

50. On the chronology see Brian Patrick McGuire, 'In Search of Jean Gerson: Chronology of His Life and Works', in *A Companion to Jean Gerson*, ed. Brian Patrick McGuire, Leiden, 2006, pp. 1–39, at pp. 21–2. On Gerson's campaign see Paul Payan, *Joseph: Une image de la paternité dans l'Occident medieval*, Paris, 2006, pp. 147–64.

51. Jean Gerson, *Œuvres complètes*, VII, ed. Palémon Glorieux, Paris, 1966, no. 300, pp. 63–94; see also 'Aultres considérations sur St Joseph', of 1414, no. 301, pp. 94–100.

52. He also discusses many questions related to Mary in his sermon of 2 February 1416, for the Purification, *Suscepimus Deus*, Brian Patrick McGuire, *Jean Gerson and the Late Medieval Reformation*, University Park, 2005, pp. 255–6.

53. Cambridge, Fitzwilliam Museum 69, fol. 48r.

54. I am grateful to Rob Wegman for taking a very good picture of this scene and generously making it available to me.

55. Gilbert Ouy, 'Discovering Gerson the Humanist: Fifty Years of Serendipity', in *A Companion to Jean Gerson*, pp. 79–132, at pp. 129–30.

56. McGuire, *Jean Gerson*, p. 297; Gerson, *Œuvres complètes* IV, 1962, pp. 31–100, at p. 44.

57. Sara Lipton, *Images of Intolerance: The Representation of Jews and Judaism in the Bible moralisée*, Berkeley, 1999, pp. 15–19.

58. See the wall painting in Mørkøv church, Denmark, c.1450; McGuire, *Jean Gerson*, figure 8, p. 235. At the end of his life Gerson also wrote a tract on the *Magnificat*, *Œuvres complètes* VIII, pp. 163–534; McGuire, *Jean Gerson*, IV, pp. 318–21.

59. V. A. Kolve, *The Play Called Corpus Christi*, London, 1966, esp. pp. 248–51. On the cultural possibilities related to a nurturing father, like Joseph, see Pamela Sheingorn, 'The Maternal Behaviour of God: Divine Father as Fantasy Husband', in *Medieval Mothering*, eds. John Carmi Parsons and Bonnie Wheeler, New York and London, 1996, pp. 77–99.

60. Alison Hunt, 'Maculating Mary: The Detractors of the N-Town Cycle's "Trial of Joseph and Mary"', *Philological Quarterly* 73 (1994), pp. 11–29; Cindy L. Carson, 'Mary's Obedience and Power in *The Trial of Mary and Joseph*', *Comparative Drama* 29 (1995), pp. 348–62.

61. On Italian representations of this scenes, the *sposalizio*, see Christiane Klapisch-Zuber, 'Zacharias, or the Ousted Father: Nuptial Roles in Tuscany between Giotto and the Council of Trent', in *Women, Family and Ritual in Renaissance Italy*, trans. Lydia Cochrane, Chicago, 1985, pp. 196–209. See also Milman, *Les Heures de la prière*, figure 149, p. 175.

62. Martial Rose and Julia Hedgecoe, *Stories in Stone: The Medieval Roof Carvings of Norwich Cathedral*, London, 1997, p. 89.

63. *Early German Painting*, 17b and 18a, pp. 94–9, reproductions on pp. 95 and 97. For similar parity see the fifteenth-century French manuscript of the *Golden Legend* in Riché and Alexandre-Bidon, *L'Enfance au Moyen Age*, p. 196.

64. Cambridge, Fitzwilliam Museum, 69, fol. 48r.

65. Antwerp, Mayer van der Bergh Museum, painted in the Meuse-Rhine region, c.1400. A cult of Joseph's hose developed at Aachen; on it see Josef de Coo, 'Addenda zum Weihnachtsmotiv der Josefhosen', *Aachener Kunstblätter* 43 (1972), pp. 249–61; also

Gail McMurray Gibson, *The Theatre of Devotion: East Anglian Drama and Society in the Late Middle Ages*, Chicago, 1989, pp. 54–9. See Rosemary Drage Hale, 'Joseph as Mother: Adaptation and Appropriation in the Construction of Male Virtue', in *Medieval Mothering*, New York, 1996, pp. 101–13. On fifteenth-century illustrated manuscripts depicting Jesus' early life with many family scenes see Elisabeth Landolt-Wegener, 'Darstellungen der Kindheitslegenden Christi in Historienbibeln aus der Werkstatt Diebolt Laubers', *Zeitschrift für schweizerische Archäologie und Kunstgeschichte* 23 (1963), pp. 212–25.

66. Siena, Pinacoteca Nazionale.

67. Liberale da Verona (1445–1525) and Girolamo da Cremona (1431–83): Siena, Libreria Piccolomini.

68. Limoges, Musée National de Porcelaine Adrien Dubouché.

69. *The York Cycle and the Worship of the City*, Woodbridge, 2006, pp.116–17.

70. Nuremberg, *c*.1450, Germanisches Nationalmuseum, Kupferstichkabinett, BP Hz372; Riché and Alexandre-Bidon, *L'Enfance au Moyen Age*, p. 124.

71. *Von der kinthait unsers hern ihesu cristi genannt vita cristi*; Bayerische Staatsbibliothek, Munich. Signatur 2° Inc.c.a.2582m, fol. XXXIr.

72. New York Pierpoint Morgan Library; John Plummer, *The Book of Hours of Catherine of Cleves*, New York, 1964, plate 23 and p. 52. See Mary spinning, with the Child Christ spinning within her womb, and Joseph in a less prominent position, in a panel from Erfurt, of *c*.1400: Ursula Weekes, *Early Engravers and Their Public: The Master of the Berlin Passion and Manuscripts from Convents in the Rhine-Maas Region*, London, pp. 180–81 (figure 176 on p. 181).

73. New York, Metropolitan Museum of Art, Cloisters. On the triptych see the excellent analysis offered in Cynthia Hahn, ' "Joseph Will Perfect, Mary Enlighten and Jesus Save Thee": The Holy Family as a Marriage Model in the Mérode Triptych', *Art Bulletin* 68 (1986), pp. 54–66.

74. Cologne, Wallraf-Richartz Museum, inv. WRM471; the image appears in *German Stoneware 1200–1900: Archaeology and Cultural History*, London, 1997, p. 2.

75. Paris, Musée de Cluny; see Riché and Alexandre-Bidon, *L'Enfance au Moyen Age*, p.15.

76. Amsterdam Rijksmuseum, Rijksprentenkabinet inv. RP-P-OB-889; van Os, *Art of Devotion*, pp. 92–4, p. 93, plate 27.

77. Like the *fort-da* play described by Freud in 'Beyond the Pleasure Principle', *The Standard Edition of the Complete Psychological Works of Sigmund Freud*, London, 2001, XVIII, pp. 14–15; I am enormously grateful to Professor Peter Brown for illuminating me with his wise comments on this image after a seminar at Princeton in April 2005.

78. Jaroslav Pelikan, *Mary through the Centuries: Her Place in the History of Culture*, New Haven, 1996, chapter XII, pp. 157–80. See also *Saint Anne in History and Art*, Oxford, 1999.

79. 'Also nam dass lieblein zu in dem leichnam der liben Anna newn monet. Do ward sie geporen auf dise werlt mit grossen freuden vnss zu trost und allen den, die sie an ruffen in ainem guten getrauen', *Das 'Marienleben' des Heinrich von St Gallen: Text und Untersuchung. Mit einem Verzeichnis deutschsprachiger Prosamarienleben bis etwa 1520*, ed. Hardo Hilg, Munich, 1981, p. 132.

80. C.1470s Hugo van der Goes, *St Anne, the Virgin and the Child with a Franciscan Donor*, Brussels, Musées Royaux des Beaux-Arts de Belgique, inv. 2748. See also the wooden sculpture within a wooden canopied niche, Helsinki, National Museum; Pamela Sheingorn, 'The Wise Mother', pp. 69–80.

81. Ingolstadt, by Hans Greif, 1472, *Musée national du moyen âge*, p. 103; and the Arhus Cathedral altarpiece of 1479, in Troels Dahlerup, *De fire stænder 1400–1500*, Copenhagen, 1989, p. 146.

82. *Treasures of the Cracow Monasteries*, eds. Janusz Tadeusz Nowak and Witold Turdza, Krakow, 2000, no. 66, p. 82; Wit Stwosz's Worskop, Krakow Cathedral Treasury, no. 122, p. 130.

83. Bernhard Strigel (1460–1528) c.1505–10; *Early German Painting*, no. 38, pp. 360–67.
84. *The Writings of Julian of Norwich*, eds. Nicholas Watson and Jacqueline Jenkins, University Park, 2006, 4.24–36; see also Kathryn Kerby-Fulton, *Books under Suspicion: Censorship and Tolerance of Revelatory Writing in Late Medieval England*, Notre Dame, 2006, pp. 320–21.
85. Van Os, *Art of Devotion*, plate 28, p. 97.
86. Anonymous, The Legend of St Anne, Bruges, Saint Salvator; Master of St Goedele, *The Legend of St Anne*, Paris, Faculté de Médicine.
87. Brussels, Musées Royaux des Beaux-Arts, *The Holy Family*, Riché and Alexandre-Bidon, *L'Enfance au Moyen Age*, p. 112.
88. Ernst Günther Grimme, 'Ein niedersächsischer Sippenaltar – Eine Neuerwerbung für das Suermondt-Museum', *Aachener Kunstblätter* 43 (1972), pp. 7–10.
89. Philadelphia Museum of Art.
90. Tom Brandenburg, 'St Anne and Her Family: The Veneration of St Anne in Connection with Concepts of Marriage and the Family in the Early-Modern Period', in *Saints and She-Devils: Images of Women in the 15th and 16th Centuries*, London, 1987, pp. 101–28.
91. Nancy Bradley Warren, 'Monastic Politics: St Colette of Corbie, Franciscan Reform and the House of Burgundy', *New Medieval Literatures* 5, Oxford, 2002, pp. 203–28.
92. *Early German Painting*, no. 46, p. 197, and about it pp. 194–201.
93. Kiss: Master of the Schottenaltar, Gerhard Jaritz, '"Serra ex ferro" – "Serra ex vitro": Medieval History – Computers – Image Meanings Reconsidered', in *History and Images: Towards a New Iconology*, eds. Axel Bolvig and Phillip Lindley, Turnhout, 2003, pp. 209–28, at p. 210; embrace: Nördlingen, Städtisches Museum, St George Altar by Friedrich Herlin; holding hands: Lyons, Visitation, Riché and Alexandre-Bidon, *L'Enfance au Moyen Age*, p. 41, by Hans or Jakob Strüb, *Early German Painting*, no. 87, pp. 379–83. On the theme see also Vera F. Vines, 'A Centre for Devotional and Liturgical Manuscript Illumination in Fifteenth-Century Besançon', in *The Art of the Book: Its Place in Medieval Worship*, Exeter, 1998, pp. 195–223, esp. at pp. 220–21.
94. Freising, Archbishop's Diocesan Museum, by Master Lienhart of Brixen.
95. Ronald G. Kecks, 'Die Jungfrau Maria am Kindbett der hl. Elisabeth', in *Musagetes: Festschrift für Wolfram Prinz zu seinem 60. Geburtstag am 5. Februar 1989*, Berlin, 1991, pp. 217–43.
96. Nuremberg, Germanisches Nationalmuseum, in Hartmut Boockmann, *Die Stadt im späten Mittelalter*, Leipzig, 1986, p. 329, no. 480.
97. Oxford, Ashmolean CD25; Miriam Milman, *Les Heures de la prière: Catalogue des livres d'heures de la bibliothèque de l'abbaye d'Einsiedeln*, Turnhout, 2003, figure 76, p. 96, and about it pp. 96–7.
98. Coral necklaces were used for the protection of children; the red colour of coral representd Christ's Passion, and Jesus is sometimes shown wearing a coral necklace or holding a branch of coral: Danièle Alexandre-Bidon, 'La Parure prophylactique de l'enfance à la fin du moyen-âge', *Razo* 7 (1987), pp. 5–35.
99. Riché and Alexandre-Bidon, *L'Enfance au Moyen Age*, p. 115.

Chapter 20: Mary: a World of Devotional Possibilities

1. Anne Winston, 'Tracing the Origins of the Rosary: German Vernacular Texts', *Speculum* 68 (1993), pp. 619–36, at pp. 624–5; Anne Winston Allen, *Stories of the Rose: The Making of the Rosary in the Middle Ages*, Unversity Park, 1997, pp. 13–30 on early rosaries.
2. A minority of rosaries were dedicated to other themes, such as the eucharist, Christ or the Stations of the Cross, see Thomas Lentes, 'Counting Piety in the Later Middle Ages', in *Ordering Medieval Society: Perspectives on Intellectual and Practical Modes of Shaping Social Relations*, trans. Pamela E. Selwyn, Philadelphia, 2001, pp. 55–91, at p. 55.

3. Anne Winston Allen, *Stories of the Rose: The Making of the Rosary in the Middle Ages*, University Park, 1997, pp. 18–22, esp. p. 19.

4. Members of the Carthusian order continued to innovate and experiment with the rosary format: see Andreas Heinz, 'Eine Variante des "Trierer Kartäuserrosenkranzes" aus dem Jahre 1482. Stadtbibliothek Trier Hs.516/1595, fol. 106–108', *Kurtrierisches Jahrbuch* 30 (1990), pp. 33–53.

5. *Einblattholzschnitte des XV. Jahrhunderts aus dem Kupferstichkabinett Basel*, Basel, 1994, figure 24, and p. 68.

6. 'Und dar noch X ave maria zů lob unser lieben frowen als sy von dem engel Gabriel den grůss enpfieng. Dar noch sprich das erste Pater noster dem liden Christi das er enpfieng an dem olberg do er schwitzet blůtigen sweiss', Jean-Claude Schmitt, 'La Confrérie du rosaire de Colmar (1485): Textes de fondation, "exempla" en allemand d'Alain de la Roche, listes des prêcheurs et des sœurs dominicaines', *Archivum fratrum praedicatorum* 40 (1970), pp. 97–124, at p. 106.

7. *Malleus maleficarum*, ed. and trans. Christopher S. Mackay, Cambridge, 2006, I, pp. 80–81; Hans Peter Broedel, *The Malleus Maleficarum and the Construction of Witchcraft: Theology and Popular Belief*, Manchester, 2003, pp. 18–19.

8. Antonio Niero, 'Ancora sull'origine del rosario a Venezia e sulla sua iconografia', *Rivista di storia della chiesa in Italia* 28 (1974), pp. 465–78, at pp. 469–74. On Venetian Marian piety see Ruth Chavasse, 'Latin Lay Piety and Vernacular Lay Piety in Word and Image: Venice, 1471–early 1500s', *Renaissance Studies* 10 (1996), pp. 319–42. By 1500 there was a Pisan translation, *Libro del rosario della gloriosa Vergine Maria*, Rome, 1965.

9. *The Commonplace Book of Robert Reynes*, pp. 287–8. On the spread in England see Paul Needham, 'The *Canterbury Tales* and the Rosary: A Mirror of Caxton's Devotions?', in *The Medieval Book and a Modern Collector: Essays in Honour of Toshiyuki Takamiya*, eds. Takami Matsuda, Richard A. Linenthal and Joan Scahill, Woodbridge and Tokyo, 2004, pp. 313–47.

10. For a colour reproduction see *The Body of Christ in the Art of Europe and New Spain 1150–1800*, Munich and New York, 1997, no. 65, pp. 142–3.

11. On the panels see *Early German Painting*, no. 57, pp. 274–9.

12. On the image and this tract see Katarzyna Zalewska, ' "Corona beatissimae Virginis Mariae": Das mittelalterliche gemalte Marientraktat aus der Bernhardinerkirche in Breslau', *Zeitschrift für Kunstgeschichte* 55 (1992), pp. 57–65.

13. Thomas Worcester, 'The Catholic Sermon', in *Preachers and People in the Reformations and Early Modern Period*, ed. Larissa Taylor, Leiden, 2001, pp. 3–37 at pp. 7–9.

14. 'Wilt ghy Maria maken eenen hoet/Van blommekins zoet/.../So sult ghy lesen/ Vichtich Aue Marien maer bouen desen/So moeter wesen tusschen elcken tiene/Een Pater nostere', Wim Hüsken, ' "Van Incommen en begheert men scat noch goet": Cornelis Everaert and the Rosary', in *European Theatre 1470–1600: Traditions and Transformations*, eds. Martin Gosman and Rina Walthaus, Groningen, 1996, pp. 119–29, at p. 121.

15. Ibid., pp. 122, 125–8.

16. June Mecham, 'Reading between the Lines: Compilation, Variation, and the Recovery of an Authentic Female Voice in the *Dornenkron* Prayer Books from Wienhausen', *Journal of Medieval History* 29 (2003), pp. 109–28, esp. at pp. 116–23. I am most grateful to Professor Mecham for enlightening conversations and exchanges on this most interesting text.

17. For such a figurine in the rubble of an English church see S. D. Harris, 'The Church of St Mary the Virgin, Stone-in-Oxney, with Particular Reference to Recent Excavation of the North Chapel and to the Fire of 1464', *Archaeologia Cantiana* 109 for 1991 (1992), pp. 121–38, at p. 128; *Visual Culture of Wales*, no. 346, p. 218.

18. Weekes, *Early Engravers and their Public*.

19. David Landau and Peter Parshall, *The Renaissance Print 1470–1555*, New Haven, 1994, no. 45, p. 66, and no. 50, p. 71.

20. Van Os, *Art of Devotion*, 25a and 25b, pp. 84–6.

21. Brussels, Royal Library. I am very grateful to Dr Peggy Smith for bringing this important early Iberian engraving to my attention. Artists were accustomed to working from pattern books and sketches; the Boxwood Sketchbook of $c.1400$ includes attempts at rendering Mary and Child, New York, Pierpoint Morgan Library M346; see William Voelkle, 'Two New Drawings for the Boxwood Sketchbook in the Pierpoint Morgan Library', Gesta 20 (1981), pp. 243–5, figure 3, p. 244.

22. London, British Museum, Annunciation; Images in Ivory, no. 76, pp. 273–4.

23. Early German Painting, pp. 95 and 97, description on pp. 94–9.

24. Boston, Museum of Fine Arts; Berlin, Gemäldegalerie.

25. James H. Marrow, 'Artistic Identity in Early Netherlandish Painting: The Place of Rogier van der Weyden's "St Luke Drawing the Virgin" ', in Rogier Van der Weyden, 'St Luke Drawing the Virgin': Selected Essays in Context, Turnhout, 1997, pp. 53–9.

26. By Jean Colombe, south-east France $c.1485$–95; Milman, Les Heures de la Prière, figure 118, p. 153 and description on p. 152.

27. Paris, BNF, 12420, fol. 86, and ms. fr. 598, fol. 86; see Stephen Perkinson, 'Engin and artifice: Describing Creative Agency in the Court of France, ca. 1400', Gesta 41 (2002), pp. 51–67, esp. at pp. 51–3, 62–3.

28. Edward Muir, 'The Virgin on the Street Corner: The Place of the Sacred in Italian Cities', in Religion and Culture in the Renaissance and Reformation, ed. Steven Ozment, Kirksville, 1989, pp. 25–42. On the abundance of images in public and private spaces see Danièle Alexandre-Bidon, 'Une foi en deux ou trois dimensions? Images et objets du faire croire à l'usage des laïcs', Annales. HSS 53 (1998), pp. 1,155–90.

29. For a detailed treatment see Dana E. Katz, 'Painting and the Politics of Persecution: Representing the Jews in Fifteenth-Century Mantua', Art History 23 (2000), pp. 475–95.

30. I am grateful to Giles Constable for kindly sharing his work on this fascinating case now published in William J. Connell and Giles Constable, 'Sacrilege and Redemption in Renaissance Florence: The Case of Antonio Rinaldeschi', Journal of the Warburg and Courtauld Institutes 61 (1988), pp. 53–92; and William J. Connell and Giles Constable, Sacrilege and Redemption in Renaissance Florence: The Case of Antonio Rinaldeschi, Toronto, 2005.

31. '. . . et per viam blasfemavit semet ipsum er nominem gloriose virginis matris Mariae, et usus fuit verbis quae pro meliori tacentur', Connell and Constable, 'Sacrilege and Redemption', p. 89. For other examples of blasphemy against Mary following gambling losses see pp. 73–4.

32. Florence, Stibbert Museum.

33. For the vast documentation that this case generated, ecclesiastical and secular, see Klaus Arnold, Niklashausen 1476: Quellen und Untersuchungen zur sozialreligiösen Bewegung des Hans Behem und zur Agrarstruktur eines spätmittelalterlichen Dorfes, Baden-Baden, 1980; for a narrative account Richard Wunderli, Peasant Fires: The Drummer of Niklashausen, Bloomington, 1992; and for analysis see John Arnold, Belief and Unbelief in Medieval Europe, London, 2005, pp. 207–16.

34. 1480s, London Lambeth Palace 474, fol. 15r; Cames, Dix siècles, figure 229, p. 135. On the Annunciation see Pelikan, Mary through the Centuries, chapter XIV, pp. 195–209.

35. Filippo Lippi: Catalogo completo, Florence, 1997, pp. 70–71.

36. Liberale da Verona, 1473–9, Siena, Piccolomini Library, fol. 33v.

37. Pierpoint Morgan, M 893, fol. 12r. This choice attracted several English illuminators throughout the century, Cambridge, Fitzwilliam Museum, 57, fol. 37r.

38. She is seated but bowing, with an arm across her chest in Zanobbi Strozzi's Annunciation panel of $c.1440$–45, London, National Gallery: Dillian Gordon, 'Zanobi Strozzi's "Annunciation" in the National Gallery', Burlington Magazine 140 (1998), pp. 517–24. On Sienese artists see H. W. van Os, Marias Demut und Verherrlichung in der senesischen Malerei 1300–1450, Rome, 1969, pp. 35–57.

39. Berlin, Gemäldegalerie; Brussels, Musées Royaux des Beaux Arts.

40. Chicago, Art Institute.

41. *Fra Angelico*, eds. Laurence Kanter and Pia Palladino, New York, 2006, figure 106, p. 184; see also figure 52, pp. 274–5.

42. See an earlier example in the Books of Hours of Gian Galeazzo Visconti decorated by the Master of the Modena Books of Hours *c.*1400, The Hague, Koninklijke Biblitoheek 76 F 6, fols. 13v–14r; see reproduction in van Os, *Art of Devotion*, p. 17.

43. Cambridge, Fitzwilliam Museum, St Lucy Altarpiece 1440s; Michael Baxendall, *Painting and Experience in Fifteenth-Century Italy*, Open University edition, Oxford, 1972, pp. 35–6, 49–57.

44. Late fourteenth-century St Saeran's church, Llanynys (Denbighshire), 71.2 cm; Lord, *The Visual Culture of Wales*, p. 155; Llanbeblig Book of Hours; E. J. M. Duggan, 'Notes Concerning the "Lily" Crucifixion in the Llanbeblig Hours', *National Library of Wales Journal* 27 (1991), pp. 39–47.

45. Tomb of Sir Wiliam ap Thomas, mid-fifteenth century, 97 × 120 cm; Lord, *The Visual Culture of Wales*, p. 154.

46. Van Os, *Art of Devotion*, p. 18; Southern Netherlands, *c.*1480–90 Antwerp, Museum Mayer van den Bergh, 41.5 × 23.5 cm. On other northern scenes see Gert Duwe, *Die Verkündigung an Maria in der niederländischen Malerei des 15. und 16. Jahrhunderts*, Frankfurt, 1994.

47. Upper Rhine late fifteenth century; Milman, *Les Heures de la Prière*, p. 36, figure 24 and on it pp. 36–7.

48. Cracow Cathedral Treasury, by 1422; *Treasures of the Cracow Monasteries*, no. 119, p. 119.

49. Kate Lowe, 'Nuns and Choice: Artistic Decision-Making in Medicean Florence', in *With and Without the Medici: Studies in Tuscan Art and Patronage 1434–1530*, Aldershot, 1998, pp. 129–53, at p. 129.

50. Claire L. Sahlin, *Birgitta of Sweden and the Voice of Prophecy*, Woodbridge, 2001, pp. 82–3.

51. 'Quasi si in corde esset puer vivus et volvens se et revolvens', *Revelaciones* ed. Birger Bergh, Stockholm, 1991, IV, p. 88.

52. 'Nam quando ego consensi angelo nuncianti michi concepcionem filii Dei, statim sensi in me mirabile quoddam et vividum'. On Birgitta's mystical experience of pregnancy see Sahlin, *Birgitta*, pp. 77–107.

53. Bridget of Sweden and Peter of Skänninge, *Officium parvum beate Marie Virginis I*, ed. Tryggve Lundén, Lund, 1976.

54. Viveca Servatius, '*Cantus sororum* – Seven Offices in Honour of the Virgin Mary within the Bridgettine Order', in *Gregorian Chant and Medieval Music: Proceedings of the Nordic Festival and Conference of Gregorian Chant: Trondheim, St Olav's Wake 1997*, Trondheim, 1998, pp. 107–18.

55. On Birgitta see also Claire M. Waters, *Angels and Earthly Creatures: Preaching, Performance and Gender in the Later Middle Ages*, Philadelphia, 2004, pp. 136–8.

56. The translation from the Latin is from Claire L. Sahlin, '*His Heart Was My Heart*: Birgitta of Sweden's Devotion to the Heart of Mary', in *Heliga Birgitta – Budskapet och Förebilden: Föredrag vid Jubileumssymposiet I Vadstena 3–7 oktober 1991*, Stockholm, 1993, pp. 213–27, at pp. 213–14.

57. Ibid., p. 223.

58. Nancy Mayberry, 'Beatriz de Silva: An Important Fifteenth-Century Visionary', *Vox Benedictina* 4 (1987), pp. 169–83, esp. at pp. 170–72.

59. Elizabeth A. Lehfeldt, *Religious Women in Golden Age Spain: The Permeable Cloister*, Aldershot, 2005, pp. 162–3.

60. Lowe, 'Nuns and Choice', pp. 130–31.

61. Cleveland, Museum of Art; he may also have designed the *Coronation of the Virgin* scene embroidered at S. Verdiana, which still survives: Lowe, 'Nuns and Choice', p. 143.

62. Jeffrey F. Hamburger, *Nuns as Artists: The Visual Culture of a Medieval Convent*, Berkeley, 1997, colour plate 7.

63. Mary inspired the visualization of settings around powerful and saintly women: Mary among saints could have suggested the scene of St Catherine among her nuns, like Matteo di Giovanni (1430–97), Virgin and Child with Saints in Siena, Museo dell'Opera, and Cosimo Rosselli, St Catherine of Siena as the Spiritual Mother of the Second and Third Orders of St Dominic, Edinburgh, National Gallery of Scotland; Lowe, 'Nuns and Choice', p. 146.

64. Jeryldene Wood, Women, Art, and Spirituality: The Poor Clares of Early Modern Italy, Cambridge, 1996, figure 89; see also figures 90 and 91.

65. I have modernized the text edited in Women's Writing in Middle English, London and New York, 1992, pp. 223–7, at pp. 224–5, lines 69–76 and 84–9.

66. By the Master of Viella; it serves as the cover picture of Jérôme Baschet's La Civilisation féodale: De l'an mil à la colonisation de l'Amérique, Paris, 2004. I am grateful to my colleague Professor Baschet for his help in understanding this image.

67. Van Os, The Art of Devotion, plate 15, p. 53, and text on p. 52.

68. 39 × 26 cm; Liège, Museum of Religious and Mosan Art. Mary's generosity was more abundant when she was depicted as Madonna delle Grazie, offering her milk to people suffering the fire of hell, as in the panel of 1508 made for the Carmelite convent of Chieti in the Abbruzzo: Susan Marti and Daniela Mondini, ' "Ich manen dich der brüsten min, Das du dem sünder wellest milte sin!" ', Himmel, Hölle, Fegefeuer: Das Jenseits im Mittelalter, ed. Peter Jezler, Zurich, 1994, figure 56, pp. 79–90.

PART VI: MARY REFORMED, MARY GLOBAL: 1500 AND BEYOND

Chapter 21: Mary of Reform and Reformation

1. Ursula Weekes, Early Engravers and their Public: The Master of the Berlin Passion and Manuscripts from Convents in the Rhine-Maas Region, ca.1450–1500, Turnhout, 2004, p. 11.

2. Contact had already extended within the Atlantic sphere as far as the Canaries around 1400; it was claimed that the Guanches, inhabitants of Tenerife, were found worshipping a figure of Mary and her child, David Abulafia, The Discovery of Mankind: Atlantic Encounters in the Age of Columbus, London and New Haven, 2008, pp. 44–8.

3. Circa 1492: Art in the Age of Exploration, ed. Jay A. Levenson, Washington, DC, 1991, no. 348, p. 489.

4. Jacques Mercier, Art that Heals: The Image as Medicine in Ethiopia, New York, 1997, fig. 85, p. 82: Mary and her son, with Gabriel and Michael from a sixteenth-century gospel book – note elongated eyes; on Africa see also Philippe Denis, The Dominican Friars in Southern Africa: A Social History (1577–1990), Leiden, 1998, chapter 1.

5. On the intricate affinities that bound Asia and Africa see Amitav Ghosh, In an Antique Land, London, 1992.

6. Robert Eric Frykenberg, 'Christians in India: An Historical Overview of their Complex Origins', in Christians and Missionaries in India: Cross Cultural Communication since 1500, with Special Reference to Caste, Conversion, and Colonialism, London, 2003, pp. 33–61. For ritual life that situates Mary as a Hindu patroness see Susan Kaufmann Bayly, 'A Christian Caste in Hindu Society: Religious Leadership and Social Conflict among the Paravas of Southern Tamilnadu', Modern Asian Studies 15 (1981), pp. 203–34.

7. For a discussion of possible meeting of eastern and western forms of mother and child imagery see A. Foucher, 'The Buddhist Madonna', in The Beginnings of Buddhist Art, trans. L. A. Thomas and F. W. Thomas, London and Paris, 1917, pp. 271–91.

8. See an ink drawing of Kannon of c.1500 in C.1492, no. 225. For a Japanese Mary shrine

worked in lacquered inlaid wood and shell, *Historía da Expansão Portuguesa*, II, eds. Francisco Bethercourt and Kirti Chaudhuri, Navarra, 1998, p. 415.

9. C. R. Boxer, *Mary and Misogyny: Women in Iberian Expansion Overseas, 1415–1815, Some Facts, Fancies and Personalities*, London, 1975, p. 105.

10. John Oliver Hand, *Joos van Cleve: The Complete Paintings*, New Haven, 2004, figure 114 (catalogue no. 91).

11. Ibid., figure 85 (catalogue no. 63).

12. Ibid., figure 14 (catalogue no. 6), figure 29 (catalogue no. 9). See the Christ Child sleeping at Mary's bare breast in Hans Baldung Grien's Mary with a Child and an Angel (Grünewaldmadonna), c.1539, Berlin, Gemäldegalerie, catalogue no. 2159.

13. Hand, *Joos van Cleve*, figure 84, (catalogue no. 58).

14. Brussels, Musées Royaux des Beaux-Arts en Belgique, inv. 3559.

15. Berlin, Gemäldegalerie, 61 × 51 cm.

16. Berlin, Gemäldegalerie, cat. no. 1732; 74.2 × 53.5 cm.

17. Rob Sulewski, 'Edited Remainders of a Nativity: Two Short, Early Polish Christmas Fragments', *European Medieval Drama* 8 (2004), pp. 205–12, at p. 209.

18. Pamela Sheingorn, 'Appropriating the Holy Kinship: Gender and Family History', in *Interpreting Cultural Symbols: Saint Anne in Late Medieval Society*, Athens, GA, 1990, pp. 169–98, at pp. 185–7. On representations of the Holy Family at the end of the fifteenth century see Klaus Arnold, 'Die Heilige Familie: Bilder und Verehrung der Heiligen Anna, Maria, Joseph und des Jesuskindes in Kunst, Literatur und Frömmogkeit um 1500', in *Maria in der Welt: Marienverehrung im Kontext der Sozialgeschichte, 10.–18. Jahrhundert*, eds. Claudia Opitz, Hedwig Röckelein, Gabriela Signori and G. P. Marchal, Zurich, 1993, pp. 153–74.

19. Paris, Musée de Cluny, Pierre Riché and Danièle Alexandre-Bidon, *L'Enfance au Moyen Âge*, Paris, 1994, p. 15.

20. Rotterdam, Museum Boymans-van Beuningen; Ruth Mellinkoff, *Outcasts: Signs of Otherness in Northern European Art of the Late Middle Ages* II, Berkeley, 1993, figure VI.71.

21. *Danske Kalkmalerier*, plate 65, and on the church pp. 80–81.

22. Nora Baráthová, Dušan Jurdík, Mikuláš Lipták, *Kežmarok*, Kežmarok, 1999, p. 63.

23. *Early German Painting 1350–1550*, ed. Isolde Lübbeke, trans. Margaret Thomas Will, no. 24, pp. 16–19.

24. *Rozmyślania Dominikańskie*, II, Wrocław, 1965, Miniatures 22, 70, 89, 102. The related image of the bleeding Christ in his weeping mother's presence was chosen as funerary image for a Polish aristocrat; Mary recommends him to her wounded son, with a gesture of her hand: *Treasures of the Cracow Monasteries*, Cracow, 2000, no. 246, p. 229.

25. Jessica A. Boon, 'The Agony of the Virgin: The Swoons and Crucifixion of Mary in Sixteenth Century Castilian Passion Treatises', *Sixteenth Century Journal* 38 (2007), pp. 3–25.

26. The music in the houses of the Brethren of the Common Life was more commonly monophonic and based on scriptural themes, as shown for a late fifteenth-century house in the Ijssel Valley, Ulrike Hascher-Burger, *Gesungene Innigkeit: Studien zu einer Musikhandschrift der Devotio moderna (Utrecht, Universiteitsbibliotheek, ms. 16 H 34, olim B 113): mit einer Edition der Gesänge*, Leiden, 2002.

27. Heiko A. Oberman, *Luther: Man between God and the Devil*, trans. Eileen Walliser-Schwarzbart, London, 1993, pp. 96–9.

28. Andries Welkenhuysen, '*Cantent epithalamium*: A Marian Christmas Carol from the Netherlandish Devotion, Edited with a Translation and Notes', in *Serta Devota in memoriam Guillelmi Lourdaux, pars prior: Devotio Windeshemensis*, Leuven, 1992, pp. 427–52, at p. 432, stanza 1.

29. Welkenhuysen, '*Cantent epithalamium*', p. 433, stanzas 21–3. Overt references to Mary

are even absent from the crib devotions of a beguine from Deventer, Sister Katherine van Arkel, the Blind, see Charles Caspers, 'De Kerstkribbe van zuster Katheryna van Arkel, "die blijnde": Jezus ende vrouwelijke Devoten in de vijftiende eeuw', in *Geen povere schoonheid: Laatmiddeleeuwse kunst in verband met de Moderne Devotie*, ed. Kees Veelenturf, Nijmegen, 2000, pp. 67–85.

30. 'Erbarm dich über vns O heilige maria bit für vns O heilige gottes gebererin bit für vns O du heilige jungfrowe Aller jungfrowen', Christel Matheis-Rebaud, ' "Die Predigt mit dem Gebet für die sieben Tage der Woche" von Johannes Geiler von Kaysersberg (1445–1510): Ein Beispiel für die religiöse und spirituelle Unterweisung von Klosterfrauen am Ende des Mittelalters', *Revue Mabillon* new series 2 (1991), pp. 207–39, at p. 218.

31. See above, pp. 314–15.

32. Harvey E. Hamburgh, 'The Problem of *Lo Spasimo* of the Virgin in *Cinquecento* Paintings of the *Descent from the Cross*', *Sixteenth Century Journal* 12 (1981), pp. 45–75, at pp. 50–51; Diarmaid Macculloch, *Reformation: Europe's House Divided, 1490–1700*, London, 2003, pp. 86–7.

33. Thomas de Vio, *Opuscula: Quaestiones et Quodlibeta*, Modena, 1529, pp. 52–4.

34. Joseph Leo Koerner, *The Reformation of the Image*, London, 2004, pp. 146–7, figure 75, p. 147. On the trial and the dissemination of news of the case see Kathrin Tremp-Utz, 'Welche Sprache spricht die Jungfrau Maria? Sprachgrenzen und Sprachkenntnisse im bernischen Jetzerhandel (1507–1509)', *Schweizerische Zeitschrift für Geschichte* 38 (1988), pp. 221–49; Kathrin Utz Tremp, 'Eine Werbekampagne für die befleckte Empfängnis: Der Jetzerhandel in Bern (1507–1509)', in *Maria in der Welt: Marienverehrung im Kontext der Sozialgeschicte, 10.–18. Jahrhundert*, eds. Claudia Opitz, Hedwig Röckelein, Gabriela Signori and G. P. Marchal, Zurich, 1993, pp. 323–37.

35. I have benefited from several illuminating conversations with Rita Copeland about the association between the education of children and pain.

36. The image was made by the Master of the Magdalen Legend, who worked in Brussels and Mechelen: Henk van Os, *Art of Devotion*, pp. 116–17, and *Essays in Context: Unfolding the Netherlandish diptych*, eds. John Oliver Hand and Ron Spronk, Cambridge (MA), 2006, pp. 158–9.

37. Berlin, Gemäldegalerie, 61 × 51 cm.

38. Cambridge, Fitzwilliam Museum, no. 908; 60.6 × 42.5 cm.

39. New York, Metropolitan Museum; Berlin, Gemäldegalerie, catalogue no. 564 A.

40. Berlin, Gemäldegalerie, on poplar wood, 91 × 76 cm. This picture inspired a version of 1530, now in Krakow: *The Treasures of the Cracow Monasteries*, figure 93, p. 107.

41. Vienna, Liechstenstein Museum, round 82 cm across; Berlin, Gemäldegalerie, catalogue no. 7; *c*.1492, 68.5 × 92.3 cm; Washington, National Gallery, Madonna and Child, *c*.1500; Perugia, Galleria Nazionale dell'Umbria, Madonna Della Consolazione; Florence, National Gallery, Madonna of Pinks, 1507; New York, Metropolitan Museum, Madonna enthroned with Saints; Dresden, Staatliche Kunstsammlungen, Gemäldegalerie Alter Meister, Sistine Madonna.

42. London, British Library Add. 35354, detached leaf; on it see Janet Backhouse, *The Illuminated Manuscript*, Oxford, 1979, p. 75.

43. Desiderius Erasmus, *The Colloquies of Erasmus*, trans. Craig R. Thompson, London, 1965, pp. 289–91.

44. Ibid., p.301.

45. Heiko A. Oberman, *The Two Reformations: The Journey from the Last Days to the New World*, New Haven and London, 2003, pp. 86–7. For criticism of pilgrimage in Hussite circles see Oto Halam, 'Die reformatorische Kritik des Marienkultus in den böhmischen Ländern', in *Wallfahrt und Reformation – Pout' a reformace: Zur Veränderung religiöser Praxis in Deutschland und Böhmen in den Umbrüchen der Frühen Neuzeit*, eds. Jan Hrdina, Hartmut Kühne and Thomas T. Müller, Frankfurt, 2007, pp. 131–7.

46. See, for example, the view of John Blumston that the pilgrimages to images of the Virgin Mary in Doncaster, Walsingham and Coventry are false, *Lollards of Coventry 1486–1522*, eds. and trans. Shannon McSheffrey and Norman Tanner, Cambridge, 2003, p. 64.

47. Peter Marshall, 'Forgery and Miracles in the Reign of Henry VIII', *Past and Present 178* (2003), pp. 39–73, at pp. 48–9.

48. Brian P. Copenhaver, 'The Historiography of Discovery in the Renaissance: The Sources and Composition of Polydore Vergil's *De Inventoribus Rerum*, I–III', *Journal of the Warburg and Courtauld Institutes 41* (1978), pp. 192–214.

49. Aston, *England's Iconoclasts*, p. 30.

50. Leipzig, Melchior Lotter, 1500; for frontispiece see http://www.hmml.org/exhibits/Trithemius/Anne.html; Klaus Arnold, *Johannes Trithemius (1462–1516)*, Würzburg, 1971, pp. 104–6. I am grateful to Anthony Grafton for an illuminating conversation on Trithemius' devotional taste. See also Virginia Nixon, *Mary's Mother: St Anne in Late Medieval Europe*, University Park, 2004, pp. 29–31.

51. Oberman, *Luther*, pp. 124–6.

52. Hans Düfel, *Luthers Stellung zur Marienverehrung*, Göttingen, 1968.

53. Beth Kreitzer, 'The Lutheran Sermon', in *Preachers and People in the Reformations and Early Modern Period*, ed. Larissa Taylor, Leiden, 2001, pp. 35–63, at p. 44.

54. Christopher Boyd Brown, *Singing the Gospel: Lutheran Hymns and the Success of the Reformation*, Cambridge, MA, 2005, p. 157.

55. 'Warumb gibt er yhn nicht die mutter Maria und Joseph zum zeychen, sondern nympt alleyn die windleen odder tuchlen und die krippen? darumb, das uns Got auff keynen heyligen wil weysen, auch zu der mutter selb nicht, darumb muß er uns ein gewiß ort anzeygen, da Christs ligte, das ist die krippen, da findt man yhn gewiß, wenn gleich Joseph und Maria nicht da wer', Düfel, *Luthers Stellung zur Marienverehrung*, p. 67.

56. 'Huc dicerem pertinere eos, qui festum Conceptionis B. Virginis volunt esse primum et summum omnium et qui novorum festorum dignitate, privilegiis, indulgentiis replent totos sermones. Nec frustra nos quoque vixisse videbit posteritas, qui novis festis fecimus vetera vera veterasse: si nihil aliud fecimus, hoc unum satis est dignum aeterna memoria . . .', ibid., p. 83.

57. Koerner, *The Reformation of the Image*, p. 215.

58. 'Beata virgo autem vidit Deum in omnibus . . . hoc autem non facit nisi cui solus Deus in visu est, cetera omnia velut evaneurunt. Non potest anima simul intenta esse magnificatione creaturae et creatori'; on it see Düfel, *Luthers Stellung zur Marienverehrung*, p. 77.

59. Martin Luther, *The Sermon on the Mount (sermons) and The Magnificat*, trans. A. T. W. Steinhaeuser, in *Luther's Works*, XXI, St Louis, 1956, pp. 299, 323; Beth Kreitzer, *Reforming Mary: Changing Images of the Virgin Mary in Lutheran Sermons of the Sixteenth Century*, Oxford, 2004, pp. 49–54. On these themes see Bridget Heal, 'Images of the Virgin Mary and Marian Devotion in Protestant Nuremberg', in *Religion and Superstition in Reformation Europe*, eds. Helen Parish and William G. Naphy, Manchester, 2002, pp. 25–46, esp. pp. 32–8. See also Bridget Heal, *The Cult of the Virgin Mary in Early Modern Germany: Protestant and Catholic Piety, 1500–1648*, Cambridge, 2008, esp. chapter 2.

60. Margaret Aston, *England's Iconoclasts: Vol. I, Laws against Images*, Oxford, 1988, p. 7.

61. Martin Luther, *An Order of Mass and Communion*, trans. Paul Zeller Strodach, Philadelphia, 1965, p. 35; on Luther and hymnody see Carl Axel Aurelius, '*Quo verbum dei vel cantu inter populos maneat*: The Hymns of Martin Luther', in *The Arts and Cultural Heritage of Martin Luther*, eds. Eyolf Østrem, Jens Fleischer and Nils Holger Petersen, Copenhagen, 2003, pp. 19–34.

62. Eyolf Østrem, 'Luther, Josquin and *des fincken gesang*', in *The Arts and Cultural Heritage of Martin Luther*, pp. 51–79, at p. 52.

63. Robin A. Leaver, 'Sequences and Responsories: Continuity of Forms in Luther's Liturgi-

cal Provisions', in *Worship in Medieval and Early Modern Europe: Change and Continuity in Religious Practice*, Notre Dame, 2004, pp. 300–328, at pp. 316–17.

64. Ibid., p. 319.

65. I am most grateful to Dr David Irving for illuminating this point.

66 Austra Reinis, *Reforming the Art of Dying: The Ars Moriendi in the German Reformation* (1519–1526), Aldershot, 2007, pp. 160–63, 252.

67. Diarmaid MacCulloch, 'Mary and Sixteenth-century Protestants', *Studies in Church History* 39 (2005), pp. 191–217, at pp. 202–5.

68. Margaret Aston, 'Relic Worship and Iconoclasm', in *The Archaeology of the Reformation 1480–1580*, Society for Post-Medieval Archaeology Monograph 1, Leeds, 2003, pp. 9–28, at p. 23.

69. Heiko Oberman, 'The Controversy over Images at the Time of the Reformation', in *The Two Reformations: The Journey from the Last Days to the New World*, New Haven and London, 2003, pp. 86–96; Diarmaid Macculloch, *Reformation: Europe's House Divided 1490–1700*, London, 2003 pp. 150–52

70. 'On Images and the Sacrament', *Luther's Works*, ed. Conrad Bergendorff, Philadelphia, 1958, XL, pp. 99–100.

71. Ibid.

72. Thomas Cramer, 'From the Word of God to the Emblem', in *Visual Culture and the German Middle Ages*, New York, 2005, pp. 251–72, at pp. 258–9; see also Horst Wenzel, 'Luthers Briefe im Medienwechsel von der Manuskriptkultur zum Buchdruck', in *Audiovisualität vor und nach Gutenberg: Zur Kulturgeschicte der medialen Umbrüche*, Vienna, 2001, pp. 185–201, at p. 193.

73. *Luther's Works* IX, ed. Jaruslav Pelikan, St Louis, 1960, p. 80; Aston, *England's Iconoclasts*, p. 6.

74. Petra Schöner, 'Visual Representations of Jews and Judaism in Sixteenth-Century Germany', in *Jews, Judaism, and the Reformation in Sixteenth-Century Germany*, Leiden, 2006, pp. 357–91, at pp. 370–72.

75. Brown, *Singing the Gospel*, pp. 86–7, with the image in figure 5.1 on p. 87. Hans Thurner's Virgin and Child statue of 1510–11 in Bern was turned in 1608 into a statue of Justice: the scales of justice in Mary's right hand replaced the Christ Child, Koerner, *The Reformation of the Image*, figure 42, p. 106.

76. Koerner, *The Reformation of the Image*, pp. 63–4, esp. figure 24, p. 64.

77. Like those described in *Luther's Works*, IX, p. 82.

78. Lee Palmer Wandel, *Voracious Idols and Violent Hands: Iconoclasm in Reformation Zurich, Strasbourg, and Basel*, Cambridge, 1999, p. 121.

79. Philip M. Soergel, *Wondrous in his Saints: Counter-Reformation Propaganda in Bavaria*, Berkeley, 1993, pp. 53–5.

80. Oberman, *The Two Reformations*, p. 91; Heiko A. Oberman, *The Roots of Anti-semitism in the Ages of Renaissance and Reformation*, Philadelphia, 1984, pp. 75–9.

81. Hans-Martin Kirn, 'Ulrich Zwingli, the Jews, and Judaism', in *Jews, Judaism, and the Reformation in Sixteenth-Century Germany*, Leiden, 2006, pp. 171–95, at pp. 181–2.

82. Koerner, *The Reformation of the Image*, p. 215.

83. 'Var der et Kors vdj Stedet, da en herlige Taffle', *Biskop Jacob Madsens Visitatsbog 1588–1604*, eds. Jens Rasmussen and Anne Riising, Odense, 1995, pp. 209–10. I am very grateful to my friend and colleague Dr Charlotte Appel for introducing me to this rich source and for translating pertinent entries from Danish.

84. 'En ung kroner Jomfruen'; 'En ny Taffle (1601) met Katekismens Ord', *Biskop Jacob Madsens Visitatsbog 1588–1604*, p. 314.

85. Axel Bolvig, 'Reformation of What? Whose and Which Reformation is Exposed in Danish Wall Paintings?', in *The Archaeology of Reformation 1480–1580*, Leeds, 2003, pp. 84–93; colour plate D, and esp. at pp. 88 and 91.

86. It is followed by the quote from II Corinthians 8:9: 'Though he was rich, yet for our sakes he became poor, that ye through his poverty might be rich', Gerald Fleming, 'On

the Origin of the Passional Christi and Antichristi and Lucas Cranach the Elder's Contribution to Reformation Polemics in the Iconography of the Passional', *Gutenberg Jahrbuch* (1973), pp. 351–68, figure 15, at p. 360.

87. Emidio Campi, 'Bernardino Ochino's Christology and "Mariology" in His Writings of the Italian Period (1538–42)', in *Protestant History and Identity in Sixteenth-century Europe*, I: The *Medieval Inheritance*, St Andrew's Studies in Reformation History, Aldershot, 1996, pp. 108–22, at p. 120.

88. Aston, *England's Iconoclasts*, p. 215.

89. Marshall, 'Forgery and Miracles', p. 51.

90. Clodagh Tait, 'Art and the Cult of the Virgin Mary in Ireland, *c.*1500–1660', in *Art and Devotion in Late Medieval Ireland*, eds. Rachel Moss, Colmán Ó Clabaigh and Salvador Ryan, Dublin, 2006, pp. 163–83, at p. 163. On Germany see Heal, *The Cult of the Virgin Mary*, chapter 4, note 99.

91. *Letters and Papers, Foreign and Domestic, of the Reign of Henry VIII*, ed. James Gairdner, London, 1887, X, no. 364, pp. 138, 139, 141.

92. Wilfrid Holme, *The Fall and Evill Successe of Rebellion from Time to Time*, London, 1572, fol. E1v; the poem was printed in 1570 as a riposte against the Catholic Northern Rebellion of 1569.

93. The story of change in England is told by Eamon Duffy, *The Stripping of the Altars: Traditional Religion in England, c. 1400–c.1580*, New Haven, 1992, part II, chapters 11–15.

94. Claire Cross, 'Excising the Virgin Mary from the Civic Life of Tudor York', *Northern History* 39 (2002), pp. 279–84, at p. 280.

95. Michael O'Connell, *The Idolatrous Eye: Iconoclasm and Theater in Early-Modern England*, Oxford, 2000, p. 22; Cross, 'Excising the Virgin', p. 281.

96. O'Connell, *The Idolatrous Eye*, p. 21.

97. Bridget Heal, 'Sacred Imagery and Sacred Space in Lutheran Germany', in *Sacred Space in Early Modern Europe*, eds, Will Coster and Andrew Spicer, Cambridge, 2005, pp. 39–59, esp. at pp. 58–9.

98. Patrick Collinson, 'Pulling the Strings: Religion and Politics in the Progress of 1578', in *The Progresses, Pageants, and Entertainments of Queen Elizabeth I*, eds. Jayne Elisabeth Archer, Elizabeth Goldring and Sarah Knight, Oxford, 2007, pp. 122–41, at pp. 129–30; Aston, *England's Iconoclasts*, p. 318. I am very grateful to my friend Anna Whitelock for discussing English queens with me.

99. Jayne Elisabeth Archer and Sarah Knight, '*Elizabetha Triumphans*', in *The Progresses, Pageants, and Entertainments of Queen Elizabeth I*, pp. 1–23, at pp. 7–9.

100. Peter McClure and Robin Hedlam Wells, 'Elizabeth I as a Second Mary', *Renaissance Studies* 4 (1990), pp. 38–70.

101. Freeman M. O'Donoghue, *A Descriptive and Classified Catalogue of Portraits of Queen Elizabeth*, London, 1894, no. 214, p. 79; on it Helen Hackett, *Virgin Mother, Maiden Queen: Elizabeth I and the Cult of the Virgin Mary*, Basingstoke, 1995, p. 213.

Chapter 22: From Europe to the Rest of the World

1. Chiyo Ishikawa, *The Retablo de Isabel la Católica by Juan de Flandes and Michel Sittow*, Turnhout, 2004, no. 7, pp. 90–94; no. 16, pp. 110–23; no. 11, pp. 106–7; no. 27, pp. 157–9.

2. Isabella was in later life a particular patron of the great Marian shrine at Guadalupe and a benefactor of the Jeronomite order, which was charged with its care: Gretchen D. Starr-LeBeau, *In the Shadow of the Virgin: Inquisitors, Friars, and Conversos in Guadalupe, Spain: Jews, Christians, and Muslims from the Ancient to the Modern World*, Princeton, 2003, p. 254.

3. Lorenzo Candelaria, 'El Cavaller de Colunya: A Miracle of the Rosary in the Choirbooks

of San Pedro Mártir de Toledo', *Viator* 35 (2004), pp. 221–64. I am most grateful to Lorenzo Candelaria for his generosity in discussing this subject with me.

4. See the analysis of retable and texts offered by Cynthia Robinson, 'Preaching to the Converted: Valladolid's *Cristianos nuevos* and the *Retablo de Don Sancho de Rojas* (1415)', *Speculum* 83 (2008), pp. 112–63.

5. Elizabeth Lehfeldt, 'Ruling Sexuality: The Political Legitimacy of Isabel of Castile', *Renaissance Quarterly* 53 (2000), pp. 31–56, esp. pp. 50–51.

6. *Circa 1492*, pp. 154–5.

7. I am most grateful to Dr Tess Knighton of the University of Cambridge for allowing me to read a draft of her paper 'Marian Devotions in Early Sixteenth-Century Spain: The Case of the Bishop of Palencia, Juan Rodriguez de Fonseca (1451–1524)'.

8. Ibid.

9. Again, I am very much indebted to Lorenzo Candelaria, musicologist and musician, who introduced me to this mass and explained it to me.

10. M. A. Ladero Quesada, *Los mudéjares de Castilla en tiempos de Isabel*, I, Valladolid, 1969, pp. 15–26.

11. I am delighted to acknowledge here the pioneering work of my first teacher of medieval history, Professor Ron Barkaï, who discovered this text and provided its first edition and interpretation in 'Une invocation musulmane au nom de Jésus et de Marie', *Revue de l'Histoire des Religions* 200 (1983), pp. 257–68, text at pp. 258–9.

12. Ibid., pp. 264–5.

13. *Jews in the Canary Islands: Being a Calendar of Jewish Cases Extracted from the Records of the Canariote Inquisition in the Collection of the Marquess of Bute*, trans. Lucien Wolf, Toronto, 2001, p. 16.

14. Ibid., p. 96.

15. Ibid., p. 23. On *moriscos* and Mary see Remensnyder, 'Christian Captives', pp. 674–5.

16. Mercedes García-Arenal, *Inquisición y moriscos: Los procesos del Tribunal de Cuenca*, Madrid, 1983, p. 107.

17. Louis Cardaillac, *Morisques et chrétiens: Un affrontement polémique, 1492–1640*, Paris, 1977, p. 222.

18. The tablet with *The History of the Seal of Salomon* has Mary as spokeswoman, conveying Salomon's words, Philippe Rousse, '*La Historia del Sello de Salomón*. Estudio, edición crítica y traducción comparada', in *Los plombos del Sacromonte: Invención y tesoro*, eds. Manuel Barrios Aguilera and Mercedes García Arenal, Valencia, 2006, pp. 141–71, at p. 161.

19. Mercedes García Arenal, 'De la autoría morisca a la antigüedad sagrada', in *Los plombos del Sacromonte: Invención y tesoro*, eds. Manuel Barrios Aguilera and Mercedes Garcia Arenal, Valencia, 2006, pp. 577–82, at p. 576; Mercedes García-Arenal, 'Orígenes sagrados y memoria del Islam: El caso de Granada', in *Europa, América y el mundo: Tiempos históricos*, eds. Roger Chartier and Antonio Feros, Madrid and Barcelona, 2006, pp. 41–66, esp. pp. 44–7.

20. On comparisons between the relative ease with which Jews and Muslims might assimilate as converts to Christianity see David Nirenberg, 'Love between Muslim and Jew in Medieval Spain: A Triangular Affair', in *Jews, Muslims and Christians in and around the Crown of Aragon: Essays in Honour of Professor Elana Lourie*, ed. Harvey J. Hames, Leiden, 2004, pp. 127–55, at pp. 150–55.

21. Norman Housley, *Religious Warfare in Europe, 1400–1536*, Oxford, 2002, pp. 81–2.

22. On the urban design of the Conquest, see Richard Kagan, *Urban Images of the Hispanic World, 1493-1793*, New Haven, 2000.

23. The artist is Alejo Fernandez, on whom see Diego Angulo Iñiguez, *Alejo Fernandez*, Seville, 1946. On the *mater misericordiae* see above p. 154.

24. Ramón Pané, *An Account of the Antiquities of the Indians: Chronicles of the New World Encounter*, trans. Susan C. Griswold, Durham, NC, and London, 1999, c. 25,

pp. 30–34. I was introduced to Pané by David Abulafia, who also kindly shared with me page-proofs of his book *The Discovery of Mankind*, pp. 131–7. For a map of the region see Irving Rouse and José Juan Arrom, 'The Taínos: Principal Inhabitants of Columbus' Indies', in *Circa 1492*, pp. 509–14, and map on p. 509.

25. Pané, *An Account of the Antiquities*, pp. 34–5.

26. Ibid., Appendix A, p. 44.

27. Ibid., Appendix C, p. 56.

28. The Codex Monteleone of *c.*1531–2, made in the Puebla region, depicts a banner of Mary in a schematic style and in local female dress: Serge Gruzinski, *Painting the Conquest: The Mexican Indians and the European Renaissance*, Paris, p. 152, figure 125.

29. Robert Stevenson, *Music in Mexico: A Historical Survey*, New York, 1952, pp. 52–4.

30. For a subtle analysis of these, as a process of 'occidentalization', see Serge Gruzinski, 'Occidentalisation', in *La Pensée métisse*, Paris, 1999, pp. 87–104. See also Serge Gruzinski, Antoinette Molinié Fiorvanati, Carmen Salazar and Jean-Michel Sallmann, 'Visions et christianisations: L'Expérience mexicaine', in *Visions indiennes, visions baroques: les métissages de l'inconscient*, ed. Jean-Michel Sallmann, Paris, 1992, pp. 117–49.

31. See the image of the arrival of the Franciscans in the Description of Tlaxcala of 1550–56, Gruzinski, *Painting the Conquest*, p. 44, figure 28. See also the mural from the convent of San Miguel: Huejutzingo, Puebla, in Samuel Y. Edgerton, *Theaters of Conversion: Religious Architecture and Indian Artisans in Colonial Mexico*, Albequerque, 2001, figure 2.1, p. 20; on it also Elizabeth Hill Boone and B. F. Cummins, 'Colonial Foundations: Points of Conflict and Compatibility', in *The Arts in Latin America 1492–1820*, ed. Joseph J. Rishel with Suzanne Stratton-Pruitt, Philadelphia, 2006, pp. 11–21, at p. 16.

32. Nicholas Griffiths, 'Introduction', in *Spiritual Encounters: Interactions between Christianity and Native Religions in Colonial America*, eds. Nicholas Griffiths and Fernando Cervantes, Birmingham, 1999, pp. 1–42, at p. 8; Inga Clendinnen, 'Ways to the Sacred: Reconstructing "Religion" in Sixteenth Century Mexico', *History and Anthropology* 5 (1990), pp. 105–41.

33. John Leddy Phelan, *The Millennial Kingdom of the Franciscans in the New World*, 2nd rev. edn, Berkeley, 1970, p. 50. On mission convents see also Edgerton, *Theaters of Conversion*, pp. 35–71.

34. Ibid., figure 5.8, p. 138; Santiago Sebastián López, José de Mesa Figueroa and Teresa Gisbert de Mesa, *Arte iberoamericano desde la colonización a la independencia* I, Madrid, 1985, pp. 183, at p. 179. See also Richard E. Phillips, 'Women and Men as Cosmic Co-Bearers at Oaxtepec, Mexico, about 1535', in *Woman and Art in Early Modern Latin America*, Leiden, 2007, pp. 99–121, esp. at pp. 115–17.

35. Othón Arróniz, *Teatro de evangelización en Nueva España*, Mexico City, 1979, pp. 51–2.

36. Penny C. Morrill, 'The Queen of Heaven Reigns in New Spain: The Triumph of Eternity in the Casa del Deán Murals', in *Woman and Art in Early Modern Latin America*, Atlantic World 10, Leiden, 2007, pp. 21–45, at pp. 41–2.

37. Susan Kellogg, *Weaving the Past: A History of Latin America's Women from the Prehispanic Period to the Present*, Oxford, 2005, pp. 78–9.

38. Jenny O. Ramírez, 'Nurture and Inconformity: Arrieta's Images of Women, Food and Beverage', in *Woman and Art in Early Modern Latin America*, Leiden, 2007, pp. 207–17, at pp. 212–14; see also Clendinnen, 'Ways to the Sacred', p. 128. Once the cult of Our Lady of Guadalupe developed she became the patron of *pulque*.

39. Dolores Aramoni Caldéron, *Los refugios de lo Sagrado: Religiosidad, conflicto y resistencia entre los Zoques de Chiàpas*, Mexico, 1992, pp. 142–3.

40. Mauricio Beuchot, *A History of Philosophy in Colonial Mexico*, trans. Elizabeth Millán, Washington, DC, 1998, p. 42.

41. For images and local cults see A. Gervase Rosser (with Jane Garnett), 'The Virgin Mary and the People of Liguria: Image and Cult', *Studies in Church History* 39 (2005), pp. 280–97.

42. Amos Megged, *Exporting the Catholic Reformation: Local Religion in Early-Colonial Mexico*, Leiden, 1996, p. 135.

43. Nora E. Jaffary, *False Mystics: Deviant Orthodoxy in Colonial Mexico*, Lincoln (NB), 2004; William A. Christian Jr, *Apparitions in Late Medieval and Renaissance Spain*, Princeton, 1989.

44. On the Iberian shrine of Guadalupe see Starr-LeBeau, *In the Shadow of the Virgin*; and on its beginnings Peter Linehan, 'The Beginnings of Santa María de Guadalupe and the Direction of Fourteenth-Century Castile', *Journal of Ecclesiastical History* 36 (1985), pp. 284–304.

45. The following year saw the publication of the Nahua version, on which see *The Story of Guadalupe: Luis Laso de la Vega's Hueitlamahuiçoltica of 1649*, eds. and trans. Lisa Sousa, Stafford Poole and James Lockhart, Palo Alto, 1998.

46. On the beginnings see David A. Brading, *Mexican Phoenix: Our Lady of Guadalupe: Image and Tradition*, Cambridge, 2001, chapter 3; Charles Gibson, *The Aztecs under Spanish Rule: A History of the Indians of the Valley of Mexico, 1519–1810*, Stanford, 1964, p. 133.

47. Images like the engraving by the Flemish artist Hieronymus Wierix (*c.*1553–1619), *Mary on the Moon-sickle*, showed the Virgin of the Apocalypse/the Immaculate Mary trampling a dragon underfoot: Gauvin A. Bailey, *The Art of Colonial Latin America*, London, 2005, p. 177 and figure 98.

48. Phelan, *The Millennial Kingdom*, p. 51.

49. Sabine MacCormack, 'Gods, Demons, and Idols in the Andes', *Journal of the History of Ideas* 67 (2006), pp. 623–47, at pp. 625–7; Maria Rostworowski, 'Pachacamac and El Señor de los Milagros', in *Native Traditions in the Post-Conquest World*, eds. Elizabeth Hill Boone and Tom Cummins, Washington, 1990, pp. 345–59, esp. pp. 346–8.

50. On Andean historical understanding see Sabine MacCormack, *On the Wings of Time: Rome, the Incas, Spain, and Peru*, Princeton, 2007, chapters 3 and 4.

51. Amy Remensnyder, 'Christian Captives, Muslim Maidens, and Mary', *Speculum* 82 (2007), pp. 642–77.

52. Sabine MacCormack, 'Gods, Demons, and Idols in the Andes', *Journal of the History of Ideas* 67 (2006), pp. 623–47, at pp. 638–9.

53. MacCormack, *On the Wings of Time*, 2007, pp. 115–17.

54. Carol Damian, *The Virgin of the Andes: Art and Ritual in Colonial Cuzco*, Miami Beach, 1995.

55. For the painting of the *Virgen del Serro* of *c.*1720 see Richard L. Kagan and Fernando Marías, *Urban Images of the Hispanic World, 1493–1793*, New Haven, 2000, colour figure 6,37; MacCormack, *On the Wings of Time*, pp. 128–9, 228.

56. Kagan, *Urban Images*, pp. 195–8; Teresa Gisbert, *Iconografía y mitos indígenas en el arte*, 1st edn, La Paz, 1980, p. 7.

57. See, for example, the life of the Ursuline nun Marie de l'Incarnation: Natalie Zemon Davis, *Women on the Margins: Three Seventeenth-century Lives*, Cambridge (MA), 1995, pp. 63–139. On women's attitudes to mission see Ramón A. Guttiérez, *When Jesus Came, the Corn Mothers Went Away: Marriage, Sexuality, and Power in New Mexico, 1500–1846*, Stanford, 1991, pp. 77–9.

58. Jose de Acosta, 'De procuranda indorum salute', in *Obras del P. José de Acosta*, Madrid, 1954, pp. 389–608, at p. 603; see also p. 566.

59. Ibid., p. 566.

60. Richard White, *The Middle Ground: Indians, Empires, and Republics in the Great Lakes Region, 1650–1815*, Cambridge, 1991, pp. 67–9; William B. Hart, ' "The Kindness of the Blessed Virgin": Faith, Succour, and the Cult of Mary among Christian Hurons and Iroquois in Seventeenth-Century New France', in *Spiritual Encounters: Interactions between Christianity and Native Religions in Colonial America*, eds. Nicholas Griffiths and Fernando Cervantes, Birmingham, 1999, pp. 65–90.

61. On this affair and the correspondence which it prompted see Richard Gray, 'A Kongo

Princess, the Kongo Ambassadors and the Papacy', in *Christianity and the African Imagination: Essays in Honour of Adrian Hastings*, Leiden, 2002, pp. 25–40.

62. Joan Meznar, 'Our Lady of the Rosary, African Slaves, and the Struggle against Heretics in Brazil, 1550–1660', in *Journal of Early Modern History* 9 (2005), pp. 371–97, at p. 377.

63. This was a strategy already tried and tested in other parts of the world; the Dominicans introduced confraternities soon after their arrival in Goa in the 1510s, *História da expansão portuguesa*, p. 427.

64. Meznar, 'Our Lady of the Rosary', p. 388. The Black Fraternity of the Rosary in Ouro Prêto supported processional festivities and in the eighteenth century built its own Baroque church there: Bailey, *The Art of Colonial Latin America*, pp. 62–5, esp. figure 28, p.63.

65. The painting of *c.*1671 *France Brings the Faith to the Indians of New France*, in the Ursuline Convent in Quebec, presents Queen Anne of Austria within a context suffused with Marian imagery; see discussion of it in F. -M. Gagnoni, 'La France apportant la foi aux Hurons de Nouvelle-France', *Journal of Canadian Studies* 18 (1983), pp. 5–20.

66. *The Jesuit Relations and Allied Documents* LIX, ed. Reuben Gold Thwaite, Cleveland, 1898, pp. 185–91, at p. 189.

67. Ibid., p. 207.

68. Ibid., pp. 207–9.

69. Jonathan D. Spence, *The Memory Palace of Matteo Ricci*, London, 1985, pp. 234–6.

70. Vitaliano R. Gorospe with R. Javellana, *Virgin of Peñafrancia: Mother of Bicol*, Manila, 1995, p. 4; and Monina A. Mercado, *Antipolo: A Shrine to Our Lady*, Manila, 1980, pp. 81–3; on the arrival of Christianity and its impact on gender relations see Carolyn Brewer, *Holy Confrontation: Religion, Gender and Sexuality in the Philippines, 1521–1685*, Manila, 2001.

71. On the *loa* see David Irving, 'Musical Politics of Empire: The *Loa* in 18th-century Manila', *Early Music* 32 (2004), pp. 383–402.

72. Ines G. Županov, 'The Prophetic and the Miraculous in Portuguese Asia: A Hagiographical View of Colonial Culture', in *Sinners and Saints: The Successors of Vasco de Gama*, Delhi and Oxford, 1995, pp. 135–61, at pp. 147–8.

73. Doreen Fernandez, '*Pompas y Solemnidades:* Church Celebrations in Spanish Manila and the Native Theater', *Philippine Studies* 36 (1988), pp. 403–26, at p. 406.

74. Ibid., pp. 406–7.

75. R. C. Boxer, *The Christian Century in Japan, 1549–1650*, Berkeley, 1951, chapters 7 and 8, esp. pp. 307–8.

76. R. Po-chia Hsia, 'Dreams and Conversions: A Comparative Analysis of Catholic and Buddhist Dreams in Ming and Qing China', *Journal of Religious History* 29 (2005), pp. 223–40, at p. 229.

77. Bailey, *The Art of Colonial Latin America*, figure 221, p. 369. On this phenomenon see Gauvin Alexander Bailey, 'Asia in the Arts of Colonial Latin America', in *The Arts in Latin America, 1492–1820*, ed. Joseph J. Rishel with Suzanne Stratton-Pruitt, Philadelphia, 2006, pp. 56–69.

78. Bailey, *The Art of Colonial Latin America*, figure 223, pp. 372–3; Gauvin Alexander Bailey, 'Creating a Global Artistic Language in Late Renaissance Rome: Artists in the Service of the Overseas Missions, 1542–1621', in *From Rome to Eternity: Catholicism and the Arts in Italy, ca. 1550–1650*, eds. Pamela M. Moss and Thomas Worcester, Leiden, 2002, pp. 225–51, at pp. 245–8.

79. Marius B. Jansen, *The Making of Modern Japan*, Cambridge, MA, 2000, pp. 80–81.

Chapter 23: Mary in a World of Neighbouring Diversity

1. *Decrees of the Ecumenical Councils*, II, ed. Norman P. Tanner, Washington, DC, and London, 1990, pp. 774*–775.

2. Ibid., session 5, 15 June 1546, Decree on Original Sin, c. 6, pp. *667–667.

3. Simon Ditchfield, 'Reading Rome as a Sacred Landscape, c.1586–1635', in *Sacred Space in Early Modern Europe*, Cambridge, 2005, pp. 167–92, at pp. 174–5.

4. Venice, Galleria dell' Accademia.

5. Jeanine de Landtsheer, 'Justus Lipsius's Treatises on the Holy Virgin', in *The Low Countries as a Crossroads of Religious Beliefs*, Leiden, 2004, pp. 65–87.

6. Robert Chambers, *Miracles Lately Wrought by the Intercession of the Glorious Virgin Marie at Mont-aigu*, Antwerp, 1606 (repr. Ilkley, 1975); Helen L. Parish, *Monks, Miracles and Magic: Reformation Representations of the Medieval Church*, London, 2005, pp. 152–3.

7. Chambers, *Miracles Lately Wrought*, p. 30.

8. Ibid., pp. 30, 33, 38.

9. Alexandra Walsham, 'Holywell: Contesting Sacred Space in Post-Reformation Wales', in *Sacred Space in Early Modern Europe*, Cambridge, 2005, pp. 211–36, at pp. 221–2.

10. Trevor Johnson, 'Gardening for God: Carmelite Deserts and the Sacralization of Natural Space in Counter-Reformation Spain', in *Sacred Space in Early Modern Europe*, Cambridge, 2005, pp. 193–210, at pp. 198–200.

11. Philip Soergel, *Wondrous in his Saints*, chapters 4 and 5.

12. Hans-Jürgen Becker, 'Der Heilige als Landsherr: Zur Staatsrechtlichen Symboldeutung des Patrons im europäischen Bereich', *Symbolon, Jahrbuch für Symbolforschung* new series 6 (1982), pp. 9–25, at pp. 21–2.

13. Marian Helm-Pirgo, *Virgin Mary Queen of Poland: Historical Essay*, New York, 1966, pp. 21–2; on Polish pilgrimage cults see also Aleksandra Witkowska, 'The Cult of the Virgin Mary in Polish Religiousness from the 15th to the 17th century', in *The Common Christian Roots of the European Nations: An International Colloquium in the Vatican*, II, Florence, 1982, pp. 467–78. The shrine of Marienzell, near Vienna, was similarly favoured in Austria, where Mary became 'Empress of Austria', see R. Po-chia Hsia, *Social Discipline in the Reformation: Central Europe 1550–1750*, London, 1989, pp. 55–6.

14. Sarah T. Nalle, *God in La Mancha: Religious Reform and the People of Cuenca, 1500–1650*, Baltimore, 1992, p. 153.

15. Glenn Ehrstine, 'Motherhood and Protestant Polemics: Stillbirth in Hans von Rüte's *Abgötterei* (1531)', in *Maternal Measures: Figuring Caregiving in the Early Modern Period*, eds. Naomi J. Miller and Naomi Yavneh, Aldershot, 2000, pp. 121–34, at p. 126. The shrine had been famous since the fifteenth century for such miracles worked by Mary's image: see p. 125. Lutheran commissioners sought out persistent pilgrims; for the case of a woman see Heal, 'Sacred Image and Sacred Space', p. 58.

16. From the edition of Florence 1620: Bernardino Amico, *Tarttato delle Piante & Immagini de Sacri Edificii di Terra Santa*, trans. David Sullivan and Commentary by Robert Halwas, Palo Alto, 1999. I am most grateful to Zur Shalev for kindly sharing this material and his expertise with me.

17. Silvana Seidel Menchi, 'Les Pèlerinages des enfants mort-nés: Des rituels correctifs pour un dogme impopulaire?', in *Rendre ses vœux: Les identités pèlerines dans l'Europe moderne (XVIe–XVIIIe siècle)*, eds. Philippe Boutry, Pierre-Antoine Fabre and Dominique Julia, Paris, 2000, pp. 139–54, at pp. 141–2.

18. Peter Marshall, *Beliefs and the Dead in Reformation England*, Oxford, 2002, pp. 202–5.

19. Menchi, 'Les Pèlerinages', pp. 144–5.

20. On the powerful pilgrimage cult to Our Lady of the Conception see Avelino de Jesus da Costa, 'O culto de Nossa Senhora de Conceição em Portugal até século XVI', in *Homenagem a Joseph M. Piel: por ocasião do seu 850 aniversário*, ed. Dieter Kremer, Tübingen, 1988, pp. 675–707.

21. Pedro Penteado, 'Pèlerinages collectifs au sanctuaire de Nossa Senhora de Nazaré (Portugal) aux XVIIe et XVIIIe siècles', in *Rendre ses vœux*, pp. 123–38, esp. at pp. 124–33.

22. Albrecht Burkardt, 'Pèlerinage et corps saints à travers les témoignages des procès de canonisation', in *Rendre ses vœux*, pp. 501–29, at p. 514.

23. Craig Harline, *Miracles at the Jesus Oak: Histories of the Supernatural in Reformation Europe*, New York, 2003, pp. 53–91.

24. Robert Maniura, *Pilgrimage to Images in the Fifteenth Century: The Origins of the Cult of Our Lady of Częstochowa*, Woodbridge, 2004, p. 146. I am grateful to Robert Maniura for his kind assistance.

25. Elizabeth Tingle, 'The Sacred Space of Julien Maunoir: The Re-christianising of the Landscape in Seventeenth-Century Brittany', in *Sacred Space in Early Modern Europe*, Cambridge, 2005, pp. 237–58, at p. 251.

26. Maureen Flynn, *Sacred Charity: Confraternities and Social Welfare in Spain, 1400–1700*, Basingstoke, 1989, p. 31.

27. Eyolf Østrem and Nils Holger Petersen, 'The Singing of the *Laude* and Musical Sensiblities in Early Seventeenth-Century Confraternity Devotion: Part I', *Journal of Religious History* 28 (2004), pp. 276–97; Nils Holger Petersen, 'The Singing of the *Laude* and Musical Sensibilities in Early Seventeenth-Century Confraternity Devotion: Part II', *Journal of Religious History* 29 (2005), pp. 163–76.

28. Østrem and Petersen, 'The Singing of the *Laude* I', pp. 286–7.

29. Nalle, *God in La Mancha*, pp. 150–51.

30. St Francis de Sales, *Introduction to the Devout Life*, 2nd edn, New York, 1966, p. 88.

31. Ibid., pp. 58–9.

32. London, National Gallery, oil on copper, 35 × 27.5 cm.

33. Worcester, 'The Catholic Sermons', p. 28.

34. Gauvin Alexander Bailey, *Between Renaissance and Baroque: Jesuit Art in Rome, 1565–1610*, Toronto, 2003, p. 78.

35. Ibid., pp. 71–3.

36. Ibid., pp. 121–2.

37. I am grateful to Louise Rice for a series of illuminating conversations about this material; see Louise Rice, 'Pietro da Cortona and the Roman Baroque Thesis Print', in *Pietro da Cortona: Atti del convegno internazionale Roma-Firenze 12–15 novembre 1997*, Milan, 1998, pp. 189–200.

38. Judith W. Mann, 'The Annunciation Chapel in the Quirinal Palace, Rome: Paul V, Guido Reni, and the Virgin Mary', *Art Bulletin* 75 (1993), pp. 113–34, at pp. 118–23.

39. Both panels are in the National Gallery in London, oil on canvas, 135 × 101.6 cm and 135.5 × 102.2 cm, respectively.

40. Francisco Pacheco, *Arte de la Pintura* II, Madrid, 1956, p. 212; Nancy Mayberry, 'Beatriz de Silva: An Important Fifteenth-Century Visionary', *Vox Benedictina* 4 (1987), pp. 169–83, at p. 181.

41. Gauvin A. Bailey, *The Art of Colonial America*, London, 2005, figure 175, pp. 296–7; Bailey, 'Creating a Global Artistic Language', pp. 225–51, at pp. 233–7.

42. Munich, Alte Pinakothek, silk, 295 × 208 cm.

43. Bailey, *The Art of Colonial Latin America*, pp. 300–301, figure 177, p. 300.

44. Ibid., pp. 173–8.

45. Sarah L. Bastow, 'The Catholic Gentlemen of the North: Unreformed in the Age of the Reformation?', in *Holiness and Masculinity in the Middle Ages*, Toronto, 2005, pp. 206–21, at pp. 208–9.

46. Anne Dillon, 'Praying by Numbers: The Confraternity of the Rosary and the English Catholic Community, c.1580–1700', *History* 88 (2003), pp. 451–71, at p. 463.

47. I am most grateful to John A. W. Lock for bringing this text to my attention and discussing it with me. The reference is to the Aragonese Dominican Juan de Monzon, around whom a Europe-wide controversy over the Immaculate Conception developed in the 1380s: Lamy, *L'Immaculée Conception*, pp. 562–75.

After Mary: A Conclusion

1. Maurice Agulhon, *Marianne into Battle: Republican Imagery and Symbolism in France, 1789–1880*, Cambridge, 1981, esp. pp. 1–7, 27–34.

2. *Culture Wars: Secular-Catholic Conflict in Nineteenth-Century Europe*, eds. Christopher Clark and Wolfram Kaiser, Cambridge, 2003.

3. Sarah Jane Boss, *Empress and Handmaid: On Nature and Gender in the Cult of the Virgin Mary*, London, 2000, pp. 146–51.

4. Ruth Harris, *Lourdes: Body and Spirit in the Secular Age*, Harmondsworth, 1999; see also Barbara Corrado Pope, 'Immaculate and Powerful: The Marian Revival in the Nineteenth Century', in *Immaculate and Powerful: The Female in Sacred Image and Social Reality*, eds. Clarissa W. Atkinson, Constance H. Buchanan and Margaret R. Miles, Boston, 1985, pp. 173–200.

5. David Blackbourn, *Marpingen: Apparitions of the Virgin Mary in Nineteenth-Century Germany*, New York, 1994. For an attempt to explain the underlying predisposition towards visionary experiences see Michael P. O'Carroll, 'Visions of the Virgin Mary: The Effect of Family Structures on Marian Apparitions', *Journal of the Scientific Study of Religion* 22 (1983), pp. 205–21.

6. Henry Adams, *The Education of Henry Adams*, ed. Jean Gooder, Harmondsworth, 1995, pp. 360–70, 531–3.

7. Griselda Pollock, *Mary Cassatt: Painter of Modern Women*, London, 1998, p. 29.

8. New Britain (CN) Museum of American Art, pastel on paper; see reproduction in Pollock, *Mary Cassatt*, plate 51, p. 101.

9. This process has been identified and discussed in Ann Douglas, *The Feminization of American Culture*, New York, 1977.

10. Jay Winter, *Sites of Memory, Sites of Mourning: The Great War in European Cultural History*, Cambridge, 1995, p. 121.

11. Colleen McDannell, *Material Christianity: Religion and Popular Culture in America*, New Haven, 1995, esp. chapter 5, on Lourdes and other shrines. See also David Morgan, *Visual Piety: A History and Theory of Popular Religious Images*, Berkeley, 1998.

12. Annette Becker, *War and Faith: The Religious Imagination in France, 1914–1930*, trans. Helen McPhail, Oxford, 1998, pp. 63–4.

13. I am grateful to Edward and Maureen Turner, who shared with me photographs of the parish memorial altar of Perignac.

14. See the poem written during the Battle of the Marne: Raymond Halter, *La Vierge Marie dans la vie et l'œuvre de Paul Claudel: Etude et anthologie*, Tours, 1958, pp. 128–9.

15. Mike Davis, *Magical Urbanism*, London, 2008, pp. 12–15; see on the image by Delilah Montoya, which expresses the Guadalupe's power to liberate and to enslave: Gauvin A. Bailey, *Art of Colonial Latin America*, London, 2005, no. 224, pp. 375–7. On the attachment of migrants to shrines and their recreation in their new locations see Gorospe, *Virgin of Peñafrancia*, esp. pp. 3–4. I am very grateful to Dr David Irving of Christ's College, Cambridge, for introducing me to this book.

16. Bailey, *The Art of Colonial Latin America*, no. 235, pp. 396–8. See also the juxtaposition of church and state in Botero's 2000 *City Street*, in *Botero: Opere*, Milan, 2007, no. 13, p. 63. In 2002 Botero was commissioned by the Commune of Siena to design the Marian banner for the Palio race.

17. James S. Donnelly Jr, 'The Marian Shrine of Knock: The First Decade', *Eire-Ireland* 28 (1993), pp. 54–99.

18. James S. Donnelly, Jr, 'The Peak of Marianism in Ireland, 1930–60', in *Piety and Power in Ireland 1790–1960*, eds. Stewart J. Brown and D. W. Miller, Notre Dame, 2000, pp. 252–83; James S. Donnelly Jr, 'Opposing the "Modern World": The Cult of the Virgin Mary in Ireland, 1965–85', *Eire-Ireland* 40 (2005), pp. 183–245. I am most grateful to Ian Green for introducing me to this area of scholarship.

19. John Martin, *Roses, Fountains, and Gold: The Virgin Mary in History, Art and Apparition*, San Francisco 1998, pp. 213–33.

20. Maria-Antonietta Macciocchi, 'Female Sexuality in Fascist Ideology', in *Feminist Review* 1 (1979), pp. 67–82; Nicholas Perry and Loreto Echeverría, *Under the Heel of Mary*, London and New York, 1988, pp. 181–93; on the military dictatorships in Argentina and Chile see pp. 281–6.

21. Maria Manuel Lisboa, *Paula Rego's Map of Memory: National and Sexual Politics*, Aldershot, 2003.

22. From an interview with John Haffenden, *Viewpoints*, London, 1981, pp. 60–61; see also Michael Parker, *Seamus Heaney: The Making of the Poet*, Basingstoke, 1993, pp. 2–5; Eamon Duffy, 'May Thoughts on Mary', in *Faith of Our Fathers: Reflections on Catholic Tradition*, London, 2004, pp. 29–37.

23. Bill Viola, *The Passions*, 2003: See *The Art of Bill Viola*, ed. Chris Townsend, London, 2004. I have benefitted from conversation with Bill Viola on the occasion of his exhibition at the National Gallery in London, 2003. See also the reflections on medieval Mary imagery in the exhibition *Mythos Mutter: Frauenmuseum, Kunstausstellung vom 5. Mai 2005 bis 28. August 2005*, ed. Marianne Pitzen, Bonn, 2005.

24. On children's visions among the Montana Salish see also Laura Peers, ' "The Guardian of All": Jesuit Missionary and Salish Perceptions of Mary', in *Reading beyond Words: Contexts in Native History*, eds. Jennifer S. H. Brown and Elizabeth Vibert, Peterborough (Ontario): Broadview Press, 1996, pp. 284–303.

25. Ian Linden with Jane Linden, *Catholics, Peasants and Chewa Resistance in Nyasaland, 1889–1939*, London, 1974, pp. 5–6, 174–6.

26. Hugo F. Hinfelaar, *Bemba-Speaking Women of Zambia in a Century of Religious Change (1892–1992)*, Leiden, 1994, pp. 138–9.

27. Ibid., pp.142–3.

28. This question was raised when the mayor of New York, Rudy Giuliani, withdrew funding from the 'Sensation' exhibition of British art of 1999, which brought *The Holy Virgin Mary* to the Brooklyn Museum of Art.

29. Popular publications have devoted space to Mary as a symbol around which a greater closeness between Christians of different traditions might be fostered: see *Newsweek*, 8 December 2003; *The Economist*, 20 December 2003–2 January 2004; *Time Magazine*, 21 March 2005.

30. Dr Ann Nichols has shared this information with me, from the Winona Diocesan Newspaper *The Courier*, September 2004.

31. I am extremely grateful to Christopher Walbank for introducing me to the world of religious chalk paintings; see www.tucsonmandonnary.com. On Mexican-American women and the cult of Our Lady of Guadalupe see Jeannette Rodriguez, *Our Lady of Guadalupe: Faith and Empowerment among Mexican-American Women*, Austin, 1994.

32. For a summary of positions see Maurice Hamington, *Hail Mary? The Struggle for Ultimate Womanhood in Catholicism*, New York and London, 1995; Marina Warner, *Alone of All Her Sex*; Ann Loades, 'The Virgin Mary and the Feminist Quest', in *After Eve*, ed. Janet Martin Soskice, London, 1990, pp. 156–78.

33. Rainer Maria Rilke, *The Life of the Virgin Mary*, translated and with an introduction by C. F. McIntyre, Berkeley, 1947, pp. 10–11.

34. W. B. Yeats, *The Collected Poems of W. B. Yeats*, London, 1933, pp. 281–2.

35. Sylvia Plath, *Collected Poems*, ed. Ted Hughes, London, 1981, p. 147.

36. Julia Kristeva, 'Stabat Mater', in *The Kristeva Reader*, ed. Toril Moi, New York, 1986, pp. 160–86, at p. 161; translation from Julia Kristeva, 'Stabat Mater', in *Histoires d'amour*, Paris, 1983, pp. 225–47.

37. See on the implications of cultural systems based on belief in 'virgin birth' Edmund Leach, 'Virgin Birth', *Proceedings of the Royal Anthropological Institute of Great Britain and Ireland* (1965–8), pp. 39–49. I have been greatly inspired by the work and writing of the Israeli artist and analyst Bracha L. Ettinger assembled in Bracha L. Ettinger, *The*

Matrixial Borderspace, Minneapolis, 2006, and especially by Griselda Pollock's introduction on pp. 10–38.

A Few Comments on Scholarship and Reading

1. Janet L. Nelson, 'Review Article: Virgin Territory: Recent Historical Work on Marian Belief and Cult', *Religion* 7 (1977), pp. 206–25, at pp. 224–5.
2. Marina Warner, *Alone of All Her Sex: The Myth and Cult of the Virgin Mary*, London, 1976.
3. Klaus Schreiner, *Maria: Jungfrau, Mutter, Herrscherin*, Munich, 1994.
4. Caroline Walker Bynum, *Holy Feast and Holy Fast: The Religious Significance of Food to Medieval Women*, Berkeley, 1988.
5. Fulton, *From Judgment to Passion*.

Index

Europe – cont.
Mary of court and rule 285–9
overview of Mary's rise to
prominence xviii–xx, 355–6
religious diversity and Mary
400–412
vernacular languages 198–9, 202
Evagrius Ponticus 23
Evangile de l'Enfance 202
Eve, Mary as antithesis to 146,
311–12
Hildegard of Bingen 148–9
in Syriac tradition 37–8, 146
Everaert, Cornelis: Play of Mary's
Chaplet 337–8
Eyck, Jan van 307
Eymerich, Nicholas 304
Eznik of Kolb 49

Fatima revelations 418
Fauré, Aude 227
feasts see Marian feasts
Fei, Giovanni 208–9
Felix V 304
Felix of Urgel 102
feminism 422
Ferdinand of Aragon 379–80
Feyerabend, Sigismund 372–3
Fishacre, Richard 270–71
flagellants 250, 254
Flémalle, Master of 344
see also Campin, Robert
Fonseca, Juan Rodríguez de 381
Fortunatus, Venantius 90–92
Fouquet, Jean 310
Francis of Assisi 197, 201
Francis de Sales 407
Franciscans xviii–xix, 197–201
Bernardines 336
and the Immaculate Conception
303–4

in the New Spain 388–9
see also friars
Franks 78–9, 100–105
Frauenlob (poet) 309
Song of Songs 211–13
Frederick of Thuringia 224
frescos of Mary 97–8, 203, 409–10
friars 197–201
confraternities and 249, 252,
254–5
in the New Spain 388–9, 392
Fulbert of Chartres 138–9, 161, 195
Fulda Sacramentary 116
Furtmeyer, Berthold 312

Gabriel, angel 6, 88
Galbius 61
Galla Placidia 49
Garcilaso de la Vega 392
gardens of Mary 310–12
Garnett, Henry 411
Gaudé Maria 97
Gautier of Coinci: Miracles de Nostre
Dame 229–32, 239, 242, 280
Geiler von Kaysersberg, Johannes
361–2
Gellone Sacramentary 102
genealogies of Jesus 5, 8, 30–31
Geoffrey of Gorham's psalter 135–6
Gerizim, Mount 54
Germanus of Constantinople 72
Gerson, Jean 309, 323–5
Gertrud the Great 262
Gilbert Crispin 162, 165
Giotto di Bondone 247
Giovanni di Paolo 326, 343–4
Glaber, Radulfus 122
Golden Fleece, Order of the 289, 298
Golden Legend 203–4
Goldene Madonna 117–18, 127–8
of Essen 121

Gonzalo de Berceo 237–8
Gorleston Psalter 245–6
Gospels
　of the Apocrypha 9–11, 13, 35,
　　202, 213–14
　Armenian book of 80
　Jewish counter-gospel, *Toledoth
　　Yeshu* 57–9
　of the New Testament 4–8
　Syriac 35 *see also Philip, Gospel of*
Goswin of Bossut 257–60
Graeculus 198
grammatica 277
Great War (1914–18) 416–17
Greccio 201
Greer, Germaine 422
Gregorian chant 145
Gregory of Nazianzus 80–81
Gregory of Nyssa 20
Gregory of Tours 90
Gregory the Great 96
Guadalupe, Virgin of 390–91, 421
Guda Homiliary 129
Guibert of Nogent 131, 163–4, 185
Guillaume de Deguileville 278
Guillaume le Clerc 273
Guta-Sintram Codex 125
Guterson, David 419

Hagia Sophia 47, 74, 79–80
Halevi, Yehudah 165
Harrison, William 411–12
Hayne de Bruxelles 298
healings 55, 185, 402–3
　monasticism and 136
Heaney, Seamus 419
Hefzibah 62
Heinrich von Mügeln 193, 274
Heischer, Lienhard 326
Helena of Constantinople 19, 28
Helinand of Froidmont 154–7

Helsin of Ramsay 183
Helvidius 29, 93
Henry II, Holy Roman Emperor
　126
Henry V, King of England 286, 287,
　346
Henry VI, King of England 286–7
Henry VIII, King of England 376
Henry of Chichester 209
Henry (Master Heinrich) of
　Constance 263
Henry of Grosmont 279–80, 286
Henry of Schaffhausen 267
Henry of St Gallen: *Life of Mary*
　328
Heraclius, Emperor 63, 67, 71
Heribert of Cologne 126–7
Herman of Tournai 185
Hermann-Joseph 266
Hesychius 54
Hikkelia 59
Hilary of Poitiers 25
Hildegard of Bingen 147–9
Hincmar of Reims 101, 104–5
History of Joseph the Carpenter
　11–12
Hoccleve, Thomas 287–8
Hodegetria iconography 81, 170–71
Holme, Wilfrid 377
Holy Family
　the European and 323–7
　Hours devoted to Anne and 329,
　　331
　Jesus and 213–14
　Mary of hearth and home 358–60
　Holy Land 19–21, 53–4, 57, 59–63
　pilgrimage sites 59–60, 169,
　　172–3, 201
Holy Spirit
　'overshadowing' of Mary 6, 15
　Syriac tradition 13, 34–5, 39

Isis cult 40–42, 64
Islam
  Mary as a Muslim-Christian
    meeting-point 382–3, 384–5
  relics and 123
  reverence of Mary 172, 173
  and the struggle over images 76
  treatment of Mary 83–8
Jacob ben Reuben, Rabbi 166–7
Jacobus da Voragine 203
Jacopone da Todi: *Donna de
  Paradiso* 252
James le Palmer 276
James, *Protogospel of* 9–11, 112
  Surat Maryam and 86
Japan 357, 398–9
Jean de Montagnac 307
Jean of Morigny 276
Jeanne d'Arc 342
Jerome 20, 30–31, 59, 126
Jesuits 394, 397, 398, 408, 411
Jesus Christ
  at the Cana wedding feast 7
  the crib, Christ the child and his
    family 201–4
  depictions within the Holy Family
    213–14
  genealogies of 5, 8, 30–31
  as hero 108–9
  Mary and the Incarnation *see*
    Incarnation, Mary's role
  Mary and the nature of Christ xvii,
    12–16, 18–19
  and Mary at the foot of the cross
    see cross of Jesus
  on true motherhood 7
Jetzer, Hans 362–3
Jewish Boy, miracle 74–5, 237
Jewish writings
  apocalyptic 62–3

trampled (*funie*) 399
  see also iconography; Marian
    representations
Immaculate Conception 303–5
  and the Counter Reformation
    408–12
  feast *see* Conception, feast of
  Franciscan/Dominican debate
    303–4
  Hesychius 54
  Iberian adoption 380
  papal affirmation as doctrine 414
  shaping of the idea 173–6
Incarnation, Mary's role
  Ambrose 27
  Anselm 134, 161
  Augustine 32
  Carolingian debates 101–2
  Christian understanding of 18
  with the crib, Christ the child and
    his family 201–4
  Fortunatus 91–2
  images and 80–81
  liturgy and 138, 147
  polemics and 161–7 *see also*
    polemics
  Rupert of Deutz 160
  theology of clothing 38
  see also 'Mother of God';
    Theotokos
Infancy Gospel of Pseudo-Matthew
  202, 213–14
intercession by Mary 116, 117, 128,
  132–4, 224
  with bared breast 211
Irene, Empress 77
Irish poetry 107–9, 423
Isabella of Portugal 289, 347
Isabella of Castile 348, 379–80
Isaiah's prophecy (Isaiah 7:14) 9, 30,
  162, 165

Jewish writings – cont.
  Christian use of 9, 15–16, 158–61, 164–5, 167, 198 see also Song of Songs
  counter-gospel (Toledoth Yeshu) 57–9
  poetry of lament (piyyutim) 165–6
  Talmud trial for blasphemies against Mary 225, 233
Jews
  anti-Jewish writings 202–3
  and the church in the thirteenth century 228–36
  and the church in the fifteenth century 301–2
  conversion of 92, 160
  crusade massacres 165–6
  and the Holy Land 53–4, 57, 59–63
  Islam and the Jews 86–7
  and Mary 55–63, 75, 152, 161–8, 226–7, 228–36, 252–5
  Prague massacre 301
  see also Judaism
Joachim, father of Mary 10, 114
Joao I of Aragon 304
Johannis libelli 267–8
John VII, Pope 98
John, abbot of St Victor priory in Paris 140–41
John of Cantimpré 259
John of Caulibus: Meditations on the Life of Christ 246–7, 261
John of Damascus 55, 73
  on images 76, 77
John of Jenstein 296
John Paul II, Pope 421
John, Gospel of 5, 7–8
Joseph 11–12, 36, 115, 220
  in sixteenth-century depictions of the Holy Family 359
  depictions of Mary with 325–7
  feast of St Joseph 356
  Gerson and 323–4, 325
Jovinian 29
Judaism
  destruction of the Jewish Temple 4, 9
  and early stories of Mary 10–12
  ecclesia-synagoga 228–9, 301
  Jewish background of Mary's life 3–4, 8, 9
  and Jews in the Holy Land 53–4
  see also Jewish writings; Jews
Julian, Emperor 27
Julian of Norwich 265, 329
Julianna of Cornillon 144
Julius II 362
Justin II 66, 67–8
Justin Martyr 13
  Dialogue with Trypho 13

Kali 356
Kalonimos, Rabbi 165
Kaloritissa cave church 81
kathisma 59
Kempe, Margery 305
Khludov Psalter 81
Kimhi, David 167
Kollwitz, Käthe 417
Konrad of Würzburg 309
kontakia 70–71
Koran 83–7, 115
Kulmbach, Hans von (Hans Suess) 335
Kwannon 357

lactation of St Bernard 350
Lambeth Apocalypse 209
Lambeth Bible 168
Lange von Wetzlar, Johannes 301
Langmann, Adelheide 264

Mary's virginity as model for nuns
92, 262
and the material Mary 124–30
around the millennium (c.1000)
116
miracles and 183
monastic song 143–9, 192–3
prayer, penance, consolation and
Mary 130–37
Saqqara complex 64
Syriac asceticism and 39–40
Visitation of the Monasteries
376–7
monoenergeia 68
Montaigu 402
Montserrat shrine 186
mosaics 66, 81, 170
Hagia Sophia 80
Roman 95, 98–9
Moschus, John 74
Mostaert, Jan 327
'Mother of God', *Theotokos*
First Council of Nicaea 19
Isis, Mary, and the mother goddess
tradition 40–42
Mary as imperial mother of God
43–9, 67–9
Nestorian controversy 43–8
the suffering mother 109, 151–2
Syriac tradition 36–40
Theotokos see *Theotokos*
see also Incarnation, Mary's role
Mother of Mercy 155–6, 286, 318,
386
mother tongue 198–9, 202, 220–21
music
Burgundy 291–2
Cantigas de Sante Maria 237
chant *see* chant
Christmas carols 360–61
Guillaume de Machaut 195–6

Hildegard of Bingen 147–9
Iberian 381–2
Lutheran 370–71
Marian feasts and 113, 178
monastic 143–9, 192–3
motets 195
musica mensurabilis 194
oratorio 407
poetry and 193
polyphonic 145, 194, 196, 381
and the rise of Mary 177–8
Mystery of the Assumption (play)
320–21
Nativity, feast of Mary's 104, 138–9
Nativity tokens 60
Nazoraeans 21
Nequam, Alexander 144, 164
Neri di Bicci 306, 348
Nestor 43–4, 46, 47, 48
Nestorian controversy 43–8
New Testament
Mary in Acts 8
Mary in the Gospels 4–8
Nicaea, First Council of (325) 18–19,
43
Nicaea, Second Council of (787) 77
Nicene Creed 53
Nicholas of St Albans 176
Nicholas of Verdun 129–30
niddah 58–9
Niklashausen 342
Norsa, Daniele da 341
Norwich cathedral 326
Notre Dame, Paris 194–5
Notre Dame of Soissons 186
Ó Dálaigh, Donnchadh Mór 211
Oberbüren shrine 404
Ocaña, Diego de 392–3
Ochino, Bernardino 376

Pontmain 416
Praise of Mary, The (Den lof van Maria) 270
prayer to Mary 67, 71
  Anselm's 134–5
  apparitions in response to 136
  monastic 131–5, 136
  rosary 332–8, 420
  as Virgin of Lourdes 417
printing technologies 339, 357
Priscilla, catacomb of 25
Proclus 44–5, 46–7, 48, 55
Protestant Reformation 356
  Lutheran critique of Mary 367–76
  Protestant England's Mary 376–8
Psalter of Queen Melisende 172
Pseudo-Evodius 55–6
'Pseudo-Jerome' of Cogitis 137
Pulcheria, Aelia 47–8
pulque 389
purgatory 132
Purification, feast of 100
Qal'at Sim'an 60
Qissat Mujadalat al-Usquf 75
Quirinal Chapel, Rome 409–10
Quiroga, Vasco de 390
Qur'an see Koran
Rabanus (Hrabanus) Maurus 103
Rahab 30–31
Rainerius of Genoa 250
Ralph of St Germer at Fly 167
Raphael 365
Ravenna 89
redemption
  and monastic prayer to Mary 131–5
  Syriac tradition 36–7
  vision spread from Constantinople 67

Iberian 184
  Marian visions and 342
  under Muslim rule 172
  see also shrines
Pionius of Smyrna 19
Pisano, Nicola 246
Pius IV, Pope 400
Planctus Mariae 246
Plath, Sylvia 423–4
plays, religious see drama
poems/poetry
  Anglo-Saxon 110
  Bergundian 290–91
  Blathmac 107–9
  Cantigas de Sante Maria 236–9
  chants of the confraternities 252–4
  Christian transformation of Latin 274–5, 288
  of the English court 287
  English devotional 248–9
  Gautier of Coinci 229–32
  of lament (piyyutim) 165–6
  liturgical 146–7
  love poetry 194
  Mary as the poetic impossible 280–82
  Middle English 278
  in parish instruction 217–18
  prayer, music and 193
  twentieth-century 423–4
polemics
  Bible commentaries and the Song of Songs 158–61
  Mary and early polemics 12–16
  Mary and the Jews 75, 161–8, 226–7 see also Jews
  miracles and 183, 403–6
  Origen 14–16
  tracts 75–6, 93 see also tracts
polyphony 145, 194, 196, 381

Vitnisvísur af Maríu 241
Vladimir of Kiev 80

wall-paintings
Chalgrove church, Oxford 203–4
Croughton church,
Northamptonshire 210
Dormition scenes 99, 170
ecclesia-synagoga 168, 229
Egypt 41
frescos 97–8, 203, 409–10
Giotto di Bondone 247
Romanesque 180–81
Rome 25–6, 95–6, 97–8, 99
Walsingham shrine 365, 376
Warmund Sacramentary 116
Warner, Marina 422
Weingarten Sacramentary 125
Werner the Swiss: *Life of Mary* 211–12
Weyden, Rogier van der 314, 315, 340, 362
William of Malmesbury 183, 188
William of Shoreham 220, 271
poem on the Five Joys of the Virgin 217–18
On the Virgin Mary 218–19
Wilton Diptych 285, 305

Winchester cathedral 317
Winchester Psalter 125
womb of Mary
female religious and 262
as a hall of purity 27, 37
monastic song and 143, 147
woodcuts 327, 331, 339, 355, 373, 375
rosary 335
Worcester cathedral 142–3, 317
Word (*logos*) 36
World War I 416–17

Ya'eqob, Zär'a, Emperor of Ethiopia 292–5
Yeats, W. B. 423

Zambia 420–21
Zamora 406
Zär'a Ya'eqob 292–5
Zend-Avesta 88
Zeno, Emperor 54
Zeno of Verona 25
Zephania 56
Zerubbabel, *Sefer* 62–3
Zwingli, Ulrich 370, 374
Zwolle, Master of 350

5/09